CANADIAN CORRECTIONS

FIFTH EDITION

CURT T. GRIFFITHS
SIMON FRASER UNIVERSITY

DANIELLE J. MURDOCH
SIMON FRASER UNIVERSITY

NELSON

NELSON

Canadian Corrections, Fifth Edition
by Curt T. Griffiths and Danielle J. Murdoch

VP, Product Solutions:
Claudine O'Donnell

Publisher, Digital and Print Content:
Leanna MacLean

Marketing Manager:
Claire Varley

Content Manager:
Suzanne Simpson Millar

Photo and Permissions Researcher:
Jessie Coffey

Senior Production Project Manager:
Imoinda Romain

Production Service:
SPi Global

Copy Editor:
Michael Kelly

Proofreader:
SPi Global

Indexer:
SPi Global

Design Director:
Ken Phipps

Higher Education Design Project Manager:
Pamela Johnston

Interior Design Modifications:
deboraH brock

Cover Design:
deboraH brock

Cover Image:
Diana Ong/Superstock/Getty Images

Compositor:
SPi Global

Library and Archives Canada Cataloguing in Publication Data

Griffiths, Curt T. (Curt Taylor), 1948–, author
        Canadian corrections / Curt T. Griffiths, Danielle J. Murdoch. — Fifth edition.

Includes bibliographical references and index.
Issued in print and electronic formats.

ISBN 978-0-17-670003-4 (softcover).— ISBN 978-0-17-682707-6 (PDF)

1. Corrections—Canada—Textbooks. I. Murdoch, Danielle J., 1983–, author II. Title.

HV9507.G75 2017   364.60971
C2017-904618-7
C2017-904619-5

ISBN-13: 978-0-17-670003-4
ISBN-10: 0-17-670003-X

BRIEF CONTENTS

Preface to the Fifth Edition xxv

**PART I   CANADIAN CORRECTIONS: SETTING
THE FRAMEWORK. 1**

Chapter 1   Perspectives on Crime and Punishment 2
Chapter 2   The Origins and Evolution of Canadian
Corrections. 23
Chapter 3   Contemporary Canadian Corrections 44
Chapter 4   Sentencing: Beginning the Corrections
Process. 72

**PART II   CORRECTIONS IN THE COMMUNITY:
ALTERNATIVES TO CONFINEMENT. 103**

Chapter 5   Alternatives to Confinement 104

PART III   INCARCERATION 137

Chapter 6   Correctional Institutions 138
Chapter 7   Working Inside: The Experience of
Correctional Officers. 175
Chapter 8   Doing Time: The Experience of Inmates 207
Chapter 9   Classification, Case Management,
and Treatment. 243

PART IV   RETURNING TO THE COMMUNITY: RELEASE, RE-ENTRY, AND REINTEGRATION . . 281

Chapter 10 Release from Incarceration 282
Chapter 11 Re-entry and Life After Prison. 322

PART V   SPECIAL POPULATIONS IN CORRECTIONS . . . 361

Chapter 12 Women Offenders. 362
Chapter 13 Indigenous Offenders 401
Chapter 14 Young Offenders. 432

PART VI   GOING FORWARD: REFORMING CORRECTIONS. 471

Chapter 15 Creating Effective Systems of Corrections . . . 472

Glossary of Key Terms 503
Index 515

CONTENTS

Preface to the Fifth Edition xxv

PART I   CANADIAN CORRECTIONS: SETTING THE FRAMEWORK 1

Chapter 1   Perspectives on Crime and Punishment 2

A Definition of Corrections 3
The Process of Correctional Change 3
The Early Days 3
   The British Legacy 4
Perspectives on Crime, Offenders, and Punishment 6
   The Classical (Conservative) School 6
   The Positivist (Liberal) School 11
   The Critical (Radical) School 11
The Functions of Punishment 12
The Objectives of Punishment 13
Corrections, Punitive Penology, and Penal Populism 15
Mass Incarceration and the Move Toward
  Decarceration in the United States 15
Summary 18
Key Points Review 18
Key Term Questions 19
Critical Thinking Exercises 19
Class/Group Discussion Exercise 20
Media Links 20
Notes 21

Chapter 2   The Origins and Evolution of Canadian Corrections 23

The Creation of the Canadian Penitentiary 23
   Local Jails and Provincial Prisons 25
Late 1800s and Early 1900s 25

The Beginnings of Modern Reform: 1930–1970 27
The Early 21st Century: The Swinging
   Pendulum of Canadian Corrections 28
The Functions and Symbolism of Canadian Prison Architecture 32
Correctional Inquiries: Facilitating Change? 36
Reflections on Corrections History 39
Summary 39
Key Points Review 40
Key Term Questions 40
Critical Thinking Exercise 41
Class/Group Discussion Exercise 41
Media Links 41
Notes 42

Chapter 3   CONTEMPORARY CANADIAN CORRECTIONS 44

The Legislative Framework of Corrections 44
   Canadian Charter of Rights and Freedoms 45
   The Constitution Act (1867) 45
   The Criminal Code 45
   The Federal Corrections and Conditional Release Act (CCRA) 45
   Provincial and Territorial Corrections Legislation 46
   International Agreements and Conventions 46
The Correctional Process 46
The Mandate and Goals of Corrections 48
Corrections in a Democratic Society 49
   Human Rights and Corrections 49
   Accountability and a Concern with the Rule of Law 49
The "Who" and the "What" of Corrections 50
   The "Who" of Corrections 50
   The "What" of Corrections 51
      Corrections as a Political Enterprise 52
      Corrections as a Philosophy for Responding to Criminal offenders . . 52
      Corrections as a Subsystem of the Criminal Justice System 52
      Corrections as a Range of Programs Delivered in Community
        and Institutional Settings 54
The Structure of Contemporary Canadian Corrections 54
   The Split in Correctional Jurisdiction 54
   The Federal System of Corrections 55
   Provincial/Territorial Corrections 55
   Parole Boards 56
   The Costs of Corrections 57

Oversight: The Federal Correctional Investigator, Provincial
    Ombudspersons, and Auditors 57
Citizen's Advisory Committees (CACs) 60
The Private, Not-for-Profit Sector 61
Corrections and the Canadian Public 62
The NIMBY Phenomenon 63
Restorative Justice: An Alternative Approach to Crime and Criminal Offenders 64
Summary 66
Key Points Review 67
Key Term Questions 68
Critical Thinking Exercise 68
Class/Group Discussion Exercises 69
Media Links 70
Notes 70

Chapter 4   Sentencing: Beginning the Corrections Process 72

The Purpose and Principles of Sentencing 73
The Goals of Sentencing: The Cases of Mr. Smith and Mr. Jones 74
Utilitarian Goals 74
Retributive Goals 74
Restorative Goals 75
What Sentences Did Mr. Smith and Mr. Jones Receive? 75
Sentencing Options 76
Sentencing Indigenous Offenders 80
Judicial Determination 81
Life Imprisonment 81
Dangerous Offenders and Long-Term Offenders 81
How Judges Decide 82
You Be the Judge 82
Specialized Problem-Solving Courts 86
The Effectiveness of Specialized Courts 88
Sentencing in a Restorative Justice Framework 88
Circle Sentencing: A Restorative Justice Approach 88
Restorative Community Justice: The Collaborative
    Justice Program, Ottawa-Carleton Judicial District 92
The Effectiveness of Sentencing 94
Summary 96
Key Points Review 96
Key Term Questions 97
Critical Thinking Exercise 97
Class/Group Discussion Exercises 98
Media Links 99
Answers for Box 4.2, "You Be the Judge" 99
Notes 100

PART II   CORRECTIONS IN THE COMMUNITY: ALTERNATIVES TO CONFINEMENT............103

Chapter 5   Alternatives to Confinement..................104

Diversion....................................... 105
   The Issue of Net-Widening 106
Intermediate Sanctions.................................. 106
   Electronic Monitoring 107
   Conditional Sentences............................... 108
Probation....................................... 109
Recruitment and Training of Probation Officers 111
Role and Responsibilities of Probation Officers 112
Types of Supervision Orders 115
Probation Case Management 116
The Dual Role of Probation Officers 118
Supervision 118
   The Application of RNR to Probation Practice:
      The STICS Initiative............................. 119
   The Use of Motivational Interviewing in Probation Practice 120
Programs for Probationers 121
Intensive Supervision Probation 122
Challenges for Probation Officers 122
   The Stress Levels of Probation Officers................ 123
   Probation Officer Safety 123
   Supervising High-Need Probationers 124
   Heavy Workloads 124
   High Caseloads 124
   A Lack of PO–Offender Contact and Intervention 124
   Increasing Needs and Risks of Probationers 125
   The Requirement to Provide Probation Services in Remote
      and Northern Regions............................. 125
   Supervising a Diverse Clientele 125
The Experience of Probationers............................... 126
The Effectiveness of Alternatives to Confinement..................... 127
Summary 130
Key Points Review 130
Key Term Questions.................................. 131
Critical Thinking Exercises 132
Class/Group Discussion Exercise............................ 133
Media Links 133
Notes....................................... 134

PART III   INCARCERATION 137

Chapter 6   Correctional Institutions...................... 138

Types of Correctional Institutions 139
    Security Levels... 139
Specialized Facilities... 139
    Forensic Psychiatric and Treatment Centres 140
    Indigenous Healing Lodges 140
Security.. 140
The Attributes of Correctional Institutions 140
    Prisons Are Asked to Pursue Conflicting Goals................. 140
    Prisons Are Political and Public Institutions 141
    Prisons Are Total Institutions 141
Roles and Responsibilities in Correctional Institutions................. 142
Incarceration in Canada.. 146
    Trends in Federal Inmate Populations, 2005 to 2015 146
The Challenges of Operating and Managing Correctional Institutions 146
    Meeting the Requirements of Legislation and Policy 146
    Increasing Accountability and the Rule of Law and Justice......... 147
    Managing Staff 147
    Conditions in Correctional Institutions 148
    The Growth in Remand Populations......................... 149
    The Changing Offender Profile 150
    Elderly Inmates 151
    The Mentally Ill 151
    Offenders Suffering from Trauma 153
    Offenders with Fetal Alcohol Spectrum Disorder 153
    Overcrowding 154
        The Impact of Overcrowding 154
    Inmate Gangs 155
    Ensuring Inmate Safety..................................... 156
    Preventing Disorder and Disturbances......................... 156
    The Use of Segregation 157
        The Use of Administrative Segregation 158
        Admissions to Segregation.............................. 158
        The Debate over Solitary Confinement 158
        The Impact of Solitary Confinement 159
    Health Issues and Infectious Diseases......................... 160
    High-Risk Behaviour....................................... 161
        Prevention Strategies 161
        Interdiction Strategies 162
    Detention and Correctional Facilities in the North.............. 163

The Effectiveness of Incarceration *163*
Summary *166*
Key Points Review *166*
Key Term Questions *167*
Critical Thinking Exercise *168*
Class/Group Discussion Exercise *168*
Media Links *169*
Notes *169*

Chapter 7   Working Inside: The Experience of Correctional Officers. 175

Roles and Responsibilities 176
Recruitment and Training 177
    Correctional Service Canada. 177
    Provincial/Territorial Training 178
Going Inside: The Socialization of New Correctional Officers. 179
Patterns of Relationships among COs 180
A Typology of COs 181
    Dualists 181
    Punishers 182
    Moral Relativists 182
CO–Inmate Relationships and Patterns of Accommodation. 183
    The Agendas of COs. 185
    Exercising Authority: COs' Discretion and Decision Making. 186
The Exercise and Abuse of Power 187
    Use of Force 188
Ethics, Professionalism, and Corruption 190
Relationships with the Prison Administration 191
Relationships with Treatment Staff. 191
Stress Among Correctional Officers. 192
    Threats to Personal Security. 192
    Lack of Support and Respect 193
    The Emphasis on Inmate Rights 193
    Multiple Tasks 194
    Inadequate Training 194
    The Impact on Personal Life 194
    Shift Work. 195
    The Impact of Prison Conditions. 195
    The Impact of Critical Incidents 195
The Experience of Women COs. 197
The Role of Correctional Officer Unions 198
Summary 198
Key Points Review 199
Key Term Questions 200

Critical Thinking Exercises *200*
Class/Group Discussion Exercise *201*
Media Links *202*
Notes 202

Chapter 8   Doing Time: The Experience of Inmates 207

A General Profile of Inmate Populations 207
    Indigenous Offenders 208
    Black Offenders 209
    Gender Identity and Sexual Orientation 209
The Health of Inmate Populations 210
Going Inside 211
Living Inside 212
    The Pains of Imprisonment 214
The Inmate Social System 215
    Inmate Sexual Orientation and Gender Identity 216
    The Inmate Code 216
    Status and Power among Inmates 218
Violence and Exploitation Among Inmates 219
    Institutional Features That Contribute to Violence 219
    Vulnerable Inmates 220
    Sexual Coercion and Rape 221
The Radicalization of Inmates 223
Parting Thoughts on the Inmate Social System 223
Coping with Confinement 224
    Drugs and Contraband 224
    Sexual Gratification 225
    Mature Coping 225
Failing to Cope with Confinement: Self-Injurious
    Behaviour and Suicide 226
    Self-Injurious Behaviour 226
    Suicide 226
Doing Life 227
Prison as "Home": The State-Raised Offender 227
Inmate Relationships and Families 228
    The Children of Inmates 228
    Maintaining Family Ties 229
    The Role of Families in Rehabilitation 230
Inmate Grievances and Complaints 231
Summary 232
Key Points Review 232
Key Term Questions 233
Critical Thinking Exercises 233

Class/Group Discussion Exercises *234*
Media Links *235*
Notes *236*

Chapter 9   Classification, Case Management, and Treatment 243

Classification and Risk Assessment 243
Case Management 245
    Classification Tools and Techniques 247
    Risk and Needs Profiles of Offenders 247
    The Correctional Plan 251
Institutional Treatment Programs 251
    The CSC Integrated Correctional Program Model 252
    Treating High-Risk Offenders: Sex Offender
       Treatment Programs 253
    Short-Changing Low-Risk Offenders? 254
    Community Involvement in Institutional Programs 254
    Inmate Community Services Projects and Activities 255
The Principles of Effective Correctional Treatment 255
Creating the Conditions for Effective Correctional Treatment 256
    Inmate Amenability to Treatment 256
    Inmate Access to Programs and Program Relevance 257
Potential Obstacles to Effective Correctional Treatment 260
    Punishment versus Treatment 260
    Doing Time and Doing Treatment 260
    The Expectations of Rehabilitation 260
    Short Periods of Confinement: Inmate Access to Programs 261
    Low Rates of Inmate Participation and Program Completion 262
    Program Fidelity, Program Drift, and Therapeutic Integrity 262
    The Importance of Throughcare 263
The Ethics of Correctional Treatment 263
Does Correctional Treatment Work? 264
    Measuring the Effectiveness of Correctional Treatment 265
    What Works in Correctional Treatment? 265
    "Nothing Works" versus "Some Things Work":
       The Legacy of Robert Martinson 266
Summary 272
Key Points Review 272
Key Term Questions 273
Critical Thinking Exercises 274
Class/Group Discussion Exercises 275
Media Links 276
Notes 276

PART IV   RETURNING TO THE COMMUNITY: RELEASE, RE-ENTRY, AND REINTEGRATION....281

Chapter 10   Release from Incarceration.................... 282

The Origins of Early Release *282*
The Purpose and Principles of Conditional Release...................... *283*
The Types of Conditional Release............................ *284*
    Judicial Recognizances for Sex Offenders...................... *289*
The Changing Face of Conditional Release *290*
Pre-release Planning *295*
The Parole File *298*
The Parole Hearing Process *300*
The Inmate and Parole Hearings *301*
The Parole Certificate *304*
Victims and Conditional Release *305*
Inmate Appeals *307*
Issues in Parole Board Decision Making *307*
    Boards May Be Subject to Public and Political Influence 307
    The Absence of Clearly Defined Release Criteria 308
    The Absence of Case Information Feedback to Parole
        Board Members.................................. 308
Summary *310*
Key Points Review *311*
Key Term Questions................................. *311*
Critical Thinking Exercises *312*
Class/Group Discussion Exercises *313*
Media Links *314*
Notes.. *318*

Chapter 11   Re-entry and Life After Prison 322

The Reintegration Process.............................. *323*
    Throughcare 324
Coming Back: The Pains of Re-entry *326*
    The Challenges of the Newly Released 327
    The Dynamic Needs of Offenders on Conditional Release 327
        Housing and Homelessness 328
        Physical and Mental Health Needs 328
    The "State-Raised" Offender and Re-entry.................... 329
Parole Officers and the Supervision of Offenders.................... *329*
    The Dual Function of Parole Supervision 331
    Parole Officer Safety: A Death in Yellowknife................. 332
Re-entry Courts: A Problem-Solving Approach *333*

Special Offender Populations on Conditional Release *333*
   High-Risk Offenders. 334
   Mentally Ill Offenders. 334
   Long-Term Offenders. 334
   Sex Offenders. 335
      Provincial/Territorial Programs for Sex Offenders. 336
      Managing the Risks of Sex Offenders 336
      Sex Offender Registries 336
Community Notification. *337*
GPS and Electronic Monitoring *339*
Suspension and Revocation of Conditional Release *339*
Making It or Going Back: Factors in the Success or Failure
  of Offenders on Conditional Release *340*
   Success on Conditional Release 340
      Re-entry and Social Support/Family Relationships 340
      Community Support. 340
      Innovations in Community Assistance
        and Supervision. 341
      Participation in Correctional Programming 341
      Utilizing the RNR Model in Community Supervision 342
Reoffending *343*
Circles of Support and Accountability (COSAs): A Restorative,
  Reintegrative Practice for High-Risk Sex Offenders *343*
Summary *349*
Key Points Review *350*
Key Term Questions *350*
Critical Thinking Exercises *351*
Class/Group Discussion Exercises *352*
Media Links *353*
Notes. *353*

PART V   SPECIAL POPULATIONS IN CORRECTIONS 361

Chapter 12 Women Offenders 362

The Evolution of Corrections Policy for Women Offenders *364*
   The Incident at the Kingston Prison for Women (P4W):
     A Watershed Event in Women's Corrections. 365
The Current State of Corrections Policy and Practice for Women Offenders . . . *367*
Alternatives to Confinement. *367*
Doing Time: Inside Women's Correctional Facilities *367*
   Violence inside Women's Institutions. 371
   A Pain of Imprisonment: Women Inmates and Their Children 371
      Mother–Child Programs 373

Psychological Health: Self-Injurious Behaviour (SIB) and Suicide . . . 374
    The Death of Ashley Smith 376
    Mental Health Issues. 378
    Physical Health 379
    Evaluation of Services for Women Offenders 381
Cross-Gender Staffing in Women's Institutions 382
Treatment Interventions. 382
    The Classification of Women Offenders 383
    Treatment Programs for Women Offenders
    and Their Effectiveness. 383
Re-entry and Life After Prison 388
Summary 391
Key Points Review 391
Key Term Questions 392
Critical Thinking Exercises 392
Class/Group Discussion Exercises 393
Media Links 394
Notes 395

Chapter 13 Indigenous Offenders 401

Indigenous Peoples in Canadian Society: The Legacy of Colonization 401
Indigenous Over-Representation in the Criminal Justice System 402
    Indigenous Women Offenders 404
Addressing Indigenous Over-Representation in the Justice System 406
Initiatives in Indigenous Corrections 406
    Indigenous Organizations 406
    Indigenous Healing Centres and Lodges 407
Indigenous Inmates and Treatment Interventions 409
    The CSC's Aboriginal Corrections Continuum of Care 411
    The CSC ICPM Initiative 412
    The Circle of Care for Indigenous Women Offenders 412
Challenges in Treatment for Indigenous Offenders. 413
Indigenous Persons and Conditional Release. 413
    Indigenous Inmates and the Parole Board 415
    Indigenous Offenders on Conditional Release. 416
*The Effectiveness of Selected Indigenous-Focused Correctional
    Programs and Interventions* 417
Summary 423
Key Points Review 424
Key Term Questions 424
Critical Thinking Exercises 425
Class/Group Discussion Exercises 425
Media Links 426
Notes 427

Chapter 14 Young Offenders 432

The Evolution of Youth Corrections *432*
    Bill C-10 and the Youth Criminal Justice System 434
A Profile of Young Offenders *435*
    Indigenous Young Offenders 436
Diversion *438*
Sentencing Young Offenders *439*
    Youth Probation 441
        Supervising Youth on Probation 442
        Risk/Needs Assessments and Case Management 443
    Custodial Sentences for Young Offenders 444
Doing Time *445*
Treatment Programs *446*
    Institutional Treatment Programs 447
    Youth–Staff Relationships 448
Risk Assessment in Youth Corrections *449*
Restorative Justice Approaches and Young Offenders *450*
Aftercare Programs *453*
    The Role of Informal Social Support Networks 453
The Journey of an Ex-Dangerous Offender *458*
Summary *459*
Key Points Review *460*
Key Term Questions *461*
Critical Thinking Exercises *461*
Class/Group Discussion Exercises *462*
Media Links *462*
Notes *463*

PART VI   GOING FORWARD: REFORMING CORRECTIONS 471

Chapter 15 Creating Effective Systems of Corrections 472

Challenges for Systems of Corrections *472*
    Developing and Implementing Evidence-Based Correctional
        Policies and Programs 473
    Addressing the Needs of Victims 473
    Providing Adequate Health Care for Inmates 473
    Addressing the Needs of Offenders with Mental Health Issues 474
    The Over-Representation of Indigenous Persons and Blacks
        in Canadian Prisons 474

Corrections in the Canadian North 474
The Systemic Failures of Corrections Systems 475
   Manitoba... 476
   British Columbia 477
   Ontario 477
Politics and Correctional Policy and Practice 478
Reforming Corrections: A Way Forward 479
Evidence-Based Policies and Programs 479
Early Intervention with At-Risk Youth...................... 480
Reducing the "Pains" Experienced by Offenders
   and Their Families.................................... 481
Addressing the Needs of Offenders 481
Addressing the Needs of Victims 482
Acknowledging the Limits of Technology 482
Adhering to the Rule of Law and Respecting the Rights
   of Offenders... 483
Improving the Effectiveness of Community Corrections 483
Reforming Correctional Institutions 484
Expanding Alternatives to Confinement 485
Addressing the Unique Challenges of Provincial/Territorial
   Systems of Corrections 486
Understanding the Experience of Offenders 486
Corrections in the Global Community....................... 486
Moving Away from a Punitive Penology 487
Expanding Effective Interventions: What Works in Corrections 487
Corrections as a Restorative Process: Time for a Rethink?........ 488
Mobilizing the Community: Maintaining Human and Helping
   Relationships 489
Developing Models of Correctional Practice for a Diverse Society .. 489
More Research on Canadian Corrections 490
Is Privatization the Answer? 491
The Unique Position of Corrections in the Criminal Justice System 492
Key Questions Going Forward 493
Final Thoughts 494
Summary 495
Key Points Review 495
Key Term Questions 496
Critical Thinking Exercises 497
Class/Group Discussion Exercises 498
Media Links 498
Notes... 499

Glossary of Key Terms 503
Index 515

List of Boxes

Box 1.1   Perspectives on Crime, Criminal Offenders,
           and the Criminal Justice System 7
Box 1.2   Sociological Perspectives on Punishment 12
Box 4.1   Factors Considered in Sentencing 83
Box 4.2   You Be the Judge 84
Box 10.1   Release Options for Federal and
           Provincial/Territorial Inmates 286
Box 13.1   Community Holistic Circle Healing Program, Hollow Water,
           Manitoba 407
Box 13.2   The Pê Sâkâstêw Centre 409

List of Figures

Figure 3.1   Flow of Cases Through the Criminal Justice System 47
Figure 3.2   The Criminal Justice Funnel 48
Figure 3.3   Admissions to Adult Correctional Services,
             by Type of Supervision and Jurisdiction, 2015–16 52
Figure 3.4   Organizational Impacts on the Adult Correctional System . . 53
Figure 3.5   Offenders Under the Responsibility of the CSC, 2015 55
Figure 3.6   The Relationships of Restorative Justice 65
Figure 3.7   Restorative Justice: Entry Points in the
             Criminal Justice System 65
Figure 4.1   Outline of the Canadian Court System 73
Figure 5.1   Components of the Pre-sentence Report 114
Figure 6.1   The External and Internal Environments
             of a Correctional Institution 141
Figure 6.2   Organizational Chart of a Federal
             Correctional Institution 143
Figure 7.1   Dynamics of the CO–Inmate Relationship 185
Figure 8.1   Federal Inmate Population, 2016 210
Figure 9.1   Offender Intake Assessment Process 245
Figure 9.2   Estimated Percentage of Identified Treatment
             Needs—Calgary Remand Centre 250
Figure 9.3   Adults in Sentenced Custody, by Type of Rehabilitative
             Need, Saskatchewan, 2010–11 250
Figure 9.4   Program Completion of a Sample of B.C.
             Provincial Inmates 259
Figure 10.1 Sentencing Milestones 285
Figure 10.2 The Federal Offender Population 290
Figure 10.3 The Percentage of Offenders Released from
             Federal Penitentiaries on Day and Full Parole 291
Figure 10.4 The Percentage of Offenders Released from
             Federal Penitentiaries at Statutory Release 292

Figure 10.5 Grant Rates for Federal and Provincial
Day Parole, 2010–11 to 2014–15 293

Figure 10.6 Grant Rates for Federal and Provincial Full Parole,
2010–11 to 2014–15 294

Figure 10.7 Participant Views on the Most Beneficial Services
Offered in IOM 297

Figure 10.8 Participant Suggestions for Other Assistance That
Could Be Added to IOM 298

Figure 11.1 The Reintegration Process for Federal Offenders 324

Figure 11.2 Federal Releases from Institutions and Graduations
to Subsequent Federal Supervision Periods 325

Figure 11.3 The Complex Web of Reintegration:
A Case Study of Releases in Ontario 330

Figure 11.4 The Key Principles of COSAs 344

Figure 11.5 Conceptual Model of a Circle of Support:
Relationships of the Circle within the Community 345

Figure 12.1 Women Federal Inmates on Psychotropic Medication 379

Figure 13.1 The 13 Phases of the Hollow Water Community
Holistic Circle Healing Process 408

Figure 14.1 Structure of the Youth Justice System under
the YCJA 435

List of Tables

Table 1.1 The Objectives of Punishment 14

Table 3.1 The "Who" of Noncarceral
and Carceral Corrections 51

Table 3.2 Per Day and Annual Costs of Supervision,
British Columbia 58

Table 3.3 Selected Recommendations Made
by Provincial Ombudspersons 60

Table 3.4 Selected Examples of Private, Not-for-Profit
Agencies and Their Activities 61

Table 3.5 Comparison of Retributive and Restorative
Justice Principles 66

Table 4.1 Sentencing Options and Case Examples 77

Table 4.2 Comparison of Traditional Courts
and Problem-Solving Courts 87

Table 4.3 The Objectives, Processes, and Effectiveness
of Specialized Courts 89

Table 4.4 Comparison of the Criminal Court Process
and Restorative Justice 90

Table 4.5 Differences between Criminal Court and
Circle Sentencing Principles 91

Table 5.1 The Uses of Probation 110

Table 5.2   Probation versus Parole: What's the Difference? 111
Table 5.3   The Activities of Probation Officers 113
Table 6.1   Positions, Roles, and Responsibilities in a Federal
             Correctional Institution 144
Table 7.1   Rank, Responsibilities, and Remuneration of Federal
             Correctional Officers 179
Table 14.1   Noncustodial Sentence Options
             for Young Offenders 440
Table 14.2   Custodial Sentences for Young Offenders 444
Table 14.3   Selected Restorative Justice Programs
             for Young Offenders 451

List of "CORRECTIONS FILE" Features

Corrections File 2.1   Entries from *The Punishment Book
                        of the Prison* (1843) 25
Corrections File 2.2   Symbol of Discipline: The Bell 26
Corrections File 2.3   A Typical Daily Menu for Inmates in the
                        Manitoba Penitentiary in the Late 1880s 27
Corrections File 2.4   The Eras of Prison Architecture and the
                        Philosophies of Corrections 33
Corrections File 2.5   Commissions and Inquiries into Systems
                        of Corrections 36
Corrections File 3.1   Inmate Access to Library Materials 59
Corrections File 4.1   Break and Enter, Possession of Credit Cards,
                        Theft Under 93
Corrections File 5.1   Types of Supervision Orders 116
Corrections File 5.2   Violence Prevention Program (VPP) 121
Corrections File 5.3   A Probation Officer's Account of the Impact of
                        Occupational Stress 123
Corrections File 5.4   Probation in the Remote North 126
Corrections File 6.1   The Case of Adam Capay 159
Corrections File 7.1   A Profile of Use-of-Force Incidents in Federal
                        Correctional Institutions, 2013–14 to 2015–16 .. 189
Corrections File 7.2   The Excessive Use of Force in Ontario
                        Provincial Institutions 189
Corrections File 8.1   A Typical Day in the Life of a Prisoner on
                        Remand in Ontario 213
Corrections File 9.1   The Five Phases of Case Management 246
Corrections File 9.2   Selected Risk Assessment Instruments 249
Corrections File 9.3   An Inmate's Responses in a Violence Prevention
                        Program: Trigger Thought Exercise 258
Corrections File 10.1   Are Parole Grant Rates Increasing or
                        Decreasing? Well, It Depends Whom You Ask 294
Corrections File 10.2   Client Feedback on B.C. Corrections'
                        Integrated Offender Management Program ... 297

Corrections File 10.3 Excerpts from a Victim's Written Submission
                       to a Parole Board 306
Corrections File 11.1 The Release and Re-entry of a Sex Offender ... 338
Corrections File 11.2 Joe and His Circle of Support 346
Corrections File 12.1 A Profile of Women Offenders in Corrections... 363
Corrections File 12.2 A Comparison of the Dynamics inside Men's
                       and Women's Correctional Institutions 370
Corrections File 12.3 The Murder of Denise Fayant 372
Corrections File 12.4 CSC and the Use of Segregation amongst Federally
                       Sentenced Women from April 2002 to
                       March 2012 373
Corrections File 12.5 CSC's Methadone Maintenance Treatment
                       Program 381
Corrections File 12.6 Buffalo Sage Wellness House 385
Corrections File 12.7 CSC's Women Offender—High Intensity
                       Program 386
Corrections File 12.8 A Profile of Women Who Sexually Offend 386
Corrections File 12.9 Two Gender-Specific Programs for Provincially
                       Sentenced Women Offenders Incarcerated in
                       British Columbia 387
Corrections File 13.1 Profile of an Indigenous Woman Serving Time
                       in a Federal Correctional Institution 405
Corrections File 14.1 A Profile of Youth Crime and Offenders 437

List of "RESEARCH FILE" Features

Research File 4.1   The Effectiveness of Sentencing 94
Research File 5.1   The Effectiveness of Alternatives to
                    Confinement................................ 127
Research File 6.1   The Effectiveness of Incarceration............... 164
Research File 7.1   Inmate Gambling: A Study of Correctional
                    Officer Discretion........................... 186
Research File 9.1   The Effectiveness of Correctional Treatment
                    Interventions............................... 266
Research File 10.1 The Effectiveness of Conditional Release 309
Research File 11.1 Perspectives of Clients and Service Providers on
                    Community Corrections Services in Hamilton,
                    Ontario: A Case Study 341
Research File 11.2 The Effectiveness of Selected Supervision/Control
                    Strategies.................................. 348
Research File 13.1 The Effectiveness of Selected Indigenous-Focused
                    Programs/Interventions 418
Research File 14.1 The Effectiveness of Selected Youth Justice
                    Interventions............................... 454

List of "CORRECTIONS PERSPECTIVE" Features

Corrections Perspective 4.1   Addiction Clinician 86

Corrections Perspective 5.1   Ex-federal Offender 105

Corrections Perspective 5.2   Probation Officer 112

Corrections Perspective 7.1   Former Correctional Officer,
Now Deputy Warden. 176

Corrections Perspective 7.2   Deputy Warden, Federal Correctional
Institution. 183

Corrections Perspective 8.1   Prison Nurse 208

Corrections Perspective 9.1   Sex Offender Treatment Therapist 253

Corrections Perspective 11.1   An Ex-offender Reflects on Re-entry . . . 322

Corrections Perspective 12.1   A Woman Offender's Perspective on
Imprisonment 369

Corrections Perspective 12.2   Treatment Therapist 384

Corrections Perspective 12.3   A Woman Offender's Concerns about
Re-entry. 389

Corrections Perspective 13.1   An Aboriginal Correctional
Program Officer 412

Corrections Perspective 14.1   An Offender's Spouse 433

PREFACE TO THE FIFTH EDITION

This text is designed to provide a comprehensive overview of corrections in Canada. It attempts to capture the dynamics of corrections in this country and to explore the unique attributes of the Canadian correctional enterprise. The materials presented in this text are descriptive and analytical. We have endeavoured to present them in a way that will stimulate your thinking about corrections and capture the intensity of the issues surrounding the response to criminal offenders by systems of corrections.

The public, criminal justice and corrections personnel, and offenders have expressed a considerable amount of frustration, anger, and disappointment with the response to criminal offenders and the operations of correctional systems in Canada over the past 200 years. It often appears that despite the expenditure of considerable time, effort, and money, we are no further ahead in our quest to find successful strategies for preventing and correcting criminal behaviour. Given the pessimism that often surrounds corrections, it would have been quite easy to write a text that focused only on the failures, of which there have been enough to fill volumes. However, to have done so would have been to tell only part of the story. In recent years, there have been some exciting initiatives in corrections, many of which hold great promise.

This text avoids the pessimism that so often characterizes discussions of corrections. It describes community-based and institutional programs and includes the latest research findings. No doubt, the text may raise more questions for you than it answers. This is the nature of scholarly inquiry and of any study of corrections.

It is also important to keep in mind that corrections systems have been assigned a very difficult role: to sanction offenders while providing programs and services designed to reduce the likelihood that the offender will return to a life of crime. The response of correctional systems to offenders in carrying out this mandate has ranged from the brutal to the humane. Nearly always, it has been controversial.

Correctional institutions continue to be beset by violence. HIV/AIDS, hepatitis, and an aging inmate population are among the more significant health-related challenges confronting systems of corrections. For correctional officers and inmates, correctional institutions continue to be unsafe places in which to work and live. The breakdown of the traditional inmate code of conduct has created more unpredictability, and a considerable amount of violence—much of it related to the illicit drug trade—continues as a feature of daily life in correctional institutions.

On the treatment side, Canada continues to be a world leader in the development of effective correctional programs, and there has been some success in implementing programs for Indigenous offenders and women offenders. The research evidence is substantial that correctional treatment programs, if properly implemented, can reduce rates of reoffending. The re-entry of offenders into the community remains an area of concern, and there is increasing scrutiny of parole board decision-making alongside efforts to meet the needs of and to manage the risk posed by special categories of offenders, including sex offenders.

STUDYING CORRECTIONS

There are many different ways to approach the study of systems of correction. The men, women, and youth who become involved in the criminal justice system represent various ethnicities as well as specific categories of offenders. Those categories include white-collar, violent, intellectually disabled, long-term, and sex offenders—and, increasingly, elderly offenders.

For many offenders, criminal behaviour is only a symptom: They may have other difficulties involving their family, peer group, and/or workplace. Although not universally true, many offenders were raised in dysfunctional homes afflicted by alcoholism and violence, and were victims of child abuse (physical, sexual, or psychological) or neglect. Many adult offenders have low levels of formal education, few marketable skills, and low self-esteem. A disproportionate number are Indigenous and Black Canadian, and are increasingly afflicted by mental illness and with fetal alcohol spectrum disorder.

Systems of corrections are not involved in the processes by which vulnerable and marginalized persons become involved in the criminal justice system; however, these systems are tasked with making every effort to provide programs and services that address the needs of these individuals—and to do so in a manner that respects their rights and ensures their safety.

The federal and provincial/territorial governments have developed a variety of programs for vulnerable persons. A number of these initiatives will be discussed throughout the text. They range from Mental Health Courts and Drug Courts that make it possible for offenders to be diverted from the justice system, to specialized post-incarceration programs. Correctional Service Canada (CSC) has developed specialized units for mentally ill offenders in several federal institutions, and probation and parole officers have received training to increase the effectiveness of their efforts.

KEY THEMES IN THE TEXT

There are a number of key themes that are woven throughout this text, discussed in the following sections.

A Critical Perspective on Corrections

In examining any component of the criminal justice system, it is important to maintain a "critical eye"—that is, to look beyond the news headlines, the pronouncements of government and systems of corrections, and other stakeholder groups. The person with a critical eye will ask questions about a particular piece of legislation, a policy, or a program, including the following:

- What were the influencing factors?
- What are the objectives of the initiative?
- Did the initiative achieve its objectives?
- To what extent have attempts to reform systems of corrections been successful, and what are the obstacles to reform?

An informed observer might also ask why, years after the issue was first identified, it was only in 2017 that steps were taken to reduce the use of solitary confinement in federal correctional institutions.

Similarly, questions will be raised about the persons who become involved in the correctional process. This includes the over-representation of Indigenous persons, racialized populations, and marginalized persons in correctional institutions. Questions might include, Is this over-representation due to these groups being more criminal than others? Or are there other forces at work, including disparities in sentencing that result in more racialized populations receiving carceral sentences, and/or the decisions of parole boards that result in these groups spending longer periods of time in confinement?

The discussion in this text will reveal that, far too often, these and other important questions are not asked. Or if they are asked and answered, changes to correctional practice are often not forthcoming.

The Influences on the Response to Crime and Criminal Offenders

How a society responds to crime and criminal offenders at any one point in history is determined in large measure by politics, economics, and sociocultural factors.

Throughout the text, we reveal how political agendas and ideology affect how criminal offenders are viewed and what responses are forthcoming in the criminal courts, in correctional institutions, and in the community. Most recently, this is illustrated by the contrasting approaches to crime and offenders taken by the previous federal Conservative government and its successor, the federal Liberal government.

Exploring the history and evolution of corrections provides insights into the factors that have influenced the different perceptions of criminal offending, the policies that have been developed by corrections in response to this offending, and the objectives of these policies. It is in reviewing correctional history that the "swinging pendulum" of perceptions of offending and the response to criminal offenders is evident.

Corrections, the Rule of Law, and the Rights of Offenders

Historically, little attention was given to the rule of law and the rights of offenders. In the past decade, this has changed. A significant development in Canadian corrections has been the increasing involvement of the courts in hearing cases relating to the rights of offenders. Inmates, for example, have become more proactive in asserting their rights under the Canadian Charter of Rights and Freedoms. This has taken the form of individual inmates suing correctional authorities, and class action suits filed on behalf of inmates alleging that their Charter rights have been violated by the manner in which they are/were treated during confinement. The courts appear to be assuming a much more activist role in hearing and ruling on these cases.

In addition, the interjection of ethics and accountability into discussions of systems of corrections is a relatively recent development. In the early 21st century, there are ongoing debates as to the ethics of correctional policies, such as the use of solitary confinement for inmates and the practice of community notification when sex offenders are released into the community. Issues of ethics and accountability arise throughout the corrections system, and these issues are discussed throughout the text.

For this edition, many of the chapters from the fourth edition have been updated and revised. There are a number of significant events that have occurred since the publication of the fourth edition of the text. This includes the election of a federal Liberal government in 2015 that seems, early its mandate, to be taking a different perspective on the response to criminal offenders.

NEW TO THE FIFTH EDITION

This edition of the textbook captures the dynamics of corrections in Canada in a descriptive and analytical manner designed to stimulate critical thinking. Various themes have been woven throughout, including approaching the topic of corrections with a critical eye by examining whether past reform efforts have been successful, how and why systems of corrections continue to experience issues that were first identified in the mid-19th century, human rights in corrections, and factors that influence the design and use of correctional strategies in Canada. The latter theme involves the examination of how policies that were implemented under the former federal Conservative government have altered the correctional landscape in Canada, and how we have seen, and will continue to see, judicial decision-making and the new federal Liberal government alter some of these policies. These themes are situated amongst earlier content and modifications that reflect the integration of empirical evidence, reports, inquiries, and case studies, amongst other sources, that have been produced since the publication of the fourth edition of the text in 2014.

Some features from the fourth edition remain, including the **Summary**, **Key Points Review**, and **Key Term Questions** sections that are located at the end of each chapter. The following *new* features are located in each chapter, designed to provide students with the opportunity to thoughtfully consider and apply the content and issues presented therein:

- **Critical Thinking Exercises** for students to complete individually and that are amenable to diverse evaluative components (e.g., written reflection activities, presentations).

- **Class/Group Discussion Exercises** typically focus on controversial topics and are amenable to learner-centred classroom activities (e.g., student debates).
- **Media Links** direct students to video and other media online, ranging from documentaries to media reports presenting contentious issues in corrections.
- **Corrections Perspectives**, short vignettes, have been included in many chapters to provide the perspectives of those involved in correctional systems—correctional personnel and offenders alike.

Most of the chapters in the fifth edition also include a new feature, **Corrections File** boxes, that highlight a variety of strategies, practices, and tools that correctional services use when "doing corrections" (e.g., risk assessment tools, Chapter 9), in addition to presenting the experiences of those involved in corrections (e.g., a participant involved in a problem-solving court, Chapter 4).

While **Research File** boxes were utilized in the fourth edition, some have been removed, others updated, and new boxes added altogether. As the title suggests, Research File boxes present up-to-date research findings highlighting various issues in Canadian corrections (e.g., the effectiveness of correctional treatment interventions, Chapter 9).

The paragraphs below provide a chapter-by-chapter review of some of the revised materials in the fifth edition.

Chapter 1 (*Perspectives on Crime and Punishment*) begins with definitions of corrections and correctional change. Discussion has been expanded on early responses to criminal behaviour, the use of imprisonment, and England's influence on the development of corrections in Canada. New content includes an overview of the functions of punishment. The rise of punitive penology and penal populism in Canada are discussed with new content documenting these issues in the United States and that country's relatively recent shift towards decarceration after a period of mass incarceration.

Chapter 2 (*The Origins and Evolution of Canadian Corrections*) presents the influences and events that resulted in the building of the first penitentiary in Canada in 1835, and early features and conditions of the penitentiary and local jails and provincial prisons, among other topics. New content includes discussion of the fiscal costs of Canadian corrections against a backdrop of the punitive legislative changes imposed by the then–federal Conservative government (2006–15), which was a marked departure from the more liberal model of corrections that had prevailed in Canada for decades. Additionally, new content documents the negative performance indicators (e.g., an increase in serious bodily injuries), overcrowding in some federal correctional institutions, and an increase in the representation of Black and Indigenous inmates that resulted from the imposition of these punitive policies.

Chapter 3 (*Contemporary Canadian Corrections*) includes updated statistics and figures describing the flow of cases through the criminal justice system, the breakdown of institutional and community corrections populations, and the fiscal costs of supervising someone in the community versus an institution. Further, new information about a number of human rights obligations and the principles of the rule of law that systems of corrections must adhere to have been included. Also integrated more extensively in this chapter is a discussion of the federal correctional investigator, provincial ombudspersons, and auditors.

Chapter 4 (*Sentencing: Beginning the Corrections Process*) begins with a discussion of the purpose and principles of sentencing and the various sentencing options available to judges. New to this edition are examples of cases where judges have imposed each of the sentencing options, and data documenting the number of dangerous offenders and long-term offenders in Canada. Further, three new cases for the activity "You Be the Judge" are included for students to choose a sentence and provide the rationale and purpose of the sentence, followed by their review of the judge's actual sentence. New content to this chapter also includes a discussion of specialized, problem-solving courts and what is known about their effectiveness.

Chapter 5 (*Alternatives to Confinement*) combines some of the content from Chapters 5 and 6 of the fourth edition of the text. Updated empirical evidence documenting the effectiveness of alternatives to confinement is provided. New content also includes information about the recruitment, training, and pay of probation officers; their professional responsibilities in preparing pre-sentence reports; police–probation partnerships in Canadian jurisdictions; strategies and techniques used by probation officers during motivational interviewing; an example of an intensive supervision probation program operating in Manitoba; stressors amongst women probation officers; and updated statistics on probation officer caseloads.

Chapter 6 (*Correctional Institutions*) describes security levels and attributes of correctional institutions. New content includes an organizational chart depicting positions, roles, and responsibilities in federal correctional institutions, and data describing incarceration in Canada and trends in the federal inmate population from 2005 to 2015. Further, in discussing the challenges of operating and managing correctional institutions, new empirical evidence, case studies, and reports, among other sources, are presented to describe the many challenges and their consequences. New challenges are discussed as well, including the use of administrative segregation and addressing the needs of offenders suffering from trauma.

Chapter 7 (*Working Inside: The Experience of Correctional Officers*) describes the roles and responsibilities of correctional officers (COs). The application process for Correctional Service Canada has been updated, and information on rank, responsibilities, and remuneration included. New research findings have been integrated throughout the chapter. New content also includes Canadian research that identifies a typology of COs in Canada based on the perceptions of former inmates, how an inmate's offence and criminal history may affect interactions between COs and inmates, the effect of communication on the inmate–CO relationship, CO perceptions of appropriate CO–inmate boundaries and relationships, and CO discretion in enforcing institutional infractions against inmate gambling. New data highlights use-of-force incidents in federal correctional institutions and in Ontario's provincial system.

Chapter 8 (*Doing Time: The Experience of Inmates*) includes an updated general profile of inmate populations in Canada with specific attention devoted to Indigenous and Black offenders, given their over-representation in various correctional populations across the country. New content includes a discussion of prisoner gender and sexual identity; the health of inmate populations; a vignette that captures a typical day in the life of a prisoner on remand in Ontario; Canadian research examining the inmate code, power dynamics, and risk mitigation strategies that offenders utilize in Canadian federal prisons; risk of victimization among Canadian prisoners; significant cases pertaining to inmate safety that have come to the attention of the courts; the radicalization of inmates; and deaths in custody. Updated information is provided about the prevalence of self-injurious behaviour and suicide within Canadian prisons, as well as the nature and frequency of inmate grievances and complaints. Updated content addresses the challenges of parental incarceration for children and families, including the obstacles to and costs of visitation.

Chapter 9 (*Classification, Case Management, and Treatment*) describes classification and risk assessment and the tools and techniques used for each. New content includes figures and statistics that highlight the rehabilitative needs of Canadian prisoners. New content also includes a critique of Correctional Service Canada practices, such as how it inadequately prepares institutional parole officers to assess offenders for early release and how it lacks guidelines about the documents required to make informed intake assessments. The discussion of differential amenability to treatment and inmate access to programming has been expanded, and current empirical evidence has been incorporated to explain the effectiveness of diverse correctional treatment interventions.

Chapter 10 (*Release from Incarceration*) begins with an overview of the origins of early release and the purpose and principles of conditional release. Content has been added to the discussion of the types of conditional release options available in Canada, providing insight into the diverse practices across jurisdictions and the practice of detention during the period of statutory release. Updated statistics highlight the changing face of conditional release in Canada, as affected by legislative changes made by the former Conservative government. The chapter also includes updated statistics and information on waivers of parole in Canada, insight into the parole hearing process for sex offenders, an examination of conditions attached to release, victim participation in conditional release hearings, and the effectiveness of various types of conditional release. New content includes a critical examination of the pre-release planning process for prisoners and legislative changes made as part of the Victims Bill of Rights Act (2015).

Chapter 11 (*Re-entry and Life After Prison*) begins with a description of reintegration and throughcare, followed by an updated discussion of recent research documenting the challenges that newly released offenders in Canada experience. More in-depth discussion is provided of the changes Correctional Service Canada made following the death of Louise Pargeter at the hands of her parolee in 2004, which emphasize parole officer safety. The discussion of special populations of offenders on conditional release has been expanded to include recent empirical evidence and current practices in their supervision, with extensive attention devoted to supervising sex offenders. Updated statistics about the success of conditional release populations and other newly released offenders and factors that contribute to success and failure on conditional release have been incorporated. The chapter concludes with an expanded discussion of suspension and revocation of conditional release and the use and effectiveness of Circles of Support and Accountability.

Chapter 12 (*Women Offenders*) presents an updated profile of women offenders in corrections. New content and findings about minimum-security facilities for federally sentenced women and women prisoners and their children, including inmate mother–child programs, has been included. Discussion of the death of Ashley Smith has been expanded to include the conclusion and recommendations of the Coroner's Inquest into her death, Correctional Service Canada's response to the report, and the Office of the Correctional Investigator's critique of CSC for failing to sufficiently address the recommendations. Current research documenting the mental, physical, and criminogenic needs of women offenders is presented, along with initiatives that are designed to address these needs and up-to-date research examining the effectiveness of some of these interventions.

Chapter 13 (*Indigenous Offenders*) includes updated statistics on Indigenous over-representation in the youth and criminal justice systems. New content includes discussion of the 2015 Truth and Reconciliation Commission (TRC) report and the calls to action the TRC has requested of various levels of government. The discussion about Indigenous healing centres and lodges has been expanded, including criticisms of their use. An updated discussion of the criminogenic needs that Indigenous inmates often present upon entry into federal correctional institutions, the treatment interventions Correctional Service Canada offers this population, and the challenges the service experiences in providing these interventions, is provided. The most recent statistics documenting the challenges Indigenous offenders experience applying for, and succeeding on, conditional release are presented.

Chapter 14 (*Young Offenders*) begins with an overview of the evolution of youth corrections in Canada. The chapter includes updated statistics on youth correctional populations in Canada and an updated profile of young offenders, with special attention devoted to Indigenous young offenders who continue to be disproportionately represented within this population.

Updated research findings are integrated throughout the chapter on a variety of practices, such as diversion, restorative justice, and the use and effectiveness of correctional programming for young offenders. By including an overview of the Structured Assessment of Violent Risk in Youth, we have expanded the discussion of risk assessments used in youth corrections.

Chapter 15 (*Creating Effective Systems of Corrections*) contains extensive revisions and new content throughout, ranging from the identification of the challenges for systems of corrections (e.g., providing adequate health care for inmates) to the systemic failures of corrections systems and how politics impact correctional policy and practice. In wrapping up the text, we identify the need to reform corrections through a variety of approaches, including implementing evidence-based policies and programs, reducing the "pains" experienced by offenders and their families, mobilizing the community, and developing models of corrections for a diverse society. We encourage our readers to think critically about corrections and whether, for example, privatization offers a viable solution to some of the systemic issues experienced by Canadian correctional systems.

FROM THE AUTHORS

Every attempt has been made to make this text student-friendly and to ensure that it complements well-taught corrections courses. At the beginning of each chapter, a number of objectives are identified. Boxes highlight research findings and present important issues. Key words are highlighted and defined in the margins and are included in the Glossary. Key Points Reviews, Key Term Questions, links to online resources, Critical Thinking Exercises, and Class/Group Discussion Exercises are located at the end of each chapter. Liberal use is made of figures and charts to illustrate important information.

We hope we have succeeded in our efforts. Should you wish to comment on any aspect of this book or have suggestions on how it can be improved, you can contact us at griffith@sfu.ca and dmurdoch@sfu.ca.

Thanks,
Curt T. Griffiths
Danielle J. Murdoch
Vancouver, British Columbia

INSTRUCTOR RESOURCES

The **Nelson Education Teaching Advantage (NETA)** program delivers research-based instructor resources that promote student engagement and higher-order thinking to enable the success of Canadian students and educators. Visit Nelson Education's **Inspired Instruction** website at www.nelson.com/inspired/ to find out more about NETA.

The following instructor resources have been created for *Canadian Corrections*, Fifth Edition. Access these ultimate tools for customizing lectures and presentations at www.nelson.com/instructor.

NETA Test Bank

This resource was written by Sheila McKinnon-Oke, Dalhousie University. It has been substantially expanded in this edition, with more than 400 multiple-choice questions written according to NETA guidelines for effective construction and development of higher-order questions.

The NETA Test Bank is available in a new, cloud-based platform. **Nelson Testing Powered by Cognero®** is a secure online testing system that allows instructors to author, edit, and manage test bank content from anywhere Internet access is available. No special installations or downloads are needed, and the desktop-inspired interface, with its drop-down menus and familiar, intuitive tools, allows instructors to create and manage tests with ease. Multiple test versions can be created in an instant, and content can be imported or exported into other systems. Tests can be delivered from a learning management system, the classroom, or wherever an instructor chooses. Nelson Testing Powered by Cognero for *Canadian Corrections*, Fifth Edition, can be accessed through www.nelson.com/instructor.

NETA PowerPoint

Microsoft® PowerPoint® lecture slides for every chapter have been created by Marlee Jordan, St. Mary's University. There is an average of 20 slides per chapter, featuring key figures, tables, and topics from *Canadian Corrections*, Fifth Edition. NETA principles of clear design and engaging content have been incorporated throughout, making it simple for instructors to customize the deck for their courses.

Image Library

This resource consists of digital copies of figures, short tables, and photographs used in the book. Instructors may use these jpegs to customize the NETA PowerPoint or create their own PowerPoint presentations. An Image Library Key describes the images and lists the codes under which the jpegs are saved. Codes normally reflect the chapter number (e.g., C01 for Chapter 1), the figure or photo number (e.g., F15 for Figure 15), and the page in the textbooks; for example, C01-F15-pg26 corresponds to Figure 1.15 on page 26.

NETA Instructor Guide

This resource was written by Joshua John Murphy, Simon Fraser University. It is organized according to the textbook chapters and addresses key educational concerns, such as an engaging "What Can I Do In Class?" section, discussion questions, and teaching ideas. Other features include a chapter summary, suggested points to consider for questions posed in the textbook, and "What Can I Do Online?"

ACKNOWLEDGMENTS

We would like to acknowledge the many people in the field of corrections who have contributed information and ideas that have been incorporated into this edition. We would also like to thank the following reviewers, whose comments and suggestions on the fourth edition of the text provided guidance in preparing the fifth edition:

- Darryl Davies, Carleton University
- Jamie Livingston, Saint Mary's University
- Eva Wilmot, Camosun College
- Rai Reece, Humber College
- Tim Williams, MacEwan University

We would also like to acknowledge the students in our corrections courses in the School of Criminology. Their curiosity and criticisms have been a continual source of inspiration. A further debt of gratitude is owed to those offenders and correctional officers and administrators who have shared their experiences and observations of corrections over the years. We would also like to acknowledge Eva Fontaine of Boise State University for her assistance compiling some of the materials for this edition of the textbook.

As always, it has been a pleasure to work with the outstanding publishing team at Nelson: Leanna MacLean, publisher; Suzanne Simpson Millar, content manager; Jessie Coffey, permissions editor; Terry Fedorkiw, marketing manager; and Imoinda Romain, senior production project manager. All brought a high level of enthusiasm, energy, and professionalism to the project and helped make it happen.

ABOUT THE AUTHORS

Curt T. Griffiths is a professor in the School of Criminology at Simon Fraser University.

Danielle J. Murdoch is a lecturer in the School of Criminology at Simon Fraser University.

PART I

CANADIAN CORRECTIONS: SETTING THE FRAMEWORK

The chapters in this opening section of the text provide the foundations for examining the various facets of Canadian corrections. Chapter 1 provides a definition of corrections, identifies the components of correctional change, explores how punishment has evolved since early times, and discusses the factors that have influenced responses to criminal offenders. Also presented are the competing perspectives on crime, criminal offenders, and the criminal justice system, as well as the features of crime and punishment in the early 21st century.

Chapter 2 describes the origins and evolution of Canadian corrections, identifying a number of eras and using prison architecture as an approach to reflect on how the philosophy of corrections has evolved over the decades.

The historical materials in Chapter 1 and Chapter 2 highlight the role that legislation, events, and personalities have played in the response to criminal offenders. The discussion highlights a critical point: Systems of corrections exist within, not apart from, the broader social context. Put another way, society's political, economic, and religious beliefs may strongly influence who is identified as criminal and/or deviant, what sanctions are imposed on those persons so identified, and the objectives of those sanctions.

The materials on the evolution of Canadian corrections will also illustrate the difficulties of using incarceration as a response to criminal offenders. While reforms have been recommended over the decades, many of the issues that confront corrections today arose nearly two centuries ago. This underscores the significant challenges in improving corrections to ensure that communities are safe and that the needs of victims and offenders are addressed.

Chapter 3 sets out the *who* and the *what* of contemporary Canadian corrections and introduces restorative justice as an alternative approach to responding to offenders. The corrections process begins at the sentencing stage of the criminal justice system, and in Chapter 4, the purposes and principles of sentencing as well as sentencing options, including restorative justice approaches, are discussed.

CHAPTER OBJECTIVES

- Define corrections and the indicators of correctional change.
- Discuss how punishment has evolved since early times and the influences on the punishment on criminal offenders.
- Compare and contrast the conservative, liberal, and radical perspectives on crime, criminal offenders, and the criminal justice system.
- Discuss the functions and objectives of punishment.
- Discuss the rise of punitive penology and penal populism.
- Discuss the experience of the United States with punitive penology and the factors that contribute to mass incarceration and to the beginning of mass decarceration.

How societies and groups have chosen to respond to those who violate norms, mores, and laws has varied over the centuries. A review of the history of punishment and corrections reveals several distinct trends. There has been increasing centralization and professionalization of punishment and corrections, with formal agents of control (i.e., police officers, judges, corrections officials) assuming responsibility for identifying, responding to, and sanctioning offenders. Concurrent with this has been an expansion of surveillance and control over offenders. This includes the increasing use of electronic monitoring of offenders in the community and extensive video surveillance in correctional institutions, as well as a diminishing role for the community in the correctional process.

Historically, responses to persons who come into conflict with the law have given little attention to the factors that precipitated the criminal behaviour. And it can be argued that, even today, systems of corrections struggle to address the issues of persons in their charge.

In this chapter, we examine the perspectives on crime, offending, and punishment. Then in Chapter 2, we look at the origins and evolution of Canadian corrections.

A DEFINITION OF CORRECTIONS

Corrections can be defined as the structures, policies, and programs delivered by governments, not-for-profit organizations, and members of the general public to sanction, punish, treat, and supervise, in the community and in correctional institutions, persons convicted of criminal offences. Note that the definition includes punishment and treatment as well as correctional institutions and the supervision of offenders in the community. Also, in this text, the sentencing stage of the criminal justice process is included in the discussion of corrections, as it is at this juncture that the decisions of judges will determine whether the offender will be under the jurisdiction of the federal or provincial/territorial system of corrections, the conditions under which the sentence will be served, and the length of the sentence.

> **Corrections**
> The structures, policies, and programs to punish, treat, and supervise persons convicted of criminal offences.

THE PROCESS OF CORRECTIONAL CHANGE

The response to persons in conflict with the law is dynamic; that is, it changes over time. We can say that correctional change has taken place when one or more of the following occurs: (1) the severity of punishment of convicted offenders is modified; (2) explanations of criminal behaviour change; (3) new structural arrangements, such as the penitentiary, are established in order to sanction offenders; and (4) the number or proportion of offenders involved in the correctional process changes.[1]

Why do these changes occur? Why, for example, did prisons become widely used as punishment in the 18th century? Scholars of penal history study correctional change from a number of perspectives. Some have focused on early reformers' humanitarian ideals; others have argued that prisons were designed primarily to control people who were perceived as threatening the emerging capitalist system of an industrializing Europe. The latter argued that prisons were not intended to be a humane alternative to the death penalty and corporal punishment; rather, they were designed for isolation and punishment.[2]

THE EARLY DAYS

Before there were nation-states and written laws, personal retaliation was the primary response to criminal behaviour. This practice was later augmented by the *blood feud*, in which the victim's family or tribe avenged themselves on the family or tribe of the offender. Before the Middle Ages (i.e., before 500 CE), the responses to criminal offenders were predicated mainly on punishment. The death penalty was carried out by hanging, live burial, stoning, boiling alive, crucifying, or drowning. Corporal punishment was also used, as were exile and fines.

It was during the Middle Ages (roughly from 500 to 1500; also often referred to as *medieval times*) that punishment took its most gruesome forms.

Societies were afflicted by feuding families and tribes.[3] It was a time of death, violence, and disease. Vengeance and blood feuds were common. Various corporal and capital punishments included flogging, branding, stretching (racking), amputations, boiling alive, and other mutilations.[4]

Many of the punishments were designed to publicly stigmatize offenders or to shame them. The historical record indicates that, in the 15th century, petty traitors in England were drawn (cut up) and hung, while in Paris, criminal offenders were burned at the stake, buried alive, or subject to other severe public punishments. The most common capital punishment administered to criminals in Europe at that time was hanging.

These punishments were inflicted primarily upon persons who had threatened the king's peace and for religious offenders.[5] These publicly administered punishments also served a symbolic function of denouncing what was considered evil conduct.

However, the historical record indicates that punishments were not always blood and gore. The majority of offenders were not subjected to these severe forms of punishment.[6] Banishment and exile were extensively used. And in the early Middle Ages, reparations were often used to settle disputes.[7] In these cases, the wrongdoer would make amends by paying money or providing other assistance to the offended party.

The history of imprisonment stretches back to the time of Confucius, circa 2000 BCE, when there is reference to political offenders being exiled and imprisoned.[8] Confinement was often used in Greece until a fine was paid, the person was exiled, or the person committed compulsory suicide.[9] Generally speaking, punishment by imprisonment was rare, confinement being employed mainly to hold those awaiting trial, execution, or corporal punishment or to compel the payment of fines. Ecclesiastical prisons run by the Catholic Church existed as early as the 6th century and were common by the 9th century. At a time when torture and execution were commonly resorted to in many countries, the Catholic Church used imprisonment as a form of punishment. Centuries later, prison design would be influenced by these church prisons, which isolated prisoners, fed them a strict diet, and provided time for self-reflection. In the 1200s, during the Inquisition, accused persons were often held for months or years. Punishment by imprisonment was rarely resorted to until the 1500s in England and the early 1600s in continental Europe.[10]

The British Legacy

Developments in England had an impact on the development of corrections in Canada. The first house of correction in England opened in a former royal palace at Bridewell, in London, in 1557. This facility operated on the principle that subjecting offenders to hard labour was the best solution to the rising population of criminals.

The 1700s saw the start of the Industrial Revolution, which led to the breakdown of England's feudal, rural-centred society. Courts increasingly resorted to the death penalty in an attempt to stem the rise of what the emerging middle class saw as the "dangerous classes." By 1780, under what had become known as the Bloody Code, more than 350 offences were punishable by death.

England disposed of a large number of offenders through transportation, a form of banishment (often resulting in death) that for centuries had been used as a sanction. Between 1579 and 1776, England sent as many as 2,000 offenders every year to her American colonies. Convicts were also confined in hulks—that is, in decommissioned sailing vessels that had been converted into floating prisons, anchored in rivers and harbours. At its peak, the hulk prison system comprised 11 ships holding more than 3,000 prisoners.[11]

There is no simple explanation for why imprisonment became such a core part of the sanctioning process. That it did can be attributed at least in part to a desire to maintain the social order, often at the expense of society's lower classes. That would explain why the use of imprisonment

The *Warrior*, a hulk anchored off Woolwich in 1848, was a floating prison.

© The Print Collector/Alamy Stock Photo

continued to expand even though there was evidence, very early on, that it did little to reduce criminal behaviour. This highlights the symbolic function of imprisonment.

During the late 1700s, John Howard pioneered efforts to reform conditions in English prisons. In his classic work, *The State of Prisons in England and Wales* (1777), he proposed a number of prison reforms, including providing single sleeping rooms for convicts, segregating women and young offenders from men, building facilities for bathing, and employing honest and well-trained prison administrators. Positive changes that resulted from Howard's work and that of other reformers included the prohibition of alcohol sales within prisons and improvements to sanitary conditions.[12]

Although well intentioned, some of Howard's proposals—for example, that offenders be placed in solitary confinement to protect them from the corrupting influences of other convicts and to provide the proper solitude for moral reflection—contributed to the deprivations that convicts experienced (and that many inmates continue to experience). Even so, his humanitarian ideals live on in Canada through the work of the John Howard Society.

PERSPECTIVES ON CRIME, OFFENDERS, AND PUNISHMENT

Punishment
Inflicting a consequence or penalty for wrongdoing, or the consequence or penalty itself.

Punishment is commonly defined as "the act of inflicting a consequence or penalty on someone as a result of their wrongdoing, or the consequence or penalty itself."[13] Who and by what means punishment has been inflicted, as well as the objectives of punishment, have continually changed over the centuries.

Criminologists have pointed out that underlying all of the justifications for punishment are certain assumptions about human nature. Explanations of crime and responses to criminal offenders have always been strongly influenced by social, political, religious, economic, and demographic factors. The types of actions defined as criminal, the explanations for criminal behaviour, the types of sanctions imposed on offenders, and the objectives of those sanctions are always changing. The particular perspective that is taken as to why individuals engage in criminal behaviour influences the sanctions imposed and the objectives of those sanctions.

There are many competing perspectives on crime and criminal offenders and on what the objectives of corrections should be. Generally, these approaches can be categorized as conservative, liberal, or radical (see Box 1.1).

The Classical (Conservative) School

During the 18th century, later known as the Age of Enlightenment, a number of ideas emerged that would strongly influence Western society's perception of and response to criminal offenders. During this time, a transition occurred from corporal punishment to imprisonment as a frequent form of punishment.

Perspectives on Crime, Criminal Offenders, and the Criminal Justice System

	Conservative	Liberal	Radical
View of capitalism and the Canadian political system	Principles are fundamentally sound.	Principles need improvement. Need greater economic and social equality.	Principles are fundamentally unsound and exploitive. Need to change to socialism.
Reason for crime	Social disorder—lack of discipline in society: Traditional institutions and values have broken down. Lenient criminal justice system—"crime pays."	Poverty, racism, and other social injustices: Society is not meeting human needs, and crime is a manifestation of this inadequacy in our system.	Capitalist exploitation: The rich exploit the poor and the poor prey on one another.
Ways to stop crime	Re-establish social order and discipline. Reassert traditional values that made Canada great. Increase the costs of crime through stiffer punishments.	Make a better social order through reform. Establish social programs to meet the needs of the disadvantaged. Establish a more humane and just criminal justice system. Focus on rehabilitation of the offender.	Eliminate the capitalist system and establish a new social order.

(continued)

	Conservative	Liberal	Radical
Focus of corrections	On the victim of crime and on innocent citizens: Offender commits crime through free will.	On the criminal: Help the disadvantaged criminal and prevent future victimization of society. Crime is a result of adverse social conditions, though increasingly, the attention is on the individual offender, who is easier to change than underlying social conditions.	On the inherent inhumanity of the system; Crime is a result of the way society is structured; any attempt to reduce crime must focus on the system rather than on individual offenders. Criminal justice system is used to repress the lower classes.
Source of crime problem	Street crime.	Street and white-collar crime.	The crime of capitalism and the rich.
Primary values	Social order—"law and order."	Protection of individual rights and humane treatment of the less advantaged—"doing justice" and "doing good."	Total economic and social equality—"no classes and no exploitation."
Historical influences	The classical and neoclassical schools of criminology; the notion of deterrence.	The positivist school of criminology.	The writings of Karl Marx and contemporary critical criminologists, including Welch and Lynch, Michalowski, and Groves.

	Conservative	Liberal	Radical
Strengths of the perspective	Focuses on efforts to maintain social order as a determinant of correctional strategies. Emphasizes the role of free will in criminal behaviour.	Considers the role of environmental factors in crime. Attempts to treat and rehabilitate offenders by giving them skills to manage their lives.	Highlights the roles of economics and politics in the development and operation of justice systems. Considers the role of race and class in crime and administration of justice and highlights the over-representation of Indigenous people and racialized groups in corrections. Examines systems of corrections as an industry.
Weaknesses of the perspective	Fails to consider any external causes of crime. Ignores the role of societal conditions such as poverty, race, and discrimination as contributors to criminal behaviour. Relies on reason alone to explain and respond to crime.	Fails to consider the role of free will in crime. Ignores the potential role of psychological and biological factors in crime. May result in net-widening and more persons under supervision in an attempt to meet their needs. Exclusive focus on individual offender may distract from an examination of broader social injustices.	Few empirical studies. Socialist agenda ignores broad public support for most laws. Gives little attention to victims.

This change was due in large measure to the writings of Enlightenment philosophers such as Montesquieu, Voltaire, Cesare Beccaria, and Jeremy Bentham, who embodied the **classical (conservative) school** of punishment and correction.

The classical school held that offenders were exercising free will and that they engaged in criminal behaviour as a result of rational choices.

In his major work, *Essay on Crime and Punishments* (1764), Beccaria argued that the gravity of the offence should be measured by the injury done to society and that certainty of punishment was the most effective deterrent against criminal behaviour. Furthermore, punishments that were too severe served only to embitter offenders and perpetuate criminal conduct.

It was Jeremy Bentham, the leading reformer of English criminal law during the 18th century, who coined the term *hedonistic calculus*. He held that the main objective of intelligent human beings was to achieve the most pleasure while receiving the least amount of pain. Sanctions, it followed, should be applied to ensure that the pain resulting from the punishment outweighed any pleasure derived from committing the offence; also, the punishment should be no greater than necessary to deter the potential offender. For Bentham, imprisonment was a more precise measure of punishment than corporal punishments: the more heinous the crime, the longer the period of confinement. In this view, criminal behaviour was not influenced by external societal factors or by deterministic forces internal to the offender; rather, the offender was responsible for their crimes.

According to the classical school, the primary goal of the criminal justice system should be deterrence, not revenge, and to be effective, punishment must be certain and must fit the crime. A person can be dissuaded from committing a crime by the spectre of certain, swift, and measured consequences. This has been the perspective of recent "tough on crime" approaches of the sort that involve mandatory minimum sentences (see Chapter 4) and mass incarceration to reduce crime rates.

A number of criticisms have been levelled at the classical school with its emphasis on free will. Foremost among them is that it ignores the role of external factors such as poverty and racism.[14] Also, there is no evidence that tougher sanctions and zero-tolerance policies in themselves contribute to specific or general deterrence, in the absence of attempts to address other, more individualized factors that may have contributed to criminality (e.g., addiction). Also, incarceration policies are expensive, especially when you consider that many offenders who thereby land in prison would otherwise have been diverted to other, less costly forms of supervision in the community. The recent fiscal crisis in the United States has prompted legislators and policy-makers to reconsider laws and policies that rely heavily on incarceration and in some cases to roll them back (see "Mass Incarceration and the Move toward Decarceration in the United States," later in this chapter).

> **Classical (conservative) school**
> A perspective on criminal offenders and punishment based on the view that offenders exercise free will and engage in criminal behaviour as a result of rational choice, and that punishment must be swift, certain, and severe.

In retrospect, Beccaria and Bentham and their contemporaries were somewhat successful in mitigating the severity of punishments imposed on offenders.

The Positivist (Liberal) School

The **positivist (liberal) school**, as set out in the writings of Cesare Lombroso, Enrico Ferri, and Raffaelo Garafalo in the 1800s, held that criminal behaviour was determined by biological, psychological, physiological, and/or sociological factors. It followed that the scientific method should be used to study criminal behaviour and identify criminal types.

From the positivist perspective, criminal offenders are fundamentally different from others in society, so explanations for crime should centre on the individual rather than on society. Sanctions should focus on treatment and be individualized so that they reflect the unique qualities of the offender. The positivist perspective calls for "selective incapacitation," whereby only serious offenders likely to commit heinous crimes are sent to prison. This is contrary to the mass incarceration that often results from laws and policies informed by the classical perspective.

One weakness of the positivist perspective is that it fails to consider the role of free will in criminal offending.

> **Positivist (liberal) school**
> A perspective on criminal offenders and punishment based on the view that criminal behaviour is determined and that offenders require individualized treatment.

The Critical (Radical) School

In contrast to the preceding, the **critical (radical) school** focuses on power and control. Its explanations of crime centre on the exploitative nature of the capitalist system, which uses the justice system to oppress the lower classes. This perspective was first set out by Karl Marx and is reflected to this day in the work of critical social theorists, including convict criminologists (i.e., those with a criminal background).

Proponents of this perspective point out that for centuries, the justice system has drawn into its clutches a disproportionate number of persons who are impoverished and who live on society's margins. These people also suffer high rates of mental illness, addiction, and homelessness and often have few skills. A prominent theme among critical social theorists has been the emergence of a prison-industrial complex that profits from laws and policies (e.g., the war on drugs) that render marginal people more susceptible to punishment. This in turn leads to mass incarceration, which does nothing to contribute to a safer society.[15]

A weakness of this perspective is that it can fail to consider individual factors that may be related to criminal behaviour. Another is that it pays little attention to the victims of crime and the impact of criminal offending on communities.

> **Critical (radical) school**
> A perspective on crime, offenders, and punishment that highlights the role of economics, politics, power, and oppression in the formulation of laws and the administration of justice.

THE FUNCTIONS OF PUNISHMENT

Historically and in contemporary times, there have been various perspectives offered on the functions of punishment. One observer, for example, has noted that the study of punishment by sociologists has been characterized by "a noisy clash of perspectives and an apparently incorrigible conflict of different interpretations and varying points of view." The works of Emile Durkheim, Karl Marx, and Michel Foucault illustrate the range of perspectives of punishment and its role in society.[16] See Box 1.2.

Sociological Perspectives on Punishment

Historically, sociologists have made significant contributions to the study of punishment and its functions in society. Three prominent scholars represented in the literature are Emile Durkheim, Karl Marx, and Michel Foucault.

For Durkheim, punishment was a moral process that served to reinforce and preserve shared values and norms in society. Punishment not only sanctioned offenders, but served to strengthen the solidarity of the social order. The criminal law, through which punishment was administered, reflected core moral values.

The rituals of punishment, including the use of incarceration, were expressive: "In reacting against violators of the conscience collective, penal institutions demonstrate the material force of basic social values and restore collective confidence in the integrity and power of the moral order. . . . Punishment is directed less at the individual offender than at the audience of impassioned onlookers whose cherished values and security had been momentarily undermined by the offender's actions."[17]

Emile Durkheim (1858–1917). French sociologist, social psychologist, and philosopher

Pictorial Press Ltd/Alamy Stock Photo

Among the critiques of Durkheim's perspective on punishment is the argument that the law and the response to offenders may serve to marginalize certain groups in the community, thereby promoting divisions rather than solidarity. This may occur, for example, when legislation criminalizes a portion of the population for behaviour such as drug use.[18]

The Marxist perspective focuses on punishment as an instrument of the ruling class to preserve the economic order and ensure maintenance of the status quo. This includes the subjugation of marginalized persons and groups. Penal policies are used to maintain class rule and are part of a wider strategy to control the poor. The high numbers of vulnerable and marginal persons in the criminal justice and corrections systems are cited in support of this perspective. On the other hand, Marx did not consider that there is broad public support for most laws.

In his book, *Discipline and Punish* (1975), Foucault documented the transition from corporal and capital punishment to the expanded use of prisons in the late 1700s. This evolution was viewed as a shift from traditional punishments focused on the crime to efforts to understand criminals and their offences in order to effect reformation. Punishment moved from the public realm into the invisible confines of the prison and experts became involved in efforts to reform individuals. In his seminal work, Foucault sought to analyze punishment in its social context, and to examine how changing power relations affected punishment. In his view, the calls for reform of punishment in the 18th century were due not to a concern for the welfare of prisoners, but to increase the efficiency of the exercise of power over individuals. The prison was a manifestation of this total control over offenders, and the so-called Enlightenment, in Foucault's view, was nothing more than increased oppression.

Karl Marx (1818–1883). German philosopher, economist, sociologist, journalist, and revolutionary socialist

Everett Historical/Shutterstock.com

Michel Foucault (1926–1984). French philosopher, historian of ideas, social theorist, philologist, and literary critic

INTERFOTO/Alamy Stock Photo

THE OBJECTIVES OF PUNISHMENT

Closely related to the perspectives on crime and criminal offenders are the objectives of punishment. There are four principal justifications for punishing criminal offenders: retribution, deterrence, incapacitation, and rehabilitation/reintegration (see Table 1.1). These, in turn, are associated with how criminal behaviour is viewed.

Table 1.1   The Objectives of Punishment

	Retribution	Deterrence	Incapacitation	Rehabilitation/ Reintegration
Justification	Moral	Prevention of further crime	Risk control	Offenders have deficiencies
Strategy	None; offenders simply deserve to be punished	Make punishment more certain, swift, and severe	Offenders cannot offend while in prison; reduce opportunity	Treatment to reduce offenders' inclination to reoffend and assist in re-entry into the community
Focus of perspective	The offence and just desserts	Actual and potential offenders	Actual offenders	Needs of offenders
Image of offenders	Free agents whose humanity we affirm by holding them accountable	Rational beings who engage in cost/benefit calculations	Not to be trusted but to be constrained	Good people who have gone astray; will respond to treatment

Source: M. Stohr, A. Walsh, and C. Hemmens. *Corrections: A Text/Reader*, p. 13. Copyright © 2009 by SAGE Publications, Inc. Reprinted by permission of SAGE Publications, Inc.

As we will see throughout the text, Canada's laws and systems of corrections have long been influenced by the various punishment perspectives. In short, ideas on punishment go in and out of fashion. There is a "swinging pendulum" wherein at certain points in history, there has been an emphasis on one punishment perspective, while at other times, other perspectives have predominated.[19] A myriad of factors may explain shifts in perspectives on punishment and its objectives, including changes in the political landscape, economics, social movements, and perceived threats to the safety and security of citizens. In Chapter 2, to illustrate these changing perspectives on crime, offenders, and punishment, we will trace the emergence of the prison in Canada and show how prison architecture reflects philosophies of corrections.

CORRECTIONS, PUNITIVE PENOLOGY, AND PENAL POPULISM

A key concept in understanding corrections is that of **punitive penology**, which is characterized by laws and correctional policies that increase the severity of criminal sanctions and that expand the control exercised over offenders by systems of corrections.

The consequences of this phenomenon may include "tough-on-crime" legislation, including an increase in mandatory minimum sentences, increased carceral populations, a de-emphasis on rehabilitation programs, and fewer resources directed toward community-based programs and services for offenders.[20]

Penal populism occurs when politicians advance "tough-on-crime" policies that appeal to the public in order to improve their chances of re-election but that do little to reduce crime rates or to ensure that justice is done. These policies often do not reflect public opinion, or they are formulated in the absence of an informed public.[21]

Penal populism is visible in calls for more severe sanctions, such as mandatory minimum sentences and American-style three-strikes-you're-out laws. Under these laws, passed in many U.S. states, persons who have three felony convictions ("three strikes") are sentenced to life in prison with no possibility of release ("you're out!"). Penal populism may make it difficult to secure funding and support for treatment and rehabilitation programs within correctional institutions and in the community.

A good example of punitive penology and penal populism is provided by the response to criminal offenders in the United States and how this has changed in recent years. The discussion in Chapter 2 will reveal that Canada has experienced a similar process whereby a punitive penology was implemented by a federal Conservative government, only to be challenged by the successor Liberal government.

MASS INCARCERATION AND THE MOVE TOWARD DECARCERATION IN THE UNITED STATES

A brief examination of law and corrections policy in the United States provides insights into the factors that influence the response to criminal offenders.

In the 1970s, criminal justice policies in the United States began to shift their focus away from rehabilitation toward retribution. This was driven by legislators, who assumed a more prominent role than criminal justice policy-makers in determining the response to criminal offenders.[22] Punishment had emerged as a political issue. As a result, indeterminate sentences were replaced with determinate (fixed) ones, including mandatory minimum sentences; also, habitual offender laws were passed, such as (in many states) "three-strikes-you're-out" laws—that is, three felony convictions meant life with no possibility of parole. A "war on drugs" was declared, and zero-tolerance charging policies were introduced.

Punitive penology
A response to criminal offenders characterized by severe criminal sanctions, including "tough-on-crime" legislation.

Penal populism
Corrections policies that are formulated in pursuit of political objectives, often in the absence of an informed public or in spite of public opinion, and that are centred on being "tough on crime."

The purpose of these initiatives was to reassure the public that something was being done about the crime problem.[23] Incapacitation, rather than rehabilitation, became the strategy whereby communities would be made safe.

From 1990 to 2010, the number of federal prison inmates in the United States rose more than 500 percent. In the early 21st century, *one in nine* black American men between 20 and 34 was a prisoner at any given time, and *one in four* either had been or was presently incarcerated.[24] The advent of mass incarceration in the United States has been extensively documented.[25] As one observer has noted, however, "Mass imprisonment is not a consequence of increased criminal activity; it is a state-made disease."[26]

By the early 21st century, however, many American states were confronting the fiscal realities associated with their "get tough" policies, and this began an era of what has been referred to as *mass decarceration*. This was due to a number of factors, including the high costs of incarcerating large numbers of offenders; court decisions holding that overcrowding in correctional institutions was unconstitutional; the efforts of advocacy groups and researchers arguing that drug laws, in particular, were discriminatory against racialized groups; and evidence that incarceration was not increasing the safety and security of communities, nor reducing the rates of reoffending. It is estimated that mass incarceration costs the United States at least $182 billion annually.[27]

Many state legislatures had found the price of incarceration too high and the deterrent value of it too low. In 2009, California's state auditor estimated that three-strikes offenders would cost the taxpayers an extra $19.1 billion for the time they spent incarcerated.[28] Around this time, a review of 49,000 of the 134,000 inmates incarcerated in California correctional institutions found that drug addiction was the major problem that these offenders were facing. Yet statistics indicated that only 15 to 20 percent of all offenders were receiving any treatment, which placed them at risk of committing further offences when they were released.

The three-strikes laws were found not to be a deterrent to serious crime.[29] Highly publicized cases of wrongful conviction have led to the reduced use of the death penalty and even to its abolition in several states. Many observers see these developments as marking the advent of "penal moderation"—that is, a shift toward less punitive and retributive sanctions.

There was also growing evidence that incarcerating mass numbers of offenders, often for drug-related offences, was not effectively addressing either the offender's or society's needs.[30] As then U.S. Attorney General Eric Holder stated in 2013, "Too many people go to too many prisons for far too long and for no truly good law-enforcement reason."[31]

Concurrent with these developments, a number of courts—including the U.S. Supreme Court—have ruled that when prison overcrowding reaches a certain threshold, it violates the constitutional rights of inmates, and have directed states to reduce prison populations. As a result, thousands of inmates have been released early, thereby overwhelming community corrections programs and their staffs. In 2009, California's prison population fell to its lowest level in 38 years, largely due to the early release of offenders from custody.[32]

Similarly, through the efforts of the police, community organizations, and reform-minded city and state officials in New York, the total local jail and state prison population declined by 55 percent between 1996 and 2014. This occurred at a time when the population of New York City grew by 1 million residents.[33]

The shift in perspective on crime and punishment was captured in the comments of a member of the Illinois State Legislature:

> *There's a real appetite for reform on both the left and the right because people are sick of watching their tax money go toward locking everybody up with no return on their investment. There are a lot of people who need to be in a prison cell; I don't deny that. But ultimately, we need to be smart on crime, not tough on crime.*[34]

The shift in corrections philosophy was also reflected in the Fair Sentencing Act of 2010 (Public Law 111-220). This legislation was passed by the U.S. Congress and signed into federal law. Among other provisions, the law eliminated the five-year mandatory minimum sentence for simple crack cocaine possession. A number of states also passed legislation designed to reduce prison populations and combat mass incarceration. This includes legislation designed to reform sentencing, resulting in reductions in the number of mandatory minimum sentences, reducing penalties for certain offences (particularly drug-related crimes), and expanding the use of probation.[35]

In the state of North Carolina, for example, the Justice Reinvestment Act was passed in 2011. This law made significant changes to sentencing and corrections in the state. In the following years, 10 prisons were closed, additional probation and parole officers were hired to provide better supervision of offenders in the community, and cognitive-behavioural and substance abuse programs were developed for those offenders at greatest risk of reoffending.[36] Many state legislatures increased opportunities for the early release of nonviolent offenders, and shifted their focus to reintegration and community-based treatment programs.[37] Significantly, in most states, these initiatives were supported by both Democrats and Republicans.

More specifically, as of 2016, the states of California, New York, and New Jersey had reduced the size of their prison populations by approximately 25 percent. The crime rates in these states have also declined faster than the U.S. national average.[38] Steep drops in prison populations, including among Blacks and Hispanics, were recorded in other states that invested heavily in community supervision, diversion programs for persons with mental illness, and other re-entry services.[39]

However, as of 2016, it was estimated that nearly 40 percent of U.S. prisoners were still unnecessarily in prison.[43] The majority of these inmates were incarcerated for nonviolent, lower-level offences and could be safely supervised in the community.

There was also a shift in attitudes of the general public. Surveys revealed strong support for a rehabilitative approach to offenders and the use of alternatives to confinement focused on treatment for nonviolent and/or drug offenders. These attitudes were found to exist even in U.S. states such as Texas, which has a history of get-tough correctional policies.[40] Polls of public opinion on crime conducted between 1994 and 2012 had revealed a decline in support for punitive policies, including the death penalty.[41]

All of these developments provide an opportunity for American correctional authorities to begin—or to continue (for those states already doing so, such as North Carolina)—implementing evidence-based programs that hold the potential to reduce reoffending and that provide a continuum of supervision and assistance between the prison and the community. These strategies are discussed in Chapters 10 and 11.

As of 2017, it is difficult to determine whether the decarceration movement in the United States will continue. The election of Donald Trump as president in 2016 may portend a shift back to "get tough" on crime policies, particularly with respect to drug offences. In addition, powerful forces, including correctional officer unions, may resist efforts to reform sentencing laws and to move away from punitive penal policies. The extent to which these factors may affect correctional policy at the state level, however, remains to be seen.[42]

SUMMARY

This chapter has examined the perspectives on crime, criminal offenders, and punishment that have been utilized in response to criminal offending. Explanations of crime and responses to criminal offenders have always been strongly influenced by social, political, religious, economic, and demographic factors and are constantly changing. The three general perspectives of crime, offenders, and the criminal justice system are the classical (conservative), positivist (liberal), and critical (radical). There are also differing views on the functions of punishment and several justifications for punishing criminal offenders.

The late 20th and early 21st centuries were marked by a move toward punitive penology in the United States, a rise in penal populism, mass incarceration, and the increasing involvement of the private sector in punishment. Ill-informed communities have generally responded negatively to offenders, and this has hindered efforts at reintegration. However, in recent years, there has been a mass decarceration, as U.S. states have found the cost of incarcerating hundreds of thousands of offenders, many for nonviolent and drug-related offences, to be cost-prohibitive and as not being effective in addressing the needs of these offenders.

KEY POINTS REVIEW

1. There are a number of explanations for correctional change.
2. How societies and groups have chosen to respond to those who violate norms, mores, and laws has varied over the centuries.
3. The history of imprisonment dates back to the time of Confucius (circa 2000 BCE).

4. Developments in England had an impact on the emergence of corrections in Canada.

5. Imprisonment became a core component of the sanctioning process in England in the 17th century (1600s).

6. There are competing perspectives on crime and criminal offenders and on what the objectives of corrections should be.

7. Both historically and during contemporary times, various perspectives have been offered on the functions of punishment.

8. The various perspectives on punishment are reflected in the works of Emile Durkheim, Karl Marx, and Michel Foucault.

9. The objectives of punishment include retribution, deterrence, incapacitation, and rehabilitation/reintegration.

10. Examining the law and corrections policy in the United States provides insights into the factors that influence the response to criminal offenders.

11. There has been a shift in correctional policy in the United States from mass incarceration to decarceration, although there are still a large number of offenders who are confined who could be safely supervised in the community.

KEY TERM QUESTIONS

1. What is the definition of **corrections** and what is included in this definition?

2. How is **punishment** commonly defined?

3. What are the basic tenets of the **classical** (conservative), **positivist** (liberal), and **critical** (radical) perspectives on crime, offenders, and the criminal justice system?

4. Discuss the concepts of **punitive penology** and **penal populism** and their role in the response to crime and criminal offenders.

CRITICAL THINKING EXERCISES

Critical Thinking Exercise 1.1

Perspectives on Crime, Criminal Offenders, and the Criminal Justice System.

Review Box 1.1 on the perspectives on crime, criminal offenders, and the criminal justice system, presented earlier in this chapter.

Your Thoughts?

1. In your view, which perspective on crime, criminal offenders, and the criminal justice system is most valid?

2. Which of the three approaches (conservative, liberal, and radical) comes the closest to your views?

Critical Thinking Exercise 1.2

Penal Populism: The Relationship between Punishment and Politics

Politics plays a key role in the ever-shifting perspectives on crime, offenders, and punishment.

Your Thoughts?

Go online and find three examples in the media that reflect various political views of criminal offenders and the most appropriate response to crime.

CLASS/GROUP DISCUSSION EXERCISE

Class/Group Discussion Exercise 1.1

The Death Penalty

Watch the film "The History of Capital Punishment," available at https://www.youtube.com/watch?v=D9DtjJFQnmY.

Your Thoughts?

1. What does the film reveal about the factors that influence punishment generally?
2. What were the key influences on the use of capital punishment historically?
3. Are any of these influences present in Canada in the early 21st century?

MEDIA LINKS

"Former Prisoner on Prison Changes," CBC News, https://www.youtube.com/watch?v=xaEa_ioDsKc

"Ancient Torture Techniques," BBC Documentaries, https://www.youtube.com/watch?v=CrFIt4BkF8Y

"Crime in the Middle Ages," https://www.youtube.com/watch?v=Y1rpnGdNNnQ

"Crime and Punishment—Industrial Britain," https://www.youtube.com/watch?v=Rj7amy5uFfQ

"Classical School of Criminology," https://www.youtube.com/watch?v=RwH1KioDtkA

"Crime and Punishment: The Story of Capital Punishment," BBC, https://www.youtube.com/watch?v=0hWcX9vZiKc

"Punishment: A Failed Social Experiment," http://topdocumentaryfilms.com/punishment-failed-social-experiment/

NOTES

1. N. Shover, *A Sociology of American Corrections* (Homewood, Ill.: Dorsey, 1979).

2. M. Foucault, *Discipline and Punish: The Birth of the Prison* (New York: Vintage, 1979); M. Ignatieff, *A Just Measure of Pain: The Penitentiary in the Industrial Revolution—1750-1850* (New York: Columbia University Press, 1978); D.J. Rothman, *The Discovery of the Asylum: Social Order and Disorder in the New Republic*, 2nd ed. (Boston: Little, Brown, 1990).

3. G. Newman, *The Punishment Response* (New York: Lippincott, 1978).

4. T.D. Miethe and J. Lu, *Punishment: A Comparative Historical Perspective* (Cambridge, UK: Cambridge University Press, 2005).

5. L.G. Mays and L.T. Winfree, *Essentials of Corrections*, 5th ed. (Malden, MA: Wiley-Blackwell, 2014).

6. R. Mills, *Suspended Animation: Pain, Pleasure and Punishment in Medieval Culture* (London, UK: Reakton Books, 2005).

7. C. Chazelle, "Crime and Punishment: Penalizing without Prisons," in *Why the Middle Ages Matter: Medieval Light on Modern Injustice*, eds. C. Chazelle, et al. (London, UK: Routledge, 2012), 15–28.

8. N. Johnston, "Evolving Function: Early Use of Imprisonment as Punishment," *Prison Journal 89*, no. 1 (2009), 10S–34S.

9. Ibid.

10. Ibid.

11. "Prison Hulks Littered British Waterways," *Intriguing History* (blog), January 2, 2012, http://www.intriguing-history.com/prison-hulks/.

12. Johnston, "Evolving Function."

13. "Punishment," *Your Dictionary*, n.d., http://www.yourdictionary.com/punishment.

14. M. Welch, *Corrections: A Critical Approach*, 3rd ed. (New York: Routledge, 2011).

15. S.J. Hartnett, *Challenging the Prison-Industrial Comple* (Urbana: University of Illinois Press, 2011).

16. D. Garland, "Sociological Perspectives on Punishment," *Crime and Justice 14* (1991), 115–65 at 121.

17. Ibid., at 123.

18. Ibid.

19. M. Tonry, "Thinking About Punishment," in *Why Punish? How Much? A Reader on Punishment*, ed. M. Tonry (New York: Oxford University Press, 1991), 9–27.

20. I. Zinger, "Human Rights and Federal Corrections: A Commentary on a Decade of Tough on Crime Policies in Canada," *Canadian Journal of Criminology and Criminal Justice 58*, no. 4 (2016), 609–27.

21. J.V. Roberts, L.J. Stalans, D. Indermaur, and M. Hough, *Penal Populism and Public Opinion: Lessons from Five Countries* (New York: Oxford University Press, 2003).

22. S. Steen and R. Bandy, "When the Policy Becomes the Problem: Criminal Justice in the New Millennium," *Punishment and Society 9*, no. 1 (2007), 5–26.

23. J. Page, "Prison Officer Unions and the Perpetuation of the Penal Status Quo," *Criminology and Public Policy 10*, no. 3 (2011), 735–70.

24. J. Forman, "The Black Poor, Black Elites, and America's Prisons," *Cardozo Law Review 32*, no. 3 (2011), 791–806 at 793.

25. See, for example, Committee on the Causes and Consequences of High Rates of Incarceration, *The Growth of Incarceration in the United States: Exploring Causes and Consequences* (Washington, D.C.: National Research Council, 2014).

26. J. Demers, *Warehousing Prisoners in Saskatchewan* (Regina: Canadian Centre for Policy

Alternatives, 2014), https://www.policyalter-natives.ca/sites/default/files/uploads/publica-tions/Saskatchewan%20Office/2014/10/warehousing_prisoners_in_saskatchewan.pdf.

27. P. Wagner and B. Rabuy, "Following the Money of Mass Incarceration," *Prison Policy Initiative* (blog), January 25, 2017, https://www.prisonpolicy.org/reports/money.html.

28. M. Lagos and R. Gabrielson, "Drug Rehab Called Key to Avoid 3rd Strike," *San Francisco Chronicle*, September 29, 2012, http://www.sfgate.com/crime/article/Drug-rehab-called-key-to-avoid-3rd-strike-3906024.php.

29. J.L. Worrall, "The Effect of Three-Strikes Leg-islation on Serious Crime in California," *Journal of Criminal Justice 32*, no. 4 (2004), 283–96.

30. J. Petersilia, "Realigning Corrections, Cali-fornia Style," *Annals of the American Academy of Political and Social Science 664*, no. 1 (2016), 8–13; H. Schoenfeld, "Penal Policy and Politics Across American States," *Annals of the American Academy of Political and Social Science 664*, no. 1 (2016), 155–74.

31. Cited in D. Klaidman, "How Eric Holder Got His Chance to Overhaul Broken Sentencing System," *The Daily Beast*, August 16, 2013, http://www.thedailybeast.com/how-eric-holder-got-his-chance-to-overhaul-broken-sentencing-system.

32. J. Petersilia, "Beyond the Prison Bubble," *Fed-eral Probation 75*, no. 1 (2011), 2–4.

33. J.A. Greene and V. Schiraldi. "Better by Half: The New York City Story of Winning Large-Scale Decarceration While Increasing Public Safety," *Federal Sentencing Reporter 29*, no. 1 (2016), 22–38, https://www.hks.harvard.edu/ocpa/cms/files/criminal-justice/research-publi-cations/fsr2901_04_greeneschiraldi.pdf.

34. From P. Yeagle, "Getting Smart on Crime: Law-makers to Reconsider Criminal Sentencing," *Illi-nois Times*, June 19, 2014, http://illinoistimes.com/article-14100-getting-smart-on-crime.html. Reprinted with permission of *The Illinois Times*.

35. J. Domanick, "The Message of California's Prop 47," *The Crime Report*, November 7, 2014, http://thecrimereport.org/2014/11/07/2014-11-the-message-of-californias-prop-47/.

36. Council of State Governments Justice Center, *Justice Reinvestment in North Caro-lina: Three Years Later* (New York: Council of State Governments Justice Center, 2014), http://jr.nc.gov/files/JRinNCThreeYears-Later.pdf.

37. A.F. Rengifo, D. Stemen, B.D. Dooley, E. Amidon, and A. Gendon, "Cents and Sensibility: A Case Study of Corrections Reform in Kansas and Michigan," *Journal of Criminal Justice 38*, no. 4 (2012), 419–29.

38. M. Mauer and N. Ghandnoosh, *Fewer Pris-oners, Less Crime: A Tale of Three States* (Wash-ington, D.C.: The Sentencing Project, 2014).

39. "Conn., N.C. and Ga. See Steep Drop in Black, Hispanic Prison Populations," *The Crime Report*, March 30, 2015, http://thecrimereport.org/2015/03/30/2015-03-conn-nc-and-ga-see-steep-drops-in-black-hispanic-pri/.

40. A.J. Thielo, F.T. Cullen, D.M. Cohen, and C. Chouhy. "Rehabilitation in a Red State: Public Support for Correctional Reform in Texas," *Crim-inology & Public Policy 15*, no. 1 (2016), 137–70.

41. M.D. Ramirez, "The Polls—Trends: Ameri-cans' Changing Views on Crime and Punish-ment," *Public Opinion Quarterly 77*, no. 4 (2013), 1006–31.

42. T. Porter, "Will the Trump Administration Jail More Drug Felons?" *Newsweek*, May 12, 2017, http://www.newsweek.com/trump-jeff-sessions-us-drugs-crime-607360.

43. J. Austin, L-B. Eisen, J. Cullen, and J. Frank, *How Many Americans Are Unnecessarily Incarcer-ated?* (New York: Brennan Center for Justice, 2016), https://www.brennancenter.org/sites/default/files/publications/Unnecessarily_Incarcerated.pdf.

THE ORIGINS AND EVOLUTION OF CANADIAN CORRECTIONS

CHAPTER OBJECTIVES

- Describe the influences and events that resulted in the building of the first penitentiary in Canada in 1835.
- Discuss the conditions of early provincial prisons and local jails across the country.
- Highlight the key developments in efforts to reform penitentiaries and the move toward a treatment model of corrections following World War II.
- Describe the models of corrections that have been developing for the past two decades.
- Discuss the various commissions of inquiry on corrections and their impact on correctional policy and practice.

This chapter discusses the origins and evolution of Canadian corrections. It examines the creation of penitentiaries in the early 1800s, traces the shifts in Canadian correctional practice from the 1800s to the present day, and discusses how the architecture of correctional institutions reflects changes in corrections philosophies.

THE CREATION OF THE CANADIAN PENITENTIARY

Recall from Chapter 1 that a key indicator of correctional change is the creation of new structural arrangements for sanctioning offenders. The events surrounding the building of Canada's first penitentiary—in Kingston, Ontario, in the early 1800s—illustrate how changes in responses to crime and criminal offenders can be influenced by social, economic, and political forces. There were influences from the United States, where, between 1790 and 1830, crime came to be viewed as a consequence of community disorder and family instability rather than a manifestation of individual afflictions. The Americans built penitentiaries in an attempt to create settings in which criminals could be transformed into useful citizens through religious contemplation and hard work. Some of these institutions operated on a "separate and silent" system, in which prisoners were completely isolated from one another in their cells—where they worked, ate, and slept. This came to be known as the **Pennsylvania model**.

In other penitentiaries, in what became known as the **Auburn model** (originating in New York State), prisoners worked and ate together during the day and slept in individual cells at night. A system of strict silence, which forbade prisoners from communicating or even gesturing to one another, was enforced at all times. Most prisons in the United States and Canada were patterned on the Auburn model.

In Canada, the building of the first penitentiary in Kingston, Ontario, was the result of a number of influences, including developments in the United States, overcrowding in the local jails (where there was also a lack of classification of inmates), and the view that corporal punishment was improper and degrading.[1] When completed in 1835, Kingston Penitentiary was the largest public building in Upper Canada. It symbolized a **moral architecture**, one that reflected the themes of order and morality.

Kingston was to be a model for those confined in it as well as for society. Among its goals were the eradication of the underlying causes of crime: intemperance, laziness, and a lack of moral values. Within the penitentiary, hard labour and a strong emphasis on religion were core elements of the reformation process.

The prisoners in Kingston were separated by gender and type of offence. They were allowed to have their own bedding, clothing, and food. Generally, however, their lives centred on hard labour and discipline. Strict silence was maintained at all times; the inmates walked in lockstep; their days were controlled by the constant ringing of bells. Breaches of prison regulations brought swift and harsh punishment, including flogging, leg irons, solitary confinement, and rations of bread and water (see Corrections File 2.1). Male inmates who violated prison regulations were generally whipped; women convicts who did so were placed in solitary confinement. The same punishments were applied to children, some as young as eight.

The conditions in Kingston led to the creation of a royal commission in 1848, 13 years after it opened. The **Brown Commission** investigated charges of mismanagement, theft, and mistreatment of convicts. It found that the warden, Henry Smith, had indeed mismanaged the institution and that there was excessive use of corporal punishment, including the flogging of men, women, and children, some as young as 11. The warden was fired and attempts were made to reform the prison. Though changes were made, corporal punishment, the silent system, and hard labour remained prominent features of life in Kingston. In retrospect, the Brown Commission is perhaps best viewed as a missed opportunity for Canadians to reconsider the use of imprisonment and to explore potentially more effective ways to prevent crime and reform offenders.

Pennsylvania model (for prisons)
A separate and silent system in which prisoners were completely isolated from one another, eating, working, and sleeping in separate cells.

Auburn model (for prisons)
A system that allowed prisoners to work and eat together during the day and housed them in individual cells at night.

Moral architecture
The term used to describe the design of the first penitentiary in Canada, the intent of which was to reflect themes of order and morality.

Brown Commission
An investigation into the operations of Kingston Penitentiary that condemned the use of corporal punishment and emphasized the need for rehabilitation.

CORRECTIONS FILE 2.1

Entries from **The Punishment Book of the Prison** (1843)

Offence	Punishment
Laughing and talking	6 lashes; cat-o'-nine-tails
Talking in wash-house	6 lashes; rawhide
Threatening to knock convicts' brains out	24 lashes; cat-o'-nine-tails
Talking to Keepers on matters not relating to their work	6 lashes; cat-o'-nine-tails
Finding fault with rations when desired by guard to sit down	6 lashes; rawhide, and bread and water
Staring about and inattentive at breakfast table	bread and water
Leaving work and going to privy when other convict there	36 hours in dark cell, and bread and water

Source: *First Report of the Commissioners of the Royal Commission on the Provincial Penitentiary*, 1849, p. 185.

In penitentiaries, the bell was the symbol of discipline and controlled the convict's day. Corrections File 2.2 presents the daily schedule of the Kingston Penitentiary in 1879. Corrections File 2.3 presents the typical coarse diet for convicts confined during the 1880s.

Local Jails and Provincial Prisons

Conditions in local jails and provincial institutions at this time were generally deplorable. Prisoners were required to pay for their meals, liquor, and rent—and, upon release, for the jailer's fee for his or her services. Those inmates unable to pay the fee were often confined for additional periods of time or allowed to panhandle on the streets to raise the necessary funds.[2]

Early county jail, Chatham, Ontario

Chatham–Kent Museum 1985.27.3.47

LATE 1800s AND EARLY 1900s

In the 1880s, efforts were made to improve the operations of prisons. Various federal laws provided for the appointment of prison inspectors and outlined their powers and duties; addressed the need for the separate confinement of

CORRECTIONS FILE 2.2

Symbol of Discipline: The Bell

5:50 a.m.	Bell. Prisoners rise, wash, dress, make beds.
6:00 a.m.	Officers parade. Keys issued, slops collected. Cells, walls, halls, and passages swept. Lamps collected and cleaned. Prisoners unlocked and escorted to work. Names of the sick taken. Night tubs [chamber pots] cleaned and placed outside the prison. Fuel distributed and ashes emptied. Random search of cells. Water pumped into tank.
7:30 a.m.	Bell. Prisoners marched to dining halls in groups of three.
7:40 a.m.	Bell. Breakfast over. Prisoners marched back to their cells and locked in. Guards had breakfast.
8:30 a.m.	Bell. Officers parade. Outside gangs unlocked and escorted outside. Inside workers escorted to their jobs. Surgeon attends the sick.
10:00 a.m.	Office hours. Convicts on report were taken to the warden.
12:15 p.m.	Bell. Prisoners marched back to their cells and locked up.
12:20 p.m.	Bell. Prisoners unlocked and marched to the dining room for lunch.
12:45 p.m.	Bell. Prisoners marched back to cells and locked up. Officers had lunch.
12:50 p.m.	Eligible prisoners unlocked for school.
1:30 p.m.	Bell. Officers parade. Prisoners unlocked and marched off to work. Random search of cells.
5:40 p.m.	Night tubs brought back into the prison.
5:50 p.m.	Bell. Prisoners marched to cells and locked up. Supper delivered to each cell. Convicts with special requests may use "signal sticks" to summon guards.
6:00 p.m.	Bell. Prisoners' clothing collected and placed outside cell door. All cells searched. Prisoners begin their meals. Guards on night shift take over. Keys collected. Chief keeper reads out daily orders.
7:00 p.m.	Patrol guards supply water to convicts who signal for it. Kitchen and dining hall locked up.
9:00 p.m.	Lights in cells turned down.
10:00 p.m.	Lights in passages turned down. Dampers of heating stoves closed. Lights out in officers' room.

(The bell, which was centrally located in the prison, was so hated by the inmates that it was destroyed during the 1971 riot at Kingston.)

Source: Reproduced from "Crime and Punishment: A Pictorial History Part III," Correctional Service of Canada. Reproduced with the permission of Correctional Service Canada.

CORRECTIONS FILE 2.3

A Typical Daily Menu for Inmates in the Manitoba Penitentiary in the Late 1880s

Breakfast	1 pint	pease coffee (sweetened with 1/2 oz. brown sugar)
	1/2 lb.	brown bread
	1/2 lb.	white bread or 1/2 lb. potatoes
	1/4 lb.	beef or pork (with beets and vinegar twice a week)
Dinner	1-1/2 pint	soup
	1/2 lb.	white bread or 3/4 lb. potatoes
	1/2 lb.	brown bread
	1/2 lb.	beef, mutton, or pork
Supper	10 oz.	white or brown bread
	1 pint	coffee (with 1/2 oz. brown sugar)

The food allowance for women inmates was generally smaller due to their lighter workload.

Source: Reproduced from "Crime and Punishment: A Pictorial History Part III," Correctional Service of Canada. Reproduced with the permission of Correctional Service Canada.

---

women offenders, mentally disordered inmates, and young offenders; and permitted the use of solitary confinement in federal penitentiaries. However, inmates continued to be subjected to a variety of physical disciplinary sanctions, many of which continued in use until the 1930s.[3]

In 1906, a Penitentiary Act was passed that included, among other provisions, the removal of youthful inmates and the mentally disordered from general penitentiary populations and expanded the powers and duties of the federal penitentiary inspectors. Despite this legislation, there was little change in the philosophy of corrections or in how prisons were operated. Punitive practices documented by the Brown Commission nearly half a century earlier continued.

THE BEGINNINGS OF MODERN REFORM: 1930–1970

During the 1930s, there were some initial signs, particularly at the federal level, that the harsh regimen of the penitentiary was changing, albeit slowly. Prisoners displaying good conduct were given lighting in their cells in order to read, were permitted to write one letter every three months to their families, and were allowed half-hour visits by relatives once a month. The strict rule of silence was modified, and inmates began to be paid for work performed in the institution at a rate of five cents per day.

Contributing to the shift in penal philosophy was the report of the Royal Commission on the Penal System of Canada (Archambault), which concluded that the goal of prisons should be not only to protect society by incarcerating offenders but also to reform and rehabilitate offenders. This increasing focus on the treatment of offenders was to provide the basis for the post-World War II era in Canadian corrections.

Following World War II, there was a shift toward a treatment model of corrections. This shift was enhanced by the findings of the Fauteux Report (1956), which recommended adoption of a correctional philosophy centred on treatment, the expansion of probation, and recruitment and training of professional staff. The federal prison system introduced vocational training, education, and therapeutic intervention techniques, such as group counselling and individual therapy. Concurrent with these developments was an increase in the numbers of psychologists and psychiatrists on prison staffs. This is an instance when a commission of inquiry did impact correctional policy and practice.

This and other reports highlighted the shift toward rehabilitation under what became known as the **medical model of corrections**. In brief, the medical model held that the offender was ill—physically, mentally, and/or socially. Criminal behaviour was a symptom of illness. As in medicine, diagnosis and treatment would ensure the effective rehabilitation of the offender.

The decade of the 1960s was the height of the treatment model in Canadian corrections. A number of new medium- and minimum-security facilities were constructed across the country, all of which were designed to hold small populations of offenders. Prisons expanded visiting privileges, as well as education and training opportunities, and included prison physicians as part of the treatment team in an attempt to address the offender's criminal behaviour. A number of other commissions of inquiry, profiled in Corrections File 2.5, contributed to this shift in correctional philosophy.

> **medical model of corrections**
> The view that criminal offenders were ill—physically, mentally, and/or socially—and that treatment and diagnosis would ensure rehabilitation.

THE EARLY 21ST CENTURY: THE SWINGING PENDULUM OF CANADIAN CORRECTIONS

In the early 21st century, there was a shift in correctional philosophy, driven in large measure by the election of a new federal government. Under the federal Conservative government (2006–2015), there was a conservative, American-style, "get tough" approach to offenders.[4] This approach was a radical departure from the more liberal model of corrections practice that had prevailed in Canada for many decades under successive Liberal governments. The primary objectives of the Conservative government were to hold offenders accountable, to address what was perceived to be leniency in sentencing, and to have "truth in sentencing"—that is, to make the sentencing process more transparent.[5]

The cornerstone of the Conservative government's approach to offenders was a series of legislative bills, which included the following provisions:

- Elimination from the Criminal Code of the "faint hope" clause, which allowed offenders convicted of first-degree murder a hearing before a jury to determine whether a reduced date for parole eligibility was possible (Bill C-48: The Protecting Canadians by Ending Sentence Discounts for Multiple Murders Act, 2011).
- Restrictions on judges as to what types of offences can be considered for a conditional sentence, which is generally served at home (see Chapter 5).
- Elimination of "two-for-one" (two days credit for one day served) for time served by offenders in pretrial custody (Bill C-25: The Truth in Sentencing Act, 2009).
- The introduction of mandatory minimum sentences for 60 criminal offences, including crimes involving guns and drugs (Bill C-10: The Safe Streets and Communities Act, 2012).
- Provisions that encouraged Crown counsel to consider adult sentences for young offenders who have committed certain offences, and changes in the rules of pretrial detention for this offender population (Bill C-10: The Safe Streets and Communities Act, 2012).
- An increase in the waiting period to apply for a record suspension (previously referred to as a "pardon") to five years for persons convicted of summary offences and ten years for indictable offences. Persons convicted of sexual offences against minors and persons convicted of three or more indictable offences were deemed ineligible for a record suspension (Bill C-23: Eliminating Pardons for Serious Crimes Act, 2010).
- Abolition of accelerated parole review, which had allowed parole boards to fast-track the release of nonviolent offenders from federal institutions (Bill C-59: The Abolition of Early Parole Act, 2011).

Also, Bill C-10 altered the wording in the Corrections and Conditional Release Act, replacing the principle that the CSC must "use the *least restrictive measures* consistent with the protection of the public, staff members, and offenders," with the principle that the measures "are limited to only what is *necessary and proportionate* to attain the purposes of this Act."[6]

In addition, prison farms operated by the CSC were closed, despite concerns that this was removing an important resource for rehabilitating offenders.[7]

The basis for this populist penology was expressed by the federal minister of justice: "Canadians have been telling us that this is what they want to see."[8] Research on public confidence in the criminal justice system, however, indicates that the public is less severe in its view of how offenders should be treated than is commonly assumed. Rather, there is among the citizenry sensitivity to the situation of the individual offender and the offence that has been committed, as well as to the costs of the justice system and to alternatives to confinement.[9] Further, surveys have found that more than 90 percent of Canadians are satisfied with their personal safety and that Canadians are generally misinformed about the nature and extent of crime.[10] There is also no evidence of a relationship between the severity of the decisions made in a province's courts and public confidence in the courts and the justice system.[11]

Bill C-10 generated a heated debate, with provincial and territorial governments arguing that the legislation would result in overcrowding, significant increases in corrections costs, and increased expenditures for criminal justice systems that the federal government would not cover.[12] The concerns regarding increased costs were borne out by a report of the federal Office of the Auditor General that found that since March 2011, CSC costs of custody have increased by $91 million. This was due primarily to the increased numbers of offenders in custody.[13]

Similarly, the legislation led to increased overcrowding in some federal correctional institutions, due primarily to a reduction in the numbers of offenders being released from confinement.[14] A report of the federal Auditor General in 2014 found that over one-half of federal prisons were operating at, or over, their rated capacity of inmates. This overcrowding led to double-bunking many inmates (two inmates placed in a cell originally designed for one) and increased violence in the institutions. The overcrowding also resulted in inmates not being able to be moved from one security level to another as they progressed through their treatment plan.[15]

The initiatives, however, did not result in mass incarceration as occurred in the United States[16] What did increase was the number of Indigenous and Black inmates. Indigenous inmates now comprise 25 percent of the inmates in federal institutions while only comprising 4.3 percent of the Canadian population; Blacks are 10 percent of prison inmates, while comprising only 3 percent of the Canadian population. The "tough-on-crime" agenda of the federal Conservatives also had a significant impact on the conditions in federal institutions. A study of key health performance indicators found increases in the following categories:

> *Use of chemical and inflammatory agents: +235.8 percent*
> *Attempted suicides: +210.3 percent*
> *Serious bodily injuries: +113.5 percent*
> *Inmate on inmate assaults: +93.0 percent*
> *Internal complaints and grievances: +63.3 percent*[17]

There was also during this time an 11 percent increase in administrative segregation placements.

There was also a significant impact on the culture of Canadian federal corrections.[18] Concerns were expressed that decision-making on criminal-justice policy in Canada had moved from professionals to politicians. A study of correctional officers (COs) in provincial correctional institutions ($N = 28$) found resistance to the idea of penal populism, one officer stating:

> [I]t's all about politics, and the popular vote wins. That leader who is gonna stand up and say, "We're gonna get tough on crime" because people wanna hear it … it's quite simple. We're going to fill our institutions with groups of [people with] mental health issues and we're gonna spend billions of dollars doing it. And in the end we're not gonna measure at all how successful it was.[19]

Ironically, the adoption of a conservative approach occurred at a time when the United States was beginning to abandon punitive penology and mass incarceration (see Chapter 1), mainly because of the costs associated with these practices and the realization that community-based treatment programs were more effective and less costly than incarceration.

Many of the legislative provisions that were brought in by the federal Conservative government during this time were subjected to court challenges, and as of late 2017, a number of them had been deemed unconstitutional by the courts. As of the end of 2016, there had been more than 100 constitutional challenges to mandatory minimum penalties.[20]

In decisions made in 2015 and 2016, the Supreme Court of Canada (SCC) rendered the following:

- Held that a provision of the Truth in Sentencing Act (2009) that prohibited judges from giving more than one-for-one pretrial credit was deemed to be unreasonable and unconstitutional (*R. v. Summers*, 2014 SCC 26).
- Struck down a provision in the Criminal Code that prevented sentencing judges from crediting more than the time the offender actually served in pre-trial detention against the sentence imposed when the offender had been denied bail because of a past criminal record (*R. v. Safarzadeh-Markhali*, 2016 SCC 14).
- Struck down the three-year minimum sentence for illegal gun possession, calling the law "cruel and unusual punishment" (*R. v. Nur*, 2015 SCC 15), and the one-year minimum term for drug traffickers with a previous conviction for trafficking (*R. v. Lloyd*, 2016 SCC 13).

In fall 2015, the Liberal party won the federal election, and the party has indicated it will soon dismantle many of the above-noted initiatives. In late 2016, the federal government announced that it was exploring the potential of introducing exceptions to mandatory minimum sentences and reinvesting in judges the discretion in sentencing.[21]

In the words of one legal observer, the shift from the position of the federal Conservative government to that of the Liberal government serves to "swing the balance away from the Conservative view that crime is a moral problem to a more modern and realistic view that crime relates to poverty and mental illness and marginalization."[22]

THE FUNCTIONS AND SYMBOLISM OF CANADIAN PRISON ARCHITECTURE

One way to track changes in corrections philosophy is by examining prison architecture. A review of the history of prison architecture in Canada reveals a number of distinct design phases that can be related to shifts in correctional philosophy. These eras are reflected in the federal correctional institutions that have been constructed, beginning with the Kingston Penitentiary in 1835 and continuing into the present.

Corrections scholars have examined the symbolism reflected in the architecture of buildings (recall the "moral architecture" of Kingston Penitentiary). It has been stated that: "every building creates associations in the mind of the beholder."[23] For prisons, this traditionally involved grandiose buildings whose exteriors contrasted starkly with the drabness and depressing conditions inside. Modern prisons are less visible and more integrated into their surroundings; however, it can be argued that the internal environments are much more sterile and desensitizing than their historical counterparts.[24]

Note that the timelines presented in Corrections File 2.4 are general rather than definite. Also, only some of the more distinctive attributes of each era have been identified.

A high proportion of federal offenders are serving sentences for violent offences, and there has been a decrease in the federal parole grant rate.[25] This means that offenders are serving longer periods of time in confinement. Also, at the provincial/territorial level, the expansion of alternatives to incarceration, such as probation and conditional sentences, has resulted in inmate populations with more-serious criminal profiles that require more-secure facilities. All of these factors have limited the ability of corrections systems to design facilities that provide increased responsibility and more freedom of movement for inmates.

A key unanswered question is whether prison architecture contributes to post-release success among inmates. There have been no evaluative studies to determine whether federal women offenders residing in the smaller regional facilities have lower rates of post-release recidivism than women who served time in and were released from the now-closed Kingston Prison for Women, which was a traditional, penitentiary-style institution. Similarly, although strong criticism has been levelled at the "big box" prisons constructed by provincial corrections systems, there is no evidence that these facilities have contributed to higher rates of reoffending upon release.

The lack of research makes it difficult to determine whether prison design has any impact on the dynamics of life inside correctional institutions as those dynamics relate, for example, to the long-standing problems of drug use and violence among inmates. The highly publicized death of a woman offender with an intellectual disability at Grand Valley Institution for Women in 2007 (see Chapter 12) suggests that while prison design may reflect changes in correctional philosophy, it may actually do little to address the needs of those who live in correctional institutions or the challenges of those who work in them.

CORRECTIONS FILE 2.4

The Eras of Prison Architecture and the Philosophies of Corrections

Design	Philosophy
Pre-1835	
Imprisonment not used as a sanction; little consideration given to the structure in which offenders were housed while awaiting trial or punishment; congregate housing with little or no separation of offenders by age, gender, or offence	Holding facility
1830s–Early 1900s	
Auburn plan—inmates worked and ate together during the day and housed separately in cells at night; rigid silent system; tiers of small, barred, windowless cells like stacked cages overlooking a tall common space	Reformation through hard labour and discipline
Early 1900s	
No change in design; punitive practices continued	Reformation through hard work and discipline

Kingston Penitentiary, 1919

Canada. Patent and Copyright Office / Library and Archives Canada / PA-030472

Design	Philosophy
1930s–1940s	
No change in design; harsh regimen of prison modified	Initial shift toward including rehabilitation as a goal of incarceration

(continued)

Design	Philosophy

1950s

Emphasis on privacy, with smaller tiers and larger cells with a solid door and a view window; static security with little staff–inmate interaction

Emerging focus on rehabilitation and treatment

1960s

Efforts to "dilute" the prison as a distinct building form; attempts to normalize the institutional environment and reduce inmates' isolation and loss of personal dignity; some facilities incorporate a campus-style layout with residential-scale buildings for living units; increase in the use of dynamic security to encourage positive staff–inmate interaction

Treatment and rehabilitation

Springhill Penitentiary

Springhill Penitentiary (Nova Scotia). Reproduced with the permission of Correctional Service of Canada.

1970s

Physical spaces are designed to increase interaction with staff; treatment, rehabilitation, and living units are overseen by a unit management team; space is provided for rehabilitation programs

Treatment and rehabilitation

Mission Institution

Mission Institution (British Columbia). Reproduced with the permission of Correctional Service of Canada.

Design	Philosophy

1980s

Mixed design; some institutions are designed to increase security and control over inmates; others, to increase inmate responsibility and staff–inmate interaction

Treatment and rehabilitation

1990s

Several federal institutions are renovated to create "neighbourhood housing"—small, autonomous housing units for five to eight inmates with reduced direct surveillance; small regional facilities are constructed for women offenders; several healing lodges are built for Indigenous offenders, incorporating elements of Indigenous cultures and spirituality

Treatment and rehabilitation

Pê Sâkâstêw Institution (Alberta). Reproduced with the permission of Correctional Service of Canada.

Pê Sâkâstêw Institution

Early 2000s

Mixed designs; some federal institutions have housing clusters in which inmates live in individual bedrooms and share a common living area; a "moral architecture" designed to facilitate positive interactions and to prepare inmates for life outside the institution; other institutions are "big boxes"—high tech, with electronic security and video-surveillance technology; reduction of staff–inmate interaction contributes to warehousing

Transition period between (1) a liberal European model emphasizing proactive intervention with inmates and treatment in the community and (2) a more punitive penology

CORRECTIONAL INQUIRIES: FACILITATING CHANGE?

At various times, governments have directed commissions of inquiry to examine correctional policy and practice. Some of the more significant of these inquiries are set out in Corrections File 2.5. Note that these investigations have generally focused on federal corrections, which involve a much smaller number of offenders than provincial/territorial corrections. There have been far fewer inquiries in the latter jurisdictions, which face many of the same challenges.

A key question is the extent to which the findings of these inquiries have impacted correctional policy and practice at the federal and provincial/ territorial level. Many of the inquiries have altered the structure of corrections. The impact on correctional policy and practice is less certain and more difficult to determine.

The impact of these investigations on federal corrections has been mixed. For example, while the Brown Commission of 1848–1849 led to the firing of Kingston's warden, few changes were made to that prison's structure and operations. However, the report *Creating Choices* (1990), produced by the Task Force on Federally Sentenced Women, resulted in a major shift in correctional policy with respect to federal women offenders—specifically, the antiquated Kingston Prison for Women was eventually closed, and several smaller regional facilities were constructed to replace it.

CORRECTIONS FILE 2.5

Commissions and Inquiries into Systems of Corrections

Year	Commission/Inquiry	Focus/Impact
1848–1849	Royal Commission of Inquiry (Brown)	Investigated charges of corruption and mismanagement at Kingston Penitentiary; identified the rehabilitation of offenders as the primary purpose of penitentiaries; impact on prison reform uncertain; most accurately viewed as a missed opportunity to rethink the concept of the penitentiary
1891	Report of the Commission Appointed to Enquire into the Prison and Reformatory System of the Province of Ontario	Documented problems with classification, poor physical facilities, and inadequate management of provincial and local institutions; contributed to early reforms in the Ontario correctional system

Year	Commission/Inquiry	Focus/Impact
1936	Royal Commission on the Penal System of Canada (Archambault)[a]	Appointed to investigate federal prisons; report (1938) concluded that the goal of prisons should be not only to protect society by incarcerating offenders but also to reform and rehabilitate offenders; gave impetus to an increasing focus on the development and expansion of vocational and educational training programs
1956	Report of a Committee Appointed to Inquire into the Principles and Practices Followed in the Remission Service of the Department of Justice of Canada (Fauteux)[b]	Recommended adoption of a correctional philosophy centred on treatment, the expansion of probation, and recruitment and training of professional staff
1969	Canadian Committee on Corrections (Ouimet)[c]	Questioned whether offenders could be rehabilitated in prisons; emphasized the importance of community corrections
1973	Task Force on the Release of Inmates (Hugessen)[d]	Examined the procedures for the release of offenders from institutions prior to the completion of their sentence; recommended the creation of five regional parole boards at the federal level and the appointment of part-time board members
1977	Report of the Parliamentary Sub-Committee on the Penitentiary System in Canada (MacGuigan)[e]	Inquiry prompted by riots in federal prisons; numerous recommendations made for improving conditions for staff and inmates
1987	Canadian Sentencing Commission	Examined sentencing and identified the purposes and principles of sentencing; proposed sentencing guidelines and revisions to the maximum and minimum sentence structure
1988	Report of the Standing Committee on Justice and Solicitor General (Daubney)	Examined sentencing and the parole process; nearly 100 recommendations, including enactment of a statement and purpose of sentencing, creation of sentencing guidelines, and greater use of community sanctions, including restorative justice approaches; informed the subsequent Corrections and Conditional Release Act (1992)

(continued)

Year	Commission/Inquiry	Focus/Impact
1990	Task Force on Federally Sentenced Women (*Creating Choices*)[f]	Examined issues surrounding correctional policies and programs for federal women offenders; recommended the closing of the Kingston Prison for Women, to be replaced by smaller regional facilities for women offenders, including a healing lodge for Indigenous women offenders (see Chapter 12); recommendations were accepted by the federal government
1996	Commission of Inquiry into Certain Events at the Prison for Women in Kingston (Arbour)[g]	In-depth examination of a critical incident at the Kingston Prison for Women, during which women offenders were stripped of clothing by male members of the Institutional Emergency Response Team; recommendations focused on women's corrections, cross-gender staffing in correctional institutions for women, the use of force and Institutional Emergency Response Teams, the needs of Indigenous women, the operation of segregation units, ways of ensuring the accountability of corrections personnel and adherence to the rule of law, and procedures for handling inmate complaints and grievances
2007	Correctional Service Canada Review Panel (Sampson)[h]	Comprehensive review of all facets of the CSC's operations, including the availability and effectiveness of rehabilitation and mental health programs, programs for Indigenous offenders, services and support for crime victims, safety and security issues, the transition of offenders into the community, and physical infrastructure; among the recommendations were that the CSC create large, regional correctional facilities

[a] J. Archambault (chair), *Report of the Royal Commission to Investigate the Penal System of Canada* (Ottawa: King's Printer, 1938).

[b] G. Fauteux (chair), *Report of the Committee Appointed to Inquire into the Principles and Procedures Followed in the Remission Service of the Department of Justice of Canada* (Ottawa: Queen's Printer, 1956).

[c] R. Ouimet (chair), *Toward Unity: Criminal Justice and Corrections: Report of the Canadian Committee on Corrections* (Ottawa: Queen's Printer, 1969).

[d] J.K. Hugessen (chair), *Task Force on Release of Inmates* (Ottawa: Solicitor General of Canada, 1972).

[e] M. MacGuigan, *Report to Parliament by the Sub-Committee on the Penitentiary System in Canada* (Ottawa: Supply and Services Canada, 1977).

f   Task Force on Federally Sentenced Women, *Creating Choices: The Report of the Task Force on Federally Sentenced Women* (Ottawa. Correctional Service Canada, 1990), http://www.csc-scc.gc.ca/women/toce-eng.shtml.

g   The Honourable L. Arbour (commissioner), *Commission of Inquiry into Certain Events at the Prison for Women in Kingston* (Ottawa: Public Works and Government Services Canada, 1996), http://www.justicebehindthewalls.net/resources/arbour_report/arbour_rpt.htm.

h   R. Sampson (chair), *Report of the Correctional Service Canada Review Panel: A Roadmap to Strengthening Public Safety* (Ottawa: Minister of Public Works and Government Services Canada, 2007), https://www.publicsafety.gc.ca/cnt/cntrng-crm/csc-scc-rvw-pnl/report-rapport/cscrprprt-eng.pdf.

Systems of correction continue to experience systemic failures in the management of offenders and these are discussed in the following chapters.

There has also not been a major review of federal corrections since 2007, although there have been numerous inquiries and panels that have examined specific areas of corrections (i.e., Indigenous offenders, women offenders). Reports have also been produced at the provincial/territorial levels. Many of these materials will be discussed throughout the text.

REFLECTIONS ON CORRECTIONS HISTORY

Systems of corrections undergo constant change driven by the ideologies of the provincial/territorial and federal governments of the day, fiscal crises, pressures exerted by public interest groups, and a variety of other influences. Many of the challenges confronting corrections systems at the beginning of the 21st century were first identified early in the 19th century. As the discussion in the following chapters will reveal, these challenges include developing structures to ensure that corrections systems are accountable, finding methods to classify offenders accurately, ensuring humane and safe conditions within institutions, establishing effective treatment and training programs, and providing the support services and programs to assist offenders released from prison to successfully reintegrate back into the community.

And as the discussion in the following chapters will illustrate, the long-ago understood needs of persons who become involved in the corrections system are still often not being met. The broader issue—*how* and *why* persons become involved in corrections systems in the first place—remains largely unaddressed.

SUMMARY

This chapter focused on the origins and evolution of corrections in Canada. The material highlighted the influence of political and economic developments as well as religious beliefs on the response to criminal offenders. The evolution of institutional corrections from the 1800s to the present was traced, as were the changing philosophies of corrections as reflected in the functions and symbolism of prison architecture. A number of inquiries into federal corrections were examined and found to have had some impact on corrections policy and practice. These results included improving the living conditions of inmates and developing correctional strategies for federal women offenders and federal Indigenous offenders. Provincial/territorial systems of corrections have received less study, and this has hindered reform in those jurisdictions.

KEY POINTS REVIEW

1. The first Canadian penitentiary was constructed in Kingston, Ontario, in 1835, and within several years, concerns were being raised regarding its effectiveness in punishing and reforming offenders.

2. The conditions in early jails and provincial institutions were generally quite bad.

3. Reforms in Canadian corrections began in the 1930s; following World War II, there was an increased emphasis on treatment.

4. Commissions of inquiry into the operation of federal corrections have had some impact on the structure of corrections and corrections policy and practice.

5. One way to trace the changing philosophy of corrections and punishment is by examining the architecture of correctional institutions over the past 200 years.

6. Many of the challenges that confront systems of corrections at the beginning of the 21st century were first identified early in the 19th century.

7. There has been concern that Canadian corrections is being Americanized although this trend is being reversed in part due to a number of SCC decisions.

KEY TERM QUESTIONS

1. Compare and contrast the *Pennsylvania model* and the *Auburn model* of prisons.

2. What is *moral architecture*, and how does it help us understand the goals of the first penitentiaries that were built in Canada?

3. What was the *Brown Commission* and why was it important in the study of Canadian corrections?

CRITICAL THINKING EXERCISE

Critical Thinking Exercise 2.1

Does the Public Really Want Tougher Laws?

Arguing in support of the "tough-on-crime" legislation, the then-federal justice minister in the Conservative government stated that the bill's provisions reflected public sentiment in favour of getting tougher on criminal offenders. Yet findings from the General Social Survey found that over 90 percent of respondents over the age of 15 were not concerned about their personal safety.

Your Thoughts?

1. What does this discrepancy indicate about how penal policy is formulated and the factors that may influence laws that affect systems of corrections?

CLASS/GROUP DISCUSSION EXERCISE

Class/Group Discussion Exercise 2.1

Inside the Kingston Pen

The CBC Doc Zone series, listed in the Media Links section below, provides key insights into life inside of Canada's first penitentiary.

Your Thoughts?

1. Watch the documentaries listed below. Then, list what you would consider to be the most significant features of the institution and the offenders who resided in it.
2. What impact do you think that the physical structure of the Kingston Pen had on the dynamics that occurred inside it?

MEDIA LINKS

CBC Doc Zone, "Tales from Kingston Pen," http://www.cbc.ca/doczone/episodes/tales-from-the-kingston-penn

CBC Doc Zone, "Tales from Kingston Pen: Timeline," http://www.cbc.ca/doczone/features/timeline

CBC Doc Zone, "Kingston Pen's 10 Most Infamous Inmates," http://www.cbc.ca/doczone/features/infamous-inmates

CBC Doc Zone, "Tales from Kingston Pen: Memoirs," http://www.cbc.ca/doczone/features/memoirs

CBC Doc Zone, "Inside the Pen: The Dome," http://www.cbc.ca/doczone/features/inside-the-pen-the-dome1

CBC Doc Zone, "Inside the Pen: The Cellblock," http://www.cbc.ca/doczone/features/inside-the-pen-the-cellblock

Prison History, https://www.youtube.com/watch?v=FKiQi90U2AU

NOTES

1. R. Baehre, "Origins of the Penitentiary System in Upper Canada," *Ontario History* 69, no. 3 (1977), 185–207.

2. D. Coles, *Nova Scotia Corrections: An Historical Perspective* (Halifax: Corrections Services Division, Province of Nova Scotia, 1979).

3. M. MacGuigan, *Report to Parliament by the Sub-Committee on the Penitentiary System in Canada* (Ottawa: Supply and Services Canada, 1977), p. 12.

4. C. M. Webster and A.N. Doob, "US Punitiveness 'Canadian Style'? Cultural Values and Canadian Punishment Policy," *Punishment & Society* 17, no. 3 (2015), 299–321.

5. J. Bronskill, "Reforms Have Compounded Pressures on Canada's Criminal Justice System: Memo," Canadian Press, December 13, 2016, http://globalnews.ca/news/3123357/reforms-have-compounded-pressures-on-canadas-criminal-justice-system-memo/.

6. *Corrections and Conditional Release Act*, S.C 1992, c. 20, http://laws-lois.justice.gc.ca/PDF/C-44.6.pdf, s. 4(c).

7. D. Mehta, "Ottawa Might Reopen Prison Farms Shut Down by the Harper Government," Canadian Press, July 10, 2016, http://www.macleans.ca/politics/ottawa/ottawa-might-reopen-prison-farms-shut-down-by-the-harper-government/.

8. K. Makin, "Canadian Crime and American Punishment," *Globe and Mail*, November 27, 2009, https://www.theglobeandmail.com/news/world/canadian-crime-and-american-punishment/article4305214.

9. K.N. Varma and V. Marinos, "Three Decades of Public Attitudes Research on Crime and Punishment in Canada," *Canadian Journal of Criminology and Criminal Justice* 55, no. 4 (2013), 549–62.

10. S. Brennan, "Canadians' Perceptions of Personal Safety and Crime, 2009," *Juristat* (Ottawa: Ministry of Industry, 2011), http://www.statcan.gc.ca/pub/85-002-x/2011001/article/11577-eng.pdf.

11. J.B. Sprott, C.M. Webster, and A.N. Doob, "Punishment Severity and Confidence in the Criminal Justice System," *Canadian Journal of Criminology and Criminal Justice* 55, no. 2 (2013), 279–92.

12. A. Rajekar and R. Mathilakath, *The Funding Requirement and Impact of the "Truth in Sentencing Act" on the Correctional System in Canada*.

13. Office of the Auditor General of Canada, *Report of the Auditor General of Canada*, Chapter 4, "Expanding the Capacity of Penitentiaries-Correctional Service of Canada" (Ottawa: Author, 2014), http://publications.gc.ca/collections/collection_2014/bvg-oag/FA1-2014-1-4-eng.pdf, p. 6.

14. I. Zinger, "Human Rights and Federal Corrections: A Commentary on a Decade of Tough on Crime Policies in Canada," *Canadian Journal of Criminology and Criminal Justice* 58, no. 4 (2016), 609–27 at 612.

15. Office of the Auditor General of Canada, *Report of the Auditor General of Canada* (2014).

16. Zinger, "Human Rights and Federal Corrections," p. 612.

17. Ibid., p. 613.

18. Ibid.

19. H. Crichton and R. Ricciardelli, "Shifting Grounds: Experiences of Canadian, Provincial Correctional Officers," *Criminal Justice Review 41*, no. 4 (2016), 427–45 at 435.

20. Bronskill, "Reforms Have Compounded Pressures on Canada's Criminal Justice System."

21. S. Fine, "Ottawa Plans to Reduce the Use of Mandatory Prison Sentences," *Globe and Mail*, November 1, 2016, http://www.theglobeandmail.com/news/national/ottawa-plans-to-reduce-use-of-mandatory-prison-sentences/article32609570/.

22. Ibid.

23. N. Pevsner, *A History of Building Types* (Princeton: Princeton University Press, 1976).

24. P. Hancock and Y. Jewkes, "Architectures of Incarceration: The Spatial Pains of Imprisonment," *Punishment and Society 13*, no. 5 (2011), 611–29.

25. Public Safety Canada Portfolio Corrections Statistics Committee, *Corrections and Conditional Release Statistical Overview: 2015 Annual Report* (Ottawa: Public Works and Government Services Canada, 2016), https://www.publicsafety.gc.ca/cnt/rsrcs/pblctns/ccrso-2015/ccrso-2015-en.pdf.

CHAPTER

3

CONTEMPORARY CANADIAN CORRECTIONS

CHAPTER OBJECTIVES

- Describe the legislative framework of Canadian corrections.
- Describe the correctional process.
- Situate the role of corrections in a democratic society.
- Describe the "who" and the "what" of corrections.
- Define corrections.
- Discuss the structure of contemporary Canadian corrections.
- Describe the role of private, not-for-profit agencies in corrections, and provide examples.
- Discuss the issues that surround corrections and the Canadian public.
- Define and describe the approach of restorative justice, noting its key principles and contrasting it with the traditional adversarial justice system.

This chapter provides an overview of the systems of corrections in Canada. The discussion is designed to get you thinking about the different dimensions of corrections and to provide a backdrop for the more detailed discussions throughout the text.

THE LEGISLATIVE FRAMEWORK OF CORRECTIONS

Correctional systems operate under a variety of federal and provincial/territorial statutes that establish the authority of correctional officials, set out jurisdiction, and provide the framework within which decisions are made and programs are administered. Among the more significant pieces of legislation are the Canadian Charter of Rights and Freedoms, the Constitution Act (1867), and the Corrections and Conditional Release Act.

Canadian Charter of Rights and Freedoms

The **Canadian Charter of Rights and Freedoms** is the primary law of the land and guarantees fundamental freedoms, legal rights, and equality rights for all citizens of Canada, including those accused of crimes. The Charter is playing a significant role with respect to systems of corrections, in particular the rights of inmates.

The Constitution Act (1867)

The **Constitution Act (1867)** sets out the respective responsibilities of the federal and provincial/territorial governments in many areas, including criminal justice. This has significant implications for Canadian corrections, as the legislation created two separate systems of corrections, one federal and the other provincial/territorial. Key themes in this text are the implications of this arrangement and the differences between the two systems. The federal government operates correctional facilities for offenders who have been sentenced to two years or more. Probation, the most widely used sanction for supervision of offenders in the community, is available only for offenders who fall under the jurisdiction of provincial/territorial corrections and to federal offenders whose sentence is exactly two years.

The Criminal Code

The **Criminal Code** is a federal statute that defines most criminal offences, the procedures for prosecuting them, and the penalties that sentencing judges can hand down.

The Federal Corrections and Conditional Release Act (CCRA)

The **Corrections and Conditional Release Act (CCRA)**, enacted in 1992, is the primary legislation under which the federal system of corrections operates. Sections in this act cover institutional and community corrections, conditional release and detention, and the Office of the Correctional Investigator (OCI).

The act also contains special provisions related to Indigenous persons in federal corrections. Sections 81 and 84 of the act are intended to assist in reducing the over-representation of Indigenous persons in federal correctional institutions while at the same time increasing the involvement of First Nations communities in assisting the release and reintegration of Indigenous offenders. Under Section 81, for example, First Nations communities can enter into agreements with the federal government to assume "care and custody" of some Indigenous inmates. Indigenous inmates in corrections are further examined in Chapter 13.

Canadian Charter of Rights and Freedoms
The primary law of the land, which guarantees basic rights and freedoms for citizens, including convicted offenders.

Constitution Act (1867)
Legislation that includes provisions that define the responsibilities of the federal and provincial/territorial governments with respect to criminal justice.

Criminal Code
Federal legislation that sets out the criminal laws of Canada and the procedures for administering justice.

Corrections and Conditional Release Act (CCRA)
The primary legislation under which the federal system of corrections operates.

Another key provision of the CCRA is a recognition of the interests of crime victims in the corrections system. The legislation includes provisions requiring that crime victims be informed about the offender's progress, review dates for conditional release, where the offender is incarcerated, and where the offender will be residing if they are released from custody. Crime victims may also provide victim impact statements to the Correctional Service of Canada (CSC) and to the Parole Board of Canada (PBC), indicating how the crime affected them.[1]

The CCRA is a "living document" and has been amended over the years. In 2015, Parliament passed legislation creating the Canadian Victims Bill of Rights. This legislation added provisions to the CCRA, including the right of registered victims to receive copies of PBC decisions, and the right of victims who do not attend a parole hearing to be able to request to listen to an audio recording of the hearing.

Provincial and Territorial Corrections Legislation

Provincial and territorial legislation includes corrections statutes that set out the framework within which provincial and territorial correctional systems operate. In Ontario, for example, the Ministry of Correctional Services Act, includes sections on the ministry, that is, duties of the minister, functions of the ministry, and agreements to provide corrective services; correctional institutions, including maximum- and medium-security custody programs, custody prior to sentencing, the use of lock-up, and rehabilitation programs, custody, and temporary absences from institutions, among others; the Ontario Parole Board, including its organization and activities; adult probation; and a variety of other provisions.[2]

International Agreements and Conventions

Finally, there are international agreements and conventions to which the Canadian government is a signatory. These include the Nelson Mandela Rules (formerly known as the United Nations Standard Minimum Rules for the Treatment of Prisoners) and the International Covenant on Civil and Political Rights. For example, the United Nations Basic Principles for the Treatment of Prisoners, Principle 9, states, "Prisoners shall have access to the health services available in the country without discrimination on the grounds of their legal situation."[3]

The response to offenders by systems of corrections in Canada has sometimes not met international standards. For example, investigations have found that Canadian inmates, particularly in provincial/territorial institutions and those on remand, often receive inadequate health care.[4]

THE CORRECTIONAL PROCESS

Persons who become involved in the criminal justice system move through a variety of stages, from initial contact with police, through the courts, and, if convicted, into corrections (see Figure 3.1). Along the way, many decisions are

Figure 3.1

Flow of Cases Through the Criminal Justice System

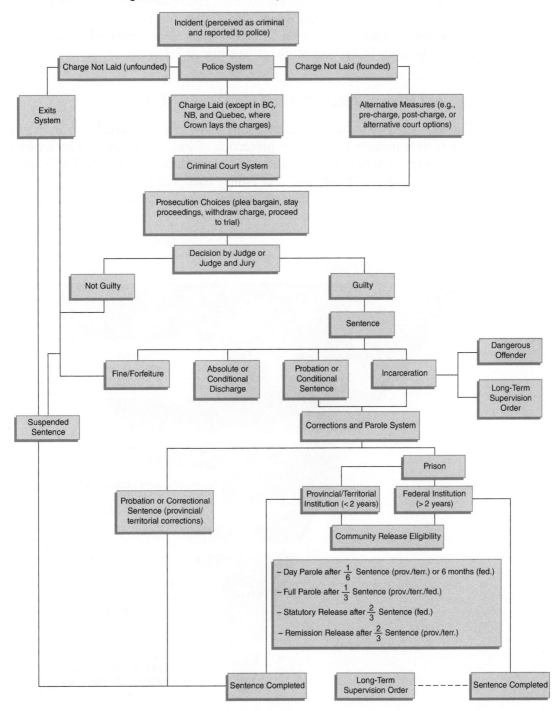

Source: From Roberts/Grossman, *Criminal Justice in Canada*, 3E. © 2008 Nelson Education Ltd. Reproduced by permission. www.cengage.com/permissions.

made by criminal justice personnel and others, all of whom are working in agencies and organizations that have specific mandates.

The flow of cases through the criminal justice system has also been characterized as a funnel; in other words, the deeper into the process, the smaller the number of cases. Fewer than 5 percent of incidents reported to the police ultimately result in a prison sentence (see Figure 3.2).

THE MANDATE AND GOALS OF CORRECTIONS

Correctional systems and the other components of the criminal justice system have as their primary mandate the protection of society. However, there is often disagreement over how this goal can best be accomplished. As discussed in Chapter 1, the correctional "pendulum" has swung back and forth between classical/conservative approaches to offenders and positivist/liberal ones. The persistence

Figure 3.2

The Criminal Justice Funnel

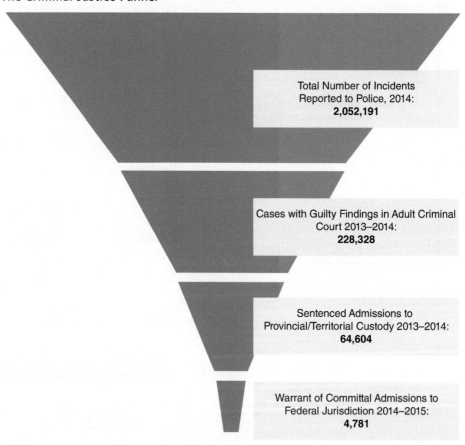

Total Number of Incidents
Reported to Police, 2014:
2,052,191

Cases with Guilty Findings in Adult Criminal
Court 2013–2014:
228,328

Sentenced Admissions to
Provincial/Territorial Custody 2013–2014:
64,604

Warrant of Committal Admissions to
Federal Jurisdiction 2014–2015:
4,781

Source: Reproduced with the permission of Public Safety Canada, 2017, https://www.publicsafety.gc.ca/cnt/rsrcs/pblctns/ccrso-2015/#c1.

of these two views of the goals of corrections—punishment versus treatment—has resulted in what is often referred to as the "split personality" of corrections.

CORRECTIONS IN A DEMOCRATIC SOCIETY

Systems of corrections, along with the police, criminal courts, and criminal law, are the primary mechanisms by which the state attempts to ensure the safety and security of the general public. In democratic societies, however, there are tensions among these systems of power and authority. Corrections systems are designed to ensure the safety and security of the community; however, at the same time, there is a need to ensure that the rights of accused and convicted persons are protected. The mission statement of the CSC, for example, reflects an attempt to balance the protection of society with the rights of offenders: "The Correctional Service of Canada (CSC), as part of the criminal justice system and respecting the rule of law, contributes to public safety by actively encouraging and assisting offenders to become law-abiding citizens, while exercising reasonable, safe, secure and humane control."

Under the Canadian Charter of Rights and Freedoms, offenders have all the same rights as other citizens except for those removed by law or incarceration. Court decisions and various commissions of inquiry have had a strong impact on correctional policies and procedures and how offenders are managed. These are discussed throughout the text.

Human Rights and Corrections

Systems of corrections must adhere to a number of human rights obligations that have been summarized in four key principles:

- The safety of correctional staff, prisoners, and society at large is paramount.
- Prisoners retain the human rights and fundamental freedoms of all members of society, except those that are necessarily removed as a consequence of sentence.
- Decisions affecting prisoners are made in a fair and forthright manner.
- Correctional authorities apply the "least restrictive measures" consistent with public safety.[5]

The materials presented in the following chapters indicate that systems of corrections have often fallen short in meeting these human rights obligations.

Accountability and a Concern with the Rule of Law

A key requirement is that criminal justice agencies be accountable and transparent. This has historically proven to be a challenge for systems of corrections.[6] There are few structures in place to ensure oversight of systems of corrections. This is in stark contrast to police services, where legislation has established numerous levels of oversight through provincial and territorial police acts, offices of police complaints commissioners, and civilian independent investigative offices.[7]

In recent years, systems of corrections and conditional release have found themselves being held more accountable. This has coincided with the increasing involvement of the courts and the Canadian Human Rights Tribunal, which are now imposing on correctional agencies and personnel a **duty to act fairly** when managing offenders. This means that decisions must be fair and equitable and that offenders must have the opportunity to respond to any assessments made by correctional personnel about their conduct and performance. In 2012, for example, a federal judge ordered a review of the inmate grievance system in federal correctional facilities, based on a finding that delays in resolving official grievances were heightening tensions and violence.[8] Court decisions have also placed limits on the use of solitary confinement and strip searches and given federal inmates the right to vote.

Correctional authorities have been the target of civil suits launched by crime victims and have also been taken to court by inmates over issues such as living conditions, disciplinary actions, and various regulations. This is discussed further in Chapter 6.

So too are systems of corrections required to abide by the **rule of law**. The universal principles of the rule of law are as follows:

1. The government and its officials and agents as well as individuals and private entities are accountable under the law.
2. The laws are clear, publicized, stable, and just; are applied evenly; and protect fundamental rights, including the security of persons, property, and certain core human rights.
3. The process by which laws are enacted, administered, and enforced is accessible, fair, and efficient.
4. Justice is delivered timely by competent, ethical, and independent representatives and neutrals who are of sufficient number, have adequate resources, and reflect the makeup of the communities they serve.[9]

The discussion in the following chapters will reveal that Canadian corrections has often not acted in accordance with these principles.

THE "WHO" AND THE "WHAT" OF CORRECTIONS

"Corrections" describes such a wide range of structures and activities that it is often difficult to determine what is being discussed. Many people make the mistake of equating corrections with prisons (and many college and university texts have pictures of prisons or inmates in cells on their covers).

The "Who" of Corrections

All correctional systems have both **noncarceral** (non-institutional) and **carceral** (institutional) components (see Table 3.1).

Duty to act fairly
The obligation of corrections to ensure that offenders are treated fairly by corrections personnel. Also, the right of inmates to be heard and to have an impartial hearing.

Rule of law
The requirement that governments, as well as individuals, be subject to and abide by the law.

Noncarceral
That portion of systems of corrections relating to offenders in non institutional settings.

Carceral
That portion of systems of corrections relating to confinement in correctional institutions.

Table 3.1 The "Who" of Noncarceral and Carceral Corrections

Noncarceral	Carceral
Judges	Judges
Probationers	Inmates
NGOs (e.g., John Howard Society and Elizabeth Fry Society)	Superintendents and wardens
Community counsellors/treatment professionals	Correctional officers; institutional parole officers
Indigenous friendship centres	Spiritual advisers (e.g., chaplains and Indigenous Elders)
Community volunteers	Indigenous prison liaison workers
Offender's family	Citizen Advisory Committees
Parole board members	Treatment professionals
Parolees	Community volunteers
Federal offenders on statutory release	Offender's family
Parole officers	
Halfway house staff	

"Community corrections" include alternatives to confinement (e.g., diversion and probation) as well as programs for offenders released from correctional institutions (e.g., offenders who are on parole). Also, both lists in Table 3.1 include criminal court judges because the correctional process actually begins when the sentence is passed (see Chapter 4).

There are more correctional personnel, offenders, and programs in noncarceral corrections, since most convicted persons are not sent to a correctional institution (although most federal correctional personnel work in institutions). Figure 3.3 presents a breakdown of Canada's adult noncarceral and carceral populations.

The "What" of Corrections

The "what" of corrections is somewhat more complicated. Correctional systems can be described in a number of ways, including the following.

Figure 3.3

Admissions to Adult Correctional Services, by Type of Supervision and Jurisdiction, 2015–16

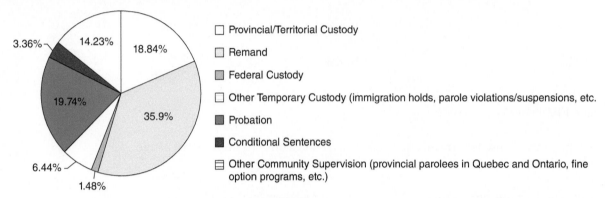

Source: Julie Reitano, "Adult Correctional Statistics in Canada, 2015/2016," *Juristat* 37, no. 1, Catalogue no. 85-002-X (Ottawa: Canadian Centre for Justice Statistics, 2017), p. 15, http://www.statcan.gc.ca/pub/85-002-x/2017001/article/14700-eng.pdf.

Corrections as a Political Enterprise

This reflects the perspective of the critical school, discussed in Chapter 1. Correctional policies and practices are influenced by laws and the government of the day. An illustration of this is the shift away from a liberal, European-influenced approach to offenders toward a more punitive penology (discussed in Chapter 2).

Corrections as a Philosophy for Responding to Criminal Offenders

Various philosophies of crime and punishment have, at different times, provided the basis for the response to persons designated as criminal. These responses have ranged from the death penalty and corporal (physical) punishments to treatment and rehabilitation.

Corrections as a Subsystem of the Criminal Justice System

Systems of corrections, together with the public, the police, and the criminal courts, are the foundation of the criminal justice system. These components of the criminal justice system are interconnected. For example, patterns of police enforcement and arrest affect the number of cases that Crown counsel must handle; the case-screening decisions of Crown counsel then determine the caseloads of criminal courts.

For another example, the sentencing decisions of criminal court judges can influence the caseloads of probation officers and determine the number of admissions to correctional institutions, while the decisions of parole boards affect the number of offenders who are incarcerated as well as the caseloads of parole officers.

Throughout the criminal justice process, various key decisions affect the likelihood that an offender will end up under the supervision of a correctional authority. Figure 3.4 shows that there are four main groups of agencies and organizations whose activities and decisions affect correctional systems: the police (apprehension), the judiciary (sentencing), correctional departments and parole boards (release from custody), and legislative bodies (the framework within which the police, the judiciary, and corrections/parole boards operate).[10]

Figure 3.4

Organizational Impacts on the Adult Correctional System

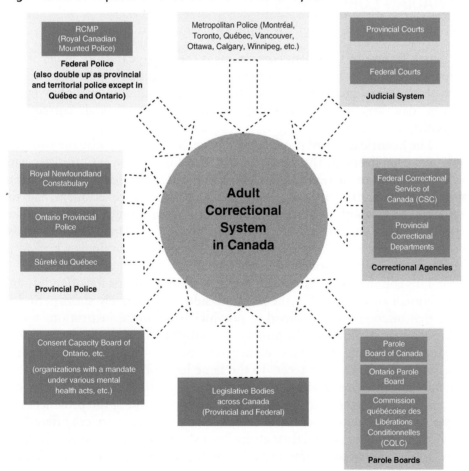

Source: From A. Rajeka and R. Mathilakath, *The Funding Requirement and Impact of the "Truth in Sentencing Act" on the Correctional System in Canada* (Ottawa: Office of the Parliamentary Budget Officer, 2010), p. 36, http://www.parl.gc.ca/PBO-DPB/documents/TISA_C-25.pdf. Reprinted by permission of the Office of the Parliamentary Budget Officer.

Corrections as a Range of Programs Delivered in Community and Institutional Settings

Most convicted offenders are not incarcerated; instead, they complete their sentences under some form of supervision in the community. This includes probation and conditional sentences, discussed in Chapter 5. There are also offenders who have been released from custody, either on parole or (for federal offenders) on statutory release (see Chapter 10). Correctional systems offer programs and services to the relatively small number of offenders who are sentenced to a period of custody (Chapter 9).

THE STRUCTURE OF CONTEMPORARY CANADIAN CORRECTIONS

The Split in Correctional Jurisdiction

Two-year rule
The basis for the division of responsibility for convicted offenders between the federal and provincial/territorial governments.

A unique feature of Canadian corrections is the **two-year rule**, under which offenders who receive sentences of two years or longer fall under the jurisdiction of the federal government, and offenders receiving sentences of two years less a day are the responsibility of provincial/territorial correctional authorities.

The historical record provides no clear explanation for why the two-year rule was established at the time of Confederation in 1867. Observers have offered a number of reasons, including these: (1) the federal government wanted to strengthen its powers; (2) only the federal government had the resources to establish and maintain long-term institutions; and (3) offenders receiving short sentences were seen as in need of guidance, whereas those receiving longer sentences were seen as more serious criminals who had to be separated from the society for longer periods.[11]

This split in jurisdiction has a number of implications for offenders and correctional authorities. On the negative side, the relatively short period of time that offenders are confined in provincial/territorial institutions means there is a high turnover of the population, which makes it difficult to provide treatment programs. There is evidence that offenders in provincial/territorial institutions may not have access to the same level of programs and services, including health care services, as their counterparts in the federal corrections system.[12] As well, there are considerable variations among the provinces and territories in the noncarceral and carceral programs and services offered.

Many offenders spend their entire "careers" in provincial/territorial facilities, while others spend time in both systems. On a more positive note, the two-year rule helps separate more serious offenders, who receive lengthier sentences and, potentially, have greater access to treatment programs, from those who have committed less serious crimes. As well, provincial/territorial offenders have access to a wide range of alternatives to incarceration, including probation and conditional sentences.

The Federal System of Corrections

The federal system of corrections is operated by the Correctional Service of Canada (CSC), an agency of Public Safety Canada. The CSC, headquartered in Ottawa, has five regions: Atlantic, Québec, Ontario, Prairie, and Pacific. It operates a variety of facilities, including federal penitentiaries, halfway houses, healing lodges for Indigenous offenders, community parole offices, psychiatric hospitals, reception and assessment centres, health care centres, and palliative care units. Also, the CSC has partnered with not-for-profit organizations to operate halfway houses across the country.

The CSC is responsible for offenders who receive a sentence of two or more years (see Figure 3.5).

Provincial/Territorial Corrections

The large majority (96 percent) of convicted offenders receive sentences that place them under the jurisdiction of provincial/territorial correctional authorities. Just more than half the custodial sentences imposed by the courts are for less than one year.[13] As a result, the larger percentage of offenders in Canada are confined in provincial/territorial facilities.

All of the provinces/territories operate a variety of noncarceral programs and services, including probation, bail supervision, fine options, community service, and diversion programs. Other programs and services include electronic monitoring (most often as a condition of probation or temporary absence), house arrest, intensive supervision probation, temporary absences,

Figure 3.5

Offenders Under the Responsibility of the CSC, 2015

Total Offender Population

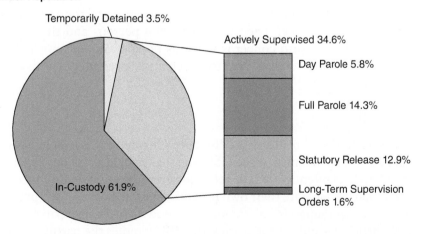

Source: Reproduced with the permission of Public Safety Canada, 2017, https://www.publicsafety.gc.ca/cnt/rsrcs/pblctns/ccrso-2015/#c1.

and parole. Most of the offenders in provincial/territorial correctional systems are on probation. The provincial/territorial governments also operate correctional facilities and remand centres.

Provincial/territorial systems of corrections have traditionally received little attention from researchers, mainly because of the diversity of programs and services they offer, the short periods that provincial offenders remain in confinement (a month, on average), and the widely held view that provincial/territorial offenders are a less serious threat in terms of their criminal behaviour—this, even though many provincial jails are faced with overcrowding, gang activity, high rates of communicable diseases (including HIV, tuberculosis, and hepatitis C), a lack of inmate safety, and poor working conditions for staff. And many offenders in provincial/territorial correctional facilities have mental health issues, may be afflicted with fetal alcohol spectrum disorder (FASD), and have significant treatment needs.

There is evidence that offenders in provincial/territorial institutions may not have access to the same level of programs and services, including health care services, as their counterparts in the federal corrections system.[14] As one observer noted about offenders in provincial/federal corrections, "A large number of people are serving a life sentence, 30 days at a time".[15]

Persons on **remand**, which include those awaiting trial or sentencing, are housed in provincial/territorial institutions. Remanded individuals (1) have been charged with an offence, and the court has ordered they be held in custody while awaiting trial, or (2) have been found guilty at trial and are awaiting sentencing.

A key feature of Canadian corrections is the increase in persons on remand. Over 60 percent of inmates in provincial/territorial jails are on remand. In the province of Ontario during 2014–15, for example, there were more admissions to remand (46,593) than sentenced offenders (25,256).[14]

Among the concerns that surround remand are the mixing of persons who have not yet been tried with convicted persons and those serving sentences. There are also concerns that this population does not have access to adequate medical services and to psychiatric assessments and treatment in some jurisdictions.[15]

Parole Boards

The Parole Board of Canada (PBC; see Chapter 10) is a federal agency that operates independently of the CSC and makes final decisions regarding when (most) federal offenders will be released from custody. Two provinces—Québec and Ontario—operate their own provincial parole boards, with provincial probation officers supervising offenders released on provincial parole. In the other eight provinces and the territories, the PBC handles the parole release of some offenders, and CSC parole officers supervise offenders.

Remand
The status of accused persons who have been charged but have been denied bail and awaiting trial or have been found guilty and are awaiting sentencing.

The Costs of Corrections

By the late 20th century, Canadian corrections had become a multibillion-dollar conglomerate, requiring massive fiscal and human resources. This has been accompanied by significant increases in the costs of housing inmates in federal prisons and in the numbers of correctional personnel. Between 2007 and 2012, the cost of the federal prison system rose 86 percent. More than 80 percent of corrections budgets are for custodial expenses, even though less than 5 percent of sentenced offenders are sent to prison.

The expenditures on adult corrections in Canada are considerable ($4.6 billion in 2014–15).[16] Custodial corrections accounted for 80 percent of the costs, while supervision in the community was 15 percent of the costs. Nearly 80 percent of CSC employees work in correctional facilities, while only 8 percent are involved in community supervision.[17] This is despite the fact that the majority of offenders under the authority of corrections are under supervision in the community.

The average cost of housing a male federal inmate in a maximum-security institution is more than $100,000 per year; for women inmates it is even higher, estimated in 2017 to be $211,000 per year. The average annual cost per federal offender for community supervision is about one-quarter that of an inmate in a minimum-security institution ($113,974 for an offender in an institution; $29,537 for an offender in the community).[18] It can be anticipated that these costs have risen. An analysis of data for one federal woman offender serving a 21.5-year sentence estimated the total cost at $7.4 million.[19] A key issue is whether these expenditures are producing positive outcomes.

Confining offenders in correctional institutions is expensive. Supervising offenders in the community is considerably less costly (see Table 3.2 for per day and annual costs of supervision of provincial offenders in British Columbia).

Oversight: The Federal Correctional Investigator, Provincial Ombudspersons, and Auditors

As noted above, a key requirement is that the criminal justice system, including corrections, be accountable and transparent, which historically has proven to be a challenge for systems of corrections.[20]

Oversight of corrections can include audits conducted by provincial auditors general and ombudspersons, and investigations conducted by the federal Office of the Correctional Investigator (OCI) and various commissions of inquiry and other bodies. The potential impact of the findings and recommendations of the correctional investigator and the provincial ombudspersons on corrections reform is limited by the fact that these are only advisory; these offices have no legal power to mandate changes in corrections policy and practice. The extent to which corrections authorities have acted on specific recommendations has been uneven, and many of the issues that have been identified,

Table 3.2   Per Day and Annual Costs of Supervision, British Columbia

Community Supervision	Custody
Average cost $6.49 per person, per day, or $2,400 per person, per year	Average cost of $202.00 per person, per day, or almost $74,000 per person, per year
• Low-risk clients: average cost of $2.65 per person, per day	
• Medium- to high-risk clients: average cost of $10.45 per person, per day	

Source: Corrections Branch, *A Profile of B.C. Corrections: Protect Communities, Reduce Reoffending* (Victoria: Ministry of Justice, 2013), p. 4, http://www2.gov.bc.ca/assets/gov/law-crime-and-justice/criminal-justice/corrections/reports-publications/bc-corrections-profile.pdf.

such as inmates not having timely access to treatment programs, have remained largely unheeded. The decisions of the courts, however, are binding, and these have been the catalyst for change in corrections policy and practice.

In the absence of a body of scholarly research on provincial correctional institutions, the reports of provincial auditors provide some insights into the issues in this under-studied component of Canadian corrections. Audits of institutional corrections generally examine all facets of operations, including fiscal expenditures, programming, strategic planning, and classification, among others. Effective oversight can play a role in improving the effectiveness of correctional institutions and their policies and programs.[21]

The OCI is an independent federal agency whose mandate is (1) to investigate the problems experienced by federal offenders in institutions, or who are under supervision in the community, and (2) to ensure that the CSC meets its obligations to manage offenders in a manner that conforms to the law and that respects the rights of offenders.[22]

The office receives and investigates issues related to inmates and correctional institutions, with a particular focus on CSC compliance with the law, the provisions of the CCRA, and Commissioner's Directives. In the 2015–16 annual report, for example, the OCI examined whether the CSC was in compliance with a Commissioner's Directive that inmates have ready access to library materials. The findings included the case study set out in Corrections File 3.1.

In its annual report, the OCI makes recommendations designed to improve the federal system of corrections. In the 2015–16 annual report, for example, there were 27 recommendations, including the following:

- I recommend that CSC develop, publicly release and implement an older offender strategy for federal corrections in 2016–17 that addresses

CORRECTIONS FILE 3.1

Inmate Access to Library Materials

During a recent visit at a maximum-security institution, the investigator noted that there was no library. Books were brought to the units on mobile library carts. Teachers exchanged books for cell studies. Acquisitions could not be determined as books were stored in various locations. General-purpose computers were available to the population, but these are not conducive for educational purposes. The warden stated that the librarian resource had been eliminated as part of recent budget cuts. At the same institution, teachers were restricted to using utility rooms in the units to hold classes as the classroom had been shuttered for over 10 years. There was a nine-month wait list for cell studies.

Source: Office of the Correctional Investigator, *Annual Report, 2015–2016*, p. 57. http://www.oci-bec.gc.ca/cnt/rpt/pdf/annrpt/annrpt20152016-eng.pdf. Reprinted by permission of the Office of the Correctional Investigator.

---

the care and custody needs of offenders aged 50 or older. This strategy should include programming, reintegration, public safety, and health care cost considerations.

- I recommend that CSC enhance harm-reduction initiatives, including the re-introduction of safe tattooing sites and the implementation of a needle exchange pilot, and assess the impacts of these measures on inmate health, institutional substance mis-use, and security operations.
- I again recommend that CSC appoint a Deputy Commissioner for Indigenous Corrections.
- I recommend that CSC significantly enhance access to the community for women residing in the minimum-security units through increased use of temporary absences, work releases, employment, and vocational skills training programs.[23]

There are also ombudspersons in all of the provinces and territories except Nunavut who have the authority to investigate citizen complaints against the decisions and actions of government agencies and employees. Such complaints include those made by offenders under the supervision and control of provincial correctional systems. Table 3.3 provides examples of the types of recommendations in the reports of provincial ombudspersons and the responses of the respective provincial corrections authorities to the recommendation.

Note that, while expenditures on corrections have increased significantly in the past decade, there has not been a corresponding increase in the budgets of correctional investigators.

Table 3.3   Selected Recommendations Made by Provincial Ombudspersons

Ombudsperson	Recommendation	Response from Corrections*
Saskatchewan Ombudsman[a]	Finding: Substandard housing for inmates. Recommendation: That the ministry repair unit 4 at the Regina Correctional Centre to ensure that it meets current building code standards, or alternatively, replace unit 4 with a new facility.	Status: Accepted. The ministry agreed with our recommendations: that unit 4 is not an appropriate place for inmates to live and that the space will be renovated or a new accommodation provided. Given the current number of inmates, the unit is being pressed into use in the short term.
Nova Scotia Office of the Ombudsman[b]	Finding: Inmates in provincial correctional facilities unable to vote in the provincial election. Recommendation: Provincial protocols outlining voting procedures for offenders in provincial facilities be developed jointly between Elections Nova Scotia and the Department of Justice, Correctional Services.	Status: The recommendation was accepted and implemented.

* Note: There may be a disconnect between accepting a recommendation and implementing a recommendation.

[a] Saskatchewan Ombudsman, "Recommendations 2010 Third Quarter Update," (2010), p. 5, https://www.ombudsman.sk.ca/uploads/document/files/rrq3-final-en-1.pdf.

[b] Nova Scotia Office of the Ombudsman, *2009–2010 Annual Report* (Halifax: Author, 2010), p. 16, https://novascotia.ca/ombu/publications/AnnualReportOmbuds-2009-10.pdf.

Citizen's Advisory Committees (CACs)

Citizen Advisory Committees (CACs) have been operating since 1965 and were subsequently enshrined in the CCRA (1992). They are designed to provide a public presence in corrections, and there are CACs for every federal institution and district parole office across the country.

CACs are composed of local citizens who volunteer their time. Attempts are made to ensure that these committees reflect the ethnic, gender, socioeconomic, and cultural diversity of the community at large. The goals of CACs include these: to promote public knowledge and understanding of corrections; to contribute to the development of correctional facilities and programs; and to increase public participation in the corrections process. They are also meant to serve as impartial observers of the CSC's day-to-day operations. CACs offer advice to CSC managers, meet regularly with correctional staff and management, and serve as liaisons between correctional institutions and the community.

In several regions of the country, the CACs have experienced challenges in recruiting and retaining volunteers. As well, there is little evidence that CACs have increased community involvement in, or oversight of, the operations of correctional institutions. This suggests that they may be more symbolic than substantive.

The Private, Not-for-Profit Sector

Private, not-for-profit organizations have long been helping deliver correctional services and programs. The organizations may be gender-focused, such as the John Howard Society (men) and the Elizabeth Fry Society (women), while others focus their efforts on specific groups of offenders, inmate families, and health issues, among others. Some of the agencies are national, while others are found in specific jurisdictions. Selected examples of these organizations and a brief synopsis of their activities are set out in Table 3.4.

Table 3.4 Selected Examples of Private, Not-for-Profit Agencies and Their Activities

Agency	Activities
John Howard Society (www.johnhoward.ca)	Operates a variety of programs across Canada, including bail supervision, community assessment and parole supervision, residential halfway housing, victim assistance, victim–offender mediation, and public and legal education. In Calgary, for example, the society operates a substance abuse program, a community conferencing program based on the principles of restorative justice, and a number of counselling, advocacy, referral, and pre-release planning programs for offenders in correctional institutions, as well as a halfway house for special needs offenders.
Elizabeth Fry Society (www.elizabethfry.ca)	The society lobbies for reform at all levels of the criminal justice system, with a particular focus on women in conflict with the law. The society advocates for correctional policy reforms, and develops and operates its own programs. It played a major role in the closing of the Kingston Prison for Women and its replacement by smaller, regional facilities. The branch in Hamilton, Ontario, operates a community service order program and provides a range of services for female offenders, including counselling and pre-release services.
Salvation Army (www.salvationarmy.ca)	The Salvation Army has been involved in Canadian corrections since the late 1880s. It provides a range of services and programs, including community service order supervision, family group conferencing, substance abuse counselling, and supervision of offenders in the community.
St. Leonard's Society (www.stleonards.ca)	Through its affiliates across the country, St. Leonard's Society sponsors a wide range of programs and facilities for offenders. St. Leonard's Society in Hamilton, Ontario, for example, operates the Emerald Street Treatment Centre, a 36-bed facility for federal offenders on conditional release. The facility also offers a number of non residential programs for federally sentenced offenders.

(continued)

Agency	Activities
Break Free Family Centre (Ontario) (www.breakfreefamily .org)	Focuses on providing a high standard of care and therapeutic counselling services to youth, family, offenders, and the community at large, regardless of religious preferences, ethnic background, gender, or race. Offers a variety of clinical programs, including individual and group counselling, trauma counselling, and anger management programs.
Canadian Families and Corrections Network (CFCN) (www.cfcn-rcafd.org)	Mission is to build "stronger and safer communities by assisting families affected by criminal behaviour, incarceration, and community reintegration." Offers programs, sponsors research, and provides resources for families.
PACT Urban Peace Program (Ontario) (pactprogram.ca)	Works with at-risk youth and youth in conflict with the law.
Pathways to Freedom Ministries (www .pathwaystofreedom.ca)	Dedicated to improving the lives of offenders by facilitating the mentorship of Christian volunteers with prison inmates and ex-offenders.
Native Counselling Services of Alberta (NCSA) (www.ncsa.ca)	Provides a wide range of programs and services for Indigenous peoples centred on Indigenous spirituality and traditions. This includes clinical, family, and youth court workers; family group conferencing; and the Stan Daniels Healing Centre and the Buffalo Sage Wellness House (see Chapter 13).
Community Justice Initiatives Association (BC) (www.cjibc.org)	Uses a restorative justice framework for conflict resolution in the criminal justice system. Facilitates victim–offender mediation and offers a variety of training programs for criminal justice professionals and other agencies and organizations.
Alberta Seventh Step Society (www .albertaseventhstep.com)	Supports prisoners and ex-prisoners to achieve and maintain their freedom, realize their potential, and grow in the community.

CORRECTIONS AND THE CANADIAN PUBLIC

The discussion in Chapter 1 revealed that in the early days, most offenders were punished in public view. Back then, community residents could actually witness sanctions, including hangings; indeed, they could often participate in the sanctioning process by showering offenders with insults (as well as the occasional rotten vegetable). Today, with a few notable exceptions—such as the involvement of community volunteers in correctional institutions, community programs, and various restorative justice programs (discussed below)— the public's role in corrections is largely reactive. Community sentiment is often expressed through interest groups that lobby for harsher sanctions for convicted persons, longer periods of incarceration, and more-stringent requirements for release.

Citizens' lack of confidence in the criminal justice system generally and their increasing feelings of insecurity are channelled by politicians into criminal laws and social policies that place an increasing emphasis on risk assessment and the management of offenders, both inside institutions and in the community. This, in turn, can lead to a punitive penology, discussed in Chapter 2.

Although there are high levels of public confidence in the police (76 percent in the most recent General Social Survey), only 57 percent of the general public has a great deal or some confidence in the justice system itself. This includes systems of correction.[24] The public generally feels that prisons do a poor job of rehabilitating offenders and releasing offenders at the right time.[25] This is often ascribed to citizens having little information about the justice and corrections system, which to some degree is a consequence of governments and systems of corrections not being proactive in providing information. This can result in the public perception that the criminal justice system is too lenient with offenders even though crime rates are in general decline.[26]

For most Canadians, the media are the primary sources of information about crime and criminal justice. However, the media tend to be biased toward sensational crimes and to simplify crime and justice issues, and the public for its part tends to generalize from specific events.[27] Research studies suggest that the media play a role in the public's fear of crime, which in turn may lead to support of punitive penal policies.[28]

As political entities, corrections systems have generally failed to work proactively to counter their media image and to correct statements made about them by politicians. This has allowed politicians and legislatures free rein to direct correctional policy based on ideological rather than empirical grounds. One could ask why corrections systems have not developed better relationships with communities and why corrections officials seem constantly to be playing defence. A cynical view would be that an uninformed public is more pliable and directs fewer questions at politicians and corrections policy-makers.

The NIMBY Phenomenon

In corrections, this lack of confidence (and lack of factual information) is often reflected in the **NIMBY (not in my back yard) syndrome**. That term refers to the resistance that communities generate to correctional systems' efforts to establish community programs and residences for offenders. Far too often, corrections personnel find themselves in crisis management mode: reacting to the accusations of citizens' interest groups; struggling to reassure a nervous public following an escape, or after the commission of a serious

NIMBY (not in my back yard) syndrome
The resistance of community residents to efforts of corrections systems to locate programming and residences for offenders in the community.

crime by an offender on parole; or attempting to justify the release of a high-risk offender into the community. This issue is discussed in Chapter 11.

There may also be concerns with high-risk offenders being held in facilities that the public perceives are not being adequately staffed and resourced, and from which there have been escapes. The federal OCI has found that many First Nations communities have been hesitant to have healing lodges situated in their region due to these concerns.[29]

However, some communities have lobbied hard to attract correctional institutions in anticipation of the jobs and other economic benefits these facilities bring. The new Okanagan Correctional Centre in Osoyoos, British Columbia, for example, was built on Osoyoos Indian Band land in 2015. Over 200 tradespeople were involved in constructing the prison, and 240 correctional officers and 60 staff will operate the facility. As Chief Clarence Louie of the Osoyoos Indian Band stated, "There's not very many $200 million projects in Oliver and Osoyoo. This is a huge project, not just for the Osoyoos Indian band, but for the entire south Okanagan."[30]

RESTORATIVE JUSTICE: AN ALTERNATIVE APPROACH TO CRIME AND CRIMINAL OFFENDERS

Concerns about the effectiveness of the traditional adversarial system of criminal justice and a variety of other influences have led to the search for alternative ways to respond to people in conflict with the law. **Restorative justice** is based on the principle that criminal behaviour injures not only victims but also communities and offenders, and that efforts to address and resolve the problems created by criminal behaviour should involve all of these parties. Key notions in restorative justice are healing, reparation and reintegration, and the prevention of future harm.

Restorative justice provides an alternative framework for responding to criminal offenders. It focuses on problem-solving, addressing the needs of victims and offenders, involving the community on a proactive basis, and fashioning sanctions that reduce the likelihood of reoffending (see Figure 3.6).

The primary objectives of restorative justice are to fully address the needs of victims of crime and to prevent reoffending by offenders reintegrating back into the community. Offenders are required to acknowledge and take responsibility for their behaviour, and efforts are made to create a "community" of support and assistance for the victim and the offender, and to address the long-term interests of the community.

There are a number of "entry" points in the criminal justice system where restorative justice approaches can be used: police (pre-charge), Crown (post-charge/pre-conviction), courts (post-conviction/pre-sentence), corrections (post-sentence), and following sentence expiry (see Figure 3.7).

Restorative justice differs in significant ways from traditional adversarial justice. The key differences are listed in Table 3.5.

Restorative justice
An approach to responding to offenders based on the principle that criminal behaviour injures victims, communities, and offenders, and that all of these parties should be involved in efforts to address the causes of the behaviour and its consequences.

Figure 3.6

The Relationships of Restorative Justice

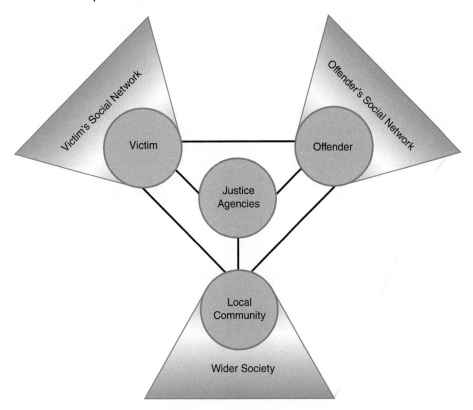

Source: Marshall, T.F. (1999). *Restorative Justice: An Overview. Home Office Occasional Paper 48.* London: Home Office.

Figure 3.7

Restorative Justice: Entry Points in the Criminal Justice System

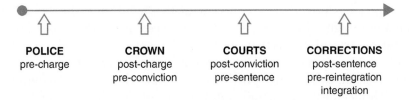

Source: *The Effects of Restorative Justice Programming,* http://www.justice.gc.ca/eng/re-pr/csj-sjc/jsp-sjp/ rr00_16/rr00_16.pdf, p. 7, Figure 2.1. Entry Points in the Criminal Justice System. Department of Justice Canada, 2000. Reproduced with the permission of the Department of Justice Canada, 2017.

Table 3.5   Comparison of Retributive and Restorative Justice Principles

Retributive Justice	Restorative/Community Justice
Crime violates the state and its laws.	Crime violates people and relationships.
Justice focuses on establishing guilt so that doses of pain can be meted out.	Justice aims to identify needs/obligations so that things can be made right.
Justice is sought through conflict between adversaries in which the offender is pitted against state rules, and intentions outweigh outcomes—one side wins and the other loses.	Justice encourages dialogue and mutual agreement, gives victims and offenders central roles, and is judged by the extent to which responsibilities are assumed, needs are met, and healing (of individuals and relationships) is encouraged.

Source: Howard Zehr, *Changing Lenses: A New Focus for Crime and Justice* (Scottsdale, Ariz.: Herald, 1990).

A key feature of restorative justice is the community's involvement in addressing the issues surrounding criminal offending. This moves residents into a proactive, participatory role, one that is not available in traditional justice processes. This involvement reflects survey findings that when provided with information, the public generally supports treatment and prevention programs.[31]

Restorative justice attempts to address both the ethical and legal dimensions of justice. The ethical objectives of justice are, ideally, achieved by all parties, including the victim, the offender, and the community, feeling that their concerns, feelings, and rights are respected. The legal objectives of justice are also addressed, in that throughout the restorative justice process, the legal rights of all parties are safeguarded.[32]

SUMMARY

This chapter has provided an overview of the "who" and the "what" of the federal and provincial/territorial corrections systems. There was a discussion of the various organizations that are involved in corrections, including the not-for-profit sector, parole boards, corrections investigators, and the community. The materials in this chapter provide the framework for the remainder of the text, which includes more detailed discussions of the different dimensions of corrections. Restorative justice was introduced as an alternative approach to addressing crime and criminal offenders. The basic principles of restorative justice were discussed and a comparison with the retributive approach of the traditional justice system was offered.

KEY POINTS REVIEW

1. Corrections systems operate under a variety of federal and provincial/territorial statutes that establish the authority of corrections officials, set out jurisdiction, and provide the framework within which decisions are made and programs are administered.

2. Correctional systems and other components of the criminal justice system have as their primary mandate the protection of society, although there is often disagreement as to the best way to accomplish this.

3. The flow of cases through the criminal justice system has been characterized as a funnel, wherein the deeper into the process, the smaller the number of cases.

4. All correctional systems have both non institutional and institutional components.

5. The "what" of corrections includes corrections as a political enterprise, a philosophy for responding to criminal offenders, a subsystem of the criminal justice system, and a range of programs delivered in the community and in institutional settings.

6. The large majority of convicted offenders receive sentences that place them under the jurisdiction of provincial/territorial correctional authorities.

7. In contrast to federal corrections, little attention and research has been focused on provincial/territorial corrections.

8. There has been an exponential growth in the number of persons on remand and often this population is larger than the sentenced population.

9. The costs of corrections are high and continue to rise, although offenders can be supervised in the community for a fraction of the cost of incarceration.

10. Among the requirements of corrections in a democratic society are a focus on human rights and the rule of law.

11. There are challenges in holding correctional authorities accountable and a key role is played by the federal Office of the Correctional Investigator, provincial ombudspersons, and auditors general.

12. The private, not-for-profit sector is very involved in the delivery of correctional services and programs.

13. Generally speaking, the Canadian public has little confidence in systems of corrections to protect communities or to help offenders become law-abiding citizens.

14. Restorative justice is an alternative approach to crime and criminal offenders that operates on principles considerably different from the adversarial system of criminal justice.

KEY TERM QUESTIONS

1. Describe the role of each of the following in providing the framework for corrections: the **Canadian Charter of Rights and Freedoms**, the **Constitution Act (1867)**, the **Criminal Code**, and the **Corrections and Conditional Release Act**.

2. Describe the components of **noncarceral** and **carceral** corrections.

3. What is the **two-year rule**, and what role does it play in corrections?

4. Define **remand** and note the issues surrounding this status.

5. What are the universal principles of the **rule of law**?

6. What is meant by the **duty to act fairly** and how does this apply to corrections?

7. What are **Community Advisory Committees** and what role do they play in corrections?

8. What is the **NIMBY** phenomena and what challenges does it present for corrections?

9. Define **restorative justice** and discuss how its principles differ from those of the "traditional" criminal justice system.

CRITICAL THINKING EXERCISE

Critical Thinking Exercise 3.1

Rethinking the Two-Year Rule

A defining feature of Canadian corrections is the "two-year" rule, wherein convicted persons who receive a sentence of two years less a day are placed under the authority of provincial/territorial correctional authorities, and convicted persons who receive a sentence of two years or more are the responsibility of federal corrections. This split is viewed as problematic by many observers, who contend that the incarcerative sentences for provincial/territorial inmates are too short to provide any meaningful programming.

Your Thoughts?

1. What is your view of the two-year rule, and the positive and less-positive features of how correctional jurisdiction is divided up in Canada?

2. Can you suggest any alternatives to the current arrangement that might address the current issues that you identified in question #1?

CLASS/GROUP DISCUSSION EXERCISES

Class/Group Discussion Exercise 3.1

Should Additional Provisions for Oversight of Corrections Be Established?

While Canadian police services are subjected to several layers of oversight—including, in many provinces, civilian-staffed agencies that investigate serious incidents involving the police—there is not a similar structure of oversight of incidents that occur in corrections. The recommendations of coroner's inquiries in the case of an inmate death in custody, for example, have no legal status, nor are the findings and recommendations of the federal OCI and provincial/territorial ombudspersons binding. Similarly, the findings from provincial audits of institutional and community correctional practice are provided to legislators, who may or may not act on them.

Your Thoughts?

1. Should provisions for independent oversight of correctional systems be established? Why or why not?
2. Should the recommendations of the federal OCI and of provincial/territorial ombudspersons be legally binding on systems of corrections? Why or why not?

Class/Group Discussion Exercise 3.2

Should the General Public Be Involved in Corrections?

Generally speaking, corrections systems have not attempted to develop community partnerships. It is often argued that responding to criminal offenders should be left to professionals. For their part, those who favour increased community involvement contend that the community is an underutilized resource.

Your Thoughts?

1. What is your view on this debate?
2. If you support the increased participation of community residents, what initiatives would you take to accomplish this?
3. If you were asked to volunteer for a program for offenders one evening a month at a halfway house or in a correctional institution, would you accept? Why or why not?
4. If the CSC proposed to construct a halfway house for offenders on parole in your neighbourhood, would you support this proposal?

MEDIA LINKS

"John Howard Society," www.johnhoward.ca

"Elizabeth Fry Society," www.elizabethfry.ca

"Solitary Confinement: CBC Interview with Howard Sapers [Canada's Prison Ombudsman]," https://www.youtube.com/watch?v=8ieWOA-F5ks

"Native Counselling Services of Alberta," www.ncsa.ca

"Recovering from Crime–Restorative Justice in Action," https://www.youtube.com/watch?v=DUyzjeOrwnw

NOTES

1. Office of the Federal Ombudsman for Victims of Crime, *Toward a Greater Respect for Victims in the Corrections and Conditional Release Act* (Ottawa: Government of Canada, 2010), http://www.victimsfirst.gc.ca/res/pub/ccra-lscmlc; Parole Board of Canada, "CVBR and Changes to the Corrections and Conditional Release Act: What This Means for Victims" (2014), https://www.canada.ca/en/parole-board/corporate/publications-and-forms/fact-sheets/the-canadian-victims-bill-of-rights-and-changes-to-the-corrections-and-conditional-release-act-what-this-means-for-victims-and-the-parole-board-of-canada.html.

2. *Ministry of Correctional Services Act*, R.S.O. 1990, c. M.22, https://www.ontario.ca/laws/statute/90m22.

3. UN General Assembly, "Basic Principles for the Treatment of Prisoners," resolution adopted by the General Assembly, 28 March 1991 (A/RES/45/111), http://www.un.org/documents/ga/res/45/a45r111.htm.

4. John Howard Society of Ontario, *Fractured Care: Public Health Opportunities in Ontario's Correctional Institutions* (Toronto: Author, 2016), http://johnhoward.on.ca/wp-content/uploads/2016/04/Fractured-Care-Final.pdf.

5. H. Sapers and I. Zinger, "The Ombudsman as a Monitor of Human Rights in Canadian Federal Corrections," *Pace Law Review 30*, no. 5 (2010), 1512–28, http://digitalcommons.pace.edu/cgi/viewcontent.cgi?article=1752&context=plr.

6. M.B. Mushlin and M. Deitch, "Opening up a Closed World: What Constitutes Effective Prison Oversight?" *Pace Law Review 30*, no. 5 (2010), 1383–1410.

7. C.T. Griffiths, *Canadian Police Work*, 4th ed. (Toronto: Nelson, 2016).

8. M. Brosnahan, "Judge Orders Judicial Review of Prison Grievance System. Ongoing Backlog Contributing to Growing Tensions, Violence," *CBC News*, August 7, 2012, http://www.cbc.ca/news/canada/judge-orders-judicial-review-of-prison-grievance-system-1.1164502.

9. World Justice Project, "What is the Rule of Law?" (n.d.), http://worldjusticeproject.org/what-rule-law. Reprinted by permission of The World Justice Project.

10. A. Rajeka and R. Mathilakath, *The Funding Requirement and Impact of the "Truth in Sentencing Act" on the Correctional System in Canada* (Ottawa: Office of the Parliamentary Budget Officer, 2010), p. 36, http://publications.gc.ca/collections/collection_2010/dpb-pbo/YN5-28-2010-eng.pdf.

11. R. Ouimet (Chair), *Toward Unity: Criminal Justice and Corrections: Report of the Canadian Committee on Corrections* (Ottawa: Information Canada, 1969).

12. J.R. Bernier and K. MacLellan, *Health Status and Health Services Use of Female and Male Prisoners in Provincial Jail* (Halifax: Atlantic Centre of Excellence for Women's Health, 2011), http://www.acewh.dal.ca/pdf/prisoner-health2011.pdf.

13. Public Safety Canada Portfolio Corrections Statistics Committee, *Corrections and Conditional Release Statistical Overview: 2015 Annual Report* (Ottawa: Public Works and Government Services Canada, 2016), https://www.publicsafety.gc.ca/cnt/rsrcs/pblctns/ccrso-2015/ccrso-2015-en.pdf.

14. John Howard Society of Ontario, *Fractured Care*, p. 14.

15. John Howard Society of Ontario, *Unlocking Mental Health Issues in Ontario*. (Toronto: Author, 2015), http://www.johnhoward.on.ca/wp-content/uploads/2015/07/Unlocking-Change-Final-August-2015.pdf; John Howard Society of Ontario, *Fractured Care*.

16. Julie Reitano, "Adult Correctional Statistics in Canada, 2015/2016," *Juristat 37*, no. 1, Catalogue no. 85-002-X (Ottawa: Canadian Centre for Justice Statistics, 2017), p. 5, http://www.statcan.gc.ca/pub/85-002-x/2017001/article/14700-eng.pdf.

17. Public Safety Canada Portfolio Corrections Statistics Committee, *Corrections and Conditional Release Statistical Overview*.

18. M. Olotu, D. Luong, C. MacDonald, M. McKay, S. Heath, N. Allegri, and E. Loree, *Report of the Evaluation of CSC's Community Corrections*, Chapter 1, "Correctional Interventions" (Ottawa: Correctional Service Canada, 2011), http://www.csc-scc.gc.ca/text/pa/ev-cci-fin/ev-cci-fin-eng.pdf, p. 106.

19. A. Rajekar and R. Mathilakath, The Funding Requirement and Impact of the *"Truth in Sentencing Act" on the Correctional System in Canada* (Ottawa: Office of the Parliamentary Budget Officer, 2010), http://www.pbo-dpb.gc.ca/files/files/Publications/TISA_C-25.pdf, pp. 99–100.

20. Mushlin and Deitch, "Opening up a Closed World."

21. S. Stojkovic, "Prison Oversight and Prison Leadership," *Pace Law Review 30*, no. 5 (2010), 1476–89.

22. Office of the Correctional Investigator (n.d.), www.oci-bec.gc.ca.

23. Office of the Correctional Investigator, *Annual Report, 2015-2016*. pp. 71–3. http://www.oci-bec.gc.ca/cnt/rpt/pdf/annrpt/annrpt20152016-eng.pdf. Reprinted by permission of the Office of the Correctional Investigator.

24. A. Cotter, *Spotlight on Canadians: Results from the General Social Survey: Public Confidence in Canadian Institutions* (Ottawa: Statistics Canada, 2015), http://www.statcan.gc.ca/pub/89-652-x/89-652-x2015007-eng.htm.

25. D. Beeby, "Study Finds Canadians Have Little Confidence in Justice System," *Canadian Press*, February 17, 2014, http://www.ctvnews.ca/canada/study-finds-canadians-have-little-confidence-in-justice-system-1.1689727.

26. M. Kennedy, "Despite Falling Crime Rates, Many Canadians Believe Justice System Is Too Lax: Pollster," *Postmedia News*, July 24, 2012, http://www.ottawacitizen.com/Canadians+feel+justice+system/6984558/story.html.

27. T.L. Dixon, "Teaching You to Love Fear: Television News and Racial Stereotypes in a Punishing Democracy," in *The Prison-Industrial Complex*, ed. S.J. Hartnett (Chicago: University of Illinois Press, 2011), 106–23.

28. J.S. Rosenberger and V.J. Callanan, "The Influence of Media on Penal Attitudes," *Criminal Justice Review 36*, no. 4 (2011), 435–55.

29. J. Gerson, "Dangerous Offender's Escape Raises Questions About Security, Effectiveness of Healing Lodges," *National Post*, August 17, 2016, http://news.nationalpost.com/news/canada/canadian-politics/dangerous-offenders-escape-raises-questions-about-security-effectiveness-of-healing-lodges.

30. A. Jung, "Rare Glimpse of New Okanagan Prison," *Global News*, May 21, 2015, http://globalnews.ca/news/2010960/rare-glimpse-of-new-okanagan-prison/.

31. K.N. Varma and V. Marinos, "Three Decades of Public Attitudes Research on Crime and Punishment in Canada," *Canadian Journal of Criminology and Criminal Justice 55*, no. 4 (2013), 549–62.

32. M. Tonry, "Restoration in Youth Justice," in *Why Punish? How Much? A Reader on Punishment*, ed. M. Tonry (New York: Oxford University Press, 1991), 319–35.

SENTENCING: BEGINNING THE CORRECTIONS PROCESS

CHAPTER OBJECTIVES

- Describe the purpose, principles, and goals of sentencing and the various sentencing options.
- Discuss the various sentencing options that are available to judges and provide an example of each option.
- Discuss the issues that surround the sentencing of Indigenous offenders, with particular reference to Section 718.2(e) of the Criminal Code.
- Describe the sanction of judicial determination and the special sentencing provisions for dangerous and long-term offenders.
- Recognize the identifying attributes of problem-solving courts, the differences between these specialized courts and traditional courts, and the effectiveness of the specialized courts.
- Discuss the dynamics of sentencing in a restorative justice framework, with particular reference to circle sentencing.
- Discuss the research findings with respect to the effectiveness of sentencing.

An often overlooked component of corrections is the sentences that are imposed by judges in the criminal courts. The criminal courts can be viewed as the beginning of the correctional process. It is here that judgments are passed on offenders and that specific sanctions are imposed through sentencing (see Figure 4.1). The decisions made by criminal court judges determine not only which system of corrections (federal or provincial/territorial) the offender will enter but also whether the offender will be under supervision and control in the community or be incarcerated.

Over the years, sentencing has been a flashpoint for public opinion and for the agenda of government. Public opinion surveys over the past three decades have consistently found that 75 percent of Canadians view sentencing

Figure 4.1

Outline of the Canadian Court System

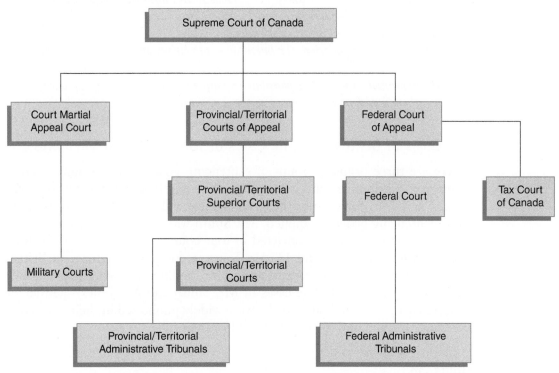

Source: *Canada's Court System*, http://www.justice.gc.ca/eng/csj-sjc/ccs-ajc/pdf/courten.pdf. "Outline of Canada's Court System," page 4. Department of Justice Canada, 2015. Reproduced with the permission of the Department of Justice Canada, 2017.

as too lenient. There appears to be widespread support for mandatory sentences, albeit with judges retaining some discretion to impose a lesser sentence in exceptional cases.[1] Reforming sentencing was a cornerstone of the government of Stephen Harper (2006–15), and the Truth in Sentencing Act (2009) contained provisions that reduced the discretion of criminal court judges and introduced mandatory minimum penalties for a number of offences (many of which have subsequently been determined by the courts to be unconstitutional).

THE PURPOSE AND PRINCIPLES OF SENTENCING

Section 718 of the Criminal Code sets out the purpose and principles of sentencing:

> *The fundamental purpose of sentencing is to protect society and to contribute, along with crime prevention initiatives, to respect for the law and the maintenance of a just, peaceful and safe society by imposing just sanctions that have one or more of the following objectives:*

(a) to denounce unlawful conduct and the harm done to victims or to the community that is caused by unlawful conduct;

(b) to deter the offender and other persons from committing offences;

(c) to separate offenders from society, where necessary;

(d) to assist in rehabilitating offenders;

(e) to provide reparations for harm done to victims or to the community; and

(f) to promote a sense of responsibility in offenders, and acknowledgment of the harm done to victims or to the community.

The Goals of Sentencing: The Cases of Mr. Smith and Mr. Jones

There are three primary groups of sentencing goals in the criminal courts: utilitarian, retributive, and restorative. The semi-fictitious cases of "Mr. Smith" and "Mr. Jones" (not their real names) will be used to illustrate how these sentencing goals are applied. Mr. Smith was a Québec police chief and swimming coach who was convicted of four counts of sexual assault for fondling two girls, aged 12 and 13. Mr. Jones, a computer engineer in British Columbia, was convicted of sexual assault for fondling his young stepdaughter over a two-year period. The cases of Mr. Smith and Mr. Jones—neither of whom had a prior criminal record—were widely publicized in their respective communities, and both men eventually lost their jobs.

Utilitarian Goals

Utilitarian sentencing goals focus on the future conduct of Mr. Smith, Mr. Jones, and others who might commit similar offences. These goals focus on protecting the public from future crimes in the following ways:

- by discouraging potential Mr. Smiths and Mr. Jones's from crime (**general deterrence**);
- by discouraging Mr. Smith and Mr. Jones from doing it again (**specific deterrence**);
- by addressing the reasons why Mr. Smith and Mr. Jones did it (*rehabilitation*); and
- by keeping Mr. Smith and Mr. Jones in jail to protect society (*incapacitation*).

Retributive Goals

The past, rather than the future, is the focus of retributive sentencing goals, which include the following:

- to express society's disapproval of Mr. Smith's and Mr. Jones's behaviour and to validate existing laws (*denunciation*); and
- to make Mr. Smith and Mr. Jones "pay" for their offences, based on the philosophy "an eye for an eye" (*retribution*).

General deterrence
An objective of sentencing designed to deter others from engaging in criminal conduct.

Specific deterrence
An objective of sentencing designed to deter the offender from future criminal conduct.

Central to the retributive goals of sentencing is the notion of proportionality—that is, the sentences received by Mr. Smith and Mr. Jones should be proportionate to the gravity of their offences as well as to their degree of responsibility.

Restorative Goals

These goals are premised on the principles of restorative justice, introduced in Chapter 3. As noted, restorative justice is based on the principle that criminal behaviour injures not only the victim but also communities and offenders. Any attempt to resolve the problems that the criminal behaviour has created should, therefore, involve all three parties. Restorative justice approaches also have a utilitarian function in that they are designed to protect the public from future criminal behaviour.

Since the victims in both these cases were children, they would be excluded from any restorative justice forum. However, the victims' families would have the opportunity to discuss the impact of the crimes, and Mr. Smith and Mr. Jones would be held accountable for their criminal behaviour.

What Sentences Did Mr. Smith and Mr. Jones Receive?

Under the Criminal Code (s. 271), everyone who commits a sexual assault is guilty of:

(a) *an indictable offence and is liable to imprisonment for a term of not more than 10 years or, if the complainant is under the age of 16 years, to imprisonment for a term of not more than 14 years and to a minimum punishment of imprisonment for a term of one year; or,*

(b) *an offence punishable on summary conviction and is liable to imprisonment for a term of not more than 18 months or, if the complainant is under the age of 16 years, to imprisonment for a term of not more than two years less a day and to a minimum punishment of imprisonment for a term of six months.*

Although neither Mr. Smith nor Mr. Jones had a prior criminal record, and both had a good job history, the offences they committed were serious and had a significant impact on the victims. One of Mr. Smith's victims suffered long-term emotional and academic problems, while Mr. Jones's former spouse and children experienced considerable emotional difficulties. The child victims in both cases had been young and vulnerable. Mr. Smith had been an authority figure in the community, and parents trusted him to supervise their children, a trust he violated. Similarly, Mr. Jones violated the trust of his stepdaughter and most likely would have continued sexually abusing her had she not informed her mother of his improper behaviour.

Mr. Smith was sentenced to two years less a day in a provincial correctional facility. The Crown appealed the sentence on the grounds that it was too lenient. But the Appeal Court upheld the sentence, in part because Mr. Smith had been fired from his job as police chief and so had already experienced a severe sanction. The Appeal Court acknowledged that child abuse typically demands a denunciatory sentence for the protection of society, but noted that each case must be judged on its merits.

Mr. Jones was not so fortunate. He was sentenced to six years in prison and sent to a federal correctional facility. In explaining the sentence, the presiding judge cited the objectives of denunciation and general and specific deterrence.

These two cases highlight the vast discretion that Canadian judges have in sentencing.

SENTENCING OPTIONS

The sentencing options from which Canadian judges may select are set out in Table 4.1. Note that offenders who receive an absolute discharge or a conditional discharge do not need to apply for a records suspension (formerly referred to as a "pardon") to have the charges removed from their records. These are the only sentences to which this proviso applies.

Most of the sentencing options set out in Table 4.1 provide alternatives to confinement (discussed in greater detail in Chapter 5). Some of these options may be mixed and matched; for example, the judge may impose a period of probation in conjunction with a sentence of two years less a day for offenders in provincial/territorial systems, or the judge may impose fines along with probation or a period of confinement.

Sentences imposed in court can be concurrent, consecutive, or intermittent. **Concurrent sentences** received by the offender are merged into one sentence and served simultaneously. Thus, an offender sentenced to two terms of nine months each will serve a nine-month sentence (not an eighteen-month sentence). With **consecutive sentences**, the sentences are served separately; one begins after the other has expired. That is, an offender sentenced to two terms of nine months each will serve 18 months. **Intermittent sentences** are served on a "part-time" basis (generally weekends, from Friday evening until Monday morning) and are no more than 90 days in length. Intermittent sentences may pose challenges for provincial/territorial systems of corrections. Many facilities are overcrowded, so it may be difficult to find appropriate accommodations for these individuals.

The Criminal Code states that all sentences are to be concurrent unless the trial judge specifies that they are to be consecutive. By contrast, sentences under the Provincial Offences Act are to be consecutive unless the sentencing judge specifies that they are to run concurrently.

Within the framework of the Criminal Code, there are special categories of offenders that judges must consider in their sentencing decisions. One is persons who are convicted of multiple murders. Under the Protecting Canadians by Ending Sentence Discounts for Multiple Murders Act (2011), offenders who are convicted of one or more murders may have their parole eligibility

Concurrent sentences Sentences that are amalgamated and served simultaneously.

Consecutive sentences Sentences that run separately and are completed one after the other.

Intermittent sentences Sentences that are served on a "part-time" basis, generally on weekends.

Table 4.1 Sentencing Options and Case Examples

Absolute discharge	The offender is found guilty but technically not convicted. The offence will appear on the offender's criminal record for one year.
	Case example: A Montréal police officer who admitted to stealing an iPhone from another officer and to possession of a large quantity of erectile dysfunction pills without a prescription was given an absolute discharge by the court. This means he will have no criminal record. The officer had pled guilty to the two charges, and the prosecutor had asked for a $1,500 fine, which would have resulted in the officer having a criminal record. Defence counsel had proposed that the officer make a donation to charity in order to avoid a criminal record and be able to return to his job as a police officer.[a]
Conditional discharge	The offender is found guilty and released upon the condition that they comply with the conditions of a probation order. If the offender fails to meet the conditions, they may be returned to court to be sentenced on the original charge. A conditional discharge remains on the offender's criminal record for three years after the completion of the probation order.
	Case example: A P.E.I. correctional officer convicted of common assault in connection with a bar fight was given a conditional discharge. The offence occurred during a bar fight, during which a local businessman suffered a serious eye injury. The defendant was sentenced to a conditional discharge for a period of six months. During this time, he would be on probation and be required to undergo an assessment, counselling, and treatment as directed. In addition, he would be required to perform 20 hours of community service and write a formal apology to the victim.[b]
Suspended sentence	The offender is convicted of the offence, but the imposition of the sentence is suspended pending successful completion of a period of probation.
	Case example: A former Manitoba Justice corrections officer was given an 18-month suspended sentence for assaulting a mentally ill inmate who verbally attacked her. The officer had been seeking a discharge, which meant she would not have a criminal record. But the provincial court judge rejected this, stating that doing so would not be in the public interest: "The public interest requires a criminal record for this offence to demonstrate the public's high expectation that, regardless of the reasons for their detention, prisoners will be kept safe by their jailers." The officer had been fired from her job in a remand centre after the inmate was struck several times in the head, suffering minor injuries.[c]
Fine	The offender must pay a specific amount of money within a specified time, or face the prospect of imprisonment for fine default.

(continued)

Absolute discharge A sentencing option wherein the offender is found guilty, but is technically not convicted.

Conditional discharge A sentencing option wherein the offender is found guilty and released upon condition that they comply with the conditions of a probation order for three years, at which time the conviction is removed from the offender's record.

Suspended sentence The offender is convicted of the offense, but the imposition of the sentence is suspended pending successful completion of a period of probation.

Fine A sentencing option wherein the offender must pay a specific amount of money within a specified time, or face the prospect of imprisonment for fine default.

Case example: A well-known Montréal activist was awarded $15,000 in damages from two Montréal police officers. The Québec Superior Court judge ruled that his rights were violated when he was arrested during a protest rally and detained for five days. The two police constables were ordered by the court to pay the activist "the sum of $15,000 in exemplary damages." The officers had testified in court that the activist and others in the crowd were behaving in a hostile fashion and yelling insults to the police. The judge noted that while being the recipient of insults was not pleasant, no threats had been made toward the officers.[d]

Intermittent sentence

The offender is sentenced to jail, generally served on weekends, and when not in custody is subject to a probation order with specific conditions. Available only for sentences that do not exceed 90 days.

Case example: A Halifax man who sexually assaulted a woman was sentenced by the Nova Scotia Supreme Court to serve 90 days on weekends. Evidence presented in court indicated that the defendant had been drinking heavily and assaulted the victim against her will.[e]

Probation

The offender is placed under supervision in the community for a specified period of time (maximum three years), must fulfill general conditions, and may be required to adhere to, or complete, specific conditions (e.g., attend alcohol or drug counselling).

Case example: A 26-year-old woman was sentenced to nine months' probation after being convicted of committing an indecent act on flight to Halifax. In addition, the defendant was given a six-month conditional sentence (see below) for assaulting a police officer, committing an act of mischief, and causing a disturbance at Halifax Stanfield International Airport. At trial, a flight attendant testified that the defendant and a male accomplice had engaged in intimate activities under a coat during the flight. Upon arrival and while in police custody, the defendant had caused damage to the interior of the airport.

The conditional sentence involved a curfew under which she would be confined to her home from 10 p.m. to 6 a.m.; also, the defendant was to submit a DNA sample and perform a total of 60 hours community service. In addition, the defendant was ordered to reimburse the airport for damage to a wall.[f]

Conditional sentence

The offender receives a term of confinement (less than two years) and is allowed to serve it in the community under the supervision of a probation officer, provided he or she meets certain specified conditions (although the offender is on a conditional sentence order and not on probation and may be imprisoned for violation of conditions).

Case example: In the Ontario Court of Justice, Criminal Division, a resident of Walpole Island received a 12-month conditional sentence, including the first 6 months under house arrest, after pleading guilty to sexual assault.

The man, who was intoxicated at the time and did not recall the incident, had broken into an apartment and climbed into bed with a man and woman at the residence. The defendant had expressed remorse for the incident, which was taken by the court to be sincere.

After serving six months on house arrest, the defendant will be subjected to a 10 p.m. to 6 a.m. curfew. He was also ordered to provide a sample of his DNA for the National DNA Data Bank and listed on the National Sex Offender Registry for 20 years.

Other requirements were that he abstain absolutely from the purchase, possession, consumption, and use of alcohol and illegal substances; attend assessment, treatment, and counselling; not associate with the man or woman; and not be present in the community where the assault occurred without the permission of his probation officers.

Following completion of this portion of the sentence, the man would be required to complete a two-year period of probation.[g]

Imprisonment The offender is sentenced to a period of confinement.

Case example: A man who killed his neighbour in a drunken dispute was sentenced to seven years in prison. The man was convicted of manslaughter after an incident in his residence in which he stabbed another man to death.[h]

---

[a] P. Cherry, "Police Officer Granted Absolute Discharge Over Erectile Dysfunction Pills, Stolen Smartphone," *Montreal Gazette*, January 14, 2016, http://montrealgazette.com/news/local-news/police-officer-granted-absolution-over-erectile-disfunction-pills-stolen-smartphone.

[b] "Prison Guard Gets Conditional Discharge for Assault," CBC News, September 18, 2009, http://www.cbc.ca/news/canada/prince-edward-island/prison-guard-gets-conditional-discharge-for-assault-1.854752.

[c] M. McIntyre, "Corrections Officer Gets 18 Month Suspended Sentence for Assaulting Inmate," *Winnipeg Free Press*, July 2, 2015, http://www.winnipegfreepress.com/local/Corrections-officer-gets-18-month-suspended-sentence-for-assaulting-inmate-311499031.html.

[d] "2 Montreal Police Officers Ordered to Pay $15,000 to Activist Jaggi Singh," CBC News, August 26, 2015, http://www.cbc.ca/news/canada/montreal/2-montreal-police-officers-ordered-to-pay-15-000-to-activist-jaggi-singh-1.3205040.

[e] B. Rhodes, "Halifax Man Sentenced to Jail on Weekends for Violent Sexual Assault," CBC News, March 10, 2016, http://www.cbc.ca/news/canada/nova-scotia/nova-scotia-sexual-assault-90-days-1.3485499.

[f] K. Doucette, "Woman Receives 9 Months Probation for Indecent Act on Halifax-Bound Flight," Canadian Press, July 14, 2015, http://www.ctvnews.ca/mobile/canada/woman-receives-9-months-probation-for-indecent-act-on-halifax-bound-flight-1.2468761.

[g] T. Peplinskie, "Man Gets 12-Month Conditional Sentence for Sexual Assault Conviction," *Pembroke Daily Observer*, October 7, 2009, http://www.thedailyobserver.ca/2009/10/07/man-gets-12-month-conditional-sentence-for-sexual-assault-conviction.

[h] M. Gilligan, "Calgary Man Who Killed Neighbour Sentenced to 7 Years in Prison," Global News, December 11, 2015, http://globalnews.ca/news/2394999/calgary-man-who-killed-neighbour-sentenced-to-7-years-in-prison.

"stacked"; that is, each murder conviction may be considered separately and the sentence for each offence served consecutively.

Sentencing Indigenous Offenders

There is a special provision in the Criminal Code (Section 718.2(e)) for the sentencing of Indigenous offenders. It is intended to reduce the over-representation of Indigenous people in correctional institutions. It was reaffirmed by the Supreme Court of Canada (SCC) in **R. v. Gladue** ([1999] 1 SCR 688). In that landmark case, the court held that where a term of incarceration would normally be imposed, judges must consider the unique circumstances of Indigenous people.

Specifically, Section 718.2(e) requires judges to consider (1) the unique systemic or background factors that may have contributed to the criminal behaviour of the Indigenous person before the court and (2) specific sentencing procedures and sanctions (including restorative justice and traditional healing practices) that may be more appropriate for the individual Indigenous offender. This includes considering colonialism, the impact of residential schools, and the marginality of Indigenous people in Canadian society.

Gladue was most recently confirmed by the SCC in *R. v. Ipeelee* (2012 SCC 13, [2012] 1 SCR 433; see Box 4.1). In 2012, the Ontario Court of Appeal ruled that two Indigenous men arrested for drug smuggling at the U.S. border should not be extradited to the United States, where their Indigenous heritage would not be considered at sentencing, as required in Canada.[2]

The involvement of Indigenous persons in systems of corrections is discussed in Chapter 13; so are policies and programs for Indigenous offenders. Despite a multitude of laws and initiatives to address the problem, Indigenous persons continue to be over-represented in the justice system and in corrections. Indeed, their over-representation has steadily increased over the past decade.

There is little evidence that the *Gladue* decision has had its intended impact. Indigenous offenders continue to be sentenced to prison and for longer periods of time at rates higher than their non-Indigenous counterparts. Critics, including Jonathan Rudin of Aboriginal Legal Services in Toronto, have argued that the *Gladue* requirements have been "virtually ignored" by many judges, particularly in the Prairie provinces where the rates of incarceration of Indigenous persons are the highest.[3] The *Gladue* principles appear to be applied most robustly in the specialized courts for Indigenous persons.[4] Others have noted that judges are often unable to sentence Indigenous offenders to alternatives to confinement due to a lack of programs and services in rural and remote areas and in cases where the Indigenous offender has committed a serious, violent offence.[5]

R. v. Gladue
A decision by the SCC that held that in cases where a term of incarceration would normally be imposed, judges must consider the unique circumstances of Indigenous people.

Judicial Determination

Section 743.6 of the Criminal Code gives sentencing judges the authority to impose, on some offenders receiving a sentence of imprisonment of two years or more, the requirement that the offender serve half the sentence or 10 years, whichever is less, before being eligible for parole, instead of the typical one-third. The main objectives of this provision—known as **judicial determination**—are denunciation and specific and general deterrence. Indigenous offenders are over-represented in the group of offenders receiving judicial determination. Offenders receiving judicial determination are more likely than other offenders to serve their entire sentence in confinement.

Judicial determination
An order by the sentencing judge that the offender serve one half of their sentence, or 10 years, whichever is less before being eligible to apply for parole.

Life Imprisonment

Under the Criminal Code, persons convicted of murder are subject to life imprisonment. This means that the offender is under sentence for life, although they may serve this sentence both in prison and upon release on parole in the community. The Criminal Code sets out the minimum number of years that an offender must serve in prison before being eligible to apply for release on parole. The key word is *apply*—there is no guarantee that the parole board will grant a release.

The death penalty was abolished by Parliament in 1976 and replaced with a mandatory life sentence without possibility of parole for 25 years in cases of first-degree murder. The debate over the death penalty continues, however.

Dangerous Offenders and Long-Term Offenders

Sections 752 and 753 of the Criminal Code set out the procedures and criteria for designating certain offenders as either **dangerous offenders** or **long-term offenders**.

On application by Crown counsel, the judge may designate a dangerous offender as a person who has been convicted of committing a serious personal injury offence (except murder) or a person who has a pattern of serious violent offences, who is deemed to present a danger to society, and who is highly likely to put the community at risk if not imprisoned. The application to designate an offender as dangerous must be made at the time of sentencing. A judge who makes a dangerous offender designation can order that person to serve an indeterminate period of time in prison. Dangerous offenders sentenced to an indeterminate period of imprisonment are eligible for a hearing before the Parole Board of Canada (PBC) every two years after serving seven years from the day they were taken into custody.

There has been a steady increase in the number of offenders designated as dangerous. In 2014–15, there were 622 federal inmates who had been designated as a dangerous offender, nearly 75 percent of dangerous offenders had

Dangerous offenders
A designation made by the judge after conviction that can result in an indeterminate term of imprisonment in a federal correctional institution.

Long-term offenders
A designation under Section 752 or 753 of the Criminal Code that requires the offender to spend up to 10 years under supervision following the expiry of their sentence.

at least one current sexual offence conviction, and nearly 90 percent were serving indeterminate sentences.[6] Of concern is the increase in the number of Indigenous offenders designated as dangerous offenders, comprising 29 percent of this group of offenders in 2016.[7] The majority of dangerous offenders were in custody in 2014–15, with a small number under supervision in the community.[8]

The long-term offender designation, designed to deal with specific sexual offences, is another option for Crown counsel, particularly where the Crown falls short of the rigid requirements or level of evidence to file a dangerous offender application. As with dangerous offenders, there must be evidence that the offender presents a substantial risk of reoffending by committing a serious personal offence. However, there must also be risk-assessment evidence demonstrating that the offender may be effectively managed in the community with appropriate supervision and treatment.

The designation is available only for those offenders who have received a sentence of more than two years. At sentencing, the judge sets the length of the long-term supervision order. This means that at the end of the sentence (which includes confinement and post-release supervision), the long-term supervision order comes into effect. This order requires that the offender be supervised by a parole officer up to 10 years.

The large majority of long-term supervision orders are for the maximum of 10 years. Just over 60 percent of offenders on long-term supervision orders in 2014–15 had at least one current sexual offence conviction. Among these offenders, some were in custody, while others were being supervised in the community.[9]

The PBC sets the conditions under which the offender will be supervised following the expiration of their sentence.

HOW JUDGES DECIDE

Criminal Court judges consider a wide range of factors when determining the sentence to be imposed on a convicted offender. The purposes of sentencing and the various sentencing options available to judges were presented earlier in the chapter. Box 4.1 sets out the additional information that judges may consider in any case. Even with the expansion of the number of offences that carry a mandatory minimum sentence, Canadian judges exercise considerable discretion in sentencing.

YOU BE THE JUDGE

To gain an appreciation of the challenges that judges face in making sentencing decisions, review the summaries of actual cases presented in Box 4.2 and place yourself in the position of the sentencing judge.

The purposes of sentencing and the various sentencing options available to judges were presented earlier in this chapter. Note that you can combine

---

BOX 4.1

Factors Considered in Sentencing

Aggravating circumstances	Facts about an offender and the offence that are considered negative and tend to increase the severity of a sentence—for example, violence.
Mitigating circumstances	Facts about the offender and the offence that may decrease the severity of a sentence—for example, being Indigenous, or being addicted.
Case law precedent	Judges consider sentencing decisions in previous, similar cases. A general principle is that there should be similar sentences in similar cases.
Pre-sentence reports (PSR)	A PSR, prepared by a probation officer, presents information on the offender's background, present situation, and risk/needs. It also sets out options for sentencing that the judge will consider.
Victim impact statements	These contain information on the harm done to the victim (psychological and physical) as well as the consequences of the victimization.
Psychological assessments	These are completed on offenders and address the mental state and treatment needs of the offender.
Indigenous offenders	Section 718.2(e) of the Criminal Code requires judges to consider alternatives to incarceration for Indigenous offenders.

---

options—that is, you can sentence the offender to a period of custody in a provincial/territorial correctional facility and, as well, add on a period of probation of up to three years. However, probation cannot be used in conjunction with a sentence of more than two years, for such sentences place the offender under the jurisdiction of federal corrections. Also discussed earlier were the various objectives of sentencing. (Note that as the judge you are not required to accept the recommendations for sentencing of either the Crown or defence counsel.)

While the case summaries in Box 4.2 do not provide all the materials that a sentencing judge would have access to, such as the PSR, the exercise does provide you with a sense of the challenges faced by sentencing judges. Note that all the offences in these cases were committed prior to the former Conservative government introducing mandatory minimum sentences for certain offences. Also, as noted, a number of the mandatory minimum penalties have been ruled unconstitutional by the courts. The penalties for the offences in the three cases presented below are maximums.

© Mike Baldwin / Cornered

"They say time is money. I had a very generous judge."

© Mike Baldwin http://www.CartoonStock.com

You Be the Judge

Read the summary of the following three cases. Then, for each case, answer the questions that are posed. Record your sentencing decisions and why you selected each particular sentence. Once you have completed all three cases, refer to the end of the chapter to see the actual sentences imposed. Then, for each question, ask yourself these questions and be prepared to discuss your answers: (1) Did my sentence match the sentence of the judge? (2) Was it more lenient or more harsh? (3) Did the judge in the actual case make a good decision?

Case #1

Appearing before you in court is a 21-year-old Indigenous man from the Atikamekw First Nation community of Wemotaci, located 270 kilometres north of Montréal. The man repeatedly burned a five-year-old girl with a cigarette and a lighter, resulting in permanent scarring on her arms, legs, face, and genitalia. The victim suffered 27 third-degree burns in the attack and was without medical treatment for some time. In court, the man denied committing the assault, although he had earlier confessed to the police.

At trial, the man was convicted of aggravated assault and is before you for sentencing. The Crown prosecutor is seeking a four-year prison term on the grounds that the seriousness of the offence requires denunciation. Defence is asking for a suspended sentence and three years probation.

Aggravated assault is an indictable offence, and the penalty as set out in the Criminal Code is a maximum of 14 years in prison. Since the offender is Indigenous, the court is required under the Criminal Code (Section 718.2(e)) to take into account the "circumstances of Aboriginal offenders" when sentencing. Although the offender was too young to have attended residential schools, he did grow up in an abusive home that was a legacy of his grandparents having been sent to the schools.

The Decision

1. What is your sentencing decision?
2. What is the rationale for the sentence?
3. What is the purpose of the sentence?

Case #2

Before you is a man who has pled guilty to assault, sexual assault, and unlawful confinement. The attacks occurred after the accused had gained entrance to the victim's apartment after scaling a wall and climbing onto a second-floor balcony. During the attack he forced himself on the victim and committed the offences. The victim was choked to blackout and suffered numerous other injuries. Both the accused and the victim knew each other prior to the attack. To date, he has already spent 30 months in pre-trial custody.

The assistant Crown attorney has asked you to consider a prison sentence of seven or eight years. With credit for time served in pre-trial custody, the accused would spend about four additional years in prison. The defence lawyer has suggested a five-year sentence, minus the time already served. The convicted man would spend two additional years in prison. The defence lawyer has stated that the offender is remorseful and has taken positive steps to change his life while in pre-trial custody. Evidence was presented that he had taken 45 counselling and self-improvement courses while in pre-trial custody. He also indicated to you that his client is a bipolar alcoholic and has pointed out that the pre-sentence report is "overwhelmingly positive."

The crime of assault can be either an indictable or a summary conviction offence. If indictable, the penalty is a maximum of 5 years in prison; if summary, a maximum of 18 months in prison. The crime of sexual assault is an indictable offence with a maximum penalty of 10 years in prison and a minimum of 1 year in prison. The crime of unlawful confinement can be either an indictable or a summary conviction offence. If an indictable offence, the offender is liable to imprisonment for a term not exceeding 10 years; if proceeded on as a summary conviction offence, the offender is punishable by a term not to exceed 18 months.

The Decision

1. What is your sentencing decision?
2. What is the rationale for the sentence?
3. What is the purpose of the sentence?   *(continued)*

Case #3

Before you is a man who has pled guilty to committing fraud over $5,000. The case in question involved selling investor units in a Mexican development called the El Golfo project. The victims were sold these units at a greatly inflated price by the man through his company, Concrete Equities, Inc. (CEI). The $23 million that was raised from nearly 1,200 investors was pocketed by the company and also transferred or lent to other CEI businesses. The ringleader is alleged to have pocketed $1 million.

One victim was the offender's father, who lost $901,000 in the scam. The offender played a supporting role in this by signing off on the offering memos and was "willfully blind" to the scam. Many of the victims lost their life savings and some lost their homes.

A joint submission by the Crown and defence to you as the judge recommends that the offender receive a conditional sentence for his participation in the fraud. The submission notes that the man pled guilty, that he did not benefit financially, and that his role was supportive rather than leading.

Fraud over $5,000 is an indictable offence in the Canadian Criminal Code. At the time the offence was committed, the penalty was punishable by a maximum sentence of 10 years. As the judge, you have the discretion to impose any of the sentencing options listed in Table 4.1.

The Decision

1. What is your sentencing decision?
2. What is the rationale for the sentence?
3. What is the purpose of the sentence?

SPECIALIZED, PROBLEM-SOLVING COURTS

CORRECTIONS PERSPECTIVE 4.1

Addiction Clinician

The current criminal justice system is flawed and people get misguided in it, because once they're labelled an addict or a drug criminal, it's hard for them to claw their way back into society. That's why we do what we do . . . . There's no reason why someone who's been charged with a crime who suffers from a drug problem can't be offered rehabilitation in tandem with their proceedings.

– Addiction clinician, Drug Court[10]

Problem-solving courts
Specialized courts designed to divert offenders with special needs from the criminal justice system.

In recent years, specialized, **problem-solving courts** have been developed that attempt to divert offenders with special needs from the criminal justice system. There are in Canada a variety of problem-solving courts, including mental health courts (MHCs), domestic violence courts (DVCs), and others. In addition, several provinces have created courts specifically for Indigenous persons. These operate on First Nations reserves, in the north, and in urban centres.

The three defining attributes of problem-solving courts are these: (1) They address the underlying problems of offenders, victims, and communities; (2) they involve collaboration among various agencies and disciplines; and (3) they are accountable to the community.[11] Unlike traditional courts, community-based courts have the potential to improve the quality of life in communities, increase residents' familiarity with the court process, and heighten community satisfaction with the response to persons in conflict with the law.[12]

These problem-solving courts abandon adversarial/legalistic approaches in favour of one that centres on treatment and rehabilitation. They develop intervention plans that address behaviours and the circumstances that contributed to them.[13] They are meant to counter the "revolving door" syndrome that affects many offenders and to improve collaboration among justice and social service agencies. Many of the principles of restorative justice are found in the practices of problem-solving courts. Table 4.2 compares traditional courts with problem-solving courts.

Specialized problem-solving courts incorporate the concept of **therapeutic justice**, which involves using the law as well as the courts' authority as change agents to promote the health and well-being of offenders, while at the same time ensuring that their legal rights are protected and that justice is done.[14]

Therapeutic justice
The use of the law and the authority of the court as change agents in promoting the health and well-being of offenders.

Table 4.2   Comparison of Traditional Courts and Problem-Solving Courts

Traditional Court	Problem-Solving Court
Adversarial/legalistic	Therapeutic/restorative
The goal is the resolution of the dispute	The goal is the resolution of the underlying problem
Anonymous/impersonal	Personalized
Backward-looking	Forward-looking
Little collaboration among criminal justice/social service personnel	Collaborative
Offence-focused	Offender-focused
Sanction-focused	Problem-focused
Generic supervision	Individualized supervision
Minimal community involvement	Community involvement, e.g., personal mentors
Judge acts as an arbiter	Judge acts as a coach
Success is measured by compliance	Success is measured by remediation of underlying problem

Source: S. Goldberg, *Problem-Solving in Canada's Courtrooms* (Ottawa: National Judicial Council, 2011), p. 4, http://www.civiljustice.info/cgi/viewcontent.cgi?article=1002&context=tj.

Critics of therapeutic justice argue that it blurs the line between treatment and enforcement and that problem-solving courts can be coercive—for example, drug treatment courts (DTCs) require abstinence by drug users instead of taking a harm reduction approach.[15]

There is considerable variation among the problem-solving courts with regard to the types of cases that are handled, their eligibility criteria, the sanctions imposed, the length and type of supervision, and the involvement of justice, social service, and community agencies.[16] Some courts only take offenders who have committed less serious crimes, while others will accept more serious offenders. DTCs in Canada, for example, will accept only those offenders who have committed nonviolent, drug-related offences.[17] As with all diversion programs, offender participation in specialized courts is voluntary. Some courts operate at the pre-plea level, while others require an admission of guilt and the acceptance of responsibility. All of the courts have established screening protocols to ensure that only those persons who meet specific criteria are selected.

The Effectiveness of Specialized Courts

There is research evidence that specialized courts can be an effective alternative to the traditional criminal justice system.[18] Problem-solving courts appear to be most effective at reducing reoffending when offenders are selected who are most suited for the program in terms of their level of risk, their needs, and their motivation and ability to complete the requirements imposed by the courts.[19] This is the risk–need–responsivity (RNR) concept of treatment intervention, discussed in Chapters 5 and 9. Persons who do not have a stable residence, who have substance abuse issues, and who have a severe mental illness are less likely to complete a program.[20]

Table 4.3 summarizes the objectives, processes, and effectiveness of a selected sample of specialized courts.

SENTENCING IN A RESTORATIVE JUSTICE FRAMEWORK

Table 4.4 compares the sentencing principles that guide the traditional criminal court process with that formed through a restorative justice approach.

Circle Sentencing: A Restorative Justice Approach

Circle sentencing was first developed in several Yukon communities as a collaboration between community residents and territorial justice personnel, primarily RCMP officers and judges from the Territorial Court of Yukon.

In circle sentencing, all of the participants, including the judge, defence lawyer, prosecutor, police officer, victim and family, offender and family, and community residents, sit facing one another in a circle. Through discussions, those in the circle reach a consensus about the best way to dispose of the case, taking into account both the need to protect the community and the rehabilitation and

Circle sentencing
An approach to sentencing based on the principles of restorative justice.

Table 4.3   The Objectives, Processes, and Effectiveness of Specialized Courts

Type of Court	Objective/Process	Outcomes
Mental health court (MHC)	Reduce the criminalization of the mentally ill; operate at pre- and post-charge stage	Reduce reoffending by 10 to 75 percent; can reduce the amount of time offenders spend in custody, increase access to treatment services, and change life circumstances (e.g., homelessness), particularly for persons who complete the program and "graduate";[a] court personnel perceive that MHCs improve clients' lives, reducing reoffending, reducing criminal court workloads, and holding offenders accountable;[b] an evaluation of the Calgary Diversion Program for mentally disordered offenders found high rates of client satisfaction, a significant reduction in charges and court appearances and in the need for acute care services;[c] potentially significant reductions in reoffending.
Drug treatment court (DTC)	Address alcohol/drug addiction of offenders and reduce reoffending; treatment-oriented approach with specified conditions (e.g., abstinence)	May significantly reduce participants' drug use and criminal offending during and following program completion;[d] helps even offenders with lengthy criminal records;[e] offenders who do not complete the program tend to lack family support, have unstable housing, and lack motivation to complete the program;[f] per-client costs are less than in traditional courts;[g] high rates of non completion; women and Indigenous people less likely to participate and to complete.[h]
Domestic violence (DV) court	Stop the cycle of domestic violence; assist victims, their families, and offenders; reduce revictimization	Cases may be heard more quickly than in traditional court; potential increase in guilty pleas; may reduce Crown stay of proceedings; evaluation of Yukon Domestic Violence Treatment Option found low rates of re-assault, effectiveness in dealing with domestic violence cases, but problems connecting with victims;[i] evaluation of the domestic violence court pilot project in Sydney, Nova Scotia, found strong support from all stakeholders, offender participation in treatment programs, but challenges in engaging victims; however, changes in offender behaviour, rates of re-offending, and the rates of re-victimization were not assessed;[j] an evaluation of the DV court pilot project in Moncton, New Brunswick, found that 69 percent ($N = 330/478$) of offenders reoffended during the three-year pilot period but that the number of victims accessing services increased throughout the pilot period.[k]

a S. Lange, J. Rehm, and S. Popova, "The Effectiveness of Criminal Justice Diversion Initiatives in North America: A Systematic Literature Review," *International Journal of Forensic Mental Health 10*, no. 3 (2011), 200–14; R.D. Schneider, "Mental Health Courts and Diversion Programs: A Global Survey," *International Journal of Law and Psychiatry 33*, no. 4 (2010), 201–6; C.M. Sarteschi, M.G. Vaughn, and K. Kim, "Assessing the Effectiveness of Mental Health Courts: A Quantitative Review," *Journal of Criminal Justice 39*, no. 1 (2011), 12–20.

b D.E. McNiel and R.L. Binder, "Stakeholder Views of a Mental Health Court," *International Journal of Law and Psychiatry 33*, no. 4 (2010), 227–35.

c C. Mitton, L. Simpson, L. Gardner, F. Barnes, and G. McDougall, "Calgary Diversion Program: A Community-Based Alternative to Incarceration for Mentally Ill Offenders," *Journal of Mental Health Policy Economics 10*, no. 3 (2007), 145–51, https://www.ncbi.nlm.nih.gov/pubmed/17890831.

d J. Roman, "Cost-Benefit Analysis of Criminal Justice Reforms," *National Institute of Justice Journal 272* (2013), 30–8, https://www.ncjrs.gov/pdffiles1/nij/241929.pdf.

e Public Safety Canada, *Toronto Drug Treatment Court Project* (Ottawa: National Crime Prevention Centre, 2007), https://www.publicsafety.gc.ca/cnt/rsrcs/pblctns/drgtrtmnt-trnt/drgtrtmnt-trnt-eng.pdf.

f B. Newton-Taylor, L. Gliksman, and J. Patra, "Toronto Drug Treatment Court: Participant Intake Characteristics as Predictors of 'Successful' Program Completion," *Journal of Drug Issues 39*, no. 4 (2009), 965–88.

g M.W. Finigan, S.M. Carey, and A. Cox, *Impact of a Mature Drug Court Over 10 Years of Operation: Recidivism and Costs* (Washington, D.C.: U.S. Department of Justice, National Institute of Justice, 2007), https://www.ncjrs.gov/pdffiles1/nij/grants/219225.pdf.

h P. Allard, T. Lyons, and R. Elliott, *Impaired Judgment: Assessing the Appropriateness of Drug Treatment Courts as a Response to Drug Use in Canada* (Toronto: Canadian HIV/AIDS Legal Network, 2011), http://www.aidslaw.ca/publications/interfaces/downloadFile.php?ref=2034.

i J.P. Hornick, M. Boyes, L. Tutty, and L. White, *The Domestic Violence Treatment Option (DVTO), Whitehorse, Yukon: Final Evaluation Report* (Ottawa: National Crime Prevention Centre, 2005), http://www.yukoncourts.ca/pdf/cwc_evaluation_june_2007_to_december_2013.pdf.

j D. Crocker, B. Crocker, and M. Dawson, *Domestic Violence Court Pilot Project, Sydney, Nova Scotia* (Halifax: Department of Justice, Nova Scotia, 2016).

k C.R. Dilworth and T.G. Dilworth, *The Domestic Violence Court (DV Court) Pilot Project, Moncton, New Brunswick* (Saint John, NB: New Brunswick Department of Public Safety, 2011), https://www.gnb.ca/0012/Womens-Issues/DomesticViolenceCourt/2011-01VictimsOffenders.pdf.

Table 4.4   Comparison of the Criminal Court Process and Restorative Justice

	Traditional Justice	**Restorative Justice**
People	Experts, non residents	Local people
Process	Adversarial state v. offender	Consensus community v. problem
Issues	Laws broken	Relationship broken
Focus	Guilt	Identify needs of victim, offender, and community
Tools	Punishment/control	Healing/support
Procedure	Fixed rules	Flexible

punishment of the offender. Circle sentencing is premised on traditional Indigenous healing practices and has number of different objectives, which include addressing the needs of communities, victims, the families of victims, and offenders through a process of reconciliation, restitution, and reparation.

At the core of circle sentencing is the idea that the sentence is less important than the process used to arrive at it. Note that the presiding judge has the final word on the sentence to be imposed; also, the final decision is informed by direct input from the community, the offender, and (often) the victim of the crime.

Table 4.5 compares the formal, adversarial criminal court system with the community-based, restorative approach as exemplified by circle sentencing.

Table 4.5   Differences between Criminal Court and Circle Sentencing Principles

Criminal Courts	Community Circles
View the conflict as the crime	View the crime as a small part of a large conflict
Hand down sentence to resolve the conflict	View the sentence as a small part of the conflict
Focus on past and present conduct	Focus on present and future conduct
Take a narrow view of behaviour	Take a broader, holistic view
Avoid concern with social conflict	Focus on social conflict
Result (i.e., the sentence) is most important	Result is least important; the process is most important, as the process shapes the relationships among all parties

Reprinted by permission of Justice Barry D. Stuart.

Symbols of Innu culture, sentencing circle table, Sheshatsui Innu First Nation, Newfoundland

It is important to note that offenders who have their cases heard in a sentencing circle may still be sent for a period of incarceration. However, a wide range of other sanctions are available, including house arrest, community service, and, for Indigenous offenders, banishment (generally to a wilderness location).

Circle sentencing is an example of how the principles of restorative justice can be applied within a holistic framework in which justice system personnel share power and authority with community residents. In contrast to the adversarial approach to justice, circle sentencing is designed to rebuild relationships within the community; to address the needs and interests of all parties, including the victim; and to focus on the causes of problems rather than just their symptoms.

Several First Nations communities have established peacemaking circles under the auspices of provincial courts.

Restorative Community Justice: The Collaborative Justice Program, Ottawa—Carleton Judicial District

It is often assumed that programs such as circle sentencing, which involve substantial community participation, are suited only to rural and remote communities with a strong cultural identity and foundation. This assertion is often used to deflect suggestions that justice personnel in suburban and urban areas should explore the potential for restorative justice approaches.

The Collaborative Justice Program operates in the Ottawa-Carleton judicial district. Cases are referred to the program by a variety of sources, which can include the judiciary, judicial pretrial, the Crown or defence counsel, the police, the probation office, and victim services. The program is a post-plea, pre-sentence restorative justice initiative.

To be eligible for the program, the accused person must display remorse and be willing to take responsibility for the crime and to work to repair the harm done, and the victim must be interested in participating.

As well as less serious cases, the program considers cases of serious offending, including robbery, break and enter, assault causing bodily harm, weapons offences, and driving offences that involve death or bodily harm, and for which a conviction would normally result in a period of incarceration.

The success of the program demonstrates that restorative justice programs can be effective in urban centres and that restorative approaches can be successfully applied to serious crimes, including crimes of violence, and may be used in conjunction with a period of incarceration. A summary of one case is presented in Corrections File 4.1.

CORRECTIONS FILE 4.1

Break and Enter, Possession of Credit Cards, Theft Under

Daniel became involved with the project after he was charged with 16 counts involving a number of break and enters, possession of property under, theft under, possession/use of credit card, loiter at night on other person's property, and fail to comply! Daniel had a long history of being involved in this kind of thing, so upon arrest he was sent to a closed custody facility prior to sentencing.

The Crown's initial position was for 10 months closed custody, followed by 2 months open custody, followed by probation. All of this would be on top of any time already served.

The caseworker met with Daniel and began the process of exploring the causes and consequences of his behaviour. Daniel seemed to take responsibility and was remorseful. Apparently, all of the charges stemmed from one evening when he became very intoxicated at a school dance. On his way home from the dance he decided to break into some houses. Being very drunk, it didn't take long for the police to catch up with him, still with the property on his person.

The victims in the case were contacted by the caseworker who then met with each of them to discuss the impact this event has had on their lives. Two asked for a letter of apology from Daniel.

Another victim asked to relay messages to Daniel. She wanted to tell Daniel that it was her little girl's property that was stolen: her CD's and her birthday money. Consequently, the little girl felt personally targeted and was very afraid even in her own home. Daniel was very surprised by this story and was deeply affected as he hadn't anticipated that his actions would harm a child. Daniel wished to do something for the little girl to show her that he hadn't meant to harm her. Unfortunately, the family chose not to participate any further in the project, fearing further retaliation from him.

Another victim talked about having seen Daniel in the upstairs hallway of his home, and in the darkness thought that Daniel was an adult. His family has been very frightened ever since. It was explained that Daniel was 15 years old at the time and very intoxicated. Although this victim chose not to participate any further, he felt much better understanding the actual circumstances of the break-in. Although the fact remained that his family home had been broken into, knowing that it was a young boy, who was remorseful, as opposed to an adult helped him to cope better with the crime.

Daniel wrote his two letters of apology. They were well written and thoughtful. Daniel had been able to put himself in the position of the victims and understand what the impact of his actions had been.

The letter to one victim was relayed and he was very touched by its content. He felt that Daniel showed promise in the literary arts and showed real insight into his own behaviour. He asked that Daniel be told that the victim feels better now and to wish Daniel well in the future. These messages were relayed to Daniel; he was very pleased and very surprised that someone he had harmed would actually wish him well.

The second letter was relayed. This victim was very moved by the letter and began to develop an almost parental concern for Daniel and his future. She asked permission to

(continued)

respond to Daniel's letter with a letter of her own. Permission was granted and she wrote the letter.

Although this case did not involve a meeting between Daniel and the victims, and there was no resolution agreement, we feel that it was extremely helpful to all the parties. The victims, because they received information and support that helped them to cope with what had happened, and because they were able to ask for what they needed.

Daniel learned about the harm that his actions had caused, in a way that allowed the victims to become "real" for him. Daniel also learned that although he had done something terrible, he could repair the harm to some extent. As a result, he unexpectedly received good wishes from a number of people he had harmed.

Daniel stayed in custody until his next court date, five months later, when he entered guilty pleas to break and enter (x2), possession of credit cards, theft under, and a breach. He was sentenced to time served (136 days), two months of open custody, followed by probation.

* Please note that identifying details and names have been changed to protect the confidentiality of the participants.

Source: Collaborative Justice Program, "Our Stories—Break & Entry, Possession of Credit Cards, Theft Under," http://www.collaborativejustice.ca/EN/our-stories/story.php?i=10&t=Break-&-Enter-Possession-of-Credit-Cards-Theft-Under. Reprinted by permission of Collaborative Justice Program.

THE EFFECTIVENESS OF SENTENCING

Despite the critical role played by sentencing in the criminal justice and corrections systems, there are questions about its effectiveness in addressing the needs of offenders and protecting the community. Some of the research on the effectiveness of sentencing is summarized in Research File 4.1.

RESEARCH FILE 4.1

The Effectiveness of Sentencing

Does increasing the severity of punishment have a deterrent effect on offenders? Generally, no. It is the certainty of punishment, rather than the severity of punishment, that has the most significant deterrent effect on offenders and others. While persons with a stake in conformity may fear lost opportunities if they are criminally sanctioned, marginal persons who perceive that they have few legitimate opportunities (and who in fact do not have many) may not engage in this calculus.[a] Persons with strong family and community ties are much more likely to be deterred by the fear of being caught than persons without those ties.[b]

Is there consistency in sentencing? Not always. With a few exceptions involving mandatory minimum sentences, most offences have only a maximum penalty, and this provides judges with considerable discretion in deciding both the objective of the sentence and the specific penalty. This makes it difficult to predict with any accuracy what type of sentence will be imposed for offences, even though judges are guided by case precedents.

Does the threat of longer prison terms reduce crime? Not likely. Mandatory minimum sentences do not appear to have a deterrent impact on criminal offending.[c]

Are sentences matched effectively to individual offenders? Often, no. Matching specific sentencing options with the needs and risks of offenders is, at best, an inexact science. Few research studies have examined which types of sentences are most effective—that is, which ones serve as a deterrent and address risk and needs—with specific types of offenders.

Is there continuity from criminal courts to corrections? Not always. Once the offender leaves the courtroom, they become the responsibility of corrections. Judicial recommendations for placement and treatment programming are not binding on correctional decision makers. However, this continuity is increased in specialized courts.

Do problem-solving courts work? Potentially. They can be effective at reducing rates of reoffending. See Table 4.2.

Are circle sentencing and peacemaking effective? Potentially. There have been few controlled evaluations of these programs. Most of the literature on circle sentencing is anecdotal, which makes it difficult to develop evidence-based practices and to determine the factors that may facilitate (or hinder) the effective use of this restorative justice strategy. This includes whether the community itself has the capacity to support circle sentencing and whether the rights of the victim will be protected.[d] Concerns have surrounded the use of circle sentencing in cases involving domestic violence, with critics arguing that the power imbalances between the accused and the accuser may result in the revictimization of women.[e]

---

[a] National Institute of Justice, "Five Things About Deterrence," (Washington, DC: U.S. Department of Justice, 2014), https://www.ncjrs.gov/pdffiles1/nij/247350.pdf; S.N. Durlauf and D.S. Nagin, "The Deterrent Effect of Punishment," in *Controlling Crime: Strategies and Tradeoffs*, eds. P.J. Cook, J. Ludwig, and J. McCrary (Chicago: University of Chicago Press, 2011), 43–94.

[b] A.E. Perry, "Sentencing and Deterrence," *What Works in Crime Prevention and Rehabilitation: Lessons from Systematic Reviews*, eds. D. Weisburd, D.P. Farrington, and C. Gill, eds. (New York: Springer, 2016), 169–91.

[c] P. Menedez and D. J. Weatherburn, "Does the Threat of Longer Prison Terms Reduce the Incidence of Assault," *Australian & New Zealand Journal of Criminology 49*, no. 3 (2015), 389–404.

[d] C.T. Griffiths and R. Hamilton, "Sanctioning and Healing: Restorative Justice in Canadian Aboriginal Communities," in *Restorative Justice: Theory, Practice, and Research*, eds. J. Hudson and B. Galaway (Monsey: Criminal Justice Press, 1996), 175–91.

[e] A. Cameron, "Sentencing Circles and Intimate Violence: A Canadian Feminist Perspective," *Canadian Journal of Women and the Law 18*, no. 2 (2006): 479–512; A. Shagufta, "Should Restorative Justice Be Used for Cases of Domestic Violence?" *International Journal of Restorative Justice 6*, no. 1 (2010): 1–48.

SUMMARY

This chapter examined the sentencing stage of the corrections process and included a description of the principles and goals underlying sentencing in the criminal courts. The sentencing decision of the judge determines whether an offender will enter the federal or provincial/territorial system of corrections; it also determines whether the offender will be under supervision in the community or incarcerated in an institution. The various factors that may influence judicial decision making were discussed, including provisions related to Indigenous offenders. Judicial discretion and the challenges that judges face when imposing appropriate sanctions were illustrated through the use of actual case summaries.

Specialized, problem-solving courts were also discussed. These specialized courts operate within a different framework than traditional criminal courts. They provide an alternative forum for accused persons with special needs, including persons with mental health issues, and for specific types of crimes, including domestic violence. The discussion revealed that these courts can be more effective in addressing the needs of offenders than their traditional court counterparts. The use of restorative justice as an alternative to the traditional, adversarial criminal court process was discussed—in particular, the restorative justice approach of circle sentencing.

KEY POINTS REVIEW

1. Sentencing in the criminal courts can be identified as the beginning of the correctional process.
2. There are three primary groups of sentencing goals in the criminal courts: utilitarian, retributive, and restorative.
3. Canadian judges have a variety of sentencing options ranging from an absolute discharge to imprisonment.
4. There are special provisions in the Criminal Code relating to the sentencing of Indigenous offenders.
5. Circle sentencing is a restorative justice approach to sentencing that differs from that of traditional criminal courts.
6. Specialized, problem-solving courts are an attempt to divert offenders with special needs from the criminal justice system and operate differently from the traditional criminal courts.
7. Evaluations of drug treatment courts, mental health courts, domestic violence, and wellness courts have found that these courts can produce positive outcomes for offenders and victims.
8. Criminal court judges consider a wide range of factors when determining the sentence to be imposed on a convicted offender.
9. Sentencing within a restorative justice framework is dissimilar from that which occurs in the traditional criminal courts.

10. It is difficult to determine the effectiveness of sentencing in reducing rates of reoffending and questionable whether sentencing assists the offender and protects the community.

11. A significant trend in diversion has been the development of problem-solving courts that incorporate therapeutic justice with elements of restorative justice.

12. Problem-solving courts, particularly those that incorporate the principles of RNR, can be an effective alternative to the traditional criminal justice system.

KEY TERM QUESTIONS

1. What is meant by **general deterrence** and **specific deterrence** in sentencing?

2. Define and contrast **concurrent sentences**, **consecutive sentences**, and **intermittent sentences**.

3. Describe each of the following sentencing options: **absolute discharge**, **conditional discharge**, **suspended sentence**, **fine**, and **intermittent sentence**.

4. What is the significance of the decision of the Supreme Court of Canada in **R v. Gladue**?

5. What is **judicial determination**, and what are its objectives?

6. Describe the process for designating offenders as **dangerous offenders** and **long-term offenders**.

7. What are **problem-solving courts** and how do they differ from traditional criminal courts?

8. What is **therapeutic justice**?

9. Describe the restorative justice approach of **circle sentencing** and note how it differs from sentencing in the traditional criminal court.

CRITICAL THINKING EXERCISE

Critical Thinking Exercise 4.1

Judicial Use of Sentencing Options

With the exception of those offences that, upon conviction, require the judge to impose a mandatory minimum sentence, Canadian judges exercise consideration discretion in sentencing. Review the case examples in Table 4.1 associated with the various sentencing options.

1. For each of the case examples, indicate whether you agree or disagree with the sentence imposed by the presiding judge.

2. What is the basis for your agreement/disagreement?

CLASS/GROUP DISCUSSION EXERCISES

Class/Group Discussion 4.1

Mr. Smith and Mr. Jones

Recall the materials on the sentencing of Mr. Smith and Mr. Jones at the outset of the chapter. Both men committed the same type of offence, but received different sentences. The presiding judges each cited different objectives of the punishment that was imposed.

It has been argued that the vast discretion that judges exercise is necessary in order to allow judges to individualize their sentencing, taking into account the unique aspects of each case that come before them. Critics counter that the wide discretion given to judges results in inconsistency in sentencing, with offenders receiving disparate sentences for committing the same type of offence.

Your Thoughts?

1. In your view, is the vast discretion exercised by Canadian criminal judges a problem?

2. What suggestions would you make as to how the need for discretion can be maintained while at the same time creating some degree of consistency in sentencing?

Class/Group Discussion 4.2

You Be the Judge

Recall the three cases presented in Box 4.2 wherein you were asked to assume the role of a presiding judge.

Your Thoughts?

1. What was your decision in each of the cases?

2. What were the rationale that you used to support your decision?

3. Now, read the decisions of the judges in the four cases below under Answers for Box 4.2, "You Be The Judge" and answer the following questions:

   a. for each case, was your decision similar or dissimilar to that of the presiding judge in the actual case?

   b. if your decision was not similar, how did it differ and why?

MEDIA LINKS

"A Day in the Life of L.A. Drug Court," https://www.youtube.com/watch?v=ncjoeNkxgdI

"Vancouver's Downtown Community Court," https://www.youtube.com/watch?v=Oiz7cy6hi-I

"Mental Health Court, King County," www.youtube.com/watch?v=DFIDmuevXQQ

"Mental Health Court Turns Lives of Chronic Offenders Around," www.youtube.com/watch?v=jFaHoEuq01M7feature=related

"Restorative Practices to Resolve Conflict/Build Relationships: Katy Hutchinson," TEDxWestVancouverED, https://www.youtube.com/watch?v=wcLuVeHlrSs

ANSWERS FOR BOX 4.2, "YOU BE THE JUDGE"

Case #1

On April 1, 2016, Alain Bellemere was sentenced to 15 months in confinement. In stating the rationale for his decision, the presiding judge noted that Bellemere's actions were impacted by the legacy of the residential schools and that the federal sentencing guidelines required him to consider this factor. The judge described Bellemere as one of the "collateral victims of the residential schools and of the cultural genocide that the Atikamekws of Wemotaci experienced." While acknowledging that the crime was "serious, revolting and must be denounced to protect other children who are victims of violence," the judge concluded that the four-year sentence proposed by the Crown was excessive given the offender's Indigenous heritage.[21]

Case #2

In this case, heard in Windsor, Ontario, the presiding judge sentenced Shawn Harold McManus to 5½ years in prison. With credit for time served in pre-trial custody, this resulted in a two-year prison term. An additional three years of probation were also added, to be completed following release from confinement. The presiding judge noted that there were gaps in the offender's lengthy record and that "he was a nice, likeable person when he was in control," but that when not in control due to his mental condition and drinking, "You were clearly someone who acts like a monster."

The judge agreed with the arguments presented by the defence lawyer that a shorter sentence would mean that the offender would serve his time in a provincial jail and allow him to remain close to his family, which would not have occurred had he received a longer sentence and been sent to a federal prison. The judge acknowledged that it was a "lenient" sentence, but stated, "If we don't hold out hope people can change...if you give up thinking that's possible, then really we've given up a certain amount of faith in the human spirit."[22]

Case #3

In this case, the Alberta Provincial Court judge agreed with the joint submission of the Crown and defence, handing Varun "Vinny" Aurora a conditional sentence of two years less a day for his role in the fraud perpetuated by Concrete Equities, Inc. For the first six months of the sentence, the offender would be under house arrest. For the next 14 months, he must abide by a curfew and perform 240 hours of community service. In passing sentence, the judge noted that there were several mitigating circumstances, including that the man had pled guilty and that he played only a limited role in the fraud.[23]

Additional Thoughts?

1. Note that the Criminal Code for this offence was subsequently amended and now provides that, upon conviction, the minimum penalty is two years in prison and the maximum is 14 years in prison. Had this been in effect, what would your sentence have been?

2. Among the comments from readers of the article on the case were the following:

"This entire case deserves to have an inquiry. 'Not only must Justice be done; it must also be seen to be done.' It's no wonder people don't trust our justice system any longer."

"HOUSE ARREST! He still has a house? The judge should keep him in his house! Another incompetent judge!"

3. How would you respond to these comments?

NOTES

1. J.V. Roberts, N. Crutcher, and P. Verbrugge, "Public Attitudes to Sentencing in Canada: Exploring Recent Findings," *Canadian Journal of Criminology and Criminal Justice 49*, no. 1 (2007), 153–84.

2. A. Jones, "Court Quashes Extradition Orders Because Men's Aboriginal Status Not Considered," Canadian Press, September 21, 2012.

3. N. Macdonald, "Canada's Prisons Are the 'New Residential Schools,'" *Maclean's*, February 18, 2016, http://www.macleans.ca/news/canada/canadas-prisons-are-the-new-residential-schools/.

4. S. April and M.M. Orsi, *Gladue Practices in the Provinces and Territories* (Ottawa: Research and Statistics Division, Department of Justice, 2013), http://www.justice.gc.ca/eng/rp-pr/csj-sjc/ccs-ajc/rr12_11/rr12_11.pdf.

5. C.T. Griffiths, *Canadian Criminal Justice: A Primer*, 5th ed. (Toronto: Nelson, 2015).

6. Public Safety Canada Portfolio Corrections Statistics Committee, *Corrections and Conditional Release Statistical Overview: 2015 Annual Report* (Ottawa: Public Works and Government Services Canada, 2016), https://www.public-safety.gc.ca/cnt/rsrcs/pblctns/ccrso-2015/ccrso-2015-en.pdf.

7. N. Macdonald, "Canada's Prisons Are the 'New Residential Schools.'"

8. Public Safety Canada Portfolio Corrections Statistics Committee, *Corrections and Conditional Release Statistical Overview*, p. 107.

9. Ibid., p. 107.

10. R. Browne, "Inside the Canadian Court That Handles Drug Crime Differently," *Vice News*, December 7, 2016, https://news.vice.com/story/inside-the-canadian-court-that-handles-drug-crime-differently.

11. R. Porter, M. Rempel, and A. Mansky, *What Makes a Court Problem-Solving? Universal Performance Indicators for Problem-Solving Justice* (Washington, DC: Center for Court Innovation, 2010), http://www.courtinnovation.org/sites/default/files/What_Makes_A_Court_P_S.pdf.

12. R. Saner, *Community Perceptions of Red Hook, Brooklyn: Views of Quality of Life, Safety, and Services* (New York: Center for Court Innovation, 2010), http://www.courtinnovation.org/sites/default/files/Community_Perceptions.pdf.

13. A.J. Lurigio and J. Snowden, "Putting Therapeutic Jurisprudence into Practice: The Growth, Operations, and Effectiveness of Mental Health Court," *Justice System Journal* 30, no. 2 (2009), 196–218.

14. S. Goldberg, *Problem-Solving in Canada's Courtrooms* (Ottawa: National Judicial Council, 2011), http://www.civiljustice.info/cgi/viewcontent.cgi?article=1002&context=tj.

15. P. Allard, T. Lyons, and R. Elliott, *Impaired Judgment: Assessing the Appropriateness of Drug Treatment Courts as a Response to Drug Use in Canada* (Toronto: Canadian HIV/AIDS Legal Network, 2011), http://www.aidslaw.ca/publications/interfaces/downloadFile.php?ref=2034.

16. F. Sirotich, "The Criminal Justice Outcomes of Jail Diversion Programs for Persons with Mental Illness: A Review of the Evidence," *Journal of the American Academy of Psychiatry and Law* 37, no. 4 (2009), 461–72.

17. E. Slinger and R. Roesch, "Problem-Solving Courts in Canada: A Review and a Call for Empirically-Based Evaluation Methods," *International Journal of Law and Psychiatry* 33, no. 4 (2010), 258–64 at 260.

18. P. Bowen and S. Whitehead, *Problem-Solving Courts: An Evidence Review* (London, UK: Centre for Justice Innovation, 2016), http://justiceinnovation.org/wp-content/uploads/2016/08/Problem-solving-courts-An-evidence-review.pdf.

19. L. Gutierrez and G. Bourgon, *Drug Treatment Courts: A Quantitative Review of Study and Treatment Quality* (Ottawa: Public Safety Canada, 2009), http://www.publicsafety.gc.ca/res/cor/rep/_fl/2009-04-dtc-eng.pdf.

20. A. Verhaaff, *Individual Factors Predicting Mental Health Court Diversion Outcome*, MA thesis, University of Ontario Institute of Technology, 2011, http://ir.library.dc-uoit.ca/bitstream/10155/164/Verehaaf_Ashley.pdf.

21. G. Hamilton, "'Collateral victim' of residential schools gets 15 months for burning child 27 times with cigarette, lighter," *National Post*, April 7, 2016, http://news.nationalpost.com/news/canada/collateral-victim-of-residential-schools-gets-15-months-for-burning-child-27-times-with-cigarette-lighter.

22. T. Wilhelm, "'Monster' rapist given 'lenient' sentence from Ontario judge in hopes offender can change," *National Post*, March 14, 2016, http://news.nationalpost.com/news/canada/monster-rapist-given-lenient-sentence-from-ontario-judge-in-hopes-offender-can-change.

23. K. Martin, "Calgary man who played role in $23M Concrete Equities fraud won't see jail," *Calgary Herald*, October 5, 2016, http://calgaryherald.com/news/crime/calgary-man-who-played-role-in-23m-concrete-equities-fraud-wont-see-jail.

PART II

CORRECTIONS IN THE COMMUNITY: ALTERNATIVES TO CONFINEMENT

Community corrections refers to programs that are alternatives to confinement and to the supervision of offenders on conditional release from correctional institutions. This part focuses on correctional strategies that are designed to serve as alternatives to custody. Chapter 5 considers diversion, intermediate sanctions, and probation. In recent years there has been an expansion of intermediate sanctions, as well as innovations in probation. These programs are under the jurisdiction of provincial/territorial governments, and there is considerable diversity in the specific programs that have been developed.

CHAPTER

5

ALTERNATIVES TO CONFINEMENT

CHAPTER OBJECTIVES

- Describe diversion and how it is used in the criminal justice system.
- Describe the differences between probation and parole.
- Discuss the recruitment, training, roles, and responsibilities of probation officers, including the dual role of probation officers in supervising offenders.
- Describe the features of intensive probation supervision.
- Describe the "pains" of probation.
- Discuss the obstacles to effective probation practice.
- Describe the objectives of intermediate sanctions and the types of programs that have been developed as intermediate sanctions.
- Describe how electronic monitoring works.
- Discuss conditional sentences as an alternative to incarceration, their use, and the issues that surround conditional sentences in Canada.
- Discuss the effectiveness of alternatives to confinement.

Alternatives to confinement play a significant role in the correctional process. A report prepared by the United Nations noted that the development of alternatives to confinement not only can address the issue of prison overcrowding but also can be an integral part of a shift in correctional philosophy from a focus on the punishment and isolation of offenders in correctional facilities, to a reintegrative and restorative approach. This approach, it is argued, holds the greatest potential for assisting offenders and protecting the community.[1]

Community corrections includes both alternatives to incarceration (discussed in this chapter) and post-release supervision and programs (discussed in Chapter 11). When used as an alternative to confinement, community corrections includes diversion and probation as well as a variety of intermediate sanctions and restorative justice initiatives. Recall from Chapter 4 that most offenders who receive a sentence of supervision remain in the community and that only a very small number of convicted persons are sent to custody.

CORRECTIONS PERSPECTIVE 5.1

Ex-federal Offender

We should be providing offenders with more alternatives than incarceration. I think that what has to be done is that we have to work with our young offenders and our youth a lot earlier. Once a youth has entered an institution, it's going to be very difficult to get that person to change their ways, because once he gets in there, he is going to be conditioned to the situation that is happening. It's a very negative environment. I know in my situation, I had been a youth in a training school. It was being conditioned to the adult person I would be for the longest time, and I would spend 23 years of my life in institutions. If you put that into dollars and cents, I think it could have been spent a lot better than it was on me.

Source: Personal communication with C.T. Griffiths.

The search for alternative measures has been driven by the escalating costs of confining offenders in correctional institutions and, to a lesser extent, by research evidence that has called into question the effectiveness of incarceration as a general and specific deterrent (see Chapter 4). In addition, the final report of the Truth and Reconciliation Commission of Canada, a wide-ranging enquiry into the impact of Indian residential schools on Indigenous culture, communities, families, and individuals, called upon the federal, provincial, and territorial governments to develop and evaluate community sanctions that could serve as alternatives to confinement for Indigenous offenders.[2]

Note, however, that the trend toward the use of alternative measures has been accompanied by the increased use of technology to provide surveillance of offenders in the community.

DIVERSION

Diversion programs have been a feature of Canadian criminal justice for decades. Offenders can be diverted from the formal criminal justice process at several points. There are diversion programs at the pre-charge, post-charge, and post-sentencing stages. The various specialized, problem-solving courts discussed in Chapter 4 are designed to divert offenders with special needs away from the adversarial court process.

The objective of all diversion programs is to keep offenders from being processed further into the formal criminal justice system, thereby reducing costs and social stigmatization and helping offenders address the specific factors that led to their offending. Most diversion programs require that offenders acknowledge responsibility for their behaviour and agree to fulfill certain conditions within a specified time. If these conditions are met, the charges are

Diversion
Programs designed to keep offenders from being processed further into the formal criminal justice system.

withdrawn and the person is not saddled with a criminal record. Traditional diversion programs focus on low-risk, first-time offenders; in recent years, however, cases involving more serious offences have been referred to diversion programs.

Many diversion programs are centred on the principles of restorative justice. A number of restorative justice approaches have as their goal to divert offenders from more extensive involvement in the justice system, including custody. Victim–offender mediation (VOM) programs (often referred to as victim–offender reconciliation [VOR] programs) take a restorative approach in which the victim and the offender are provided with the opportunity to express their feelings and concerns. With the help of a neutral mediator, the offender and the victim resolve the conflict, address the consequences of the offence, and, ultimately, come to understand each other. In recent years, VOM and VOR programs have been extended to cases involving crimes of violence and have included incarcerated offenders.

Diversion is being increasingly used to keep persons with mental illness (PwMI) out of the criminal justice system and into mental health programs and services.[3] At the pre-charge phase, the police can divert PwMI through referrals to local mental health services, while court support services can be used to divert these persons at the post-charge stage. Post-conviction/post-incarceration treatment can be made part of the offender's supervision plan.

Although there are no recent Canadian studies, research in the United States suggests that diversion programs can be an effective strategy and can reduce the seriousness and frequency of reoffending.[4] The factors associated with successful outcomes for offenders involved in diversion programs include stable employment and a supportive environment.[5]

The Issue of Net-Widening

A major concern with diversion programs is **net-widening**—that is, involving offenders who would otherwise have been released outright by the police or not charged by Crown counsel. Another concern is that diversion programs can be punitive. Also, there is some ambiguity regarding the notion of "choice" in the operation of diversion programs and whether diversion programs may infringe on the rights of accused persons.

The issue of net-widening has also been raised with respect to the specialized, problem-solving courts discussed in Chapter 4.[6]

INTERMEDIATE SANCTIONS

Intermediate sanctions, often referred to as *alternative sanctions* or *community sanctions*, encompass a variety of correctional programs that fall between traditional probation and incarceration, although specific initiatives may include either of these penalties. Intermediate sanctions include fines, community

Net-widening
A potential, unanticipated consequence of diversion programs in which persons who would otherwise have been released outright by the police or not charged by Crown counsel are involved in the justice system.

Intermediate sanctions
A wide range of correctional programs that generally fall between probation and incarceration, although specific initiatives may include either of these penalties as well.

service, day attendance centres, home detention with or without electronic monitoring (EM), intensive probation supervision, strict discipline camps (boot camps), conditional sentence orders (CSOs), and halfway houses. Intermediate sanctions have two sets of objectives:

- *Offender*-oriented objectives, which include the assurance of real punishment, retribution, and some degree of incapacitation and control of offenders
- *System*-oriented objectives, which include reducing institutional populations and the costs of corrections, as well as rates of recidivism[7]

The primary objective of intermediate sanctions is to hold offenders responsible for their behaviour through restrictive and intensive intervention. Treatment and rehabilitation are generally secondary, although usually a component of these sanctions. Studies that have queried offenders about their perceptions of the severity of intermediate sanctions as opposed to incarceration have found that alternatives to incarceration can be effective at sanctioning and managing offenders.[8]

Examples of intermediate sanctions are presented below.

Electronic Monitoring

A key trend in punishment and corrections is the increasing surveillance of offenders under supervision in the community. This has been made possible by technologies that allow authorities to track offenders through various forms of **electronic monitoring (EM)** and global positioning systems (GPSs). These technologies may provide alternatives to confinement and allow the offender to remain in the community.

There are "front end" and "back end" EM programs, referring to the stage of the correctional process at which the strategy is used. In some provinces, EM is imposed by the sentencing judge, while in others, such as Ontario, EM is a condition of early release from incarceration, although offenders with a history of sex offences or domestic abuse are not eligible for EM.

Where EM is used in support of an alternative to confinement, its main objective is to ensure public safety while allowing the offender to remain in the community. Generally, only offenders who have been convicted of less serious, nonviolent offences and who have a stable residence and a telephone are eligible to participate in EM programs.

More recent GPS technology can track an offender's movements on an ongoing basis. This provides greater protection for crime victims, who can thus be notified if the offender travels outside pre-established boundaries. GPS monitoring makes it possible to determine where an offender is at any given moment. In addition, GPS makes it possible to "customize" tracking by specifying the boundaries of an offender's movements and establishing locations where the offender is not permitted (e.g., a sex offender may be prohibited from going near schools and/or playgrounds). A monitoring program can be

Electronic monitoring (EM) A correctional strategy that involves using electronic equipment to ensure that the conditions of supervision are fulfilled.

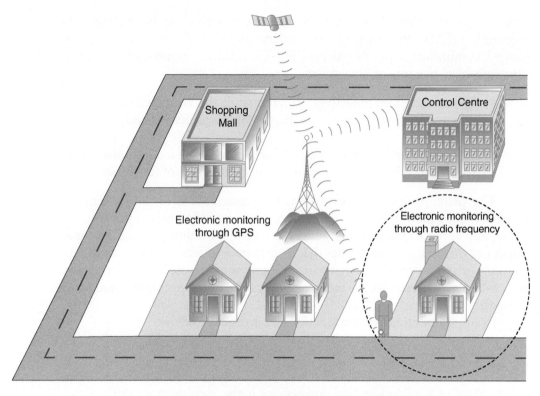

Global Positioning System Monitoring Components

designed that will alert both the offender and the agency if the offender violates certain area restrictions.

In Canada, Bill C-10, passed in 2012, has a provision that allows the Correctional Service Canada (CSC) and the Parole Board of Canada (PBC) to require that offenders on temporary absence (TA), work release, parole, statutory release, or long-term supervision wear a monitoring device (see the discussion in Chapter 10).

Conditional Sentences

Section 742 of the Criminal Code states that a convicted person who would otherwise be incarcerated for less than two years can be sentenced to a conditional term of imprisonment, to be served in the community rather than in custody. Under this **conditional sentence**, the offender is required to fulfill certain conditions. Failure to comply with the conditions of a conditional sentence order (CSO) results in the offender being returned to court, where the sentencing judge has a variety of options, including sending the offender to prison.

> **Conditional sentence**
> A sentence imposed on an offender who would otherwise be incarcerated for a period of less than two years but whose risk is determined to be manageable in the community.

Offenders on conditional sentences are supervised in the community by probation officers; however, *these offenders are not on probation*. The Supreme Court of Canada (SCC) has delineated the differences between a conditional sentence and probation (*R. v. Proulx*, [2000] 1 SCR 61). The main difference is that probation focuses on rehabilitation, whereas a conditional sentence embraces the principles of rehabilitation *and* punitive justice. This means that the conditions attached to a conditional sentence are generally more onerous and more restrictive than the conditions attached to a probation order. The SCC in *Proulx* directed that two factors be taken into account in determining whether a conditional sentence is appropriate: (1) the risk that the offender will reoffend, and (2) the amount of harm the offender would cause in the event of offending again.

All CSOs contain standard, compulsory conditions that are similar to those contained in probation orders. Optional conditions may also be set down and may be added to or reduced by the court over time. These may include abstaining from alcohol or drugs, providing for the support or care of dependents, performing community service work, and/or attending a treatment program.

Noncompliance with the conditions of a CSO can result in the offender being incarcerated. If an allegation is made that a condition has been breached, the offender may have to appear in court to prove that the allegation is false. This is a reverse onus situation; in other words, it is up to the offender to prove that the breach did *not* occur.

Federal legislation prevents judges from imposing a conditional sentence in cases where the offender has been convicted of an offence involving bodily harm, drug trafficking, or the use of a weapon (along with a variety of other offences in which the Crown had proceeded by indictment). As of late-2017, it remains to be seen whether these restrictions on the use of conditional sentences will be overturned by the courts.

Offenders who are given a CSO and placed under house arrest are often viewed by the media and the general public as having received a "slap on the wrist" and as having escaped the negative experiences of incarceration. Yet adhering to a CSO's requirements, which may include 24-hour house arrest, presents challenges for offenders that are no less intense than those of incarceration. In interviews, offenders on CSOs mention the negative impact on their working lives and on those who are close to them, including their children.[9]

PROBATION

Section 731 of the Criminal Code provides that in cases in which no minimum penalty is prescribed, the sentencing judge may place the offender on probation for up to three years. **Probation** is the most common strategy for supervising

Probation
A sentence imposed on an offender by a criminal court judge that provides for the supervision of the offender in the community by a probation officer, either as an alternative to custody or in conjunction with a period of incarceration.

offenders in the community as an alternative to incarceration, although it can be used in conjunction with other sanctions as well.

The proportion of cases receiving a sentence of probation has remained stable over the years (around 45 percent), as has the average length of probation orders (around a year).[10] When probation follows a term of confinement, probation supervision begins either at the time of release or on the expiration of parole.

There are a number of ways that adult offenders can be placed on probation. See Table 5.1.

Probation differs in significant ways from parole. See Table 5.2.

Probation is popular largely because it is so versatile. The length and conditions of a probation order can be tailored to the individual needs and circumstances of the offender. Intensive probation supervision is often used to manage the risk presented by high-risk offenders. Some of the statutory conditions of a probation order, including to obey the law and keep the peace, are mandatory. However, the sentencing judge may attach further conditions, such as requiring the offender to abstain from drugs and/or alcohol or to attend a treatment program. The frequency of reporting and intensity of supervision may be set by the court or determined by the supervising probation officer. Note that offenders who receive a period of custody to be followed by supervised probation (which would follow the completion of parole if this were granted) present a different risk/needs profile than offenders who have been placed on probation as an alternative to confinement.

Probation conditions must be reasonable, and ideally, they are designed with an eye to preventing the offender from committing further crimes. During the period of supervision, the probation officer may ask the sentencing judge to increase, decrease, or eliminate additional conditions or to reduce (but not lengthen) the total period of the probation order.

An adult probationer who, without a reasonable excuse, fails or refuses to comply with a condition, or who commits a new offence, *may* be charged with breach of probation. A breach of probation is an elective (or hybrid) offence and carries a maximum penalty of four years' imprisonment if proceeded by indictment, or a term of imprisonment of not more than 18 months if a summary conviction (Criminal Code, s. 733.1(1)).

Table 5.1   The Uses of Probation

Adult offenders can be on probation in the following circumstances:
- as part of a conditional discharge (mandatory)
- as a condition of a suspended sentence (mandatory)
- as part of an intermittent sentence (mandatory)
- as a sentence on its own (the most common)
- following a prison term of two years less a day (provincial/territorial offenders)
- following a prison term of exactly two years (federal offenders; rarely imposed by sentencing judges)
- in conjunction with a conditional sentence

Table 5.2   Probation versus Parole: What's the Difference?

Probation	Parole
Imposed by a criminal court judge	Granted by an administrative tribunal (a parole board)
Available only for provincial/territorial offenders (except federal offenders who received a sentence, or sentences, totalling exactly two years)	Available to federal and provincial/territorial offenders
Maximum length is three years	Continues until warrant expiry date (end of sentence)
May be used in conjunction with a period of confinement in a provincial/territorial institution (and following a sentence of exactly two years in a federal correctional facility)	A form of conditional release from confinement in a provincial/territorial/federal correctional facility
Requires offender to abide by general conditions (e.g., obey the law and keep the peace) and perhaps specific conditions tailored to the offender's individual risk factors (e.g., abstain from alcohol)	Requires offender to abide by general and perhaps also specific conditions that are designed to reduce risk factors (e.g., no-contact provisions)
Breach of condition can be a charge under the Criminal Code that requires evidence for conviction of breach of probation; additional conditions may be imposed and the terms of probation extended; offenders found in breach of conditions rarely incarcerated	Breach of condition may result in suspension or revocation, resulting in a return to custody; the offender may be re-released with additional conditions, or returned to custody pending the next parole eligibility date, statutory release date, or warrant expiry

RECRUITMENT AND TRAINING OF PROBATION OFFICERS

As noted earlier, probation falls under the authority of the provinces/territories. Each jurisdiction has developed its own procedures and standards for recruiting and training probation officers, although there are similar qualifications. Applicants for probation officer positions are often required to hold a university degree and have strong verbal and written communication skills, among others. In Alberta, applicants must demonstrate a number of core competencies, including managing information and people, organizational skills, and problem-solving, among others.[11]

In Ontario, to apply for the position of probation officer, an applicant must

- hold a degree, from an institution authorized by the province to grant degrees, in one of the following disciplines: social work, psychology, sociology, and criminology; or a degree from an institution authorized by the province to grant degrees; and experience, greater than five years in total, in a social services or correctional organization, in a role(s) that involves the formal assessment of human behaviour and the application of structured interventions aimed at supporting the changing of human behaviour;

- possess strong verbal and written communication skills, as well as counselling and assessment skills; and,
- be able to establish and maintain client and stakeholder relationships.[12]

Most often there is pre-employment training, during which potential applicants must complete a number of courses (many of which are offered online), often at their own expense, before being eligible to apply for a position as a probation officer.

There are also ongoing in-service training courses for probation officers. These focus on the supervision of special populations (such as sex offenders and the mentally disordered) and the use of assessment instruments.

Probation officer salaries vary between the provinces/territories. In Ontario in 2016, the median salary was $37.98 per hour, while in Saskatchewan, the hourly wage ranges from $27.22 to $34.11 per hour. In Manitoba, probation officer salaries range between $45,335 and $71,775 per year.

ROLE AND RESPONSIBILITIES OF PROBATION OFFICERS

The activities of probation officers largely involve assessing clients with respect to their needs and the risks they pose, providing individualized case management with the objective of reducing criminal behaviour, and supervising offenders on probation as well as persons who have been released on bail while awaiting trial. In Québec and Ontario, probation officers

CORRECTIONS PERSPECTIVE 5.2

Probation Officer

I think it is our responsibility to try to help individuals and to identify the issues that they have, so they can begin working on themselves. For the offenders on my caseload, I try to help them with basic needs, such as food, shelter, employment training, and core programming that will help them develop their self-confidence and address their issues. It is important to have empathy and to understand the client's needs while also having realistic expectations of them. I try to see that the conditions of the probation order are followed while at the same time respecting the person.

Source: Personal communication with C.T. Griffiths.

supervise offenders who have been released on provincial parole; in the other provinces and territories, these offenders are supervised by federal parole officers. Some probation officers supervise offenders involved in diversion programs (i.e., who have been diverted from the criminal justice system). The myriad activities of probation officers are listed in Table 5.3.

Probation officers help prepare PSRs on adult offenders who have been convicted. The PSR contains a wealth of information on the offender's background and offence history, as well as victim impact information and assessments completed by treatment professionals. For Indigenous offenders, there are special considerations that the PSR must address. For

Table 5.3   The Activities of Probation Officers

Officer of the Court

Preparing the **pre-sentence report (PSR)**; attending court proceedings; applying to change conditions of probation orders; writing progress reports; consulting with Crown counsel

Investigation

Preparing pre-sentence reports; preparing community assessments (for provincial parole boards in Ontario and Québec); preparing case files

Assessment

Risk assessment and case management planning (e.g., interviewing clients and collateral contacts); making evidence-based assessments of offender; determining appropriate interventions to address risk and need areas

Counselling

Conducting initial interviews; motivational interviewing; challenging difficult client attitudes and behaviours; individual supervision; group counselling; facilitating core programs (in provinces where POs play this role) such as Respectful Relationships and Substance Abuse Management

Service Coordination

Collaborating with police and social services; identifying educational, vocational, and employment goals; providing treatment opportunities; assisting with locating housing; addressing family, financial, and other issues

Surveillance and Enforcement

Monitoring compliance with conditions of probation; monitoring compliance with conditions of provincial parole (in Ontario and Québec); conducting home visits; documenting violations; preparing violation reports and recommendations; preparing violation reports for provincial parolees (in Ontario and Québec)

Source: Copyright © 2011 From *Corrections: Foundations for the Future* by J.B. Stinchcomb. Reproduced by permission of Taylor and Francis Group, LLC, a division of Informa plc.

Pre-sentence report (PSR) A document prepared by the probation officer for the sentencing judge that contains information on the convicted offender, including socio-biographical information, offence history, victim impact, and risk assessments.

example, it must include information on the offender's background and community, as well as on available community-based programs and services, including restorative justice programs such as sentencing circles and Elder-assisted interventions (see Figure 5.1).

No information can be included in the PSR that was not presented in court, and the PSR's summary cannot include any information that is not contained in the body of the report. In many provinces, as a matter of policy, probation officers are prohibited from making sentencing recommendations to the judge, although the PSR will generally set out available community and institutional programs for the judge to consider in determining the sentence. Where probation officers do make sentencing recommendations, they are generally accepted.[13]

In *R. v. Junkert* (2010 ONCA 549), the Ontario Court of Appeal reaffirmed that probation officers are held to high standards of professionalism. The presiding judge stated, "A pre-sentence report is intended to be an accurate, independent, and balanced assessment of an offender, his background,

Figure 5.1

Components of the Pre-sentence Report

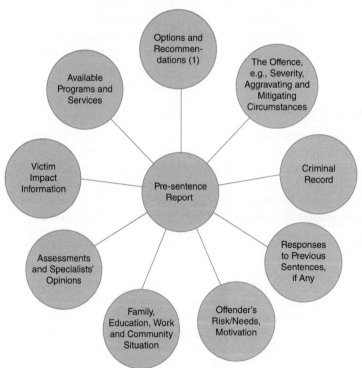

[1]In some jurisdictions, probation officers can make recommendations to the sentencing judge.

and his prospects for the future." The comments made by the appeal court judge were in relation to a case where the pre-sentence report prepared by the probation officer on an offender omitted significant information, relied upon the statements of one police officer, and misrepresented the offender's degree of remorse for the crime.[14]

For an example of how a PSR is used by judges at sentencing, see the case of *R. v. Pauchay* (2009 SKPC 35), accessible at http://www.thestarphoenix.com/pdf/09skpc35pauchay.pdf.

A typical workday for a probation officer involves writing reports, meeting with offenders, and reporting their findings to judges or other criminal justice personnel. While probation officers may have contact with offenders on their caseload in the community, the majority of their work is done in the office. These offices are located in community corrections buildings or local courthouses. Certain job duties may force the officer to work well into their evenings and weekends, for example, when conducting interviews with offenders' friends, families, and employers. Additionally, the officer will often deal with dangerous offenders. These individuals may suffer from various forms of mental illness or drug and alcohol issues. Parole officers frequently use computers and other communication tools to compile reports, organize and schedule their caseload, and provide information to colleagues and the court system.

Increasingly, probation officers are working in an interdisciplinary context. Most community police stations in Alberta, for example, have probation and parole officers working out of them. There is also in Alberta the Priority Prolific Offender Program (PPOP), wherein probation officers work with the police and the courts. The personnel collaborate to prosecute and rehabilitate repeat offenders.[15] The role of probation officers includes ensuring that prolific offenders have access to appropriate treatment resources and working with offenders to implement a plan for successful re-entry into the community.

Probation officers in Alberta also participate in the Integrated Justice Services Project (IJSP), wherein probation officers are paired with Alberta Health and Alberta Human Services professionals, police, and other municipal professionals in a single office.[16]

These partnerships assist in breaking down the silos that have traditionally existed between criminal justice and social service and health agencies and can be a more effective and efficient approach to addressing the needs of probation clients as well as facilitating information sharing on materials related to serious and prolific offenders.

TYPES OF SUPERVISION ORDERS

Probation officers are responsible for a variety of supervision orders. These are set out in Corrections File 5.1.

CORRECTIONS FILE 5.1

Types of Supervision Orders

Type of Order	Maximum Custody	Maximum Community
Conditional discharge or suspended sentence	None	3 years
Fine plus probation	None	3 years
Conditional sentence plus probation	None	3 years
Probation	None	3 years
Intermittent prison plus probation	90 days	3 years
Prison plus probation	2 years less a day (provincial)	3 years
	Exactly 2 years (federal)	3 years
Section 810 recognizance	None	12 months

PROBATION CASE MANAGEMENT

Effective case management requires that the risks and needs of offenders be identified so that the appropriate level of supervision can be determined (i.e., more intensive supervision for higher risk/needs offenders and less supervision for lower risk/needs offenders). This process also identifies services to address the needs of offenders.[17]

In recent years, the principles of Risk–Need–Responsivity (RNR) have gained prominence in systems of corrections. The **risk principle** states that correctional interventions have a greater chance of success when they are matched with the offender's level of risk because higher risk offenders benefit more than medium- and low-risk offenders. The **need principle** holds that correctional interventions should target the criminogenic needs (i.e., dynamic risk factors) of offenders, which can include substance abuse, peer relations, and pro-criminal attitudes. The **responsivity principle** says that correctional interventions should be matched to the learning styles and abilities of individual offenders, with particular emphasis on cognitive-behavioural interventions.

Risk principle
Correctional interventions are most effective when matched with the offender's level of risk, and higher risk offenders benefit from interventions more than medium- and low-risk offenders.

Need principle
To be effective, correctional interventions must address the criminogenic needs of offenders.

Although RNR is most frequently associated with institutional treatment programs (discussed in Chapter 9), it is now recognized that this model may be effective in community corrections and in providing supervision and programs for offenders who have avoided a custodial sentence and those released into the community following confinement.[18] Programs and interventions that utilize RNR have been proven to be more successful than those based on traditional practice.

A core component of the probation officer's work is completing assessments, which are designed to identify the offender's needs, to evaluate risk, and to help formulate plans of supervision. These assessments are used not only during the case management process but also at parole hearings, where provincial parole boards determine whether to grant conditional release to offenders in custody (see Chapter 9).

Two of the more common instruments are the Level of Service Inventory-Revised (LSI-R) and the Level of Service/Case Management Inventory (LS/CMI); these are used for adult offenders. The LSI-R is a 54-item, interview-driven assessment that measures risk factors in relation to a number of areas, including criminal history, education/employment, financial status, and drug problems. The LS/CMI measures risk and need factors, taking basically the same approach. In Saskatchewan, probation officers use the Saskatchewan Primary Risk Assessment instrument for case and risk management. In Alberta, the Service Plan Instrument (SPIn), a standardized risk assessment tool, is used to assess offenders under supervision in the community. This instrument measures the level of risk presented by the offender's criminal history, response to supervision, aggression/violence, substance use, social/cognitive skills, and mental health, among others.[19]

There are also assessment instruments for specific groups of offenders, including sex offenders (Sex Offender Risk Assessment [SORA]) and offenders convicted of spousal assault (Spousal Assault Risk Assessment [SARA]).

The scores developed through these assessment instruments allow probation officers to target specific risk/needs areas and to devise case management and supervision plans. All of these instruments have been effective in identifying needs and in predicting the likelihood of reoffending.

Research studies have found that these instruments are valid for both genders and different ethnicities. Some observers have questioned the objectivity of risk assessment instruments such as the LSI-R, arguing that probation officers exercise considerable discretion when conducting these assessments and developing plans of supervision.[20]

It has also been argued that the role of probation officers has become more restricted and rule-bound. This points to efforts to standardize probation practices and to hold probation officers accountable for adhering to evidence-based practice standards. The use of risk assessment instruments as the basis for case management also allows probation officers to "externalize responsibility" for their decisions and to avoid criticism if an offender reoffends.[21]

Responsivity principle Correctional interventions should be matched to the learning styles of individual offenders.

Although risk assessment instruments are now a core component of probation practice; there is evidence that individual probation officers continue to exercise considerable discretion in their supervisory practices. A study conducted in an open-custody facility for young offenders found that the staff employed a variety of strategies to subvert the results of risk assessments; they also applied their experience and subjective assessments when constructing and implementing case management plans.[22]

THE DUAL ROLE OF PROBATION OFFICERS

Probation officers play a dual role: They provide assistance and support for offenders and at the same time they enforce the conditions of probation orders. In carrying out the assistance and support role, the probation officer may help the offender address issues that have contributed to the offence and identify resources in the community such as alcohol and drug treatment programs, education upgrading courses, and mental health services. However, the probation officer must at the same time ensure compliance with the general and specific conditions of the probation order. For offenders who are less cooperative, an approach based on control may be effective; for offenders who are motivated to change, the probation officer can provide encouragement, support, and assistance. Probation officers have the discretion to tailor their style of supervision to the needs and risk of the individual probationer.

It is often difficult for probation officers to handle both roles, and this can be a barrier to effective case management. For example, a probationer with a history of drug addiction who has relapsed and started "using" again (or who never ceased using drugs) may want to ask their probation officer for help finding a treatment program. However, that person could trigger a charge of breach of probation by disclosing the illegal drug use to the probation officer. On the other hand, failing to disclose the drug relapse could result in the commission of further criminal acts to support the addiction.

A probation officer who becomes aware that the probationer is not adhering to the conditions of the probation order often has considerable discretion in deciding whether to revoke probation. This decision making may be affected by a number of factors, including the organization in which the probation officer works, the individual style of the officer, and the severity of the violation.[23]

SUPERVISION

Over the past decade there has been a strong shift in the role and orientation of probation officers toward control and surveillance.[24] This shift has been due in large measure to increasing caseloads, the focus on risk assessment in order to ensure accountability and reduce liability, and the increasing number of higher risk categories of offenders—such as sex offenders and assaultive male offenders—who are receiving sentences of probation.

The probation officer–client relationship has been found to be critical to the success of this correctional strategy. A study of probationers' perspectives on probation found that relationships built on trust, mutual respect, and the pursuit of mutually agreed upon goals were directly related to the offender's perceptions of the helpfulness of probation.[25]

To be effective, a probation officer must, to the greatest extent possible, balance enforcement with treatment and balance a client-centred approach with organizational requirements (e.g., completing assessments and other paperwork).[26] Successfully implementing RNR-based probation practice requires organizational and policy changes as well as a commitment by both management and probation staff.[27]

Many probation offices now have specialized supervision units composed of specially trained officers for offenders convicted of spousal assault, sex offences, and other specific types of crime. Studies suggest that specially trained probation officers are less likely to be punitive in responding to violations of a probation order, perhaps because of their more in-depth understanding of the cognitive thinking patterns and behaviours of specific groups of offenders.[28]

Key to PO–offender relationships is **continuity of supervision**. Offenders who are supervised by many different probation officers during their probation period are at a higher risk to reoffend. One study ($N = 5{,}134$) found that offenders who were supervised by just one probation officer while on probation were nearly 60 percent more likely to complete their probation sentence successfully.[29]

Little is known about the impact of gender in probation supervision. For example, we know little about the challenges that women face when working with certain groups of offenders (e.g., male sex offenders), or how women probation officers cope with offenders' gender stereotypes. In one study ($N = 10$), women probation officers described how their male probationers often attempted to manipulate the supervisory relationship to undermine the officer's authority. Techniques ranged from flirting to physical and psychological intimidation.[30] Similarly, women probation officers may experience a heightened sense of vulnerability and, for officers who are mothers, a heightened sense of risk. It can be anticipated that racialized probation officers may also experience unique challenges in carrying out their roles, although this remains to be explored.

Continuity of supervision
The requirement that, to be effective, offenders be supervised by the same probation officer during their term of probation.

The Application of RNR to Probation Practice: The STICS Initiative

A core component of probation practice in several jurisdictions is the Strategic Training Initiative in Community Supervision (STICS) program. The STICS program focuses on principles of RNR and teaches probation officers ways to utilize those principles when supervising probationers, with particular attention to criminogenic factors such as relationships with peers and criminal-thinking patterns. The STICS approach is centred on relationship building and establishing trust between the probation officer and the client. The probation officer assumes the role of a change agent, as opposed to merely "managing" the offender and ensuring compliance with conditions.

The STICS initiative is a good example of applying evidence-based correctional strategies—in this case, the principle of RNR—to correctional practice—in this instance, probation. As one observer has noted, "The STICS directive allows probation officers to 'think outside the box' and as a consequence, allows them the ability to exercise creativity with policy in regard to the responsivity needs of offenders and subsequent service delivery."[31] This is particularly important when the probation officer is supervising persons with impairments, including fetal alcohol spectrum disorder (FASD). For these individuals, the cognitive-behavioural approach that is widely used in correctional interventions may not be effective, requiring the probation officer to adapt to the needs of the probationer.

In the words of one probation officer:

> *My STICS program tells me that I am going to try something else. I am going to go out of the box a little bit. I'm going to say, "Listen, I do have to breach you on this, but I am going to recommend that no action be taken." Or I might not breach at all and I am going to tell him, "You know what? I want you to go to AA for maybe about 2 months and then I will re-refer you and we will see how that works'… and I am willing to go out of the box like that."[32]*

Research studies have found that probation officers who utilize STICS have better outcomes with their probationers and that there are lower levels of reoffending.[33]

Key elements of successful probation supervision include establishing and maintaining rapport, considering the risk/needs of the offender, and adjusting the balance between control and assistance as required. The efforts of the probation officer will be enhanced if probationers are able to speak openly about their issues and challenges, while at the same time understanding what is expected of them. Probation officers have identified interpersonal communication and interviewing skills, knowledge of community resources, and the ability to cope with the offender's emotions as required core competencies for effective supervision.[34] When the probation officer can focus on addressing the problems the probationer is experiencing, there is often a reduction in reoffending.[35]

The Use of Motivational Interviewing in Probation Practice

Motivational interviewing (MI)
An interview technique used by probation officers designed to empower offenders to change their attitudes and behaviour.

An evidence-based practice that many probation officers follow is **motivational interviewing (MI)**. This approach uses empathy and other non confrontational strategies to improve the relationship between the probation officer and the offender and to strengthen the offender's motivation to change.[36] This is accomplished by engaging the offender in a positive dialogue through the use of open questions, affirmation, reflective listening, and summary reflections (OARS).[37]

Through the use of MI, the probation officer facilitates a client-centred conversation that empowers the probationer to make positive changes in their life.[38] The evidence is mixed as to whether MI lowers rates of reoffending; however, it is viewed as a central component of an RNR approach to probation supervision.[39]

PROGRAMS FOR PROBATIONERS

Provincial/territorial systems of corrections and not-for-profit organizations offer probationers a variety of programs and services. In British Columbia, officers are actively involved in several programs for their probationers. These include violence prevention, substance abuse management, respectful relationships, living skills, cognitive skills, and educational upgrading, as well as a program for sex offenders. The components of the violence prevention program are set out in Corrections File 5.2.

CORRECTIONS FILE 5.2

Violence Prevention Program (VPP)

Rationale	Offenders learn to differentiate between violence and anger.
	Offenders explore sources of anger.
	Offenders identify nonviolent ways to express and resolve anger.
	Participants learn about their cycle of violence.
	Participants develop self-management techniques to behave in a healthy manner.
Objectives	Practise stress management skills.
	Identify positive communication skills.
	Learn problem-solving skills.
Trained facilitators	Correctional staff in correctional centres
	Correctional staff in community corrections offices
Targeted population	Offenders assessed as medium or high risk to reoffend.
	Offenders convicted of domestic violence attend respectful relationship (RR), not VPP.
Duration	Ten 150-minute sessions.
	Recommended participation: one to two sessions/week.

These programs are offered by community corrections offices throughout the province and are available for both probationers and provincial parolees. Participation is generally stipulated on the offender's probation order, although the programs also accept persons other than probationers.

INTENSIVE SUPERVISION PROBATION

Intensive supervi-
sion probation
(ISP)
An intermediate
sanction (between
the minimal
supervision of tra-
ditional probation
and incarceration)
that generally
includes reduced
caseloads for
probation officers,
increased surveil-
lance, treatment
interventions, and
efforts to ensure
that probationers
are employed.

Intensive supervision probation (ISP) is meant to be an intermediate sanction between traditional probation practice—which generally involves minimal supervision—and incarceration. ISP programs entail increased surveillance of probationers, various treatment interventions, efforts to ensure that offenders are employed, and reduced caseloads for probation officers. In Canada, ISP is used for both adult and youth offenders.

Offenders in ISP programs are monitored closely and rigorous conditions are imposed on them, such as multiple weekly reporting, strict enforcement of the probation order's mandatory and optional conditions, and the requirement that offenders secure and maintain employment. ISP is more suited to offenders who pose a greater risk to reoffend. A premise of these programs is that they can help reduce the number of prison admissions, cut operational costs, and protect the public, while providing increased supervision of more serious offenders.

An example of an ISP is the Criminal Organization and High Risk Offender Unit (COHROU) program in Manitoba. The COHROU targets high-risk offenders and involves intensive supervision and programming for serious, high-risk offenders, most of whom have committed violent offences and are assessed as being high risk. An evaluation of the COHROU found relatively high rates of reoffending among a sample ($N = 409$) of probationers in the program, including breaches of probation conditions, and only 27.4 percent of the offenders did not commit an offence during the program or during the two-year follow-up. On the other hand, if violations of probation conditions are not included, 57.5 percent of the offenders successfully completed the COHROU without committing a new offence, while 46.2 percent did not commit a new offence either during their entire period of supervision or during the two-year follow-up.[40]

CHALLENGES FOR PROBATION OFFICERS

The perspectives and experiences of correctional officers have been studied extensively; little attention has been paid to those of probation officers. What studies have been done have found that the most satisfying part of a probation officer's job is working with offenders, and that the least satisfying part is the ever-increasing burden of administrative duties, including paperwork and dealing with agency management.[41]

The Stress Levels of Probation Officers

Studies have found that probation officers face higher stress levels than the general population. Women probation officers may have higher levels of stress than their male counterparts because of the issues noted earlier regarding their supervision of male probationers.[42] The work of probation officers may also expose them to trauma that can contribute to their levels of stress[43] (see Corrections File 5.3).

Women probation officers, particularly those with children, may be particularly vulnerable to the impact of occupational stresses. A Canadian study ($N = 106$) of women probation officers found high levels of stress-related symptoms, including interpersonal issues both in work and home domains, physical and self-esteem problems, panic disorder, and depression, anxiety, and chronic physical health concerns. Overall, the reported areas of distress were generally found to be more prevalent for women probation officers with children.[44]

Probation Officer Safety

An issue that has recently emerged is officer safety: There is evidence that incidents involving probation officers are vastly under-reported. Many probation officers do not conduct visits to the homes of their probationers. Often this is

CORRECTIONS FILE 5.3

A Probation Officer's Account of the Impact of Occupational Stress

As a probation officer, part of my job is to write pre-sentencing reports. To do so I pore over documents related to crimes committed. I've always thought of myself as a tough guy. Lately though, when I deal with cases where the victim was a child, I can't shake the anger I feel. I find myself wanting to punch something. Sometimes I've even felt like crying, but I just won't allow myself to do that, because I'm not weak. Instead I end up hating the world. More than once I've caught myself putting off looking through files. Frequently on my way home I buy a six-pack. I then go to take care of my horses, drinking while I do that. I stay away from my family's happy chatter as much as I can. They are so naïve and ignorant! I don't want to burst their bubble, so I don't talk to them about my work. But I worry constantly about my children's safety. I am very strict with them, especially about where they go and who they hang out with. I get into arguments with my wife who objects to my repetitive coaching of my kids to not trust anyone outside immediate family. I often fantasize about what I would do to an offender if he hurt one of my kids.

Source: C. Spinaris, "Occupational Exposure to Primary and Secondary Trauma in Corrections," corrections.com, January 7, 2013, http://www.corrections.com/news/article/31682-occupational-exposure-to-primary-and-secondary-trauma-in-corrections. Reprinted by permission of the author.

because they don't have enough time or because they worry for their safety. Still other officers believe that home visits are an intrusion on probationers and their families.[45]

Supervising High-Need Probationers

Probation officers often struggle to access services for their clients, especially probationers who face mental impairments and/or addictions, or who are afflicted by FASD or other challenges. There may be challenges in liaising with other agencies to secure support services and access to programs.

Compounding this is that probation officers may not have had sufficient training to recognize and intervene with high-need clients. In a study of FASD probationers, it was noted that, "There remains a strong suspicion that FASD is, by and large unrecognized by professionals working in the criminal justice system including judges, lawyers, police, community corrections workers (probation), parole officers and institutional correctional workers and as a result, fair judicial treatment is less than forthcoming."[46]

Heavy Workloads

The duties of probation officers have continued to expand and now include providing bail supervision for adult criminal courts, preparing PSRs for sentencing courts, supervising offenders on conditional release orders, and liaising with social services, the police, and the courts.

High Caseloads

Probation officers in many jurisdictions have experienced increases in their caseloads, some of which are in the 100+ range per officer. In Ontario, probation officers have the highest average caseload, among their counterparts in other jurisdictions, with 66.5 clients per officer. There are approximately 800 probation and parole officers in Ontario who are charged with supervising 50,000 offenders (note that in Ontario, these officers supervise offenders on probation and those offenders on provincial parole).[47] In British Columbia, the average caseload is 64 clients per officer, an increase of 28 percent since 2005–2006.[48] The impact of caseload size on the quality of supervision provided and on rates of violations of probation orders and reoffending, however, is unknown.

A Lack of PO–Offender Contact and Intervention

Depending on other commitments and responsibilities, probation officers may have only limited in-person contact with the individual offenders on their caseloads. Contact may be by telephone, and when the officer does meet with the offender, the session may be short. When probation services shift to more of a managerial approach, focusing on risk assessments and away from client-centred practice, it may be even more difficult for probation officers to find adequate time for their clients.

Close supervision is particularly important for offenders on probation who are designated as high risk. The issue of high-risk offenders on probation was highlighted in 2015, when an offender killed three women in eastern Ontario: One was his ex-girlfriend, whom he had previously been convicted of assaulting, and another of the victims was a woman he had been convicted of threatening. The offender had refused to sign a probation order requiring him to have no contact with one of the victims.[49] A spokesperson for the probation officers' union stated that this incident was a reflection of the probation service being understaffed and unable to conduct offender home visits and provide proper supervision.[50]

Increasing Needs and Risks of Probationers

In recent years, there has been an increase in the needs and risk levels of offenders placed on probation and in the numbers of offenders who are mentally disordered or who have been convicted of sex-related crimes and crimes of violence. Today, more probationers have been convicted of a violent crime and many probationers have been assessed as being high risk.[51]

The Requirement to Provide Probation Services in Remote and Northern Regions

Unique challenges are involved in providing effective probation services in remote and northern areas of the country. For example, community resources are absent, and it is difficult to recruit and retain probation officers. These difficulties are particularly acute given the high rates of crime and violence that afflict many northern and remote communities (see Corrections File 5.4).

Supervising a Diverse Clientele

An unstudied dimension of probation practice in Canada is the challenge presented by factors such as language, culture, religion, and ethnicity. Most probation officers in Canada are Caucasian, yet these officers carry out their tasks in a diverse society. English- or French-speaking probation officers can expect to encounter difficulties when supervising newly arrived Canadians, who may have limited language skills; similarly, cultural differences may impede the development of therapeutic relationships with probationers as well as with community partners. Research in the United States found that probationers who were supervised by an officer of their own race had more positive perceptions of that officer.[52] This question has not yet been explored in Canada.

CORRECTIONS FILE 5.4

Probation in the Remote North

There are unique challenges in probation practice in northern and remote communities. These communities often lack the capacity to provide programs for probationers, especially those who are high-risk violent offenders or sex offenders and those suffering from a mental illness, addiction issues, and/or FASD. Concerns have been raised regarding whether probation is overused or being used inappropriately and whether probation orders protect communities. Also, programs and services for probationers are severely lacking, and, in some communities, so is adequate supervision.

Concerns about the effectiveness of probation were reflected in the comments of an Inuit woman who had been the victim of violence in one of the communities:

> *He was charged with assault. Then, a few weeks later, he was in JP court and he got six months' probation. I thought it was going to be okay because after the JP court he said he would quit beating me up. But after one month he started again. That was against his probation. He'd go see his probation officer every month and when he still had six or eight months to go, he quit going. Nobody said anything and nothing happened. He was still drinking when he was on probation. It's just a lot of words, no action.*[a]

Circuit court judges, who hold court in northern and remote communities, may be reluctant to sentence offenders to custody in correctional institutions that may be hundreds of kilometres from the offender's home community.

---

[a] C.T. Griffiths, E. Zellerer, D.S. Wood, and G. Saville, *Crime, Law, and Justice Among Inuit in the Baffin Region, N.W.T., Canada* (Burnaby, B.C.: Criminology Research Centre, Simon Fraser University, 1995).

THE EXPERIENCE OF PROBATIONERS

Few studies have examined the experiences of persons on probation. However, there is some evidence that many probationers believe that their sentence served as a deterrent and that being on probation was beneficial.[53] A survey (N = 1,121) conducted in British Columbia found that probationers had a positive overall experience of probation (81 percent); that most of them (90.5 percent) felt their probation officer treated them fairly; and that they did not have difficulty accessing programs (91.3 percent). Similarly, most of the probationers surveyed (63.5 percent) indicated that they were involved in their supervision plan.[54]

With respect to continuity of supervision, most of the respondents had only one (48 percent) or two (32 percent) different probation officers in the course of their sentence/supervision.[55] Overall client satisfaction did not vary with the gender or Indigenous status of the probationer, nor did it with the region of the province in which they resided.

Despite these findings from B.C., there is evidence that some offenders experience **pains of probation**. Depending on the specific conditions attached to the probation order, these pains may include loss of autonomy, having to change daily routines, the stigma associated with probation, and possible difficulties with employment. The pains experienced by inmates in correctional institutions are often physical; by contrast, those associated with probation tend to be economic and emotional.[56] Intensive supervision programs, in particular, may place restrictions on the probationer, who as a result may view probation negatively.

American researchers found that some offenders rate being on probation as more punitive than a short-term prison sentence.[57] Offenders' perceptions of probation may be partly a function of their past experiences of prison and probation: Offenders who have been incarcerated in the past may not find confinement as punitive as close supervision in the community.

> **Pains of probation**
> The emotional and economic challenges that probationers may experience while under probation supervision in the community.

THE EFFECTIVENESS OF ALTERNATIVES TO CONFINEMENT

Community corrections agencies often do not gather the information required to determine the effectiveness of probation practices.[58] Few of the more common programs for probationers, including those operated by private contractors, have been evaluated.

For a summary of research on the effectiveness of alternatives to confinement, see Research File 5.1.

RESEARCH FILE 5.1

The Effectiveness of Alternatives to Confinement

Does traditional diversion work? Inconclusive. There have been few formal evaluations. It may "widen the net" by focusing on low-risk, first-time offenders. There is no evidence that diversion has any impact on correctional populations; in fact, it may increase the justice system's workload and costs.[a]

Do conditional sentences work? Potentially. Historically, the violation rates of conditional sentences were high (up to 40 percent of cases). This may change with restrictions that have been placed on its use by Bill C-10, although there are concerns that such sentences are being used inappropriately by judges.[b] Research evidence suggests that conditional sentences may be more effective than imprisonment in reducing recidivism.[c]

(continued)

Do electronic monitoring and GPS work? Potentially. EM can play a significant role in reducing rates of recidivism, even among more serious offenders, including sex offenders.[d] There is, though, no evidence that EM programs reduce prison admissions or that they are less costly than incarceration. The perception among probation officers and offenders in an American study was that EM had a negative impact on the offender's personal and family relationships and hindered efforts to secure housing and employment.[e] Also, it may increase the workload for probation and parole officers and may cause net-widening and raise privacy issues. There is evidence that EM in Canada has not generally been used as a true alternative to confinement.[f]

Do restorative justice alternatives work? They can. There is evidence that some restorative justice programs, succeed at reducing rates of reoffending and at addressing the needs of victims, offenders, and communities.

Does probation supervision reduce reoffending? Potentially. There is no evidence that traditional probation practices reduce reoffending.[g] This is for a variety of reasons, including the lack of training of probation officers in strategies that may improve probation outcomes, in particular the absence of the principles of RNR in probation practice. It also depends to some extent on the criminality of the group being studied. Many probationers who have committed less-serious crimes successfully complete; less-positive results are reported for offenders with lengthy criminal records and who have additional issues, such as addiction and mental illness.[h] The STICS approach to the delivery of probation services and the use of motivational interviewing have produced positive outcomes.

Do the principles of RNR improve the effectiveness of probation? Generally, yes. There is growing evidence that incorporating RNR into probation practice improves the quality of supervision as well as case outcomes.[i] A study ($N = 192$) of youth probationers in Saskatchewan found that case management centred on the "need principle" and on the criminogenic needs of youth resulted in lower rates of reoffending.[j] The results of the STICS initiative are promising.

Does ISP work? Yes. These programs can manage risk while providing probationers with access to treatment. ISP may be more cost-effective than incarceration and produce better outcomes.[k]

Do collaborative partnerships between probation and other agencies, including police services, improve probation outcomes? Collaboration may improve information sharing and the quality of supervision, but it is uncertain whether this results in more-effective probation outcomes and reduced reoffending. Concerns have been expressed that probation–police partnerships may blur the roles and mission of the two agencies, with probation officers abandoning their treatment and assistance role for one of enforcement and control.[l] It may also increase the role ambiguity of probation officers as they attempt to balance the enforcement and assistance roles discussed above.[m]

What factors may compromise successful probation outcomes? The effectiveness of probation may be compromised by low program completion rates by offenders. A random sample of 60 offenders on probation in British Columbia found that only 35 percent of offenders with a condition on their probation order to complete a treatment program did so.[n] (See a slide presentation on this investigation at http://www.bcauditor.com/pubs/2011/report10/bc-community-corrections-cccp.) The reasons why probationers fail to complete mandated programs are many, but they certainly include a lack of access to programs and weak motivation. Furthermore, the guiding principle of RNR that program efforts should focus on high-risk probationers may prove to be unworkable if these offenders have needs that exceed the capacity of community-based programs.[o] In such cases, programs for low- and medium-risk probationers may be more effective.

It is important that the supervision strategies the officer employs match the needs and risk of the individual offender. However, there is often a disconnect between the risk assessment and the intervention plan developed by the supervising probation officer.[p] Probation agencies may also lack the capacity to assess effectiveness, determine gaps in program delivery, and ensure that probationers receive the interventions identified as required by the risk assessment.

For which offenders is probation most effective? Research studies suggest that probation is most effective for offenders who are in a stable personal relationship, are employed, have higher levels of education, and do not have an extensive criminal record. Specialized supervision units can be effective in increasing offender accountability and reducing rates of reoffending; they also have a positive impact on victim satisfaction.[q]

---

[a] J. Bonta, "Adult Offender Diversion Programs: Research Summary," *Corrections Research and Development 3*, no. 1 (Ottawa: Solicitor General Canada, 1998), http://www.publicsafety.gc.ca/res/cor/sum/_fl/cprs199801-eng.pdf; J. Nuffield, *Diversion Programs for Adults* (Ottawa: Solicitor General Canada, 1997).

[b] D. North, "The Catch-22 of Conditional Sentencing," *Criminal Law Quarterly 44*, no. 3 (2001), 342–74.

[c] Cf. J. Cid, "Is Imprisonment Criminogenic? A Comparative Study of Recidivism Rates Between Prison and Suspended Prison Sanctions," *European Journal of Criminology 6*, no. 6 (2009), 459–80.

[d] W. Bales, K. Mann, T. Blomberg, G. Gaes, K. Barrick, K. Dhungana, and B. McManus, *A Quantitative and Qualitative Assessment of Electronic Monitoring* (Washington: National Institute of Justice, U.S. Department of Justice, 2010), http://www.ncjrs.gov/pdffiles1/nij.grants/230530.pdf; S. Bottos, *An Overview of Electronic Monitoring in Corrections: Issues and Implications* (Ottawa: Correctional Service Canada, 2007), http://publications.gc.ca/site/eng/381780/publication.html#.

[e] Bales et al., *A Quantitative and Qualitative Assessment*.

[f] J. Bonta, S. Wallace-Capretta, and J. Rooney, "Can Electronic Monitoring Make a Difference? An Evaluation of Three Canadian Programs," *Crime and Delinquency 46*, no. 1 (2000), 61–75.

[g] J. Bonta, G. Bourgon, T. Rugge, T-L. Scott, A.K. Yessine, L. Gutierrez, and J. Li, "An Experimental Demonstration of Training Probation Officers in Evidence-Based Community Supervision," *Criminal Justice and Behavior 38*, no. 11 (2011), 1127–48 at 1129.

[h] M. DeLisi and P.J. Conis, *American Corrections: Theory, Research, Policy, and Practice*, 2nd ed. (Burlington: Jones and Bartlett Learning, 2013), 248.

[i] Bonta et al., "An Experimental Demonstration of Training Probation Officers in Evidence-Based Community Supervision."

[j] D. Luong and J.S. Wormith, "Applying Risk/Need Assessment to Probation Practice and Its Impact on the Recidivism of Young Offenders," *Criminal Justice and Behavior 38*, no. 12 (2011), 1177–99 at 1197.

[k] DeLisi and Conis, *American Corrections*.

(continued)

l B. Kim, J. Gerber, and D.R. Beto, "Listening to Law Enforcement Officers: The Promises and Problems of Police–Adult Probation Partnerships," *Journal of Criminal Justice 38*, no. 4 (2010), 625–32.

m D. Murphy and F. Lutze, "Police–Probation Partnerships: Professional Identity and the Sharing of Coercive Power," *Journal of Criminal Justice 37*, no. 1 (2009), 65–76.

n B.C. Office of the Auditor General, *Effectiveness of BC Community Corrections* (Victoria: Author, 2011), http://www.bcauditor.com/sites/default/files/publications/2011/report_10/report/OAGBC-BC-Community-Corrections%20for%20print.pdf.

o D.A.S. Pearson, C. McDougall, M. Kanaan, R.A. Bowles, and D.J. Torgerson, "Reducing Criminal Recidivism: Evaluation of Citizenship: An Evidence-Based Probation Supervision Process," *Journal of Experimental Criminology 7*, no. 1 (2011), 73–102.

p J. Bonta, T. Rugge, B. Sedo, and R. Coles, *Case Management in Manitoba Probation*, 27–28 (Ottawa: Public Safety Canada, 2004), https://www.publicsafety.gc.ca/cnt/rsrcs/pblctns/cs-mngmnt-mntb/cs-mngmnt-mntb-eng.pdf.

q Luong and Wormith, "Applying Risk/Need Assessment to Probation Practice."

SUMMARY

This chapter has provided an overview of the various strategies used by systems of corrections as alternatives to confinement. These include traditional practices such as diversion and probation, as well as more recent innovations such as the electronic surveillance of offenders. Many diversion programs use a restorative justice approach.

Probation is the most widely used alternative to incarceration and is popular because of its versatility. Probation officers are involved in a range of activities, including preparing PSRs, conducting risk and need assessments, and supervising offenders. Probation officers confront a number of challenges in carrying out their mandate, many of them related to the dual role of providing support while also enforcing the conditions of probation orders. Probation officers are susceptible to a variety of stressors that may impact them on a personal and professional level.

The STICS initiative is an example of how the principles of RNR have been successfully applied in probation practice and produced positive outcomes. Probationers can experience challenges while being supervised in the community.

KEY POINTS REVIEW

1. When used as an alternative to confinement, community corrections includes diversion, intermediate sanctions, the use of electronic monitoring, and probation.

2. Offenders can be diverted from the criminal justice process at several points: pre-charge, post-charge, and post-sentencing.

3. There is concern that traditional diversion programs may "widen the net" and be coercive and punitive.

4. Probation is the most widely used strategy for supervising offenders in the community as an alternative to incarceration.

5. There are significant differences between probation and parole.

6. Probation officers have a variety of roles and responsibilities, including preparing pre-sentence reports, assessing offender risk and needs, and providing supervision and assistance.

7. The supervision strategies used by probation officers must match the need, risk, and responsivity of the individual offender; that is, the principles of RNR must be followed.

8. Probation officers play a dual role: They provide assistance and support for offenders, and they enforce the conditions of the probation order.

9. The STICS initiative is a good example of applying evidence-based correctional strategies to correctional practice.

10. There are a number of challenges in probation practice, including officer stress, safety, heavy workloads and high caseloads, limited PO–client interaction, and the increasing risk/needs levels of offenders on probation.

11. Providing probation services in northern and remote communities is a particular challenge.

12. Probation appears to be most effective with offenders who are employed, have stable family relationships, and do not have an extensive criminal record.

KEY TERM QUESTIONS

1. Identify and discuss the objectives of *diversion* programs.

2. What is *net-widening* and why is it a concern associated with diversion programs?

3. Identify and discuss the objectives of *intermediate sanctions* and provide examples of these types of sanctions.

4. Describe the use of *electronic monitoring*, including the potential role of GPS technology, as a corrections strategy.

5. Describe the following sentencing options: *conditional sentence* and *probation*.

6. What is a *pre-sentence report (PSR)* and how is it used in the correctional process?

7. Discuss the *risk principle*, the *need principle*, and the *responsivity principle* and their importance in the study of corrections.

8. What is meant by *continuity of supervision* and why is it important in probation practice?
9. Describe the objectives and approach of *motivational interviewing (MI)*.
10. What is *intensive supervision probation (ISP)*?
11. Describe the *pains of probation* and how these may affect an offender and their family.

CRITICAL THINKING EXERCISES

Critical Thinking Exercise 5.1

Should Electronic Monitoring Be Expanded to Include Behavioural Surveillance of Offenders?

It is likely that in the not-too-distant future, technology will be able to track offenders as well as provide surveillance/control of the offender's behaviour. It may soon be possible to monitor heartbeat, brain activity, and other vital signs. When paired with chemical implants, it may soon be possible to monitor—and where required, control—an offender's behaviour.

Your Thoughts?

1. Would you support the use of such technology for these purposes? What arguments could be made for and against this type of surveillance?
2. If you were convicted of a crime and were offered the opportunity to be placed under a 24-hour GPS tracking system rather than being sent to custody, which would you choose, and why?

Critical Thinking Exercise 5.2

How Much Discretion Should Probation Officers Have in Supervising Offenders?

In recent years, the emergence of evidence-based practices and predictive risk assessment instruments has reduced the broad discretion traditionally exercised by probation officers. Proponents argue that this has helped standardize probation practices and increase effectiveness. Critics counter that probation officers should be able to use professional discretion and adapt their supervisory practices to the requirements of individual offenders.

Your Thoughts?

1. What is your view on how much discretion probation officers should have?

Class/Group Discussion Exercise 5.1

The Role of Technology in Probation Supervision

In several U.S. states, low-risk probationers are allowed to report in to their supervising probation officers at a kiosk. The kiosks are similar to ATMs and are located in probation offices, courthouses, or police departments. The kiosk contains a biometric reader that identifies the probationer who then is prompted to provide information that would be discussed in a face-to-face meeting with their probation officers. The kiosks are designed to be a low-cost alternative to traditional supervision. This allows probation officers to spend more time on high-risk, high-needs offenders on their caseload.[59] The kiosk program is premised on the principles of risk–need–responsivity, which include the provision that lower-risk offenders do not require close attention. Evaluations of kiosk programs have found reductions in rates of reoffending ranging from 3 to 10 percent. Probation officers have generally favourable views of these programs, which allow them to spend more time with probationers with higher risks and needs. In 2017, several probation offices in B.C. were using kiosks on a trial basis.

Your Thoughts?

1. In your view, should probation services across Canada pilot the use of kiosks for low-risk probationers?

2. What would be the benefits, and challenges of the use of this technology?

MEDIA LINKS

"See How the 'Buddi' Electronic Monitoring System Works," Global News, http://globalnews.ca/video/2486798/see-how-the-buddi-electronic-monitoring-system-works

"Risky Business: Calgary Police Unit Monitors City's Most Dangerous Criminals," Postmedia, http://www.sprucegroveexaminer.com/2016/03/19/risky-business-calgary-police-unit-monitors-citys-most-dangerous-criminals

"Motivational Interviewing" https://www.youtube.com/watch?v=67I6g1I7Zao

"Vancouver Intensive Supervision Unit—Finding the Person within the Illness," https://www.youtube.com/watch?v=1q3x9-2EgQ4

NOTES

1. M. Weinrath, M. Doerksen, and J. Watts, "The Impact of an Intensive Supervision Program on High-Risk Offenders: Manitoba's COHROU Program," *Canadian Journal of Criminology and Criminal Justice* 57, no. 2 (2015), 253–88.

2. Truth and Reconciliation Commission of Canada, *Calls to Action* (Winnipeg: Author, 2015), p. 3, http://www.trc.ca/websites/trcinstitution/File/2015/Findings/Calls_to_Action_English2.pdf.

3. Canadian Association of Mental Health, *Evidence Summary: Mental Health Diversion Frameworks in Canada* (Ottawa: Author, 2014), http://eenet.ca/wp-content/uploads/2014/04/Mental-Health-Diversion-Policy-Frameworks_April2014-Final.pdf.

4. L. Butler, J. Goodman-Delahunty, and R. Lulham, "Effectiveness of Pre-Trial Community-Based Diversion in Reducing Reoffending by Adult Intrafamilial Child Sex Offenders," *Criminal Justice and Behavior 39*, no. 4 (2012), 493–513; D.E. Roe-Sepowitz, K.E. Hickle, M.P. Loubert, and T. Egan, "Adult Prostitution Recidivism: Risk Factors and Impact of a Diversion Program," *Journal of Offender Rehabilitation 50*, no. 5 (2011), 272–85.

5. A. Verhaaff and H. Scott, "Individual Factors Predicting Mental Health Court Diversion Outcome," *Research on Social Work Practice 25*, no. 2 (2015), 213–28.

6. E. Miller, "Embracing Addiction: Drug Courts and the False Promise of Judicial Interventionism," *Ohio State Law Journal 65*, no. 6 (2004), 1479–1576.

7. J. Junger-Tas, *Alternatives to Prison Sentences: Experience and Developments* (New York: Kugler, 1994), pp. 11, 13.

8. J. Petersilia and E.P. Deschenes, "What Punishes—Inmates Rank the Severity of Prison vs. Intermediate Sanctions," *Federal Probation 58*, no. 1 (1994), 3–8.

9. J.V. Roberts, "Serving Time at Home: The Conditional Sentence of Imprisonment," in *Criminal Justice in Canada: A Reader*, 4th ed., eds. J.V. Roberts and M.G. Grossman (Toronto: Nelson, 2012), 178–86.

10. A. Maxwell, "Adult Criminal Court Statistics in Canada, 2013/2014," *Juristat 35*, no. 1, Catalogue no. 85-002-X (Ottawa: Minister of Industry, 2015), p. 9, http://www.statcan.gc.ca/pub/85-002-x/2015001/article/14226-eng.htm#a6.

11. "Probation Officer," Alberta Justice and Solicitor General website, n.d., https://www.solgps.alberta.ca/careers/probation_officer/Pages/default.aspx.

12. Ontario Ministry of Public Safety and Correctional Services, "Careers in Corrections: Becoming a Probation and Parole Officer," https://www.mcscs.jus.gov.on.ca/english/corr_serv/careers_in_corr/careers_pp_officer/careers_pp_officer.html. © Queen's Printer for Ontario, 2016. Reproduced with permission.

13. J. Bonta, G. Bourgon, R. Jesseman, and A.K. Yessine, *Presentence Reports in Canada* (Ottawa: Public Safety Canada, 2005), http://www.publicsafety.gc.ca/res/cor/rep/_fl/2005-03-presntnce-eng.pdf.

14. J. Melnitzer, "Appeal Court's Attack on Pre-Sentence Report Signals Larger Issue," *Law Times*, August 22, 2010, http://www.lawtimesnews.com/20100823991/headline-news/appeal-courts-attack-on-pre-sentence-report-signals-wider-issue.

15. "Priority Prolific Offender Program," Alberta Justice and Solicitor General website, n.d., https://www.solgps.alberta.ca/safe_communities/community_awareness/ppop/Pages/Default.as.

16. P. Thompson and J. Schutte, *Integrated Justice Services Project: Implementing Problem-Solving Justice* (Edmonton: Government of Alberta, 2010), http://www.courtinnovation.org/sites/default/files/documents/Integrated%20Justice%20Service%20Project.pdf.

17. J. Bonta, T. Rugge, B. Sedo, and R. Coles, *Case Management in Manitoba Probation* (Ottawa: Public Safety and Emergency Preparedness Canada, 2004), http://www.publicsafety.gc.ca/res/cor/rep/_fl/2004-01-cse-mana-eng.pdf.

18. J. Bonta, G. Bourgon, T. Rugge, T-L Scott, A.I. Yessine, L. Gutierrez, and J. Li, "An Experimental Demonstration of Training Probation Officers in Evidence-Based Community

Supervision," *Criminal Justice and Behavior 38*, no. 11 (2011), 1127–48.

19. Thompson and Schutte, *Integrated Justice Services Project: Implementing Problem-Solving Justice*.

20. K. Bullock, "The Construction and Interpretation of Risk Management Technologies in Contemporary Probation Practice," *British Journal of Criminology 51*, no. 1 (2011), 120–35.

21. D. Ballucci, "Subverting and Negotiating Risk Assessment: A Case Study of the LSI in a Canadian Youth Custody Facility," *Canadian Journal of Criminology and Criminal Justice 54*, no. 2 (2012), 203–28 at 205.

22. Ibid.

23. J.J. Krebs, M. Jones, and J.M. Jolley, "Discretionary Decision Making by Probation and Parole Officers: The Role of Extralegal Variables as Predictors of Responses to Technical Violations," *Journal of Contemporary Criminal Justice 25*, no. 4 (2009), 424–41.

24. R. Burnett and F. McNeill, "The Place of the Officer–Offender Relationship in Assisting Offenders to Desist from Crime," *Probation Journal 52*, no. 3 (2005), 221–42.

25. B. DeLude, D. Mitchell, and C. Barber, "The Probationer's Perspective on the Probation Officer-Probationer Relationship and Satisfaction with Probation," *Federal Probation 67*, no. 1 (2012), 35–39.

26. J. Matthews, "'People First: Probation Officer Perspectives on Probation Work'—A Practitioner's Response," *Probation Journal 56*, no. 1 (2009), 61–67.

27. D.A. Andrews, "The Impact of Nonprogrammatic Factors on Criminal Justice Interventions," *Legal and Criminological Psychology 16*, no. 1 (2011), 1–23.

28. J. Louden, J.L. Skeem, J. Camp, and E. Christensen, "Supervising Probationers with Mental Disorder: How Do Agencies Respond to Violations?" *Criminal Justice and Behavior 35*, no. 7 (2008), 832–47.

29. J. Clark-Miller and K.D. Stevens, "Effective Supervision Strategies: Do Frequent Changes of Supervision Officers Affect Probationer Outcomes?" *Federal Probation 75*, no. 3 (2011), 11–18.

30. M. Petrillo, "Power Struggle: Gender Issues for Female Probation Officers in the Supervision of High Risk Offenders," *Probation Journal 54*, no. 4 (2007), 394–406.

31. B.L. Gerger, "'Now You See Me, Now You Don't'—Service Delivery of Fetal Alcohol Spectrum Disorder (FASD) Offenders: A Study of Policy and Practice in Saskatchewan Community Corrections," unpublished M.A. thesis (Regina: Justice Studies, University of Regina: 2011), p. 102, http://ourspace.uregina.ca/bitstream/handle/10294/3540/Gerger_Bonny_Lynn_192303351_MA_JUST_Spring2012.pdf?sequence=1.

32. Ibid.

33. G. Bourgon, L. Gutierrez, and J. Ashton, *From Case Management to Change Agent: The Evolution of "What Works" in Community Supervision* (Ottawa: Public Safety Canada, 2012), https://www.publicsafety.gc.ca/cnt/rsrcs/pblctns/2012-01-cmc/index-en.aspx.

34. D. Bracken, "Skills and Knowledge for Contemporary Probation Practice," *Probation Journal 50*, no. 2 (2003), 101–14.

35. J. Bonta, T. Rugge, T.-L. Scott, G. Bourgon, and A.K. Yessine, "Exploring the Black Box of Community Supervision," *Journal of Offender Rehabilitation 47*, no. 3 (2008), 248–70.

36. M. McMurran, "Motivational Interviewing with Offenders: A Systematic Review," *Legal and Criminological Psychology 14*, no. 1 (2009), 83–100.

37. L.C. Sobell and M. Sobell, "Motivational Interviewing Strategies and Techniques: Rationales and Examples," 2008, http://www.nova.edu/gsc/forms/mi_rationale_techniques.pdf.

38. J. Paul and L. Feuerbach, "A Changing Role: Perspectives from Two Officers," *Federal Probation 72*, no. 2 (2008), 77–79.

39. D.A. Andrews, "The Impact of Nonprogrammatic Factors on Criminal Justice Interventions."

40. M. Weinrath, M. Doerksen, and J. Watts, "The Impact of an Intensive Supervision Program on

High-Risk Offenders: Manitoba's COHROU Program."

41. J. Annison, T. Eadie, and C. Knight, "People First: Probation Officer Perspectives on Probation Work," *Probation Journal 55*, no. 3(2008), 259–71.

42. C. Simmons, J.K. Cochran, and W.R. Blount, "The Effects of Job-Related Stress and Job Satisfaction on Probation Officers' Inclination to Quit," *American Journal of Criminal Justice 21*, no. 2 (2007), 213–29; R.N. Slate, T.L. Wells, and W.W. Johnson, "State Probation Officer Stress and Perceptions of Participation in Workplace Decision Making," *Crime and Delinquency 49*, no. 4 (2003), 519–41.

43. K.R. Lewis, L.S. Lewis, and T.M. Garby, "Probation Officers' Stress and Burnout Associated with Caseload Events," *Corrections & Mental Health*, September 9, 2013, http://community.nicic.gov/blogs/mentalhealth/archive/2013/09/09/probation-officers-stress-and-burnout-associated-with-caseload-events.aspx.

44. H. Ratti, "Female Probation Officers: The Challenge of Work-Life Balance in the Context of Traumatic Stress," unpublished M.A. thesis (Athabasca, AB: Athabasca University, 2011), http://dtpr.lib.athabascau.ca/action/download.php?filename=gcap/jenniferrattaiProject.pdf.

45. Personal communication with C.T. Griffiths.

46. B.L. Gerger, "'Now You See Me, Now You Don't,'" p. 2.

47. J. Hamilton-McCharles, "Insight into Probation and Parole," *The Nugget*, January 5, 2015, http://www.nugget.ca/2015/01/05/insight-into-probation-and-parole.

48. Auditor General of British Columbia, *Effectiveness of BC Community Corrections* (Victoria: Author, 2011), http://www.bcauditor.com/sites/default/files/publications/2011/report_10/report/OAGBC-BC-Community-Corrections%20for%20print.pdf.

49. "Ontario Probation Officers Say Workload is Too Great to Do Home Visits," CBC News, September 26, 2015, http://www.cbc.ca/news/canada/ottawa/ontario-probation-officers-understaffed-1.3245289.

50. Ibid.

51. L. Landry and M. Sinha, "Adult Correctional Services in Canada, 2005/2006," *Juristat 28*, no. 6, Catalogue no. 85-002-X (Ottawa: Minister of Industry, 2008), http://www.statcan.gc.ca/pub/85-002-x/2008006/article/10593-eng.htm.

52. N.F. Springer, B.K. Applegate, H.P. Smith, and A.H. Sitren, "Exploring the Determinants of Probationers' Perceptions of Their Supervising Officers," *Journal of Offender Rehabilitation 48*, no. 3 (2009), 210–27.

53. B.K. Applegate, H.P. Smith, A.H. Sitren, and N.F. Springer, "From the Inside: The Meaning of Probation to Probationers," *Criminal Justice Review 34*, no. 1 (2009), 80–95.

54. R.A. Malatest and Associates Ltd, *BC Community Corrections Client Survey Research: Client Satisfaction—Community Corrections Services* (Victoria: B.C. Ministry of Public Safety and Solicitor General, 2008).

55. Ibid.

56. I. Durnescu, "Pains of Probation: Effective Practice and Human Rights," *International Journal of Offender Therapy and Comparative Criminology 55*, no. 4 (2011), 530–45.

57. B.M. Crouch, "Is Incarceration Really Worse? Analysis of Offender's Preferences for Prison Over Probation," *Justice Quarterly 10*, no. 1 (1993), 67–88; J. Petersilia and S. Turner, "Intensive Probation and Parole," in *Crime and Justice: A Review of the Research*, ed. M. Tonry (Chicago: University of Chicago Press, 1993), 281–335.

58. Auditor General of British Columbia, *Effectiveness of BC Community Corrections*.

59. E.M. Ahlin, C.A. Hagen, M.A. Harmon, and S. Crosse, "Kiosk Reporting Among Probationers in the United States," *The Prison Journal 96*, no. 5 (2016), 688–708.

PART III

INCARCERATION

The discussion of the origins and evolution of punishment and corrections in Chapter 2 revealed that the use of incarceration for punishment is a relatively recent development. A review of Canadian correctional history found that the difficulties surrounding prisons emerged very soon after Canada opened its first penitentiary in 1835. Many of these difficulties have yet to be overcome; corrections officials and inmates are still struggling to build institutional environments that promote positive change, protect the community, and reduce reoffending.

The dynamics that develop in correctional institutions are complex and present challenges for administrators, correctional officers, treatment staff, and the inmates themselves. Chapter 6 examines the attributes of correctional institutions and the complexities of operating and managing these facilities; Chapter 7 explores the experiences of correctional officers (COs) and the important role they play in the daily life of institutions.

But it is the lives of the inmates themselves that have received the most attention from scholars and in the popular media. Chapter 8 examines life in custody for inmates, the relationships among them, and the various strategies they use to survive in custody. Most of the materials in Chapter 8 relate to male inmates. Women inmates are discussed in Chapter 12.

Chapter 9 explores the strategies and interventions used by systems of corrections to classify, manage, and address the risk and needs of inmates. The discussion reveals that while a number of programs hold promise, there are many obstacles to effective treatment in correctional institutions.

CHAPTER

6

CORRECTIONAL INSTITUTIONS

CHAPTER OBJECTIVES

- Identify the types and attributes of correctional institutions.
- Discuss the structure, operations, and management of institutions.
- Discuss the roles and responsibilities of personnel in correctional institutions.
- Identify and discuss the challenges of operating and managing correctional institutions.
- Discuss the general trends in the federal prison population and in remand populations.
- Discuss the changing offender profile and the challenges this presents for corrections.
- Discuss overcrowding and its impact on staff and inmates in correctional institutions.
- Describe the issues surrounding inmate safety and the role of inmate gangs in correctional institutions.
- Discuss the use of administrative segregation and the issues surrounding its use in correctional institutions.
- Describe the various prevention and interdiction strategies used by correctional systems to prevent the spread of HIV/AIDS and infectious diseases, as well as the issues that surround harm reduction efforts.
- Discuss the effectiveness of incarceration.

For 150 years, correctional institutions (as they are now called) have been a core component of the response to criminal offenders. These facilities have endured despite ongoing challenges, many of which emerged within the walls of Canada's first penitentiary in the 1830s—overcrowding, the lack of classification, and inmate safety, among others. As previously noted, only a small percentage (around 5 percent) of convicted offenders are sentenced to a period of custody. Generally speaking, correctional facilities house those offenders who present the highest risks and have the greatest needs.

TYPES OF CORRECTIONAL INSTITUTIONS

The federal and provincial/territorial governments operate a wide variety of facilities. These include correctional institutions and correctional centres that house sentenced offenders, jails and detention centres for short-term offenders who are awaiting sentencing, remand centres for accused persons awaiting trial, and correctional camps, treatment centres, and community residences that house lower-risk inmates in a minimum-security setting as well as those on conditional release.

Security Levels

Federal correctional facilities have three security levels:

- **Minimum-security institutions** generally have no perimeter fencing and allow unrestricted inmate movement, except at night.
- **Medium-security institutions** are surrounded by high-security perimeter fencing and place some restrictions on inmate movements.
- **Maximum-security institutions** have highly controlled environments and high-security perimeter fencing, and strictly control and monitor inmates' movements through video surveillance.

Canada has one **Special Handling Unit (SHU)** located in Ste-Anne-des-Plaines, Québec, for inmates who present such a high level of risk both to staff and to other inmates that they cannot be housed even in maximum-security facilities. There are also **multilevel institutions**, which contain more than one of the above security levels. Within the same institution, there may be distinct inmate populations that, for security and safety reasons, cannot be allowed to commingle. Finally, Correctional Service Canada (CSC) operates a number of regional health centres, which house violent offenders and offer treatment programs that focus on violence and anger management.

The provinces and territories operate facilities with various levels of security, though there are no uniform designations. These jurisdictions make more extensive use of maximum-security institutions than the CSC, mainly because they are responsible for housing persons who are on remand awaiting trial or sentencing. These individuals present a broad range of security risks, and in the absence of time to assess individual offenders, all are detained in maximum security. Provincial correctional systems also operate treatment facilities for special populations, such as sex offenders.

SPECIALIZED FACILITIES

The CSC and the provinces and territories operate a number of facilities for special populations of inmates.

Minimum-security institutions Federal correctional facilities that generally have no perimeter fencing and allow unrestricted inmate movement except at night.

Medium-security institutions Federal correctional facilities that have a less highly controlled institutional environment than maximum-security institutions and in which the inmates have more freedom of movement.

Maximum-security institutions Federal correctional institutions with a highly controlled institutional environment.

Special Handling Unit (SHU) A federal correctional facility that houses inmates who pose such a high risk to inmates and staff that they cannot be confined in maximum-security institutions.

Forensic Psychiatric and Treatment Centres

The provincial/territorial and federal governments operate forensic psychiatric facilities for offenders who have serious psychological disorders. The CSC operates a number of regional psychiatric and treatment centres. These are generally multilevel security facilities.

The provinces and territories also operate specialized institutions for offenders with severe mental health issues. For an inside look at one facility in Ontario, view the documentary film *Out of Mind, Out of Sight: Inside the Brockville Psych*, listed in Media Links section at the end of the chapter.

Indigenous Healing Lodges

Healing lodges are designed to provide culturally sensitive and appropriate treatment programs for Indigenous offenders and are operated by both the CSC and provincial/territorial corrections. These facilities continue to be constructed; in 2016, the province of Ontario announced the building of a new healing lodge for Garden River First Nation to serve communities located from Sudbury to Sault Ste. Marie.[1]

SECURITY

All correctional facilities have two types of security: (1) **static security**, which includes things such as perimeter fencing, video surveillance, and alarms, as well as fixed security posts staffed by correctional officers (COs), and (2) **dynamic security**, which includes ongoing interactions (beyond observation) between COs and inmates. This includes working with and speaking with inmates, making suggestions, providing information, and being generally proactive.

THE ATTRIBUTES OF CORRECTIONAL INSTITUTIONS

Correctional institutions are impacted by both their internal and external environments (Figure 6.1). These features determine the daily challenges that confront correctional managers as well as the patterns of interaction among the various groups who live and work inside correctional facilities. Three of the more significant features are described in the sections below.

Prisons Are Asked to Pursue Conflicting Goals

The primary goal of correctional institutions is to protect society by housing offenders who pose a serious risk to the community. But these same institutions are also expected to prepare offenders for eventual release into the community as law-abiding and contributing members of society. These two goals underscore the split personality of corrections.

Multilevel institutions Federal correctional institutions that contain one or more security levels (minimum, medium, and maximum) in the same facility or on the same grounds.

Static security Fixed security apparatus in correctional institutions, including fixed security posts to which correctional officers are assigned, such as a control room.

Dynamic security A variety of ongoing, meaningful interactions between staff and inmates.

Figure 6.1

The External and Internal Environments of a Correctional Institution

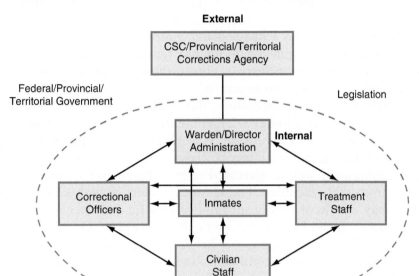

Prisons Are Political and Public Institutions

The impact of social, political, and economic forces on Canadian prison systems was discussed in Chapter 2. Those forces continue to determine the goals of incarceration and the extent to which those goals are achieved. Politicians, legislatures, and bureaucrats exercise considerable control over how correctional institutions are operated, the goals they are asked to pursue, and the resources that are made available to corrections personnel. For example, the discussion in Chapter 2 revealed how the federal Conservative government (2006–15) had an impact on crime-related legislation and on the correctional process. And the courts have been active, in a number of instances ruling that some of the legislation was unconstitutional. These are components of the external environment.

Prisons Are Total Institutions

More than four decades ago, the sociologist Erving Goffman introduced the concept of the prison as a **total institution**, that is, "a place of residence and work where a large number of like-situated individuals, cut off from the wider society for an appreciable period of time, together lead an enclosed, formally

Total institution
Correctional institutions, mental hospitals, and other facilities characterized by a highly structured environment in which all movements of the inmates/patients are controlled 24 hours a day by staff.

administered round of life."[2] Goffman outlined the principal attributes of life inside total institutions (which, for him, also included mental hospitals and military installations). They included the fact that all aspects of life are conducted in the same place; also, the activities of persons with similar status (inmates, in the case of prisons) are tightly scheduled and controlled by an administrative hierarchy.[3] Compare this regimen with the one set out in Box 2.2. For many inmates, little has changed over the past century, though in minimum-security facilities, the daily regimen is less structured.

In modern correctional institutions, this control has been extended by advanced technologies that allow ever-larger numbers of inmates to be housed, monitored, and controlled by fewer staff. While high-tech institutions are less expensive to operate, the end result may be *higher* costs because of disturbances and riots by inmates as well as increased rates of recidivism when inmates are released from these facilities. The reduced contact in high-surveillance institutions may also have significant implications for treatment interventions (see Chapter 9) and for positive interactions between COs and inmates (see Chapter 7). High-tech regimens may heighten the pains of imprisonment, reduce staff–inmate contact and communication, and increase the stress levels and isolation of COs.[4]

While all correctional institutions are total institutions, some are more "total" than others. That is, they vary in terms of their security classification, affiliation (federal/provincial/territorial), size, management style, inmate characteristics, and other factors that affect the dynamics of institutional life. To reflect this variability, a **continuum of correctional institutions** can be constructed, based on the extent to which individual institutions reflect Goffman's description. At one end of such a continuum would be minimum-security and community correctional facilities; at the other end would be maximum-security facilities. Clearly, the dynamics of life inside institutions at either end of the continuum will be considerably different. And even institutions at the same security level have their own "personalities," which are a function of their history, the attitudes and behaviour of administrators and staff, the attributes of the inmate population, and other, less tangible factors.

> **Continuum of correctional institutions**
> The differences in institutional environments among correctional institutions located at either end of the security spectrum—minimum to maximum.

ROLES AND RESPONSIBILITIES IN CORRECTIONAL INSTITUTIONS

The organizational chart for a federal medium-security institution is presented in Figure 6.2. There are a number of key roles in correctional institutions. These are set out in Table 6.1. Note that this table does not include all of the positions that may be found in a particular federal institution and that there may be variations of these positions in provincial/territorial institutions.

The leadership in a correctional institution has a powerful impact on the quality of life for staff and inmates inside correctional institutions and may have a direct impact on levels of violence and misconduct among the inmates.[5] Recall from the discussion of Canadian correctional history in Chapter 2 that an

Figure 6.2

Organizational Chart of a Federal Correctional Institution

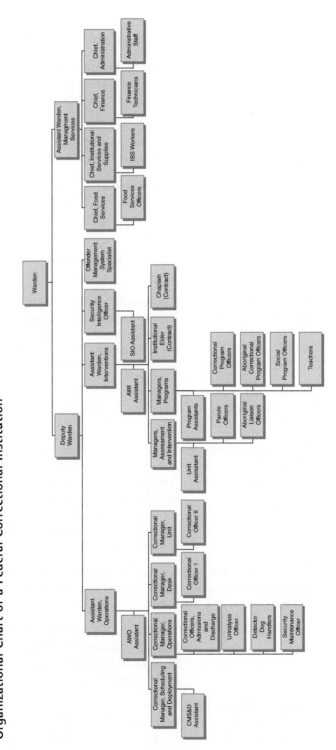

Table 6.1   Positions, Roles, and Responsibilities in a Federal Correctional Institution

Position	Role/Responsibilities
Warden	Has overall responsibility for the operations of the institution, ensuring that procedures and policies, legislation, and Commissioner's Directives are adhered to.
Deputy warden	Has the authority and accountability for operations, interventions, and security intelligence in the institution, and is considered the second-in-command.
Assistant warden, operations (AWO), or manager, operations (MO)	Responsible for all security operations within the institution.
Correctional manager (CM)	Responsible for the daily operations in the institution.
Assistant warden, interventions (AWI)	Responsible for managing all professional correctional interventions in the institution (i.e., human, financial, and material resources related to programs, case management, psychology, education, volunteers' activities, chaplaincy, and Indigenous spiritual activities).
Manager, assessment and intervention (MAI)	Responsible for the administration of case management and sentence management duties in the institution.
Manager, programs (MP)	Responsible for managing programs (i.e., financial management; needs planning; supervising program facilitators, including psychologists assigned to program delivery; and ensuring program availability) and social activities for offenders (volunteers and socio-cultural activities), and making decisions on offender pay and work assignments.
Manager, intensive intervention strategy (MIIS)	Responsible for the implementation and management of the National Intensive Intervention Strategy in a women's institution.
Correctional officers (COs)	Responsible for providing static and dynamic security, being the main point of contact with inmates, and being involved in the management of offenders at the line level (see Chapter 7).
Primary worker (PW) and Older Sister (Indigenous healing lodges)	Primary workers are front-line staff in women's institutions, and responsibilities include case management and program support; Older Sisters work at the Okimaw Ohci Healing Lodge (see Chapter 12).

Position	Role/Responsibilities
Correctional program officer (CPO)	Responsible for identifying the offenders' risk factors, their deficits and their strengths; developing the self-management plan; and delivering correctional programs (see Chapter 9).
Aboriginal correctional program officer (ACPO); Aboriginal liaison officer (ALO)	ACPOs work with Indigenous offenders to fulfill the components of their healing plan; ALOs work with the offender's case management team and provide support and assistance to offenders with their healing and release plans (see Chapter 13).
Treatment/medical staff	Includes psychologists, nurses, and other professionals who are involved in providing counselling and programs in the institution.
Institutional parole officer	Coordinates the offender's release plans and liaises with parole officers and other agencies in the community to ensure a smooth transition from the institution to the community.
Security intelligence officers	Responsible for gathering intelligence on the inmate population, detecting and investigating the smuggling of contraband into the institution, gang-related activities, and potential risks to the inmate population.

Sources: Correctional Service of Canada, 2016a; 2016b. Correctional Service of Canada. 2016a. "Guidelines. Institutional Management Structure: Roles and Responsibilities". http://www.csc-scc.gc.ca/acts-and-regulations/005-1-gl-eng.shtml#annexA

1848–49 investigation into the Kingston Penitentiary centred on the warden, Henry Smith. Fast forward to 2010, when a government report about a riot at the Central Nova Scotia Correctional Facility described "veteran guards shaken by filthy prison cells, chaotic behaviour of inmates and lack of leadership for staff."[6]

Researchers have identified a number of "types" of senior managers in corrections, ranging from "Operators," who are highly skilled in operations and have forceful personalities, to "Managerialists," who are more focused on administration and driven by performance metrics, and "Entrepreneurs," who are more likely to be innovators and risk-takers.[7]

Many provincial/territorial institutions are structured around the **unit management model** (also often referred to as the living unit model). Under this model, each unit in the institution has a manager, who reports to a deputy warden and supervises the unit's COs, classification officers, and support staff. The unit manager's responsibilities include security, case management, programming, and health and safety. One group of COs works directly with the inmates; the other group provides static security.

Unit management model
The supervisory arrangement in many provincial/territorial correctional institutions.

Provincial and territorial institutions have found it a challenge to develop effective management models. This has had a significant impact on the role of COs and on quality of interactions with inmates (see Chapter 7).

INCARCERATION IN CANADA

Canada's incarceration rate (106 per 100,000) is high compared to Western European countries, including Italy (86 per 100,000), Germany (78 per 100,000), and Denmark (61 per 100,000), although lower than Australia (151 per 100,000 population) and England and Wales (148 per 100,000), and much lower than the U.S. rate (689 per 100,000).[8]

Nearly 50 percent of federal offenders are serving a sentence of less than five years.[9] Indigenous offenders accounted for 24.6 percent of the in-custody population and 16.8 percent of the community population in 2014–15.[10] Nearly 70 percent of federal offenders in custody were serving a sentence for a violent crime.[11]

Trends in Federal Inmate Populations, 2005 to 2015

During the decade from 2005 to 2015, the overall federal inmate population increased by just under 14 percent. Other notable trends during this time included the following:[12]

- A significant increase (+77.4 percent) in the number of women incarcerated as compared to males (+11.6 percent)
- A significant increase in the incarcerated Indigenous population (+52.4 percent) compared to non-Indigenous people (+4.9 percent)
- A significant increase in the Black population (+77.5 percent) as compared to the Caucasian population (+6.8 percent)

Needless to say, the significant increases in the number of women, Indigenous people, and Blacks are of concern and require the attention of both scholars and governments.

THE CHALLENGES OF OPERATING AND MANAGING CORRECTIONAL INSTITUTIONS

Meeting the Requirements of Legislation and Policy

The legal framework within which correctional systems operate has become increasingly complex. Senior correctional personnel must stay abreast of changes in law and policy and ensure that the operations of the institution and the activities of its staff comply with those laws and policies. The violent confrontation that occurred between women offenders and correctional staff at the Kingston Prison for Women (now closed) in 1994 occurred because the staff and administration did not follow the rule of law and administrative policies. This incident is discussed in Chapter 12. Institutions are also subject to periodic external audits to ensure that they are following proper administrative and fiscal procedures.

Increasing Accountability and the Rule of Law and Justice

There has been an increase in the accountability of systems of corrections and conditional release, although as the discussion in this chapter will reveal, there are still significant shortcomings. This has coincided with the increasing involvement of the courts, which are now imposing on correctional agencies and personnel a duty to act fairly in managing offenders, to ensure that decision making is fair and equitable, and that inmates' Charter rights are not violated. In addition, the Corrections and Conditional Release Act (CCRA) provides that an independent chairperson from outside the institution (often a lawyer) is to preside over the disciplinary hearings involving serious allegations against an inmate.

More and more crime victims are filing civil suits against correctional authorities. Also, millions of dollars have been paid out by correctional systems to settle lawsuits filed by inmates over a range of issues, from violations of regulations to unsafe living conditions. There have also been civil suits filed by the parents of inmates who have been severely injured or killed by another inmate. In 2011, the parents of Jeremy Phillips filed an $11 million suit (later settled out of court for an undisclosed sum) against the CSC alleging negligence after their son was murdered by a serial killer with whom he had been double-bunked.[13] The coroner's jury in the Phillips case recommended that serial killers be housed in separate, single cells. Note, however, that the recommendations of coroner's juries are not binding on correctional services.

Managing Staff

Wardens and other senior correctional administrators often spend as much time on staff issues as they do on the inmates. The smooth functioning of an institution requires good morale and a shared sense of purpose among staff, including COs and program staff. A failure of leadership can result in a poor working environment that, if nothing is done, can lead to incidents and disruptions.

Research studies have identified the importance of the organizational climate of a correctional institution. This may have a significant impact on the interactions that occur within the institution, the morale of correctional staff, and the relationships within the inmate population. It has been noted that, even in higher security level institutions, good leadership, training, and resources can create a positive organizational environment.[14]

The organizational environment can also play an important role in the success of prison-based programs and treatment. Effective management can reduce the rates of institutional misconduct and post-release recidivism.[15] Conversely, a poor organizational climate may serve as a barrier to successful treatment of inmates.[16]

Conditions in Correctional Institutions

The first was the deplorable physical condition of the penitentiary. The cleanliness or lack of it is horrendous. There is a build-up of dirt and grime throughout the Penitentiary . . . It appeared that the interior of the Penitentiary had not been painted for years as there were areas where the paint was literally peeling off the walls and ceilings . . . Washrooms were filthy and staff often had to resort to cleaning them on their own. While some cells had been renovated, others had been plastered at some point and had gaping holes in the walls.[17]

A description of a Canadian prison in the 1800s? No—that quote comes from a provincial report dated 2008 on a provincial penitentiary in Nova Scotia that was built in 1903. Remember the Kingston Penitentiary, Canada's first prison? It did not close until 2014.

Similarly, here is a description of the Baffin Correctional Centre in Nunavut from a report completed in 2013 by the OCI who was asked to review the institution:

Because of repeated flooding incidents, there is extensive damage to the bottom of walls—paint is peeling, plaster showing or the drywall has been removed entirely and not replaced. . . Many inmates and some staff complained about the lack of heat in the facility. . . Due to the lack of bed space, some inmates sleep on mattresses directly on the cold cement floor. . . Some cells and the gymnasium have no toilets or running water.[18]

This report provided the impetus for the government to plan a new correctional centre, scheduled to open by 2021.

Her Majesty's Penitentiary in St. John's, Newfoundland, opened in 1859 and added on to over the decades, has been described as a "tinderbox," with overcrowding, a lack of programs, and understaffing. Assaults in the institution doubled between 2014 (20) to 2016 (40).[19] Critics have called the institution "a Victorian-era throwback that should be bulldozed."[20]

The physical condition of a correctional facility can have a significant impact on relations among inmates and between inmates and staff.[21] In a potentially precedent-setting case, a Québec judge in 2012 reduced an offender's sentence from 53 to 44 months after calling a provincial correctional facility "unhygienic" and commenting, "There are rats and vermin (in the jail)." The judge also cited gang activity and the high rate of drug use in the prison as imposing unnecessarily severe punishment on offenders there.[22]

The Growth in Remand Populations

Remand refers to accused individuals who have been charged and detained in custody and have either been denied **bail**, have yet to appear before a judge, or are awaiting sentencing or the commencement of a custodial sentence. Bail is the release of a person who has been charged with a criminal offence, prior to trial or to sentencing.

The number of persons detained on remand in provincial jails has tripled in the past three decades, and this population now represents nearly 60 percent of persons in provincial/territorial institutions.[23] The number of persons on remand outnumber sentenced offenders in confinement in most jurisdictions. There has also been an increase in the length of time spent on remand.[24]

There are a number of issues surrounding the use of bail, which it has been argued, fails those persons who require legal aid.[25] Among the findings of a report on bail were that "legally innocent persons are processed through a bail system that is chaotic and unnecessarily risk-adverse and disproportionately penalizes and frequently criminalizes—poverty, addiction, and mental health issues."[26]

All prisoners on remand are held in maximum-security facilities, regardless of the alleged offence and their criminal record, and have minimal access to programs and services.[27]

Nearly one-quarter of those on remand are in prison for offences against the administration of justice—for example, breach of probation or bail conditions, or failure to appear in court.[28] Because offenders on remand are housed in provincial/territorial institutions, the increase in their numbers is straining resources and leading to overcrowding. (Facilities in British Columbia and Manitoba have been as high as 200 percent overcapacity.)

The costs of keeping a person awaiting trial in remand are high: A report in Ontario found that the per diem cost of incarcerating an adult on remand was about $183 per day, as opposed to about $5 per day if the person was on bail and under supervision in the community.[29]

An investigation by the OCI found that 70 percent of the 106 inmates in the Baffin Correctional Centre in Nunavut were on remand status, while the remaining 30 percent were convicted offenders. Due to the physical facility, the two groups were not separated, which the correctional investigator noted was contrary to human rights standards.[30]

In commenting on the high remand populations in Manitoba (64 percent of the total institutional population), the provincial auditor general called on the province to develop more programs that would allow persons to be released on bail and supervised in the community while awaiting trial without increasing the risk to the community.[31]

Remand populations include persons charged with violent offences but also persons with mental health and addiction problems. This presents challenges to correctional staff, whose role is generally limited to custody-type activities. It has been argued that the conditions faced by persons in remand

Remand
The status of accused persons who have been charged and detained in custody and have either been denied bail, have yet to appear before a judge, or are awaiting sentencing or the commencement of a custodial sentence.

Bail
The release of a person who has been charged with a criminal offence, prior to trial or to sentencing.

violate international human rights standards, which require that those on remand who have not been convicted of a crime be held in conditions better than those for sentenced offenders.[32] According to one ex-offender who spent time in the Calgary Remand Centre, conditions in these facilities can be horrible:

> *I have been to CRC twice. The staff treat you like animals. Remand is a place where you go before you are convicted. Needless to say, if you are in remand, you are still innocent until proven guilty. Not in CRC. In CRC you are guilty until proven innocent. You are belittled, and battered by staff. You are stuck in conditions that the SPCA wouldn't allow animals to be placed in.*

Of concern is the revolving door of pre-trial detention, wherein accused persons are granted bail with conditions that may set the person up to fail, for example, conditions that require abstinence by persons addicted to alcohol or drugs, residency requirements for persons who are homeless, and reporting requirements for persons who may have a mental illness or otherwise have difficulty attending an office at a specific time or location.[33] Since the failure to comply with the conditions of bail is a criminal offence, this often creates a situation wherein accused persons are criminalized for behaviour that is otherwise not a crime.[34] These infractions are categorized as "administrative of justice" charges and the number of these offences has also increased in recent years, due in large measure to violations of bail conditions.

The Changing Offender Profile

More and more federal offenders are being classified as maximum security at admission, and a higher proportion of them are serving a sentence for a violent offence. Although most of the offenders committed to provincial/territorial institutions have been convicted of nonviolent offences, these populations pose challenges as well. For example, inmates in this group have high rates of alcohol and drug abuse and unstable work histories. Inmates in both jurisdictions have high rates of communicable diseases, including HIV/AIDS, tuberculosis, and hepatitis B and C. An inquiry in Saskatchewan found that provincial correctional facilities were sorely lacking in programs to address inmates' substance abuse, weak job skills, and family/marital problems.[35]

Inmates in custody are likely to be single and poorly educated and to have a variety of treatment needs. Over 90 percent have been assessed as requiring treatment for substance abuse. Almost 90 percent of inmates in federal custody have treatment needs in the personal/emotional domain.[36] There are also groups of offenders who require special attention, which are discussed in the following sections.

Elderly Inmates

The number of inmates over the age of 50 has doubled over the past decade: 25 percent of federal inmates and 30 percent of federal offenders under supervision in the community are more than 50 years old.[37] In one Ontario federal institution, more than half of the inmate population is over the age of 50. This institution has four dialysis machines, which are used for inmates with failing kidneys.

Elderly offenders are more likely to have been convicted of more serious violent offences or sexual offences, although many of their cases involve "cold cases" or "historical" crimes, which makes them a lower risk to the community.

Chronic illnesses, disabilities, hearing and vision loss, incontinence, mental disorientation, and Alzheimer's disease require special attention and resources. Older inmates—especially those serving their first prison term—may have difficulty adjusting to the prison regimen and may also be susceptible to psychological and physical victimization by younger inmates.[38] While in earlier decades, older inmates commanded respect from other inmates, in the contemporary prison these offenders may be isolated and afraid.

Most correctional facilities were not designed to address the needs of elderly offenders. It has been suggested that separate correctional facilities be constructed for elderly inmates, although given the trend toward "big box" institutions, this is not likely to happen.

The Mentally Ill

Commenting on the increasing numbers of inmates in correctional institutions with mental health issues, a prison nurse stated, "Overwhelmingly, prisoners are dealing with mental health issues. The correctional staff and the nursing staff have to work together to monitor their behaviours, to listen when they're having problems, and to identify when they might be having an acute mental health crisis that will need more frequent monitoring."[39]

The number of offenders entering correctional institutions with mental health issues is growing: It is estimated that 40 percent of inmates in Ontario provincial institutions have at least one severe mental health symptom and 13 percent have two or more symptoms. Women and Indigenous offenders in the province are more likely to have two or more current severe mental health symptoms.[40] These offenders present unique challenges for provincial/territorial corrections, given the short amount of time that the offenders are confined and the absence of screening protocols.[41]

It is further estimated that 35 percent of federal inmates have a mental impairment that requires treatment.[42] There are much higher rates of mental health disorders such as schizophrenia, major depression, and bipolar disorder among carceral and noncarceral populations than among the general population. More than half of all federal women inmates have an identified mental health need, as compared to 26 percent of federal male inmates.[43]

In the absence of community services and facilities, correctional institutions have become the "asylums of the 21st century."[44] A study of federal corrections found "limited services and programs" for mentally ill inmates.[45]

The CSC has made slow progress on addressing the mental health needs of offenders. The death of Ashley Smith in a federal women's correctional centre has helped spotlight deficiencies in the system's response to mentally ill persons who become involved in the justice and corrections systems.

Provincial and territorial governments have only recently begun to develop strategies for managing mentally ill offenders. Generally, there has been an absence of screening and assessment for identifying mental health issues.[47]

In Nova Scotia, the development of a provincial mental health and addictions strategy was precipitated by the death of Howard Hyde in the Central Nova Scotia Correctional Facility in 2007, where he had been remanded awaiting a court appearance. Hyde had lived for many years with severe, chronic schizophrenia and was being held following arrest on a charge of domestic assault. Physicians who had examined him had assumed that he would be sent for a psychiatric assessment (he wasn't). A judicial inquiry into his death documented his involvement with medical and corrections personnel and made a number of recommendations. For example, it called for a provincial mental health strategy to ensure continuity of care between the mental health and criminal justice systems.[47]

Correctional managers find it a challenge to provide treatment programs for inmates with mental health issues. Inmates with a mental illness may have difficulty following institutional rules, may be highly susceptible to victimization by other inmates, and may lack access to treatment programs, especially in provincial/territorial correctional facilities.[48]

The challenges are especially acute in provincial/territorial institutions, given the short periods of confinement and the lack of program resources. The Québec ombudsman investigated the conditions facing mentally ill offenders in detention and found that they had lengthier records of probation and detention than other inmates. Newly committed inmates were being evaluated for suicide risk, but otherwise, there was no screening for mental health problems. In addition, personnel in the detention facilities received little support in managing these offenders, who had difficulty accessing psychological and psychiatric services.[49] In Ontario, it was found that offenders with a mental illness were more likely to face discipline than to receive treatment and that this had a significant impact on their opportunities for conditional release and their ultimate success in the community.[50]

An example of how some provinces are attempting to address the special needs of mentally ill offenders is the St. Lawrence Valley Correctional and Treatment Centre in Ontario. In this joint initiative, the Ministries of Corrections and Community Services provide correctional staff, and Royal

Ottawa Hospital provides doctors, nurses, and treatment programs. The 100-bed facility offers treatment in a secure setting.

Offenders Suffering from Trauma

There is increasing evidence that a large number of offenders in correctional institutions are suffering from some type of trauma. This may be related to critical physical and psychological abuse as a child, exposure to traumatic events, and physical injuries, including traumatic brain injury as a result of head injuries.[51] This disability may have a significant effect upon the ability of the inmate to adjust to life in the institution and to participate in, and benefit from, correctional programs and services.

Offenders with Fetal Alcohol Spectrum Disorder

Fetal alcohol spectrum disorder (FASD) is a consequence of a woman drinking alcohol while pregnant and often results in irreversible brain damage to the fetus. The defining symptoms of persons suffering from FASD include impulsive violence and an inability to control aggressive, harmful behaviour.[52] Persons with FASD tend not to learn from their mistakes and do not connect "cause and effect." They also tend to be egocentric, to minimize the impact of their actions on others, and to blame their victims.[53]

Research studies have established a link between FASD and youth delinquency and adult crime.[54] Persons with FASD are at heightened risk of alcohol and substance abuse, repeated inappropriate sexual behaviour, and involvement in the criminal justice system.[55]

It is estimated that between 10 and 23 percent of federal inmates are afflicted with FASD. Reliable figures are difficult to obtain, as the CSC does not have in place a reliable system to screen offenders for this disorder when they enter the prison system.[56] There are concerns that many of these offenders remain undiagnosed.[57] Systems of corrections have only recently begun to develop screening protocols.[58]

To diagnose FASD requires multidisciplinary teams of medical professionals, and these are not present in Canadian correctional institutions. A study in Manitoba at the Stony Mountain Institution found that inmates there were 10 times more likely than the general population to have FASD. Nearly all of the offenders diagnosed with FASD had poor problem-recognition abilities and were unaware of the consequences of their actions; all were described as having poor stress-management and conflict-resolution skills.[59]

Individuals afflicted with FASD may have only a limited ability to benefit from correctional treatment programming designed to alter their attitudes and behaviour.[60] They may also be subject to victimization and manipulation by other inmates. Inmates with FASD require special

Fetal alcohol spectrum disorder (FASD)
A condition of mental impairment due to the birth mother drinking alcohol while pregnant.

programming while in custody and extensive support when they are released into the community.

Overcrowding

Overcrowding has plagued correctional institutions since the Kingston Penitentiary was constructed in 1835. Today, many Canadian prisons are beyond 100 percent capacity; for example, Saskatchewan facilities are operating at twice their capacity, and in 2013, the overall occupancy rate in Manitoba adult correctional centres was 128 percent (and ranged from 110 to 145 percent in different correctional facilities). The Manitoba situation existed even after the province had increased bed capacity by 52 percent over the previous five years at a cost of $182 million.[61]

In 2016, it was reported that the Ottawa-Carleton Detention Centre was so overcrowded that some inmates were forced to sleep in the showers.[62] Some federal institutions are double-bunking inmates in segregation cells.[63] This results in the warehousing of offenders (two inmates in a cell originally designed for one) to the extent that the focus is on managing the prison populations rather than on rehabilitation.[64]

There are many factors that cause overcrowding in correctional institutions, including changes in legislation, mandatory minimum sentences, inmates remaining in custody longer due to parole board decisions, the decision of offenders not to apply for release at their eligibility date, and the absence of new facilities. In the federal system, an increase in the number of long-term prisoners, including lifers (who represent 20 percent of the inmate population), also contributes to overcrowding.[65]

Another potential contributor to overcrowding is the extensively documented challenges that systems of corrections have in strategic planning. Audits of provincial corrections have found a lack of capacity to plan for long-term needs, to produce reliable inmate population forecasts, and to devise strategic plans to address overcrowding.[66]

In provincial/territorial institutions, overcrowding is also related to increases in the number of offenders on remand. Some steps have been taken by provincial/territorial authorities to reduce overcrowding. To address overcrowding at the Elgin-Middlesex Detention Centre (EMDC) and to improve staff and inmate safety, for example, the province of Ontario in 2016 opened a stand-alone Regional Intermittent Centre (RIC) for those offenders serving their sentence on an intermittent basis, primarily on weekends.[67]

The Impact of Overcrowding

Overcrowding in correctional institutions has significant consequences for inmates and staff. It can affect daily prison life by heightening tensions among inmates and between inmates and COs; it can also compromise security and overburden treatment programs.[68] Inmate gangs are more difficult to keep separated in overcrowded institutions. Access to programs and services may be restricted, and inmates may spend longer periods of time in their cells. It may be difficult to keep separate persons on remand with the convicted inmate population.[69] Double-bunking is now considered standard practice in federal institutions and in most provincial/territorial institutions.[70] Double-bunking violates the Nelson Mandela Rules (formerly titled the UN Standard Minimum Rules for the Treatment of Prisoners).

Overcrowding can also result in increasing levels of violence in institutions. Inmate-on-inmate assault in federal prisons increased 93 percent from 2006–07 to 2014–15.[71] In many provinces, there have been double-digit increases in inmate-on-inmate violence.[72] In Manitoba, for example, where provincial institutions are as much as 145 percent over capacity, there was a 43 percent increase in "serious incidence" security events between 2009 and 2012.[73] There were also significant increases in staff overtime costs. These problems persisted despite corrections increasing bed capacity by 52 percent since 2008.

Academic studies on the relationship between overcrowding and inmate–staff assaults, however, have generated mixed results, suggesting that much depends on prison management, the "mix" of inmates, and the competence of the correctional staff, among other factors.[74]

In Ontario, overcrowding in provincial institutions has resulted in a significant increase in lockdowns, wherein inmates are confined in their cells for lengthy periods of time.

Inmate Gangs

Yet another challenge facing prison administrators is the growing prevalence of inmate gangs that are based in communities and that import their affiliations and tactics into correctional institutions. Estimates are that one in six federal inmates is affiliated with a known gang or with organized crime.[75]

There seems to have been an increase in gang activity in many provincial and federal institutions, especially in the Prairie provinces. This is partly a result of legislative and enforcement efforts that have targeted gangs in communities. There has been exponential growth in Indigenous gangs in urban and rural areas of the Prairie provinces. Indigenous youth are especially susceptible to gangs' recruiting efforts—a consequence of poverty as well as disenfranchisement from family, school, and the community.[76]

Among the most notorious gangs in the Prairie provinces are the Alberta Warriors, Indian Posse, Redd Alert, Native Syndicate, and Manitoba Warriors. Other gangs include the Asian Crazy Dragons in Alberta, the U.N. and Red Scorpion gangs in B.C., and the multinational Hells Angels.

Gang-affiliated inmates are at risk for the most serious forms of misconduct in correctional institutions.[77] Gang members involve themselves in a variety of activities, including smuggling, drug dealing, and extortion. Gang members often resort to assault and intimidation in order to secure and maintain power and influence within the prison. Conflicts between gang members within institutions are a major cause of riots and disruptions, and the CSC often transfers gang-affiliated inmates to other institutions in an attempt to control their activities.[78]

The following is a posting by a member of the Garden City Renegades in Manitoba, putting down other gangs (Garden City is a First Nations Reserve): "Garden Hill Renegades and STP Soldiers in a rise together, holding down Island Lake. Down with Manitoba Warriors. Fuck the krazies and localz, and who the hell are the wpg krazies? They are just hairspray-drinking rubies (sic) from the rez, wannabe fukks" (www.insideprison.com). For a look inside the culture of Indigenous gangs, visit the video links provided in this chapter.

Ensuring Inmate Safety

The accountability of corrections officials extends to ensuring the safety of inmates in their charge—an onerous task, especially in federal maximum-security institutions. Wardens have little say in how many inmates are sent to their facility, the types of inmates they receive, and when inmates will leave their institution via transfer, conditional release, or statutory release. They are, however, responsible for the safety and security of the inmates once they have arrived.

Canadian courts have become more active in addressing inmates' rights, which include the right to serve time in a safe and secure environment. The federal government is being sued more and more frequently by inmates who have been victimized while serving their time.

Preventing Disorder and Disturbances

A primary objective of prison wardens is to maintain "good order" in the institution, ensuring that the staff and inmates move through the daily routine or schedule with no or minimal conflict.[79] This routine consists of "long standing patterns of social relations where participants have common expectations (e.g., chow is at 11:30), as well as a typical level of inmate involvement in work assignments, education, rehabilitative programming, and so forth."[80]

A number of factors may influence the level of order or disorder in an institution, including the composition of the inmate population, the behaviour of COs, the prison's physical design, and the management style of prison administrators. The presence of inmates from rival gangs and tensions between ethnic groups can spark inmate-on-inmate attacks. As noted earlier, overcrowding can generate strained relationships within a correctional facility. Inmates who are confined in institutions that have a higher proportion of violent offenders are more likely to become involved in misconduct; inmates who have work responsibilities inside the facility may be less likely to violate regulations. This suggests that there are specific measures that correctional managers can take to reduce the levels of prison misconduct.[81]

Riots continue to be a feature of Canadian federal and provincial correctional facilities, including a six-hour riot in the maximum-security Central North Correctional Centre in Ontario in June 2015, and a riot at the federal Saskatchewan Penitentiary in December 2016, during which one inmate was killed and several injured.[82] The causes of prison disturbances and riots are multifaceted and may involve the inmates being provoked by correctional officers, mismanagement of the institution, overcrowding, disputes between rival gangs, and poor quality and quantity of food, among other reasons.

The Use of Segregation

One strategy that is used by correctional managers is **segregation** (also often referred to as **solitary confinement**). While the terms may vary, solitary confinement is also known as "segregation," "isolation," "separation," "cellular," "lockdown," "Supermax," "the hole," or "Secure Housing Unit."[83] These may involve different regulations and processes, but the net result is that the inmate spends the large majority of time locked in a small space.

The United Nations Istanbul Statement on the Use and Effects of Solitary Confinement defines solitary confinement as the physical isolation of individuals who are confined to their cells for 22 to 24 hours a day.[84] Key features of solitary confinement are social isolation, minimal environmental stimulation, and little opportunity for social interaction.

The United Nations has noted that the justifications provided by States for the use of solitary confinement fall into five general categories: (a) to punish an individual (as part of the judicially imposed sentence or as part of a disciplinary regime); (b) to protect vulnerable individuals; (c) to facilitate prison management of certain individuals; (d) to protect or promote national security; (e) to facilitate pre-charge or pretrial investigations."[85] Under the so-called "Mandela Rules," prisoners are not to be confined to their cells for 22 hours a day without meaningful human contact for longer than 15 consecutive days.

Solitary confinement has a long history in Canadian corrections. Segregation is used to maintain the security of the institution or to discipline an inmate for misconduct. Inmates placed in segregation may be locked in a cell for 23 hours a day and generally do not have access to programming or to normal inmate privileges. The CCRA includes provisions for two types of segregation: disciplinary and administrative. **Disciplinary segregation** is imposed in cases where an inmate has been found in violation of an institutional rule, whereas **administrative segregation** is imposed when an inmate has attempted or intends to act in a way that is deemed to threaten the prison population.

Note that solitary confinement is a *place*, not a correctional strategy; solitary confinement may be used for inmates who are placed in administrative segregation.

Segregation
The physical isolation of individuals who are confined to their cells for 22 to 24 hours a day; also often referred to as *solitary confinement*.

Disciplinary segregation
An inmate is placed in solitary confinement after being found in violation of an institutional rule.

Administrative segregation
The separation of an inmate to prevent association with other inmates, when specific legal requirements are met, other than pursuant to a disciplinary decision.

The Use of Administrative Segregation

The purpose and regulations of administrative segregation are set out in the CCRA.

While there are strict guidelines for the use of disciplinary segregation, including time limits and mandatory independent oversight, these safeguards do not apply to inmates who are in administrative segregation. Many inmates who have been held in solitary confinement for lengthy periods of time, and some who have died while in solitary (including Ashley Smith, whose case is discussed in Chapter 12), were classified as being in administrative segregation.

Admissions to Segregation

A review of the 10-year trend (2005–06 to 2014–15) in the use of administrative segregation in CSC custody revealed increases in the number of Indigenous and Black admissions to segregation and decreases in the number of Caucasian inmates admitted to segregation. Indigenous inmates are represented in segregation in federal institutions at a rate that is approximately eight times that of their proportion of the Canadian population (30 percent in segregation; 4.3 percent of the Canadian population). Among federal offenders, the large majority (95 percent) of admissions to administrative segregation are men and just over 30 percent are Indigenous.[86]

Although the number of federally sentenced women (FSW) admitted to segregation has fluctuated, 2014–15 saw the highest number of FSW admissions for the time period 2005–15.[87] The majority (67 percent) of admissions to administrative segregation in federal institutions were for 30 days or less, although 7 percent were longer than 120 days.[88]

The reasons for these increases have not been explored by researchers. It could be due to discriminatory decision making by correctional officers and/or the behaviour of the inmates themselves. The decline in Caucasian admissions to administrative segregation while the rates of others were increasing does raise concerns.

The Debate over Solitary Confinement

The use of solitary confinement in federal and provincial/territorial correctional institutions is the focus of ongoing controversy.[89] There are concerns that segregation is increasingly being used to manage overcrowding in provincial institutions and as a management strategy to deal with inmates with physical and mental health issues.[90]

There are also concerns about whether procedures are being followed in the use of solitary confinement. Although there are provisions for reviews, it is often the *quality* of reviews that is most often the issue.[91] And, there appears to be considerable variability between the provinces and territories in the provisions for, and the use of, solitary confinement. Until 2016, for example, the province of New Brunswick did not track the number of inmates being sent to isolation in provincial facilities.[92]

In another case, an Indigenous inmate was held in solitary confinement in an Ontario provincial institution for 1,560 consecutive days before being "discovered" during a visit by the chair of the Ontario Human Rights Commission (see Corrections File 6.1).

The Impact of Solitary Confinement

There is considerable evidence that solitary confinement causes "psychotic disturbances," the symptoms of which include "anxiety, depression, anger, cognitive disturbances, perceptual distortions, paranoia and psychosis and self-harm."[93] Inmates who are placed in solitary confinement for prolonged

CORRECTIONS FILE 6.1

The Case of Adam Capay

Adam Capay, a 24-year-old member of the Lac Seul First Nations in northwestern Ontario, spent four-and-a-half years in solitary confinement in a provincial jail in Thunder Bay, Ontario, while awaiting trial. His trial had been delayed three times. During this time:

> Capay said he spent much of his time in a kind of half sleep, drifting in and out of consciousness. The lights were on 24 hours a day. Reality was difficult to discern. He was constantly hungry. He went into the yard once or twice a month. A psychiatrist talked to him for a couple of minutes every few months, mostly to approve his continued segregation. He'd engaged in self-harm, and had lacerations on his wrists and puncture wounds on his scalp. He'd recently been restrained after bashing his head against the wall.[a]

Adam Capay was detained in solitary for this lengthy period of time despite provincial regulations requiring a review every 5 days and a formal report to senior correctional managers in the provincial government every 30 days. During the time that Capay was in solitary, the province produced statistics indicating that the longest time that an inmate had spent in segregation in a correctional institution was 939 days. Capay's name never appeared in the list of inmates in solitary provided by corrections to the provincial ministry.

The length of time that Adam Capay was held in solitary violated UN standards. Evidence subsequently emerged that ministry personnel had known for years of Mr. Capay's lengthy confinement in solitary, although the government of Ontario argued that it was "administrative segregation," not solitary confinement. The revelations in the Capay case contributed to the resignation of the Ontario Minister of Community Safety and Correctional Services in late 2016.

View the film *Inside Canada's Corrections System. Prisons: The Case of Adam Capay*, at http://tvo.org/video/programs/the-agenda-with-steve-paikin/inside-canadas-corrections-system.

---

[a] M. Patriquin, "Why Adam Capay has spent 1,560 days in solitary," *Maclean's*, November 2, 2016, http://www.macleans.ca/news/why-adam-capay-has-spent-1560-days-in-solitary/

periods of time, defined by the United Nations as any period in excess of 15 days, may be particularly at risk.[94] The United Nations Special Rapporteur has denounced prolonged, indefinite solitary confinement—of the kind taking place every day in Canadian prisons—as torture.[95]

Given these adverse effects, the use of solitary confinement can constitute a violation of the UN Convention against cruel, inhuman, or degrading punishment.[96] The Canadian Medical Association has labelled the placement of inmates in solitary confinement as "cruel and unusual punishment" and recommended that the practice be severely restricted.[97]

In 2016, the province of Ontario announced that there would be a limit of 15 days per stay for inmates in segregation, although other provinces do not have limits.

The CSC now conducts mandatory reviews of every segregated inmate's case file after 5 days, and then at 30-day intervals. In addition, at-risk inmates, including those who are suicidal, have a serious mental illness, or who are actively engaging in serious self-harm cannot be sent to solitary confinement in federal institutions.

Furthermore, pregnant inmates, inmates in palliative care, and inmates with significant mobility issues cannot be placed in administrative segregation unless exceptional circumstances exist. It is likely that provincial/territorial systems of correction will follow suit.

The issue of solitary confinement continues to be at the forefront of discussions about Canadian corrections. In some quarters, including the Ontario Human Rights Commission, there have been increasing calls for its abolition.[98] Others have called on authorities to adopt the recommendations of the federal correctional investigator and various provincial inquiries. How governments and correctional authorities will respond to these calls remains uncertain.

Health Issues and Infectious Diseases

Correctional systems face challenges providing short- and long-term health care, dispensing medication, and developing policies to combat high-risk behaviours. Compounding these problems are the challenges faced by corrections in attracting and retaining medical staff. In 2015–16, for example, some of Québec's correctional facilities were hard-pressed to provide adequate medical services because of the shortage of general practitioners working within the correctional system.[99]

Perhaps the most critical challenge facing correctional authorities is the spread of communicable diseases, including HIV/AIDS, tuberculosis, and hepatitis B and C.[100] There are alarmingly high rates of infection among Canadian inmates. Estimates are that the rate of HIV/AIDS infection in federal prisons is 15 times higher than in the general population; for Indigenous offenders, the rate is even higher.[101] It is a serious concern that these rates are continuing to rise. Moreover, these figures are based on cases *known* to correctional authorities; many offenders may not have disclosed their medical condition, may not be aware that they are infected, or refuse to be tested. This places other inmates and correctional staff at risk in the institution, as well as in communities and families when the offender is released from custody.

There are also high rates of infection among provincial/territorial inmates, with those rates especially high among Indigenous offenders incarcerated in provincial facilities in the three Prairie provinces. As many as 75 percent of the women in the Edmonton Prison for Women are known to be HIV-positive, compared to less than 1 percent of the Canadian population.

Inmates living with HIV face numerous challenges, including in ostracism from correctional officers and other inmates if it becomes known that they are HIV-positive, and gaining access to treatment and ongoing medical services.[102]

High-Risk Behaviour

High rates of HIV/AIDS are a result of high-risk behaviours before and during incarceration. The ways in which the HIV virus can be transmitted include blood-to-blood, via unprotected intercourse, and sharing contaminated needles and/or syringes. Other blood-borne diseases such as hepatitis B and C are also transmitted by the pens, pencils, and wire instruments that inmates use for body piercing and tattooing. In addition to this, many offenders are already infected by the time they enter systems of corrections. The incarceration of offenders who are injection drug users has contributed to an increase in HIV transmission.[103] As one woman ex-offender recalled:

> I would say about 80 percent of the women in the prison were using drugs. 35 percent would have to do sexual favors for drugs. And 25-50 percent of the women would be injecting drugs. To inject, we would use used needles from the nurse's office, which we stole. Anywhere from 10 to 15 people would share one needle over a months' time . . . I also got a tattoo. I know the needle for my tattoo had been used a lot; I don't know where it came from or who had used it. Back then, we were not allowed to bleach, so we never used it to clean our needles. We were aware of getting hepatitis C and HIV from sharing needles, but we didn't care. Being in there, we felt our lives sucked so it didn't matter anyway.

—Woman formerly incarcerated in the Prison for Women in Kingston, Ontario[104]

Prevention Strategies

Systems of corrections have developed a number of **prevention strategies** in their efforts to prevent and reduce high-risk behaviours among inmates and to reduce levels of infection. For example, the CSC provides inmates with condoms, lubricants, dental dams, and bleach kits for needles (though not needles). In several federal institutions, inmates have been trained as peer health counsellors to educate others on how to reduce the risk of infection. The federal government has also expanded its methadone maintenance program

Prevention strategies Efforts to prevent and reduce high-risk behaviour among inmates and to reduce the levels of infection of HIV/AIDS and other infectious diseases.

for heroin-addicted offenders. Provincial/territorial systems of correction have undertaken similar efforts, though there is considerable variation in the harm-reduction resources provided to inmates. The challenges are considerable, given the higher turnover of inmates in the latter system and the short periods of confinement.

The non-profit Prisoners' HIV/AIDS Support Action Network (PASAN) (www.pasan.org) has been instrumental in advocating for changes in correctional policy and for inmate rights in this area. This includes providing support services for prisoners and their families, conducting HIV-prevention programs in correctional institutions in Ontario, and advocating to change correctional policies with respect to HIV/AIDS issues. Another organization that is active in this area is the Canadian AIDS Treatment Information Exchange (CATIE) (www.catie.ca).

The Canadian Human Rights Commission has expressed concern that the absence of needle exchange programs is denying inmates harm-reduction strategies that are available to the outside community.[105] In 2012, a federal inmate launched a lawsuit against the federal government for failing to provide clean needles to inmates in correctional institutions. The argument presented was that this was a violation of the right to life, liberty, and security of the person as set out in the Charter of Rights and Freedoms, besides denying the right to health care.[106]

Research studies have found that in those countries that provide clean needles and syringes to inmates, those programs do not lead to increased drug use. They do, however, increase referrals to drug treatment programs. But they have *not* increased the risk to COs from inmates using needles and syringes as weapons.[107] However, it is not yet clear whether providing condoms and bleach kits reduces either the risk or the level of infection among inmate populations.

An in-depth study of the actions taken on HIV/AIDS found considerable variation in the initiatives undertaken by Canada's systems of corrections. Federal institutions have developed intensive support units (ISUs) that can be accessed by inmates who have substance abuse issues as well as by inmates who wish to reside in a "drug-free" environment. Preliminary evaluations indicate that these units have strong support both from the inmates who utilize them and from correctional staff, although the long-term effectiveness of these units on both drug use and recidivism is uncertain.[108]

The CSC also has health education programs to educate inmates about the risks of hepatitis C virus (HCV) and HIV; these programs seem to have succeeded in reducing high-risk behaviour, such as sharing needles and injecting with a dirty needle.[109] Public health officials have noted that since one in nine persons with hepatitis C is incarcerated at some point, this provides an opportune time to focus on prevention and treatment.[110]

> **Interdiction strategies** Efforts to reduce the use of illegal drugs and other high-risk behaviours in order to prevent HIV/AIDS and other infectious diseases.

Interdiction Strategies

The general public would be surprised to learn how prevalent illegal drugs are in correctional institutions. The CSC uses a number of **interdiction strategies** to reduce the use of illegal drugs and other high-risk behaviours, such as tattooing. These strategies include frequent searches, a urinalysis program, drug-sniffing dogs, video surveillance, and ion scanners that can detect drug residue on visitors' clothing and on the clothes of inmates returning from absences in the community.

The effectiveness of interdiction strategies is uncertain. One concern is that the various drug detection strategies may lead to an *increase* in hard drug use in institutions, because drugs such as marijuana and hashish remain in the bloodstream for many days, whereas heroin stays in the body's system for around 48 hours. This makes the chances of being caught by a random urinalysis test higher for those inmates who use "soft" drugs. While mandatory drug testing may reduce levels of marijuana use in prisons, there is no evidence that these programs reduce the use of opioids such as heroin.[111] Canadian research has found that the length of time that inmates are incarcerated, the security level of the institution, the nature and extent of drug use prior to incarceration, and drug availability are all related to drug use during confinement.[112]

Detention and Correctional Facilities in the North

A key theme in this text is the challenges faced by systems of corrections in northern and remote areas of the country. Poor or non-existent facilities for detention and confinement mean that offenders who are detained on remand are often kept in inadequate facilities or are transferred hundreds of kilometres away to the nearest correctional facility.

The logistical issues are considerable and the result is that Indigenous accused may spend more time in pre-trial detention than had been sentenced initially on the charge.[113]

An investigation by the Québec ombudsperson into the detention conditions in the northern Québec region of Nunavik (an area the size of the state of California) found that the conditions in which persons who were arrested were held in detention were below current standards and did not always respect the fundamental rights of inmates.[114] In the absence of correctional facilities in the region, persons are held in cells in police stations. These arrangements were found to lead to overcrowding (e.g., seven persons held in a cell designed for two).

THE EFFECTIVENESS OF INCARCERATION

Research has found that, generally, there is little evidence that increasing the severity of punishments have an impact on deterring persons from offending.[115] What does serve as a deterrent to criminal behaviour is certainty of punishment.[116] The deterrent effect appears to be strongest for those persons who have a stake in conformity, an attribute that many persons who are marginal may not possess.

A number of questions surround the use of incarceration as a response to criminal offenders. Several of these are discussed in Research File 6.1.

The Effectiveness of Incarceration

Does incarceration reduce reoffending? It depends. The research evidence suggests that prisons should not be used with the expectation of reducing reoffending and that the excessive use of incarceration as a sanction can have substantial cost implications as well as increase criminal behaviour among some offenders.[a] Individuals sent to prison may be further marginalized and socially and economically stigmatized.[b] As one group of researchers has noted, very little is known about whether incarceration reduces recidivism.[c]

The threat of custody is unlikely to deter "state-raised" offenders. However, some research suggests that incarceration can be effective in interrupting the crime trajectory of individual offenders and result in reduced offending upon release. This seems to depend on the criminal history and age of the offender: Offenders with lengthy criminal records may continue offending upon release; older inmates with a criminal history are less likely to reoffend.[d]

Can incarceration increase offending? Potentially. Sentencing to custody persons with little or no prior involvement in crime and the justice system may result in increased criminality when they return to the community, particularly if they are confined in higher-security institutions.[e] There is some evidence that, all things being equal, inmates housed in higher levels of security and in harsh conditions are more likely to reoffend upon release.[f]

Is incarceration more effective in reducing reoffending than community supervision? Maybe not. There is evidence that offenders who spend their time under supervision in the community have lower rates of reoffending than offenders released from correctional institutions, even considering the types of offences committed.[g]

How does incarceration compare to community supervision in terms of cost? It's more expensive. Imprisonment is much more costly than supervision in the community and may not make the community safer or increase the potential of offenders to return to the community as law-abiding citizens.

Can prisons, generally, be considered change agents? Generally speaking, no. But it is difficult to measure the impact, positive or negative, that confinement may have on the individual offender, and particularly on offenders who do not have a lengthy history of incarceration in youth and adult facilities. Some offenders, especially those who are "state-raised," may view correctional institutions as "home" and as providing safe sanctuary from a hectic outside world. Ironically, rather than serving as a deterrent to future criminal behaviour, for many inmates the correctional institution may be a marked improvement over their quality of life in the outside community. For many of these offenders, surviving in the outside, free community often poses far greater challenges than doing time in prison (state-raised offenders are discussed in Chapter 8).[h]

Do all offenders view prison negatively? No. "State-raised" offenders and offenders with lengthy criminal histories may not be deterred by a sentence of confinement and may find it preferable to non-incarcerative options such as probation or intermediate sanctions.[i] Offenders who are unemployed, who have no family and no permanent living address, who are drug addicted, and/or who are living with a medical conditions such as HIV/AIDS or hepatitis C may view confinement as a way to get three meals a day and a bed (often referred to as "three hots and a cot"), a paid job, and plenty of rest.

In the words of one inmate incarcerated in a provincial correctional facility: "A lot of the guys who come in here are drug sick. They had served their sentence, or been granted parole, went back out on the street, and got right back into the drug life. They come back, get well, put on a few pounds, and they are ready to go out and start it all over again" (personal communication with C.T. Griffiths). Offenders from remote communities may view a trip out to a correctional institution as a welcome break from boredom and isolation.[j] Recall from the discussion in Chapter 5 that alternatives to incarceration, including conditional sentence orders (CSOs), electronic monitoring (EM), and probation, may impose "pains" on offenders and their families.

---

[a] F.T. Cullen, C.L. Jonson, and D.S. Nagin, "Prisons Do Not Reduce Recidivism: The High Cost of Ignoring Science," *Prison Journal 91*, no. 3 (2011), 48–65.

[b] S.N. Durlauf and D.S. Nagin, "The Deterrent Effect of Punishment," in *Controlling Crime: Strategies and Tradeoffs*, eds. P.J. Cook, J. Ludwig, and J. McCrary (Chicago: University of Chicago Press, 2011), 43–94.

[c] D.P. Mears, J.C. Cochran, and F.T. Cullen, "We are still largely in the dark as to whether incarceration reduces recidivism," *American Politics and Policy* [blog], October 1, 2015, http://blogs.lse.ac.uk/usappblog/2015/10/01/we-are-still-largely-in-the-dark-as-to-whether-incarceration-reduces-recidivism/.

[d] A.S. Bhati and A.R. Piquero, "Estimating the Impact of Incarceration on Subsequent Offending Trajectories: Deterrent, Criminogenic, or Null Effect?" *Journal of Criminal Law and Criminology 98*, no. 1 (2008), 207–54.

[e] S.D. Bushway and R. Paternoster, "The Impact of Prison on Crime," in *Do Prisons Make Us Safer? The Benefits and Costs of the Prison Boom*, eds. S. Raphael and M.A. Stoll (New York: Sage, 2009), 119–50.

[f] M.K. Chen and J.M. Shapiro, "Do Harsher Prison Conditions Reduce Recidivism? A Discontinuity-Based Approach," *American Law and Economics Review 9*, no. 1 (2007), 1–29.

[g] J. Cid, "Is Imprisonment Criminogenic? A Comparative Study of Recidivism Rates Between Prison and Suspended Sentence Sanctions," *European Journal of Criminology 6*, no. 6 (2009), 459–80.

[h] Cullen et al., "Prisons Do Not Reduce Recidivism."

[i] D.C. May and P.B. Wood, "What Influences Offenders' Willingness to Serve Alternative Sanctions?" *Prison Journal 85*, no. 2 (2005), 145–67.

[j] C.T. Griffiths, E. Zellerer, D.S. Wood, and G. Saville, *Crime, Law, and Justice Among Inuit in the Baffin Region, N.W.T., Canada* (Burnaby, B.C.: Criminology Research Centre, Simon Fraser University, 1995).

SUMMARY

Correctional institutions have endured since the first prison was built in Kingston in the early 1800s. The task of these facilities is to house offenders to protect the community while preparing them for life outside the walls.

Among the challenges in operating and managing correctional institutions are these: meeting the requirements of legislation and policy, ensuring adherence to the rule of law, and dealing with changing and diverse inmate populations. Correctional institutions are housing an increasing number of Indigenous, Black, and women inmates, as well as inmates who are elderly and inmates with mental health issues. There has also be an exponential growth in remand populations.

Many correctional institutions are overcrowded, and this has a negative impact on both staff and inmates and is a primary cause of violence and disturbances. The use of segregation (solitary confinement) is extensive and has demonstrable negative effects on inmates, particularly those with mental health issues. Correctional authorities face challenges in dealing with health issues and infectious diseases in institutions and a number of prevention strategies have been developed in an attempt to address these issues. It is not certain that correctional institutions are effective in protecting the community or addressing the needs and risks of inmates.

KEY POINTS REVIEW

1. Only a very small percent (around 5 percent) of convicted offenders are incarcerated in correctional institutions.

2. A wide variety of correctional facilities are operated by the federal government and provincial/territorial governments.

3. The dynamics inside correctional institutions are impacted by their internal and external environments.

4. There are a variety of roles and responsibilities for personnel inside correctional institutions.

5. Operating correctional institutions has a number of inherent challenges, including these, among others: meeting the requirements of legislation and policy, managing staff, addressing overcrowding, combating inmate gangs, ensuring inmate safety, and meeting the needs of special inmate groups.

6. In recent years, there have been significant increases in the numbers of Blacks, Indigenous people, and women in correctional institutions.

7. The number of persons on remand outnumber sentenced offenders in correctional institutions in most provincial/territorial jurisdictions.

8. The changing offender profile, including increases in the number of elderly inmates, inmates with mental illness, offenders suffering from trauma, and inmates with fetal alcohol spectrum disorder, present challenges for institutional staff.

9. Overcrowding is a key feature of Canadian correctional institutions and has significant consequences for inmates and correctional staff.

10. Ensuring inmate safety, controlling gangs, and preventing disorder and disturbances are major challenges for correctional staff.

11. The use of administrative segregation is surrounded by controversy.

12. Solitary confinement can have a significant impact on the mental health of inmates.

13. Correctional authorities have developed a number of prevention and interdiction strategies in an attempt to reduce the transmission of HIV/AIDS and other infectious diseases.

14. Incarceration should not be used with the expectation that reoffending will be reduced.

KEY TERM QUESTIONS

1. Describe the attributes of the *minimum-*, *medium-*, and *maximum-security facilities* and the *multilevel institutions* and *Special Handling Unit,* operated by the federal Correctional Service of Canada.

2. Compare and contrast *static security* and *dynamic security*.

3. Why are prisons viewed as *total institutions*?

4. What is the *continuum of correctional institutions* and how does this concept assist our understanding of life inside prisons?

5. Describe the *unit management model* in correctional institutions.

6. Discuss the issues surrounding *remand* in Canadian corrections.

7. What are some of the challenges that inmates with *FASD* experience while incarcerated?

8. What are the issues surrounding the use of *segregation* and *solitary confinement* in Canadian corrections?

9. Describe the difference between *disciplinary segregation* and *administrative segregation*.

10. Discuss the *prevention strategies* and *interdiction strategies* that correctional systems have implemented in their efforts to reduce the rates of HIV/AIDS and other infectious diseases inside correctional institutions.

CRITICAL THINKING EXERCISE

Critical Thinking Exercise 6.1

The Use of Solitary Confinement/Administrative Segregation

Despite research findings on the impact of solitary confinement and recommendations that its use be restricted, particularly for inmates with mental health issues, some corrections authorities continue the practice.

Your Thoughts?

1. Should there be mandatory limits on the amount of time that an inmate can be held continuously in solitary confinement/administrative segregation?

CLASS/GROUP DISCUSSION EXERCISE

Class/Group Discussion Exercise 6.1

Should Governments Initiate/Expand Harm-Reduction Programs in Prisons?

Proponents of harm-reduction programs argue that needle exchanges and related measures reflect the reality that drugs are widely available to inmates; in their view, inmates should be provided with clean needles to help reduce infection rates. Also, it is cheaper to implement strategies to prevent HIV infection than to treat persons who have become infected. The costs of HIV treatment are estimated to be $29,000 per year.[117] The position of the B.C. Civil Liberties Association is that drug users in prison have a legal right to sterile supplies, a spokesperson stating, "People should not be given a death sentence simply because they are in prison and don't have the same community harm-reduction supplies that exist outside of prison."[118] Opponents of such programs counter that harm-reduction measures encourage drug use and the violation of institutional regulations and the law, and that needles can be used as weapons against corrections staff.

Your Thoughts?

1. To what extent should the government be involved in harm-reduction initiatives, such as providing condoms and bleach kits?
2. How can such initiatives be reconciled with the requirement to enforce institutional regulations against drug use and sexual relationships between inmates?
3. Should clean needles and syringes be provided?

MEDIA LINKS

"A Tour of the New Toronto South Detention Centre," http://torontoist.com/2013/10/a-tour-of-the-new-toronto-south-detention-centre/

"Revealed in Photos: Take a Tour Inside Ottawa's Notorious Jail," http://ottawacitizen.com/news/local-news/inside-the-ottawa-jail-tour-of-the-ocdc

"Institutionalized: Mental Health Behind Bars," https://www.youtube.com/watch?v=-fQ50a-m92Y

Out of Mind, Out of Sight: Inside the Brockville Psych, http://tvo.org/video/documentaries/out-of-mind-out-of-sight-inside-the-brockville-psych

"Death Behind Bars," http://globalnews.ca/news/1301910/investigation-canadas-psychiatric-prisons-have-highest-death-assault-rates/

"Behind Bars: Overcrowded Prisons in Canada," www.youtube.com/watch?v=2mDOof6H6cc

"Beyond the Fence: A Virtual Tour of a Canadian Penitentiary," http://www.csc-scc.gc.ca/csc-virtual-tour/index-eng.shtml

"code red diss," www.youtube.com/watch?v=0IFqwiJ9OJA

"12 Block Code Red," www.youtube.com/watch?v=AbQHjmn6yJQ

"represent your set (AW-SW-MW)," https://www.youtube.com/watch?v=KDz9K_pui30

"N.W. Prison Attack Highlights 'A Problem Right Across the Country,'" http://thechronicleherald.ca/canada/1423643-video-n.s.-prison-attack-highlights-a-problem-right-across-the-country

NOTES

1. "Ontario Funding New Healing Lodge for Garden River First Nation," Ontario Ministry of Community and Social Services [news release], June 28, 2016, https://news.ontario.ca/mcss/en/2016/06/ontario-funding-new-healing-lodge-for-garden-river-first-nation.html.

2. E. Goffman, *Asylums: Essays on the Social Situation of Mental Patients and Other Inmates* (Garden City: Doubleday, 1961), p. 11.

3. Ibid., p. 6.

4. P. Hancock and Y. Jewkes, "Architectures of Incarceration: The Spatial Pains of Imprisonment," *Punishment and Society 13*, no. 5 (2011), 611–29.

5. W.W. Franklin, C.A. Franklin, and T.C. Pratt, "Examining the Empirical Relationship between Prison Crowding and Inmate Misconduct: A Meta-Analysis of Conflicting Research Results," *Journal of Criminal Justice 34*, no. 4 (2006), 401–12.

6. "N.S. Prison Report Describes Filthy Conditions," CBC News, December 7, 2010, http://www.cbc.ca/news/canada/nova-scotia/n-s-prison-report-describes-filthy-conditions-1.943078.

7. B. Crewe and A. Liebling, "Are Liberal-Humanitarian Penal Values and Practices Exceptional?" in *Penal Exceptionalism? Nordic Prison Policy and Practice*, eds. T. Ugelvik and J. Dullum (New York: Routledge, 2011), 175–98 at 179.

8. Public Safety Canada Portfolio Corrections Statistics Committee, *Corrections and Conditional Release Statistical Overview: 2015 Annual Report* (Ottawa: Public Works and Government Services Canada, 2016), p. 8, https://www.publicsafety.gc.ca/cnt/rsrcs/pblctns/ccrso-2015/ccrso-2015-en.pdf.

9. Ibid., p. 41.

10. Ibid., p. 53.

11. Ibid., p. 61.

12. "Administrative Segregation in Federal Corrections: 10 Year Trends," Office of the Correctional Investigator, May 28, 2015, p. 7, http://www.oci-bec.gc.ca/cnt/rpt/pdf/oth-aut/oth-aut20150528-eng.pdf.

13. G. Hamilton, "Natural Born Killer," *National Post*, November 30, 2011, p. A3, http://www.pressreader.com/canada/national-post-latest-edition/20111130/281603827283219.

14. M. Lugo, "Measuring Organizational Climate in Prisons," *Journal of Contemporary Criminal Justice 32*, no. 4 (2016), 357–82 at 374–5.

15. N.A. Landenberger and M.W. Lipsey, "The Positive Effects of Cognitive-Behavioral Programs for Offenders: A Meta-Analysis of Factors Associated with Effective Treatment," *Journal of Experimental Criminology 4*, no. 4 (2005), 451–476.

16. S. Belenko, I.D. Johnson, F.S. Taxman, and T. Rieckmann, "Probation Staff Attitudes Toward Substance Abuse Treatment and Evidence-Based Practices," *International Journal of Offender Therapy and Comparative Criminology*, advance online publication, May 23, 2016, at 375–76.

17. S. Poirier (chair), *Decades of Darkness: Moving Towards the Light. A Review of the Prison System in Newfoundland and Labrador* (St. John's, NL: Ministry of Justice, 2008), p. 17, http://www.justice.gov.nl.ca/just/publications/ac_report.pdf.

18. Office of the Correctional Investigator, *Report of the Office of the Correctional Investigator (Canada) on the Baffin Correctional Centre and the Legal and Policy Framework of Nunavut Corrections* (Iqaluit: Nunavut Corrections, 2013), p. 8, http://assembly.nu.ca/library/GNedocs/2013/001193-e.pdf.

19. "'It's a Tinderbox': Assaults Soar in 158-Year Old Prison," Canadian Press, January 15,2017, http://www.edmontonsun.com/2017/01/15/its-a-tinderbox-assaults-soar-in-158-year-old-prison.

20. Ibid.

21. D.M. Bierie, "Is Tougher Better? The Impact of Physical Prison Conditions on Inmate Violence," *International Journal of Offender Therapy and Comparative Criminology 56*, no. 3 (2012), 338–55.

22. "'Unhygienic' Prison Conditions Leads to Less Time for Prisoner," QMI Agency, October 12, 2012, http://cnews.canoe.com/CNEWS/Canada/2012/10/13/20280551.html.

23. Correctional Services Program, "Trends in the Use of Remand in Canada, 2004/2005 to 2014/2015," *Juristat 37*, no. 1, Catalogue no. 85-002-X (Ottawa: Canadian Centre for Justice Statistics, 2017), http://www.statcan.gc.ca/pub/85-002-x/2017001/article/14691-eng.htm.

24. Julie Reitano, "Adult Correctional Statistics in Canada, 2015/2016," *Juristat 37*, no. 1, Catalogue no. 85-002-X (Ottawa: Canadian Centre for Justice Statistics, 2017), http://www.statcan.gc.ca/pub/85-002-x/2017001/article/14700-eng.pdf.

25. *A Legal Aid Strategy for Bail*, Legal Aid Ontario (Toronto: Author, 2016), http://www.legalaid.on.ca/en/publications/paper-legal-aid-strategy-for-bail-2016-11.asp.

26. A. Deshman and N. Myers, *Set Up to Fail: Bail and the Revolving Door of Pre-Trial Detention* (Ottawa: Canadian Civil Liberties Association, 2014), p. 1, https://ccla.org/dev/v5/_doc/CCLA_set_up_to_fail.pdf.

27. P. George, T.N. Gopal, and S. Woods, "Look at My Life: Access to Education for the Remand Population of Ontario," *Canadian Review of Social Policy 70*, (2013/2014), 34–47, https://www.researchgate.net/publication/272830977_Look_at_my_Life_Access_to_Education_for_the_Remand_Population_in_Ontario.

28. L. Porter and D. Calverley, "Trends in the Use of Remand in Canada," *Juristat*, vol. 31, no. 1, Catalogue no. 85-002-X (Ottawa: Minister of Industry, 2011), http://www.statcan.gc.ca/pub/85-002-x/2011001/article/11440-eng.htm.

29. D. Drummond, *Public Services for Ontarians: A Path to Sustainability and Excellence* (Toronto: Government of Ontario, 2012), p. 353, http://www.fin.gov.on.ca/en/reformcommission/chapters/report.pdf.

30. Office of the Correctional Investigator, *Report of the Office of the Correctional Investigator (Canada) on the Baffin Correctional Centre*, p. 4.

31. Office of the Auditor General Manitoba, *Managing the Province's Adult Offenders* (Winnipeg:

Author, 2014), p. 251, http://www.oag.mb.ca/wp-content/uploads/2014/03/Chapter-6-Managing-the-Provinces-Adult-Offenders-Web.pdf.

32. Standing Committee on Prison Conditions in Ontario, *Remand in Ontario: Second Report to the Board* (Toronto: John Howard Society, 2007), p. 9, http://www.johnhoward.on.ca/wp-content/uploads/2014/09/remand-in-ontario-second-report-to-the-board-december-2007.pdf.

33. Deshman and Myers, *Set Up to Fail: Bail and the Revolving Door of Pre-Trial Detention.*

34. Ibid.

35. M. Dauvergne, *Adult Correctional Statistics in Canada, 2010–2011* (Ottawa: Minister of Industry, 2012), http://www.statcan.gc.ca/pub/85-002-x/2012001/article/11715-eng.pdf.

36. D. Calverley, "Adult Correctional Services in Canada, 2008-2009," *Juristat*, vol. 30, no. 3, Catalogu no. 85-002-X (Ottawa: Minister of Industry, 2010), http://www.statcan.gc.ca/pub/85-002-x/2010003/article/11353-eng.htm.

37. Office of the Correctional Investigator, *Annual Report, 2015-2016* (Ottawa: Author, 2016), http://www.oci-bec.gc.ca/cnt/rpt/pdf/annrpt/annrpt20152016-eng.pdf; "Canadian Prisons Strained by Aging Population," *Metro*, April 6, 2014, http://www.metronews.ca/news/canada/2014/04/06/canadian-prisons-strained-by-aging-population.html.

38. P. Edwards, "Times Tough for Older Inmates in Canada's Prisons," *Toronto Star*, January 3, 2014, https://www.thestar.com/news/crime/2014/01/03/times_tough_for_older_inmates_in_canadas_prisons.html.

39. T. Thompson, "What It's Like Working as a Prison Nurse," Vice.com, June 8, 2016, https://www.vice.com/en_ca/article/8gebkv/what-its-like-working-as-a-prison-nurse.

40. G.P. Brown, J.P. Hirdes, and B.E. Fries, "Measuring the Prevalence of Current, Severe Symptoms of Mental Health Problems in a Canadian Correctional Population: Implications for Delivery of Mental Health Services for Inmates," *International Journal of Offender Therapy and Comparative Criminology 59*, no. 1 (2015), 27–50.

41. D. Lafortune, "Prevalence and Screening of Mental Disorders in Short-Term Correctional Facilities," *International Journal of Law and Psychiatry 33*, no. 2 (2010), 94–100.

42. K. Makin, "Senator Fights for Mentally Ill in Prison," *Globe and Mail*, November 19, 2010, p. A9; K. Makin, "Why Canada's Prisons Can't Cope with Flood of Mentally Ill Inmates," *Globe and Mail*, January 21, 2011, http://www.theglobeandmail.com/news/national/why-canadas-prisons-cant-cope-with-flood-of-mentally-ill-inmates/article563604/?page=all.

43. Office of the Correctional Investigator, *Annual Report, 2015–2016.*

44. Mental Health Commission of Canada, *Changing Directions, Changing Lives: The Mental Health Strategy for Canada* (Calgary: Author, 2012), http://strategy-mentalhealthcommission.ca/pdf/strategy-images-en.pdf.

45. J. Bronskill, "'Limited programs' in Criminal Justice System for Aboriginal People," Canadian Press, April 11, 2016, http://www.cbc.ca/news/indigenous/limited-programs-in-criminal-justice-system-for-indigenous-1.3530177.

46. Schizophrenia Society of Ontario, *Provincial Correctional Response to Individuals with Mental Illnesses in Ontario: A Review of Literature* (Toronto: Author, 2012), http://www.schizophrenia.on.ca/get-media/c2af5aea-1bf8-40fd-86ad-1fd9b928f40a/Provincial_.

47. The Honourable A.S. Derrick, *In the Matter of a Fatality Inquiry Regarding the Death of Howard Hyde. Halifax, Nova Scotia* (Halifax: Department of Justice, 2010), http://www.courts.ns.ca/hyde_inquiry/hyde_inquiry_report.pdf.

48. K. Adams and J. Ferrandino "Managing Mentally Ill Inmates in Prisons," *Criminal Justice and Behavior 35*, no. 8 (2008), 913–27; C.L. Blitz, N. Wolff, and J. Shi, "Physical Victimization in Prison: The Role of Mental Illness," *International Journal of Law and Psychiatry 31*, no. 5 (2008), 385–403.

49. Le Protecteur du Citoyen, *A Special Report by the Québec Ombudsman–Toward Services That Are Better Adjusted to Detainees with Mental Disorders*, May 11, 2011, https://protecteurducitoyen.qc.ca/en/news/press-releases/a-special-report-by-the-qu%C3%A9bec-ombudsman-toward-services-that-are-better-adjusted-to-detainees-with-mental-disorders-pdf-102-ko.

50. Schizophrenia Society of Ontario, *Provincial Correctional Response to Individuals with Mental Illnesses in Ontario: A Review of Literature.*

51. Centers for Disease Control, "Traumatic Brain Injury in Prisons and Jails: An Unrecognized Problem" (Atlanta: Author, 2009), https://www.cdc.gov/traumaticbraininjury/pdf/prisoner_tbi_prof-a.pdf.

52. L. Burd, "Fetal Alcohol Syndrome," *Addiction Biology 9*, no. 2 (2006), 115–18; L.M. Caley, C. Kramer, and L.K. Robinson. "Fetal Alcohol Syndrome Disorder," *Journal of School Nursing 21*, no. 3 (2005), 139–46.

53. D.K. Fast and J. Conry, "The Challenge of Fetal Alcohol Syndrome in the Criminal Legal System," *Addiction Biology 9*, no. 2 (2006), 161–6 at 162.

54. F.J. Boland, R. Burrill, M. Duwyn, and J. Karp, *Fetal Alcohol Syndrome: Implications for Correctional Service* (Ottawa: Correctional Service Canada, 2011), http://www.csc-scc.gc.ca/research/r71e-eng.shtml; Fast and Conry, "The Challenge of Fetal Alcohol Syndrome in the Criminal Legal System."

55. A.P. Streissguth, F.L. Brookstein, H.M. Barr, P.D. Sampson, K. O'Malley, and J.K. Young, "Risk Factors for Adverse Outcomes in Fetal Alcohol Syndrome and Fetal Alcohol Effects," *Developmental Behavioral Pediatrics 25*, no. 4 (2004), 228–38.

56. Office of the Correctional Investigator, *Annual Report, 2015–2016*, p. 14.

57. S. Popova, S. Lange, D. Bekmuradov, A. Mihic, and J. Rehm. "Fetal Alcohol Spectrum Disorder Prevalence Estimates in Correctional Systems: A Systematic Literature Review," *Canadian Journal of Public Health 102*, no. 5 (2011), 336–40.

58. L. Burd, D.K. Fast, J. Conry, and A. Williams "Fetal Alcohol Spectrum Disorder as a Marker for Increased Risk of Involvement with Correction Systems," *Journal of Psychiatry and Law 38*, no. 4 (2010), 559–83.

59. P. MacPherson and A.E. Chudley, *FASD in a Correctional Population: Preliminary Results from an Incidence Study* (Montague, P.E.I.: Addictions Research Centre, 2007).

60. Boland et al., *Fetal Alcohol Syndrome: Implications for Correctional Service.*

61. Office of the Auditor General Manitoba, *Managing the Province's Adult Offenders*, p. 237.

62. T. Khandaker, "A Canadian Jail is so Over-Crowded That Inmates Have Been Sleeping in Showers," *Vice News*, March 30, 2016, https://news.vice.com/article/a-canadian-jail-is-so-overcrowded-that-inmates-have-been-sleeping-in-showers.

63. J. Demers, *Warehousing Prisoners in Saskatchewan* (Regina: Canadian Centre for Policy Alternatives, 2014), https://www.policyalternatives.ca/sites/default/files/uploads/publications/Saskatchewan%20Office/2014/10/warehousing_prisoners_in_saskatchewan.pdf.

64. "Prison Double-Bunking Used in Segregation Cells," CBC News, November 22, 2011, http://www.cbc.ca/news/canada/prison-double-bunking-used-in-segregation-cells-1.1120279.

65. Office of the Correctional Investigator, *Annual Report, 2015–2016*.

66. Auditor General of British Columbia, *An Audit of the Adult Custody Division's Correctional Facilities and Programs* (Victoria: Author, 2015), https://www.bcauditor.com/sites/default/files/publications/2015/special/report/AGBC%20Corrections%20report%20FINAL.pdf; Office of the Auditor General Manitoba, *Managing the Province's Adult Offenders*, p. 237.

67. "New Elgin-Middlesex Regional Intermittent Centre Opens," Ontario Ministry of Community Safety and Correctional Services [news release], September 13, 2016, https://news.ontario.ca/mcscs/en/2016/09/new-elgin-middlesex-regional-intermittent-centre-opens.html.

68. Office of the Correctional Investigator, *Annual Report, 2009–2010* (Ottawa: Author, 2010), http://www.oci-bec.gc.ca/rpt/annrpt20092010-eng.aspx.

69. Office of the Auditor General Manitoba, *Managing the Province's Adult Offenders*, p. 248.

70. Demers, *Warehousing Prisoners in Saskatchewan*, p. 11.

71. M. Tutton, "Inmate Violence Steadily Increasing Throughout Canadian Prison System," *Globe and Mail*, December 12, 2016, http://www.theglobeandmail.com/news/national/inmate-violence-steadily-increasing-throughout-canadian-prison-system/article33295905/.

72. Ibid.

73. Office of the Auditor General Manitoba, *Managing the Province's Adult Offenders*, p. 248.

74. Franklin et al., "Examining the Empirical Relationship Between Prison Crowding and Inmate Misconduct."

75. R. Sampson (chair), *Report of the Correctional Service of Canada Review Panel: A Roadmap to Strengthening Public Safety* (Ottawa: Minister of Public Works and Government Services Canada, 2007), http://publications.gc.ca/collections/collection_2008/ps-sp/PS84-14-2007E.pdf.

76. R. Sinclair and J. Grekul "Aboriginal Youth Gangs in Canada: (De)contructing an Epidemic," *First Peoples Child & Family Review* 7, no. 1 (2012), 8–28.

77. M. DeLisi, J.O. Spruill, D.J. Petters, J.W. Caudill, and C.R. Trulson, "Half In, Half Out: Gang Families, Gang Affiliation, and Gang Misconduct," *American Journal of Criminal Justice 38*, no. 4 (2013), 602–15.

78. L. Stone, "Gangs Starting to 'Infect' Women's Prisons," *Calgary Herald*, May 25, 2012, http://www.calgaryherald.com/news/alberta/gangs+starting+infect+women+prisons/5553864/story.html.

79. B. Steiner, *Maintaining Prison Order: Understanding Causes of Inmate Misconduct within and Across Ohio Correctional Institutions* (unpublished doctoral dissertation), University of Cincinnati, July 2008, p. 10.

80. Ibid.

81. M. Solinas-Saunders and M. J. Stacer, "Prison Resources and Physical/Verbal Assault in Prison: A Comparison of Male and Female Inmates," *Victims and Offenders* 7, no. 3 (2012), 279–311.

82. H. Alam, Hina, "Inmate Dead, Others Injured after Riot in Saskatchewan Prison," *Toronto Star*, December 15, 2016, https://www.thestar.com/news/canada/2016/12/15/inmate-dead-others-injured-after-riot-in-saskatchewan-federal-prison.html; V. Ferreira, "Six-hour inmate riot at Penetanguishene superjail under investigation," *Barrie Examiner*, June 21, 2015, http://www.thebarrieexaminer.com/2015/06/19/six-hour-inmate-riot-at-penetanguishene-super-jail--under-investigation.

83. United Nations, "Torture and Other Cruel, Inhuman or Degrading Treatment or Punishment," General Assembly 66th session, item 69 (b), August 5, 2011, pp. 8–9, http://solitaryconfinement.org/uploads/SpecRapTortureAug2011.pdf.

84. Ibid., p. 8.

85. Ibid., p. 12.

86. Public Safety Canada Portfolio Corrections Statistics Committee, *Corrections and Conditional Release Statistical Overview*, p. 65.

87. "Administrative Segregation in Federal Corrections: 10 Year Trends," Office of the Correctional Investigator, pp. 4–6.

88. Public Safety Canada Portfolio Corrections Statistics Committee, *Corrections and Conditional Release Statistical Overview*, p. 67.

89. M. Warzecha, "'Solitary Horrors': The Grim History of Solitary Confinement and Its Modern-Day Comeback," *National Post*, April 14, 2016, http://nationalpost.com/g00/news/world/solitary-horrors-the-grim-history-of-solitary-confinement-and-its-modern-day-comeback/.

90. John Howard Society of Ontario, *Unlocking Change. Decriminalizing Mental Health Issues in Ontario* (Toronto: Author, 2015), http://www.johnhoward.on.ca/wp-content/uploads/2015/07/Unlocking-Change-Final-August-2015.pdf.

91. CSC senior correctional manager, personal communication with C.T. Griffiths.

92. K. Donkin and J. Hazelwood, "New Brunswick Wasn't Tracking Segregation in Jails until This Year," CBC News, October 24, 2016, http://www.cbc.ca/news/canada/new-brunswick/new-brunswick-segregation-tracking-1.3816211.

93. United Nations, "Torture and Other Cruel, Inhuman or Degrading Treatment or Punishment," pp. 17–18.

94. Ibid., p. 22.

95. Ibid.

96. Ibid., pp. 19–20.

97. D. Kelsall, "Cruel and Usual Punishment: Solitary Confinement in Canadian Prisons," *Canadian Medical Association Journal 186*, no. 18 (2014, December 9), 1345.

98. West Coast Prison Justice Society, *Solitary: A Case For Abolition* Vancouver: Author, 2016), https://prisonjusticedotorg.files.wordpress.com/2016/11/solitary-confinement-report.pdf.

99. Le Protecteur du Citoyen, *2015–2016 Annual Report* (Québec: Author, 2016), p. 82, https://protecteurducitoyen.qc.ca/sites/default/files/pdf/rapports_annuels/2015-2016-annual-report-ombudsman.pdf.

100. R. Jurgens, M. Novak, and M. Day, "HIV and Incarceration: Prisons and Detention," *Journal of the International AIDS Society 14*, no. 1 (2011), 26–42.

101. "HIV and Hepatitis C Crisis in Federal Prisons, According to New CSC Report," Canadian HIV/AIDS Legal Network [news release], April 21, 2010, http://www.aidslaw. ca/site/wp-content/uploads/2013/04/April-21NewsRel-CSCreport-ENG.pdf.

102. D. McLay and A. Silversides, "Behind the Walls: Living with HIV in Prison Comes With Its Own Set of Challenges, and Some Aren't the Ones You'd Expect," *The Positive Side*, Canadian AIDS Treatment Information Exchange, winter 2011, http://www.catie. ca/en/printpdf/positiveside/winter-2011/behind-walls.

103. D. Werb, T. Kerr, W. Small, K. Li, and J. Montaner. "HIV Risks Associated with the Incarceration Among Injection Drug Users: Implications for Prison-Based Public Health Strategies," *Journal of Public Health 30*, no. 2 (2008), 126–32.

104. "Women in Prison, HIV and Hepatitis C," Canadian HIV/AIDS Legal Network [info sheet], 2012, p. 1, http://www.aidslaw.ca/site/women-and-hiv-women-in-prison-hiv-and-hepatitis-c.

105. Canadian Human Rights Commission, *Protecting Their Rights: A Systematic Review of Human Rights in Correctional Services for Federally Sentenced Women* (Ottawa: Author 2003), p. 3, http://www.chrc-ccdp.ca/eng/content/protecting-their-rights-systemic-review-human-rights-correctional-services-federally.

106. A. Mehler-Paperny, "Prison Inmate Takes Ottawa to Court Over Access to Clean Needles," *Globe and Mail*, September 25, 2012, http://www.theglobeandmail.com/news/politics/inmates-take-ottawa-to-court-over-access-to-clean-needles/article4566054/.

107. Ibid.

108. R. Jurgens, A. Ball, and A. Verster, "Interventions to Reduce HIV Transmission Related to Injecting Drug Use in Prison," *Lancet Infectious Diseases 9*, no. 1 (2009), 57–66; D.D. Varis, "Intensive Support Units for Federal Inmates: A Descriptive Review," *Forum on Corrections Research 13*, no. 3 (2001), http://www.csc-scc.gc.ca/research/forum/e133/e133m-eng.shtml.

109. D. Zakaria, M. Thompson, and F. Borgatta, *The Relationship between Knowledge of HIV and HCV, Health Education, and Risk and Harm-Reducing Behaviours among Canadian Federal Inmates* (Ottawa: Correctional Service Canada, 2010), http://www.csc-scc.gc.ca/text/rsrch/reports/r195/r195-eng.shtml.

110. F. Kouyoumdjian and K.E. McIsaac, "Persons in Correctional Facilities in Canada: A Key Population for Hepatitis C Prevention and Control," *Canadian Journal of Public Health 106*, no. 6 (2015), E454–E456.

111. Jurgens, Ball, and Verster, "Interventions to Reduce HIV Transmission Related to Injecting Drug Use in Prison."

112. C. Plourde and S. Brochu, "Drugs in Prison: A Break in the Pathway," *Substance Use & Misuse 37*, no. 1 (2002), 47–63.

113. Deshman and Myers, *Set Up to Fail: Bail and the Revolving Door of Pre-Trial Detention*, p. 3.

114. Le Protecteur du Citoyen, *Special Report by the Quebec Ombudsman. Detention Conditions, Administration of Justice and Crime Prevention in Nunavik* (Québec: Author, 2016), p. 2, https://protecteurducitoyen.qc.ca/sites/default/files/pdf/rapports_speciaux/2016-02-18_detention-conditions-in-Nunavik.pdf.

115. S.N. Durlauf and D.S. Nagin, "The Deterrent Effect of Punishment," in *Controlling Crime: Strategies and Tradeoffs*, eds. P.J. Cook, J. Ludwig, J. McCrary (Chicago: University of Chicago Press, 2011), 43–94.

116. Ibid.

117. S. Chu and K. Peddle, *Under the Skin: A People's Case for Prison Needle and Syringe Programs* (Toronto: Canadian HIV/AIDS Legal Network, 2009), http://www.aidslaw.ca/publications/interfaces/downloadFile.php?ref=1990.

118. A. Woo, "Inmate Access to Clean Needles Draws Debate in B.C.," *Globe and Mail*, August 22, 2016, http://www.theglobeandmail.com/news/british-columbia/inmate-access-to-clean-needles-draws-debate-in-bc/article31501785/.

WORKING INSIDE: THE EXPERIENCE OF CORRECTIONAL OFFICERS

CHAPTER OBJECTIVES

- Discuss the roles and responsibilities of correctional officers (COs).
- Discuss the arrangements for the recruitment and training of COs.
- Describe the process of socialization of new COs and CO interaction in correctional institutions.
- Describe the normative code that exists among COs.
- Describe the different "types" of COs.
- Examine the relationships between COs and inmates.
- Describe the attitudes and orientations that COs have toward inmates and toward the organizations in which they work.
- Speak to the decision making of COs and the issues surrounding the abuse of power and use of force by COs.
- Identify and discuss the sources of stress for COs.
- Discuss CO ethics, professionalism, and corruption.

The responsibilities of correctional officers (COs) have grown more complex in recent years and also more challenging. Their duties centre on providing static and dynamic security and include carrying out motorized and foot patrols, staffing control posts, counting and escorting offenders, searching for contraband, enforcing institutional regulations, and providing emergency response. COs mediate conflicts, control inmate movement within the facility, admit and process new arrivals, and serve as information and referral sources for inmates. In many institutions, COs play an active role in case management. In some provincial institutions, they help provide core programming to inmates. In general terms, they have four main tasks: (1) security, providing surveillance inside the prison, (2) service, looking after inmate needs, (3) helping inmates adjust to life inside, and (4) helping inmates prepare to re-enter the community.

CORRECTIONS PERSPECTIVE 7.1

Former Correctional Officer, Now Deputy Warden

When you step into the world of the prison for the first time, the thing that always stays with you is the sound of the door clanging behind you. When I first went to work as a correctional officer, everything inside seemed to be in chaos. You wonder what the heck is going on. It takes a few months to get in tune with the place. After you've been there awhile you get to know who the major players are, how different correctional officers approach situations. You develop a rapport with the inmates and begin developing relationships with them. I've always said that being a correctional officer is an art . . . to know how to balance the authority you have with the realities of life inside.

Source: Personal communication with C.T. Griffiths.

In federal institutions, correctional officers are responsible for dynamic and static security, establishing working relationships with inmates and other staff, and supporting case management. The CO1's priority is security. CO2s, by contrast, focus on case management and on facilitating and encouraging inmate participation in programs. In provincial/territorial institutions, the role of COs is more multifaceted.

ROLES AND RESPONSIBILITIES

COs play a pivotal role in correctional institutions. It is COs who have the most daily contact with the inmates. Although systems of corrections make extensive use of advanced technology, such as video surveillance and various warning devices (static security), COs are the primary mechanism by which institutional policies and regulations are implemented and by which the inmates are controlled (dynamic security). COs are also a key part of efforts to rehabilitate offenders. All CSC correctional officers are uniformed and are designated as federal peace officers under Section 10 of the Corrections and Conditional Release Act, and provincial/territorial correctional officers have peace officer status as well. This gives them powers of arrest and the authority to use force, among other authorities.

The authority of COs in prisons is both legal and moral. With respect to legal authority, COs do not have the power to discipline inmates, but in enforcing the institution's policies and regulations, they are able to initiate the punishment process. Equally important is their moral authority, which is based on establishing functional relationships with the inmates.[1]

The desirable attributes of COs, as identified by correctional managers, COs, and the inmates themselves, include these: setting consistent boundaries, communicating well, showing moral integrity, exercising power and authority fairly, understanding the challenges faced by inmates, and being optimistic in a difficult environment.[2]

RECRUITMENT AND TRAINING

Ensuring that suitable candidates are recruited for the position of CO and providing training that prepares the recruits for work inside correctional institutions are key to COs successfully meeting the challenges of working inside. A feature of Canadian corrections is the variability between the training for federal correctional officers and their provincial/territorial counterparts. Another is the lack of diversity among COs, despite the fact that Indigenous people and Blacks are over-represented in prison populations.

Correctional Service Canada

At the federal level, each of the CSC's five regions (Atlantic, Québec, Ontario, Prairies, Pacific) recruits, selects, assesses, and hires its own COs according to national standards. Those who are seeking an entry-level CO position must apply to the region where they want to work (www.jobs.gc.ca). Applicants are screened for experience and education and must provide the following documentation: a driver's licence, proof of citizenship, proof of education, and automated external defibrillator (AED), cardiopulmonary resuscitation (CPR), and First Aid certification. They must pass a general aptitude test, the Bona Fide Occupational Requirements (BFOR) for COs, and a set of medical and physical standards, including the Correctional Officer Physical Abilities Test (COPAT).

Persons with an interest in a career as a federal CO are encouraged by the CSC to complete the self-assessment questionnaire for the position of CX-01. The questionnaire can be found at http://www.csc-scc.gc.ca/careers/092/003001-3021-eng.pdf.

Federal correctional officers belong to the Union of Canadian Correctional Officers, which advocates on their behalf (https://ucco-sacc-csn.ca/). This includes negotiating with the federal Treasury Board for wages and benefits.

The online application is followed by electronic screening, enhanced suitability screening, written tests, an interview and reference check, and a psychological assessment. Candidates who successfully navigate the aforementioned stages are placed in the partially qualified pool and are then eligible to participate in the Correctional Training Program (candidates are not paid and do not receive an allowance while completing the training).[3]

The in-depth interview focuses on the applicant's background and personal integrity. The CSC has dropped the requirement that applicants have a university degree; it now requires only a high school diploma or high school equivalency.

Successful applicants are required to complete the Correctional Training Program, which has three stages:

Stage 1: Up to four weeks of online learning.

Stage 2: Four to five weeks of online written assignments (as preparation for stage 3).

Stage 3: 10 to 11 weeks of training at one of the CSC Staff Colleges or the Training Academy. Focuses on "law and policy, use of firearms and chemical agents, fire safety, self-defence and arrest and control techniques, use of batons, suicide prevention, the situation management model."[4]

The CSC has developed a special process for selecting and training staff to work in institutions for federally sentenced women. Correctional officers who work in women's institutions are referred to as primary workers or Kimisinaw (Cree for "older sister"); Kimisinaw work exclusively in the Okimaw Ohci Healing Lodge.[5] Specific criteria are used to identify personnel who are sensitive to women's issues, their life histories, and their unique needs. Besides the training provided to all new COs, staff selected to work in women's facilities must complete a "women-centred training" course. That course has a number of modules covering areas such as women's criminality and its links to personal history, self-injury, and suicide; same-sex relationships; cultural sensitivity; and dealing effectively with lifers.

One of the most ambitious studies of Canadian COs examined how the attitudes of officers changed between the training phase and the field. It was found that new recruits held positive views about correctional work generally and about the idea of rehabilitation and that these attitudes persisted after one year on the job. After starting the job, however, officers experienced stress associated with shift work, threats to their safety, the lack of challenges in their work, and COs' low degree of decision-making autonomy.[6]

Table 7.1 sets out the ranks of federal correctional officers and the responsibilities/remuneration for each rank. Note that the salary figures are estimates and do not include overtime or benefits.[7]

The salary for COs in provincial/territorial institutions varies by jurisdiction and is most often expressed in terms of an hourly wage. In Ontario in 2015, newly hired COs began at $24.02 per hour and could progress to a maximum $31.79 an hour. In Alberta, the hourly rate is somewhat higher, at between $25 and $37 per hour. These salaries are exclusive of pensions and benefits.[8]

Provincial/Territorial Training

In contrast to federal corrections, there are no national standards for recruiting and training COs for provincial/territorial systems of corrections. Each province and territory has its own procedures, standards, and training courses, some of which are more thorough than others. A review of training in Nova

Table 7.1   Rank, Responsibilities, and Remuneration of Federal Correctional Officers

Rank	Responsibilities/Remuneration
CX-01(or COI)	Responsible for institutional security functions including static security posts, patrolling the perimeter of the institution, first response, and providing inmate escorts. Salary range is about $55,000 to $75,000 per year.
CX-02 (or COII)	More experienced COs who work in living units, and engage in dynamic security, case management, and casework. Known as primary workers in institutions for federally sentenced women. Salary range is about $60,000 to $75,000 per year.
CX-03	A supervisory role over other officers. Salary range is about $65,000 to $82,000 per year.
CX-04 (CM)	Correctional manager who functions as the institutional supervisor or a correctional facility manager. Salary range is about $70,000 to $89,000 per year.

Scotia, for example, found gaps in training for front-line staff and no centralized capacity to monitor training requirements.[9]

Many CO recruits to provincial/territorial corrections are trained using some combination of initial and on-the-job training. They must generally complete a multistage process that includes (among other things) a physical activities test, a background check, and a medical exam. Increasingly, potential recruits are required to pay the costs of their own training. Some jurisdictions offer pre-employment courses through community colleges.

In Ontario, for example, recruits must complete the Correctional Officer Training and Assessment (COTA) program, an eight-week training and assessment program containing theory and practical skills based on job-related topics. It includes behavioural and skills-based assessment of recruits.[10]

In most jurisdictions, someone who is interested in a career as a CO can enroll in a certificate course offered by a community college or justice training centre. These courses may enhance an applicant's chances of being hired, but they do not guarantee a successful application.

GOING INSIDE: THE SOCIALIZATION OF NEW CORRECTIONAL OFFICERS

A number of challenges confront new COs, not the least of which is a lack of knowledge of what it will be like working inside a prison. A new CO probably has not visited a correctional institution in any capacity before being hired.

Indeed, most new COs have been exposed to prison life solely through movies and sensational media reports.

If they are to exercise discretion properly and carry out their tasks effectively, new COs must learn the subtle nonverbal cues that will help them "read" individual inmates. They must also become familiar with the intricacies of the inmate social system, the methods they use to distribute drugs and other contraband, and other inmate activities such as gambling, strong-arming, and debt collection. Inmates will "test" new COs to determine how they will exercise their discretion and authority. Adapting to prison life, learning how it works, and developing strategies to cope with its pressures and demands is much the same process for COs as for the inmates themselves.[11]

Another challenge confronting new COs is gaining acceptance from co-workers. New officers must demonstrate their solidarity through their actions. There is often a "probationary" period during which the neophyte must prove that they can be trusted and can perform the job.

PATTERNS OF RELATIONSHIPS AMONG COs

It has long been assumed that COs, much like police officers, have developed an occupational subculture. The foundations for the **normative code of behaviour** among COs are said to include the following: always assisting another officer who is in real or potential danger; don't rat on fellow officers; not becoming overly friendly with the inmates; and deferring to the experience of veteran officers.[12] This is similar to the code among inmates (see Chapter 8).

Among the factors that have been identified as contributing to solidarity among COs are these: the ever-present potential for injury on the job; the hostility directed toward COs by inmates; the often-conflicting demands made on COs, largely as a consequence of shifting correctional philosophies; a work environment where rewards and recognition are few and far between; and the reliance of officers on one another.[13]

The resulting normative code of behaviour provides a mechanism for COs to cope with the demands of both inmates and the prison administration. However, it may also foster a "code of silence" among officers with respect to officer misconduct, harassment of staff and women COs, and abuse of authority. As well, officers who are deemed to be too friendly with inmates may be considered by other COs as untrustworthy.[14] Similarly, it may undermine the potential of COs to serve as change agents for inmates.

On closer examination, however, the subculture of COs seems not to be monolithic. Indeed, COs as a work group may be as fragmented as the inmates are. Line-level security personnel build friendship networks, which may be gender-based or centred on shared experiences, such as completing a university degree. The extent to which COs exhibit solidarity depends on a number of factors, including the security level of the institution; the age, gender, and backgrounds of the officers; the relations between officers and the administration; and other factors that are less tangible, including the extent to which the COs

Normative code of behaviour (among correctional officers) The behavioural rules that guide interaction and contribute to solidarity among correctional officers.

in any one institution perceive that they are threatened by the inmates or by administrative policies.

In fact, for many COs it is their *colleagues,* not the inmates, who are the main source of job-related stress. COs who gossip among themselves, who share information with inmates, and who are perceived as too authoritarian are potential sources of stress for line-level personnel. Conflict may also arise when certain officers are viewed as "slackers"—for example, because they sleep during graveyard shifts and fail to make their rounds at the appointed times.

There are attributes of the CO subculture that may contribute to officers abusing their authority and mistreating inmates. The solidarity of officers may make it difficult to detect, investigate, and prosecute officers who are involved in activities that violate professional standards, institutional regulations, or the law.

A TYPOLOGY OF COs

Attempts have been made to categorize COs based on their attitudes toward the inmates, their co-workers, their occupation, and the institutional environment. Such efforts are fraught with difficulty, since it is unlikely that any single officer will exhibit all of the attitudinal and behavioural features of one particular type. But these attempts do sensitize one to the fact that not all COs think and act the same way.

Individual COs can be placed on a continuum based on how they exercise their discretionary authority. At one end are those who are rigid and who attempt to enforce all the rules at all times; at the other end are officers who do little or no rule enforcement. This latter group may include officers who are close to retirement. In the middle are officers who are consistent in their decision-making and straightforward with inmates, who do not make arbitrary decisions, and who temper their authority with common sense and a respect for the law. These officers have good judgment and communication skills, are able to mediate potentially explosive behavioural situations, and are good judges of character.[15]

A typology of Canadian COs, based on the perceptions of former inmates, has been developed.[16] Interviews with former federal male inmates (N = 56), who were on parole, revealed several CO orientations, as reflected in how they carried out their role in the institution.

Dualists

Dualists are those COs who took both a security and a harmony-oriented approach in their work. Dualists were viewed by the ex-inmates as being both compassionate and strict in their interactions with inmates, which often presents challenges for inmates who are uncertain how a CO will respond in any particular instance. The ex-inmates further distinguished between *harmonious dualists* who are motivated towards 'fairness' yet take into account the experience of prisoners beyond being law-breakers (e.g., as fathers, sons, spouses).[17]

This is reflected in the comments of one ex-inmate, who stated, "I saw a lot of good guards that were very nice to me. Laugh, joke with me, and guards that told me they were proud of me."[18] There were also COs identified by the ex-inmates as "security dualists" whose actions reflected more of a security orientation, an emphasis on control and rule-following, and as often abusing their authority in an attempt, as one ex-inmate commented, "to control your every movement."[19]

Punishers

Punishers were COs who were perceived by the ex-inmates to be enforcement-oriented and punitive in their interactions with inmates. This orientation was manifested by disrespect toward the rights of inmates, verbal harassment, ignoring requests, withholding food, and other behaviours designed to harass and intimidate inmates. These COs were viewed by the ex-inmates as the most difficult COs to deal with in the institutional environment, as the punishers made life inside even more challenging. In the words of one ex-inmate, "Their attitude really sucked . . . it's sick . . . they treated us like a piece of shit."[20] Another inmate recounted an encounter with a CO who he described as a punisher:

> You see a guard coming; "Sir, sir, can I speak to you for a minute?" "No." Keeps walking. It's unnecessary. I'm not asking you to let me out. I'm not asking to date his sister. I'm asking: "Can you call my parole officer to take care of this, or can you mail this letter for me?" And they just take it from me and drop it on the floor . . . It's antagonizing.[21]

Moral Relativists

These were COs who, in the view of the ex-inmates, exhibited ambivalence in carrying out their tasks and a weak commitment to either a security or a harmony approach.[22] These officers are viewed as not having either passion or ambition for their jobs, described by the ex-inmates as "ready to retire," as motivated primarily by their paycheque, and as "ambivalent about their occupational responsibilities to prisoners, colleagues, and management."[23]

Little is known about the trajectories of CO orientations, that is, whether an individual CO began their career as a dualist and, over the years, became a relativist. Or began as a dualist and subsequently transformed into a punisher, perhaps due to occupational stress, or PTSD. Additional research remains to be done on the orientations of COs so as to better understand the role of the organizational environment, correctional leadership and managers, and work/life balance (or imbalance) on the way in which COs carry out their roles and responsibilities in the institution and their interactions with inmates (and other corrections personnel). It has been suggested that various orientations can emerge during the course of a CO's career.[24]

CO–INMATE RELATIONSHIPS AND PATTERNS OF ACCOMMODATION

Even though a core principle among COs is "never trust an inmate," the exigencies of daily life inside institutions generate unique pressures for COs and inmates to develop accommodative relationships. For inmates, this helps reduce the pains of imprisonment; for COs, it ensures daily stability and order.

Relations with inmates are generally not a source of stress for COs, though the officers realize they are outnumbered by the inmates and that peace and order in the institution require the inmates' cooperation. Inmates and COs have a mutual interest in ensuring that order and routine are maintained in the institution. An unstable environment characterized by disruptions and unpredictable events increases stress levels for both inmates and COs and places everyone at risk.[25]

The specific patterns of interaction that develop between COs and inmates depend on a variety of factors, including the individual CO, the size of the inmate population, the security level of the facility, and the policies and management style of the senior administration. In Chapter 2, the changing philosophies of corrections as reflected in prison architecture were discussed. Research studies have found that the design of a prison can have a significant impact on inmate–staff and inmate–inmate relationships. Newer institutions and those in which there were few inmates who were double-bunked evidenced more positive relationships and interactions.[26]

CORRECTIONS PERSPECTIVE 7.2

Deputy Warden, Federal Correctional Institution

In terms of the inmates, the long-term inmates are more manageable than the short-term inmates. They understand they are going to have to get along with other inmates and the staff. There is an adjustment period . . . When they first come in, they get really depressed and we have them on suicide watch. They lose hope. After they've been in a few weeks, they come to terms with the fact that they are going to be in jail for a long time. That's when you begin to see more prosocial behaviour out of these guys. The long-term guys are the ones that end up being on the inmate committees and taking a more balanced view of things.

It's the short-term guys that are the most difficult to manage. They are part of the 20 percent of inmates in the prison who are difficult to manage and it's this group that causes all of the problems. That's the 20 percent you always see coming back. They go out on statutory release and screw up, or they serve to their warrant expiry date and they go out and commit another crime and end up coming back. And those are the guys who can make you cynical—that nothing is working.

(continued)

> It's the quiet guys that are there, doing their own time, working their way through the programs, getting out on parole and not coming back—those are the guys you don't even remember and that's the vast majority of guys. The 20 percent are the guys who commit serious offences in the community—like a guy goes out of prison and commits an armed robbery three days later. Then the public and the politicians get up in arms about the system not being tough enough. Meanwhile, the other 80 percent who are going out and not getting into trouble don't get any attention.

Source: Personal communication with C.T. Griffiths.

Generally, inmates serving life sentences (25-year minimums) are the easiest group to deal with. By contrast, many younger offenders (often referred to as for COs "new school inmates"), because they have a "get high today, the hell with tomorrow" attitude, are a source of instability in the institution for both COs and other inmates. Ironically, then, even though conditions in correctional institutions have improved, life has become more unpredictable for COs and other staff. Figure 7.1 illustrates the "push–pull" nature of interactions between COs and inmates and the factors that may come into play.

The boundaries that are set between COs and inmates ensure there is a routine and predictability in the daily life of the institution. New COs may inadvertently violate the boundaries by being manipulated by inmates (often referred to as "being set up"). One CO in a federal institution noted that officers are trained not to trust inmates, "So, whenever they say something, you don't want to just take it at face value."[27] Inmates can be very adept at gleaning personal information from COs during everyday conversations, one federal CO noting, "I think an inmate can find out a lot of information on staff if we are not aware of it. I think it goes back to remembering where you work."[28] Maintaining boundaries with inmates may be difficult, particularly in federal institutions where inmates are serving long sentences and increased communication with the same inmates may be longstanding and frequent.

The interactions between COs and inmates may also be affected by the inmate's offence and criminal history. A study of Canadian male and women COs in several provinces ($N = 100$) found that sex offenders were viewed negatively by COs and as objects of fear and distrust.[29] A predominant view among the COs was that the institutional environment was not sufficiently punitive for sex offenders, one officer stating, "It should be a punishment to be in here, not a privilege."[30] The disgust felt toward sex offenders by many of the COs is

Figure 7.1

Dynamics of the CO–Inmate Relationship

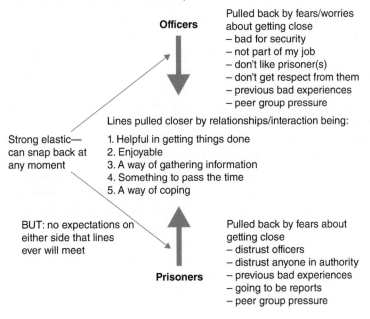

Source: From *The Prison Officer*, 2nd edition, A. Liebling, D. Price, and G. Shefer, Copyright © 2011, Willan Publishing. Reproduced by permission of Taylor & Francis Books UK.

reflected in the following comments in response to the question "How do you feel about sex offenders?":

> *"I hate that, well, I got no use for that shit."*

> *"Yeah it bothers me it's actually one of the worst feelings ever to give a guy a meal who you know sexually assaults people."*[31]

The Agendas of COs

Studies have revealed that COs can have one of two agendas: custodial or correctional. The **custodial agenda** of COs centres on control and the enforcement of regulations. Historically, this agenda included the excessive use of force against inmates, although these types of incidents have decreased in recent years. According to some observers, the prison environment itself, with its features of a total institution, contributes to many of the problems that arise between COs and inmates.[32]

By contrast, the **correctional agenda** involves COs functioning as change agents by referring inmates to programs and other resources, by helping them resolve problems and personal crises related to their incarceration, and by serving as intermediaries between the inmate and the institutional bureaucracy.[33]

Custodial agenda (of correctional officers)
The activities of correctional officers that centre on control and enforcement of regulations.

Correctional agenda (of correctional officers)
The activities of correctional officers as change agents using their authority to help inmates cope with the problems of living in confinement.

COs have considerable discretion to help inmates and ease the difficulties they encounter so often in their daily lives.

There are COs who are oriented more towards a custodial approach, while others are involved in activities reflective of a correctional agenda.

Canadian researchers have found that CO communication style can have a significant impact on the relationship between COs and inmates.[34] A study (*N* = 42) of male and women COs in provincial institutions across the country found that the communication style of "relational but secure" presented an opportunity for relationships based on trust and respect that would, in turn, assist efforts at rehabilitation.[35]

Officers who develop a rapport with inmates beyond the basic "keeper and the kept" level are generally more effective at maintaining order in the units. A positive relationship with inmates may also increase the amount of information that "snitches" or "information providers" pass along to officers, as well as encourage inmates to tell officers about problems that are developing in the unit. It seems that generally speaking, most inmates "get along" with COs.

The institution's management model can have a significant impact on CO–inmate interactions. A review of correctional institutions in Newfoundland and Labrador found that they followed a paramilitary model wherein the COs focused on rule enforcement. These officers had little interaction with the inmates.[36]

Exercising Authority: COs' Discretion and Decision Making

COs have considerable discretion in carrying out their daily activities and in determining when and how they will enforce the institution's rules and regulations. Officers are well aware that full enforcement of all institutional regulations at all times would make life unbearable both for themselves and for the inmates. A former CO recalled that a general principle was this: "Read the book, but don't throw the book. Do not go prescriptively into any situation."[37] Correctional officers are generally focused on those inmate behaviours that might disrupt the prison routine.[38]

RESEARCH FILE 7.1

Inmate Gambling: A Study of Correctional Officer Discretion

A study of COs (*N* = 24) in provincial institutions in Québec explored how the officers exercised their discretion in enforcing institutional restrictions against inmate gambling (Beauregard, et al., 2013). The study found that formal enforcement was rarely used to counter this activity, and when the COs did intervene, it was most often related to inmate misconduct associated with gambling, such as causing a disturbance. Gambling was viewed by the COs as a leisure activity that kept the inmates occupied and helped to maintain peace and quiet in the living areas. In contrast, the COs indicated that they were much more aggressive in enforcing regulations against intoxicants, which were viewed as having a potentially negative, and harmful, impact on the COs and other inmates.

Source: V. Beauregard, V. Chadillon-Farniacci, S. Brochu, and M-M. Cousineau, "Enforcing Institutional Regulations in Prison Settings: The Case of Gambling in Quebec," *International Criminal Justice Review 23*, no. 2 (2013), 170–84.

COs also know that there are limits to the use of incident reports as a means to secure inmate compliance. Thus, they may resort to "informal punishments" such as refusing or "forgetting" to provide certain services for the inmate (e.g., "misplacing" an inmate's paperwork).[39]

THE EXERCISE AND ABUSE OF POWER

COs exert various types of power in the institution. These include *coercive power* (rule enforcement, disciplinary charges, and searches), *reward power* (awarding certain inmates privileges, providing favourable reports), *legitimate power* (the officer's formal authority), *exchange power* (the informal system of rewards, under-enforcement of regulations), and *expert* or *"professional" power* (the use of expertise to resolve conflicts).[40]

Following is an exchange between a woman ex-offender and a CO from Nova Scotia Institution for Women, a federal institution, on the website insideprison.com:

> *Woman ex-offender: I really don't have anything good to say about this place. I believe the guards are rude and enjoy controlling the inmates, and the women are treated poorly. If they put themselves in our situation for once and gave us some empathy they would probably get more respect from inmates.*

> *Correctional officer: I really don't think you understand what it is like to be a guard, either. Think about just one person having to run a unit that is overcrowded with inmates who have no respect and treat you like crap all day. You would realize how much of a thankless job it really is . . . So I'm guessing the only piece of advice to someone who doesn't like the way they are being treated in jail would be to not break the law.*

The low visibility of daily life inside correctional institutions, combined with the broad discretion exercised by COs, may lead to situations where COs abuse their authority and sometimes even violate the law. Racialized group inmates, in particular, may perceive that COs are abusing their discretionary powers. Interviews ($N = 73$; 30 women, 43 men) with Black inmates in Canadian federal institutions found that nearly all had experienced discrimination by corrections officials, the report finding, "Their needs did not appear to be a priority; their concerns were often ignored and many felt as though there were a 'different set of rules' for Black inmates."[41] The Black inmates also reported feeling targeted for infractions of institutional regulations more frequently than other inmates, and institutional records revealed that these inmates were over-represented in categories of infractions where COs had discretion, such as "being disrespectful to staff" or "jeopardizing the safety/security of the institution or another person."[42] Conversely, Black inmates were under-represented in categories of infractions that required evidence, such as possession of stolen property or having unauthorized items.[43]

Use of Force

More and more attention is being paid to the use of force by COs. This is for several reasons, including greater accountability and oversight and a number of recent high-profile incidents. Statistics on use-of-force incidents are often sketchy or, in the case of many provincial/territorial institutions, non-existent.[44]

In general terms, COs are permitted to use only the level of force required to carry out their duties. The use of force in correctional institutions can easily generate controversy, because of the low visibility of CO interactions with inmates. With the advent of social media and cameras in correctional facilities, the use of force against inmates is now more visible.

Statistics suggest that the number of CO–inmate incidents has increased, but that increase may be due to more stringent reporting requirements: Incidents that in the past would not have been recorded now *must* be recorded. There was a time when COs were not required to report all physical contacts with inmates.

Figures on reported incidents of use of force in federal correctional institutions during 2015–16 as compiled by the Office of the Correctional Investigator are presented in Corrections File 7.1.

The excessive use of force has also been an issue in provincial correctional institutions. See Corrections File 7.2.

It is worth noting that COs have access to a wider variety of control options than police officers; they also have a better idea of whom they are dealing with—that is, they may have extensive knowledge of the inmates and their behaviour. Further, there is no evidence of differences between male and women COs in their response to inmate challenges and misbehaviour.[45]

Increasingly, COs are being held civilly and criminally liable for their actions. In a number of incidents, COs have been fired following riots or inmate deaths.

CORRECTIONS FILE 7.1

A Profile of Use-of-Force Incidents in Federal Correctional Institutions, 2013–14 to 2015–16

From 2013–14 to 2015–16, the following were reported:

- There was a 22 percent increase in use-of-force incidents.
- Indigenous offenders (25 percent of the prison population) accounted for 30 percent of all use-of-force incidents reviewed, similar to the previous year.
- Black offenders (10 percent of the population) accounted for 18 percent of all use of force incidents reviewed, a 3 percent increase from the previous year.
- 14 percent of use-of-force interventions were in response to incidents of self-injury.
- 39 percent of all use-of-force incidents reviewed occurred in the offender's cell.
- 36.6 percent of all incidents involved offenders with a mental health issue identified by the service.
- 41 percent of use-of-force incidents at the CSC's treatment centres included the use of pepper spray.

Of concern were the deficiencies associated with the use of force, including the following:

- Decontamination procedures were not followed in 31 percent of all incidents reviewed.
- Post–use-of-force health care assessments deficiencies were noted in 54 percent of all reviews.
- Video recording procedures were deficient in 77 percent of all reviews.
- Strip search procedures were not followed in 30 percent of all interventions.

Source: From Office of the Correctional Investigator, 2016. *Annual Report, 2015-1016,* http://www.oci-bec .gc.ca/cnt/rpt/pdf/annrpt/annrpt20152016-eng.pdf. Reprinted by permission of the Office of the Correctional Investigator.

CORRECTIONS FILE 7.2

The Excessive Use of Force in Ontario Provincial Institutions

In response to a high number of inmate complaints, the ombudsman of Ontario conducted a formal investigation into allegations of the excessive use of force by COs in Ontario provincial institutions. The investigation included interviews with inmate complainants and meetings with corrections officials.

Among the findings of the review was that there was a "code of silence" among COs that protected officers who engaged in the excessive use of force and resulted in officers "conspiring to lie, destroy, and falsify records" (p. 9).

Numerous cases of excessive use of force were documented and revealed instances in which officers failed to report use-of-force incidents as required by regulations, colluded in

(continued)

preparing reports on incidents, and did not intervene when other officers engaged in physical brutality against inmates. One officer who recanted their original report of an incident recalled:

> One of my fellow officers kicked him in the back of the head and his head went off the track, splitting his head open, and blood started spilling out from underneath him . . . I was shocked. I was stunned. I stood there and the same officer booted him . . . for the second time. (p. 30)

Source: Ombudsman Ontario, *The Code: Investigation into the Ministry of Community Safety and Correctional Services' Response to Allegations of Excessive Use of Force Against Inmates* (Toronto: Author, 2013), https://www.ombudsman.on.ca/Files/sitemedia/Documents/Investigations/SORT%20Investigations/The-Code-EN.pdf.

ETHICS, PROFESSIONALISM, AND CORRUPTION

Little attention has been paid to ethics and professionalism among COs (i.e., far less than among police). Because of the "closed" nature of correctional institutions and the frequent contact between inmates and COs, there are many opportunities for officers to be compromised.

There are attributes of the CO subculture that may contribute to officers abusing their authority and mistreating inmates. The solidarity of officers may make it difficult to detect, investigate, and prosecute officers who are involved in activities that violate professional standards, institutional regulations, or the law (see Corrections File 7.2). The code of silence among officers may serve as a deterrent to COs reporting wrongdoing.[46] A violation of peer trust may serve to isolate a CO who no longer has the support of fellow officers. A former CO recalled being in that situation, stating, "If an incident went down, there was no one to cover my back. That's a very important lesson to learn. You need your back covered and my back wasn't covered there at all. And, at one point, I was in fear of being set up by guards. I was put in dangerous situations purposely."[47]

Corrupt conduct can range from minor violations of regulations to criminal acts such as theft, trafficking in contraband, smuggling items into the institution, having sexual relations with inmates, covering up incidents in the institution, and the misuse of authority (including taking gratuities from inmates). Misconduct can involve individual officers or groups of officers.[48] Corrupt COs have sometimes joined forces with organized criminal groups such as Hells Angels. COs have also been dismissed for violating regulations; some have even been convicted of criminal offences.

Among the recent incidents: A provincial CO in British Columbia was sentenced to three years in prison for helping an inmate escape. Soon after that, another CO in the same facility was sentenced to four years in prison for trafficking drugs, after being caught on a surveillance camera passing drugs to an inmate. A federal CO was fired for having an inappropriate sexual relationship with an inmate, and another for smuggling drugs into the institution.

Correctional officers often find themselves in situations that present ethical dilemmas. These may involve situations where COs may violate institutional regulations by behaving inappropriately with inmates, such as excessive use of force, having sexual relations with inmates, or more complex situations in which COs may be caught between the directive of senior management in the institution and "doing the right thing." For their (in)actions/actions, COs can receive a verbal or written reprimand, be demoted, be suspended without pay, or be terminated for cause. COs can also be charged criminally.

An example of COs caught in an ethical dilemma who were ultimately charged criminally is the case of Ashley Smith, a federal inmate who died while in solitary confinement. Her case is discussed in detail in Chapter 12, and the ethical dilemma of the COs who were present when she passed away in her cell is presented in Class/Group Discussion 12.1.

RELATIONSHIPS WITH THE PRISON ADMINISTRATION

Research on COs' orientation and attitudes has revealed that a key source of stress and alienation is the relationship between COs and the prison administration. Administrators may be viewed with distrust and cynicism, as being distant from the everyday realities of the prison, and as being overly concerned about fiscal and administrative issues that have little relevance to line-level officers. COs are especially critical of administrators who fail to provide clear and consistent operational policies.

COs may have particular problems with operational directives, such as those related to the disciplinary process and the use of segregation, wherein it would be the CO who would be held responsible and reprimanded should things go awry. As one provincial CO stated, "I'm scared to do a mistake and to get the finger."[49] This occurred in the case of the death of Ashley Smith, discussed in Chapter 12.

RELATIONSHIPS WITH TREATMENT STAFF

Many COs hold a dim view of rehabilitation programs, believing that they are a waste of time and money. The COs' view that few inmates have the ability, resources, and motivation to make significant changes in their attitude and behaviour may limit their potential to be effective change agents. There is also the perception that many inmates become involved in treatment programs primarily to improve their chances of release on parole, rather than for self-improvement.

In federal facilities, officers at the CO2 level are involved in case management; in provincial/territorial facilities, most COs have little input into case management and indeed often find themselves at odds with case managers.

This conflict is in part a consequence of the different roles that COs and case management officers play in the institution: The primary role of many COs is security, whereas case managers are charged with developing, implementing, and monitoring the offender's plan of treatment.

STRESS AMONG CORRECTIONAL OFFICERS

There is considerable evidence that COs experience high levels of stress and burnout.[50] This may have a significant impact on COs' lack of support for treatment programs, the amount of sick leave they take, and their degree of support for management, as well as on how they interact with the inmates.[51] Further, surveys of COs have revealed that those who are suffering from burnout are more likely to be more punishment-oriented in their views.[52] These findings indicate that CO burnout has negative consequences for themselves, the institution, and the inmates.

The organizational environment in which correctional officers work has been found to have a significant impact on the stress levels of correctional officers.[53] It may also play a more important role than the attributes of individual officers.[54] Work environments in which correctional officers have high levels of job satisfaction, commitment to the organization, and feel a sense of accomplishment in their work are less likely to create stress for COs.[55] Positive working environments can be developed through improved communication between COs and management and giving voice to the concerns of COs.[56]

Threats to Personal Security

The threat of physical violence is always present in correctional institutions. Interviews with COs who worked in provincial remand centres and correctional institutions ($N = 100$) revealed that the threat and presence of physical violence are omnipresent in institutions. Overcrowding contributed to this, one CO stating, "The place was fit for fifty-seven inmates and you got to come [into work] with ninety-two [prisoners]."[57] Another commented, "When you have, instead of ten, thirty in each area and one officer outside and one officer inside, it's a big difference."[58] The study also found that the COs' concerns with security extended to their personal lives, including the threat of victimization of themselves and their family.[59] This included the fear of being followed and being watched by ex-inmates.

The fears of victimization may be greater among women COs.[60] A U.S. study found that women COs working in male correctional institutions expressed greater levels of fear of victimization, in particular, in institutions with a poor organizational climate.[61]

Concerns about personal security are a leading cause of stress among COs.[62] There has been an increase in inmate assaults on COs in federal institutions.[63] Many COs feel that the institution's policies and procedures are inadequate to ensure their personal security. Among the safety concerns of

COs is the danger of exposure to inmates who are infected with HIV/AIDS, hepatitis, and tuberculosis. There is no mandatory testing of inmates for HIV/AIDS, and as a matter of policy, COs are not told which inmates are HIV-positive. This means that officers must assume that every inmate with whom they have contact is infected with a communicable disease. As first responders to incidents that occur in the institution, COs may be exposed to the blood and bodily fluids of infected inmates.[64]

A survey of provincial COs in British Columbia (N = 205) found that the majority had been exposed to blood (90 percent); feces, spit, and urine (75 percent); and inmate threats to their personal safety (66 percent); also, 20 percent of them had witnessed the death of an inmate.[65] More than 90 percent of the officers surveyed stated that their work had become more stressful in recent years. Among the major causes of this stress were overcrowding and understaffing.[66]

Lack of Support and Respect

COs may feel that senior managers, the media, and the general public neither understand nor respect their profession. This view is reflected in the words of one officer: "We are asked to work in an environment that imposes a heavy personal toll on us, and we get no recognition for it. We do not feel valued by management, and we certainly are not valued by either the inmates or the general public. We're the only ones who understand the difficult environment."[67]

Research in the United States has found that media depictions of correctional officers are most often inaccurate and portray COs negatively.[68] There is some evidence in Canada, however, that COs may underestimate the public's regard for them. In a survey in Alberta (N = 1,200), the large majority of respondents (85 percent) said they respected correctional centre staff for the work they do.[69]

A related source of frustration for COs is the absence of communication with and support from management, which too often develops policies without consulting front-line workers. Uncertainty among officers as to their roles, lack of direction and guidance, and unreasonable expectations of senior management are significant stressors.[70]

The Emphasis on Inmate Rights

A key trend in corrections has been an increasing focus on accountability, the rule of law, and the rights of inmates under the Canadian Charter of Rights and Freedoms. This may lead to COs feeling that the new emphasis on inmate rights has come at the expense of their own rights. Some officers perceive that the inmates are now running the institutions. In the words of one CO: "No two ways about it, we can do nothing to them now. Absolutely nothing. At one point, at least we had the threat of being able to lock them up and charge them, or some type of control. Now you tell them you are going to charge them— they laugh at you."[71]

Correctional officers may also perceive that their jobs have become more onerous due to the increased regulations and reporting requirements and advocates for inmate rights.[72] One provincial correctional officer in Alberta stated, "The human rights, they bring lawyers in and everything, so now discipline is sure less and less. You charge or violate inmates in the system, but in the end you are doing all of the paperwork and you are getting questioned. 'Did you actually see that?' 'Did this actually happen?' 'Did they really say that?'"[73]

Multiple Tasks

The duties of federal COs may include not only patrolling, conducting searches, and intervening in inmate disturbances, but also issuing permits and passes; performing casework and reclassification; briefing volunteers, visitors, and professionals; escorting inmates within the institution; transferring and processing inmates; and answering the telephone. In short, in addition to the requirement to provide security, COs are being called on to play the multiple roles of "nurse, psychologist, parole officer, administrator, police, criminologist, fireman, and teacher."[74] Owing to resource constraints, this multitasking may be even more prevalent among COs in provincial/territorial institutions.

A source of considerable stress is the conflicting demands of casework and security. In the words of one CO:

> *A difficulty is handling the two philosophies of corrections right now, which is security and rehabilitation. Having a caseload and security. The caseload … it's hard to be a guard and hug him in the morning and then mace him in the afternoon because he's been a bad person. Don't laugh, it happens.*[75]

Inadequate Training

A common complaint among COs is that the training they receive is insufficient for the variety of tasks they are required to perform. As a consequence, a considerable amount of learning occurs "on the job." A review of training for federal COs found that training needs and requirements have not kept pace with the increased knowledge and skills required of COs. Given the broad range of tasks that COs perform, it is likely that experience on the job will remain a key feature of the position.

The Impact on Personal Life

Many COs find it difficult to separate their work life from their personal life. At the same time, many of them are unwilling or unable to talk about their work experiences with people outside the profession. In the words of one CO:

> *[The job] screws up your relationships. You limit the friends that you've got. How many people are you going to talk to about [it], other than a cop or an ambulance driver, what kind of mayhem you went through that day … It's indescribable.*[76]

Shift Work

COs generally work rotating shifts. For federal officers, the most common schedule is 12-hour shifts on a 2-day, 2-night, 5-days-off rotation. Shift work often results in loss of sleep and a disruption of the circadian rhythm (or biological clock), which controls the body's sleep, wake, and arousal periods. Disruptions of the circadian rhythm result in a feeling similar to jet lag: fatigue, nausea, irritability, and loss of appetite. Shift workers may be more prone to poor performance, accidents, and health problems.[77]

Shift work can also affect a CO's private life and make the management of family and other personal relationships more difficult. It may limit the opportunities for officers to interact with their children during non-school hours and to participate in community activities. A survey of federal CO1s and CO2s ($N = 2,000$) found that over 70 percent of officers at each level felt that shift work had a negative or very negative impact on their family life. The level of job satisfaction was lower (and stress higher) among those who reported highly negative impacts of shift work on family relations.[78]

The Impact of Prison Conditions

An increase in prison populations has coincided with overcrowding and double-bunking and a rise in violent incidents. These conditions may increase the stress levels of COs and result in an increased number of sick days taken, as well as alcohol and substance abuse. Prison conditions have been found to have a significant impact on the job satisfaction of COs.[79]

There is some evidence that stress levels among COs are related to the specific correctional environment in which the officer is employed. Maximum-security institutions, as well as the more "secure" medium-security facilities, may be more tense environments with, it follows, greater potential for violence both between inmates and against COs by inmates. The stress levels among COs may be particularly high in institutions that house inmates with multifaceted mental health issues, including the five CSC treatment centres that are located across the country. The inmates in these facilities often have multiple needs, including mental health issues, personality disorders, substance-abuse issues, and a history of trauma.[80]

The Impact of Critical Incidents

In addition to organizational and operational stressors, the exposure to potentially dangerous circumstances and to violent incidents plays a significant role in the mental health issues faced by COs.[81]

During the course of their careers, COs may be exposed to a wide variety of critical incidents, including disturbances and riots, hostage takings, inmate murder, inmate self-mutilation and suicide, threats to the officer's safety, and injury to the officer. These incidents may result in symptoms associated with **post-traumatic stress disorder (PTSD)**, an extreme form of critical incident

Post-traumatic stress disorder (PTSD)
An extreme form of critical incident stress that includes nightmares, hypervigilance, intrusive thoughts, and other forms of psychological distress.

stress, the symptoms of which include nightmares, hypervigilance, intrusive thoughts, and other forms of psychological distress.[82] In its most extreme forms, such as are found among combat veterans, sufferers experience flashbacks during which they relive the trauma as if they were there.

As one CO stated:

"I didn't know how to release the stuff I kept dreaming about. You're doing tier count and you're watching a human being die in front of your eyes because he's coughing up lungs and screaming with his eyes for help and there's nothing you can do . . . Even though he's an inmate, he's still human; you're still human."[83]

Research has found that 36 percent of male federal COs are suffering from PTSD, compared to between 1.1 and 3.5 percent of the Canadian general population.[84] These rates are similar to those reported in a U.K. study of COs, which found that 34 percent of COs were afflicted by PTSD. A study of federal COs in Ontario ($N = 122$), conducted over 25 years ago, found that 95 percent had experienced severe impacts on their personal life, including sleep disturbances, nightmares, and exaggerated startle response (i.e., hypervigilance). Only 40 percent of the officers had sought professional help for their problems.[85] It can be anticipated that these rates are even higher today, given the increasing challenges faced by COs. A survey of corrections employees in Saskatchewan ($N = 271$) found that nearly 80 percent of those surveyed had experienced a traumatic event in their work and that 25 percent reported PTSD symptoms. These levels are comparable to those experienced by combat veterans and emergency service personnel.[86]

The results of surveys highlight the need for correctional systems to develop policies for critical incident stress management centred on **critical incident stress debriefing (CISD)**. This technique involves on-scene debriefing of the CO by a trained intervenor after a critical incident has occurred; "defusing" by a mental health professional or trained peer, during which the symptoms of stress are identified and strategies for stress management are provided; a formal critical incident stress debriefing; and, if required, a follow-up critical incident stress debriefing. The objective of CISD is to protect and support the CO, while imparting information and strategies that will help the officer cope with any symptoms of critical incident stress that might later arise.

COs also have access to employee assistance programs, which provide financial support and legal assistance as well as help with substance abuse, mental and physical health, and family- and work-related issues. The culture of COs may be a barrier to accessing these sources of assistance. As one CO stated, "Much like police officers, COs may view any disclosure of stress as "emotional weakness." Another CO commented, "Prison staff learn to apply a thin layer of 'Machismo'" as a result of each incident they respond to. It's like a Band-Aid. But this type of Band-Aid doesn't protect the wound from infection or aid in the healing process. Instead it covers and seals in your emotions and your feelings; otherwise you're weak, a punk, or a sissy."[87]

Critical incident stress debriefing (CISD)
A procedure for assisting COs following a critical incident.

This has often led officers to deny that corrections work has had any impact on their well-being. Officers may also fear that disclosing the mental health challenges they are facing may affect their career prospects.[88]

The stressors that COs experience in their work can have a negative impact on their personal life and can lead to work/life conflicts.[89] One CO stated, "My wife tells me that I've become hard, cold, uncaring. The other day she asked me how I can possibly deal with inmate murders and suicides and not blink an eye. She said, 'Does this come with the job or are you just heartless?'"[90]

As of late-2017, the provinces of Ontario and Manitoba have recognized that front-line responders, including COs, are prone to PTSD and have created protocols to ensure that, in cases of a PTSD diagnosis, treatment is made available.

THE EXPERIENCE OF WOMEN COs

Historically, the role of women in correctional facilities was largely confined to clerical and noncustodial positions. In many institutions, especially provincial and territorial ones, women COs are still far outnumbered by male COs. Women encountered strong resistance from men when they were first hired as COs. Women COs work in a largely male-dominated environment that has traditionally valued toughness and physicality over communication skills and tact.

They were (and often still are) perceived by male co-workers and supervisors as lacking the mental and physical toughness to survive the rigours of institutional life, to control inmates when required, and to back up male officers in crisis situations. In addition, male COs may believe that women are more prone to being victimized and manipulated by inmates. There is also the issue of the privacy of male inmates, especially in relation to frisks and strip searches. In *Conway v. Canada* ((1993) 2 SCR 872), however, the Supreme Court of Canada reaffirmed the right of women to be employed as COs in male institutions.

Research studies have found that the resistance—indeed, sometimes outright hostility—of male officers tends to diminish as women demonstrate their abilities. Research on the experiences of women COs in the United States has revealed that they have a positive impact on the management of inmates in maximum-security institutions, that they are less likely than their male counterparts to be assaulted by inmates, and that they are less confrontational and often better able to defuse explosive situations.[91]

Historically, internal surveys conducted by the CSC have found a high incidence of sexual harassment, discrimination, and abuse of authority in many federal institutions. And there is evidence that this continues in many correctional institutions. A former woman federal CO referred to a "hush-or-hurt culture," where women victims of harassment often did not report it due to fear of reprisal.[92] In one case, allegations of harassment and related threats at the federal Edmonton Institution reflected what employees referred to as a "culture of fear," where women COs did not feel safe.

A series of sexually explicit phone calls between male COs, relating to women COs in the institution, were downplayed by authorities, and the women were not initially informed of the sexually explicit conversations. A survey revealed that 53 percent of the staff at Edmonton Institution had experienced harassment and 75 percent indicated that the source of the harassment was a co-worker.[93]

Similarly, gay and lesbian COs may experience harassment from co-workers. A gay CO at the Ottawa-Carleton Detention Centre resigned his position after being subjected to repeated bullying, taunting, and homophobic comments.[94] In 2013, the former CO was awarded $100,000 after the provincial Grievance Settlement Board determined that the provincial government had failed to protect him from a "poisoned" workplace.

THE ROLE OF CORRECTIONAL OFFICER UNIONS

The role that CO unions play in correctional policy at the federal and provincial/territorial levels in Canada has remained largely unexamined. Unions in the United States and Canada have lobbied effectively for changes in laws relating to mandatory minimum sentences. The U.S. unions, however, may be impeding the shift away from mass incarceration as a result of their lobbying for more correctional facilities and for restrictions on the movements of high-risk offenders.[95]

In Canada, the Union of Canadian Correctional Officers (UCCO; www.ucco-sacc-csn.ca) advocates on behalf of federal COs. Among the issues the UCCO has addressed are inmate attacks on COs with bodily fluids and the impact of Bill C-10 (see Chapter 2). The UCCO was pleased that Bill C-10 contained provisions making it a disciplinary infraction to assault others with bodily fluids. But at the same time, the UCCO opposed many of the bill's provisions, contending that by worsening overcrowding, they will increase the number of inmate-on-inmate attacks as well as inmate assaults on COs. See Class/Group Discussion Exercise 7.1.

SUMMARY

The discussion in this chapter has centred on the pivotal role that COs play in institutions. The provisions for the recruitment and training of COs were examined. It was noted that the authority of COs in the institution is both moral and legal. New COs undergo a period of socialization into the daily life of the institution and must develop functional relations with other COs as well as the inmates. It is possible to develop a typology of COs, based on how they carry out their tasks, how they exercise discretion, and their attitudes toward inmates and other COs.

COs develop accommodative relationships that ensure that order and routine are maintained in the institution. There are instances in which COs have abused their power and authority, often with respect to the excessive use of force against inmates. Given their position in the institution, COs may be susceptible to being compromised, by acting unethically, violating regulations, or engaging in criminal activity.

There are a number of potential sources of stress for COs which, if unaddressed, can affect their mental health. Women COs experience these stressors and may also be the victims of discrimination and harassment by male COs.

KEY POINTS REVIEW

1. The responsibilities of COs have become more complex and challenging in recent years.
2. COs play a pivotal role in correctional institutions.
3. While training for federal COs is standardized and involves online and in-class sessions, there are no nationwide standards for recruiting and training provincial/territorial COs.
4. COs have the most extensive contact with inmates and are in the position to act as change agents in assisting inmates.
5. Among the challenges confronting new COs is learning the subtle, nonverbal cues that will help them interact with inmates and gain the acceptance of their co-workers.
6. COs vary in how they exercise their discretionary authority, in their attitudes toward inmates, and in their level of commitment to the organization.
7. COs develop accommodative relationships with inmates that are characterized by "push–pull" interactions.
8. The authority of COs is both legal and moral, and they use several different types of power to carry out their role in the institution.
9. Research studies have found that some COs are more rule and enforcement oriented, while others rely on communication skills and common sense to solve problems.
10. COs exert various types of power in correctional institutions and, in certain instances, may abuse their power and authority, particularly with respect to the use of force against inmates.
11. There may be among COs a code of silence that protects unprofessional and unlawful behaviour.
12. COs may have strained relationships with correctional administrators, and may hold a dim view of treatment programs.
13. Among the sources of stress for COs are threats to their personal security, a perceived lack of support and respect from corrections

officials and the general public, the impact of the job on their personal lives, and critical incidents.

14. Women COs are susceptible to sexual harassment and discrimination by male COs.

KEY TERM QUESTIONS

1. What is the *normative code of behaviour* of COs, and what factors may mitigate against officer solidarity?

2. Compare and contrast the *custodial agenda* with the *correctional agenda* of COs.

3. What is *post-traumatic stress disorder (PTSD)* and why is it a potential source of stress for COs?

4. Describe *critical incident stress debriefing (CISD)* and its objectives.

CRITICAL THINKING EXERCISES

Critical Thinking Exercise 7.1

Correctional Officer Respect for Inmates

Among the findings from an internal survey conducted by the CSC in 2013 were the following: "Apparently social values around respect toward offenders have not been encouraged within CSC to the same extent as values of respect toward the organization and co-workers—leaving this aspect to each individual's discretion." Responses to the survey also indicated that corrections staff felt that they did not receive sufficient training in how to support and assist inmates.[96]

Your Thoughts?

1. What initiatives might be taken to address these findings?

2. What should systems of corrections do to ensure that inmates are treated with respect?

Critical Thinking Exercise 7.2

A Death in Custody: The Case of Matthew Hines

On May 27, 2015, Matthew Hines, an inmate in Dorchester Penitentiary, a federal prison in New Brunswick, died while in the custody of several COs and medical staff. Read about the case on the Internet, including the following articles:

K. Donkin, "Public must know what happened to Matthew Hines: public safety minister," CBC News, August 24, 2016, http://www.cbc .ca/news/canada/nova-scotia/matthew-hines-dorchester-penitentiary-cape-breton-pepper-spray-prison-1.3734785.

K. Donkin, "Prison guards in N.B. used 'inappropriate' force on inmate, report says," CBC News, August 22, 2016, http://www.cbc.ca/news/thenational/report-says-prison-guards-in-n-b-used-inappropriate-force-on-inmate-1.3731773.

K. Donkin, "Correctional service admits 'staff misconduct' in inmate's death," CBC News, September 23, 2016, http://www.cbc.ca/news/canada/nova-scotia/correctional-service-staff-misconduct-hines-1.3774555.

K. Donkin, "Prison watchdog investigates death of N.B. inmate pepper-sprayed 5 times by guards," CBC News, August 23, 2016. http://www.cbc.ca/news/canada/new-brunswick/prison-death-pepper-spray-1.3728443.

Your Thoughts?

1. From these and other materials you locate, describe the key issues in this case with respect to 1) the inmate Matthew Hines, 2) the response of the COs and medical staff, and 3) the response of the correctional authorities.

2. What actions could have been taken to avoid this incident from occurring in the first place?

3. What lessons are to be learned from this case?

CLASS/GROUP DISCUSSION EXERCISE

Class/Group Discussion Exercise 7.1

Should Correctional Officers Unions be Involved in Political Activities?

In 2015, the union representing federal correctional officers in the Fraser Valley region, east of Vancouver, urged residents in the area not to vote for the Conservative Party in the forthcoming federal election. The Fraser Valley is the location of seven federal correctional facilities housing a total of around 2,000 federal inmates. Members of the union went door-to-door as part of the campaign. The union was upset with the then-Conservative government's punitive penal policies, which increased the number of mandatory sentences (and thereby, potentially, the number of offenders in prison), and reduced inmate programs.[97] Among the comments posted following the article were the following:

> *Good for them! I wouldn't vote Conservative anyway, but hopefully they'll get the message out and change some minds. Best of luck. It would be nice to see some broader news coverage of this. — June 16.*

> *It is a difficult spot, though. While I fully concur with the Union on this issue, I do worry about the consequences for Canada when the civil service becomes anything other than politically neutral. This important principle*

has provided Canada with very good and politically neutral civil service throughout history, and we need to be careful about how it is affected through such activities. — June 16.

Your Thoughts?

1. What is your position on the correctional officer union activities in this case?

MEDIA LINKS

"B.C. Corrections COPAT—Correctional Officer Physical Abilities Test," www.youtube.com/watch?v=ZCIqSiIC-s8

"Shocking Video Released of Canadian Prison Riot," www.youtube.com/watch?v=YLLdJJA6QwY

"Prison Beatings Caught on Video at Ontario and Quebec Jails," http://www.cbc.ca/news/canada/prison-beatings-caught-on-video-at-ontario-and-quebec-jails-1.2426904

"BC Public Service Corrections—North Fraser Pretrial Centre," https://www.youtube.com/watch?v=j8P8qy4lkqU

"Prison Guards and PTSD: High Rates with Little Attention," https://www.youtube.com/watch?v=y3sggkw-X3Y

"Are There Good Correctional Officers? Prison Talk 8.16" (an ex-inmate comments on correctional officers; although it is from the United States, the clip provides some insights into prison life and correctional officer-inmate interaction), https://www.youtube.com/watch?v=16by1GPX2kE

"We Are Also Doing Hard Time," https://www.youtube.com/watch?v=oObCGCWqkDM&feature=youtu.be

"Working at CSC—Why People Love It," http://www.csc-scc.gc.ca/careers/003001-7001-eng.shtml

"Bloody Cells," https://www.youtube.com/watch?v=1R5a4eNCq_A&feature=youtu.be

NOTES

1. A. Liebling, D. Price, and G. Shefer, *The Prison Officer* (New York: Willan, 2011).

2. Ibid.

3. "Training & Appointment," Correctional Service Canada website, May 22, 2014, http://www.csc-scc.gc.ca/careers/003001-3004-eng.shtml.

4. Ibid.

5. "Primary Worker/Kimisinaw," Correctional Service Canada website, May 22, 2014, http://www.csc-scc.gc.ca/careers/003001-3010-eng.shtml.

6. P. Bensimon, *Correctional Officer Recruits During the College Training Period: An Examination* (Ottawa: Correctional Service Canada, 2005), http://www.csc-scc.gc.ca/research/r165-eng.shtml; P. Bensimon, *Correctional Officers and Their First Year: An Empirical Investigation* (Ottawa: Correctional Service Canada, 2005), http://www.csc-scc.gc.ca/research/r179-eng.shtml.

7. J. Lindzon, "I want to be a correctional officer. What will my salary be?" *Globe and Mail*, May 6, 2015, http://www.theglobeandmail.com/report-on-business/careers/career-advice/i-want-to-be-a-correctional-officer-what-will-my-salary-be/article24214927/.

8. Ibid.

9. Deloitte & Touche, *Report on Nova Scotia's Adult Correctional Facilities* (Halifax: Department of Justice, 2008), https://www.novascotia.ca/just/global_docs/Deloitte%20Report%20-%20NS%20Correctional%20Facilities%20Nov08.pdf.

10. "Becoming a Correctional Services Officer," Ontario Ministry of Community Safety and Correctional Services website, February 8, 2016, http://www.mcscs.jus.gov.on.ca/english/corr_serv/careers_in_corr/become_corr_off/COTraining/cs_cotraining.html.

11. M. Welch, *Corrections: A Critical Approach*, 3rd ed. (New York: Routledge, 2011).

12. M.A. Farkas, "The Normative Code Among Correctional Officers: An Exploration of Components and Functions," *Journal of Crime and Justice 20*, no. 1 (1997), 23–36; J.M. Pollock, *Ethical Dilemmas in Criminal Justice*, 8th ed. (Belmont, Calif.: Wadsworth, 2014), pp. 342–43.

13. E.L. Grossi and B.L. Berg, "Stress and Job Dissatisfaction Among Correctional Officers: An Unexpected Finding," *International Journal of Offender Therapy and Comparative Criminology 35*, no. 1 (1991), 73–81.

14. Pollock, *Ethical Dilemmas in Criminal Justice*, p. 356.

15. M.A. Farkas, "A Typology of Correctional Officers," *International Journal of Offender Therapy and Comparative Criminology 44*, no. 4 (2000), 431–49.

16. R. Ricciardelli, "Canadian Prisoners' Perceptions of Correctional Officer Orientations to their occupational responsibilities," *Journal of Crime and Justice 39*, no. 2 (2014), 324–43.

17. Ibid., p. 332.

18. Ibid., p. 332.

19. Ibid., p. 333.

20. Ibid., p. 335.

21. Ibid., p. 335.

22. Ibid.

23. Ibid., p. 336.

24. Ibid., p. 335.

25. S. Tait, "A Typology of Prison Officer Approaches to Care," *European Journal of Criminology 8*, no. 6 (2011), 440–54.

26. K.A. Beijersbergen, A.J.E. Dirkzwager, P.H. van der Laan, and P. Nieuwbeerta "A Social Building? Prison Architecture and Staff—Prisoner Relationships," *Crime & Delinquency 62*, no. 7 (2016), 843–74.

27. M. Weinwrath, *Behind the Walls: Inmates and Correctional Officers on the State of Canadian Prisons* (Vancouver: UBC Press, 2016), p. 177.

28. Ibid., p. 178.

29. D. Spencer and R. Ricciardelli, "'They're a Very Sick Group of Individuals': Correctional Officers, Emotions, and Sex Offenders," *Theoretical Criminology 21*, no. 3 (2017), 380–94.

30. Ibid., p. 8.

31. Ibid., p. 9.

32. K. Kauffman, *Prison Officers and Their World* (Cambridge, Mass.: Harvard University Press, 1988).

33. R. Johnson, *Hard Time: Understanding and Reforming the Prison* (Belmont, Calif.: Wadsworth, 1996).

34. R. Ricciardelli and K. Perry, "Responsivity in Practice: Prison Officer to Prisoner Communication in Canadian Provincial Institutions,"

Journal of Contemporary Criminal Justice 32, no. 4 (2016), 401–25.

35. Ibid., p. 409.

36. S. Poirier (chair), *Decades of Darkness: Moving Towards the Light. A Review of the Prison System in Newfoundland and Labrador* (St. John's, NL: Ministry of Justice, 2008), p. 12, http://www.justice.gov.nl.ca/just/publications/ac_report.pdf.

37. J.M. Yates, *Line Screw: My Twelve Riotous Years Working Behind Bars in Some of Canada's Toughest Jails* (Toronto: McClelland & Stewart, 1993), p. 115.

38. V. Beauregard, V. Chadillon-Farniacci, S. Brochu, and M-M. Cousineau, "Enforcing Institutional Regulations in Prison Settings: The Case of Gambling in Quebec," *International Criminal Justice Review 23*, no. 2 (2013), 170–84.

39. Union of Canadian Correctional Officers, *Towards a Policy for Canada's Penitentiaries: The Evolution of Canada's Prison System and the Transformation of the Correctional Officer's Role (1950–2002)* (Montréal: Author, 2002), p. 123, http://www.ucco-sacc-csn.ca/wp-content/uploads/2015/05/Towards-a-policy-for-Canada_s-Penitentiaries1.pdf.

40. Liebling et al., *The Prison Officer*.

41. Office of the Correctional Investigator, *Annual Report 2012–2013* (Ottawa: Author, 2013), p. 9, http://www.oci-bec.gc.ca/cnt/rpt/pdf/annrpt/annrpt20122013-eng.pdf.

42. Ibid.

43. Ibid.

44. Ombudsman Saskatchewan, *My Brother's Keeper: A Review of Electronic Control Devices in Saskatchewan Correctional Centres Housing Male Inmates* (Regina: Author, 2008), p. 23, http://www.ombudsman.sk.ca/uploads/document/files/my-brothers-keeper-en.pdf.

45. R. Tewksbury and S.C. Collins, "Aggression Levels Among Correctional Officers: Reassessing Sex Differences," *The Prison Journal 86*, no. 3 (2006), 327–43.

46. Pollock, *Ethical Dilemmas in Criminal Justice*, p. 344.

47. Ibid., p. 343.

48. T.E. Barnhart, "Deviance and Corruption," Corrections.com, February 15, 2010. http://www.corrections.com/articles/23579-deviance-and-corruption.

49. H. Crichton and R. Ricciardelli, "Shifting Grounds: Experiences of Canadian Provincial Correctional Officers," *Criminal Justice Review 41*, no. 4 (2016), 427–45 at 436.

50. G. Keinan and A. Malach-Pines, "Stress and Burnout Among Prison Personnel: Sources, Outcomes, and Intervention Strategies," *Criminal Justice and Behavior 34*, no. 3 (2007), 380–98.

51. E.G. Lambert, N. L. Hogan, I. Altheimer, S. Jiang, and M.T. Stevenson, "The Relationship Between Burnout and Support for Punishment and Treatment: A Preliminary Examination," *International Journal of Offender Therapy and Comparative Criminology 54*, no. 6 (2010), 1004–22.

52. E.G. Lambert, N.L. Hogan, M.O. Griffin, and T. Kelley, "The Correctional Staff Burnout Literature," *Criminal Justice Studies 28*, no. 4 (2015), 397–443.

53. C. Finney, E. Stergiopoulos, J. Hensel, S. Bonato, and C.S. Dewa, "Organizational Stressors Associated with Job Stress and Burnout in Correctional Officers: A Systematic Review," *BMC Public Health 13*, no. 1 (2013), 1–13.

54. E.G. Lambert, S.M. Barton-Bellessa, and N.L. Hogan, "The Consequences of Emotional Burnout Among Correctional Staff," *Sage Open 15*, no. 2 (2015), 1–15.

55. Ibid.

56. Finney et al., "Organizational Stressors Associated with Job Stress and Burnout in Correctional Officers."

57. R. Ricciardelli and A. Gazso, "Investigating Threat Perception Among Correctional Officers in the Canadian Provincial Correctional System," *Qualitative Sociology Review IX*, no. 3 (2013), 96–120 at 106.

58. Ibid.

59. Ibid., p. 111.

60. J.A. Gordon, B. Proulx, and P.H. Grant, "Trepidation Among the 'Keepers': Gendered Perceptions of Fear and Risk of Victimization Among Correctional Officers," *American Journal of Criminal Justice 38*, no. 2 (2013), 245–65.

61. J. Gordon and T. Baker, "Examining Correctional Officers' Fear of Victimization by Inmates," *Criminal Justice Policy Review*, advance online publication, June 4, 2015, at 17.

62. W. Millson, "Predictors of Work Stress Among Correctional Officers," *Forum on Corrections Research 14*, no. 1 (2002), 45–7, http://www.csc-scc.gc.ca/research/forum/e141/141l_e.pdf.

63. M. Brosnahan, "Record-high prison numbers sparking violence," CBC News, August 27, 2012, http://www.cbc.ca/news/canada/record-high-prison-numbers-sparking-violence-1.1260764.

64. L.F. Alarid, "Risk Factors for Potential Occupational Exposure to HIV: A Study of Correctional Officers," *Journal of Criminal Justice 37*, no. 2 (2009), 114–22.

65. N. Boyd, *Abnormal Working Conditions: Correctional Officers in British Columbia* (Burnaby: B.C. Government Employees Union, 2011), http://www.bcgeu.ca/sites/default/files/FINAL%20Boyd-Report-2011.pdf.

66. Ibid.

67. Joint Committee on Federal Correctional Officers, *Joint Committee Report on Federal Correctional Officers* (Ottawa: Public Service Alliance of Canada, Treasury Board Secretariat, and Correctional Service Canada, 2002), p. 54, https://opseu.org/sites/default/files/2000_federal_report.pdf.

68. S.G. Vickovic, M.L. Griffin, and H.F. Fradella, "Depictions of Correctional Officers in Newspaper Media: An Ethnographic Content Analysis," *Criminal Justice Studies 26*, no. 4 (2013), 455–77.

69. Alberta Solicitor General and Public Security, *Survey of Albertans* (Edmonton: Author, 2011), http://open.alberta.ca/publications/alberta-solicitor-general-and-public-security-survey-of-albertans.

70. N.L. Hogan, E.G. Lambert, M. Jenkins, and S. Wambold "Impact of Occupational Stressors on Correctional Staff Organizational Commitment: A Preliminary Study," *Journal of Contemporary Criminal Justice 22*, no. 1 (2006), 44–62.

71. M. Harris, *Con Game: The Truth About Canada's Prisons* (Toronto: McClelland and Stewart, 2002), p. 49.

72. Weinwrath, *Behind the Walls: Inmates and Correctional Officers on the State of Canadian Prisons*, p. 191.

73. Ibid.

74. Environics Research Group, *Focus Group Report to the Joint Committee of the Public Service Alliance of Canada, Treasury Board, and Correctional Service of Canada on the Jobs and Working Environment of Federal Correctional Officers and RCMP Officers* (Ottawa: Public Service Alliance of Canada, Treasury Board, and the Correctional Service Canada, 2000), p. 7, https://opseu.org/sites/default/files/2000_federal_report.pdf.

75. *Joint Committee Report on Federal Correctional Officers*, Treasury Board of Canada Secretariat, 2017.

76. Environics Research Group, *Focus Group Report to the Joint Committee*, p. 15.

77. D.X. Swenson, D. Waseleski, and R. Hartl "Shift Work and Correctional Officers: Effects and Strategies for Adjustment," *Journal of Correctional Health Care 14*, no. 4 (2008) 299–310.

78. B. Grant, "The Impact of Working Rotating Shifts on the Family Life of Correctional Staff," *Forum on Corrections Research 7*, no. 2 (1995), 40–42; R.A. Venne, "The Impact of the Compressed Work Week on Absenteeism: The Case of Ontario Prison Guards on a Twelve Hour Shift," *Industrial Relations 52*, no. 2 (1997), 382–400.

79. V.W. Mahfood, W. Pollock, and D. Longmire "Leave It at the Gate: Job Stress and Satisfaction in Correctional Staff," *Criminal Justice Studies 26*, no. 3 (2013), 308–25.

80. B.A. Adam, "PTSD high among prison workers, union says," *Saskatoon Star Phoenix*, April 18, 2016, http://thestarphoenix.com/

news/local-news/ptsd-high-among-prison-workers-union-says.

81. C. Spinaris, M. Denhof, and G. Morton, *Impact of Traumatic Exposure on Corrections Professionals* [white paper], December 21, 2013, retrieved from National Institute of Corrections, https://info.nicic.gov/virt/sites/info.nicic.gov.virt/files/06Impact_of_Traumatic_Exposure.pdf.

82. L. Rosine, "Critical Incident Stress and Its Management in Corrections," in *Forensic Psychology—Policy and Practice in Corrections*, eds., T.A. Leis, L.L. Motiuk, and J.R.P. Ogloff (Ottawa: Correctional Service Canada, 1995), 213–26.

83. D. Lisitsina, "Prison guards can never be weak": the hidden PTSD crisis in America's jails," *The Guardian*, May 20, 2015, https://www.theguardian.com/us-news/2015/may/20/corrections-officers-ptsd-american-prisons.

84. G. Galloway, "PTSD affects 36 percent of male prison officers, federal data reveal," *Globe and Mail*, July 27, 2016, http://www.theglobeandmail.com/news/politics/ptsd-prevalent-among-male-prison-officers-federal-data-reveal/article31145169/.

85. L. Rosine, "Exposure to Critical Incidents: What Are the Effects on Canadian Correctional Officers?" *Forum on Corrections Research* 4 no. 1 (1992), 31–37, http://www.csc-scc.gc.ca/research/forum/e041/e041m-eng.shtml.

86. B.L. Stadnyk, "PTSD in Corrections Employees in Saskatchewan," M.A. thesis, University of Regina, 2002, http://rpnascom.jumpstartdev.com/sites/default/files/PTSDInCorrections.pdf.

87. Spinaris et al., *Impact of Traumatic Exposure on Corrections Professionals*, p. 5.

88. Lisitsina, "Prison guards can never be weak."

89. G. Kinman, A.J. Clements, and J. Hart, "Working Conditions, Work-Life Conflict, and Well-Being in UK Prison Officers," *Criminal Justice and Behavior 44*, no. 2 (2017), 226–39.

90. Spinaris et al., *Impact of Traumatic Exposure on Corrections Professionals*, p. 7.

91. K.A. Cheeseman and R. A. Downey, "Talking 'Bout My Generation: The Effect of 'Generation' on Correctional Employee Perceptions of Work Stress and Job Satisfaction," *Prison Journal 92*, no. 1 (2011), 24–44.

92. M. Warnica, "Edmonton prison guards' taped sexual phone chats highlight 'culture of fear,'" CBC News, November 24, 2016, http://www.cbc.ca/news/canada/edmonton/edmonton-prison-guards-taped-sexual-phone-chats-highlight-culture-of-fear-1.3865242.

93. Ibid.

94. J. Rankin, "Gay Ontario jail guard Bob Ranger suffered poisoned workplace," *Toronto Star*, May 18, 2013, https://www.thestar.com/business/2013/11/18/gay_ontario_jail_guard_bob_ranger_suffered_poisoned_workplace.html.

95. J. Page, "Prison Officer Unions and the Perpetuation of the Penal Status Quo," *Criminology and Public Policy 10*, no. 3 (2011) 735–70.

96. W. Campbell, "Prison guards lack, 'common understanding' on basic respect for inmates: Survey," *Canadian Press*, March 31, 2013, https://www.theglobeandmail.com/news/national/prison-guards-lack-common-understanding-on-respect-for-inmates-survey/article10599481/.

97. T. Olsen, "Fraser Valley prison guards take political stance," *Mission City Record*, June 16, 2015, http://www.missioncityrecord.com/news/307653941.html.

DOING TIME: THE EXPERIENCE OF INMATES

CHAPTER OBJECTIVES

- Provide a general profile of inmate populations.
- Discuss the experience of inmates entering and living inside correctional institutions.
- Discuss the inmate social system, the inmate code, and the extent to which these are operative in correctional institutions.
- Describe how inmates attempt to cope with incarceration.
- Describe the challenges that confront offenders serving long-term sentences.
- Discuss the patterns of violence and exploitation among inmates and the strategies that inmates use to reduce their risk of being victimized.
- Describe the challenges that confront the inmate family.
- Discuss the inmate grievance system and the work of provincial ombudspersons and the Office of the Correctional Investigator.
- Discuss the issues surrounding self-injurious behaviour and suicide among inmates in correctional institutions.
- Comment on the issues that arise relating to inmate rights in prison.

A GENERAL PROFILE OF INMATE POPULATIONS

Offenders confined in correctional institutions tend to be male, young, single, poorly educated, and marginally skilled. They are disproportionately Indigenous and Black and are likely to have lived unstable lives. Many were raised in dysfunctional families and experienced traumatic events, including family violence. Nearly one-half of inmates report a history of physical, sexual, and/or emotional abuse during their childhood.[1]

Their problem-solving skills are minimal. Most of them are serving time in provincial/territorial institutions, and more than half of their sentences are for less than one month.[2]

Many inmates were homeless or under-housed prior to their incarceration.[3] A large percentage have a lengthy criminal history. Their treatment

CORRECTIONS PERSPECTIVE 8.1

Prison Nurse

You see a lot of really sad things. And it's very challenging too because, obviously, it's a jail, we have people that come in that have done terrible things. That have done awful things that turn your stomach, that make you feel sick. But you have to treat them the same way that you treat any other inmate in there. You have to treat somebody who molested children, you have to provide them with the same access to healthcare and the same rights as somebody who blew over, or was a breach of probation, or stole a pack of smokes from Mac's. It's hard. It's really hard to do that. As a nurse, we have to treat everyone equally. Regardless of what kind of a person you might think they are that should have nothing to do with your job as a nurse. If you're unable to do that, you shouldn't work in corrections.

Source: T. Thompson, "What It's Like Working as a Prison Nurse," *Vice*, June 8, 2016, http://www.vice .com/en_ca/read/what-its-like-working-as-a-prison-nurse. Reprinted with permission from Vice Studio Canada Inc.

needs are high: Many of them suffer from alcohol and/or drug addiction, and many have a mental impairment or other affliction such as fetal alcohol spectrum disorder (FASD).

Generally speaking, women offenders share with their male counterparts a marginalized background of poverty, alcohol and/or drug dependency, limited education, and minimal employment skills. In addition, women offenders may have suffered sexual and physical abuse and may be responsible for children or stepchildren (see Chapter 12).

These offenders often have few connections to "mainstream" Canadian society. In this way, they are very similar to their predecessors in previous centuries. They have needs and present risks that place significant demands on systems of corrections, and especially on provincial/territorial institutions, which tend to have fewer resources than their federal counterparts and must attempt to respond in a highly compressed time frame.

Indigenous Offenders

Indigenous people are over-represented in federal and in provincial/territorial institutions and the number of Indigenous offenders in custody has increased significantly in recent years (see Chapter 13). The average age of admission to federal correctional facilities is lower for Indigenous offenders than for non-Indigenous offenders. In 2014–15, 50 percent of Indigenous offenders were under the age of 30, compared to 36 percent of non-Indigenous offenders.[4]

Black Offenders

Only recently has the dramatic rise in the number of Black Canadians in federal prisons been the subject of concern. While Black Canadians comprise 3 percent of the general population, they represent 10 percent of the federal inmate population. This is a 70 percent increase from a decade ago.[5] Blacks are also over-represented in many provincial institutions. In Nova Scotia, for example, Blacks represent only 2.1 percent of the population, but 14 percent of all provincial prison admissions.[6] The majority of Black federal inmates are incarcerated in Ontario and Québec, and 96 percent are male. Approximately 50 percent are under the age of 30; nearly 50 percent are foreign-born, with the largest percentage being from Jamaica; and 50 percent are incarcerated for a violent or drug-related offence. Black inmates are twice as likely than the general inmate population to have a gang affiliation, although the majority (80 percent) are not gang members.[7]

A variety of explanations have been offered for this dramatic increase, including poverty, racism, racial profiling by police, and disproportionate sentencing for Black-Canadian offenders as compared to Whites committing similar crimes.[8]

Figure 8.1 presents a breakdown of the federal prison population in 2016. Note the high percentages of Indigenous and Black offenders in relation to their percentages in the Canadian population (Indigenous people, 4.3 percent; Black, 3 percent). A key attribute of Canadian inmate populations is diversity. This has implications for institutional policies and practices; for the training provided to corrections staff, including COs; for correctional programming; and for the inmates themselves.

Gender Identity and Sexual Orientation

Recall Figure 3.4 in Chapter 3, which depicts the external influences on correctional institutions. Events in the larger community can have an impact on correctional policies and life inside prisons. The issue of gender and sexual identity of inmates is an excellent example. As the LGBTQ community secures rights in Canadian society, so too, it is argued, should offenders who are incarcerated.

In Canada, governments and corrections authorities are in the early stages of giving attention to the needs of transgendered inmates. Historically, transgendered persons and others who identified as non-gender were assessed based on their primary sexual characteristics. This often resulted in these inmates being subjected to violence and intimidation, resulting in them being placed in segregation, which, as discussed in this chapter, has its own negative impacts.[9] In 2015, Ontario became the first jurisdiction to implement a policy whereby inmates will be assessed and housed based on their gender identity, rather than their anatomy.[10] This was followed the same year by British Columbia. In 2017, the CSC announced that inmates would be placed in institutions based on their gender identity rather than their genitalia. It is likely that other provincial/territorial correctional authorities will follow suit.

Figure 8.1

Federal Inmate Population, 2016

Total inmate population: 14,615 (average daily count)
Inmate Population Diversity

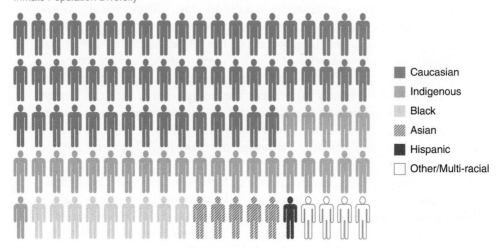

Caucasian

Indigenous

Black

Asian

Hispanic

Other/Multi-racial

$111,202
Average annual cost (2013–14) of incarcerating a male inmate
(women inmates cost twice as much)

1 in 4
inmates are Indigenous
(36% of women inmates are Indigenous)

1 in 4
inmates are over the age of 50

Almost 60%
of inmates are classified as medium security

1 in 5
inmates are serving a life sentence

More than half
of all women inmates have an identified mental health need
(compared to 26% of male inmates)

4 in 10
inmates are serving a sentence of 2 to 4 years

Source: From Office of the Correctional Investigator, 2016, *Annual Report, 2015–2016,* http://www.oci-bec. gc.ca/cnt/rpt/pdf/annrpt/annrpt20152016-eng.pdf. Reprinted by permission of the Office of the Correctional Investigator.

It can be anticipated that the authorities will come under increasing pressure to ensure that the rights and security of this group of inmates are protected. Some jurisdictions, including B.C., have produced materials for transgendered inmates (https://prisonjusticedotorg.files.wordpress.com/2012/11/trans-rights-federal1.pdf). The coping strategies of these inmates are only now beginning to be studied and understood.[11]

THE HEALTH OF INMATE POPULATIONS

The overall health status of inmates is poor compared with the general population as measured by a range of indicators including mortality, mental health, substance use, communicable diseases, and sexual and reproductive health.[12] For federally sentenced men:

- Eighty percent have a serious substance abuse problem.
- Over 16 percent are diagnosed with latent tuberculosis.
- Twenty percent have cardiovascular conditions.
- Over 34 percent have a head injury.
- Sixty-four percent are overweight or obese.[13]

Health data on provincial inmates in Ontario indicates the following:

- *Hepatitis C*: Rate is 28 percent, compared to 0.8 percent in the general population.
- *HIV*: Rate is 1.2 percent, which is seven to ten times higher than the Canadian population.
- *Mental health issues*: Two to three times more prevalent than in the general population.
- *Mortality*: Inmates die of natural causes 15 years younger than people in the community.[14]

A study ($N = 125$) conducted in a provincial institution in Ontario found that many of the inmates did not have access to adequate primary health care prior to their incarceration and had more unmet health care needs than the general Canadian population (54 percent versus 8.8 percent in the general population).[15]

A feature of many correctional institutions is the widespread prescribing of psychotropic drugs to inmates. An investigation by the OCI found that the prescribing rates for inmates (30 percent) were much higher than for the general Canadian population (8 percent). The most commonly prescribed drugs were anti-depressants. Women inmates were prescribed drugs at a much higher rate than their male counterparts.[16]

GOING INSIDE

> *I remember the day that I came in; the first time I went to the cafeteria and I could feel a hundred sets of eyes on me. I could see everybody wondering who you are, what you're in for, how long you're doing.*[17]

The specific impact that entry into prison has on the individual offender depends on a variety of factors, including his or her personality, offence history, and previous incarcerations. First-time offenders may experience severe culture shock. See the documentary film, *How to Prepare for Prison*, listed in the Media Links section at the end of this chapter. The film, produced by TV Ontario, follows three persons facing prison for the first time.

Conversely, those offenders with long criminal histories and previous confinements are likely to be relatively unaffected. For these inmates, the experience of confinement is well-known, as are many of the correctional officers

(COs) and inmates in the facility. Indeed, returning to prison may be more of a homecoming than a banishment. For the uninitiated inmate, however, adjusting to prison life can be stressful and frightening.

Regardless of background, the individual on entering prison is materially and psychologically stripped down. This involves a series of **status degradation ceremonies**, which include the issuing of prison clothing, the assignment of an identification number, the loss of most personal possessions, and the end of unhindered communication with the outside community.[18] These are the mechanisms by which the offender is moved from the community, with its attendant freedoms, to the world of the prison, with its rules, regulations, informal economy, and social system.

It can be argued that many of those who are entering correctional institutions have already had their "status" degraded, through a life of poverty, addiction, mental health problems, and dysfunctional environments. Degradation is closely associated with marginalization, and the above-noted profile of offenders suggests that it is persons from vulnerable groups who are most likely to end up incarcerated. As one long-time inmate related to Canadian corrections scholar Rose Ricciardelli, "I've done ten federal sentences. I've got thirty-six years of substance abuse correlated to thirty-two years of incarceration in total since the age of twelve."[19]

All incoming inmates are provided with a copy of the institution's regulations and with an orientation; beyond that, each inmate is left to their own devices (and wits) when it comes to adjusting to life inside and to developing a survival strategy. Below is part of the advice one inmate gave another who had just arrived at Millhaven, a federal facility in Ontario:

> *Drugs and alcohol are everywhere and I urge you to avoid that trip. Ninety percent of all killings revolve around the dope scene. . . . Don't accept anything from anyone, because you don't want to put yourself in a position where you'll have to repay the favour. Nothing is free. It's in your best interest to avoid cliques. You'll be spending a lot of time on your own—it's much safer that way. . . . Don't encourage conversation with anyone. Be brief and polite. . . . Don't promise anyone anything. . . . Stay quiet and mind your own business.[20]*

Unfortunately, though systems of corrections have perfected the mechanisms for transforming citizens into inmates, there are no "status restoration" ceremonies at the end of confinement that might convert them back into citizens. Chapter 11 explores the consequences of this for the reintegration of offenders released from correctional institutions.

LIVING INSIDE

> *The cells are filthy. The walls are pocked with the carcasses of dead flies. During the day, the roaches visit, at night the mice. The door and door frames to the cells are solid steel, and every time they close, steel against steel,*

Status degradation ceremonies The processing of offenders into correctional institutions whereby the offender is psychologically and materially stripped of possessions that identify them as a member of the "free society."

the sound is deafening. It seems as if there is a contest among the guards to determine who can make the doors bang loudest on closing. A constant reminder, if you need one, of where you are and the role you have to play.[21]

In Corrections File 8.1, a former inmate on remand describes the daily routine in an Ontario provincial institution.

CORRECTIONS FILE 8.1

A Typical Day in the Life of a Prisoner on Remand in Ontario

6:00 a.m., Wake-up: You are woken up in your prison cell, designed for one person, and look over at the other one or maybe even two cellmates you have. If you have another cellmate, you may have to step over one sleeping on the floor to use the uncovered, stainless steel toilet. Forget privacy. This is also where you eat your meals.

Range time: For several hours during the day, you are locked out of your cell for "range time" with all of the other prisoners in your unit. The range is one big common area cell, that all of the individual prisoner cells open into. It is typically quite noisy, and you might pass the time playing cards or watching TV. This is your chance to use the phone. Usually the guards are outside of the range, looking in. Note: Prisoners in segregation and protective custody can spend up to 23 hours a day isolated in their cells.

Bernard Weil/Toronto Star via Getty Images

The interior of a jail cell in the Toronto South Detention Centre

(continued)

Yard time and/or programming: Provincial prisons do not offer recreational programming, and have not for some time. At best, prisoners receive about 20 minutes a day for yard time or "fresh air." The availability of programming options in prisons for remand prisoners varies across institutions, but often Alcoholics Anonymous and Narcotics Anonymous are available. Prisoners are also entitled to religious services where requested. Work opportunities inside are very limited, and tend to only be available for sentenced prisoners.

Visits: Depending on what day of the week it is—visitation hours vary—you may be entitled to have a visit with a loved one. If you are in a prison that is far away from your home, it is likely much more difficult for them to get out to see you, and even then you can only speak through a telephone and see each other through a glass wall. As part of your time out of your cell each day, you are afforded a shower. Prisoners are given a toothbrush, toothpaste, and shower gel, which functions as both soap and shampoo.

Dinner and lockdown: You are then returned to your cell for the nightly lockdown. You are most likely served a "cook-chilled" dinner—food that is prepared in a factory and re-heated in the prison kitchen—which is served to you in your cell. If you require special dietary considerations for religious or medical reasons, you will be accommodated. You are locked in your cell for the rest of the evening with your cellmates, until you fall asleep.

You are woken up the next morning and do it all over again.

Source: John Howard Society of Ontario, 2013, "A Day in the Life of a Prisoner in Ontario," http://johnhoward .on.ca/wp-content/uploads/2014/09/counter-point-3-a-day-in-the-life-of-a-prisoner-in-ontario.pdf. Reprinted by permission of the John Howard Society of Ontario.

The Pains of Imprisonment

If I come out at fifty-six, as a thirty-one-year-old, after twenty-five years in prison, I'll be the same mental age as my children. How do you deal with that? Assuming that I make it through this sentence, if I'm fortunate enough to, and I pray that I am, I don't want to die any more than any other person, I like living just as much as anybody else and if I make it through, I still wouldn't see my children. I would make a point of not seeing them. It's far better for them to have me not interfere with their life in any way, shape, or form.[22]

Pains of imprisonment
The deprivations experienced by inmates confined in correctional institutions, including the loss of autonomy, privacy, security, and freedom of movement and association.

A core concept in understanding the carceral experience is the **pains of imprisonment.** In *Society of Captives*, his classic study of a maximum-security prison, Gresham Sykes identified a number of deprivations that inmates experience. These included the loss of liberty, loss of access to goods and services, and loss of access to heterosexual relationships, as well as the loss of personal autonomy and personal security.[23]

Of all the pains of imprisonment, the loss of liberty is perhaps the most devastating for most offenders, especially when we consider that our society places a high premium on citizens' rights and freedoms. In prison, inmates must find ways to cope with the loneliness, boredom, and hopelessness associated with the loss of freedom. Although Canada's correctional systems operate family visit programs, many inmates are not visited by anyone. An inmate may go for years without receiving a letter, much less a personal visit. The pains of imprisonment may be especially acute for Indigenous inmates, who are often incarcerated hundreds or even thousands of kilometres from their home community (see Chapter 13).

The pains of imprisonment are also brought about by correctional policies and practices. Pains and insecurities are associated with indeterminate sentences, which leave inmates uncertain when they will be released from confinement and what the conditions will be. The inconsistent application of institutional regulations by COs, risk assessments that categorize inmates and that result in loss of personal integrity, and the dangers associated with institutional decisions, all contribute to insecurity in individual inmates.[24] In newer correctional institutions, the use of high-tech surveillance has made the experience of incarceration "'deeper' and more burdensome . . . less directly oppressive, but more gripping—*lighter but tighter*."[25]

THE INMATE SOCIAL SYSTEM

Every correctional institution has an **inmate social system**, often referred to as the *inmate subculture*. For decades, criminologists have attempted to determine the origins, components, and functions of the inmate social system. These efforts have provided insights into prison life and the experience of incarceration. Two explanations have long been offered for the evolution of inmate social systems: the **deprivation theory**, which holds that the inmate social system exists to provide inmates with access to illicit goods and services, and the **importation theory**, which holds that the attitudes and behaviours that characterize the inmate social system are imported into the institution by offenders who had criminal careers on the outside.[26]

Research studies have found that both theories are useful for understanding the origins of these systems, with the combined impact referred to as the **integration model**.[27]

A number of other concepts can help us understand the inmate social system. One of these is **prisonization**, defined as the process whereby inmates become socialized into the norms, values, and culture of the prison.[28] This is not a uniform process; those inmates with extensive carceral experience are likely to already have developed antisocial, criminally oriented attitudes and behaviours. Offenders are said to be **institutionalized** when they have become prisonized to such a degree that they are unable to function in the outside, free community. Many of these persons are **state-raised offenders**; that is, they have spent most of their youth and adult lives confined in correctional institutions.

Inmate social system
The patterns of interaction and the relationships that exist among inmates confined in correctional institutions; often referred to as the *inmate subculture*.

Deprivation theory
An explanation that holds that the inmate social system develops as a consequence of inmates' attempts to mitigate the pains of imprisonment.

Importation theory
An explanation that holds that the inmate social system develops as a consequence of pre-prison attitudes and behaviours that are brought by inmates into the institution.

Integration model
An explanation of inmate behaviour inside correctional institutions that considers both the environmental features of the institution and the attributes of the individual offender as affecting behaviour.

Prisonization
The process by which inmates become socialized into the norms, values, and culture of the prison.

Institutionalized
Inmates who have become prisonized to such a degree that they are unable to function in the outside, free community.

State-raised offenders
Inmates who have spent most of their youth and adult lives confined in correctional institutions.

The longer an inmate is confined, the more difficult it may be for that person to retain prosocial attitudes and behaviours, especially when confined with offenders with even more hardened criminal orientations.

A major challenge confronting correctional systems is preventing offenders from becoming so immersed in the prison's culture that the efforts of correctional staff to promote positive values and behaviours cannot succeed. Another challenge is how to "unprisonize" inmates as they move closer to their release date. Unfortunately, many of the attitudes and values that become embedded in inmate social systems are antithetical to those of the outside, law-abiding community.

Inmate Sexual Orientation and Gender Identity

LGBTQ inmates may face challenges in their interaction with staff and other inmates in correctional institutions although there has been little research into the issues surrounding sexual orientation and gender identity in inmate populations. While there are no published Canadian studies, research in the U.S. has found that LGBTQ inmates may be targeted for physical and sexual abuse and may also be deprived of rights given to other inmates, including visitation.[29]

Interviews with a sample ($N = 56$) of federal offenders who had served time in federal institutions in Ontario revealed that the prison is largely a homophobic environment, the study finding that "prisoners' attitudes toward homosexuality are overwhelmingly negative and conversations about sexuality are laced with derogatory language directed toward gay men."[30]

The Inmate Code

Inmate code
A set of behavioural rules that govern interactions among inmates and with institutional staff.

Another core component of the inmate social system is the **inmate code**, defined as a set of rules governing interactions with other inmates and with institutional staff.[31] Canadian research has identified the following tenets of the inmate code: (1) never rat on a con and don't get friendly with the staff; (2) be dependable (not loyal); (3) follow daily behavioural rules or else; (4) I won't see you, don't see me, and shut up already; and (5) be fearless or at least act tough.[32] Research has found that inmates give at least verbal adherence to the tenets of the inmate code, regardless of whether they and other inmates' behaviour may be to the contrary.[33] A primary reason that inmates adhere to the code is to mitigate their risk of being victimized, rather than for solidarity.[34]

One inmate described doing your own time as follows:

> It means keep yourself separate from everything and everybody. Don't comment, interfere, or accept favours. Understand that you are "fresh meat" and need to learn the way of the joint. You have to deal with the "Vikings" (slobs, applied to both guards and cons), "booty bandits" (someone

looking for ass to fuck), and the "boss," "hook," "grey suit" or "cookie" (all terms for prisons officials of various ranks) without "jeffing" (sucking up) to the staff. You have to deal with other cons who want you as a "punk" or a "fuck boy." Anybody can be carrying a "shank" (homemade knife) made out of a toothbrush and a razor blade or a piece of sharpened steel. Probably the more innocent someone looks, the more you have to worry.[35]

A number of **social (or argot) roles** are associated with the inmate social system. These roles are based on the inmate's friendship networks, sentence length, current and previous offences, degree of at least verbal support for the inmate code, and participation in illegal activities such as gambling and drug distribution.

For example, "square johns" exhibit prosocial behaviour and a positive attitude toward staff and the administration. "Right guys," by contrast, are antisocial and have a negative attitude toward authority. "Snitches" ("rats" or "squealers") play a risky game of providing correctional staff with information about other inmates and their activities.[36] That these types of roles exist in inmate populations is strong evidence that the inmate code is not the defining feature of inmate behaviour. In fact, inmate relations are characterized by considerable fear, intimidation, violence, and manipulation; how much this is so depends on the "vibe" of the particular correctional institution and the types of offenders housed in it.

A related feature of inmate society is its specialized vocabulary: A "bit" is the inmate's sentence (e.g., a five-year "bit"); a "beef" is the crime committed; a "fish" is a new inmate; and a "goof" is an inmate who behaves inappropriately in the institution—for example, who violates the inmate-imposed prohibition against whistling anywhere in the facility. Most inmates pay at least lip service to the code, but even when they do, an inmate's greatest source of danger is other inmates. It can be anticipated that adherence to the code is more prevalent in high-security institutions, where inmates are likely to be prison veterans with more entrenched criminal attitudes and behaviours.

Contributing to the lack of loyalty and solidarity among inmates is the rat (or snitch) system, by which inmates improve their own position and prospects with COs and the administration at the expense of fellow inmates. Reflecting on the breakdown of the inmate code, a provincial inmate commented, "The unwritten rules of jail are basically gone. There's so much rattin' and shit on these ranges. It's fuckin sickening."[37]

Inmates and correctional staff distinguish between "convicts" and "inmates" (or "new school kids"). The latter are perceived as not respecting the traditional inmate social system. As a deputy warden in a federal correctional facility stated, "These 'new school kids' think nothing of going into another inmate's cell in groups of four or five and punching out the inmate and taking his TV. That would never happen in the past, and it makes life in the institution much more unpredictable than in previous years" (personal communication with C.T. Griffiths). This view was echoed by a provincial correctional officer:

Social (or argot) roles
Roles that inmates assume based on their friendship networks, sentence length, and other factors related to their criminal history and activities in the institution.

I think that it is there, but definitely not as big as before. Years back, there used to be an inmate code of conduct and they respected each other's privacy. Now, there is a very limited code because they are pretty much stealing from each other—unheard of back in, say the early eighties.[38]

Another ex-inmate stated, "In the old days, you fought one guy if you had a problem with somebody. If you lost, you just licked your wounds. Now, gangs attack."[39]

Status and Power among Inmates

The days when one inmate "boss" controlled an entire population in an institution are over. That said, there is still a hierarchy of status and power among inmates, with higher status being accorded to inmates who are serving life sentences, who are intelligent and are able to articulate the concerns and issues of the inmate population, and whose pre-prison status and activities are well-known and admired.[40] Other inmates exercise power based on gang affiliation, their ability to control illicit goods and services within the institution (including drugs and gambling), and their sheer physical strength.[41]

Despite the status that individual inmates may have, interviews with ex-inmates suggest that no one is safe in the institution. As one ex-inmate stated:

I don't think anybody feels safe when they're in there. You always got to look over your shoulder. You don't know what could happen at any time. A guy could be angry and just want to come and stab you in the neck for nothing . . . Even when you're in your cell at nighttime and your cell's locked, you still don't feel safe.[42]

Generally speaking, inmates convicted of sex offences, transgendered inmates, inmates who have been tagged as snitches (rats) by other inmates, and those with gambling or drug debts are all vulnerable to physical and perhaps sexual abuse. These inmates may be placed in protective custody (PC) for their protection. Then there are other inmates who, because of their personality, offence, or physical weakness, have little or no power and influence. Inmates confined for sexual offences, especially against children, have low status in most institutional populations and may be subject to victimization. Sex offenders have the double stigma of being criminals and sex offenders.[43]

A defining feature of life in contemporary correctional institutions is that inmates tend to group themselves into niches or friendship networks. These networks may be based on associations formed during previous incarcerations or in the outside community (e.g., gangs); on shared ethnicity or culture (e.g., Black or Indigenous groups); or on length of sentence (e.g., lifers). It is the friendship group, rather than the inmate population as a whole, that provides the individual inmate with security and support and that is the recipient of the inmate's loyalty. The result is an inmate population characterized by pluralism rather than by uniformity of thought and action.

VIOLENCE AND EXPLOITATION AMONG INMATES

Despite the tenets of the inmate code, the prison can be a place of violence and exploitation.

The level of violence in correctional institutions is a function of many factors, including living conditions, the actions of COs and administrators, the demographics of the inmate population (e.g., age), the security level of the institution, overcrowding, and competition among inmate gangs for turf. Some of these factors are related to one another—for example, overcrowding may increase inmate misconduct if there are a large number of younger inmates who are having difficulty adjusting to prison life.[44]

Institutional Features That Contribute to Violence

For inmates in many correctional institutions, the potential for violence and exploitation is a fact of daily life, although only a small percentage of inmates are a threat to others. Inmates convicted of more serious crimes such as murder do not account for a disproportionate share of prison violence or involvement in misconduct in the institution.[45] Prison assaults are disproportionately committed by younger inmates (under the age of 25) and in institutions that are overcrowded.[46] Often, violent incidents occur because of gambling debts, conflict over the drug market inside the institution, or previous on-the-street relationships. Or, the inmate who was assaulted was a snitch.

As one ex-federal offender stated, "Prison is not safe. Like when you're in their care, you're supposed to be safe. And you're not. Nobody's safe."[47] Many inmates live in constant fear for their safety. Given the patterns of violence in prison, this fear is most likely justified. Issues related to inmate safety have come to the attention of the courts. In 2004, the Supreme Court of Canada acquitted a former inmate on a charge of possessing a dangerous weapon. Jason Kerr had stabbed another inmate to death with a homemade knife. The court found that Kerr had been carrying the knife for self-defence after he was threatened with harm by the victim and that possession of the weapon did not endanger the public (*R. v. Kerr*, 2004 SCC 44).

In another case, an inmate was charged with four counts of assault after defending himself from an attack by a number of other inmates, one of whom was slashed several times and sent to hospital. In dismissing all of the charges at trial, the judge indicated that the inmate was justified in defending himself, stating, "The system put him in this situation, and the system cannot blame him for resorting to his own means of defence" (*R. v. Short*, 2016 ONSC 4594).

Institutions with large populations and higher-security institutions tend to have higher rates of violent victimization.[48] At the provincial level, institutions that house persons on remand and those holding longer-term inmates may have a higher number of inmate-on-inmate assaults.[49] Male inmates in Canadian federal institutions are more likely to be murdered than males in the outside, free community. And the rates of inmate assaults and deaths are higher in the federal psychiatric centres than in other federal institutions.[50] For example, an inmate in the Ontario Regional Treatment Centre is 260 percent more likely to die than an inmate in the (now closed) Kingston Penitentiary.[51]

The security level of the correctional institution is a strong predictor of the level of violence that occurs and not in a way that might be anticipated. Canadian research with ex-inmates has found that the threat of violence is greater in higher-security prisons due to a reliance on formal, coercive controls, and lesser in lower-security facilities where there is a more informal routine and inmates are engaged in remunerative activities, including work and programming.[52]

The level of violence between inmates is also often related to the amount of gang activity in an institution because there may be conflicts between gang-affiliated inmates. For example, at Joyceville Institution, a federal facility in Ontario, it is estimated that one in ten inmates is affiliated with a gang and that as many as 25 percent of incidents in correctional institutions are gang-related.[53] This creates challenges for prison administrators to keep "incompatibles" separate from one another in order to prevent gang-precipitated violence.

Vulnerable Inmates

Sex offenders and LGBTQ inmates may be particularly at risk, given the role of masculinity in the prison. In 2016, a sexual predator on remand awaiting trial, who was beaten by other inmates and, in one instance, by a CO, had his 12-year sentence reduced by one-half and given more than three days credit for each day in pre-trial custody, despite a federal law that caps pre-trial custody credit at 1.5 days per day served. The judge determined that his rights had been violated, stating, "Criminals are still people entitled to basic human rights and the Charter [of Rights and Freedoms] extends to that environment the way that it extends to all environments."[54]

Interviews with ex-inmates has revealed that sex offenders employ a variety of strategies to avoid being identified by other inmates and live in a constant state of fear of being victimized.[55] Their challenges are compounded by a lack of trust that the correctional staff will protect them.

Inmates who are in debt in the prison economy, who lend money to other inmates, or who lack sufficient resources to obtain illicit goods and services are more likely to be victimized by other inmates. "Similar to the free world, those who are poor are more likely to be victimized."[56] Inmates with a mental health disability and lower functioning may be especially vulnerable to exploitation.

Younger inmates appear to be more vulnerable to victimization than older inmates, as are inmates who have a history of misconduct. Weak and vulnerable inmates may be coerced to provide sexual services, to pay money or goods for protection, to repay loans or favours at high interest, or to persuade family members to bring drugs into the institution.

Toughness is a central feature of inmate identity, and inmates may use extreme violence for self-protection, to achieve and maintain power and status, and to retaliate against snitches. Though COs are sometimes the source of brutality inflicted on inmates, other inmates present the greatest danger to their safety.

Inmates use both individual strategies and alliance strategies to cope with the threat of victimization.[57] Individual coping strategies may involve passive precautions, including spending more time in one's cell, or aggressive precautions, including keeping a weapon.[58] In a study ($N = 56$) of how inmates managed the threat of violence, an ex-inmate relayed an example of an aggressive precaution, stating, "There were times that I had to literally call a guy to fight, hoping that it didn't go there, but I had to say, 'Well, Sal? You're going to have to do this or else.'"[59]

Another coping strategy is for inmates to develop "alliance strategies," which involve developing a network of support with other inmates. The inmate's actions in these alliances may be either passive or aggressive, although the difference may be indistinguishable.[60] Alliances in prison, particularly those centred on gang membership, can be a powerful and potentially disruptive force in a correctional institution. As an ex-inmate stated, "They're so many of them [alliance members] and they just run the prison. It's not like they run the prison to say what happens and what does not happen. But not a lot of people fuck with the [gang]."[61]

Because gang membership may provide inmates with a level of security and safety, inmates are vulnerable to gang recruiting efforts inside the institution. Ironically, a gang-affiliated inmate may feel safer inside prison than on the street. As one inmate commented with respect to his life inside, "Last time I came to prison, I felt like I was coming home. Sometimes when you get out of jail, you don't want to get out. Out there, it's like, you gotta be more cautious. You've got your homies backing you up here."[62]

In contrast to the physical aggression that characterizes life inside institutions for male offenders, in women's facilities such aggression appears to be more indirect and to take the form of verbal bullying, threats, ostracism, intimidation, and gossip.[63]

Sexual Coercion and Rape

Sexual coercion and rape are two brutal realities of prison life, yet there is very little information about the perpetrators and victims of this type of violence or about its prevalence in Canadian institutions. Canadian scholars have noted that non-consensual sexual assault is rare in Canadian institutions.[64] A study of

CP PHOTO/Paul Chiasson

Federal CO in Québec shows a display of homemade weapons seized from inmates.

former federal inmates ($N = 56$) in Ontario found that not one of the inmates in her sample had been the victim of non-consensual sex, the view being that, "if someone is having sex in prison, he wants to be having sex in prison."[65]

The reluctance of inmate victims to report victimization, combined with the assumption among many correctional observers that most inmate sexual activity is consensual, has hindered an understanding of this important area of institutional corrections.[66] More attention has been given to this topic in the United States (e.g., the website of "Just Detention International: Rape Is Not Part of the Penalty"; http://www.spr.org).

Perpetrators use a variety of tactics to coerce sex, including inflicting direct physical harm or threatening to do so, intimidating the target physically, and applying persuasion. An inmate may succeed in taking another inmate as his "punk"—an exploitative relationship that nevertheless provides a measure of security and protection for the weaker inmate. Depending on the circumstances, such as whether there are multiple perpetrators, the target can often prevent the attack by avoiding the perpetrators, consistently refusing, using defensive threats, fighting, or launching a pre-emptive attack.[67]

There are, however, a number of factors that mitigate against inmates sexually assaulting even weaker inmates in the prison, including the threat of being investigated by prison authorities, the possibility of disciplinary sanctions, and potential criminal and civil charges.

THE RADICALIZATION OF INMATES

A number of high-profile terrorist-related incidents and attempted attacks have highlighted the issues surrounding offenders convicted of terrorist-related crimes, their incarceration, and their potential influence on other inmates who may be vulnerable to being radicalized.[68]

Religion is one strategy used by inmates to cope with the conditions of confinement.[69] In recent years, there are concerns that some inmates may be vulnerable to being radicalized into views that may lead to terrorist activities upon their release. Other jurisdictions, including Australia, have developed de-radicalization programs that are designed to rehabilitate offenders convicted of terrorism-related offences. The effectiveness of these programs is uncertain.[70]

There are no programs in Canadian correctional institutions designed for inmates who have been convicted of terrorism-related offences or for inmates who may be susceptible to radicalization. Fahim Ahmad was convicted in 2010 of three terrorism charges and given a 16-year sentence. He and several accomplices were charged with plotting to set off bombs in downtown Toronto and at a military base. Ahmad indicated in 2016 that he had been denied parole because the board was unable to assess his progress toward rehabilitation; yet, there are no programs specifically designed for this type of offender, placing him and others in a Catch-22 situation.

Muslim prison chaplains have described the current initiatives for inmates who have been or are at risk of being radicalized as inadequate and that sufficient attention has not been given to this issue.[71] A number of observers have called for corrections authorities to develop CVE (countering violent terrorism) programs.[72]

PARTING THOUGHTS ON THE INMATE SOCIAL SYSTEM

It is likely that the most highly developed inmate social systems are in federal facilities, which house offenders with more extensive criminal records for longer periods of time. The more rapid turnover of inmates in provincial/territorial institutions would seem to work against the development of inmate social systems. On the other hand, many provincial/territorial inmates have been incarcerated in the past and may be well schooled in the various facets of doing time.

While some type of social system always develops among inmates, there are variations in the specific form that system takes—for example, in the extent to which an inmate code takes hold, and how powerful social roles are. For many inmates, adherence to the code is done out of self-interest—to mitigate their own level of risk.

Despite verbalizing support for an inmate code, snitching, acts of violence, and intimidation are regular features of institutional life. Disruptions and critical incidents in correctional institutions may be in part a result of the erosion of the "inmate code." That erosion has brought about changes in how inmates relate to one another.

Not so long ago, some inmates functioned as "elder statesmen," exerting control over the units and helping keep peace and stability in the institution as a whole. Today, in the words of one CO, "it's all intimidation, and brute force, and who has the most drugs to sell."[73] This attitudinal shift among inmates was noted by a correctional staff member in a Saskatchewan provincial institution: "Before, there were tough guys [inmates] and you [the inmate] knew to stay away from them. There was a code. Now everyone gets beat on."[74]

COPING WITH CONFINEMENT

While incarcerated, inmates expend considerable energy trying to reduce the pains of imprisonment. Consensual sexual relationships may be entered into. They often become involved in obtaining, distributing, and/or using illicit goods and services, including drugs and other contraband. Participation in the underground economy is not without risk, however. As noted, inmates who incur gambling debts may risk being physically harmed or may be pressured to have family members smuggle drugs and contraband into the prison. To protect themselves, these inmates may request placement in a protective custody unit, where their freedom of movement in the institution and access to programs are severely curtailed.

Drugs and Contraband

> *Illicit drugs and alcohol are the central driving force in the lives of inmates: they not only supply ways of escaping the deadening routine of doing time but also confer currency, collateral, and power on their dealers. Just as on the street, substance abuse in prison leads to violence and further crime.*[75]

In most Canadian correctional facilities, drugs are as freely available as they are on the street. Inmates use drugs or alcohol to cope with their environment, forget their problems, or just relax. Many offenders become addicted to drugs while in confinement.

The smuggling networks in correctional facilities are extensive and sophisticated. Organized gangs play a major role in importing and distributing drugs, especially in federal institutions. Drugs in prison—their distribution and use—are commonly associated with intimidation, extortion, and staff corruption. Moreover, violence and victimization among inmates are often the result of nonpayment for illicit drugs. This presents a risk to the safety and security of both inmates and staff. Of particular concern is "homebrew," a concoction made by inmates with ingredients (bread, fruit, or vegetables) stolen from the kitchen or dining hall. Most illicit drugs in prison have the effect of "downing out" inmates; by contrast, homebrew consumption can precipitate violence.

The problem of illicit drugs and contraband inside prisons might seem surprising at first glance, given the strict regimen of correctional institutions, the various static and dynamic security arrangements, and the multitude of drug interdiction strategies. The latter include metal detectors, ion scanners, nonintrusive searches of all visitors, drug-sniffing dogs, cell searches and physical searches of inmates, and, at the federal level, a national random-urinalysis program that tests the urine samples of 5 percent of the inmate population each month. In reality, however, it is almost impossible for correctional staff to eliminate the flow of drugs and contraband. There is extensive contact between inmates and outside visitors; offenders leave institutions on temporary absences and day parole; and inmate labour is used in a variety of noninstitutional settings, including community service, forestry work, and firefighting.

Additionally, tennis balls or dead birds can be tossed over the fence; visitors and sometimes corrections staff can walk them in. Increasingly, and what occurred in Regina at the Regional Correctional Centre in February 2017, drones are being used to drop drugs into prison facilities.[76]

Sexual Gratification

Inmates who have been deprived of heterosexual relationships still seek sexual gratification. Masturbation and consensual sexual relations with another inmate are the two most common types of sexual activity in correctional institutions. Consensual sex, while technically homosexual, is an adaptation to a unique circumstance; inmates revert to heterosexual sexual activity when they return to the community. The extent to which prison authorities should tolerate sexual relations between inmates is a topic of ongoing discussion. A less common means of sexual release, which is also a manifestation of power and control in the inmate social system, is the rape of an inmate (see "Sexual Coercion and Rape").

Mature Coping

Inmates encounter many opportunities to participate in illegal activities during their confinement but may choose instead to mitigate the pains of imprisonment through more constructive means. **Mature coping** is a positive approach to adapting to life inside. Inmates who take this route avoid using violence and deception in addressing problems, are altruistic in their relationships with other inmates, and use their time in confinement for positive growth through participation in treatment programs.[77]

There are obstacles to mature coping: The prison regimen may not encourage independent judgment, other inmates may seek to disrupt the prison environment, and inmates who try to cope maturely may find themselves victimized by others.

Mature coping
A positive approach taken by inmates to adjust to life inside correctional institutions.

FAILING TO COPE WITH CONFINEMENT: SELF–INJURIOUS BEHAVIOUR AND SUICIDE

The pains of imprisonment, combined with the challenges faced by individual inmates, which may include mental health issues and experiences of trauma, may lead to **self-injurious behaviour (SIB)** and, in some cases, to suicide.[78]

> **Self–injurious behavior (SIB)** Deliberate self-inflicted bodily harm or disfigurement.

Self–Injurious Behaviour

SIB refers to any deliberate action that involves bodily harm or disfigurement; it includes head banging and skin cutting.[79] SIB is distinct from suicide, as people engage in SIB without "conscious suicidal intent."[80] Only in recent years have correctional systems paid attention to these issues.

Rates of SIB are higher among inmates than in the general population and much higher (estimated to be 23 percent) among women inmates.[81] Women offenders are at higher risk of SIB as a way to cope with isolation, distress, emotional pain, and negative emotions. Indigenous offenders also account for a disproportionate number of all self-harm incidents in federal prisons.[82]

The CSC has a number of initiatives designed to reduce the incidence of SIB. These include health assessments at intake, policies for managing inmates who are deemed at risk, and various behavioural interventions.[83]

Suicide

The most frequent causes of inmate death are natural ones, followed by drug or alcohol abuse, accident, and suicide.[84] The suicide rate among incarcerated federal offenders (68 per 100,000) and for provincial offenders (40 per 100,000) are considerably higher than for the Canadian general population (10.2 per 100,000).[85] Male inmates are more at risk of suicide, and as noted above, women offenders are more likely to engage in SIB. Most inmates who commit suicide (most often by hanging) were serving a longer sentence, suffered from a psychological disorder, or had a history of violence.[86]

Inmates who are mentally disordered or have compromised mental health have an elevated risk of suicide of self-harm.[87] A recent CSC study found that 22 percent of suicides occurred in segregation or segregation-like conditions of confinement.[88]

There is still considerable work to be done to prevent suicides and self-harm among inmates. In recent years, correctional systems have been developing screening protocols to identify inmates at risk of suicide. To reduce the incidence of suicide and self-harm, the CSC has implemented inmate peer-support programs in all maximum- and medium-security institutions. The Samaritans program, which operates in several federal facilities, is a peer-support program through which a community-based organization provides suicide prevention training for inmate peer counsellors.

DOING LIFE

Picture yourself falling into a tunnel, totally dark, and it's going to take you twenty-five years to walk out … one step at a time. *

—P.J. Murphy and Loyd Johnsen, *Life-25: Interviews with Prisoners Serving Life Sentences,* 1997

The death penalty was abolished by Parliament in 1976 and replaced by a mandatory life sentence without possibility of parole for 25 years in cases of first-degree murder. Under the Criminal Code, persons convicted of murder are subject to life imprisonment. This means that the offender is under sentence for life, although he or she may serve this sentence both in prison and upon release on parole in the community. The Criminal Code sets out the minimum number of years that an offender must serve in prison before being eligible to apply for release on parole. The key word is "apply"—there is no guarantee that the parole board will grant a release. An offender serving life offered the following observation:

> *I've been in for two and a half years, just about going on three years. Seems like forever already. It's hard to remember what it's like out there. So many things can happen in three years. It's a terrible transition period; it's a terrible thing to go through. Especially when you don't see a light at the end of the tunnel anywhere. You're just stuck here and you're herded into your cell every few hours for a count. You feel like cattle. You get a feeling like you're helpless. Herd you in, lock the door. They count you like diamonds and treat you like shit.*[89]

Long-term sentences pose challenges not only to correctional systems with regard to housing and programming but also to individual inmates. It is highly unlikely that most long-term offenders will be able to sustain their pre-prison relationships, especially if relations with a spouse and/or children were already unstable.

Long-term confinement may not produce the predicted negative impacts on inmates, but neither does it promote positive changes. Most inmates seem to eventually adjust to life in prison, but this may make it more difficult for them to survive in the outside, free community on release. Ironically, those inmates who adjust well to the highly structured environment of a correctional institution may be the ones who encounter the most difficulties upon release.

PRISON AS "HOME": THE STATE-RAISED OFFENDER

Some offenders have spent most of their youth and adult lives in correctional institutions. These state-raised offenders have experienced only limited periods of freedom in the community and may have neither the social skills nor the ability to function outside the total institutional world of the prison. Many of them are frightened at the prospect of having to cope with the fast pace of modern life. For the state-raised offender, the prison provides security, friends, room and board, and a predictable routine; none of these are guaranteed in the outside community. The prison, not the community, is their home. State-raised offenders present challenges to systems of corrections, especially when these offenders re-enter the community.

INMATE RELATIONSHIPS AND FAMILIES

Discussions of corrections often overlook the fact that many inmates are fathers or mothers, husbands or wives, or in relationships. Little attention has been given to the dynamics and needs of inmate families, either during the inmate's confinement or following release. This is surprising, given that nearly half of offenders in confinement were married at the time of admission and that most have children or stepchildren. Furthermore, inmate mothers are likely to be sole caregivers for their children (see Chapter 12).

Correctional systems were not designed to consider the needs of inmate families, and family members may feel isolated and neglected by correctional authorities.[90] Also, the families of inmates may be stigmatized and marginalized in the community.[91] This societal indifference increases the challenges faced by the families of inmates. Other concerns relate to finances, housing, and fears related to the offender's return to the community.[92]

The partners of offenders may experience trauma, shame, isolation, and depression.[93] For one person's memoir of her relationship with an offender, read *This Is Not My Life: A Memoir of Love, Prison, and Other Complications* (2016) by Diane Schoemperlen and the documentary featuring her, "In Love with an Inmate: Navigating the Prison System" listed in the Media Links section at the end of the chapter.

Attention has recently been given to the mental health and well-being of families affected by crime and incarceration. A study ($N = 140$ survey responses; 44 in-person interviews) found that concerns with mental health and wellness increased over time, while there was a decline in seeking assistance.[94] Positive coping strategies of family members included seeking professional assistance, exercise, and peer support, while negative coping responses included alcohol, the misuse of prescription drugs, and attempted suicide.[95] The study also documented the difficulties that inmate families had in accessing information and support services.

The Children of Inmates

Children whose parents are incarcerated can suffer from emotional, behavioural, and academic problems; their type and severity vary with the child's age, gender, and length of separation from the parents.[96] The symptoms can mirror those evidenced by children who have experienced the death of a parent. The children of inmates may feel responsible for their parents' incarceration, be embarrassed among their peers, and worry that they may be sent to prison one day. In the words of an inmate spouse: "David, my son, he was afraid of people knowing about his step-dad because they, you know, parents wouldn't let their kids play with him and those kind of things. That was very, very difficult."[97]

Research studies indicate that children of incarcerated parents are at a high risk of antisocial behaviour.[98] In Canada, it is estimated that the children of federal inmates are two to four times more likely to have conflict with the law as compared to other children.[99]

Maintaining Family Ties

For the inmate, the loss of regular family contact is one of the pains of imprisonment. The CSC has a family visit program that provides an opportunity for married and common law partners to spend time alone in a separate facility on the grounds of the institution. Not all inmates qualify for these visits, and even when the inmate is eligible for a family visit, the spouse or partner may be unable to travel to the institution, because of the distance involved or for financial or other personal reasons.

Similarly, maintaining contact via telephone is costly.[100] Interviews with Black women in Canadian federal institutions ($N = 30$), most of whom were foreign nationals and many from Jamaica, found that the high cost of long-distance calls made it difficult to maintain contact with their families.[101]

As one woman inmate in a provincial institution in Saskatchewan stated, "Women don't get visits. And it's really hard to get visits. They put us so far away that there's no way our families can afford to come. Women have children and yet we're the farthest they place. What are our families supposed to do?"[102]

A woman inmate's partner commented on the distance and expense of visiting her in a provincial institution:

$45 to come from the bus depot to the jail just to have a visit with your wife. For an hour. It might cost you $300 just to take the trip. To get a one hour visit. You can't even kiss them—you can't even touch them or anything. No contact. Travelling six hours to visit, and then they can't even kiss you or touch you. How insulting can you be? I don't know anybody that's that bad. No contact is everywhere now.[103]

A number of factors hinder efforts to maintain and strengthen the family ties of incarcerated offenders, including limited visiting hours, poor visiting facilities, the obstacles imposed by geographic distance, and the difficulties of maintaining family ties over the course of a long-term sentence. To address this issue many US states, including the State of New York have launched programs that allow inmates to "meet" with their families via videoconference.[104] Correctional services in Canada are also using video visitation systems.

Alberta, for example, has "visitation centres" that are designed for families to make video calls to family members who are incarcerated.[105]

Inmates and their families have complained about the "high-tech, low-touch" arrangements for family visits that exist in many correctional institutions, particularly the expanding use of "visits" via video link.

The challenges for Indigenous families may be particularly acute. Inmates from northern and remote communities may be placed in correctional facilities thousands of kilometres from their families. Inuit offenders from northern Québec, for example, are incarcerated in correctional facilities in the "southern" regions of the province and are deprived of family and community support, as well as experiencing other challenges, including language-related barriers.[106] An Indigenous provincial inmate in Headingley Correctional Centre (Manitoba) stated, "I've been in two months—no visits. I am far away from home—Tadoule Lake, up north. It's kinda hard sometimes. It gets lonely. No communication with my people."[107] (Tadoule Lake is the Seyisi Dene First Nation and is an isolated community in northern Manitoba accessible only by air, snowmobile, and dog sled team; the community is approximately 1,000 km from Headingley Correctional Centre where this inmate was incarcerated.)

The OCI has been particularly critical of how the CSC communicates with families of inmates who die in custody.[108] In a review of cases ($N = 8$) in which an inmate had died in custody, the correctional investigator found that the CSC only reluctantly shared information with the family about the circumstances of the death, and "had little interest in doing so."[109] The CSC was found to have withheld as much information as possible for as long as possible at all stages of the process, from the notification of the death to the investigation of the circumstances surrounding it.[110] When materials were provided, they were often heavily censored. The overall impact of this was to deepen the grief of families.

The Role of Families in Rehabilitation

The challenges faced by inmate families assume even greater importance in view of research studies that suggest that prison visits by families of inmates may reduce recidivism and increase survival rates in the community.[111] Research suggests that family visit programs and the emotional support provided by family members have a positive impact on the inmate's family life, reduce institutional misconduct, and lower rates of reoffending.[112] There is evidence that inmates in correctional institutions located far from home are more likely to violate prison regulations than offenders confined closer to home.[113]

The failure of correctional systems to address the needs of inmate families has undermined the potential for the inmate's partner and family to play a positive role in reintegrating the offender back into the community upon release.[114]

Most correctional institutions also host volunteer programs that provide inmates an opportunity to interact with residents from the outside community. These programs are often sponsored by service organizations and religious groups and can have a number of benefits for the inmates, staff, and volunteers who participate.[115] A Toronto organization, Book Clubs for Inmates, runs 17 book clubs in 17 federal institutions, which involves volunteers leading monthly discussions with inmates.[116]

INMATE GRIEVANCES AND COMPLAINTS

The Corrections and Conditional Release Act (CCRA) sets out the procedures for ensuring that official grievances filed by federal inmates are dealt with in a fair, equitable, and timely manner and at the lowest possible level.[117]

Federal inmates must make every attempt to resolve their grievances through the internal grievance procedure in the institution before filing a written complaint with the OCI. Similar grievance procedures and requirements are in place for inmates in provincial/territorial institutions.

Thousands of complaints and grievances are filed every year by inmates in Canadian correctional facilities. The most common complaints received by the OCI relate to health care, conditions of confinement, and institutional transfers.[118] In the federal system, a few inmates file hundreds of complaints every year, many that might be considered frivolous.[119] In an attempt to address this situation, a provision in Bill C-10, enacted in 2012, made it a disciplinary offence for an inmate to knowingly make a false claim for compensation from the Crown. The danger is that this will deter inmates with legitimate complaints from exercising their rights.

The OCI investigates issues related to federal offenders; provincial ombudspersons focus on provincial cases. Following is a case investigated and resolved by the Ontario Ombudsman:

> *An inmate called the Ombudsman because he was eligible for parole in one week and he was afraid his request for a parole hearing would not be submitted on time. His Institutional Liaison Officer had not met with him to begin the process, which takes four to six weeks. Ombudsman staff discovered that delays in processing parole hearing requests were routine at the institution. As a result of the Ombudsman's inquiries, the responsible manager was directed to clear up the backlog to ensure that inmates were given the opportunity for parole hearings before their parole eligibility dates. Additional staff were hired and two senior probation and parole officers were assigned to work with the Institutional Liaison Officer to help improve their performance.[120]*

SUMMARY

The discussion in this chapter has centred on the experiences of offenders who are sentenced to a period of custody. Offenders in correctional institutions tend to be from the margins of society and to have limited education and skill sets. On entering the institution, the offender must develop strategies for coping with life inside. Inmates face a number of challenges, including the pains of imprisonment, learning their way around the inmate social system, and avoiding abuse and exploitation. It is likely that this process is easier for state-raised offenders who have spent much of their youth and adult life in custody.

Generally speaking, systems of corrections have given little attention to the needs of inmates' families, and this has made it difficult for inmates to maintain their relationships with spouses, partners, and children. There are procedures by which inmates can file grievances and complaints, and the OCI and provincial ombudspersons are involved in investigating inmate grievances as well.

KEY POINTS REVIEW

1. Persons confined in correctional institutions tend to have low levels of education, limited employment skills, and addiction issues, and are disproportionately Indigenous or Black.

2. The overall health status of inmates is poor compared with the general population.

3. The specific impact that entry into prison has on an individual offender depends on a number of factors, including personality, offence history, and previous incarcerations.

4. The loss of liberty is perhaps the most significant impact on inmates.

5. There is a social system among inmates in every correctional institution.

6. There is a hierarchy of status and power among inmates.

7. While incarcerated, inmates expend considerable energy attempting to reduce the pains of imprisonment, and this often involves contraband.

8. For inmates in many correctional institutions, the potential for violence and exploitation is a fact of daily life.

9. The degree to which an inmate is vulnerable to attack and exploitation by other inmates depends in large measure on his or her status, power, and friendship networks.

10. The challenges of doing time may lead to inmates engaging in self-injurious behaviour or even suicide.

11. Rates of self-injurious behaviour are higher among inmates than in the general population and are much higher for women offenders.

12. Little attention has been given to the dynamics and needs of inmate families.

13. Correctional systems have formal inmate grievance procedures. They also have ombudspersons who may investigate inmate complaints.

KEY TERM QUESTIONS

1. Define and discuss the importance of the following concepts for the study of corrections and life inside correctional institutions: (1) *status degradation ceremonies*; (2) *pains of imprisonment*; and (3) *state-raised offenders*.

2. Discuss the attributes of the *inmate social system/inmate subculture* and what is known about its existence in correctional institutions.

3. Describe and contrast the *importation theory* of the inmate social system and the *deprivation theory* of the inmate social system.

4. What is the *integration model* of the inmate social system?

5. Discuss the concept of *prisonization* and describe what is meant when it is said that an inmate has become *institutionalized*.

6. Identify the tenets of the *inmate code* and discuss whether the code still exists among inmates in correctional institutions.

7. What role do *social* (or *argot*) *roles* play inside correctional institutions?

8. Describe what is meant by *mature coping* by inmates, identify the components of mature coping, and note the obstacles that inmates may encounter in their efforts to engage in this practice.

9. Why is it important to understand *self-injurious behaviour (SIB)* among inmates?

CRITICAL THINKING EXERCISES

Critical Thinking Exercise 8.1

Responding to a Particular View of Prisons

In any discussion of prison conditions, there are persons who take the perspective that life inside correctional institutions should be harsh. Following is a comment that was made online in response to an article that indicated that the policies of the former federal Conservative government had led to overcrowding and increased violence:

Are you kidding me? This article actually made me facepalm. Just what the devil did you THINK prisons were? Mr. Dressup's trunk filled with feather boas and sparkly slippers? Tea parties with tiny cakes and finger sandwiches? Good grief, I'm having a hard time believing this article made it to the media. Prisons are for CRIMINALS. Bad people who do BAD things! Take away the rights to a free education, where inmates become lawyers, and give that free education to a deserving child. Take away the tennis courts, swimming pools, televisions, computers and everything else ANYONE feels they deserve to keep them calm. Prison isn't about criminal rights. They chose to forego those when they broke the law and prison is PUNISHMENT for their actions.[121]

Your Thoughts?

1. If you were on a panel session on corrections with this person, how would you respond?

Critical Thinking Exercise 8.2

Being Inside: An Inmate's Perspective

1. Access the article "What It's Really Like to Spend Time in a Canadian Prison," written by Karim Martin (http://www.vice.com/en_ca/read/what-its-really-like-to-spend-time-in-a-canadian-prison).

2. Identify the features of his experience that may compromise the ability of incarceration to effect change in an offender.

CLASS/GROUP DISCUSSION EXERCISES

Class/Group Discussion Exercise 8.1

Should Inmates Have the Right to Defend Themselves in Correctional Institutions?

In the discussion of violence in correctional institutions, a case was cited wherein an Ontario judge dismissed assault charges against an inmate, ruling that the inmate was justified in warding off his attackers. The judge heard evidence from the inmate's attacker who stated that most of the inmates in the Toronto East Detention Centre (where the attack occurred) carried a weapon. In his ruling, the judge blamed correctional authorities for putting the inmate in the position of having to defend himself against attack. This included COs who the judge indicated had not intervened in a timely manner to stop the fight and who had contributed to the unsafe conditions in the prison.

Read the court's decision in the case of *R. v. Short* (2016 ONSC 4594) at http://canlii.ca/t/gshr6.

Responding to the ruling, a representative of the union that represents COs noted that while the judge was correct in noting that weapons had become pervasive in institutions, the ruling set a dangerous precedent. The representative stated, "It sends a message to inmates that it's okay to carry these types of weapons."[122]

A Queen's University law professor noted that the ruling in the case "sets out contradictory demands for inmates. . . . On the one hand, Mr. Short would have been charged for possession of a weapon if guards had discovered the shank prior to the altercation. On the other hand, he could have been killed without it."[123]

Your Thoughts?

After reading the judgment in this case:

1. Do you agree with the judge's decision and the rationale presented for the decision?
2. What is your response to the concerns of the CO union representative?
3. Considering the points made by the Queen's University law professor, is there any way to resolve the situation where inmates are placed in this "contradictory" situation?

Class/Group Discussion Exercise 8.2

Untapped Talent in Prison

Observers have often pointed out that there is among inmate populations a vast and generally untapped reservoir of talent, be it artistic, entrepreneurial, or spiritual. Watch the TED talk, "Lessons in business . . . from prison," at https://www.ted.com/talks/jeff_smith_lessons_in_business_from_prison.

Your Thoughts?

1. What is your response to the presenter's ideas?
2. What policy and programmatic initiatives might be taken to implement some of the suggestions made by the speaker?

MEDIA LINKS

"Kingston Pen: Secrets and Lies," https://www.youtube.com/watch?v=f5oEe8r2fYs

"Tales from Kingston Pen," http://www.cbc.ca/doczone/episodes/tales-from-the-kingston-penn

"*How to Prepare for Prison*," http://tvo.org/video/documentaries/how-to-prepare-for-prison-feature-version

"Myths and Facts About Prisons," http://tvo.org/video/programs/the-agenda-with-steve-paikin/myths-and-facts-about-prison

"State of Incarceration: Life in Prison," http://www.cbc.ca/doczone/features/life-in-a-maximum-security-prison

"State of Incarceration," http://www.cbc.ca/doczone/episodes//new-season-state-of-incarceration

"Surviving Supermax," www.youtube.com/watch?v=tQNGrb3xUWo

"NCR: Not Criminally Responsible," http://www.cbc.ca/doczone/episodes/not-criminally-responsible

"Holiday Prison Visit," http://www.cbc.ca/news/holiday-prison-visit-1.2877985

"TheStar.com: A Canadian Prisoner's Perspective," http://www.dailymotion.com/video/x2mq5mg

"In Love with an Inmate: Navigating the Prison System," http://tvo.org/video/programs/the-agenda-with-steve-paikin/in-love-with-an-inmate

"The Devil You Know," http://www.cbc.ca/fifth/episodes/2010-2011/the-devil-you-know

"The Prisons Video Trust Families of Prisoners," www.youtube.com/watch?v=R_QFU7Au5mo

"Visiting Day: The Unrelenting Stress of Family Prison Visits," https://www.theatlantic.com/video/index/415560/visiting-day-the-unrelenting-stress-of-family-prison-visits/

"Life in Prison for a Sex Offender," https://www.youtube.com/watch?v=n8e9UmXKRKk

"Corrections Investigator Raises Alarm Bells Over Prisoner Self-Harm," http://aptnnews.ca/2012/10/24/corrections-investigator-raises-alarm-bells-over-prisoner-self-harm/

NOTES

1. A.L. Schuler, F.L. Matheson, and S.W. Hwang, "Health Status of Prisoners in Canada Narrative Review," *Canadian Family Physician* 62, no. 3 (2016), 215–22, http://www.cfp.ca/content/62/3/215.full.pdf.

2. A. Maxwell, "Adult Criminal Court Statistics in Canada, 2014/2015," *Juristat* 37, no. 1, Catalogue no. 85-002-X (Ottawa: Minister of Industry, 2017), http://www.statcan.gc.ca/pub/85-002-x/2017001/article/14699-eng.htm.

3. John Howard Society of Toronto, *Homeless and Jailed: Jailed and Homeless* (Toronto: Author, 2010), http://johnhoward.ca/wp-content/uploads/2016/12/Amber-Kellen-Homeless-and-Jailed-Jailed-and-Homeless.pdf.

4. Public Safety Canada Portfolio Corrections Statistics Committee, *Corrections and Conditional Release Statistical Overview: 2015 Annual Report* (Ottawa: Public Works and Government Services Canada, 2016), p. 45, https://www.publicsafety.gc.ca/cnt/rsrcs/pblctns/ccrso-2015/ccrso-2015-en.pdf.

5. Office of the Correctional Investigator, *A Case Study of Diversity in Corrections: The Black Inmate Experience in Federal Penitentiaries* (Ottawa: Author, 2013), http://www.oci-bec.gc.ca/cnt/rpt/pdf/oth-aut/oth-aut20131126-eng.pdf.

6. A. Owusu-Bempah and S. Wortley, "Race, Crime, and Criminal Justice in Canada," in *Ethnicity, Crime, and Immigration*, eds. S.M. Bucerius and M. Tonry (New York: Oxford University Press, 2014), 281–319.

7. Office of the Correctional Investigator, *A Case Study of Diversity in Corrections: The Black Inmate Experience in Federal Penitentiaries*, p. 8.

8. Owusu-Bempah and Wortley, "Race, Crime, and Criminal Justice in Canada."

9. M. McNamara, "Better to Be Out in Prison Than Out in Public: LGBTQ Prisoners Receive More Constitutional Protection if They Are Open About Their Sexuality While in Prison," *Law & Sexuality 23* (2014), 135–54.

10. T. Lupick, "Living nightmare for transgender inmate at all-male prison," *Toronto Star*, December 13, 2015, https://www.thestar.com/news/canada/2015/12/13/living-nightmare-for-transgender-inmate-at-all-male-prison.html.

11. L. Strapagiel, "Ontario will now assess transgender inmates based on identity, not anatomy," *National Post*, January 26, 2015, http://news.nationalpost.com/news/canada/ontario-will-now-assess-transgender-inmates-based-on-identity-not-anatomy.

12. P. Moskowitz, "How LGBTQ prisoners use art to survive incarceration," *VICE*, November 4, 2016, https://www.vice.com/en_us/article/how-lgbtq-prisoners-use-art-to-survive-incarceration.

13. S. Green, J. Foran, and F.G. Kouyoumdjian, "Access to Primary Care in Adults in a Provincial Correctional Facility in Ontario," *BMC Research Notes 9*, no. 1 (2016), 1–8.

14. John Howard Society of Ontario, *Fractured Care: Public Health Opportunities in Ontario's Correctional Institutions* (Toronto: Author, 2016), p. 9, http://johnhoward.on.ca/wp-content/uploads/2016/04/Fractured-Care-Final.pdf.

15. Ibid., p. 5.

16. Green et al., "Access to Primary Care in Adults in a Provincial Correctional Facility in Ontario."

17. Office of the Correctional Investigator, *Annual Report, 2015–2016* (Ottawa: Author, 2016), p. 10, http://www.oci-bec.gc.ca/cnt/rpt/pdf/annrpt/annrpt20152016-eng.pdf.

18. P.J. Murphy and L. Johnsen, *Life 25: Interviews with Prisoners Serving Life Sentences* (Vancouver: New Star, 1997).

19. R.A. Cloward, "Social Control in the Prison," in *Prison Within Society: A Reader in Penology*, ed. L. Hazelrigg (Garden City, NY: Doubleday, 1969), pp. 78–112.

20. R. Ricciardelli, *Surviving Incarceration: Inside Canadian Prisons* (Waterloo, ON: Wilfred Laurier Press, 2014a), p. 39.

21. R. Dube, *The Haven: A True Story of Life in the Hole* (Toronto: HarperCollins, 2002) pp. 238–39.

22. F.W. Ault, Inmate's Description of Life in the Reception Centre at Millhaven Institution, Ontario, "Imprisoned by an Uncaring Public," *Globe and Mail*, April 21, 1997, A14.

23. Murphy and Johnsen, *Life 25*, p. 79.

24. G.M. Sykes, *Society of Captives—A Study of a Maximum Security Institution* (Princeton, NJ: Princeton University Press, 1958).

25. B. Crewe, "Depth, Weight, Tightness: Revisiting the Pains of Imprisonment," *Punishment and Society 13*, no. 5 (2011), 509–29.

26. Ibid., p. 524.

27. J. Irwin and D. R. Cressey, "Thieves, Convicts, and the Inmate Culture," *Social Problems 10*, no. 1 (1962), 142–55.

28. R. Ricciardelli, "An Examination of the Inmate Code," *Journal of Crime and Justice 37*, no. 2 (2014b), 234–55 at 237.

29. Ricciardelli, *Surviving Incarceration: Inside Canadian Prisons*, p. 57.

30. D. Clemmer, *The Prison Community* (Boston: Christopher, 1940).

31. Office of the Correctional Investigator, *Annual Report, 2015–2016*.

32. G.M. Sykes and S. L. Messinger, "The Inmate Social System," in *Theoretical Studies in the Social Organization of the Prison*, eds. R. A. Cloward et al. (New York: Social Science Research Council, 1960).

33. Ricciardelli, "An Examination of the Inmate Code," pp. 243–48.

34. Ibid., p. 243.

35. Ibid., p. 249.

36. S. Thompson, *Letters from Prison: Felons Write About the Struggle for Life and Sanity Behind Bars* (New York: HarperCollins, 2002), pp. 15–16.

37. M. Welch, *Corrections: A Critical Approach*, 3rd ed. (New York: Routledge, 2011), pp. 137–38.

38. M. Weinwrath, *Behind the Walls: Inmates and Correctional Officers on the State of Canadian Prisons* (Vancouver: UBC Press, 2016), p. 103.

39. Ibid.

40. R. Richmond, "Behind Bars: 'The Law of the Jungle,'" *London Free Press*, November 16, 2013, http://www.lfpress.com/2013/11/15/behind-bars-the-law-of-the-jungle.

41. Ricciardelli, "An Examination of the Inmate Code."

42. P.L. Faulkner and W.R. Faulkner, "Effects of Organizational Change on Inmate Status and the Inmate Code of Conduct," *Journal of Crime and Criminal Justice 20*, no. 1 (1997), 55–72.

43. Ricciardelli, "An Examination of the Inmate Code," p. 242.

44. R. Ricciardelli and M. Moir, "Stigmatized among the Stigmatized: Sex Offenders in Canadian Penitentiaries," *Canadian Journal of Criminology and Criminal Justice 55*, no. 3 (2013), 353–85.

45. W.W. Franklin, C.A. Franklin, and T.C. Pratt "Examining the Empirical Relationship Between Prison Crowding and Inmate Misconduct: A Meta-Analysis of Conflicting Research Results," *Journal of Criminal Justice 34*, no. 4 (2006), 401–12.

46. D.M. Perez, A.R. Gover, K.M. Tennyson, and S.D. Santos, "Individual and Institutional Characteristics Related to Inmate Victimization," *International Journal of Offender Therapy and Comparative Criminology 54*, no. 3 (2010), 378–94; B. Steiner, J.M. Ellison, H.D. Butler, and C.M. Cain "The Impact of Inmate and Prison Characteristics on Prisoner Victimization," *Trauma, Violence, & Abuse 18*, no. 1 (2017), 17–36.

47. L. Throness, *Standing Against Violence: A Safety Review of BC Corrections* (Victoria: Government of British Columbia, 2014), http://www2.gov.bc.ca/assets/gov/law-crime-and-justice/criminal-justice/corrections/reports-publications/standing-against-violence.pdf.

48. J. Sorensen and M.D. Cunningham, "Conviction Offense and Prison Violence: A Comparative Study of Murderers and Other Offenders," *Crime and Delinquency 56*, no. 1 (2011), 103–25.

49. K.F. Lahm, "Inmate-On-Inmate Assault: A Multilevel Examination of Prison Violence," *Criminal Justice and Behavior 35*, no. 1 (2008), 120–37.

50. Ricciardelli, *Surviving Incarceration: Inside Canadian Prisons*, p. 67.

51. S. Fine, "Alberta judge cuts sex predator's sentence in half after beating in jail," *Globe and Mail*, November 24, 2016, http://www.theglobeandmail.com/news/national/alberta-judge-cuts-sex-predators-sentence-in-half-after-beating-in-jail/rticle33042363/.

52. R. Ricciardelli and D. Spencer, "Exposing 'Sex' Offenders: Precarity, Abjection and Violence in the Canadian Federal Prison System," *British Journal of Criminology 54*, no. 3 (2014), 428–48 at 445.

53. J. Copes, G.E. Higgins, R. Tewksbury, and D.A. Dabney, "Participation in the Prison Economy and Likelihood of Physical Victimization," *Victims and Offenders 6*, no. 1 (2011), 1–18.

54. A.M. Paperny, "Investigation: Canada's psychiatric prisons have highest death, assault rates," Global News, March 19, 2015, http://globalnews.ca/news/1301910/investigation-canadas-psychiatric-prisons-have-highest-death-assault-rates/.

55. Ibid.

56. R. Ricciardelli and V. Sit, "Producing Social (Dis)Order in Prison: The Effects of Administrative Controls on Prisoner-on-Prisoner Violence," *The Prison Journal 96*, no. 2 (2016), 210–31.

57. Richmond, "Behind Bars: 'The Law of the Jungle.'"

58. R. Ricciardelli, "Coping Strategies: Investigating How Male Prisoners Manage the Threat of Victimization in Federal Prisons," *The Prison Journal 94*, no. 4 (2014c), 411–34.

59. R.C. McCorkle, "Personal Precautions to Violence in Prisons," *Criminal Justice and Behavior 19*, no. 2 (1992), 160–73.

60. Ricciardelli, "Coping Strategies: Investigating How Male Prisoners Manage the Threat of Victimization in Federal Prisons," p. 422.

61. Ricciardelli, "Coping Strategies: Investigating How Male Prisoners Manage the Threat of Victimization in Federal Prisons."

62. Ibid., p. 426.

63. Weinwrath, *Behind the Walls: Inmates and Correctional Officers on the State of Canadian Prisons*, p. 244.

64. J. Ireland and J. Archer, "Descriptive Analysis of Bullying in Male and Female Adult Prisoners," *Journal of Community and Applied Social Psychology 6* (1996), 35–47.

65. Ricciardelli, *Surviving Incarceration: Inside Canadian Prisons*.

66. Ibid., p. 56.

67. T.R. Jones and T.C. Pratt, "The Prevalence of Sexual Violence in Prison," *International Journal of Offender Therapy and Comparative Criminology 52*, no. 3 (2008), 280–95.

68. I. O'Donnell, "Prison Rape in Context," *British Journal of Criminology 44*, no. 2 (2004), 241–55.

69. M.S. Hamm, *The Spectacular Few: Prison Radicalization and the Evolving Terrorist Threat* (New York: NYU Press, 2013).

70. E. Mulcahy, S. Merrington, and P. Bell, "The Radicalisation of Prison Inmates: Exploring Recruitment, Religion and Prisoner Vulnerability," *Journal of Human Security 9*, no. 1 (2013), 4–14.

71. J. Horgan and K. Braddock, "Rehabilitating the Terrorists? Challenges in Assessing the Effectiveness of De-radicalization Programs," *Terrorism and Political Violence 22*, no. 2 (2010), 267–91.

72. "Muslim prison chaplains plea for more time with federal inmates to curb radicalization," CBC News, January 18, 2016, http://www.cbc.ca/news/canada/montreal/federal-prison-imam-chaplain-radicalization-1.3408765.

73. M. Shepard, "Toronto 18 plotter reflects on a decade in prison," *Toronto Star*, May 29, 2016, https://www.thestar.com/news/atkinsonseries/generation911/2016/05/29/toronto-18-plotter-reflects-on-a-decade-in-prison.html.

74. M. Harris, *Con Game: The Truth About Canada's Prisons* (Toronto: McClelland and Stewart, 2002), p. 48.

75. Ombudsman Saskatchewan, *My Brother's Keeper: A Review of Electronic Control Devices in Saskatchewan Correctional Centres Housing Male Inmates* (Regina: Author, 2008), p. 23, http://www.ombudsman.sk.ca/uploads/document/files/my-brothers-keeper-en.pdf.

76. Harris, *Con Game: The Truth About Canada's Prisons*, p. 185.

77. "Regina police investigate after drone used to drop drugs into prison," Canadian Press, February 17, 2017, https://www.thestar.com/news/canada/2017/02/17/regina-police-investigate-after-drone-used-to-drop-drugs-into-prison.html.

78. R. Johnson, *Hard Time: Understanding and Reforming the Prison* (Belmont, Calif.: Wadsworth, 1996).

79. J. Power and S.L. Brown, *Self-Injurious Behaviour: A Review of the Literature and Implications for Corrections* (Ottawa: Correctional Service

Canada, 2010), http://www.csc-scc.gc.ca/text/rsrch/reports/r216/r216-eng.shtml.

80. Ibid.

81. A. Favazza, "Why Patients Mutilate Themselves," *Hospital and Community Psychiatry 40*, no. 2 (1989), 137–45.

82. Power and Brown, *Self-Injurious Behaviour: A Review of the Literature and Implications for Corrections*.

83. C.A. Dell and T. Beauchamp, "Self-Harm Among Criminalized Women," Canadian Centre on Substance Abuse [fact sheet], 2006, http://www.ccsa.ca/Resource%20Library/ccsa-011338-2006-e.pdf\#search=Self%2DHarm%20Among%20Criminalized%20Women.

84. Power and Brown, *Self-Injurious Behaviour: A Review of the Literature and Implications for Corrections*.

85. Office of the Correctional Investigator, *Annual Report, 2011–2012* (Ottawa: Author, 2012), p. 36, http://www.oci-bec.gc.ca/cnt/rpt/annrpt/annrpt20112012-eng.aspx?texthighlight=annual+report+2011.

86. A. Usher, J. Power, and G. Wilton, *Assessment, Intervention, and Prevention of Self-Injurious Behaviour in Correctional Environments* (Ottawa: Correctional Service Canada, 2010), http://www.csc-scc.gc.ca/research/005008-0220-01-eng.shtml.

87. Office of the Correctional Investigator, *Annual Report, 2011–2012*.

88. Public Safety Canada Portfolio Corrections Statistics Committee, *Corrections and Conditional Release Statistical Overview: 2015 Annual Report*, p. 69.

89. J. Power and D.L. Riley, *A Comparative Review of Suicide and Self-Injury Investigative Reports in a Canadian Federal Correctional Population* (Ottawa: Correctional Service Canada, 2010, http://www.csc-scc.gc.ca/text/rsrch/reports/r221/r221-eng.shtml.

90. Office of the Correctional Investigator of Canada, A *Three Year Review of Federal Inmate Suicides (2011–2014)* (Ottawa: Author, 2014), p. 4, http://www.oci-bec.gc.ca/cnt/rpt/pdf/oth-aut/oth-aut20140910-eng.pdf.

91. Ibid., p. 7.

92. Murphy and Johnsen, *Life 25*, p. 30.

93. R. Light and B. Campbell, "Prisoners' Families: Still Forgotten Victims?" *Journal of Social Welfare and Family Law 28*, no. 3–4 (2006), 297–308.

94. S. Hannem, "Stigma and Marginality: Gendered Experiences of Families of Male Prisons in Canada," in *Critical Criminology in Canada: New Voices, New Directions*, eds. A. Doyle and D. Moore (Vancouver: UBC Press, 2011), 183–217.

95. D. Braman, *Doing Time on the Outside: Incarceration and Family Life in Urban America* (Ann Arbor: University of Michigan Press, 2007).

96. Light and Campbell, "Prisoners' Families: Still Forgotten Victims?"; S. Moroney, *Through the Glass* (Toronto: Doubleday Canada, 2011).

97. S. Hannem and L. Leonardi, *Forgotten Victims: The Mental Health and Well-Being of Families Affected by Crime and Incarceration* (Kingston, ON: Canadian Families and Corrections Network, 2016), pp. 2–3, http://www.cfcn-rcafd.org/text/FamilyMentalHealth-FinalReport.pdf.

98. Ibid., p. 3.

99. R.C. Johnson, "Ever-Increasing Levels of Parental Incarceration and the Consequences for Children," in *Do Prisons Make Us Safer? The Benefits and Costs of the Prison Boom*, eds. S. Raphael and M.A. Stoll (New York: Sage, 2009), 177–206; J. Murray, "The Cycle of Punishment: Social Exclusion of Prisoners and Their Children," *Criminology and Criminal Justice 7*, no. 1 (2010), 55–81.

100. Hannem, "Stigma and Marginality: Gendered Experiences of Families of Male Prisons in Canada," p. 200.

101. J. Murray, D.P. Farrington, and I. Sekol, "Children's Antisocial Behavior, Mental Health, Drug Use, and Educational Performance After Parental Incarceration: A Systematic Review and Meta-Analysis," *Psychological Bulletin 138*, no. 2 (2012), 175–210.

102. L. Withers and J. Folsom, *Incarcerated Fathers: A Descriptive Analysis* (Ottawa: Correctional Service Canada, 2007), http://www.csc-scc.gc.ca/text/rsrch/reports/r186/r186-eng.pdf.

103. J. Demers, *Warehousing Prisoners in Saskatchewan* (Regina: Canadian Centre for Policy Alternatives, 2014), p. 24, https://www.policyalternatives.ca/sites/default/files/uploads/publications/Saskatchewan%20Office/2014/10/warehousing_prisoners_in_saskatchewan.pdf.

104. Office of the Correctional Investigator, *A Case Study of Diversity in Corrections: The Black Inmate Experience in Federal Penitentiaries*, p. 12.

105. Demers, *Warehousing Prisoners in Saskatchewan*, p. 26.

106. Ibid.

107. O. Yaniv, "Videoconference prison visit programs set to quadruple in size this fall," *New York Daily News*, August 28, 2012, http://www.nydailynews.com/new-york/videoconference-prison-visit-program-set-quadruple-size-fall-article-1.1146718.

108. Z. Todd, "Canada's prison visitation system 'high-tech, low-touch,' says correctional investigator," CBC News, September 25, 2016, http://www.cbc.ca/news/canada/edmonton/canada-s-prison-visitation-system-high-tech-low-touch-says-correctional-investigator-1.3777990.

109. Le Protecteur du Citoyen, *Special Report by the Quebec Ombudsman: Detention Conditions, Administration of Justice and Crime Prevention in Nunavik* (Québec City: Author: 2016), https://protecteurducitoyen.qc.ca/sites/default/files/pdf/rapports_speciaux/2016-02-18_detention-conditions-in-Nunavik.pdf.

110. Weinwrath, *Behind the Walls: Inmates and Correctional Officers on the State of Canadian Prisons*, p. 113.

111. Office of the Correctional Investigator, *In the Dark: An Investigation of Death in Custody Information Sharing and Disclosure Practices in Federal Corrections* (Ottawa: Author, 2016b), http://www.oci-bec.gc.ca/cnt/rpt/pdf/oth-aut/oth-aut20160802-eng.pdf.

112. Ibid., p. 12.

113. Ibid.

114. K. De Claire and L. Dixon, "The Effects of Prison Visits from Family Members on Prisoners' Well-Being, Prison Rule Breaking, and Recidivism: A Review of Research Since 1991," *Trauma, Violence, & Abuse 18*, no. 2 (2017), 185–99.

115. D. Derkzen, R. Gobeil, and J. Gileno, *Visitation and Post-Release Outcome Among Federally Sentenced Offenders* (Ottawa: Correctional Service Canada, 2009), http://www.csc-scc.gc.ca/text/rsrch/reports/r205/r205-eng.shtml; C.J. Taylor, "The Family's Role in the Reintegration of Formerly Incarcerated Individuals: The Direct Effects of Emotional Support," *The Prison Journal 96*, no. 3 (2016), 331–54.

116. M. Solinas-Saunders and M.J. Stacer, "Prison Resources and Physical/Verbal Assault in Prison: A Comparison of Male and Female Inmates," *Victims and Offenders 7*, no. 3 (2012), 279–311.

117. J. Christian, J. Mellow, and S. Thomas, "Social and Economic Implications of Family Connections to Prisoners," *Journal of Criminal Justice 34*, no. 4 (2006), 443–52.

118. H.E. Duncan and S. Balbar, "Evaluation of a Visitation Program at a Canadian Penitentiary", *Prison Journal 88*, no. 2 (2008), 300–27.

119. K. Taylor, "The book club at the big house: How reading makes a difference in prison," *Globe and Mail*, November 21, 2014, https://www.theglobeandmail.com/arts/books-and-media/the-book-club-at-the-big-house-how-reading-makes-a-difference-in-prison/article21691700/.

120. "Commissioner's Directive: Offender Complaints and Grievances," Correctional Service Canada website, January 13, 2014, http://www.csc-scc.gc.ca/acts-and-regulations/081-cd-eng.shtml.

121. T. Lupick, "Stephen Harper's Tough-on-Crime Agenda Linked to Increasingly Dangerous Prisons," *Georgia Straight*, August 23, 2014, http://www.straight.com/news/307446/stephen-harpers-tough-crime-agenda-linked-increasingly-dangerous-prisons.

122. P. White, "Inmate was Justified in Stabbing Other Prisoner, Ontario Judge Says," *Globe and Mail*, July 19, 2016, http://www.theglobeandmail.com/news/toronto/inmate-was-justified-in-stabbing-other-prisoner-ontario-judge-says/article31003398/.

123. Ibid.

CHAPTER 9

CLASSIFICATION, CASE MANAGEMENT, AND TREATMENT

CHAPTER OBJECTIVES

- Discuss the process of classification and risk assessment.
- Discuss the tools and techniques used in classifying inmates.
- Describe the five phases of case management.
- Describe the CSC's Integrated Correctional Program Model.
- Identify and discuss the principles of effective correctional treatment.
- Discuss what is known about the effectiveness of various types of correctional treatment programs.
- Discuss the difficulties that surround attempts to assess the effectiveness of correctional treatment programs.
- Identify and discuss the potential obstacles to effective correctional treatment.
- Discuss what the research says about the effectiveness of correctional treatment.

There are three major trends in offender classification and treatment: (1) the increasing use of sophisticated risk/needs assessment instruments; (2) the increasing domination of treatment research, policy, and programs by a psychological perspective—in particular, a cognitive-behavioural approach; and (3) differentiated treatment approaches for women, Indigenous people, and specific categories of offenders such as sex offenders.

CLASSIFICATION AND RISK ASSESSMENT

Classification is the process by which inmates are subdivided into groups based on a variety of factors. In each region of Correctional Service Canada (CSC), there are reception centres where offenders spend a period of time after sentencing. Classification is used to determine the appropriate custody and security level, program placement, and assignment to housing units within the institution.

> **Classification**
> Using various assessment instruments to categorize inmates in order to determine the appropriate security level and programs.

Classification involves gathering documentation on the offender from a variety of sources, including the family, corrections, the courts, the police, and the victim. Then, at the reception centre, the inmate is evaluated for health, mental health, security concerns, and suicide risk. Also, a risk and needs assessment is conducted. During the initial classification process, the factors considered in determining the inmate's security level include institutional adjustment; the offender's escape risk and risk to the public; where the institution is located; the seriousness of the offence; outstanding charges; the offender's social, criminal, and (where available) young offender history; potential for violence; and any physical or mental illness.

On the basis of all these, an institutional placement is decided on and programming recommendations are made. The classification of offenders, with a strong emphasis on risk and needs, is a core component of correctional treatment.

There is considerable variation in the quality of classification across the country and even between the federal and provincial systems within the same jurisdiction. Federal inmates in Newfoundland and Labrador, for example, gave that province's classification process high marks; inmates in the provincial system, however, viewed it as inadequate.[1]

Early in a federal inmate's sentence, a reintegration potential rating is established, based on information gleaned from a number of risk assessment instruments as well as various static and dynamic risk factors. This rating places the individual inmate in one of three categories: high, medium, or low reintegration potential. Most inmates with high reintegration potential will not require core programming. The existence of this category reflects the concern that some inmates are being steered into programs unnecessarily, which is a waste of their time and the system's resources.

Assessment continues throughout the offender's sentence, from intake through incarceration and release from custody and up to sentence expiry. Inmates are reclassified periodically in the course of their confinement based on their progress and performance in treatment programs and work assignments and on their behaviour in the institution. Both at the initial classification stage and in later classification decisions, correctional personnel consider security and risk concerns as well as the inmate's abilities and program needs. The assessment process for federal offenders is set out in Figure 9.1.

Offenders have a variety of criminogenic needs that must be addressed both within the institution and later in the community. These relate variously to education, social networks, employment, accommodation, drugs and alcohol, attitudes, and cognitive skills. All of these criminogenic needs are *dynamic* in the sense that they are amenable to change. All have been found to be important in reducing the likelihood of reoffending.[2]

Given the high number of inmates who are suffering from mental health issues, it has been recommended that a standardized mental health assessment/ screening tool be administered at admission to all offenders.[3]

Figure 9.1

Offender Intake Assessment Process

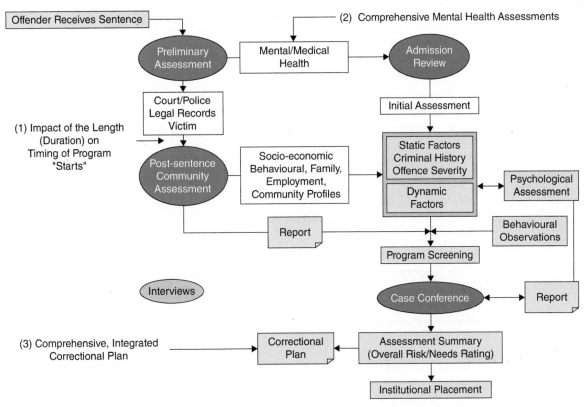

Source: A Road Map to Strengthening Public Safety. http://www.johnhoward.ca/media/A%20Roadmap%20to%20Strengthening%20 Public%20Safety%20-%20English%20Report.pdf Canada, 2007). Reproduced with the permission of the Minister of Public Works and Government Services Canada, 2013.

CASE MANAGEMENT

Correctional **case management** is the process by which the needs and abilities of offenders are matched with correctional programs and services. The primary goals of case management are (1) to enable systematic monitoring of the offender during all phases of confinement, (2) to balance the need for rehabilitation with community protection, (3) to prepare the inmate for successful reintegration into the community, and (4) to contribute to the effective supervision of the offender in the community.

Corrections File 9.1 provides an overview of the case management process. Note that case management is carried out both during the inmate's confinement and after release from the institution.

Because most of the offenders in provincial/territorial correctional systems spend a very short time in confinement, the case management that does occur

> **Case management**
> The process by which the needs and abilities of offenders are matched with correctional programs and services.

CORRECTIONS FILE 9.1

The Five Phases of Case Management

I. Initial Assessment and Institutional Placement
  - Identification of inmate risks/needs
  - Development of correctional plan

II. Correctional Planning and Institutional Supervision
  - Correctional plan initiated
  - Institutional programs (work, treatment, skills upgrading)
  - Institutional transfers
  - Institutional releases (temporary absences, work releases)
  - Ongoing monitoring of inmate progress

III. Preparing Cases for Release Decisions
  - Institutional progress reports
  - Community assessments

IV. Parole Board Decision and Release
  - Temporary absences, day/full parole, statutory release

V. Community Supervision

tends to focus on release planning. For many of these inmates, there is little or no case planning or access to treatment programs. In federal institutions, by contrast, case management generally involves a much longer time frame. Regular reviews are conducted during which program requirements are identified and decisions are made about transferring inmates from one institution to another and, eventually, releasing them.

In federal institutions, a key role in case management is played by institutional parole officers (IPOs), who have the primary responsibility for case management and who work on teams that include COs, psychologists, and the offender, among others. Their duties include the following: assessing offenders' needs as well as behaviour or attitudes that have contributed to their criminal behaviour; developing intervention plans to address those attitudes and behaviours; and helping offenders undertake and complete their intervention plans.

The IPOs also make recommendations concerning offender transfers, temporary absences, and other forms of conditional release, including parole. In many institutions, IPOs spend most of their time completing paperwork rather than supervising and counselling inmates; this may make it harder for them to help offenders.

A review found that while the IPOs were involved in determining when an offender was ready for early release from the institution, these officers had only limited tools and guidelines to assist them in this assessment.[4] It was also found that there was considerable variation in the number of face-to-face visits between IPOs and inmates, and that there were not more frequent meetings with high-risk offenders than low-risk offenders.[5]

Classification Tools and Techniques

The classification procedures applied by Canadian systems of corrections generally involve psychological, personality, and behavioural inventories. At the federal level, the procedure is referred to as the Offender Intake Assessment (OIA), during which extensive information on the offender's criminal history and patterns is gathered. The majority of offenders in federal custody are classified as "medium" risk, although Indigenous offenders at this risk level are more likely to be held in a medium- or maximum-security institution than their non-Indigenous counterparts.[6]

Concerns have been expressed about the "over-classification" of Indigenous offenders at intake. In 2015, a Federal Court judge ordered the CSC to stop using its risk assessment tools on Indigenous offenders, ruling that the assessments did not adequately consider the special needs of Indigenous offenders and were susceptible to cultural bias.[7] In 2016, however, this decision was overturned by the Federal Court of Appeal, which held that there was insufficient evidence presented at the original trial to indicate that the assessments produced inaccurate or unreliable results.[8]

The provinces and territories vary considerably with regard to their capacity to conduct classification. A review of Nova Scotia corrections, for example, found that there was no system in place to assess the risk that an offender might pose while incarcerated.[9]

Risk and Needs Profiles of Offenders

Risk assessment and risk management are the mantras of contemporary corrections, and the assessment of risk is central to classification and case management. Risk assessments are designed to identify those offenders who are most likely to reoffend upon release from the institution if no treatment intervention occurs.[10]

Risk analysis is used to determine which facility the offender should be confined in or moved to; to identify the offender's treatment needs; to identify those offenders who require higher levels of support, intervention, and supervision upon release; and to assist in release decisions. Since an inmate's criminal history is strongly related to success (or failure) on conditional release, the assessment of both risk and needs improves predictions about which offenders will recidivate.

Risk determination, then, involves combining static criminal history information with dynamic (or criminogenic need) factors. This determination plays a role in decisions to release offenders from confinement (see Chapter 10). Risk assessments are also used to assign offenders to a specific level of security, to inform program decisions, as information for release authorities, and to determine supervision requirements.

In assessing the degree of risk posed by an offender, corrections personnel generally consider both **static risk factors** and **dynamic risk factors**. Static risk factors include the offender's criminal history (including prior convictions), the seriousness of prior offences, and whether the offender has successfully completed previous periods of supervision in the community. Dynamic risk factors focus on those attributes of the offender that can be altered through intervention; they include addiction issues, attitude and motivation, cognitive abilities, and education and job skills. As is not the case with static factors, it is possible to change dynamic factors—for the better or, if not addressed, for the worse. Many risk/needs factors are **criminogenic**—that is, if they are not addressed, future criminal behaviour may occur.

All correctional personnel, from institutional staff to parole board members to parole officers, have access to theoretically and/or empirically based assessment instruments and tools. These instruments provide them with information with which to develop effective management and treatment plans; they also reduce the liability and culpability of personnel should the offender later commit serious crimes in the community.

Corrections File 9.2 describes several of the more common risk assessment instruments used by the CSC, as well as one used in Ontario and other provinces for provincial offenders. Many of these instruments can also be used by community corrections personnel, including probation officers and parole officers.

Presumably, these instruments have replaced what has been referred to as "structured professional judgment" (more traditionally, "discretion"). However, corrections personnel can subvert the objective results of risk assessments by exercising discretion.[11] Considerable controversy has surrounded the risk assessment and classification of women offenders (see Chapter 12).

Research studies have identified eight factors (i.e., the "Central Eight") that reliably predict involvement in criminality and that need to be targeted to reduce recidivism. These are composed of the "Big Four"—(1) antisocial peers, (2) antisocial temperament/personality, (3) antisocial attitudes, and (4) history of antisocial behaviour—and the "Moderate Four"—(1) lack of attachment to family/marital supports, (2) social/employment problems, (3) lack of prosocial leisure or recreation activities, and (4) substance abuse.[12] Note that this list includes both static and dynamic risk factors.

Figure 9.2 presents information on the identified treatment needs of persons in the Calgary Remand Centre, while Figure 9.3 presents data on the rehabilitative needs of offenders admitted to correctional facilities in Saskatchewan in 2010–11. The majority of offenders in Saskatchewan had five of the six rehabilitative needs. Note the high percentage of offenders with substance abuse issues and social interaction deficits among this population.[13]

There appears to be considerable variability in the extent to which corrections systems gather information on inmate needs. An audit of adult provincial corrections in Manitoba found a lack of statistical information on the needs

Static risk factors
Attributes of the offender that predict the likelihood of recidivism and that are not amenable to change, including criminal history, prior convictions, seriousness of prior offences, and performance on previous conditional releases.

Dynamic risk factors
Attributes of the offender that can be altered through intervention, including level of education, employment skills, addiction issues, and cognitive thinking abilities.

Criminogenic risk factors
Risk/needs factors that contribute to a person's propensity to commit criminal offences, including substance abuse problems and the acceptance of antisocial values. See also dynamic risk factors.

CORRECTIONS FILE 9.2

Selected Risk Assessment Instruments

- OIA—Revised: Information is gathered at intake on the offender's criminal history and from post-sentence community assessment; measured are static and dynamic risk factors, as well as the offender's accountability, motivation, and responsivity; information is entered into the Offender Management System.
- Custody Rating Scale: Determines the initial risk and classification level of male offenders; used to make an initial placement of new inmates; includes information on offence, sentence length, history of disciplinary infractions, substance use, number of prior convictions (after age 16), age at sentencing and at time of first federal admission, escape history, conditional release history, and indicators of social stability.
- Security Reclassification Scale (SRS for men) (SRS–W for women): A multipoint scale used to inform decisions on the inmate's security level; includes information on the inmate's behaviour in the institution, and participation and progress in treatment programs.
- Statistical Information on Recidivism Scale Revised: A 15-item scale used to estimate the probability of an offender reoffending within three years of release from custody; includes age and criminal history; not administered to women or Indigenous offenders.[a]
- STATIC-99/STATIC-2002: Designed to estimate the probability of sexual and violent recidivism among men who have been convicted of at least one sexual offence against a child or nonconsenting adult; includes items on general criminal history and information specific to the sex offence.
- Level of Service Inventory—Ontario Revised: Standardized interview relating to the offender, including offence history, substance abuse, and employment history; used in Ontario and several other provinces.
- LS/CMI: A risk assessment and case management tool; assesses the risk and needs factors of offenders; scales cover criminal history, family/marital, alcohol/drug issues, pro-criminal attitudes/orientation, and barriers to release, among others; used in several provinces.
- Spousal Assault Risk Assessment (SARA): A 20-item set of risk factors used to predict the risk of future violent offending among men convicted of spousal assault.
- Psychopathy Check List: A 20-item scale used to predict recidivism and violent reoffending.

---

[a] M. Nafekh and L.L. Motiuk, *The Statistical Information on Recidivism—Revised 1 (SIR-R1) Scale: A Psychometric Examination* (Ottawa: Correctional Service Canada, 2002), http://www.csc-scc.gc.ca/research/092/r126_e.pdf.

of offenders who were incarcerated. The report noted that the corrections department "did not know the average educational level of its offenders. Nor did it know the percentage of offenders employed, lacking adequate housing, suffering from a mental disorder, or reporting substance abuse or mental health problems."[14]

Figure 9.2

Estimated Percentage of Identified Treatment Needs—Calgary Remand Centre

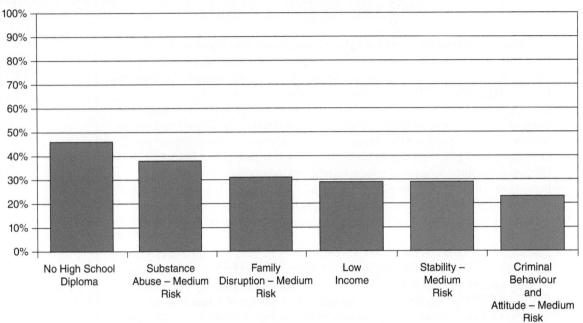

Source: Adapted from P. Thompson and J. Schutte, *Integrated Justice Services Project: Implementing Problem-Solving Justice* (Edmonton: Government of Alberta, 2010), p. 32, http://www.courtinnovation.org/sites/default/files/documents/Intergrated%20 Justice%20Service%20Project.pdf.

Figure 9.3

Adults in Sentenced Custody, by Type of Rehabilitative Need, Saskatchewan, 2010–11

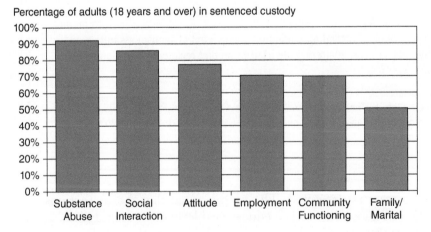

Source: M. Dauvergne, *Adult Correctional Statistics in Canada, 2010–2011* (Ottawa: Minister of Industry, 2012), p. 13. http://www.statcan. gc.ca/pub/85-002-x/2012001/article/11715-eng.pdf.

The extensive use of risk assessment instruments can have a significant impact on offenders, by defining them in ways that hinder efforts at self-determination. Many of these instruments have validity as predictors of risk and the likelihood of reoffending; too often, though, they are not accompanied by an equal amount of attention to the development of personal relationships with offenders.[15] "Assessment is simply 'done to them' in the interests of public protection, and they have very limited opportunities to present alternative versions of life events and self-identity."[16] Offenders with specific challenges such as addiction, mental illness, and/or fetal alcohol spectrum disorder (FASD) may have little ability to counter the identity created by correctional professionals.

The Correctional Plan

At the core of case management is the **correctional plan**. One of these is developed for most inmates, the exception being those who are serving short sentences. This plan determines the offender's initial institution placement, specific treatment and training opportunities, and release plan.

The correctional plan is based on the risk/needs profile of the inmate and is used to guide all decisions made about the inmate. The plan identifies program needs, based in part on the dynamic factors discussed above. For example, if substance abuse is a contributing factor to the inmate's pattern of criminality, then the offender should be referred to a substance abuse program. The correctional plan also sets out benchmarks, including parole eligibility dates and likely program entrance dates.

A review of the process by which CSC officials develop correctional plans found a lack of guidelines as to which documents must be obtained and reviewed to ensure the integrity of the intake assessment process. Key official documents were often not available for use in determining the offender's security level.[17] This included timely access to information on the offender's criminal history.

> **Correctional plan**
> A key component of the case management process that determines the offender's initial institution placement, specific treatment or training opportunities, and preparation for release.

INSTITUTIONAL TREATMENT PROGRAMS

The programs most frequently offered in correctional institutions address substance abuse, family violence, and anger management. Also offered are GED (high school equivalency) courses and various vocational programs. Still other programs target specific groups of offenders, such as sex offenders. Some programs are facilitated by outside groups such as Alcoholics Anonymous and Narcotics Anonymous. And there are specific programs for women offenders (see Chapter 12) and Indigenous offenders (see Chapter 13).

Provincial/territorial institutions vary considerably in the programs they offer. The short time that most offenders spend in these institutions makes it difficult to address alcohol, drug, and mental health issues or to develop specialized programs (e.g., for offenders with FASD). Over one-half of the custodial sentences that are handed down by judges are one month or less.[18]

Overcrowding often limits inmate access to programs, with the consequence that many offenders leave the institution without completing a full course of treatment. Although many provincial/territorial programs are modelled on the CSC's, severe time constraints require authorities to compress the program timelines, and this may compromise program integrity. The maintenance of program integrity has been found to be associated with reduced rates of reoffending among inmate participants.[19]

It is valid to ask whether treatment is a priority for correctional authorities. The CSC, for example, spends less on correctional programming than on staff overtime—about 2 percent of its multibillion-dollar budget. Programs for inmates in provincial/territorial facilities are often limited and are the first item to be reduced in times of fiscal restraint.[20] This despite the fact that offenders in custody are generally higher risk and have more needs than those under supervision in the community.

The CSC Integrated Correctional Program Model

The CSC has developed the **Integrated Correctional Program Model (ICPM),** which consists of three distinct program streams: (1) a multi-target program; (2) a sex offender program; and (3) an Aboriginal multi-target program. The ICPM integrates best practices from programs that had previously been offered separately, including anger management, cognitive skills, and violent offender programs.[21] The ICPM includes the most effective components of these programs while continuing to target the dynamic risk factors of offenders through social-learning, cognitive-behavioural, and structured-behavioural practices.

> **Integrated Correctional Program Model (ICPM)**
> An interdisciplinary approach to correctional programming operated by the CSC.

Reflecting what is known about the risk principle, the ICPM is delivered according to the offender's likelihood of reoffending. Higher risk offenders participate in high-intensity programs that involve approximately 100 two-hour sessions, whereas moderate risk offenders receive moderate-intensity programs that involve approximately 50 two-hour sessions. These hours do not reflect the number of additional hours that offenders may spend in the primer and maintenance components of ICPM. The Multi-Target Program–High Intensity, for example, is designed for high-risk offenders. It contains five modules and is centred on the good lives model and the principles of risk–need–responsivity (RNR). There are approximately 100 two-hour sessions, delivered to groups no larger than 12 inmates. There are modules on relationships, clear thinking, living a healthy lifestyle, conflict resolution skills, and the challenges of self-management.

The ICPM also attempts to provide inmates with more timely access to treatment programs, to deliver interventions in a more effective manner, to increase the rates of program completion, and to decrease the rates of readmission for new convictions.

Evaluations of the ICPM have found that inmates under this model experience shorter wait times to access programs and have higher completion rates.

Also, Indigenous inmates have significantly higher rates of program completion and access their first program earlier in their sentence—within six months of admission.[22]

However, with respect to outcomes, the ICPM was no more effective than traditional programming approaches in reducing reoffending. For Indigenous offenders, the rates of reoffending were higher among those who participated in the ICPM. The reasons for this are unknown.

An exception was that inmates with convictions for spousal assault who participated in the ICPM program had lower levels of readmission to prison than those who participated in other programs.[23]

Treating High-Risk Offenders: Sex Offender Treatment Programs

The treatment of sex offenders has become a focal point of correctional systems, in large measure because of growing public and political concern about this group of offenders and their growing numbers in institutional populations.

Sex offenders are difficult to treat, especially those classified as high risk. Their patterns of deviance are often deeply entrenched. Furthermore, to a greater extent than other offender groups, sex offenders tend to deny having committed an offence, to minimize the impact of the crime on the victim(s), and to attribute their behaviour to the actions and wishes of the victim(s). Sex offenders may not be motivated to participate in treatment programs and to engage in the self-change.[24]

CORRECTIONS PERSPECTIVE 9.1

Sex Offender Treatment Therapist

In discussing treatment, I will always separate out sex offenders in terms of the dynamics of offending and treatment intervention. Sex offenders are the ones who have the greatest difficulty taking responsibility for what they have done. Groups are a good way to get to them. When you facilitate a group of sex offenders, there is a certain dynamic that goes on. A sex offender might say that the only reason that he fondled the five-year-old is because he was drunk; another sex offender across the room will say, "I wasn't drunk when I fondled my victim." Sex offenders in the group have an understanding of behaviour that I will never have. With sex offenders, the biggest strength of the group was their being able to help each other accept responsibility for their behaviour. Sometimes it would get very intense in the groups, and the language would be very colourful. They would get into each other's faces and say, "You are lying to yourself. You can lie to us, but don't lie to yourself."

Source: Personal communication with C.T. Griffiths.

As a group, and in contrast to the general inmate population, sex offenders tend to represent a broad spectrum of society: educated professionals, skilled tradespeople, and persons who, except for their sexual deviance, may live stable lives. This may present challenges for treatment staff, who will be wary of being manipulated.

Most treatment interventions for sex offenders take a multidisciplinary approach that involves psychiatrists, psychometrists, social workers, physicians, nurses, chaplains, recreational staff, and volunteers. These programs are designed to reduce the likelihood that sex offenders will recidivate upon release from the institution. Programs focus on identifying the nature and pattern of the offender's behaviour and on providing skills in self-management and self-control. Many treatment programs for sex offenders take a cognitive-behavioural approach and emphasize relapse prevention. This involves having sex offenders become aware of the thoughts, feelings, and behaviour that are related to their offending. In this way, they learn to identify the "triggers" for their sex offending and to develop strategies for managing these triggers. For some sex offenders, this may include not being alone in the company of a minor or not being near schools and playgrounds.

Short-Changing Low-Risk Offenders?

Following the principles of RNR, the CSC focuses its treatment interventions on high-risk offenders and, in so doing, gives less attention to the needs of low-risk offenders. As of 2009, federal inmates who are classified as low risk no longer have access to correctional programming.[25] This decision was made based on research that indicated that correctional programs were most effective with high-risk offenders.

This may result in low-risk inmates having less access to programs than their higher-risk counterparts. However, low-risk inmates have needs as well. Compounding this situation is that many low-risk federal inmates remain in custody after their parole eligibility date.[26]

A review of casework files ($N = 50$) of institutional parole officers found that few of the inmates who were classified as low risk were recommended for release when they were first eligible.[27]

Community Involvement in Institutional Programs

Community volunteers are involved in a wide range of activities in Canadian institutions. Many volunteers represent community service clubs and various religious organizations; others work one-on-one with inmates both during confinement and following release. The most active programs of this type are M2 (Man to Man) and W2 (Woman to Woman). In these programs, a citizen from the community is matched with an offender. Across the country, college and university students are actively involved in institutional programs. One is the Inside-Out program, in which students go into institutions and study with inmates in a post-secondary class.[28]

Inmate Community Services Projects and Activities

The media's focus on the more sensational events in corrections, such as escapes, riots, and heinous crimes committed by offenders under supervision in the community, tends to obscure the extensive involvement of federal and provincial/territorial inmates in community service projects. Inmates are involved in snow removal for seniors (Peace River Correctional Centre in Alberta), making wooden toys that are donated to non profit organizations (Fort Saskatchewan Correctional Centre), and cleaning up provincial parks and fighting forest fires (B.C. provincial institution).[29]

These activities benefit various groups of community residents; at the same time, they provide an outlet for the energies and talents of inmates and engage them in community-focused endeavours. Participation in community projects may help inmates develop prosocial attitudes and behaviours.

THE PRINCIPLES OF EFFECTIVE CORRECTIONAL TREATMENT

There is conclusive evidence that effective correctional interventions (1) are based on empirically supported models of behavioural change; (2) incorporate the principles of RNR; (3) are focused on the dynamic, that is, changeable factors related to criminal behaviour; (4) are geared to the learning style of the offender; (5) are monitored, evaluated, and accredited; and (6) are implemented by well-trained, dedicated program staff.[30]

Recall that the risk principle holds that treatment interventions have a greater chance of success when they are matched with the risk level of the offender. Higher levels of service are reserved for higher-risk inmates; lower-risk inmates do not require the same level of service to benefit from treatment interventions and may, in fact, be negatively affected by intensive service delivery. Treatment programs have little impact on reoffending among low-risk offenders. Higher-risk inmates benefit from treatment programs that focus on criminogenic factors.[31]

The need principle holds that to be effective, treatment interventions must address the criminogenic needs of inmates. As described earlier, research indicates that to see the greatest reductions in recidivism, interventions must target the Central Eight.

And the responsivity principle refers to the "how" of intervention and includes both general and specific responsivity. General responsivity holds that treatment interventions are most effective when offered using social-learning and cognitive-behavioural techniques where prosocial behaviour can be promoted and reinforced.[32] Specific responsivity holds that treatment interventions must be matched to the learning styles and abilities of individual inmates.[33] This presents challenges to correctional systems, for many offenders have disabilities that present obstacles to learning. The responsivity principle is associated with the notion of **differential treatment effectiveness**: that not all programs will work with all offenders.

Differential treatment effectiveness The requirement that, to be effective, treatment interventions be multifaceted and matched to the specific needs of individual offenders.

CREATING THE CONDITIONS FOR EFFECTIVE CORRECTIONAL TREATMENT

Corrections personnel must create conditions that increase the potential effectiveness of treatment programs. In any prison population, there is considerable variability regarding how inmates adapt to confinement and how closely they adhere to institutional rules and display an interest in participating in prosocial activities and programs. One challenge confronting correctional administrators is how to accommodate those inmates who are interested in making positive changes, while at the same time controlling the more negative influences of those inmates who are engaged in illicit and disruptive behaviour. Similarly, correctional staff may be challenged to remain optimistic when high-risk offenders who are disruptive and unmotivated to change are given priority access to treatment programs.[34]

As noted in Chapter 7, the relations between prison staff (including COs) and inmates are an important factor in correctional treatment. It is important that COs and other staff support the efforts of treatment personnel in their daily interactions with the inmates.

Inmate Amenability to Treatment

The inmate is a key component of the treatment process. For any program to have a significant impact, the offender must be amenable to treatment. Among the inmates in any institutional population, there is a **differential amenability to treatment**. In other words, not all inmates are receptive to treatment. This can be for a variety of reasons, including mental deficiency or learning disability, a deeply rooted attitudinal and behavioural pattern centred on a criminal lifestyle, an extensive history of confinement in institutions, and/or a general lack of interest in making the effort to change.

Many offenders are in a state of denial about the offence for which they have been convicted, and this frame of mind may make effective treatment intervention more difficult. In the words of one treatment professional:

> *Embarrassment and shame are two major issues you have to deal with. And denial. And wanting to blame others: "It's not really my fault. If I hadn't been dating Joe, this would never have happened." Accepting responsibility for what they did, and the fact that they made choices to deal drugs, or whatever, is important. Yes they were involved in prostitution. Yes they were abused and addicted. But that does not give them permission to hurt somebody, to do a home invasion.*

Personal communication with D. Murdoch

Other inmates may not see the relevance of treatment programs. One ex-inmate commented:

> *If I could improve the system at all, if I could contribute, it would be lose the programs. The violence prevention program was a joke. You go to a*

Differential amenability to treatment
The notion that, for a variety of reasons, not all inmates are receptive to treatment, and/or that they require interventions tailored to meet their specific needs, abilities, and interests.

classroom every day for two months or whatever, and they tell you not to use violence, how to stop and breathe, stop and think, and they toss you a ball: "Are you a green ball today? Yellow ball today? Or a red ball today?" It's absolutely ridiculous. Right after, you go back to the range, somebody calls you a goof, and it's like, "Are you going to stop and think or are you going to fight the guy?"[35]

In contrast, the criminologist Michael Weinrath found that most of the federal and provincial Canadian inmates he interviewed held positive views toward vocational programs and treatment programs, although they noted that the inmate had to be ready to change. One inmate stated, "Programs are important. If you want to change, the programs are there and they work. But I'm only seeing that now, you know."[36] Another noted, "Programs are important. Our teachers are excellent. But you have to be ready for them. Because you're not going to learn until you shut up and listen."[37]

Research has found that inmates who are "treatment ready" were more than two times likely to complete programs.[38]

Inmates who are receptive to treatment may struggle to alter deeply engrained attitudes and behaviour. An Aboriginal Programs Officer related how he conducted his violence prevention groups for federal Indigenous offenders:

I give a lot of examples to the guys in my group: the rent's due; your girlfriend's telling you to find a job; she's telling you the diapers are low; the baby needs food. Are you going to do what you did before? Or are you going to find a new way to move forward? You need to tell me what it is about the way of moving forward that is healthy and that's not going to harm anybody.

Personal communication with D. Murdoch

These challenges are illustrated in Corrections File 9.3, in the responses of one inmate in a "Trigger Thought Exercise" in a violence prevention program (VPP).

In this exercise, the inmates in the VPP are being taught to recognize their triggers for violence. The approach reflects the reality that many offenders have few coping skills or alternative methods for resolving stressful situations they become involved in and may have few nonviolent conflict resolution skills.

Inmate Access to Programs and Program Relevance

That inmates have timely access to treatment programs is a key requirement for effective interventions. Once the inmate's correctional plan has been created, it is important that it be actioned. An audit of CSC programming found that the CSC has improved the timeliness of program delivery; however, it also found that a large number of offenders (65 percent in

CORRECTIONS FILE 9.3

An Inmate's Responses in a Violence Prevention Program: Trigger Thought Exercise

Instructions: Read each example. If you were the person in the example, what would you be thinking? Write down your response. What thoughts would go through your mind?

Example 1: You are driving down the highway and are cut off by another driver. You slam on your brakes to avoid hitting him. If this were you, what would you be thinking?

Response: "What an asshole."

Example 2: The guy next to you bumps into you in a line-up. He looks at you and says, "Hey Buster, watch out." If this were you, what would you be thinking?

Response: "What a fucking loser. It's his fault."

Example 3: Your ex-spouse/partner promises to drop your children off for a visit, but doesn't show up again. If this were you, what would you be thinking?

Response: "Fucking bitch. She did it on purpose."

Example 4: You are financially desperate and have applied for income assistance. Your financial assistance worker sets a meeting up for you in two weeks. When the date comes, you are told that you do not qualify for income assistance. What would you be thinking?

Response: "This is bullshit. I'm being put into a situation where I can't win."

Example 5: Your next-door neighbour leaves a note on your door saying if you are noisy at night again, she's calling the police. If this were you, what would you be thinking?

Response: "Fucking rat."

Source: Anonymous.

2013–14) had not completed their programs prior to being first eligible for consideration for early release.[39]

An investigation by the federal Auditor General, found that Indigenous offenders waited, on average, five months after their admission to custody to start their correctional programs in fiscal year 2015–16, and only one-fifth of short-term offenders (those sentenced to four years or less) completed their correctional programs by the time of their first conditional release eligibility date.[40]

Inmates in provincial/territorial institutions may have difficulty accessing programs in a timely manner, and they are often released from custody before completing their programs. Provincial inmates often identify a lack of programming as a major issue. Access to and completion of treatment programs may be especially problematic for sex offenders, who may be released before

Figure 9.4

Program Completion of a Sample of B.C. Provincial Inmates

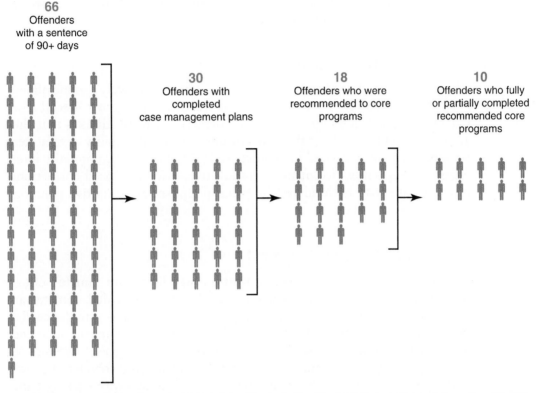

66
Offenders
with a sentence
of 90+ days

30
Offenders with
completed
case management plans

18
Offenders who were
recommended to core
programs

10
Offenders who fully
or partially completed
recommended core
programs

Source: Office of the Auditor General of British Columbia, *An Audit of the Adult Custody Division's Correctional Facilities and Programs* (Victoria: Author, 2015), p. 29, http://www.bcauditor.com/sites/default/files/publications/2015/special/report/AGBC%20Corrections%20 report%20FINAL.pdf.

they have completed a multi-month treatment program. A review of correctional programming in B.C. provincial institutions found low rates of program completion (see Figure 9.4).

Even if inmates have timely access to programs and are amenable to treatment, there is the issue of the relevance of treatment interventions, particularly as it relates to Indigenous and Black inmates and to inmates of different ethnicities.

An investigation by the OCI found that Black inmates were exposed to culturally inappropriate educational materials; had difficulty securing work positions in the institution, particularly those that involved an element of "trust" or provided training in a trade; and had a lack of access to community support groups from the Black community.[41]

In recognition of the importance of culture in treatment programming, the CSC has developed a number of programs specifically designed for Indigenous offenders. These are discussed in Chapter 13.

POTENTIAL OBSTACLES TO EFFECTIVE CORRECTIONAL TREATMENT

There are a number of potential obstacles to the delivery of effective treatment programs in correctional institutions.

Punishment versus Treatment

The primary mandate of correctional institutions—to securely confine offenders—often undermines the objectives of treatment programs. Recall from Chapter 6 that a defining attribute of correctional institutions is that they are public and political entities. This means that the availability of treatment resources may be restricted by politicians, legislatures, and community interest groups. Attempts to introduce innovative, evidence-based correctional interventions may be hindered by penal populism and punitive penology (see Chapters 1 and 2).

Doing Time and Doing Treatment

The dynamics of life inside the institution may hinder an inmate's efforts to participate in treatment programs. As Chapter 8 revealed, inmates are confronted with a variety of pains of imprisonment, as well as with the need to develop coping and survival strategies for doing time. Though inmate adherence to the convict code has eroded in recent years, the inmate social system, with its attendant illicit goods and services, and the violence and coercion that exist in many institutions, may be a major obstacle to treatment within the system.

Inmates who must expend a considerable portion of their time and energy coping with confinement and avoiding victimization may find it difficult to pursue self-change through participation in treatment programs. They may also be intimidated by other inmates not to participate in correctional programming.[42] Ironically, one of the biggest obstacles to the delivery of effective correctional treatment may be the institution itself and the dynamics of life inside correctional institutions.[43]

The Expectations of Rehabilitation

Rehabilitation is a value-laden process in which a key question is this: Just what is correctional intervention attempting to accomplish? The answers to that question may include the following: to develop in the offender prosocial attitudes and behaviour; to address the issues associated with criminal behaviour; to stabilize and strengthen inmates' personal lives and relationships; or—the most common measure—to prevent reoffending.

The challenges facing offenders who want to significantly alter their attitudes and behaviour should not be underestimated. Many offenders have grown up in marginalized, dysfunctional circumstances, with little contact with law-abiding citizens. Often they have few if any noncriminal friends. They may suffer from addiction, mental health disability, or FASD, and they may have limited skills. The expectation that participation in a compressed treatment program in a provincial/territorial institution will begin to address what are often long-standing difficulties is unrealistic, especially in the absence of follow-up programs and services in the community.

The challenges for offenders may be compounded by treatment staff who bring to their work professional and middle-class values that influence the decisions they make about offenders. The chasm between treatment professionals, as the providers of service, and offenders, as clients of that service, may hinder the development of positive therapist–offender relationships and compromise the effectiveness of interventions. Conversely, treatment professionals may be labouring under legislation and correctional policies that reflect a punitive penology.

Short Periods of Confinement: Inmate Access to Programs

Offenders who are sent to provincial/territorial institutions spend only a very short period of time in confinement. Nearly 60 percent of adult offenders served a term of one month or less in 2014–15.[44] In Ontario, 76 percent of persons sentenced to provincial correctional facilities in 2015 received a sentence of three months or less.[45]

The challenges of providing treatment programs in provincial/territorial institutions are especially acute, given the short periods of confinement. There is a shortage of programs in many of these institutions, and existing programs must be delivered within an extremely compressed time frame.[46] Yet offenders in these facilities face many of the same problems as federal inmates, including low levels of education, anger management problems, a propensity to violence, mental disabilities, FASD, and substance abuse problems. It is unlikely that an offender with a long-standing drug addiction is going to even begin to address this issue during a six-week program inside the institution.

For provincial/territorial offenders, the use of probation, either as an alternative to confinement or following a period of confinement, may hold the most promise for effective treatment interventions (see Chapter 5).

Even federal offenders may face a very short timeline for completing programs so that evidence of treatment success can be presented to the parole board as part of the inmate's application for conditional release. The federal ICPM, discussed earlier, was designed specifically to provide inmates with timely access to programs.

There is **differential treatment availability** in correctional institutions. This results in situations where, for example, a high-risk sex offender receives one year of treatment in a specialized program in one CSC region, while a sex offender in another region completes only a six-month nonresidential program. The newly minted ICPM is designed to increase inmate access to programs in federal institutions.

Differential treatment availability
The recognition that, within systems of corrections, not all inmates have equal access to treatment programs.

There are unique challenges in delivering effective treatment programs for women offenders (see Chapter 12) and Indigenous offenders (see Chapter 13).

Low Rates of Inmate Participation and Program Completion

Although the classification process can determine the programming needs of inmates, many offenders either never enroll in programs or fail to complete the ones that have been recommended. Non-completion rates appear to be higher among Indigenous inmates, higher-risk inmates, and inmates with less education.[47]

Only about 50 percent of federal inmates who have a treatment component in their correctional plan actually participate in a treatment program.[48] A large study of federal offenders ($N = 24,315$) found that between 35 and 50 percent of the offenders did not complete assigned programs prior to their release. Reasons for non-completion included transfers, the limited capacity of programs, and short sentences.[49] This finding is in line with other research studies on inmate completion/non-completion of treatment programs, which have also found that negative perceptions of treatment, staff, and peers, as well as an inability of the inmate to control behaviour and a lack of support from corrections staff, were associated with non-completion.[50]

Program Fidelity, Program Drift, and Therapeutic Integrity

A key factor in the development of effective correctional treatment programs is program implementation.[51] Correctional authorities must ensure that there is **program fidelity**—that is, that the treatment program is delivered in the way it was originally designed.

Program fidelity can be assured by providing a clear program manual as well as appropriate training and supervision to treatment staff. This is closely related to the principle of program integrity noted earlier.

Program fidelity may be compromised in institutions where COs are involved in facilitating core treatment programs, as has occurred in some provincial institutions. One can imagine the challenges of having a CO facilitate a treatment group of offenders, which requires the inmates to speak openly and honestly about their issues. There is also the issue of **program drift**, where for a variety of reasons, including a lack of qualified staff and effective administrative oversight, a treatment initiative moves away from its original design and objectives. This compromises the integrity and potential effectiveness of the intervention.

Closely associated with this is the **therapeutic integrity** of programs. This concept underscores the importance of treatment staff having adequate training, appropriate skill sets, and competent supervision.[52] The therapeutic integrity of programs is enhanced if both staff and inmates view the environment of the institution as conducive to and supportive of change.[53] This highlights the importance of the "social climate" of the institution, which has been

Program fidelity
The extent to which a treatment program is delivered in accordance with the original program design.

Program drift
The extent to which a treatment program as delivered has moved away from the original design, with a potential impact on program effectiveness.

Therapeutic integrity
The importance of the training, skill sets, and supervision of treatment staff for the effectiveness of correctional treatment programs.

described as "being supportive, offering a safe environment and opportunities for personal growth and development."[54]

The following comments of staff and inmates in a sex offender treatment program in a U.K. prison reflect a positive view toward the institutional climate and staff–inmate relationships:

> **Inmate:** *It comes down to respect, they treat us like human beings. I haven't seen an officer here who thinks of me as just a number, that's Mr. X, you're not just a number here you're a person and that's the feeling you get.*[55]

> **Staff:** *I feel clear about what our objective is or what our objectives are and that what we are about really. I think we are very different to other prisons in that our sole purpose here is about helping people who are locked up here to address their offending and reasons for their offending. . . . . I think it's important to have that level of purpose for a prison direction.*[56]

The Importance of Throughcare

A long-standing challenge for correctional systems has been to ensure continuity between treatment interventions in institutional settings and those in the community following release. This is the concept of **throughcare**. Studies have found that the effectiveness of institution-based treatment programs is enhanced when there is a "seamless" transition to community-based treatment when the offender is released from confinement (see Chapter 11).[57] For provincial/territorial offenders who are not released on parole, there are generally no programs and services provided unless the offender has a term of probation to complete.

The absence of resources, a lack of communication between institutional treatment personnel and their community-based counterparts, and the loss of eligibility to participate in community-based programs on warrant expiry (end of sentence) all contribute to the lack of treatment continuity. Throughcare is especially problematic in cases where Indigenous people return to their remote northern communities. As well, continuity of care is a problem once the offender's sentence has expired. Except for offenders on long-term supervision orders, corrections authorities do not have the authority to provide services beyond the end of an offender's sentence. There may also be problems in jurisdiction: A federal offender, for example, may experience challenges in accessing provincial health care.[58]

> **Throughcare**
> The notion that there should be continuity between institutional treatment programs and community-based services for offenders.

THE ETHICS OF CORRECTIONAL TREATMENT

In the past, inmates had no power to resist the sanctions imposed on them, and a wide variety of punishments have been inflicted on inmates under the guise of treatment. At one time, these punishments included electroshock "therapy," which psychiatrists administered to many inmates without their consent until

"It's interesting——with each conviction I learn a little more about myself."

the 1980s. Throughout the 1960s and 1970s, prison inmates were used as subjects in a variety of experiments conducted by drug companies, federal agencies, and universities, including studies of the effects of LSD. The inmates in this series of studies did provide "consent"; the issue is whether a captive person is able to provide informed consent.

The Canadian Charter of Rights and Freedoms guarantees all persons the right to life, liberty, and security of the person—rights that would most likely be violated by any provision of mandatory treatment.[59] The CCRA states that inmates must provide informed consent, both at the outset and during treatment, and that they have the right to refuse treatment or to withdraw from a treatment program at any time. Research suggests that mandated (coerced) participation in treatment programs is ineffective at reducing reoffending, although it may promote behavioural change within the institution.[60]

DOES CORRECTIONAL TREATMENT WORK?

Since the introduction of treatment programs into correctional institutions in the 1950s, there has been an ongoing debate over their effectiveness. The debate has involved politicians, community interest groups, correctional scholars, and senior-and line-level corrections personnel.

Measuring the Effectiveness of Correctional Treatment

The traditional approach for determining the success of treatment programs has been **recidivism rates**—that is, the number of offenders who, once released from confinement, are returned to prison either for a technical violation of their parole or statutory release or for the commission of a new offence.

There are few attempts to measure any changes in attitudes and behaviour of offenders released into the community, short of law-breaking.[61] Little, if any information is gathered on employment record, educational achievement, family stability, or other facets of an offender's life in the community.

Using recidivism rates as a measure of success prevents an assessment of the "relative" improvement in the offender. For example, an offender who previously committed serious crimes and is subsequently returned to confinement for a relatively minor offence could be viewed as a "relative success" rather than as a failure. Offenders have also noted that official measures of recidivism do not capture what they view as "success," which is captured in the following quote: ". . . accomplishing a little a day, it is not accomplishing nothing big, it is just . . . to me success is just everyday making it through the day, whatever your struggles are, and getting over it every day . . . I struggle with addiction and being a Mom. If I can make it through the day, I've succeeded."[62]

Or if that inmate succeeds, it may have been for reasons unrelated to the treatment intervention. There are many reasons why an individual might cease violating the law, including the efforts of a supportive family and/or spouse, success in securing stable employment, maturation, and the availability of programs and services in the community. On the other hand, the offender may have returned to criminal activity without being detected.

The success or failure of an offender upon release may also depend on the level and type of supervision they receive on the outside. Among parole officers, there are a variety of supervision styles, ranging from officers who have a more punitive orientation to those who focus on providing services and assistance (see Chapter 11).

What Works in Correctional Treatment?

Determining "what works" in correctional treatment is very difficult. Historically, systems of corrections, especially provincial/territorial corrections, have done a poor job at assessing the effectiveness of their treatment interventions. Most programs do not contain an evaluative component, and studies typically do not use random assignment of inmates to experimental and control groups.

Investigations have found that, especially in provincial/territorial institutions, there is a paucity of information on inmate access to programs, completion rates, the integrity of correctional programs, and whether the programs are achieving their intended objectives.[63]

An audit of provincial corrections in Manitoba found, for example: "In general, the Department had no means of determining if rehabilitation programs were achieving positive outcomes for offenders. Tracking of program

Recidivism rates
The number of offenders released from confinement who, once released from confinement, are returned to prison.

offerings, enrolments, completions, and outcomes was limited and, in some cases, non-existent."[64]

It has been suggested that systems of corrections develop a broader range of recidivism measures and track offenders who are released from institutions for a longer period of time than is currently practised. Most corrections systems track offenders only for a maximum of two years following release, or only until their warrant expiry date, at which time their sentence ends. Further, gathering and analyzing data on the relationship between outcomes in the community and the particular treatment programs that offenders participated in while confined, as well as examining treatment outcomes by level of risk and by status (i.e., gender, ethnicity, etc.), would provide greater insights into the effectiveness of correctional interventions.[65]

The absence of evidenced-based policies and programs is a challenge for corrections and is discussed in Chapter 15.

"Nothing Works" versus "Some Things Work": The Legacy of Robert Martinson

No discussion of the effectiveness of correctional treatment would be complete without mention of Robert Martinson, a scholar who, over 40 years ago, conducted a survey of more than 200 treatment programs and concluded that, with a few exceptions, none of them had an impact on reoffending.[66] Although scholarly research, historically, had little impact on correctional policy, this finding was seized on by politicians and used as a premise to not vigorously develop and support treatment programs. No mind that Martinson, on the basis of further analysis, recanted his original conclusion.[67]

A number of scholars have argued that the "nothing works" mantra still prevails, despite evidence to the contrary.[68] A review of some of what we know about the effectiveness of correctional treatment interventions is presented in Research File 9.1.

RESEARCH FILE 9.1

The Effectiveness of Correctional Treatment Interventions

Do correctional treatment programs work? They can. The general consensus among researchers is that some programs work to reduce reoffending for some offenders and that treatment programs are more likely than criminal sanctions to reduce recidivism. Effective treatment programs follow the principles of RNR and utilize a cognitive-behavioural approach.[a] If the principles of RNR are adhered to, reductions in recidivism can range from 10 to 40 percent. For example, family violence prevention programs for male offenders based on RNR have been found to diminish attitudes among inmate participants that supported violence against women, to develop prosocial skill sets that assist in the inmate being in non-abusive relationships, and to reduce offending related to spousal violence upon release and violence generally.[b]

Significant reductions in reoffending are possible if key factors are targeted, including criminal attitudes, criminal peer groups, and the attitudes and behaviours associated with antisocial personalities.[c] Inmates who complete treatment programs have higher success rates in terms of successful reintegration than offenders who do not acknowledge their level of risk.[d] In the words of one scholar, "offenders are good judges of their need for treatment."[e] The preliminary results from the federal ICPM are encouraging.

Do correctional programs successfully address the risk and needs of offenders? Perhaps not. A large study of federal offenders ($N = 24,315$) on conditional release between 2005 and 2010 found little change in their risk levels (93.5 percent at no change) or in their needs (88.2 percent at no change) from intake to release from custody. This suggests that whatever programming these offenders received while incarcerated did not alter their risk/needs ratings.[f]

Do education programs reduce reoffending? Potentially. Obtaining a secondary degree (GED, or equivalent) in prison can significantly increase the odds of securing post-release employment, while inmates who achieve a post-secondary degree in prison have lower rates of reoffending.[g] Medium-and high-risk federal inmates who participate in educational programming recidivate less than their counterparts who do not participate in programming.[h] The effectiveness of education programs is improved if there is more continuity between prison education and post-release follow-up and support (the notion of throughcare).[i]

Do vocational and work programs reduce reoffending? Participation in vocational and work programs can reduce levels of misconduct in the institution, increase the likelihood that the offender will find employment when released, and increase the chances of success in the community.[j] A key requirement is throughcare—continuity between the institutional program and programs and services in the community (discussed in Chapter 11). There is some evidence that vocational programs are most effective for inmates classified as high risk, reinforcing one of the key principles of RNR: that higher-risk offenders are most likely to benefit from treatment interventions.[k]

CORCAN, the industries program that operates in federal institutions, provides employment opportunities for inmates. However, a review of institutional employment programs in federal institutions found that the CSC does not have guidelines to prioritize inmate access to these programs nor did CORCAN employ those inmates whose identified needs included improving their employability skills. Further, since the CSC eliminated incentive pay for inmates employed in CORCAN in 2013, fewer inmates are participating in the CORCAN program, which is operating at nearly less than half of its capacity.[l]

Do cognitive-behavioural-based treatment programs work? Cognitive-behavioural centred interventions focus on the inmate's maladaptive or dysfunctional thought

(continued)

processes and teach problem-solving skills and coping strategies.[m] These programs are successful in reducing reoffending.[n] Studies have found that these programs can increase critical reasoning skills, the capacity for optional thinking, and interpersonal problem solving.[o]

A review of the impact of CSC programming on recidivism found that participating in treatment programs centred on a cognitive-behavioural approach reduces the risk of reoffending and that this impact held across all ethnic groups, including Indigenous people, Blacks, Caucasians, and others.[p]

Do programs for offenders with mental health issues work? Potentially. An evaluation of the CSC mental health strategy, which was designed to provide a continuum of care from the institution to the community, found that offenders who had access to mental health specialists were less likely to have their conditional release revoked or suspended.[q] Challenges to providing effective interventions for this population include a lack of institutional resources and the fact that inmates with mental health issues are more likely to be held in segregation, limiting their access to programs.[r]

Do substance abuse programs work? Programs that are centred on a therapeutic community, wherein inmates in the program are separated from the general population, are effective in reducing post-release recidivism.[s] Drug maintenance programs, such as methadone maintenance, have been found to increase program participation and reduce drug dependence, although not to reduce reoffending once the inmate is released into the community.[t] Federal inmates who reside in "drug-free" Intensive Supervision Unit (ISU) programs are less likely to be returned to custody than other offenders and are less likely to be returned to custody for a new offence.[u] Multi-stage residential programs that provide a bridge between the prison and the community have also been found to reduce post-release reoffending.[v]

Do sex offender treatment programs work? Some do. Some interventions, including programs that are cognitive-behavioural based, appear to reduce reoffending among certain groups of sex offenders.[w] Part of the problem in determining the effectiveness of programs is the wide variety of offenders who are classified as "sex offenders." Offenders who participate in treatment programs generally have lower rates of reoffending than those in comparison groups who received no intervention (in one meta-analysis of 23 studies [$N = 6,746$ offenders], 11 versus 19 percent).[x] The reductions in sexual and violent reoffending have been found to extend for two years; after that, treatment impact may dissipate.[y] Programs for sex offenders based on the principles of RNR are the most effective at reducing reoffending; as noted above, cognitive–behavioural interventions that focus on dysfunctional thoughts and feelings have also had some success.[z]

Do programs for Indigenous offenders work? Potentially, although there are few studies, the research conducted to date suggests that culturally appropriate treatment programs can impact attitudes and behaviour.[aa] The In Search of Your Warrior Program combines Western treatment interventions with Indigenous cultures and traditions and includes Indigenous Elders as part of the treatment team. An evaluation found that Indigenous inmates had a positive view of the program and that, although the rates of reoffending were no different from those of Indigenous offenders who did not participate in the program, fewer of the program participants committed a violent offence.[bb] The Tupiq Program for Inuit Sex Offenders, also offered by the CSC, involves Inuit Elders in program delivery and includes individual and group sessions. An evaluation found high completion rates, positive attitude changes, and reduced sexual offending (although not general offending) upon release.[cc] The Aboriginal Offender Substance Abuse Program (AOSAP), another program offered to federal offenders, and which includes a strong cultural component, has been found to reduce reoffending.[dd]

Do religious programs work? Although the research to date has been Christian-centric, these programs have been found to mitigate the pains of imprisonment and to alter somewhat the values and behaviours of inmates while in confinement.[ee] There is no clear evidence, however, that these programs reduce reoffending.[ff]

Do treatment programs in provincial/territorial institutions work? Unknown. Even though most offenders in confinement are in these facilities, program evaluations are virtually nonexistent.

Are risk assessment instruments effective at predicting future reoffending? Generally, yes. Research studies have validated the effectiveness of risk assessment instruments, including the LSI-OR and the Static-99R/Static-2002R.[gg]

Does effective correctional treatment save money? Yes. A CSC evaluation of programs in federal institutions found the following returns on a per-dollar investment: $1 of correctional programming = return of $1 to $8; $1 of sex offender programming = return of $6.59; and $1 of substance abuse programming = return of $2.69. Note that "returns" here refers to cost savings associated with achieved correctional outcomes (i.e., offenders are supervised in the community and do not reoffend). In addition, the "cost of participating in institutional employment programs = $779 in terms of good correctional outcomes vs. offenders not participating in institutional employment programs in terms of poor correctional outcomes = $15,662."[hh]

[a] J. Bonta, *Offender Rehabilitation: From Research to Practice* (Ottawa: Department of the Solicitor General of Canada, 1997), https://www.publicsafety.gc.ca/cnt/rsrcs/pblctns/ffndr-rhblttn-rsrch/ffndr-rhblttn-rsrch-eng.pdf; L.W. Sherman, D. Gottfredson, D. MacKenzie, J. Eck, P. Reuter, and S. Bushway, *Preventing Crime: What Works, What Doesn't, What's Promising* (Washington: Office of Justice Programs, U.S. Department of Justice, 1997), https://www.ncjrs.gov/pdffiles/171676.pdf; P. Smith, P. Gendreau, and K. Swartz, "Validating the Principles of Effective Intervention: A Systematic Review of the Contributions of Meta-Analysis in the Field of Corrections," *Victims and Offenders 4*, no. 2 (2009), 148–69.

[b] L.A. Stewart, N. Gabora, and P.R. Kropp, "Effectiveness of Risk-Needs-Responsivity-Based Family Violence Programs with Male Offenders," *Journal of Family Violence 29* (2014), 151–64.

[c] J. Bonta and D.A. Andrews, "Viewing Offender Assessment and Treatment Through the Lens of the Risk–Need–Responsivity Model," in *Offender Supervision: New Directions in Theory, Research, and Practice*, eds. F. McNeil, P. Raynor, and C. Trotter (New York: Willan, 2010), 19–40.

[d] M. Nafekh, N. Allegri, A. Fabisiak, D. Batten, Y. Stys, H. Lie et al., *Evaluation Report: Correctional Service Canada's Correctional Programs* (Ottawa: Correctional Service Canada, 2009), http://www.csc-scc.gc.ca/text/pa/cop-prog/cp-eval-eng.shtml; C.T. Griffiths, Y. Dandurand, and D. Murdoch, *The Social Reintegration*

(continued)

of Offenders and Crime Prevention (Ottawa: National Crime Prevention Centre, Public Safety Canada, 2007), https://www.publicsafety.gc.ca/cnt/rsrcs/pblctns/scl-rntgrtn/scl-rntgrtn-eng.pdf.

e S. Levenson, "'But I Didn't Do It!': Ethical Treatment of Sex Offenders in Denial," *Sexual Abuse: A Journal of Research and Treatment 23*, no. 3 (2011), 346–64.

f M. Olotu, D. Luong, C. MacDonald, M. McKay, S. Heath, N. Allegri, and E. Loree, *Report of the Evaluation of CSC's Community Corrections*, Chapter 1, "Correctional Interventions" (Ottawa: Correctional Service Canada, 2011), p. 48, http://www.csc-scc.gc.ca/publications/092/005007-2008-eng.pdf.

g J.H. Esperian, "The Effect of Prison Education on Recidivism," *Journal of Correctional Education 61*, no. 4 (2010), 34; John Howard Society of Alberta, *Inmate Education* (Edmonton: Author, 2002), http://www.johnhoward.ab.ca/pub/old/respaper/educa02.pdf; G. Duwe and V. Clark, "The Effects of Prison-Based Educational Programming on Recidivism and Employment," *The Prison Journal 94*, no. 4 (2014), 454–78; D.B. Wilson, "Correctional Programs," in *What Works in Crime Prevention and Rehabilitation. Lessons from Systematic Reviews*, eds. D. Weisburd, D.P. Farrington, and C. Gill (New York: Springer, 2016), 193–217.

h Correctional Service Canada, *2015–16 Departmental Performance Report* (Ottawa, Author: 2016), http://www.csc-scc.gc.ca/publications/005007-4500-2015-2016-eng.shtml.

i Correctional Service Canada, *Evaluation Report: Offender Education Programs and Services* (Ottawa: Author, 2015), http://www.csc-scc.gc.ca/publications/092/005007-2014-eng.pdf.

j C.A. Gillis, L.L. Motiuk, and R. Belcourt, *Prison Work Program (Corcan): Impact on Post-Release Employment and Recidivism* (Ottawa: Correctional Service Canada, 1998), http://www.csc-scc.gc.ca/research/r69e-eng.shtml.

k D. Newton, A. Day, M. Giles, J. Wodak, J. Graffam, and E. Baldry, "The Impact of Vocational Education and Training Programs on Recidivism: A Systematic Review of Current Experimental Evidence," *International Journal of Offender Therapy and Comparative Criminology* (2016), 1–21.

l Office of the Auditor General of Canada, *Preparing Male Offenders for Release—Correctional Service Canada* (Ottawa: Author, 2015), http://www.oag-bvg.gc.ca/internet/docs/parl_oag_201504_06_e.pdf.

m H. Milkman and K. Wanberg, *Cognitive-Behavioral Treatment: A Review and Discussion for Corrections Professionals* (Washington, DC: National Institute of Corrections, 2007), https://s3.amazonaws.com/static.nicic.gov/Library/021657.pdf.

n C.R. Hollin, M.J. Palmer, and R.M. Hatcher, "Efficacy of Correctional Cognitive Skills Programmes," in *What Works in Offender Rehabilitation: An Evidence-Based Approach to Assessment and Treatment*, eds. L.A. Craig, L. Dixon, and T.A. Gannon (Hoboken, NJ: Wiley, 2013), 117–28; Wilson, "Correctional Programs."

o D. Robinson, *The Impact of Cognitive Skills Training on Post-Release Recidivism Among Canadian Federal Offenders* (Ottawa: Correctional Service Canada, 1995), http://publications.gc.ca/collections/collection_2010/scc-csc/PS83-3-41-eng.pdf; J. Vennard, D. Sugg, and C. Hedderman, "Changing Offenders' Attitudes and Behaviour: What Works?" *Home Office Research Study 171* (London, UK: Home Office Research and Statistics Directorate, 1997), http://w3.unisa.edu.au/hawkeinstitute/sprg/documents/what-works.pdf.

p A. Usher and L. Stewart, *The Effectiveness of Correctional Programs with Diverse Offenders: A Meta-Analytic Study* (Ottawa: Correctional Service Canada, 2011), http://www.csc-scc.gc.ca/005/008/092/005008-0246-eng.pdf.

q N. Allegri, K. Delveux, D. Loung, H. Li, T. Jensen, D. Batten, K. Barney, E. Loree, and M. Henighan, *Evaluation Report: Community Mental Health Initiative* (Ottawa: Correctional Service Canada, 2008), http://www.csc-scc.gc.ca/publications/092/005007-2012-eng.pdf.

r Olotu et al., *Report of the Evaluation of CSC's Community Corrections*.

s Wilson, "Correctional Programs."

t Wilson, "Correctional Programs."

u D.D. Varis, D. Lefebvre, and B.A. Grant, "Intensive Support Units for Federal Offenders with Substance Abuse Problems: An Impact Analysis," *Forum on Corrections Research 18*, no. 1 (2006), http://www.csc-scc.gc.ca/research/r151-eng.shtml.

v B. Pelissier, W. Rhodes, W. Saylor, G. Gaes, S. Camp, S. Vanyur, and S. Wallace, *TRIAD Drug Treatment Evaluation Project, Final Report of Three-Year Outcomes: Part 1* (Washington, DC: Federal Bureau of Prisons, 2000), https://www.bop.gov/resources/pdfs/TRIAD/TRIAD_pref.pdf; N. Allegri et al., *Evaluation Report: Community Mental Health Initiative.*

w Wilson, "Correctional Programs."

x R.K. Hanson and M.T. Bussiere, "Predicting Relapse: A Meta-Analysis of Sexual Offender Recidivism Studies," *Journal of Consulting and Clinical Psychology 66*, no. 2 (1998), 348–62; F. Losel and M. Schmucker, "The Effectiveness of Treatment for Sexual Offenders: A Comprehensive Meta-Analysis," *Journal of Experimental Criminology 1*, no. 1 (2005), 117–46.

y M.E. Olver, T.P. Nicholaichuk, D. Gu, and S.C.P. Wong, "Sex Offender Treatment Outcome, Actuarial Risk, and the Aging Sex Offender in Canadian Corrections: A Long-Term Follow-Up," *Sexual Abuse: A Journal of Research and Treatment 25*, no. 4 (2012), 396–422.

z F. Cortoni and K.L. Nunes, *Assessing the Effectiveness of the National Sexual Offender Program* (Ottawa: Correctional Service Canada, 2007), http://www.csc-scc.gc.ca/research/r183-eng.shtml; P. Corabian, M. Ospina, and C. Harstall, *Treatment for Convicted Adult Male Sex Offenders* (Edmonton: Institute of Health Economics, 2010), http://www.inahta.org/upload/Briefs_12/11127%20Treatment%20for%20Convicted%20Adult%20Male%20Sex%20Offenders.pdf; R.K. Hanson, G. Bourgon, L. Helmus, and S. Hodgson, *A Meta-analysis of the Effectiveness of Treatment for Sexual Offenders: Risk, Need, Responsivity* (Ottawa: Public Safety Canada, 2009), https://www.publicsafety.gc.ca/cnt/rsrcs/pblctns/2009-01-trt/2009-01-trt-eng.pdf.

aa J. Thakker, "The Role of Cultural Factors in Treatment," in *What Works in Offender Rehabilitation: An Evidence-Based Approach to Assessment and Treatment*, eds. L.A. Craig, L. Dixon, and T.A. Gannon (Hoboken, NJ: Wiley, 2013), 389–407.

bb S. Trevethan, J.-P. Moore, and N. Allegri, *The "In Search of Your Warrior" Program for Aboriginal Offenders: A Preliminary Evaluation* (Ottawa: Correctional Service Canada, 2005), http://www.csc-scc.gc.ca/research/r172-eng.shtml.

cc S. Trevethan, J.-P. Moore, and L. Naqitarvik, *The Tupik Program for Inuit Offenders: A Preliminary Investigation* (Ottawa: Correctional Service Canada, 2004), http://www.csc-scc.gc.ca/research/092/r153-eng.pdf.

dd D. Kunic and D.D. Varis, *The Aboriginal Offender Substance Abuse Program (OASAP): Examining the Effects of Successful Completion on Post-Release Outcomes* (Ottawa: Correctional Service Canada, 2009), http://www.csc-scc.gc.ca/005/008/092/rs13-03-eng.pdf.

ee L. Schaefer, T. Sams, and J. Lux, "Saved, Salvaged, or Sunk: A Meta-Analysis of the Effects of Faith-Based Interventions on Inmate Adjustment," *The Prison Journal 96*, no. 4 (2016), 600–22.

ff Wilson, "Correctional Programs."

gg K.M. Babchishin, R.K. Hanson, and L. Helmus, *The RRASOR, Static-99R and Static-2002R All Add Incrementally to the Prediction of Recidivism Among Sex Offenders* (Ottawa: Public Safety Canada, 2011); R. Hanson and K.E. Morton-Bourgon, "The Accuracy of Recidivism Risk Assessments for Sexual Offenders: A Meta-Analysis of 188 Prediction Studies," *Psychological Assessment 21*, no. 1 (2009), 1–21; S.M. Hogg, "The Level of Service Inventory (Ontario Revision) Scale Validation for Gender and Ethnicity: Addressing Reliability and Predictive Validity," unpublished MA thesis (Saskatoon: University of Saskatchewan, 2011), https://ecommons.usask.ca/bitstream/handle/10388/etd-04112011-085608/Hogg_MA_Thesis.pdf?sequence=1&isAllowed=y; C.M. Langton, "Actuarial Assessment of Risk for Reoffense Among Adult Sex Offenders: Evaluating the Predictive Accuracy of the Statti-2002 and Five Other Instruments," *Criminal Justice and Behavior 34*, no. 1 (2007), 37–59.

hh Olotu et al., *Report of the Evaluation of CSC's Community Corrections.*

SUMMARY

This chapter has focused on the strategies and programs in correctional institutions that are designed to assess and address the risk and needs of offenders. There is a question as to whether incarceration is effective in addressing the identified risk and needs of offenders during the period from intake to release. To be effective, correctional interventions must adhere to the principles of risk, need, and responsivity and must overcome a number of obstacles, including the dynamics of life inside correctional institutions, the limited skill sets of inmates, and the challenges of providing inmates with timely access to programs. The issue as to "what works" in correctional treatment is complex, although there is evidence that some programs work with some offenders and that there are successful interventions with specific groups of offenders.

KEY POINTS REVIEW

1. Three major trends in offender classification and treatment are the increasing use of risk assessment instruments, the use of psychological approaches to treatment, and the development of differentiated treatment approaches for women, Indigenous people, and specific categories of offenders.

2. Offenders have a variety of criminogenic needs that must be addressed within the institution and later in the community.

3. The classification procedures used by corrections generally involve psychological, personality, and behavioural inventories.

4. The assessment of risk is a key component of classification and case management.

5. Case management is a process that occurs both in the institution and after the inmate is released from confinement, although post-release planning is more common for federal inmates given the short length of time that provincial/territorial inmates are confined.

6. There is considerable variability among the provinces/territories in the institutional treatment programs that are available.

7. Sex offenders, particularly those classified as high risk, are difficult to treat.

8. Among the requirements of successful treatment programs is adherence to the principles of risk, need, and responsivity, the involvement of highly trained staff, and a focus on the dynamic risk factors associated with the inmate's criminal behaviour.

9. The conditions required for effective correctional treatment include supportive COs and staff, the matching of inmates' needs/amenability to programs, and continuity of treatment from the institution to the community.

10. Recidivism rates are an inadequate measure of the effectiveness of correctional treatment programs.

11. Among the potential obstacles to effective correctional treatment are the conflict between punishment and treatment; the dynamics of life inside prisons; unrealistic expectations of offenders with respect to changes in attitudes and behaviour; inmate access to programs; low rates of inmate participation and completion; an absence of therapeutic integrity; and the lack of continuity between prison treatment programs and community treatment programs.

12. Inmates must provide informed consent at the outset and during treatment and may refuse or withdraw from participation in treatment programs.

13. The general consensus among corrections researchers is that some programs work to reduce reoffending among some offenders and that higher-risk inmates are more likely to benefit from correctional treatment than low-risk inmates.

14. There is some question as to whether incarceration and institutional programs are effective in reducing the risk/needs levels of offenders.

KEY TERM QUESTIONS

1. Define *classification* and its role in corrections.

2. Compare and contrast *static risk factors* and *dynamic risk factors*, and note the role of each type of factor in the classification process.

3. What are *criminogenic risk factors*?

4. Define and discuss the goals of correctional *case management*.

5. What is the *correctional plan* and what role does it play in correctional treatment?

6. Describe the approach and components of the *CSC Integrated Correctional Program Model (ICPM)*.

7. What is meant by (1) *differential treatment effectiveness* and (2) *differential amenability to treatment*, and how does each of these notions contribute to our understanding of correctional treatment for inmates?

8. What are the issues that surround the use of *recidivism rates* as a measure of the success of correctional treatment programs, and what alternatives have been suggested that may more accurately reflect treatment success?

9. What is meant by *differential treatment availability*?

10. Define these concepts—*program fidelity, program drift, therapeutic integrity*, and *throughcare*—and discuss why these concepts are important in the study of correctional treatment.

CRITICAL THINKING EXERCISES

Critical Thinking Exercise 9.1

Should Prison Inmates Have the Right to Refuse Treatment?

Consider the following scenario: An inmate convicted of a sex offence is sentenced to 15 years in prison. During confinement, he refuses to participate in treatment programs. As a consequence, he does not receive any form of conditional release, is denied statutory release after having served two-thirds of the sentence, and serves his entire sentence in prison. On his warrant expiry date, he is released, untreated, from the correctional institution, at high risk of reoffending.

A provision of the CCRA states that inmates must provide informed consent, both at the outset and during treatment, and that the inmate has the right to refuse treatment or to withdraw from a treatment program at any time. The Canadian Charter of Rights and Freedoms also guarantees that all persons have the right to life, liberty, and security of persons, rights that would most likely be violated by any provision of mandatory treatment.

Research has established that high-risk offenders gain the most benefit from treatment programs; however, this group is less likely to voluntarily participate in programming. A U.S. study found that high-risk inmates who participated in a "nonvoluntary" treatment program were generally hostile at the outset, but came to see the benefits of the program for facilitating change.[69]

Your Thoughts?

1. What is your view on the right of inmates to refuse treatment?
2. If personal change is viewed as a multi-step process, should inmates be initially forced into treatment programs to begin that process?
3. Do you feel that it is unethical to force inmates to participate in treatment programs?

Critical Thinking Exercise 9.2

One Offender's Rehabilitation

The discussion of correctional treatment and the rehabilitation of offenders often focuses on specific programs and interventions. This often obscures the role that the individual offender and their decisions play in addressing their issues and leading a law-abiding life after release from confinement. This is the notion of "amenability" to treatment discussed in this chapter. The journey for each offender is different.

View the video "A Prison Rehab Interview: JAVIER" at https://www.youtube.com/watch?v=E8iS5WJx1NA.

Your Thoughts?

1. From the interview with Javier, identify the key elements that played a role in his movement out of a criminal lifestyle.

2. What does this interview tell us about "rehabilitation"?

CLASS/GROUP DISCUSSION EXERCISES

Class/Group Discussion 9.1

To Treat or to Punish

Throughout the history of corrections, there has been an ongoing debate as to whether offenders should be punished or treated. Access online the article: "The old debate: punish prisoners, or rehabilitate them?" (http://www.telegraph.co.uk/news/uknews/crime/10514678/The-old-debate-punish-prisoners-or-rehabilitate-them.html). Then, scroll down through the "Comments" following the article. Although the article speaks to correctional institutions in the United Kingdom, the same issues can be raised about Canadian corrections.

Your Thoughts?

1. In your view, should the primary objective of correctional institutions be to punish, or to treat, inmates?

2. Are there lessons to be learned from the example of Norwegian corrections? Why or why not?

Class/Group Discussion Exercise 9.2

Civil Commitment for Sex Offenders

In some U.S. states, there are provisions in law to civilly commit sex offenders who are deemed by a panel of psychologists to be so dangerous as to pose a risk to the community should they be released, even after serving their entire sentence in prison. Upon the recommendation of the panel, the offender is committed to an indefinite period of "involuntary" confinement, with their case reviewed on a periodic basis.

View the following materials:

"What Is Civil Confinement?" https://www.youtube.com/watch?v=hM1yq88rO7Y

"Inside Wisconsin Sex Offender Treatment Facility," https://www.youtube.com/watch?v=wTbpZsFVfIg

Your Thoughts?

1. There is no provision in the Canadian Criminal Code for this type of civil commitment of sex offenders. In your view, should consideration be given to including this provision in the Criminal Code?

2. What arguments could be presented in support of, or in opposition to, such a provision?

MEDIA LINKS

"What Is Cognitive-Behavioral Therapy?" https://www.youtube.com/watch?v=yCKcFhnMhPw

"Prisoner Throughcare: Townsville." https://www.youtube.com/watch?v=yCKcFhnMhPw

NOTES

1. S. Poirier (chair), *Decades of Darkness, Moving Towards the Light: A Review of the Prison System in Newfoundland and Labrador* (St. John's: Government of Newfoundland and Labrador, 2008), p. 27, http://www.justice.gov.nl.ca/just/publications/ac_report.pdf.

2. G. Harper and C. Chitty, *The Impact of Corrections on Re-Offending: A Review of What Works* (London, UK: Development and Statistics Directorate, Home Office, 2005), http://webarchive.nationalarchives.gov.uk/20110218135832/rds.homeoffice.gov.uk/rds/pdfs04/hors291.pdf.

3. John Howard Society of Ontario, *Unlocking Change. Decriminalizing Mental Health Issues in Ontario* (Toronto: Author, 2015), http://www.johnhoward.on.ca/wp-content/uploads/2015/07/Unlocking-Change-Final-August-2015.pdf.

4. Office of the Auditor General of Canada, *Preparing Male Offenders for Release—Correctional Service Canada* (Ottawa: Author, 2015), p. 13, http://publications.gc.ca/collections/collection_2015/bvg-oag/FA1-2015-1-6-eng.pdf.

5. Ibid., p. 12.

6. Public Safety Canada Portfolio Corrections Statistics Committee, *Corrections and Conditional Release Statistical Overview: 2015 Annual Report* (Ottawa: Public Works and Government Services Canada, 2016), p. 55, https://www.publicsafety.gc.ca/cnt/rsrcs/pblctns/ccrso-2015/ccrso-2015-en.pdf.

7. D. Quan, "Tests to Predict if Inmates will Reoffend Unreliable for Aboriginal Offenders, Judge Rules," *National Post*, September 24, 2015, http://news.nationalpost.com/news/canada/tests-to-predict-if-inmates-will-reoffend-unreliable-for-aboriginal-offenders-judge-rules.

8. L. Britten, "Federal Appeal Court Overturns Ruling on Psychological Tests for Aboriginal Prisoners," CBC News, August 4, 2016, http://www.cbc.ca/news/canada/british-columbia/psychological-test-prison-aboriginal-1.3708405.

9. Deloitte & Touche, *Report on Nova Scotia's Adult Correctional Facilities* (Halifax: Department of Justice, 2008), p. 92, http://www.novascotia.ca/just/global_docs/Deloitte%20Report%20-%20NS%20Correctional%20Facilities%20Nov08.pdf.

10. G. Taylor, "Implementing Risk and Needs Classification in the Correctional Service of Canada," *Forum on Corrections Research 9*, no. 1 (1997), 32–35, http://www.csc-scc.gc.ca/research/forum/special/espe_g-eng.shtml.

11. D. Ballucci, "Subverting and Negotiating Risk Assessment: A Case Study of the LSI in

a Canadian Youth Custody Facility," *Canadian Journal of Criminology and Criminal Justice 54*, no. 2 (2012), 203–28.

12. D.A. Andrews and J. Bonta, *The Psychology of Criminal Conduct*, 5th ed. (New Providence, NJ: Matthew Benders, 2010).

13. M. Dauvergne, *Adult Correctional Statistics in Canada, 2010–2011* (Ottawa: Minister of Industry, 2012), p. 12, http://www.statcan.gc.ca/pub/85-002-x/2012001/article/11715-eng.pdf.

14. Office of the Auditor General Manitoba, *Managing the Province's Adult Offenders* (Winnipeg: Author, 2014), p. 273, http://www.oag.mb.ca/wp-content/uploads/2014/03/Chapter-6-Managing-the-Provinces-Adult-Offenders-Web.pdf.

15. B. Crewe, "Depth, Weight, Tightness: Revisiting the Pains of Imprisonment," *Punishment and Society 13*, no. 5 (2011), 509–29.

16. Ibid., p. 517.

17. Office of the Auditor General of Canada, *Preparing Male Offenders for Release*, p. 16.

18. Public Safety Canada Portfolio Corrections Statistics Committee, *Corrections and Conditional Release Statistical Overview*, p. 11.

19. C.T. Lowenkamp, E.J. Latessa, and P. Smith, "Does Correctional Program Quality Really Matter? The Impact of Adhering to the Principles of Effective Intervention," *Criminology and Public Policy 5*, no. 3 (2006), 575–94.

20. Office of the Correctional Investigator Canada, *Annual Report, 2010–2011* (Ottawa: Author, 2012), p. 32, http://www.oci-bec.gc.ca/cnt/rpt/pdf/annrpt/annrpt20102011-eng.pdf.

21. Correctional Service Canada, *Integrated Corrections Program Model* (Ottawa: Author, 2014), http://www.csc-scc.gc.ca/correctional-process/002001-2011-eng.shtml.

22. Correctional Service Canada, *Departmental Performance Report, 2010–2011* (Ottawa: Author, 2011), http://publications.gc.ca/collections/collection_2011/sp-ps/PS81-5-2011-eng.pdf.

23. Correctional Service Canada, *A Study of the Efficiency and Effectiveness of the Integrated Correctional Program Model (ICPM): Executive Summary* (Ottawa: Author, 2016), http://www.csc-scc.gc.ca/publications/005007-9012-eng.shtml; L. Motiuk and B. Vuong, "Effectiveness of the Integrated Correctional Program Model (ICPM) for Federal Offenders Identified as Perpetrators of Spousal Assault," *Research in Brief*, May 2016, http://www.csc-scc.gc.ca/005/008/092/005008-rb-16-02-eng.pdf.

24. K.L. Nunes, R.K. Hanson, P. Firestone, H.M. Moulden, D.M. Greenberg, and J.M. Bradford, "Denial Predicts Recidivism for Some Sexual Offenders," *Sexual Abuse: A Journal of Research and Treatment 19*, no. 2 (2007), 91–105.

25. Office of the Auditor General of Canada, *Preparing Male Offenders for Release*, p. 12.

26. Ibid., p. 11.

27. Ibid., p. 13.

28. "Women See the Other Side," *Toronto Star*, December 27, 2011, https://www.thestar.com/opinion/editorials/2011/12/27/women_see_the_other_side.html.

29. L. McKay-Panos, "Prisoners and Work," *Law Now Magazine*, January 5, 2016, http://www.lawnow.org/prisoners-and-work/.

30. Andrews and Bonta, *The Psychology of Criminal Conduct*; J. Bonta and D.A. Andrews, *Risk-Need-Responsivity Model for Offender Assessment and Rehabilitation* (Ottawa: Public Safety Canada, 2007), https://www.publicsafety.gc.ca/cnt/rsrcs/pblctns/rsk-nd-rspnsvty/rsk-nd-rspnsvty-eng.pdf; Office of the Correctional Investigator Canada, *Annual Report, 2010–2011*, p. 33.

31. P. Smith and P. Gendreau, "The Relationship Between Program Participation, Institutional Misconduct, and Recidivism Among Federally Sentenced Adult Male Offenders," *Forum on Corrections Research 19*, no. 1 (2007), http://www.csc-scc.gc.ca/research/forum/Vol19No1/v19n1b-eng.shtml.

32. D.L. Polaschek, "An Appraisal of the Risk-Need-Responsivity (RNR) Model of Offender Rehabilitation and Its Application in Correctional Treatment," *Legal and Criminological Psychology 17*, no. 1 (2012), 1–17.

33. Ibid.

34. J.S. Wormith, "Principles of Effective Correctional Treatment: Musing of a Former Clinician and Administrator," *Forum on Corrections Research 19*, no. 1 (2007), http://citeseerx.ist.psu.edu/viewdoc/download;jsessionid=680E843D0337B38FFF7FD338197E1DAA?doi=10.1.1.533.763&rep=rep1&type=pdf.

35. R. Ricciardelli, *Surviving Incarceration. Inside Canadian Prisons* (Waterloo, ON: Wilfred Laurier Press, 2014), pp. 190–91.

36. M. Weinwrath, *Behind the Walls. Inmates and Correctional Officers on the State of Canadian Prisons* (Vancouver: UBC Press, 2016), p. 214.

37. Ibid., p. 215.

38. A. Bosma, M. Kunst, J. Reef, A. Dirkzwager, and P. Nieuwbeerta, "Prison-Based Rehabilitation: Predictors of Offender Treatment Participation and Treatment Completion," *Crime & Delinquency 62*, no. 8 (2016), 1095–1120.

39. Office of the Auditor General of Canada, *Preparing Male Offenders for Release*, p. 8.

40. Auditor General of Canada, *Report 3 – Preparing Indigenous Offenders for Release – Service Canada* (Ottawa: Author, 2016), http://www.oag-bvg.gc.ca/internet/English/parl_oag_201611_03_e_41832.html#.

41. Office of the Correctional Investigator, *Annual Report 2012–2013* (Ottawa: Author, 2013), http://www.oci-bec.gc.ca/cnt/rpt/pdf/annrpt/annrpt20122013-eng.pdf.

42. Personal communication with a deputy warden, federal correctional institutions.

43. A. Day and T. Ward, "Offender Rehabilitation as a Value-Laden Process," *International Journal of Offender Therapy and Comparative Criminology 54*, no. 3 (2010), 289–306.

44. Julie Reitano, "Adult correctional statistics in Canada, 2015/2016," *Juristat 37*, no. 1, Catalogue no. 85-002-X (Ottawa: Canadian Centre for Justice Statistics, 2017), p. 5, http://www.statcan.gc.ca/pub/85-002-x/2017001/article/14700-eng.pdf.

45. John Howard Society of Ontario, *Fractured Care: Public Health Opportunities in Ontario's Correctional Institutions* (Toronto: Author, 2016), p. 14, http://johnhoward.on.ca/wp-content/uploads/2016/04/Fractured-Care-Final.pdf.

46. Poirier, *Decades of Darkness, Moving Towards the Light*, p. 195.

47. K.L. Nunes and F. Cortoni, *The Heterogeneity of Treatment Non-Completers* (Ottawa: Correctional Service Canada, 2006), http://www.csc-scc.gc.ca/research/092/r176_e.pdf; J.S. Wormith and M.E. Olver, "Offender Treatment Attrition and Its Relationship with Risk, Responsivity, and Recidivism," *Criminal Justice and Behavior 29*, no. 4 (2002), 447–71.

48. Office of the Correctional Investigator Canada, *Annual Report 2010–2011*, p. 32.

49. D. Luong, C. MacDonald, M. McKay, M. Olotu, S. Heath, N. Allegri, and E. Loree, *Report of the Evaluation of CSC's Community Corrections. Chapter 1: Correctional Interventions* (Ottawa: Correctional Service Canada, 2011), p. 52, http://www.csc-scc.gc.ca/publications/092/005007-2008-eng.pdf.

50. D. Sturgess, J. Woodhams, and M. Tonkin, "Treatment Engagement from the perspective of the Offender: Reasons for Noncompletion and Completion of Treatment – A Systematic Review," *International Journal of Offender Therapy and Comparative Criminology 60*, no. 6 (2016), 1873–96.

51. P. Gendreau, C. Goggin, and P. Smith, "The Forgotten Issue in Effective Correctional Treatment: Program Implementation," *International Journal of Offender Therapy and Comparative Criminology 43*, no. 2 (1999), 180–87; Lowenkamp et al., "Does Correctional Program Quality Really Matter?"

52. P. Smith, P. Gendreau, and K. Swartz, "Validating the Principles of Effective Intervention: A Systematic Review of the Contributions of Meta-Analysis in the Field of Corrections," *Victims and Offenders 4*, no. 2 (2009), 148–69.

53. N. Blagen, B. Winder, and C. Hames, "'They Treat Us Like Human Beings'—Experiencing a Therapeutic Sex Offenders Prison: Impact on Prisoners and Staff and Implications for Treatment," *International Journal of Offender Therapy and Comparative Criminology 60*, no. 4 (2016), 371–96.

54. Ibid., p. 373.

55. Ibid., p. 384.

56. Ibid., pp. 380–81.

57. A.L. Solomon, K.D. Johnson, J. Travis, and E.C. McBride, *From Prison to Work: The Employment Dimensions of Prisoner Reentry* (Washington, DC: Urban Institute, 2004), http://www.urban.org/sites/default/files/publication/58126/411097-From-Prison-to-Work.pdf.

58. Luong et al., *Report of the Evaluation of CSC's Community Corrections*, p. 52.

59. C. McKinnon, "The Legal Right of Offenders to Refuse Treatment," *Forum on Corrections Research* 7, no. 3 (1995), 43–47, http://www.csc-scc.gc.ca/research/forum/e073/e073n-eng.shtml.

60. N.L. Hogan, S.M. Barton-Bellessa, and E.G. Lambert, "Forced to Change: Staff and Inmate Perceptions of Involuntary Treatment and Its Effects," *Applied Psychology in Criminal Justice 11*, no. 1 (2015), 19–39; K.K. Parhar, J.S. Wormith, D.M. Derkzen, and A.M. Beauregard, "Offender Coercion in Treatment: A Meta-Analysis of Effectiveness," *Criminal Justice and Behavior 35*, no. 9 (2008), 1109–35.

61. Office of the Auditor General Manitoba, *Managing the Province's Adult Offenders*, p. 278.

62. G. Heidemann, J.A. Cederbaum, and S. Martinez, "Beyond Recidivism: How Formerly Incarcerated Women Define Success," *Journal of Women and Social Work 31*, no. 1 (2016), 24–40 at 33.

63. Office of the Auditor General of Ontario, *Annual Report, 2008* (Toronto: Author, 2008), http://www.auditor.on.ca/en/content/annualreports/arbyyear/ar2008.html.

64. Office of the Auditor General Manitoba, *Managing the Province's Adult Offenders*, p. 238.

65. Ibid.

66. R.M. Martinson, "What Works? Questions and Answers About Prison Reform," *Public Interest 35* (1974), 22–54.

67. R.M. Martinson, "New Findings, New Views: A Note of Caution Regarding Sentencing Reform," *Hofstra Law Review* 7 (1979), 243–58.

68. Smith, Gendreau, and Swartz, "Validating the Principles of Effective Intervention."

69. Hogan et al., "Forced to Change: Staff and Inmate Perceptions of Involuntary Treatment and Its Effects."

PART IV

RETURNING TO THE COMMUNITY: RELEASE, RE-ENTRY, AND REINTEGRATION

One of the most important decisions in the criminal justice system is when to release an offender from custody and what conditions—if any—will be attached to the release. Chapter 10 discusses the purpose and principles of conditional release, the release options available to offenders, and the various issues that surround the decision-making of parole boards. The decision to release an inmate from custody is often more art than science, with parole boards having to balance the interests of the offender with the protection of the community. Given the significance of the parole board's decision to release an offender on parole, it is this form of conditional release that is the focus of Chapter 10.

Chapter 11 examines reintegration and the challenges that offenders experience when re-entering the community. Many offenders returning to the community were marginal before their incarceration and will experience considerable difficulties finding their way in the absence of supports and services, and in the face of negative responses from their communities and the media. Like their probation officer counterparts, parole officers must balance the dual roles of providing assistance and maintaining surveillance. Restorative justice approaches, including Circles of Support and Accountability, are evidence that the community can be mobilized in proactive ways to help offenders and reduce their risk of reoffending.

CHAPTER
10

RELEASE FROM INCARCERATION

CHAPTER OBJECTIVES

- Discuss the purpose and principles of conditional release.
- Identify the types of conditional release.
- Discuss the release options for provincial/territorial and federal inmates.
- Define statutory release and the detainment practice known as detention during the period of statutory release.
- Discuss the changing face of conditional release in Canada.
- Describe the issues surrounding crime victims and conditional release.
- Describe the dynamics of parole board decision-making and the issues that surround it.

It was noted in the opening pages of this text that nearly everyone who is sent to a correctional institution will eventually be released. Most inmates are released sooner rather than later in their sentence. It is the small percentage of offenders who receive sentences of two years or more who present the greatest challenges. This chapter examines the decisions surrounding the timing, type, and conditions of conditional release.

THE ORIGINS OF EARLY RELEASE

The practice of releasing offenders before the end of their sentence—today called *conditional release*—originated in the days when English convicts were transported to penal colonies in Australia. For centuries, the only avenue for early release had been to petition the king or queen for a Royal Prerogative of Mercy. That is, the monarch could grant a pardon or remission for humanitarian reasons or because the severity of the sentence far exceeded the severity of the crime.

The work of 19th-century penal reformers such as Alexander Maconochie was rooted in the observation that the harsh and brutalizing conditions in prisons did little to encourage convicts to be good citizens and, in fact, did much to ensure that they would become hardened criminals. Maconochie was the superintendent of Norfolk Island (off the coast of Australia), a penal colony where offenders thought to be incorrigible and irredeemable were sent. He developed a "mark system" whereby a day's labour earned the offender 10 marks, and ten marks shortened the sentence by one day. A day's rations and supplies cost between three and five marks, so inmates could earn one day toward early release for every two days of work.

Alexander Maconochie

In the 1890s, some jurisdictions in Canada began adopting indeterminate sentences and a mark system for juvenile offenders. For adults, reforms found expression in the concept of "ticket of leave." The Act to Provide for the Conditional Liberation of Penitentiary Convicts, known as the Ticket of Leave Act, was passed in 1899. This legislation allowed federal convicts to be at large from prison under specified conditions.

The Prison Gate Section of the Salvation Army undertook to help those on tickets of leave, there being no equivalents to the modern-day parole officers to supervise and assist reintegrating offenders. The first Dominion parole officer, a brigadier in the Salvation Army, was appointed in 1905.

An enormous change to the parole system occurred after a commission of inquiry in the mid-1950s.[1] The commission wanted an independent body affiliated with neither the penal system nor government to make release decisions. The National Parole Board, now known as the Parole Board of Canada (PBC), came into being with the passage of the Parole Act in 1959.

THE PURPOSE AND PRINCIPLES OF CONDITIONAL RELEASE

Section 100 of the Corrections and Conditional Release Act (CCRA) states:

> *The purpose of conditional release is to contribute to the maintenance of a just, peaceful and safe society by means of decisions on the timing and conditions of release that will best facilitate the rehabilitation of offenders and their reintegration into the community as law-abiding citizens.*

Section 100.1 emphasizes, "the protection of society is the paramount consideration for the Board and the provincial parole boards in the determination of all cases."

Section 101 of the act sets out a number of principles to be followed by parole boards in pursuing the objectives of conditional release. These include that the protection of society is the primary consideration in every case, that the board must consider all relevant case information when making decisions, and that offenders are to be provided with relevant information and reasons for decisions.

With respect to parole release, which is just one type of conditional release available to offenders in Canada, Section 102 of the CCRA outlines the criteria that parole boards must consider before granting parole to an offender:

The Board or a provincial parole board may grant parole to an offender if, in its opinion,

>   a. *The offender will not, by reoffending, present an undue risk to society before the expiration according to law of the sentence the offender is serving; and*
>   b. *The release of the offender will contribute to the protection of society by facilitating the reintegration of the offender into society as a law-abiding citizen.*

Because the guidelines are broad, parole board members have considerable discretion in making decisions to grant or deny parole.

The process of determining which inmates qualify for conditional release has been described as an inexact science at best; it is forward looking, predictive, and often difficult for board members to be certain how offenders will respond if released into the community. The board is required to ask two basic questions: (1) If released, will the inmate commit an offence that they would not have committed if kept in confinement? (2) Will release with supervision reduce the risk for reoffending, compared to a **cold turkey release** with no supervision?

THE TYPES OF CONDITIONAL RELEASE

The premise of conditional release programs is that the likelihood of recidivism is reduced if the offender is reintegrated back into the community under supervision. Various studies, including those conducted by CSC, have found that certain types of offenders, particularly medium- and high-risk offenders, who are gradually released from prison on conditional release are more likely to become law-abiding citizens than those who stay in prison until the end of their sentence.[2]

Conditional release is also believed to minimize the pains of imprisonment and provide offenders with incentive to behave in the institution, contributing to institutional order and security. Further, early release can lead to reductions in institutional overcrowding and cost savings given that it costs less to supervise someone in the community than an institution.[3] To illustrate, the Auditor General of Canada observed that the CSC could have saved $26 million in fiscal year 2013–14 alone had low-risk offenders incarcerated in minimum-security facilities been released at their first parole eligibility date.[4]

The release of an offender from custody can occur at one of three points in the sentence: (1) the parole eligibility date; (2) the statutory release date (applicable to federal offenders) or the earned release date (applicable to provincial/territorial offenders), which is usually at the two-thirds point in a sentence; or (3) the **warrant expiry date**, which marks the end of the sentence imposed by the court.

Cold turkey release
The discharge of an offender at the end of a sentence when no conditional release or supervision is possible, such as when an offender has served their entire sentence in federal custody, or when provincial/territorial offenders are released early due to earned remission.

Warrant expiry date
The end of an offender's sentence as imposed by the court at the time of sentencing.

The specific conditional release options available to an inmate depend on the length of the sentence and on whether he or she is under the supervision and control of a provincial/territorial or federal system of corrections. See Box 10.1 for the release options for federal and provincial/territorial inmates.

Figure 10.1 illustrates the sentencing milestones for federal offenders serving fixed sentences. Note: Those sentenced to an indeterminate sentence, such as dangerous offenders who receive an indeterminate sentence, are eligible for a full parole hearing after serving seven years, and are eligible to apply for day parole three years prior.[5] Further, life-sentenced prisoners can only be released from prison if granted parole by the Parole Board of Canada. Unlike most inmates who are serving a sentence of fixed length (e.g., 2 years, 10 years, or 20 years), lifers are not entitled to statutory release. If granted parole they will remain subject to the conditions of parole and the supervision of a CSC parole officer for the rest of their lives.

The PBC can also grant parole by exception at any point in an offender's sentence so long as they do not assess the applicant to be a risk to his or her community, and the offender is not serving an indeterminate sentence or a sentence for first- or second-degree murder. Parole by exception can be granted in the following circumstances: (1) if a prisoner has a terminal illness; (2) if the prisoner's "physical or mental health is likely to suffer serious damage if . . . [the prisoner is] made to stay in prison"; or (3) it would be an extreme hardship that was not reasonably foreseeable when sentenced to keep [the prisoner] in prison.[6]

Figure 10.1

Sentencing Milestones

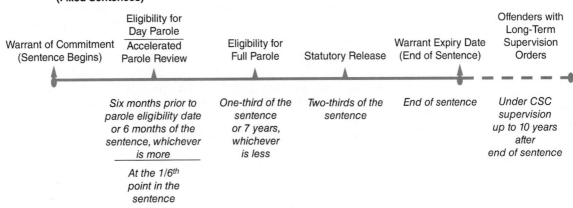

Source: Reproduced with the permission of Public Safety Canada, 2017, https://www.publicsafety.gc.ca/cnt/cntrng-crm/csc-scc-rvw-pnl/report-rapport/toc-en.aspx.

BOX 10.1

Release Options for Federal and Provincial/Territorial Inmates

Temporary absences (TAs)
A type of conditional release that allows an inmate to leave the institution for a reason that adheres to their correctional plan, including for employment and education. May be either escorted or unescorted, or a work release.

Work release
A type of conditional release that allows inmates to leave the institution to participate in community-service or employment opportunities.

Type of Release	Federal	Provincial/Territorial
Temporary absences (TA)	Usually the first type of release granted; escorted (ETA) or unescorted (UTA); CSC has discretion to grant ETAs except to life-sentenced prisoners (a PBC decision); used for medical, administrative, parental responsibility, rehabilitation, family contact, community service, employment, or compassionate purposes. Medical TAs for an unlimited number of days; maximum of 15 days for reasons other than medical. **Work release**, another type of TA; supervised by a staff member or authorized person or organization to allow offenders to work or participate in community service outside of the penitentiary; can be up to 60 days.	Most common type of release; use and duration varies by jurisdiction (e.g., prisoners in Nova Scotia, Ontario, and British Columbia can apply for medical, humanitarian, and rehabilitation TAs for up to 60 days; those in Saskatchewan can apply for humanitarian and rehabilitation TAs for up to 15 days);[7] in Ontario, the superintendent of the institution grants TAs of less than 72 hours whereas the Ontario Parole Board grants TAs of 72 hours or more.
Eligibility	ETA at any time. UTA varies with length and type of sentence—Maximum-security inmates not eligible for UTAs • Sentences of three years or more: May apply for UTA after serving one-sixth of sentence • Sentences of two to three years: May apply for UTA six months into sentence • Life sentences: May apply for UTA three years before full parole eligibility date. Offenders eligible for UTAs are also eligible to apply for work release.	Varies; in some jurisdictions inmate can apply immediately (e.g., in Nova Scotia); others require waiting period (e.g., Saskatchewan requires prisoners serve one-third or one-half of their sentence (depending on the crime); in Québec, the parole board can grant inmates TAs between one-sixth and one-third of their sentence; may require EM.

Day parole	Prepares offender for release on full parole by allowing participation in community-based activities; offender must return nightly to an institution or halfway house unless otherwise authorized by the PBC.		**Day parole** The authority granted by a parole board that provides an opportunity for inmates to be at large to complete community-based activities in preparation for full release (e.g., for job search) while returning at night to an institution or, more typically, to a community residential facility or halfway house.
Eligibility	Sentences of two years or more: six months prior to full parole eligibility or six months, whichever is greater; life sentences: eligible to apply three years before full parole eligibility date	Day parole does not exist for provincial inmates in Ontario and Québec. Provincial/territorial inmates serving sentences of six months or more in the remaining jurisdictions are eligible for day parole after serving one-half of the portion of the sentence that must be served before full parole may be granted.	
Full parole	Provides an opportunity for offenders to serve remainder of the sentence under supervision in the community; usually follows successful completion of day parole (where available); parolees usually reside in a private residence; parolee must report to a parole supervisor on a regular basis and abide by conditions.		**Full parole** The authority granted by a parole board for an inmate to be at large under supervision in the community for the remainder of their sentence.
Eligibility	After serving one-third of sentence or seven years, whichever is less (except for offenders serving life sentences for murder) after 25 years if serving a life sentence for first-degree murder; between 10 and 25 years (set by judge at sentencing) for offenders serving life sentences for second-degree murder (exception: judges *may* order individuals convicted of multiple murders to serve the parole ineligibility periods for each murder conviction consecutively, resulting in lengthier periods of ineligibility, e.g., 50 years)	Inmates sentenced to less than six months in Ontario may apply for parole at any time, but those sentenced to six months or more must serve one-third of their sentence for eligibility; prisoners sentenced to six months to two years less a day in Québec and the remaining jurisdictions are eligible for parole release after serving one-third of their sentence.	**Statutory release** A provision that allows incarcerated federal offenders to be released at the two-thirds point in their sentence (unless PBC accepts CSC's recommendation to detain an offender during their period of statutory release) and to serve the remaining one-third of their sentence under supervision in the community.
Statutory release	Mandatory conditional release of federal offenders by law (i.e., not a decision made by PBC) who have not applied for parole or who have not been granted parole that provides structure and support to offenders to increase the likelihood offenders will successfully reintegrate into the community. Standard, mandatory conditions: report to a parole officer, remain within a certain area, and obey the law and keep the peace. The parole board can impose special conditions tailored to the offender; sometimes this includes a requirement to stay at a halfway house or community correctional centre.		

(continued)

Earned remission date
A provision that allows incarcerated provincial/territorial offenders to earn early release through good behaviour at a rate of 15 days for every month served.

Detention during the period of statutory release
A decision by the Parole Board of Canada (after an application by the CSC) that a federal inmate be denied statutory release and be detained in the institution until the warrant expiry date.

One-chance statutory release
When CSC recommends to PBC detention during the period of statutory release but the PBC decides to release the offender who has been convicted of serious crime(s) at their statutory release date, wherein if the offender is revoked, they must complete the remainder of their sentence in prison.

Eligibility	By law, for most federal offenders after serving two-thirds of their sentence; offenders serving life or indeterminate sentences not eligible; CSC may recommend that an offender be denied statutory release if it believes the offender is likely to (a) commit an offence causing death or serious harm to another person; (b) commit a sexual offence against a child; or (c) commit a serious drug offence before the end of the sentence.[a]	Not applicable to provincial/territorial inmates
Earned remission date	Not applicable to federal offenders.	Provincial/territorial offenders may serve their entire sentence in custody unless they earn remission through good behaviour at a rate of 15 days for every month served.
Eligibility	Not applicable	The earned release date can be as early as the two-thirds point of the sentence. Unless the offender has a probation order, there will be no supervision upon release.

[a] The PBC may detain the offender if the Board is satisfied "that the offender is likely, if released, to commit an offence causing the death of or serious harm to another person, a sexual offence involving a child, or a serious drug offence";[8] this is **detention during the period of statutory release**. Inmates detained in this manner will have their case reviewed on an annual basis or bi-annual basis (the latter is reserved for offenders who are serving a sentence for a Schedule I offence that involved the death or serious harm of another person).[9] If PBC does not order detention, the offender will be released on regular statutory release, or on "**one-chance statutory release**." The latter means that if the offender's statutory release is revoked (revocation to be discussed in Chapter 11), the offender is prohibited from being released again on statutory release prior to the warrant expiry date; thus, the offender will be incarcerated until that time.[10]

Source: National Parole Board, 2010. Fact Sheet: Types of Release. https://www.canada.ca/en/parole-board/services/parole/types-of-conditional-release.html. Contains information licensed under the Open Government Licence - Canada.

Prisons and Reformatories Act (1985). Retrieved from http://laws.justice.gc.ca/PDF/P-20.pdf; Corrections and Conditional Release Act (1992). Retrieved from http://laws-lois.justice.gc.ca/PDF/C-44.6.pdf; Ministry of Correctional Services Act (1990). Retrieved from https://www.canlii.org/en/on/laws/regu/rro-1990-reg-778/latest/rro-1990-reg-778.html; Commission des liberations conditionelles Québec (2016). Conditional release programs: Steps and procedure to follow. Retrieved from https://www.cqlc.gouv.qc.ca/fileadmin/Documents/depliant-contrevenant-EN.pdf; Government of Canada (2016). Types of conditional release. Retrieved from https://www.canada.ca/en/parole-board/services/parole/types-of-conditional-release.html; Correctional Service Canada (2016). Commissioner's Directive 712-5: Pre-release case preparation for provincial/territorial offenders and federal offenders incarcerated in provincial/territorial facilities. Retrieved from http://www.csc-scc.gc.ca/acts-and-regulations/712-5-cd-eng.shtml#d1; Correctional Service Canada (2014). Types of release. Retrieved from http://www.csc-scc.gc.ca/parole/002007-0003-eng.shtml; Ontario Parole Board (2013). Ontario Parole Board 2012–2013 annual report. Retrieved from http://www.ontla.on.ca/library/repository/ser/100632/2012-13.pdf

Judicial Recognizances for Sex Offenders

Federal sex offenders not released on either parole or statutory release remain in custody until warrant expiry. These offenders are then released "cold turkey" and are not required to inform law enforcement or correctional agencies of their location. One response to this problem has been the use of community notification, discussed in Chapter 11. Another is the use of Section 810.1 of the Criminal Code to force the individual to enter into a **judicial recognizance**, often referred to in this context as a peace bond.

Judicial recognizance is most commonly used with pedophiles who have reached warrant expiry but who remain at a very high risk of offending against children under 16.[11] The applicant—who can be a police officer—need only have reasonable grounds to fear that the subject of the order may commit one of the designated offences in the near future. In other words—and this is somewhat unique in legal terms—it is applied proactively for offences that may be committed rather than in reaction to offences that have been committed.

The application is heard in a provincial court, where the judge can order the subject to enter into a recognizance to comply with set conditions, which can include a prohibition from engaging in any activity that involves contact with persons under 16. For example, the subject will not be permitted to visit a daycare centre, a schoolyard, a playground, or any public park or swimming area where children are present or can reasonably be expected to be present.

Other conditions include refraining from use of the Internet and requiring the defendant to engage in treatment programming. Section 810.1(3) provides that if the judge is satisfied that the applicant has reasonable grounds for the fear, "the judge may order the defendant enter into a recognizance to keep the peace and be of good behaviour for a period that does not exceed 12 months." Section 810.1(3.01) authorizes provincial court judges to impose the order for up to 24 months if they are satisfied the defendant was previously convicted of an offence involving a person under the age of 16.

A person who refuses to enter into the recognizance can be sent to prison for up to 12 months for the refusal. An offender who violates a condition of the order commits an offence for which they are liable for up to four years in prison if proceeded by way of indictable offence and 18 months if proceeded by way of summary offence.[12]

Section 810.1 raises the issue of how to balance the rights of ex-offenders with the need to protect the community. Note that Section 810.2 includes a similar

Judicial recognizance An order of the court, often referred to as a peace bond, that requires offenders (most often sex offenders) to adhere to set conditions beyond the expiry of their sentence, including most often avoiding places where there are children.

procedure for issuing a judicial recognizance to individuals at risk of committing a serious personal offence. Section 810.2 judicial recognizances are the same length as those issued under Section 810.1 and have similar consequences for failure to enter into the recognizance and for breaching the conditions of the recognizance.[13]

THE CHANGING FACE OF CONDITIONAL RELEASE

Release on parole is not a statutory right—it is a privilege. Although inmates have the right to apply for parole when eligible, there are no guarantees that an application will succeed. Although the federal offender population has increased in recent years, as Figure 10.2 shows, the conditional release population has not grown at the same pace. PBC partially attributes this change to the abolition of accelerated parole review (see discussion below) that has resulted in non-violent offenders serving more of their sentences in custody rather than in the community.[14] Offenders are also serving more of their sentences before being released on full parole than when Stephen Harper came into power in 2006 (46 percent versus 42 percent).[15]

A former director general of corrections and criminal justice at the Department of Public Safety noted that statistics on federal parole were inaccurate due to recent changes in how the statistics are calculated (including the retroactive removal of data), resulting in a "presentation that is not telling the whole story"[16] and that "what we're seeing is really the demise of parole in Canada."[17] See Corrections File 10.1 for additional insight on this topic.

Figure 10.2

The Federal Offender Population

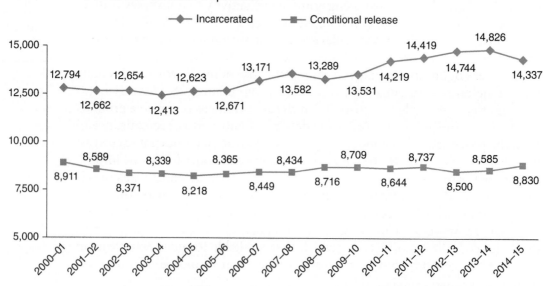

Source: Parole Board of Canada. (2016). *Performance monitoring report 2014–2015,* page 7. https://www.canada.ca/content/dam/canada/parole-board/migration/005/009/093/005009-3000-2015-en.pdf. Contains information licensed under the Open Government Licence - Canada.

Figure 10.3 shows that although the percentage of federal offenders released on day and full parole has increased in the past two years, this number is still less than 10 years ago. Figure 10.4 illustrates how the percentage of federal offenders released at their statutory release date has decreased in the past two years though this number has increased over the past 10 years (from 66.6 percent to 70.8 percent).[18] The Auditor General of Canada observed that in 2013–14, the majority of offenders released on statutory release (N = 2,000) went from medium- (64 percent) or maximum-security (11 percent) institutions directly into the community. Those released on statutory release are more likely to engage in violent recidivism before their warrant expiry date than those released on parole.[19]

Figures 10.5 and 10.6 show that there has been an increase in the number of offenders granted federal day parole (71 percent grant rate in 2014–15, up 8 percent from 2010–11) and federal full parole (30 percent, up 13 percent from 2010–11).[20] Figures 10.5 and 10.6 also show that the number of offenders granted provincial day parole (in the jurisdictions where PBC grants parole) has increased (57 percent grant rate in 2014–15, up 14 percent from 2010–11), although the number of offenders granted provincial full parole has remained consistent (32 percent grant rate in 2014–15,

Figure 10.3

The Percentage of Offenders Released from Federal Penitentiaries on Day and Full Parole

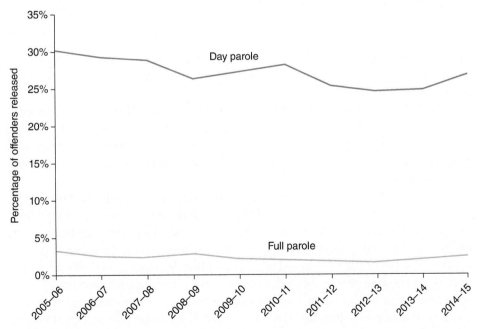

Source: Reproduced with the permission of Public Safety Canada, 2017, https://www.publicsafety.gc.ca/cnt/rsrcs/pblctns/ccrso-2015/index-en.aspx.

Figure 10.4

The Percentage of Offenders Released from Federal Penitentiaries at Statutory Release

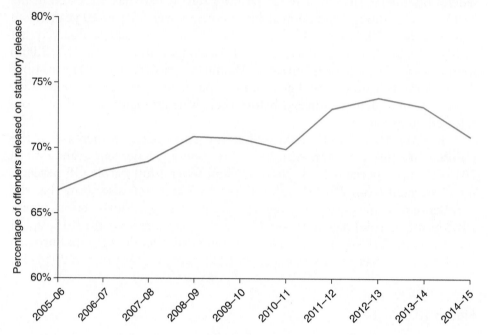

Source: Reproduced with the permission of Public Safety Canada, 2017, https://www.publicsafety.gc.ca/cnt/
rsrcs/pblctns/ccrso-2015/index-en.aspx.

up 1 percent from 2010–11). As noted above, extreme caution should be exercised when interpreting this data due to changes in the reporting practices of the PBC.

In 2012–13, the grant rate for the Québec Parole Board (i.e., Commission québécoise des libérations conditionnelles) was 44 percent, and in 2013–14, the Ontario Parole Board held over 1,000 parole hearings and granted parole in 35 percent of cases, with the average parolee serving seven months on parole.[21]

From 2005–06 through 2014–15, women were more likely than men to be granted federal day and full parole. During that time the grant rate for federal full parole for Indigenous offenders remained lower than for non-Indigenous offenders. The federal day parole grant rate for Indigenous offenders has been consistently lower than for non-Indigenous offenders since 2008–09. Over the past 10 years, Indigenous offenders have served a higher proportion of their sentences prior to day or full parole release than their non-Indigenous counterparts. Indigenous offenders were also more likely to be released on statutory release than other types of release, and were more likely than non-Indigenous

Figure 10.5

Grant Rates for Federal and Provincial Day Parole, 2010–11 to 2014–15

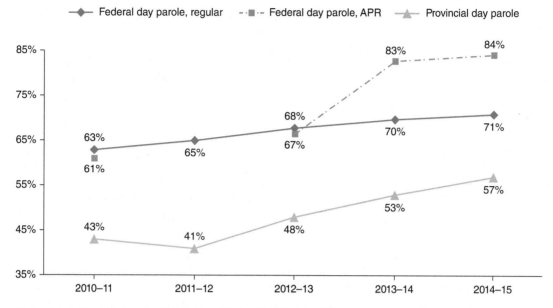

Source: Parole Board of Canada, *Performance Monitoring Report 2014/2015*, page 27. https://www.canada
.ca/content/dam/canada/parole-board/migration/005/009/093/005009-3000-2015-en.pdf. Contains information licensed under the Open Government Licence - Canada.

offenders to be released on statutory release.[22] The reasons for these disparities in grant rates have yet to be thoroughly explored.

In 2013–14, CSC recommended fewer inmate-applicants be granted parole than in 2011–12, including fewer recommendations for lower-risk offenders, which has led to this offender population serving more time in prison and less time supervised in the community. This is despite CSC acknowledging that low-risk offenders are more likely to successfully reintegrate when they have served a greater portion of their time under supervision in the community setting.[23]

The practice of CSC making recommendations for parole release is itself somewhat controversial; CSC is not required by legislation to make recommendations, and the argument is that if PBC is to be a true, independent administrative tribunal, CSC should not be providing recommendations as to whether parole should be granted. While the high concordance rate between CSC recommendations and PBC release decisions—for example, 86 percent of day parole cases in 2013–14[24]—could simply reflect the fact that both agencies have access to the same documentation and prioritize public safety when making their decisions, a more critical perspective suggests that PBC is risk averse and agrees with CSC to shift accountability to that organization should an offender reoffend.[25]

Figure 10.6

Grant Rates for Federal and Provincial Full Parole, 2010–11 to 2014–15

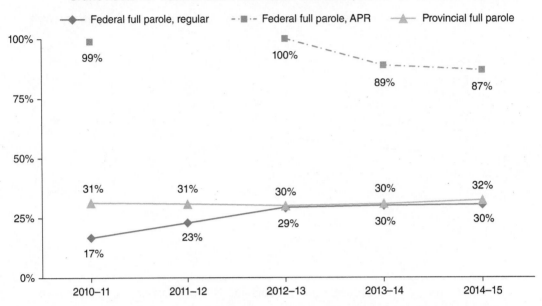

Source: Parole Board of Canada, *Performance Monitoring Report 2014/2015*, page 30. https://www.canada.ca/content/dam/canada/parole-board/migration/005/009/093/005009-3000-2015-en.pdf. Contains information licensed under the Open Government Licence - Canada.

CORRECTIONS FILE 10.1

Are Parole Grant Rates Increasing or Decreasing? Well, It Depends Whom You Ask

The information outlined in the section above highlights parole grant rates documented in PBC's Performance Monitoring Report, and yet when one reads the annual report for the Office of the Correctional Investigator (OCI), the picture is different. The OCI cautions that parole grant rates are on the decline in Canada, observing that in the past 10 years, day parole grant rates have decreased by 15 percent and full parole grant rates by 40 percent. Of concern for the OCI is that the majority of offenders who are released into our communities are those on statutory release—the very individuals who often pose the highest risk and needs and could benefit the most from supervision.

The discrepancy in information available and published about parole grant rates highlights the challenges that are often faced by researchers in determining what is actually happening in corrections, and suggests that greater transparency is required.

Changes in legislation have affected conditional release. For example, Stephen Harper and his Conservative government abolished accelerated parole review (APR) in 2011 with the passage of the Abolition of Early Parole Act (AEPA) and applied the legislation retroactively. APR was designed to provide a mechanism for releasing non-violent, first-time federal offenders from custody after serving one-sixth of their sentence if deemed unlikely to commit a violent crime.

In 2014, the Supreme Court of Canada ruled the retroactive nature of the legislation infringed Section 11 of the Charter and ruled the legislation could not be applied to offenders sentenced prior to the date the AEPA was passed.[26] The Supreme Court has not addressed the issue of whether the legislation infringes Section 11 for offenders who committed their offences pre-AEPA but were sentenced post-AEPA; however, several lower courts, including the Ontario Court of Appeal, have ruled in favour of prisoners.[27]

The then-federal Conservative government also passed the Protecting Canadians by Ending Sentence Discounts for Multiple Murders Act in 2011, allowing judges to impose consecutive rather than concurrent parole ineligibility periods for multiple murderers. In 2013, Travis Baumgartner, the 21-year-old who murdered three co-workers in an armoured-car heist, was sentenced to life with no possibility of parole for 40 years, the most severe sanction imposed by the Canadian courts since Canada's last execution in 1962.[28]

Given how recent these changes have been, it is difficult to determine the impact they will have on prison populations, corrections costs, and rates of reoffending in the long term. What *is* clear is that there is an increasing emphasis on punishment rather than rehabilitation and that there are ever fewer opportunities for conditional release, resulting in increased costs and capacity issues for CSC.[29]

PRE-RELEASE PLANNING

Pre-release planning is an important part of the inmate's correctional plan and is directed toward managing the risk posed by offenders and, ideally, toward providing access to programs and services in the community. Despite its importance in the correctional process, pre-release planning is often minimal in provincial/territorial institutions. There may also be a lack of pre-release planning for inmates with particular challenges, such as mental illness. This hinders successful reintegration into the community upon release.[30]

A small sample ($N = 12$) of provincial inmates in Nova Scotia, some of whom had also served federal time, found that they did not feel they were prepared for release. One respondent commented: "Because there is no support, you're back on the street and then soon back in the system."[31] The inmates indicated that there was no pre-release planning, and no information provided on support services in the community, and that they were not generally aware of the assistance that was available to them.

The Auditor General of Ontario criticized the Ontario Parole Board for low parole participation rates in 2013–14, as the number of inmate-applicants had decreased by half since 2000–01. The Auditor General attributed the low participation rates to the challenging and lengthy (about 60 days) nature of applying for a parole hearing, low grant rates in recent years (averaging approximately 32 percent) that discourage offenders from applying, and inconsistent staff resources available to assist offenders with the application process.[32]

Federal inmates, who are incarcerated for longer periods of time than their provincial counterparts, have greater access to pre-release assistance. However, results from the 2015 Office of the Auditor General audit of the timeliness of CSC correctional interventions provided to facilitate an offender's safe release into the community highlighted significant issues. The Office of the Auditor General examined release rates from March 2011 onward for non-Indigenous, male offenders and found that although CSC has improved the timeliness of programming, it has not led to earlier release. In fact, 80 percent of offenders released from CSC custody had been incarcerated beyond their first parole eligibility date, and only 20 percent of offenders had their cases prepared in time for their earliest parole eligibility date.

As noted above, the Auditor General estimated that CSC spent approximately $26 million providing custodial supervision for low-risk offenders in 2013–14 due to its inability to prepare these offenders for their earliest parole eligibility date.[33] Low-risk offenders were typically released on parole eight months after their first parole eligibility date, with 39 percent of this population entering the community on statutory release rather than parole. The Auditor General of Canada also noted that most offenders did not complete their programs by their first parole eligibility date.[34]

Institutional parole officers (IPOs) play a vital role in assisting offenders with their reintegration and preparing offenders for their first eligibility date (pre-release planning), and yet CSC does not specify contact guidelines based on the offender's level of risk (contrary to existing guidelines for community parole officers (CPOs)).[35]

Of further concern is that IPOs have considerable discretion in recommending an offender's early release, and yet CSC provides "little guidance and tools . . . to support the parole officer to make an objective assessment of the impact of interventions on an offender's progress toward safe reintegration, particularly for low-risk offenders."[36] These issues indicate federal offenders face systemic barriers to successfully participating in correctional programming and engaging in pre-release planning as they work toward applying for parole.

International research has found that the development of high-quality release plans for violent offenders and sex offenders may decrease an offender's risk of quick reimprisonment (within 12 months of release).[37] These plans involved risk management and positive life planning (e.g., employment).[38]

Corrections File 10.2 highlights B.C. Corrections' Integrated Offender Management program and the services that inmates who participated in the program identified as beneficial and those that should be incorporated into programming.

CORRECTIONS FILE 10.2

Client Feedback on B.C. Corrections' Integrated Offender Management Program

B.C. Corrections designed and implemented the Integrated Offender Management (IOM) program to facilitate collaboration between its institutional and community corrections branches. This collaboration is vital for case planning and management purposes to develop a reintegration plan, informed by the Risk–Need–Responsivity model, for offenders who are being released from institutional supervision to community corrections supervision.

Participants surveyed in this study were males sentenced to a minimum of 135 days, females sentenced to 90 days or more, those who would be subject to a minimum of six months community supervision to follow their custodial sentence, those previously sentenced to a community or custodial sanction, and those who were assessed "an overall high supervision and high needs assessment rating" (p. 6). Some of the clients surveyed were also participants of the OIM/Homelessness Intervention Project implemented in 2010 to assist vulnerable populations in their transition to the community.

In total, 466 surveys were analyzed and the findings were positive. Ninety-seven percent of the participants understood the purpose of the program, 96 percent found the case planning process useful, 91 percent agreed or strongly agreed that working with both jail and probation staff on their case was beneficial, 87 percent said the assistance they had received made them feel more comfortable returning to the community, and 79 percent indicated they believed this assistance would reduce their likelihood of returning to jail (pp. 8–12). Figure 10.7 highlights what the participants viewed as being the most beneficial services offered in IOM, and Figure 10.8 highlights assistance the participants suggested could be added to the program.

Figure 10.7

Participant Views on the Most Beneficial Services Offered in IOM

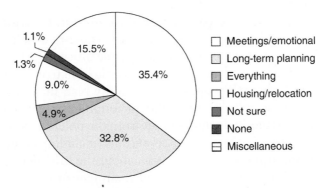

Source: BC Corrections Performance, Research and Evaluation Unit. (2014). *Integrated Offender Management participant exit survey report,* page 10. http://www2.gov.bc.ca/assets/gov/law-crime-and-justice/criminal-justice/corrections/research-evaluation/iom-client-exit-survey-report.pdf. Reprinted by permission of the Strategic Operations Division, B.C. Corrections, Ministry of Public Safety & Solicitor General.

Figure 10.8

Participant Suggestions for Other Assistance That Could Be Added to IOM

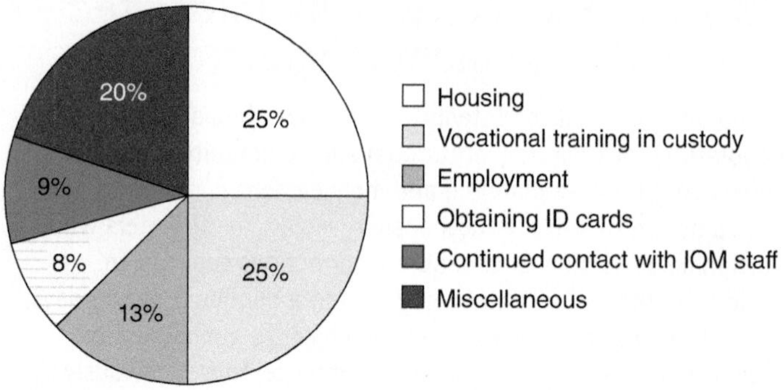

- ☐ Housing
- ☐ Vocational training in custody
- ▨ Employment
- ☐ Obtaining ID cards
- ▨ Continued contact with IOM staff
- ■ Miscellaneous

Source: BC Corrections Performance, Research and Evaluation Unit. (2014). *Integrated Offender Management participant exit survey report*, page 13. http://www2.gov.bc.ca/assets/gov/law-crime-and-justice/criminal-justice/corrections/research-evaluation/iom-client-exit-survey-report.pdf. Reprinted by permission of the Strategic Operations Division, B.C. Corrections, Ministry of Public Safety & Solicitor General.

THE PAROLE FILE

In its deliberations, the parole board considers a number of documents contained in the inmate-applicant's parole file. These generally include, but are not limited to, police reports, an official record of convictions, classification reports, custody reports from institutional staff on the inmate's behaviour and performance, correctional plan progress reports, victim impact statements, pre-sentence reports, letters of support, and a document prepared by a probation or community parole officer assessing the offender's release plan and proposing a supervision strategy for the offender.

A key document in the parole file is the **community strategy guide**, also sometimes referred to as a community assessment, which is prepared by community parole officers (probation and parole officers (PPOs) in Québec and Ontario). This file is best described as an investigation to evaluate the feasibility of the inmate-applicant's proposed community plan in terms of the level of supervision required and the availability of community resources.

The report typically includes input from the police as well as the inmate's response to previous corrections interventions (including community supervision), if any. And it includes information about the offender's family relationships and friendship network, proposed treatment or counselling programs, and an assessment of the components of the proposed release plan, including the proposed residence and education/employment activities. The CPO may recommend that special conditions be attached to the release certificate that will help manage the level of risk the offender poses to the community and facilitate the offender's rehabilitation.

Community strategy guide
A document prepared by probation and parole officers (in Ontario and Québec) or community parole officers for the parole board and containing information on the feasibility of the inmate-applicant's proposed community plan in terms of the level of supervision required, employment/residential/education plans, and the availability of community resources.

"*Bad news. The mailman is going to attend the parole-board hearing.*"

Leo Cullum/The New Yorker Collection/www.cartoonbank.com

Parole officers are also responsible for writing the report, **Assessment for Decision**. This report presents their recommendation for release and/or the inclusion of special conditions; is based on a thorough, current review of major correctional documents (e.g., criminal profile, correctional plan, and community strategy guide); addresses how successful the offender's correctional plan has been in changing the offender's attitudes and behaviours; and whether the parole officer thinks the proposed release plan and accompanying community supervision will adequately address the offender's risk in the community and promote their reintegration.[39]

It is believed POs can be influenced easily by the ideology of those in power above them; for example, a PO might be risk-averse in their assessments to appease regional headquarters management personnel if he or she is concerned about future employment opportunities.[40]

Many offenders find it a challenge to develop a viable release plan. Family support may be lacking, and there may be no arrangements for employment or accommodation. Also, access to specialized community-based treatment programs for addiction, sex offending, and mental health issues may be limited, particularly for provincial/territorial inmates and for offenders from rural and remote communities. Because many treatment programs will not accept offenders who have a history of violence, it is often difficult to ensure throughcare for high-risk offenders.

> **Assessment for Decision**
> A document prepared by an institutional or community parole officer that addresses the offender's criminal and conditional release history, institutional and community behaviour, correctional plan progress and offender engagement, release plan and supervision strategy, and their recommendations for conditional release and special conditions.

THE PAROLE HEARING PROCESS

Parole hearings are usually presided over by two board members and a parole board hearing assistant and are generally convened at the institution where the inmate is being held. In federal parole hearings, a CSC representative, usually an IPO, accompanies the inmate-applicant to provide the board with their reasons for either supporting or not supporting the inmate-applicant's release. Inmate-applicants may also have Elder support to provide information on the inmate-applicant's culture, among other information, and an assistant, whose role is to help the inmate understand PBC questions and summarize their case at the end of the hearing. Lawyers may attend hearings on the inmate's behalf (as an assistant), but there is no provision for the adversarial approaches found in criminal courts. Lawyers may provide additional information to the board, clarify the PBC's questions for the inmate-applicant, and/or speak in support of the inmate's application. It is also possible for observers to attend (e.g., students, media, other CSC or PBC staff, victims, and/or friends and relatives of the inmate-applicant and/or the victims).[41]

Before the hearing, the board members review the parole file and make notes on key points. During the hearing, the board members ask the inmate about the release plan and strategies to succeed in the community (and other questions) to ascertain suitability for release. The board may pay a great deal of attention to the inmate's version of the offence, looking for some insight into why it was committed and why it would not happen again. (The inmate's participation in treatment programs and skills/trades training, as well as any other positive steps taken while in custody, are key factors here.) Board members are interested in the insights the offender has gained about the offence, the decisions that led to the criminal behaviour, and the steps the offender has taken to address the issues that were associated with the criminal activity. Often, this involves addressing issues related to alcohol or drug abuse, anger management, or life skills. Indications of remorse and of empathy for the victim are considered important by board members. The file review and the interview are meant to determine whether the offender can be managed at an acceptable level of risk in the community.

To conduct an effective interview with the inmate-applicant, the board members must be aware of their own biases and avoid moralizing. As well, they must appreciate the pressure that is on the inmate-applicant. Most applicants appear without assistants or family members present and may have limited verbal skills. Parole boards are administrative tribunals, not courts of law. That said, the onus is on these boards to be fair, and they must follow specific procedures (see the grounds for appeal, discussed below).

After the interview, the inmate is asked to wait outside the hearing room while the members deliberate and decide. The inmate returns to the room to be told the outcome—whether the release has been granted, denied, or deferred pending the gathering of additional information. If it has been denied, specific reasons must be given so that the inmate can understand how to increase the likelihood of success if another application is made—for example, by participating in a treatment program or developing a different release plan. Provincial parole boards in Ontario and Québec follow a decision-making process similar to that of the PBC, except that victims who attend hearings of the Québec board cannot make oral statements to the board.

If the parole board determines that the level of risk the inmate-applicant presents is not manageable in the community, the application for release on day parole or full parole will be denied. A decision of the Ontario Parole Board to grant parole is presented in Appendix 10.1.

American research investigating parole decision-making has identified factors that significantly predict parole release decisions: aggressive disciplinary incidents while incarcerated; correctional personnel recommendations for release; confirmed residence in the community; actuarial measures of risk to reoffend; offender characteristics (e.g., age, substance use, and ethnicity); offence characteristics (e.g., the type of offence); inmate visitation history, type, and frequency; criminal history; and participation in treatment programs (i.e., perceived parole readiness).[42]

Analyses of parole denials made in 2013–14 by the Ontario Parole Board were attributed to a lack of suitable housing on release, the gravity of the original offence, the inmate's minimization of the offence, and a lack of suitable employment, support networks, and/or appropriate programming.[43]

THE INMATE AND PAROLE HEARINGS

For inmates applying for conditional release, the appearance before the parole board can be stressful, intimidating, and anxiety-provoking. Even inmates who have previously appeared before a parole board are uncertain what questions will be asked and how individual board members will weigh the information contained in the parole file and the responses provided by the inmate during the interview. There are often great socio-economic disparities between board members and inmates; there may also be cultural differences (including language barriers) that make it difficult for board members and the inmate to communicate. Many inmates have little or no understanding of the parole board's role and may be intimidated by the more sophisticated language skills of board members. Parole board members, for their part, may not realize that the inmate-applicant is mentally disordered or is still in withdrawal following a relapse into drug use while on conditional release.

In contrast, some inmate-applicants play the parole "game"—that is, they manipulate the system to create the impression that they are addressing their issues and moving toward a law-abiding life. There is more knowledge of the role of the parole board and of the dynamics of parole hearings among federal offenders who have served multiple terms in custody. A lifer on parole who had appeared before the parole board on many occasions offered the following opinion:

> *Parole hearings for me now are old hat. I know how to present myself, what to do, what they want to hear, why they want to hear it. I have a good understanding of what their role is, and what they think their role is and how to approach that . . . I think they have a really difficult job in trying*

*to gauge the threat to society of the people who are there. They're respon-
sible for the decisions they make. Just looking at a file doesn't give you a
very good indicator of who people are. But if you put a person in a stressful
situation and crank them up a bit and see how they react and see how they
handle a situation, then you get a pretty good view of who that person is. I
think the board does that quite often. . . . If you're able to handle yourself
in those situations and still be able to supply the things that are necessary,
and make them feel comfortable with the idea of actually letting the person
out, then you've done your job as a presenter to the board of your case.*[44]

As noted above, board members can ask the inmate-applicant literally
anything. The questions may relate to past criminal activities and convictions,
the present offence, and participation in treatment programs. Also within
bounds are more personal questions about family members and current friendships. For most inmates who plead guilty in criminal court, this is the first
time they have been asked detailed questions about their crimes, their personal
history, and their future intentions. The severe time constraints under which
many parole boards operate place an added burden on both board members and
the inmate-applicant, and this may lead to superficial coverage of some topics.

Below is an excerpt of a transcript from a PBC day parole hearing involving a federal sex offender. The board focused its questions on the offender's
management of his sexual fantasies and arousal by asking him to discuss his
crime cycle and relapse prevention plan to ascertain whether he recognized
how these contribute to his offending.[45]

35. PB1: What did you learn in [the latest sex offender treatment program]?

*36. Alan: I learned to look at my high risks. I learned to manage them.
I keep a fantasy log.*

*37. PB1: I have lots of questions about the program. What are your high
risks?*

*38. Alan: It's your crime cycle: your feelings, thoughts, behaviour that will
make you reoffend. I know I cannot go to malls, public pools, places where
there are children.*

. . . .

*45. PB1: Okay, so being where children are is high risk. Drinking is high
risk. What else?*

*46. Alan: Being in malls, places where there are children. Hanging out
with women with children is a high risk. I have to stay away from that.*

47. PB1: Anything else? You said something about a fantasy log?

48. Alan: Yes, I look for my triggers.

49. PB1: What's a trigger?

50. Alan: It means more or less if you have problems. A trigger builds up your crime cycle.

51. PB1: Do you remember your triggers?

52. Alan: I have to be careful whom I associate with.

53. PB1: Are fantasies a trigger for you?

54. Alan: Yes, I know that I cannot watch certain shows on TV, shows with children. I cannot look at books with pictures of children.

...

108. PB2: Do you think it would be safe to be in a room with a child?

109. Alan: I would not want to be alone with a child. I would ask for someone to accompany me.

110. PB2: Let us say you are at your M2's* house and a neighbour comes over with his ten-year-old boy. The M2 and the neighbour decide to go the garage and leave the kid in the kitchen while you watch TV in the living room. What would you do?

111. Alan: It would be better for me to avoid the situation. I would get up and go to the garage with the two adults to avoid being with the child.

112. PB2: Mr. S. when you are out in the community there will be children. Let us say, you're in a bus, how much risk will you be?

113. Alan: Well, I have done sex offender programming. I know my triggers.

114. PB2: How do you know that the program worked? What makes you think that you will act differently this time?

115. Alan: I know my danger points.[46]

Of concern is that in jurisdictions where the PBC is responsible for provincial/territorial parole hearings (i.e., everywhere but Ontario and Québec, which operate their own parole boards for provincially sentenced prisoners), "paper decisions" are common and there is no hearing. This denies inmate-applicants the opportunity to meet face to face with the board and discuss their application. It also denies the victims of crime the chance to appear before the

---

* Man to Man, a mentorship program

parole board and to discuss the impact of the crime and to offer their opinion on the application.

Many provincial/territorial inmates do not even apply for parole; instead, they serve out their sentences in custody. These inmates are eligible to be released after serving two-thirds of their time in custody, at their earned remission date. In contrast to federal offenders released on statutory release, provincial/territorial inmates released at their earned remission date are not supervised by parole officers. This can discourage provincial/territorial offenders from applying for parole if they do not want to be subject to supervision.

Another factor discouraging provincial/territorial offenders from applying for parole is that those who are granted parole are subject to supervision until their warrant expiry date. This means they are under correctional supervision up to one-third of their sentence longer than if they had waited for release at their earned remission date. Provincial parole boards often must decide between releasing an offender on parole who may present a risk, or whose plan is not optimal, or having the inmate leave at their earned remission date and re-enter the community with no plan or supervision.

Depending on which parole board has jurisdiction of the offender, the length of the prisoner's sentence, and the type of parole being considered (full or day parole), a prisoner can withdraw their parole application, postpone their hearing, or waive their hearing, with different consequences. The Auditor General of Canada found that 65 percent of offenders waived or postponed their PBC full parole hearings in 2013–14 and explained that these decisions could have been motivated by personal reasons (e.g., fear and anxiety regarding the parole process) but could also reflect CSC's inability to prepare offenders' files in time for their hearing.[47]

Waiver rates were also high for the Ontario Parole Board in 2012–13; 68 percent of prisoners serving sentences of six months or more waived their right to a parole hearing. During the same year, the waiver rate for the Québec Parole Board was 50 percent. The Auditor General of Ontario analyzed the data and found that the top three reasons inmates gave for waiving their parole hearings were (1) applied for/was accepted into custodial work program or correctional program (26 percent), (2) did not want parole or wanted to avoid community supervision by waiting for the earned remission date (40 percent), and (3) did not have a parole release plan or residence (14 percent).[48]

THE PAROLE CERTIFICATE

Parole certificate
A document that contains the standard and, often, special conditions of a conditional release.

If parole is granted, a certificate of parole is prepared. The **parole certificate** contains both standard conditions and special ones the board deems reasonable and necessary to protect society and facilitate the offender's rehabilitation.[49] Standard conditions include reporting regularly to a parole officer, obeying the law, not owning or possessing a weapon, and securing permission from the supervising parole officer prior to leaving a specified geographic area.

The parole board may add special conditions to the parole certificate to address issues specific to the offender. These conditions may require the parolee to participate in a treatment program as directed by their parole officer, to inform the parole officer of certain types of relationships, to abstain from all intoxicants, to maintain employment, not to have contact with certain persons, and to live in an approved residence. A parole certificate issued by the Ontario Parole Board and Earned Release Board is presented in Appendix 10.2.

A review of statutory release offenders who were released or re-released on statutory release during 2006 revealed that in comparison to statutory release offenders without a residency condition, those who had an imposed residency condition "were more likely to have: (a) committed a violent and/or serious offence, (b) a current or prior mental health diagnosis, (c) higher risks and needs, and (d) rated lower on motivation and reintegration potential."[50]

Experts recommend that conditions of release should be realistic (i.e., few—two to three at a time), relevant (i.e., individualized to each offender's unique risk and needs profile), and evidence based (i.e., they will reduce the likelihood of reoffending and increase public safety).[51] CPOs should consider "front loading" services for when recidivism risk is the greatest (i.e., 6 to 12 months post-release).[52]

High rates of revocation for breach of conditions in Canada might indicate risk-aversion amongst parole officers, and further, that parole conditions are burdensome and hard for offenders to successfully navigate in the community.

VICTIMS AND CONDITIONAL RELEASE

The role of crime victims in the conditional release process has been tenuous. Victims of crime in Québec can make written statements for use by the Québec Parole Board when the board is considering the release of offenders on TAs or parole. The Ontario Parole Board and PBC provide the victim of the offence committed by the inmate-applicant with the opportunity to observe the hearing and make a statement in person or in writing. PBC also allows victims to submit a pre-recorded video or audio recording of their statement in lieu of attending the inmate-applicant's hearing.[53]

It is not common for victims to submit statements to parole boards or to attend hearings. The Ontario Parole Board heard 1,021 cases for parole release in 2012–13; victim impact statements were submitted in only 100 of them, and victims attended only 24 parole hearings.[54] This is quite dissimilar to restorative justice approaches, where the victim is a key player in the discussions.

There are a variety of factors that might contribute to low victim participation in parole hearings; for example, the victim may not have access to a victim support worker, or the institution where the parole hearing is held may be a considerable distance from the victim's home. To address this barrier, the Ontario government has a fund to help victims attend Ontario Parole Board hearings, and victims of crimes committed by inmate-applicants being heard by PBC can apply for Department of Justice Victims Fund support for travel and accommodation for themselves and a support worker (if they choose to have one) and child care.[55]

Most victims have little knowledge of the parole process or of how hearings are conducted. Besides this, it can also be very intimidating for them to sit in a hearing room with the offender present and to speak candidly about the offender's potential release. The victim may fear reprisals if and when the offender is released. For these and a variety of other reasons, some victims choose to make a written submission to the parole board to be considered during the hearing; a smaller number submit videotaped statements for parole board members to view. Corrections File 10.3 presents an excerpt from a victim's written submission to a parole board.

It is possible the passage of the Canadian Victims Bill of Rights Act (2015) will result in an increase in victim participation in parole hearings in the years ahead. The Act created the following statutory rights for victims of crime: the right to information, participation, protection, and restitution.[56] CSC and PBC operate an online system called the Victims Portal to disseminate information to victims of crime: notification of parole hearings, conditional release dates and conditions, an updated photo of the offender prior to release, information about the offender's progress toward their correctional plan, and disciplinary infractions.[57] This is also where victims of crime can upload information for

---

CORRECTIONS FILE 10.3

Excerpts from a Victim's Written Submission to a Parole Board

I have just received notification that [Mr.____], if granted parole, will be released as soon as [____]. I am writing this letter to express my opposition to his parole. I am the victim of the crimes for which [Mr.____] was convicted. I was in an on-off relationship with [Mr. ____] that spanned for six months. During that time he was severely emotionally abusive and increasingly physically abusive. My last encounter with him resulted in a serious concussion, multiple bruises and lacerations, and my fleeing the province. Several incidents prior to that last one also resulted in physical injury of varying severity. The emotional wounds were far more severe and it took a long time for me to recover from them.

If [Mr.____] claims that he must be released from the correctional facility to receive treatment, he is merely being manipulative. I am absolutely certain that [Mr.____] will reoffend. I believe that he should, at least, fulfill his entire sentence. I believe that the more time he is kept from society, then the safer it will be. It is only a matter of time before he will appear before the courts again. If [Mr.____] is released early, then it will reaffirm to him that he is able to act inappropriately without any significant fear of punishment.

Source: Anonymous. Provided to the authors.

CSC and PBC to consider when making decisions about the offender's case management and conditional release.[58]

INMATE APPEALS

Section 147 of the CCRA sets out a number of grounds for appeal by the inmate-applicant. Parole boards are not courts of law, but they are bound by policies relating to administrative tribunals. In cases where the proper procedures are not followed, the inmate may have grounds for an appeal. The appeal division may reverse or vary the decision.

A review of successful appeals (68) of PBC decisions in 2014–15 follow, culled for the top five reasons for their being modified: offender's right to be heard was not met (19); PBC failed in duty to provide reasons (12); PBC failed to provide thorough analyses and review of risk assessment (9); relied on erroneous or incomplete information (8); or PBC made an error of law (6).[59]

ISSUES IN PAROLE BOARD DECISION MAKING

The decision of a parole board to release an inmate back into the community is, along with the verdict of the criminal court, perhaps the most important decision that is made in the correctional process. Yet little attention has been given to the composition of parole boards, the relationship between member characteristics and conditional release decisions, how board members use the information contained in offender case files, and the consequences of decisions for the offender, the victims, and the community. A number of issues surrounding parole board decision making are discussed in the following sections.

Boards May Be Subject to Public and Political Influence

Parole board members are appointed by governments (e.g., PBC members are Governor in Council appointments finalized by the Governor General upon recommendation from the Cabinet), and positions on parole boards have long been patronage appointments—that is, rewards for supporters of the government. Experts advise that appointment decisions should be upon the recommendation of a nonpartisan panel.[60] Members are not required by legislation to have any special training or expertise in law, criminology, psychology, or corrections. Proponents of parole have argued that there is a need to staff parole boards with persons with specialized competence in corrections, criminology, and evidence-based practices and actuarial tools to ensure they make informed decisions.[61]

At the time of writing (late-2017), PBC applicants are required to submit a cover letter, their CV, and the three-page application. The application requests information on topics such as their ability to travel, language capabilities, highest level of educational achievement, and professional and employment history (i.e., "work experience in decision-making at a senior level related to sensitive and complex issues . . . experience in the interpretation and application of legislation, regulations and policies . . . community involvement, membership, interests . . . [and] any additional information").[62] Note the absence of questions specific to corrections and criminology, and the applicants' ability to interpret evidence-based practices and actuarial risk assessment tools.

A notable trend on the PBC is the appointment of retired police officers as parole board members. Some observers contend that this is meant to inject more conservatism into the board's decision making . Critics argue that it is yet another expression of the former federal government's "get tough" approach to crime. In the Conservatives' first two years in office (2006–2008), they appointed 8 retired police officers and 15 former corrections staff.[63] There is little doubt that the move toward a punitive penology in Canada has had a significant impact on the provisions for releasing offenders from correctional institutions.

The Absence of Clearly Defined Release Criteria

One criticism often levelled against parole boards is that too much discretion has been vested in nonjudicial, unscrutinized decision-makers. Board members have access to a great deal of information on each inmate-applicant—including police reports, pre-sentence reports, the presiding judge's reasons for the sentence, materials produced by case managers (including risk/needs assessments), and parole officers' community strategy guides—yet it is often difficult for them to prioritize this information. This lack of guidance, combined with the discretion exercised by board members, can result in individual styles of decision making that may, in turn, lead to disparity in decisions on applications for conditional release between boards as well as among board members, even within the same jurisdiction. Whether a particular inmate-applicant is successful may depend upon which board members happen to be sitting at the hearing.

As of 2014, 80 percent of American parole boards rely on data software to calculate a parole applicant's likelihood of reoffending, curbing concern that "parole board members rely too much on their personal experiences and make inconsistent decisions."[64] The software calculates a parolee's risk to offend by comparing offender profiles; this approach appears to be successful, as analyses indicate it reduces the proportion of parolees who reoffend by approximately 15 percent.[65] The use of computer software to grant or deny parole might be something to consider to curb the lack of clearly defined release criteria in Canada.

The Absence of Case Information Feedback to Parole Board Members

Few if any mechanisms are in place for parole board members to receive feedback on the outcomes of their decisions—that is, on what happens to offenders while they are under supervision in the community and after warrant expiry and the end of supervision. This prevents individual board members from developing their knowledge of the factors that may facilitate, or hinder, successful reintegration with the community. Generally, parole board members learn of an inmate's behaviour on conditional release only when that person commits a high-profile crime, or by happenstance, reappears during a parole suspension hearing before one of the board members involved in the original decision.

Research on the effectiveness of conditional release is presented in Research File 10.1.

RESEARCH FILE 10.1

The Effectiveness of Conditional Release

Do TAs work? Yes. The rates of successful completion of UTAs have consistently been in the 95 percent+ range.[a]

Is day parole an effective conditional release option? Yes. It provides inmates with access to community services, employment, and educational opportunities. The successful completion rates for day parole are around 90 percent.[b]

Is parole an effective conditional release option? Yes. Supervision in the community provides offenders with the best chance to address their needs, while at the same time managing the risk posed to the community. Federal and provincial/territorial offenders who are released on some form of conditional release do quite well. Over the past 10 years, 93 percent of offenders released by PBC on day and full parole have not committed a new offence while on parole, and 99 percent of offenders have not committed a violent offence during their parole release.[c]

It could be argued that these high rates of completion are due in part to the more restrictive release policies of federal and provincial parole boards, although this perspective has yet to be validated by research. Further, there is little information on whether the needs of offenders have been addressed and whether their quality-of-life issues (e.g., addiction issues, housing, family stability, employment) have been addressed. Ex-offenders may remain marginal and vulnerable. The primary measure is recidivism rates, which consider none of these items. There is a need for studies on post-supervision recidivism and other measures of success.

Which offenders benefit most from parole? Lower risk offenders. Success rates are generally higher for low-risk offenders without lengthy criminal histories and those who have not committed a crime of violence. There is evidence from American studies that low-risk offenders benefit most from parole supervision and community programs, while those offenders with lengthy criminal histories and who had committed crimes of violence were the least impacted by parole.[d]

Is statutory release (SR) a useful strategy? Yes. Although the PBC is generally not involved in this decision, SR does provide for supervision of the highest-risk offenders. Without SR, these offenders would serve their entire sentence in custody and be released without any supervision (unless they are subject to a long-term supervision order). The successful completion rate of offenders on SR is around 63 percent. The success rate of SR releasees who had a period of day parole or full parole

(continued)

supervision prior to SR is 12 percent higher. This indicates the value of providing offenders, even those who are high risk, the opportunity for community supervision.[e]

Which categories of offenders' breach conditional release for the commission of new and/or violent offences? Over the past 10 years, offenders released on statutory release have been more likely to commit a new offence while under supervision and have been ten times more likely than federal offenders on full parole and four times more likely than federal offenders on day parole to commit a violent offence on release. Provincial parolees are more likely to breach a condition of release than to commit a new offence and have very few revocations of parole resulting from the commission of a violent offence.[f]

Are parole boards effective in their decision making? Hard to tell. The effectiveness of parole boards should be measured by more than rates of reoffending. The lack of standardized criteria for board membership, the potential impact of public and political influences, the absence of feedback, and broad decision-making guidelines all potentially undermine the effectiveness of parole boards. As well, offenders with fetal alcohol spectrum disorder (FASD) or mental illness, or who are a visible minority or who are Indigenous, may be at a disadvantage in parole hearings.

[a] Parole Board of Canada, *Performance Monitoring Report 2010–2011* (Ottawa: 2012), xi, http://pbc-clcc.gc.ca/rprts/pmr/pmr_2010_2011/pmr_2010_2011-eng.pdf; Public Safety Canada, Portfolio Corrections Statistics Committee, *Corrections and Conditional Release Statistical Overview* (Ottawa: Ottawa: Public Works and Government Services Canada, 2010), http://www.publicsafety.gc.ca/res/cor/rep/_fl/2010-ccrso-eng.pdf.

[b] Parole Board of Canada (2016). *Performance Monitoring Report 2014–2015*. Retrieved from https://www.canada.ca/content/dam/canada/parole-board/migration/005/009/093/005009-3000-2015-en.pdf

[c] Government of Canada. (2016). Parole in Canada. Retrieved from https://www.canada.ca/en/parole-board/services/parole/what-is-parole.html

[d] B.M. Huebner and M.T. Berg, "Examining the Sources of Variation in Risks for Recidivism," *Justice Quarterly* 28, no. 1 (2011), 146–73; A.L. Solomon, V. Kachnowski, and A. Bhati, Does Parole Work? Analyzing the Impact of Postprison Supervision on Rearrest Outcomes (Washington, DC: Urban Institute, 2005), http://www.urban.org/publications/311156.html.

[e] Parole Board of Canada (2016). Performance Monitoring Report 2014–2015. Retrieved from https://www.canada.ca/content/dam/canada/parole-board/migration/005/009/093/005009-3000-2015-en.pdf

[f] Parole Board of Canada, *Performance Monitoring Report* 2014–2015.

SUMMARY

This chapter has focused on one of the most important stages of the corrections process: the release of offenders from confinement. The purpose and principles of conditional release, which are set out in the CCRA, provide only a broad framework for release decisions. A variety of types of release have been designed to reintegrate offenders back into the community. For inmate-applicants, the parole hearing can be intimidating, and there are often socio-economic and cultural disparities between board members and inmate-applicants. A number of issues surround parole board decision making , which makes it, at best, an inexact science.

KEY POINTS REVIEW

1. The purpose and principles of conditional release are set out in the CCRA.

2. The specific conditional release options available to inmates depend on the length of the offender's sentence and whether they are under the supervision and control of provincial/territorial or federal systems of corrections.

3. There is often little pre-release planning for provincial/territorial offenders.

4. Federal inmates, who are incarcerated for longer periods of time than their provincial counterparts, tend to be released in gradual stages, and long-term studies show that offenders who are gradually released from prison are more likely to become law-abiding citizens than offenders who remain in prison until the end of their sentence.

5. The role of crime victims in conditional release is sporadic and is most often limited to providing written impact statements to the board.

6. The parole file contains many types of information, including the community strategy guide and assessment for decision that board members use in reaching a decision.

7. Parole certificates contain both standard and special conditions to which the inmate must adhere.

8. Issues surrounding parole board decision making include these: Boards may be subject to public and political influence; there is an absence of clearly defined release criteria; and there is a lack of feedback on case decisions to parole board members.

9. Predicting which offenders will reoffend upon release is a difficult task.

10. The consequences of parole board decisions can be significant if the offender reoffends.

KEY TERM QUESTIONS

1. What is the *warrant expiry date?*

2. Define the following types of conditional release: *temporary absences, day parole, full parole, earned remission date*, and *statutory release.*

3. What is *cold turkey release* and what issues does it raise?

4. Describe the procedures and objectives of *detention during the period of statutory release* and **one chance statutory release.**

5. Describe the purpose and conditions of a *judicial recognizance.*

6. Discuss the role of the *community strategy guide* and *Assessment for Decision* in the conditional release process.

7. Describe the *parole certificate.*

CRITICAL THINKING EXERCISES

Critical Thinking Exercise 10.1

Should statutory release be abolished?

While 63 percent of offenders on SR successfully complete their period of supervision, offenders serving schedule I non-sex offences on SR have been responsible for nearly 75 percent of all revocations with violent offences over the past five years.* Supporters contend that SR provides supervision for high-risk offenders that would not be available if they served their entire sentence in custody. Critics of SR point to the high rates of violent reoffending among offenders released on SR as evidence that it neither contributes to the rehabilitation of offenders nor protects the community, and that offenders "play the clock" until the two-thirds mark of their sentence, cause disruptions in the prison, and are not motivated to participate in treatment programs.

Your Thoughts?

1. In your view, should SR be abolished?

* Parole Board of Canada. (2016). Performance monitoring report 2014–2015. Retrieved from https://www. canada.ca/content/dam/canada/parole-board/migration/005/009/093/005009-3000-2015-en.pdf

Critical Thinking Exercise 10.2

Should parole be abolished?

Many American states have abolished parole, replacing it with fixed sentences. The majority of offenders are released at the two-thirds point of their sentence. High-risk offenders are generally required to be under supervision, including GPS monitoring for sex offenders. Proponents of parole argue that it provides a way to reintegrate offenders back into the community under the supervision of a parole officer who can help the offender access programs and services. Also, the discretionary decisions of parole boards can be improved with the appointment of persons with specialized professional competence. Critics of parole contend that abolishing the parole board eliminates uncertainty and discretionary decision making, which may be politically influenced, and that there is no evidence that jurisdictions without parole have higher rates of reoffending than those with parole.

Your Thoughts?

1. What additional arguments could be made in support of, or in opposition to, parole?
2. Which arguments do you find most persuasive?

CLASS/GROUP DISCUSSION EXERCISES

Class/Group Discussion Exercise 10.1

Judicial Recognizance for Sex Offenders

What are your thoughts about the practice of imposing a judicial recognizance on sex offenders proactively for behaviour they might commit rather than as a reaction to offences they have committed? Do you think this practice promotes public safety? Do you have any concerns with respect to the offender's rights and ability to reintegrate into the community?

Class/Group Discussion Exercise 10.2

Justice Shouldn't Be Political

The following editorial was published in the *Ottawa Citizen* on February 23, 2011, following the then-federal Conservative government's announcement that new members had been appointed to the Parole Board of Canada:

The recent appointment of eight new members to the National Parole Board of Canada by the Minister of Public Safety, Vic Toews, raises important questions about the appointment process to administrative boards and tribunals in Canada. Of the eight new appointees, five are former police officers.

There is no reason to believe that all the appointees are not "highly qualified and committed people" as claimed by the minister. There is also no reason why former police officers are not deserving candidates to serve on this important federal board.

What is troubling about the appointments is the apparent attempt to create a perception that the current federal government is going to be tough on prospective parolees by putting their fate in the hands of enforcement-minded individuals. . . . The role of appointed members of the tribunal is not to be tough or lenient but to be fair and objective.

Federal and provincial boards and tribunals have long been a repository for politicized appointments. . . . These quasi-judicial tribunals play an extremely important role in deciding critical issues of life, liberty and public safety. Any perception by the public that the impartiality or competence of these rights-oriented boards and tribunals has been compromised by partisan political appointments will necessarily bring the administration of justice into disrepute.

Reprinted by permission of James C. Morton

Your Thoughts?

1. What is your response to this editorial?
2. What reforms could be undertaken to address the issues that are raised in the editorial?

MEDIA LINKS

"A Day in the Life of a Parole Board Member," Parole Board Canada, https://www.canada.ca/en/parole-board/services/board-members/a-day-in-the-life-of-a-board-member.html

"Virtual Tour of a Hearing Room," Parole Board of Canada, https://www.canada.ca/en/parole-board/services/parole/virtual-tour-of-a-hearing-room.html

"Presentation of a sitting before the Commission to enable offenders to better prepare for their parole hearing," Commission des liberations conditionelles Québec, https://www.cqlc.gouv.qc.ca/english-section/video.html

"Victim Services," Parole Board of Canada, https://www.youtube.com/watch?v=RN5TcrXtXIA

"Your Guide to Parole," Parole Board of Canada, https://www.youtube.com/watch?v=Nrxhl3sU5gM

"What You Need to Know About Parole If You're in Provincial/Territorial Custody," Parole Board of Canada, https://www.youtube.com/watch?v=FgfbtxKJAyA

"Elder Assisted Hearings," Parole Board of Canada, https://www.youtube.com/watch?v=1GPOfCfPFIU

APPENDIX 10.1

Ontario Parole Board

Commission ontarienne des libérations conditionelles

Parole Decision of Board
Décision de la Commission
En matière de libération
Conditionnelle

Last Name, First, Middle/ Nom de famille, Prénom, deuxième	Client ID/ N° matricule	DOB/ Date de naissance	FPS No./ Numéro de SED

Institution/Établissement *Monteith Correctional Centre*	Date of Decision/Date de décision

Parole Eligibility Date d'admissibilité à la libération conditionnelle 09/15/2007	Discharge Possible Date Date possible de libération 11/17/2007	Final Warrant Expiry Date Date d'échéance finale du mandat 01/16/2008

After careful review of all available information about your case, the Ontario Parole Board has decided:
/Après avoir étudié attentivement tous les renseignements disponibles sur votre cause, la commission ontarienne des libération conditionnelles et des mises en libertés méritées a conclu la décision suivante:

☒	Parole Granted/ Libération conditionnelle accordée	☐	Parole Terminated/ Libération conditionnelle Terminée	☐	Hearing Denied/ Audience refusée
☐	Parole Denied/ Libération conditionnelle refusée	☐	Parole Continued/ Libération Conditionnelle prolongée	☐	Parole Granted Decision Rescinded/ Décision de libération conditionnelle annulée
☐	Parole Decision Deferred/ Décision ajournée	☐	Hearing Granted/ Audience accordée	☐	Conditions Varied/ Conditions modifiées
☐	Parole Revoked/ Libération conditionnelle révoquée	☐	Hearing Rescheduled/ Audience remise à une autre date	☐	Conditions Not Varied/ Conditions maintenues
Details/Détails Parole Granted effective September 26, 2007				☐	Remission Recredited/ Remise de peine reportée au dossier
				☐	Remission Not Recredited/ Remise de peine non reportée au dossier

REASON FOR DECISION/RAISONS QUI MOTIVENT LA DÉCISION:

a)   Risk to society by re-offending/Danger de récidive pour la société :

Your custody sentence relates to a very serious assault offence that occurred while you were under the influence of alcohol after a lengthy period of consumption. You have no prior convictions and you have maintained a successful and lawful interim release period prior to coming into custody. It is apparent that the offence and related charge caused you to realize that you required assistance in dealing with personal issues which include alcohol consumption and anger management. In response to your issues, you have completed an anger management program and additional, more intensive, counselling sessions at the North of Superior Community Mental Health Programs. It is also noted by the Board that you have maintained institutional program invlovement and institution work while in custody.

b)   Protection of society through reintegration/Protection de la société grâce à la réinsertion sociale :

Your release plan includes sponsor support and your plans to return to your employment. You also intend to continue counselling sessions with the North of Superior Community organization. The Board believes that your plan contains sufficient support to ensure a successful parole release. Your request is granted to become effective September 26, 2007.

Standard Parole Conditions
/Conditions générales de libération conditionnelle

You have agreed to the following standard conditions/Vous avez accepté les conditions générales suivantes:

Pursuant to Section 48 ss(a) to (e) of the Ministry of Correctional Services Act and Regulations (1990)/Conformément aux alinéas a) à c) de la *Loi de 1990 sur le ministère des Services correctionnels* et ses règlements.

48.   It is a condition of every grant of parole, unless the Board orders otherwise that the parolee shall/ À moins d'avis contraire par la Commission, tout libéré conditionnel doit respecter les conditions suivantes:

1)   remain within Jurisdiction of the Board/vous devez rester dans la juridiction territoriale de la Commission

Ontario Parole Board

Commission ontarienne des libérations conditionelles

Parole Decision of Board
Décision de la Commission
En matière de libération
Conditionnelle

2) keep the peace and be of good behaviour/vous ne devez pas troubler l'ordre public et vous devez vous conduire convenablement

3) obtain the consent of the Board or the parole supervisor for any change of residence or employment/vous devez obtenir l'autorisation de la commission ou de votre surveillant de libération conditionnelle pour tout changement de domicile ou d'emploi

4) report immediately upon release to your parole supervisor and the local police force. Report thereafter as required by your parole supervisor./ vous devez vous présenter au bureau de votre surveillant de libération conditionnelle et au poste de police immédiatement après liberation. Et par après vous presenter tel que convenu avec votre surveillant de liberation conditionnelle.

5) refrain from associating with any person who is engaged in criminal activity or unless approved by the parole supervisor, with any person who has a criminal record/Il vous est interdit de fréquenter des personnes ayant des activités criminelles ou, sauf avec autorisation du surveillant de libération conditionnelle, des personnes ayant un casier judiciaire

6) carry your parole certificate at all times and present it to any police officer or probation and parole officer upon request./Porter sur vous,en tout temps, votre document de liberation conditionnelle et le presenter à tout agent de probation et liberation conditionnelle ou à tout agent de police qui vous le demande

Special Parole Conditions
/Conditions spéciales de libération conditionnelle

You have also agreed to the following special conditions/Vous avez aussi accepté les conditions spéciales suivantes:

1. Upon release abide by your approved travel plan.
2. Abstain from the purchase, possession or consumption of alcohol or other intoxicating substances.
3. Not to enter or be found in any establishment whose primary source of business is the sale of alcohol.
4. Not to associate or hold any communication directly or indirectly with (named individual) except within circumstances approved of by the Parole Officer in writing.
5. Abstain from owning, possessing or carrying any weapon as defined by the criminal code.
6. Continue to attend for and actively comply with any counselling program for anger management issues and substance use issues with the North of Superior Community Health Program and provide written verification of same to your Parole Officer, or any such programming as may be recommended by your Parole Officer and provide proof of same to your Parole Officer.

Release Plans/Plans de Libération

Residence/Domicile	
Employment/Education/Other/Emploi, éducation et autre(s)	
Parole Supervisor/Name & Address	
Police Reporting	
Vice Chair or Designate / Vice-président ou mandataire	**Member Signature/Signature du membre**

PROVISO: The Board's decision to grant parole is conditional upon your good behaviour and the continuation of your Board approved release plan.
/La Commission accorde la libération temporaire à la condition que votre comportement demeure convenable et que vous vous conformiez à votre plan de libération approuvé par la Commission.

DISTRIBUTION: Inmate/Parolee
Board Case File
I.L.O./Parole Supervisor
Superintendent

Source: © Queen's Printer for Ontario, 2011. Reproduced with permission.

APPENDIX 10.2

Ontario Parole Board

Commission ontarienne des libérations conditionnelles

Certificate of Parole/
Certificat de mise en liberté conditionnelle

Date(s) Issued/ Date d'émission	Warrant Expiry/ Expiration du mandat	Release Date/ Date de mise en liberté
	01/16/2008	09/26/2007
Supervision Service Sector/ Secteur de Service superviseur	Released from/Mise en liberté de	

Under the **Ministry of Correctional Services Act 1990**, and the regulations, the Ontario Parole Board releases:
/En vertu de la **Loi de 1990 sur le ministère des services correctionnels** et des réglements y afférents, la commission des libération conditionnelles et des mises en liberté méritées libère:

Last Name/ Nom de famille	First, Middle/ Prénom, deuxième	Client ID/ N° matricule	DOB/ Date de naissance	FPS No./ Numéro de SED

Under the following standard conditions/sous réserve du respect des conditions normales suivantes:

1) Remain within jurisdiction of the Board.
   /Vous devez rester dans la jurisdiction de la Commission des libérations conditionnelles.
2) Keep the peace and be of good behaviour.
   /Vous ne devez pas troubler l'ordre public et vous devez vous conduire convenablement.
3) Obtain the consent of the Board or the Parole Supervisor for any change of residence or employment.
   /Vous devez obtenir l'autorisation de la commission ou de votre surveillant de libération conditionnelle si vous désirez changer d'emploi ou de résidence.
4) Report immediately upon release to your Parole Supervisor and local Police force. Report thereafter as required by your parole supervisor.
   /Vous devez vous présenter au bureau de votre surveillant de libération conditionnelle et au poste de police immédiatement après votre libération. Et par après vous presenter tel que convenu avec votre surveillant de libération conditionnelle.
5) Refrain from associating with any person who is engaged in criminal activity or unless approved by the Parole Supervisor with any person who has a criminal record.
   /Il vous est interdit de fréquenter des personnes impliquées dans des activités criminelles. D'autant plus, vous ne devez fréquenter des personnes ayant un casier judiciare, sans l'autorisation du surveillant de libération conditionnelle.
6) You must carry your parole certificate at all times and present it to any police officer or Parole Supervisor upon request.
   /Vous devez porter votre certificat de libération conditionnelle en tout temps et le présenter, sur demande, à tous officier de police ou agent de probation.

Special Conditions/ Conditions spéciales

1. Upon release abide by your approved travel plan.
2. Abstain from the purchase, possession or consumption of alcohol or other intoxicating substances.
3. Not to enter or be found in any establishment whose primary source of business is the sale of alcohol.
4. Not to associate or hold any communication directly or indirectly with (named individual) except within circumstances approved of by the Parole Officer in writing.
5. Abstain from owning, possessing or carrying any weapon as defined by the criminal code.
6. Continue to attend for and actively comply with any counselling program for anger management issues and substance use issues with the North of Superior Community Health Program and provide written verification of same to your Parole Officer, or any such programming as may be recommended by your Parole Officer and provide proof of same to your Parole Officer.

Upon Release you shall
/Lors de votre libérations vous devrez

Report immediately to a Parole Supervisor/ Lors de votre libération vous devrez vous présenter immédiatement à surveillant de libération
Reside at address/ Adresse d'habitation
Report to Police at/ Vous présenter au poste de police de

Parole Declaration/Déclaration de mise en libérté conditionnelle

I have carefully read or had read to me the conditions of this certificate. I understand the conditions and contents of this certificate of Parole. I accept my release and pledge myself honestly to comply with the conditions. I also understand that if I violate the conditions of my Parole, I may be returned to a correctional institution to serve the portion of my term of imprisonment, including any remission that remained unexpired at the time Parole was granted less the period of time spent on Parole.
/Je déclare avoir lu attentivement ce certificat ou en avoir reçu lecture. Je déclare voir lu attentivement ce certificat ou en avoir reçu lecture. Je comprends les conditions et la teneur de ce certificat de mise en liberté conditionnellle. J'accepte ma libération en ces termes et je promets en toute honnêteté d'observer ces conditions. Je sais également que, si je commets une infraction aux conditions stipulées pour ma libération conditionnelle, on peut me renvoyer dans un établissement corrrectionnel pour y purger le reste de ma peine d'emprisonnement, y compris toute réduction de peine, non encore purgée au moment où la libération conditionnelle m'a été accordée, moins la période de liberté conditionnelle.

Valid only when signed by Parolee/Ce certificat n'est valide que s'il est signé par la personne en liberté conditionnelle Parolee's Signature/Signature de la personne en liberté conditionnelle
Date

Given in triplicate by the authority of the Ontario Parole Board.
/Établi en triple exemplaire avec l'autorisation de la commission ontarienne des libérations conditionnelles et des mises en liberté méritées.
Vice Chair or Designate/Vice-Président ou mandataire

Signature _____ Date _____

DISTRIBUTION: Parolee (after signing)
                 Probation and Parole Office
                 Board Case File

Source: © Queen's Printer for Ontario, 2011. Reproduced with permission.

NOTES

1. G. Fauteux, *Report of a Committee Appointed to Inquire into the Principles and Procedures Followed in the Remission Service of the Department of Justice of Canada* (Ottawa: Queen's Printer, 1956).

2. M.D. Schlager and K. Robbins, "Does Parole Work - Revisited: Reframing the Discussion of Postprison Supervision on Offender Outcome," *The Prison Journal* 88, no. 2 (2008), 234–51; Office of the Auditor General, *Report 6 – Preparing Male Offenders for Release – Correctional Service Canada* (Ottawa: Author, 2015), http://www.oag-bvg.gc.ca/internet/English/parl_oag_201504_06_e_40352.html#hd2c.

3. Office of the Auditor General, *Report 6 – Preparing Male Offenders for Release*.

4. Ibid.

5. Government of Canada, *Decision-Making Policy Manual for Board Members* (Ottawa: Author, 2016), https://www.canada.ca/en/parole-board/corporate/publications-and-forms/decision-making-policy-manual-for-board-members.html#annex_a.

6. Prisoners' Legal Services, *Information for Federal Prisoners in British Columbia: Conditional Release* (Burnaby, BC: Author, 2015), p. 8, https://prisonjusticedotorg.files.wordpress.com/2012/11/federal-parole1.pdf.

7. Canadian Association of Elizabeth Fry Society, *Human Rights in Action: Handbook for Provincially Sentenced Prisoners in Saskatchewan* (Ottawa: Author, 2015), http://www.caefs.ca/wp-content/uploads/2013/05/Human-Rights-in-Action-Handbook-for-Provincially-Sentenced-Prisoners-in-Saskatchewan-June-2015-1.pdf; Correction Act (2004), http://www.bclaws.ca/civix/document/id/complete/statreg/04046_01#section22; Province of Nova Scotia, Correctional Services, *Offender Handbook: Adult Offender Correctional Facilities* (Halifax: Author, 2016), http://www.novascotia.ca/just/corrections/_docs/adult_offender_handbook_en.pdf.

8. Corrections and Conditional Release Act (1992), Section 130(3), http://laws-lois.justice.gc.ca/PDF/C-44.6.pdf.

9. Ibid., Section 131(1-1.1).

10. Ibid., Section 130(4)

11. P. Lussier, N. DesLauriers-Varin, and T. Ratel, "A Descriptive Profile of High-Risk Sex Offenders Under Intensive Supervision in the Province of British Columbia, Canada," *International Journal of Offender Therapy and Comparative Criminology* 54, no. 1 (2010), 71–91.

12. Criminal Code of Canada (1985), Section 811, http://laws-lois.justice.gc.ca/PDF/C-46.pdf.

13. Ibid., Section 810.2.

14. Parole Board of Canada, *Performance monitoring report 2014–2015* (Ottawa: Author, 2016), https://www.canada.ca/content/dam/canada/parole-board/migration/005/009/093/005009-3000-2015-en.pdf.

15. S. Fine, "Inside Out: The Decline of Parole and the Fundamentals of Canada's Penal System," *Globe and Mail*, September 26, 2016, http://www.theglobeandmail.com/news/national/inside-out/article32027038/.

16. E. Loop, "Parole Numbers don't Paint Accurate Picture, Expert Says," *Ottawa Citizen*, December 14, 2014, http://ottawacitizen.com/news/politics/parole-numbers-dont-paint-accurate-picture-expert-says.

17. J. Winter, "Fix Broken Parole System, Experts Urge as AG Prepares Prison Report," *Ottawa Citizen*, April 26, 2015, http://ottawacitizen.com/news/politics/fix-broken-parole-system-experts-urge-as-ag-prepares-prison-report.

18. Public Safety Canada Portfolio Corrections Statistics Committee, *Corrections and Conditional Release Statistical Overview: 2015 Annual Report* (Ottawa: Public Works and Government Services Canada, 2016), https://www.publicsafety.gc.ca/cnt/rsrcs/pblctns/ccrso-2015/ccrso-2015-en.pdf.

19. Office of the Auditor General, *Report 6 – Preparing Male Offenders for Release*.

20. Parole Board of Canada, *Performance Monitoring Report 2010–2011* (Ottawa: Author, 2012), xi, http://pbc-clcc. gc.ca/rprts/pmr/pmr_2010_2011/ pmr_2010_2011-eng.pdf; Public Safety Canada Portfolio Corrections Statistics Committee, *Corrections and Conditional Release Statistical Overview* (Ottawa: Public Works and Government Services Canada, 2010), http://www.publicsafety.gc.ca/res/ cor/rep/_fl/2010-ccrso-eng.pdf.

21. Ministries of Community Safety and Correctional Services, and the Attorney General. (2014). *Annual report of the Office of the Auditor General of Ontario* (Toronto: Author, 2014), http://www.auditor.on.ca/ en/content/annualreports/arreports/ en14/301en14.pdf.

22. Public Safety Canada Portfolio Corrections Statistics Committee, *Corrections and Conditional Release Statistical Overview*.

23. Office of the Auditor General, *Report 6 – Preparing Male Offenders for Release*.

24. Ibid.

25. I. Zinger, "Conditional Release and Human Rights in Canada: A Commentary," *Canadian Journal of Criminology and Criminal Justice 54*, no. 1 (2012), 117–35.

26. *Canada (Attorney General) v. Whaling*, (2014), case number 35024, http:// scc-csc.lexum.com/scc-csc/scc-csc/en/ item/13543/index.do.

27. R. Mendelson, "Ontario's Top Court Makes Inmates Eligible for Early Parole," *Toronto Star*, July 5, 2015, https://www. thestar.com/news/crime/2015/07/05/ ontarios-top-court-makes-inmates- eligible-for-early-parole.html.

28. S. Fine, "Five Fundamental ways Harper has Changed the Justice System," *Globe and Mail*, May 7, 2014, http:// www.theglobeandmail.com/news/ politics/five-fundamental-ways-harper- has-changed-the-justice-system/ article18503381/?page=all.

29. Zinger, "Conditional Release and Human Rights in Canada," p. 120; Office of the Auditor General, *Report 6 – Preparing Male Offenders for Release*.

30. Schizophrenic Society of Ontario, *Provincial Correctional Response to Individuals with Mental Illnesses in Ontario: A Review of Literature* (Toronto: Author, 2012), p. 4, http://cefso.ca/wwdnews/uploads/ Provincial_Corrections_Literature_ Review_Final_March_2012.pdf.

31. C. Marshall, *HIV/AIDS and Hepatitis in Correctional Facilities: Reducing the Risks* (Halifax: Nova Scotia Advisory Commission on AIDS, 2008), p. 26, http://www.gov.ns.ca/AIDS/ documents/HIV-AIDS-Hepatitis-C- Correctional%20Facilities.pdf.

32. Office of the Auditor General of Ontario, *Adult Community Corrections and Ontario Parole Board* (Toronto: Author, 2016), http://www.auditor.on.ca/en/content/ annualreports/arreports/en14/301en14. pdf.

33. Office of the Auditor General, *Report 6 – Preparing Male Offenders for Release*.

34. Ibid.

35. Ibid.

36. Ibid., p. 13

37. S.R. Dickson, D.L.L. Polaschek, and A.R. Casey, "Can the Quality of High- risk Violent Prisoners' Release Plans Predict Recidivism following Intensive Rehabilitation? A Comparison with Risk Assessment Instruments," *Psychology, Crime & Law 19*, no. 4 (2013), 371–89.

38. S.R. Dickson and D.L.L. Polaschek, "Planning to Avoid Risk or Planning for a Positive Life: The Relationship Between Release Plan Valence and Reoffending," *International Journal of Offender Therapy and Comparative Criminology 58*, no. 12 (2014), 1431–48. G. Duwe, "Does Release Planning for Serious and Persistent Mental Illness (SPMI) Offenders Reduce Recidivism? Results from an Outcome Evaluation," *Journal of Offender Rehabilitation 54* (2015), 19–36.

39. "Commissioner's Directive: Pre-Release Decision Making," Correctional Service Canada website, Commissioner's Directive 712-1 (2015), http://www.csc-scc.gc.ca/politiques-et-lois/712-1-cd-eng.shtml#s2a.

40. Fine, "Inside out: The Decline of Parole and the Fundamentals of Canada's Penal System."

41. Prisoners' Legal Services, *Information for Federal Prisoners in British Columbia.*

42. G. Bonham, G. Janekseala, and J. Bardo, "Predicting Parole Decision in Kansas Via Discriminant Analysis," *Journal of Criminal Justice 26* (1986), 205–81; M.R. Pogrebin, E.D. Poole, and R.M. Regoli, "Parole Decision Making in Colorado," *Journal of Criminal Justice 14* (1986), 147–55; L. Carroll and M.E. Mondrick, "Racial Bias in the Decision to Grant Parole," *Law and Society Review 11* (1976), 93–107; J.S. Carroll, "Causal Attributions in Expert Parole Decisions," *Journal of Personality and Social Psychology 36*, no. 12 (1978), 1501–11; J.L. Proctor, "The 'new parole': An Analysis of Parole Board Decision Making as a Function of Eligibility," *Journal of Crime and Justice 22*, no. 2 (1999), 193–217; B.M. Huebner and T.S. Bynum, "An Analysis of Parole Decision Making using a Sample of Sex Offenders: A Focal Concerns Perspective," *Criminology 44*, no. 4 (2006), 961–91; E.R. Vilcica, "The Influence of Inmate Visitation on the Decision to Grant Parole: An Exploratory Study," *Journal of Criminal Justice 43* (2015), 498–509, J.L. Mooney and M. Daffern, "Elucidating the Factors that Influence Parole Decision-Making and Violent Offenders' Performance on Parole," *Psychiatry, Psychology and Law 21*, no. 3 (2013), 385–405.

43. Office of the Auditor General of Ontario, *Adult Community Corrections and Ontario Parole Board.*

44. P.J. Murphy, L. Johnsen, and J. Murphy, *Paroled for Life: Interviews with Parolees Serving Life Sentences* (Vancouver: New Star, 2002), p. 93.

45. D. Lacombe, "'Mr. S., You Do Have Sexual Fantasies?' The Parole Hearing and Prison Treatment of a Sex Offender at the Turn of the 21st Century," *Canadian Journal of Sociology 38*, no. 1 (2013), 33–63 at 58 and 61, https://ejournals.library.ualberta.ca/index.php/CJS/article/view/14844/14896. Reprinted with permission from the Canadian Journal of Sociology.

46. Ibid.

47. Office of the Auditor General, *Report 6 – Preparing Male Offenders for Release.*

48. Office of the Auditor General of Ontario, *Adult Community Corrections and Ontario Parole Board.*

49. Corrections and Conditional Release Act (1992), Section 133.

50. T.L. Scott, "At Risk for Residency: A Profile of Statutory Release Offenders with a Residency Condition," Correctional Service Canada, Research at a glance R-261, November 2012, http://www.csc-scc.gc.ca/research/005008-0261-eng.shtml.

51. C. Wickland, *Evaluation of Re-Entry Initiatives: What is Missing?* Paper Presented at the Justice Research and Statistics Association Conference, St. Petersburg, FL, October 27, 2005, as cited in E.E. Rhine, J. Petersilia, and K.R. Reitz, "The Future of Parole Release: A Ten-Point Reform Plan," Forthcoming in *Crime and Justice: A Review of Research*, ed., M. Tonry (2016).

52. Rhine et al., "The Future of Parole Release: A Ten-Point Reform Plan."

53. "Presenting a Statement at a Parole Hearing," Government of Canada website, last modified May 2017, https://www.canada.ca/en/parole-board/services/victims/participating-in-the-parole-process-as-a-victim/presenting-a-statement-at-a-parole-hearing.html; "Victims and the Ontario Parole Board," Ontario Parole Board website (n.d.), http://www.slasto.gov.on.ca/en/OPB/Pages/Victims-and-the-Ontario-Parole-Board.aspx.

54. Ontario Parole Board, *2012–2013 Annual Report* (Toronto: Ministry of Community Safety and Correctional Services, 2013), p. 12. http://www.ontla.on.ca/library/repository/ser/100632/2012-13.pdf.

55. "Financial Assistance to Attend a Parole Hearing," Government of Canada website, last modified September 2016, https://www.canada.ca/en/parole-board/services/victims/participating-in-the-parole-process-as-a-victim/financial-assistance-to-attend-a-parole-hearing.html; "Victims and the Ontario Parole Board."

56. "Frequently Asked Questions: Canadian Victims Bill of Rights," Correctional Service Canada website, last modified June 2016, http://www.csc-scc.gc.ca/victims/003006-1003-eng.shtml#q1.

57. Ibid.

58. Ibid.

59. Parole Board of Canada, *Performance monitoring report 2014-2015*.

60. Rhine et al., "The Future of Parole Release: A Ten-Point Reform Plan."

61. Ibid.; M.A. Paparozzi and R. Guy, "The Giant That Never Woke: Parole Authorities as the Lynchpin to Evidence-Based Practices and Prisoner Reentry," *Journal of Contemporary Justice 25*, no. 4 (2009), 397–411.

62. "Governor in Council Appointment Application form: Full-Time and/or Part-Time Member," Parole Board of Canada (n.d.), https://www.canada.ca/content/dam/canada/parole-board/board-members/appform-en.pdf.

63. Fine, "Inside out: The Decline of Parole and the Fundamentals of Canada's Penal System."

64. "Parole and Technology: Prison Breakthrough," *The Economist*, April 19, 2014, http://www.economist.com/news/united-states/21601009-big-data-can-help-states-decide-whom-release-prison-prison-breakthrough.

65. Ibid.

CHAPTER
11
RE-ENTRY AND LIFE AFTER PRISON

CHAPTER OBJECTIVES

- Describe reintegration as a process rather than as an event.
- Discuss what is meant by the pains of re-entry.
- Describe the activities of parole officers and, in particular, their dual function in supervision.
- Discuss the unique challenges of supervising high-risk offenders, long-term offenders, mentally ill offenders, and sex offenders on parole.
- Discuss the key issues that surround the practice of community notification (CN).
- Describe the structure and dynamics of circles of support and accountability (COSAs).
- Describe the procedures that apply when a parolee commits a new offence or violates the conditions of the parole certificate.
- Address the issue of the effectiveness of supervision and control strategies used for offenders re-entering the community.

CORRECTIONS PERSPECTIVE 11.1

An Ex-offender Reflects on Re-entry

The moment offenders step off the bus, they face several critical decisions. Where will they live, where will they be able to find a meal, where should they look for a job, how will they get to a job interview, and where can they earn enough money to pay for necessities? These returning inmates are also confronted with many details of personal business, such as obtaining identification cards and documents, making medical appointments, and working through the many everyday bureaucratic problems that occur during any transition. These choices prompt feelings of intense stress and worry over the logistics of their return to the outside world. To those who have had no control over any aspect of life for many years, each of these problems can be difficult. In accumulation, they can be overwhelming.

My own experience is a good example. Shortly after my release from prison to the halfway house, some friends took me to lunch at a local deli. The waiter came over to take our orders. Everyone else told him what they wanted, but I kept poring over the menu. My eyes raced over the columns of choices. I knew that I was supposed to order, but the number of options overwhelmed me. My friends sat in embarrassed silence. I was paralyzed. The waiter looked at me impatiently. I began to panic. How ridiculous that I wasn't able to do such a simple thing as order lunch. Finally, in desperation, I ordered the next item my eyes landed on, a turkey sandwich. I didn't even want it, but at least it put an end to this embarrassing incident.

For two years I hadn't been able to make any choices about what I ate. Now I was having a hard time making a simple choice that most people make every day. If I had this much difficulty after only a couple of years in prison, think how hard it is for those inmates who haven't made any choices for 5, 10, or 15 years. And what about those who didn't have the wonderful home, the loving family, the strong faith, and the good education that I had? They face a baffling array of options and little preparation. Is it any surprise that so many newly released prisoners make some bad choices and end up back in prison? If we do not prepare these inmates for their return to the community, the odds are great that their first incarceration will not be their last.

Source: P. Nolan, "Prepared Statement Presented to the Committee on the Judiciary, U.S. House of Representatives," November 3, 2005, http://www.gpo.gov/fdsys/pkg/CHRG-109hhrg24372/pdf/CHRG -109hhrg24372.pdf.

THE REINTEGRATION PROCESS

Reintegration is a process, not an event. It has been defined as "all activity and programming conducted to prepare an offender to return safely to the community as a law-abiding citizen."[1]

It begins with the intake assessment that leads to the development of a correctional plan and participation in treatment programs, as described in Chapter 9, and includes the development of a release plan that sets out where the inmate will live, work, and, if required, go to school and participate in post-release treatment programs. The John Howard Society of Ontario and the University of Guelph identified inadequate discharge planning as a barrier to successful re-entry for offenders released in Ontario. Discharge planning involves creating a release plan that addresses the offender's assessed risks and needs and identifying community providers to take over an offender's care upon release (see the concept of throughcare, discussed next). This process promotes public safety by improving releasees' access to community-service providers and decreasing the likelihood they will reoffend.[2] The goal of reintegration is to avoid recidivism in the short term (i.e., until the warrant expiry date (WED)) as well as afterward. When required, yet another goal is to address the interests of crime victims.

> **Reintegration**
> The process whereby an inmate is prepared for and released into the community after serving time in prison.

The term "reintegration" is problematic, for it suggests that offenders had been successfully integrated into the community before their incarceration. In fact, many inmates come from marginalized backgrounds and have never acquired the attitudes and behaviours necessary to live as productive members of society.[3]

Throughcare

For reintegration to succeed, there should be continuity between institutional programs and the services an offender receives on conditional release in the community.[4] This is the concept of throughcare (discussed in Chapter 9). To illustrate, continuity between participation in employment training and education programming while incarcerated and upon release into the community has been found to reduce recidivism.[5]

A seamless transition in treatment from the institution to the community is especially important for offenders with special needs, such as substance-abuse issues.[6]

The reintegration process for federal offenders is illustrated in Figure 11.1. Figure 11.2 breaks down the federal correctional release population in

Figure 11.1

The Reintegration Process for Federal Offenders

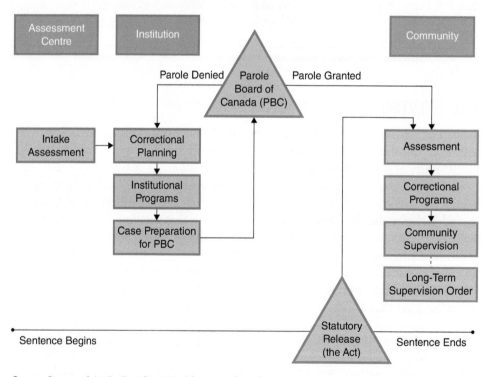

Source: Report of the Auditor General of Canada - (1996), Office of the Auditor General of Canada. Reproduced with the permission of Her Majesty the Queen in Right of Canada, as represented by the Auditor General of Canada, 2017.

Figure 11.2

Federal Releases from Institutions and Graduations to Subsequent Federal Supervision Periods

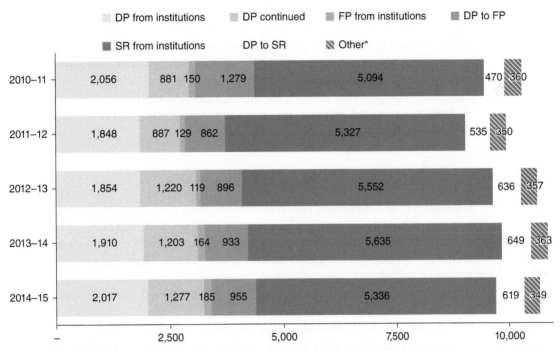

*Includes releases from institutions at warrant expiry, at warrant expity with a long-team supervision order, graduation from federal supervision periods to a long-team supervision order upon warrant expiry, deaths, transfers to foreign countries, and so on.

Source: Board of Canada. (2016). *Performance Monitoring Report 2014–2015*, page 17. https://www.canada.ca/content/dam/canada/parole-board/migration/005/009/093/005009-3000-2015-en.pdf. Contains information licensed under the Open Government Licence - Canada.

2014–15. Note the high number of offenders who are on statutory release, who, like federal parolees, require supervision from parole officers.

The Integrated Correctional Program Model (ICPM) in federal corrections (see Chapter 9) is one initiative that has been designed to provide continuity of care from the institution to the community. The short time that provincial/territorial offenders spend in custody works against this type of planning. There is often also a lack of continuity between the institution's programs and those in the community. Offenders who were in a methadone maintenance program in the institution, for example, may not have access to this program in the community. All of this is especially true for offenders from rural and remote communities.[7] There is often also a lack of resources, especially for groups with special needs. Additional challenges may exist owing to mental illness and the presence of fetal alcohol spectrum disorder (FASD).[8] A study (*N* = 671) of offenders with mental illness in detention in Québec found, for example, that these individuals were poorly prepared to re-enter the community and had difficulty accessing services; also, there was little program continuity between the institution and the community.[9]

Other valuable recommendations for the resettlement of prisoners reflect what was discussed in Chapter 9 about case management (i.e., where the reintegration process begins) and the use of the risk–need–responsivity model. This includes tailoring programming and services to the individual's risk and needs rather than assuming all offenders require the same supervision and services; addressing the offender's practical needs (e.g., residence, employment) and criminogenic thinking (i.e., thoughts, attitudes, emotions, and behaviour); and ensuring trained practitioners provide the programming as it was designed to be delivered.[10]

COMING BACK: THE PAINS OF RE-ENTRY

Chapter 8 noted that many inmates in confinement experience pains of imprisonment. Similarly, on being released from confinement, offenders may experience **pains of re-entry**. Persons who are sent to custody undergo a variety of status degradation ceremonies as they enter prison. Unfortunately, there are no status *restoration* ceremonies and "rituals of reintegration" that would build on the offender's accomplishments while incarcerated; instead, the focus is solely on risk to the community.[11]

Newly released offenders carry the shame and stigma of their past lives; a prominent researcher who studies re-entry says that for offenders to be successful upon re-entering their communities, they must develop a new, positive self-narrative.[12]

Put another way, a prison sentence triggers a process whereby individuals are extracted from society and forced to adjust to a closed, structured, and artificial environment, one in which an antisocial value system predominates and inmates have little responsibility. Then, upon release, these same inmates are expected to resume/assume law-abiding lives in the community and to hold prosocial values, exercise independence of thought and decision-making, and display life skills that enable them to cope with the complexities of daily life in a fast-paced society. A transition this dramatic would challenge even the most gifted individual, and it is especially difficult for marginalized and socially isolated offenders who have been incarcerated for long periods.

One long-term offender told C. T. Griffiths, "The values, attitudes, and behaviours that I learned inside were just the opposite of what I needed to make it in the free world." Complicating this, offenders tend to have few, if any, noncriminal friends and little access to legitimate opportunities. As a consequence, newly released offenders are left largely to their own devices as they attempt to adapt and survive in the community.

There are also the "collateral effects" of confinement, which often include the loss of personal relationships and social networks, the acquisition of self-defeating habits and attitudes, and the loss of personal belongings.[13] It is likely that these had been problems even before they were incarcerated.

Pains of re-entry
The difficulties that inmates released from correctional institutions encounter in attempting to adjust to life in the outside, free community.

A newly released offender can feel like the proverbial "stranger in a strange land"—embarrassed and inadequate, and convinced that every person on the street can tell at a mere glance that he or she has been in prison. One woman parolee with a life sentence commented: "I didn't feel like I was back. I didn't feel like I belonged ... I didn't feel part of this world anymore, I was still inside. In some respects, part of me will always be inside."[14] Ironically, offenders may experience paranoia and fear for their safety upon re-entering the community. Another offender commented, "I was always more nervous getting out than going in."[15]

The Challenges of the Newly Released

Various studies have documented the criminogenic effect of imprisonment; analyses consistently demonstrate that offenders sentenced to a term of imprisonment have higher rates of reoffending one, two, and three years post-release than offenders sentenced to prison diversion programs.[16]

While additional research is needed, and in Canadian prisons, a recent American study indicates that parolees who experienced medium to high levels of prison overcrowding had higher rates of parole violations, particularly for drug charges, than parolees who were subject to low-level crowding.[17]

Combined, these findings suggest the experience of imprisonment itself is a major obstacle to the successful reintegration of offenders.

The Dynamic Needs of Offenders on Conditional Release

Most federal offenders on conditional release have difficulties associated with one or more of these seven dynamic need domains: attitudes, community functioning, employment, marital/family, personal and emotional, associates, and substance abuse.[18] Newly released offenders may face social, economic, and personal challenges that make it difficult for them to avoid returning to criminal activity. Offenders often find themselves in a catch-22 situation. One released individual explained: "You need to meet with a worker first to get money, you need to get out of jail to meet with a worker ... You need an address to get a cheque, and a cheque to get an address."[19]

To address these, and other challenges experienced by federally incarcerated males in Ontario, the John Howard Society of Kingston and District operates a six-phase module on release planning: module one provides information on types of release options; module two provides information on halfway-house residency and obtaining identification in the community; in module three, an employment consultant provides the men with information about employment opportunities upon their release; the fourth module addresses personal finances; and the fifth and sixth modules provide information on parole and incorporate a mock parole trial.[20]

In one study, the John Howard Society of Ontario and the University of Guelph identified five key challenges that releasees face in Ontario: inadequate discharge planning; the inability to secure housing, which often results in homelessness; barriers to employment and education; inadequate social supports to address complex needs (e.g., mental health, addiction, and family reunification); and stigma that results in social exclusion.[21] These, and other barriers to re-entry, are discussed in the paragraphs that follow.

Housing and Homelessness

It is estimated that 30 percent of released offenders are homeless and have no stable residence to go to after they are released.[22] Compounding this problem are provincial laws that allow landlords to deny accommodation to persons with a criminal record.[23] Homelessness poses a severe challenge to newly released offenders and certain populations—women, Indigenous people, and those who have a mental illness or mental illness and substance abuse issue— are more at risk of becoming homeless upon release.[24]

There is evidence that homelessness is related to reoffending, including parole revocations, readmission to prison, and new offences.[25] A Canadian study found that four out of ten homeless persons admitted to one Toronto-area jail during one year were returnees.[26]

Research has found that providing housing services (e.g. subsidized housing) and other services can result in fewer re-admissions to custody and decreased costs.[27] Ironically, studies show that providing social housing would have been cheaper than providing offenders with medical and social services.[28]

Physical and Mental Health Needs

Post-incarceration syndrome (PICS) A condition of offenders in custody and in the community that is caused by prolonged exposure to the dynamics of life inside correctional institutions.

There is concern that offenders who have been incarcerated for lengthy periods of time may suffer from **post-incarceration syndrome (PICS)**. The symptoms of this include post-traumatic stress, which arises from trauma experienced prior to incarceration and during confinement, and an institutionalized personality, which develops as a result of life inside the prison.[29]

Formerly incarcerated individuals have high physical and mental health care needs and substance abuse issues to be addressed throughout the process of reintegration.[30] Research indicates that probationers and parolees' behavioural and health care needs can impede their success in the community, compromising public safety goals.[31]

Canadian research examining rates and deaths in custody and after release for individuals who had been admitted to provincial correctional facilities in Ontario in 2000 found that over the 12-year follow-up period, individuals in the sample population were four times more likely to die than people in the general population, were nearly twice as likely to die while in custody, and had lower life expectancy rates than men and women in the general population, and that many of the deaths were due to "preventable and treatable causes" (e.g., death due to overdose and death due to suicide or self-inflicted injury).[32]

There are also high rates of mortality amongst offenders within the first few weeks of their release into the community; contributing factors include high rates of substance use (i.e., deaths are often due to overdoses) and the absence of throughcare between institutional health care initiatives and community health care services.[33]

See Figure 11.3 for facts about social reintegration amongst a population of offenders released in Ontario.

The "State-Raised" Offender and Re-entry

The stress of re-entry may be especially acute for state-raised offenders (see Chapter 8). These individuals have very little experience living in the outside community, have few or no family ties, and—a key point—have no "stake" in the community. Their friends, identity, status, and power are all inside the correctional institution. Out in the community, they have no guarantees of status, of security, or of a routine that will provide for their basic needs. For these people, the pull of the institution may be stronger than that of the outside world.

Close friendships forged in the prison are in danger of being lost; indeed, the inmate may feel that he or she is abandoning close friends, confidants, and/ or lovers. One ex-offender who had spent many years in federal prisons confided to C. T. Griffiths: "I have never had the intensity of friendships, the trust, the companionship, in the outside community that I had when I was incarcerated." These feelings may be especially acute when the soon-to-be-released inmate realizes that he or she has no friends on the outside who can be relied on for help, protection, and security.

Even offenders who, prior to confinement, had relatively conventional lifestyles (except for their law-breaking) can find it hard to unlearn the automatic responses they have acquired in an environment where physical aggression is necessary for survival.

To cope with the pains of re-entry, formerly incarcerated persons may revert to high-risk behaviour, including heavy drinking, drug use, resuming friendships with former criminal associates, and spending time with old friends from prison. Although most will complete their period of conditional release without committing a new offence, many will be convicted of another criminal offence within three years of release.[34]

PAROLE OFFICERS AND THE SUPERVISION OF OFFENDERS

Federal offenders on statutory release and parole are generally required to report regularly to a correctional agent, such as a parole officer. Parole officers employed by, or under contract to, Correctional Service Canada (CSC) supervise all federal parolees and offenders released on statutory release. Parole officers are also involved in supervising offenders who are placed on long-term supervision orders by the court. By agreement, the CSC also supervises provincial parolees released by the Parole Board of Canada (PBC) in those jurisdictions that do not have their own provincial parole boards. In two jurisdictions—Ontario and Québec— provincial probation and parole officers provide supervision for offenders on parole as well as for many inmates on temporary absences.

Figure 11.3

The Complex Web of Reintegration: A Case Study of Releases in Ontario

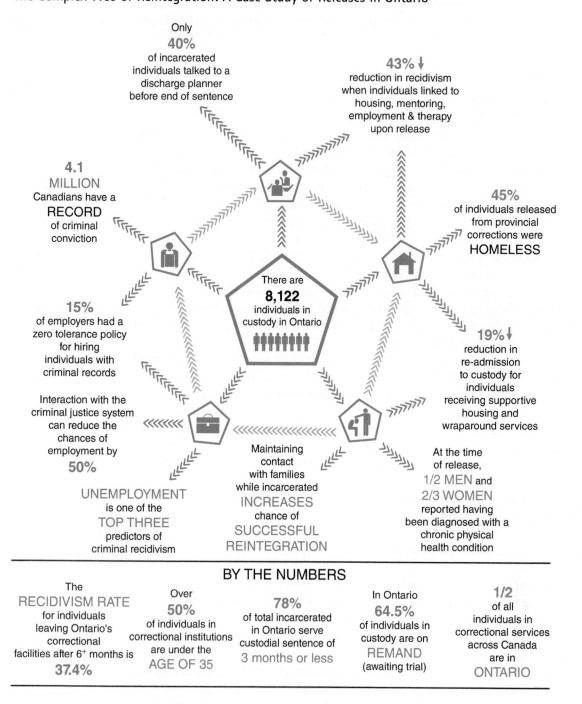

Only **40%** of incarcerated individuals talked to a discharge planner before end of sentence

43% ↓ reduction in recidivism when individuals linked to housing, mentoring, employment & therapy upon release

4.1 MILLION Canadians have a **RECORD** of criminal conviction

45% of individuals released from provincial corrections were **HOMELESS**

There are **8,122** individuals in custody in Ontario

15% of employers had a zero tolerance policy for hiring individuals with criminal records

Interaction with the criminal justice system can reduce the chances of employment by **50%**

19% ↓ reduction in re-admission to custody for individuals receiving supportive housing and wraparound services

UNEMPLOYMENT is one of the **TOP THREE** predictors of criminal recidivism

Maintaining contact with families while incarcerated **INCREASES** chance of **SUCCESSFUL REINTEGRATION**

At the time of release, 1/2 MEN and 2/3 WOMEN reported having been diagnosed with a chronic physical health condition

BY THE NUMBERS

The **RECIDIVISM RATE** for individuals leaving Ontario's correctional facilities after 6+ months is **37.4%**

Over **50%** of individuals in correctional institutions are under the **AGE OF 35**

78% of total incarcerated in Ontario serve custodial sentence of **3 months or less**

In Ontario **64.5%** of individuals in custody are on **REMAND** (awaiting trial)

1/2 of all individuals in correctional services across Canada are in **ONTARIO**

Source: John Howard Society in Ontario. (2016). *Reintegration in Ontario: Practices, Priorities, and Effective Models.* Retrieved from http://johnhoward.on.ca/wp-content/uploads/2016/11/RiO-Infographic-Final-1.pdf. Reprinted by permission of the John Howard Society of Ontario.

In provincial/territorial corrections, few distinctions are made between parole and probation, except with regard to provisions for enforcement. For example, the breach of a probation condition is a new offence, whereas the violation of a parole condition can (but does not always) lead to suspension of the release and to a return of the parolee to custody.

Not all offenders who are released into the community require the same level of supervision. An assessment is made to determine the offender's need and risk levels—low, medium, or high—and the results are used to determine the level and intensity of supervision. Supervision by parole officers may range from periodic telephone calls to the offender's residence to the requirement that the offender reside in a community-based residential facility with 24-hour monitoring and attend frequent face-to-face meetings with a parole officer.

Parole officers are involved in a myriad of activities, including conducting risk assessments and case management planning for offenders on release; case preparation in relation to specific offender populations, for example, Section 84 planning for those Indigenous offenders who have applied for such a release type; enforcement of the conditions of parole; and assisting parolees to access programs and services.

The Dual Function of Parole Supervision

Similar to probation officers, parole officers have a dual role in their relations with clients. The first involves being a resource person and confidant to counter the pains of re-entry. The supportive activities of parole officers can include offering job search advice, referring clients for counselling, and advocating with welfare authorities on their behalf. The second role involves monitoring and enforcing parole and statutory release conditions.

Each parole officer has their own style of supervision. Some are more lenient and give the offenders assigned to them a longer "leash"; others are much stricter. The style of supervision also depends on the level of risk the offender poses to the community. Ideally, a balance between the two roles is achieved, with more control/surveillance during the early phases of release and more assistance as the supervision period draws to an end. Not surprisingly, research studies have found that parole officers with more authoritarian attitudes are more inclined to enforce the conditions of parole and to send an offender to a parole board revocation hearing.[35]

To be effective, a parole officer must adapt their supervision style to the offender's risk and needs. A number of factors may damage the relationship between the two, including the perceptions that each brings to the relationship. Parole officers may believe, for example, that offenders make a rational choice to follow (or not) the conditions of their release. A parole officer who treats the offender with disrespect can actually hinder the latter's good-faith efforts to succeed in the community.[36] Offenders, on the contrary, may perceive that parole officers don't understand "where they're coming from" and that they are not able to appreciate the pressures and challenges they face.[37] High-risk offenders, such as sex offenders, may be unlikely to disclose their urges to reoffend to their parole supervisor for fear of being returned to custody.

The increasing emphasis on risk management in corrections may soon transform the role of parole officers into one of monitoring and enforcing compliance with release conditions and periodically reassessing changes in risk and need.[38] The paperwork burden of conducting these assessments and recording them in computerized, centralized databases has had a strong impact on the amount of time that parole supervisors can spend in face-to-face contact with clients. Similar to their probation officer counterparts, parole officers may also experience stress and may be affected by the emotional intensity of their work.[39]

Parole Officer Safety: A Death in Yellowknife

The death of a federal parole officer in Yellowknife highlighted issues surrounding the safety of parole officers as well as the decision-making of the PBC. On October 6, 2004, CSC parole officer Louise Pargeter went to the home of Eli Ulayuk, one of the parolees she supervised. She failed to return to her office as scheduled, and her co-workers were unable to locate her. The following day, the RCMP made a gruesome discovery: They found her body at Ulayuk's apartment. During the trial, the court learned that Ulayuk had wanted to kill Pargeter since 2001 when she revoked his day parole. The court heard that Ulayuk had struck Pargeter with a hammer five times, strangled her with twine, and had sex with her body. In February 2006, Ulayuk was found guilty of second-degree murder and sentenced to life in prison, with the recommendation that he be ineligible for parole for 25 years.

A CSC inquiry into the incident identified a number of factors that may have led to Pargeter's death.[40] Earlier, Ulayuk had been convicted of the murder of a woman in his home community of Igloolik, Nunavut, and had been diagnosed as a necrophiliac, a form of sexual deviance. The sentencing judge in that case commented that Ulayuk was one of the most dangerous offenders ever to have come before the court. The Board of Investigation (BOI) found that while Ulayuk was in confinement, the CSC had not completed sufficient clinical assessments of him, nor had sufficient attention been given to his sexual deviancy in the treatment plan. The BOI also stated that there had not been sufficient analysis of Ulayuk's case file prior to his release; it then made numerous recommendations with respect to the CSC's information-gathering process, case preparation for PBC hearings, and the supervision of offenders in the community.

After Louise Pargeter's death, the CSC modified its regulations, which now require that two officers conduct home visits "for offenders who have a criminal history involving any sexual offence and/or death and are assessed as high risk at intake (level of intervention based on static risk factors) [or who] are classified as maximum security upon release (offender security level)."[41] The BOI also recommended that the PBC change the format of its decisions to make it more structured, with a focus on specific risk factors. Further, when an offender has experienced a revocation of his or her parole, the decision to re-release an offender should clearly state the Board's justifications for re-release and their risk assessment. The BOI also recommended providing CSC and PBC staff with cultural sensitivity training for Inuit culture and history, and encouraged the CSC to develop an Inuit-specific risk assessment tool.[42]

In the days and years that followed this incident, the PBC reduced the number of hearings that board members hear per day and expanded training for new and existing employees. The CSC also made changes to its community safety procedures, including encouraging community parole officers (CPOs) to notify local police authorities of their upcoming home visits, request additional support from their colleagues (or police) for home visits, revisit supervision measures for individual cases through ongoing dialogue with their supervisors, and complete the training course, "Community Supervision Safety Training."[43]

RE-ENTRY COURTS: A PROBLEM-SOLVING APPROACH

In Chapter 4, we discuss the emergence of problem-solving courts as an alternative to the traditional criminal justice process. The research evidence suggests that this approach can be effective in addressing the needs of offenders while providing protection to the community and reducing reoffending.

A similar approach could be taken with respect to offenders re-entering the community following incarceration. Re-entry courts have been established in a number of American jurisdictions. These courts hold offenders accountable; promote family and individual responsibility; review the progress and problems of offenders; assist in the continuity of treatment from the institution to the community; monitor compliance with release conditions; and apply sanctions when offenders do not comply with treatment requirements to promote public safety through reduced reoffending, improve parole outcomes, and reduce the use of incarceration.[44]

In re-entry courts, judges actively involve themselves in the offender's transition from prison to the community, either by retaining jurisdiction over the offender from sentencing to warrant expiry or by assuming jurisdiction once the offender is released. The activities of re-entry courts include designing reintegration plans based on offenders' assessed needs, providing active oversight, and coordinating services (e.g., access to drug treatment, health and mental health treatment, vocational services) and community supports. The courts can be especially helpful for women offenders who are attempting to reunite with their children following a period of incarceration.[45]

SPECIAL OFFENDER POPULATIONS ON CONDITIONAL RELEASE

As noted earlier in the chapter, offenders vary in the specific types of problems they encounter on re-entry. This disparity requires that correctional systems adapt their policies and programs to meet the needs of special offender populations and to manage the risks they present.

High-Risk Offenders

One Canadian program for high-risk offenders is a collaborative effort between the CSC and several police departments across the country (including the Regina Police Service and the Hamilton Police Service). It involves police officers being hired as community corrections liaison officers (CCLOs). These officers monitor the activities of high-risk/high-needs offenders in the community and liaise between police officers and parole officers.[46]

Mentally Ill Offenders

Mentally disordered parolees returning to the community face special challenges: They tend to be socially isolated and to be more prone to substance abuse, and they have even more difficulty finding suitable employment and housing. As is often the case, provincial/territorial programs for these populations are less developed than federal ones. Mentally ill offenders released to northern and remote communities are likely to face particular challenges, though corrections scholars have done little research on this.

Interventions designed to improve criminal justice and mental health outcomes amongst populations of criminally involved adults reduce future involvement with the criminal justice system although they have not been found to have a positive effect on breach of conditional release.[47] Programs that are particularly valuable include institutional and community programming and services, which again highlights the importance of throughcare.[48]

Further, programming for mentally disordered offenders that targets the central eight risk factors (i.e., criminal history, antisocial associates, antisocial attitudes and cognitions, antisocial personality patterns, education/employment, family/marital, substance abuse, and leisure/recreation) in both institutional and community settings has been found to increase their likelihood of success upon release into the community.[49]

Long-Term Offenders

As we note in Chapter 4, at sentencing, a judge can order an offender who is perceived to be at high risk of reoffending to a period of long-term community supervision, known as a long-term supervision order (LTSO). This period of supervision begins once the offender is released from custody at his or her warrant expiry date. The PBC pursues two objectives in creating conditions for offenders who are on LTSOs: promoting public safety and aiding the offender's rehabilitation. Offenders can challenge the conditions of their LTSO, such as a residency condition, through the courts.[50]

Similar to the procedure for suspending other forms of conditional release, supervising parole officers can suspend an LTSO if they believe the offender is at risk to breach a condition, a suspension is believed to be in the public's best interests, or the officer suspects the offender has breached a condition. If any of the above standards are met, the first step is for the officer to suspend the LTSO, which is followed by the offender's commitment to prison, a community residential facility, or a mental health facility for up to 90 days. The parole officer has 30 days to cancel the suspension or refer it to the PBC. The PBC can also cancel the suspension and, in the process, reprimand the offender, modify the conditions of the LTSO, and delay the offender's release for up to 90 days during which time he or she is required to participate in programming.[51]

Where the post-suspension hearing outcomes differ for those subject to LTSOs is in the consequences for violating the conditions of these orders; the consequences are much more severe than for breaching a condition of parole or statutory release. The PBC "may make a decision to proceed with recommending to provincial Crown counsel the laying of information for breach of a LTSO."[52] If the offender is charged and found guilty by the courts, a sentence of up to 10 years of imprisonment can be imposed for the breach with the LTSO commencing at the expiration of any new sentence that is imposed on the offender.[53]

Ste. Anne Residence, located in Ottawa, Ontario, has 25 beds and admits those released on statutory release with a residency condition and those who are designated a long-term or dangerous offender. This halfway house provides a variety of supports for offenders reintegrating into the community: motivational and supportive counselling, life skills programming (e.g., personal finances), and case management. The expectation is that individuals residing here are employed, pursuing educational goals, and participating in treatment programming.[54]

Sex Offenders

No group of offenders has attracted more interest from the public, politicians, and correctional authorities than sex offenders. Their release from prison is often front-page news in the local press or even announced over the Internet. Citizen protests and resistance to released offenders occur despite research studies that have consistently found that sex offenders have low recidivism rates for sexual reoffending upon re-entry.[55]

The CSC operates a high-risk offender program as well as a maintenance program for managing sex offenders on release in the community. The National Sex Offender Program (comprised of the High Intensity National Sex Offender Program, Moderate Intensity National Sex Offender Program, National Sex Offender Maintenance Program, and the Tupiq Program for Inuit men offenders) is cognitive-behaviour oriented and includes individual and group counselling.

Group therapy is used to address the four Fs related to sexual offending: feelings, fantasy, future, and follow-through. This multidisciplinary program involves monthly case conference meetings attended by the supervising parole staff, treatment staff, and the program director. These case conferences provide an opportunity to discuss supervision of the offender and any concerns relating to the offender's no-contact orders, family relationships, employment, and attitude and behaviour. Sex offenders who have admitted their guilt and who require lower-intensity relapse prevention participate in the National Sex Offender Maintenance Program. These offenders receive individual or group therapy designed to maintain their institutional treatment gains.

Provincial/Territorial Programs for Sex Offenders

In provincial/territorial programs, the potential effectiveness of sex offender treatment programs may be severely compromised by the short period of time these offenders are confined. Inmates may not be able to access programs in a timely manner and may not complete all of the prescribed sessions of a treatment intervention prior to being eligible for parole or reaching their earned remission date (as early as the two-thirds point in their sentence). There may also be a lack of throughcare due to the absence of community-based resources. Provincial/territorial offenders who are discharged at their earned remission date do not have access to corrections programs and services in the community.

Managing the Risks of Sex Offenders

Correctional systems use a variety of techniques to manage the risks of this offender group. These techniques include programming (see above and Chapter 9), drugs such as anti-androgens to reduce sex drive, electronic monitoring, community notification (CN), registration, and supervision and monitoring strategies, including polygraph testing.[56] Residency conditions can also be imposed as part of a sex offender's conditional release (this, despite the absence of empirical evidence conclusively documenting the effectiveness of residency conditions in preventing future crime, and further, the existence of evidence that suggests these conditions can have negative outcomes, such as reoffending).[57]

Research has found that there are lower rates of recidivism for sex offenders who are supervised via a case management approach and who are offered individualized treatment services in combination with an appropriate level of parole supervision.[58]

Sex Offender Registries

The federal government and several provinces (including British Columbia and Ontario) have established sex offender registries to track high-risk sex offenders. The purpose of the federal Sex Offender Information Registration Act (SOIRA;2004) is to "help police services prevent and investigate crimes of a sexual natureby requiring the registration of certain information relating to sex offenders."[59] Sex offenders subject to a SOIRA order must register within 7 or 15 days depending on the registration centre they are referred to—prior to release into the community (or upon conviction if they receive a noncustodial sentence), and must then re-register annually as well as 15 days prior to any change of address.

The registry database includes information on the offender, such as name, date of birth, current address, and identifying marks, as well as photographs.

While the RCMP is responsible for administering and maintaining the National Sex Offender Registry, all police jurisdictions collect data for the registry and enforce registration. The maximum length of the sentence for which an offender is sentenced dictates how long the offender is required to be registered, whether for 10 years, 20 years, or life.[60]

Individuals convicted of sexual offences against children must inform their local police of all international travel, whereas all others must inform police only of international travel exceeding seven days.[61] Currently, in contrast to many sex offender registries in the United States, the public does not have access to the National Sex Offender Registry.

COMMUNITY NOTIFICATION

We noted in Chapter 10 that the victims of incarcerated offenders have the right to request that they be informed of the timing of their release. In some cases this information can help the victims take the necessary steps to ensure their safety. The large majority of crime victims are not harassed or threatened by offenders on conditional release; however, some victims are at great risk. It is in these cases that victim notification is most crucial, for both officially sanctioned releases and unauthorized absences from community supervision.

The use of **community notification (CN)** when high-risk offenders are released into the community is a key component of various attempts to manage risk and protect the community. This strategy may also be viewed as a hardening of attitudes against certain categories of offenders and as reflective of a punitive penology. Decisions about CN are most often made by a committee composed of a police representative, a private citizen, a specialist in medical/therapeutic interventions, and representatives from provincial and federal corrections.

The premise of CN policies is that when potential victims and the community at large are warned, the community is better able to protect itself; also, offenders who know they are being watched will be deterred from reoffending.[62] The negative aspects of CN are that it limits the amount of social capital available to sex offenders, preventing the offender from re-establishing a stable residence, employment, and relationships in the community, and increasing the strains they experience and their notoriety, which may lead to victimization, thereby increasing the possibility of reoffending.[63]

An example of CN that ended tragically is the case of Raymond Lee Caissie, who was released at sentence expiry after serving a 22-year sentence for sexually assaulting a 21-year-old woman. Three months after his release, in June 2013, B.C. Corrections issued a community notification for Caissie with his physical description, some of the conditions he was subject to, and his city of residence. Despite being subject to this public warning, and a Section 810.2 judicial recognizance (see Chapter 10), Caissie was charged in September 2014 with second-degree murder in the death of 17-year-old Serena Vermeersch.[64] See Corrections File 11.1 for a discussion of the release and re-entry of a high-risk sex offender in British Columbia.

> **Community notification**
> The practice, usually carried out by police agencies, of making a public announcement that a high-risk offender has taken up residence in an area.

CORRECTIONS FILE 11.1

The Release and Re-entry of a Sex Offender

James Conway, a high-risk sex offender, was released into the community of Abbotsford, British Columbia, in 2015. Conway had a history of committing offences against children, and his return to the community was well-publicized (i.e., he was subject to community notification). He was greeted with citizen protests, and his residence was vandalized multiple times (e.g., community residents threw rocks at his home and climbed the outside of the house, placing a running hose in the attic which flooded the residence).

Community residents protest against a sex offender released from prison taking up residence in their neighbourhood.

The City of Abbotsford launched a lawsuit against the property owners who had leased the home to a company, which violated the zoning bylaws in place. The adjacent City of Mission, where Conway moved to a halfway house following his departure from Abbotsford, also filed a lawsuit in the B.C. Supreme Court. The lawsuit was filed against the company running the halfway house and challenged Conway's residence due to city bylaw infractions. This example—and the public outcry that occurred in two cities in the Lower Mainland of British Columbia—highlights the challenges sex offenders face in reintegrating into the community.

Sources: A. Judd, "Mission residents file lawsuit to remove sex offender from their community," Global News, October 12, 2016, http://globalnews.ca/news/2997733/mission-residents-file-lawsuit-to-remove-sex-offender-from-their-community/; V. Hopes, "Child sexual offender leaves Abbotsford, comes to Mission," Abbotsford News, August 3, 2016, http://www.missioncityrecord.com/news/389084611.html; F. Bucholtz, "Mission residents hold protest outside of sex offender's home," *Mission City Record*, August 8, 2016, http://www.missioncityrecord.com/news/389546231.html.

GPS AND ELECTRONIC MONITORING

As we discussed in Chapter 5, correctional services utilize GPS and electronic monitoring to supervise diverse populations of offenders in the community to monitor their compliance with special geographical conditions included on their release—for example, to avoid/remain in certain locations and to adhere to curfews.[65]

SUSPENSION AND REVOCATION OF CONDITIONAL RELEASE

There are several ways in which the supervision of an offender on conditional release comes to an end: (1) successful completion of sentence to the end of the supervision period; (2) revocation for a breach of a condition of release ("a positive intervention, which reduces the risk of reoffending"); (3) revocation as a prevention measure due to the belief an offender is at risk of breaching a condition of his or her release; (4) revocation due to a conviction for a new offence ("a negative end to the supervision period, which results in a new conviction"); and (5) termination of the conditional release due to circumstances beyond the client's control.[66]

A **suspension of conditional release** can occur if a client fails to abide by any of the set conditions, including failing to adhere to the conditions of the parole certificate, or if the parole officer "is satisfied that it is necessary and reasonable to suspend the parole or statutory release [of their client] to prevent a breach of any condition thereof or to protect society."[67]

The supervising parole officer suspends the conditional release and issues a Canada-wide warrant for their client's rearrest and return to custody. When the client is back in custody, the community parole officer has a decision to: (1) cancel the suspension and release the person from custody, or (2) refer the case back to the provincial parole board or PBC for a post-suspension review. During the post-suspension review, the parole board reviews the post-suspension report prepared by the community parole officer and decides whether to:

1. cancel the suspension (but reprimand the offender, modify the release conditions, or, if the offender has previously been suspended on conditional release, require that release from custody be delayed for up to 30 days)[68]
2. terminate the parole or statutory release ("if the undue risk is due to circumstances beyond the offender's control"),[69] or,
3. revoke the parole or statutory release. A **revocation of conditional release** can be the outcome of the post-suspension hearing if the board decides an offender is no longer a manageable risk in the community.

Parole officers have considerable discretion in the use of suspensions. The law states that officers *may* suspend a parolee for violating a parole condition, when they believe an offender is a risk to breach a condition, or when new offences are alleged. The number of cases in which technical violations occur or new offences are alleged but a suspension is not imposed is unknown.

An under-studied area of corrections is the decision-making of staff in community corrections centres and other facilities where offenders may reside

Suspension of conditional release
A process initiated by the supervising parole officer (or in some instances by the parole board) in cases where the releasee has allegedly failed to abide by the conditions of release, is believed to be at risk of breaching a condition, or is at risk of re-offending.

Revocation of conditional release
A decision by a releasing authority, such as a parole board, made in connection with an offender whose release has been suspended.

while on release. These staff may facilitate or hinder an offender's efforts to abide by conditions of release. A staff member at a federal halfway house stated: "Sometimes a staff member won't like the offender and will find any little reason to have them violated and returned to prison. There is definitely favouritism at work" (personal communication with C. T. Griffiths).

MAKING IT OR GOING BACK: FACTORS IN THE SUCCESS OR FAILURE OF OFFENDERS ON CONDITIONAL RELEASE

Even the most institutionalized state-raised inmate does not leave a correctional institution with the intent of returning. Furthermore, correctional systems have as a primary objective the reduction of recidivism among offenders released into the community. And yet, research consistently demonstrates that imprisonment has a criminogenic effect, as offenders subject to imprisonment rather than an alternative sanction, have higher recidivism rates.[70]

Success on Conditional Release

Among the factors that increase the likelihood of success on parole are a supportive network of family and friends, stable housing and employment, participation in treatment programs (in both institutional and community settings), and a conscious decision to move out of a criminal lifestyle.[71]

Re-entry and Social Support/Family Relationships

The families of offenders can provide significant support and assistance both while the offender is confined and upon release; it has been found to contribute to the successful reintegration of offenders into the community.[72] Family support has been found to contribute to positive re-entry outcomes in the following areas: accommodation, alcohol and drugs, coping abilities, and stronger family relationships.[73]

Given the importance of social support and family ties for offender re-entry, correctional services should remove barriers to visitation for prisoners' support networks and promote programming to facilitate the maintenance of social and family ties.

Community Support

Community volunteers may also play a vital role in the re-entry process, providing returning offenders with prosocial support that they do not receive from family members. Mentors have been found to provide support for mentees, empower them, and assist them with navigating services and appointments, among other functions, providing overall value in the lives of the mentees as they re-enter society.[74]

Receiving visits from community volunteers—clergy members and mentors—has also been found to decrease recidivism for rearrest, reconviction, and reincarceration.[75]

Innovations in Community Assistance and Supervision

Across the country, a number of programs have been developed to increase community involvement in helping released offenders. These programs are generally staffed by trained volunteers, whose activities include assisting parole officers and offenders and participating in COSAs (discussed later).

Research File 11.1 highlights the work of various community organizations in providing services to offenders in Hamilton, Ontario.

Participation in Correctional Programming

Participation in correctional education has been found to contribute to successful re-entry (i.e., reduced recidivism, employment opportunities, and achievement test scores). Further, providing correctional education programs has been found to be cost-effective given reduced incarceration costs (due to less recidivism).[76]

Participation in substance abuse programming—CSC's National Substance Abuse Program-High Intensity (NSAP-H) and Moderate Intensity Program (NSAP-M)—has also been found to contribute to successful re-entry, reducing the likelihood of offenders returning to custody within 24 months of their release. Participation in community aftercare was found to be important for an offender's success amongst those in both the NSAP-H and NSAP-M groups.[77]

RESEARCH FILE 11.1

Perspectives of Clients and Service Providers on Community Corrections Services in Hamilton, Ontario: A Case Study

Interviews with clients (N = 35 [16 men, 19 women]) of a number of community corrections organizations in Hamilton, including the Elizabeth Fry Society, the St. Leonard's Society, the John Howard Society, and the Native Women's Centre, identified a number of challenges for offenders returning to the community. Housing was one of these challenges: Many offenders had nowhere to go upon release and relied on family and friends for shelter. Other needs they identified were for drug-free shelter, employment opportunities, mental health and counselling supports, and addiction services.

(continued)

One client stated, "I didn't overcome these challenges. I went back to sex trade work. Most girls, that's what they do." Another commented on what happens when the ex-offender's needs are not met, noting, "They wander the streets. They don't know how to address their needs." One particular challenge was staying away from old friendship networks. Comments on this from the clients included the following:

> *People have big plans coming out of jail but they don't happen because of the time lag between being released from jail and arriving at the first service provider.*

> *A girl gets out of jail, she wants to get into rehab right away. She can't go so she gets frustrated and decides, "Well, if I can't get clean now I might as well still do drugs."*

Personnel in community corrections organizations noted the need for housing, for gender-specific programs and services, and for more collaboration and sharing of resources among agencies. Many of their clients had multiple issues, one of these often being addiction. It was proposed that a "wrap-around model" of services be developed so that one facility could provide addiction counselling, mental health services, and housing and employment assistance.

Source: Social Planning and Research Council of Hamilton, *Hamilton Community Correctional Services Needs Assessment* (Hamilton: Author, 2010), pp. 15, 16, http://www.sprc.hamilton.on.ca/wp-content/uploads/2010/02/Hamilton-Community-Correctional-Services-Needs-Assessment-February-2010.pdf.

Utilizing the RNR Model in Community Supervision

To promote offender success in the community, the CSC strives to provide community supervision consistent with the RNR model discussed in Chapter 9, which involves identifying those who are higher risk and who require "closer supervision and more intensive intervention [and the dynamic risk factors that] should be targeted for change during supervision."[78] This is because CSC research demonstrates variability across groups in the risk factors for revocation in the community and the need to tailor supervision and programming to their unique risks/needs.

To illustrate, women who have been found to be most at risk for revocation require substance abuse treatment, have a history of institutional infractions, and are released from higher security facilities and on statutory release.[79] In contrast, men who have been found to be most at risk for revocation are young, have needs in employment and community functioning, did not adjust well to institutional life, and are released on statutory release.[80] Research File 11.2 provides a review of the effectiveness of selected supervision/control strategies for offenders in the community.

REOFFENDING

Most inmates who reoffend do so within the first three years following release from a correctional institution.[81] The first year upon re-entering the community is the highest risk period for rearrest amongst the returning offender population.[82] CSC analyses have documented the need to provide offenders with throughcare, support, and supervision during the first year of release, as the majority (80 percent; $N = 12,690$) of the revocations of conditional release for offenders released from CSC custody between 2010 and 2013 occurred within the first 12 months in the community.[83]

Contrary to the impression given by media reports, the rate of reconviction for violent offences for offenders under community supervision has declined over the past decade. Unfortunately, it is a small number of offenders who commit heinous crimes again who receive the attention of the media. It is they who often have a strong impact on corrections policies and practices—who encourage tougher sentencing laws and tighten the decision-making of parole boards. The "silent majority" of offenders who successfully complete conditional release is invisible to the community. When asked about the connotations attached to the word "parolee," community residents tend to respond in one of two ways: "got out too soon," or "dangerous to the public." These responses reflect the fact, noted in Chapter 3, that most citizens get their information on crime, criminal justice, and corrections from the media.

The highest failure rate is among those offenders who were not granted parole but instead were released on statutory release after serving two-thirds of their sentence. As a group, these offenders are at high risk to reoffend, which perhaps is one reason why they were not granted release on parole.

There are challenges in studying the reoffending (or recidivism) of offenders who have been released from confinement. Recidivism can be measured in various ways, such as rearrest rates, parole revocation (due to a technical violation or for the commission of a new offence), reconviction, and reincarceration. How recidivism is measured can affect conclusions about the effectiveness of parole supervision and the success of correctional programs.[84]

CIRCLES OF SUPPORT AND ACCOUNTABILITY (COSAs): A RESTORATIVE, REINTEGRATIVE PRACTICE FOR HIGH–RISK SEX OFFENDERS

COSAs were first developed by the Canadian Mennonite community in the early 1990s, and they are used in countries worldwide (e.g., the United States, the United Kingdom, New Zealand, and Australia).[85] They are based on the traditional Indigenous practice of healing circles. COSAs provide support for sex offenders who are released from federal institutions at warrant expiry or whose period of supervision on conditional release has ended due to warrant expiry. COSAs are a counterweight to the professionalization of corrections and penal populism.[86] These offenders are the most

Circles of support and accountability (COSAs) Community-based committees composed of criminal justice personnel and community members that provide mentoring for high-risk sex offenders whose sentences have expired.

likely targets of judicial recognizances and CN. Any offender who participates in the program does so on a voluntary basis; there is no legal mechanism that can compel him or her to be subject to monitoring.

COSAs are centred on the principles of restorative justice, including the importance of positive relationships that can facilitate positive change in the offender while at the same time address the injury caused to the victim and the community.[87] COSAs are designed to extend contact with the offender beyond the warrant expiry date (end of sentence and conditional supervision) and to engage the community in efforts to reintegrate high-risk offenders.[88] Figure 11.4 sets out the four key principles on which COSAs are based: reintegration/restoration, support, monitoring, and maintenance. Figure 11.5 illustrates the relationships of COSAs.

A circle of support is a team of five or six volunteers assigned to assist an offender as they take up residence in their community. Volunteers can include teachers, social workers, police officers, businesspeople, and other

Figure 11.4

The Key Principles of COSAs

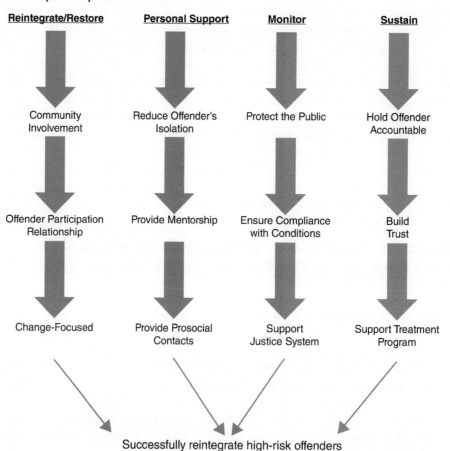

Reintegrate/Restore	Personal Support	Monitor	Sustain
Community Involvement	Reduce Offender's Isolation	Protect the Public	Hold Offender Accountable
Offender Participation Relationship	Provide Mentorship	Ensure Compliance with Conditions	Build Trust
Change-Focused	Provide Prosocial Contacts	Support Justice System	Support Treatment Program

Successfully reintegrate high-risk offenders

Figure 11.5

Conceptual Model of a Circle of Support: Relationships of the Circle within the Community

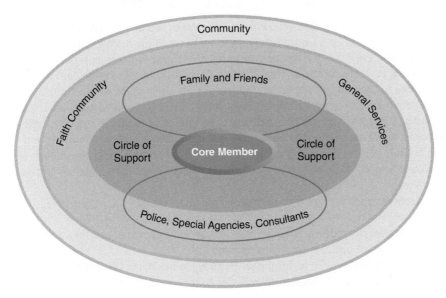

Source: E. Heise, L. Horne, H. Kirkegaard, H. Nigh, I. P. Derry, and M. Yantzi, *Community Reintegration Project* (Toronto: Mennonite Central Committee, 1996), p. 14. Reprinted by permission of Mennonite Central Committee Ontario.

community residents. They help with all facets of reintegration, including housing, employment, budgeting and financial management, spiritual development, and moral support. The offender may call only in times of stress or may have daily contact with the circle members. Circle members can also mediate between the offender and the community, as suggested in the conceptual model in Figure 11.5.

In Ontario, the Mennonite Central Committee operates the Community Reintegration Project (CRP), which provides the Circles of Support and Accountability program, which in turn offers support for sex offenders who are released from federal institutions at warrant expiry. Mediation took place in the case of Joe, whose arrival in the community was the subject of a CN (see Corrections File 11.2).

Despite evaluations that have demonstrated the effectiveness of COSAs, the federal Conservative government eliminated its funding support in 2015. As of late-2017, the original funding levels had not been restored by the federal Liberal government, although the COSAs continue to operate.

The effectiveness of selected supervision/control strategies for offenders in the community are summarized in Research File 11.2.

CORRECTIONS FILE 11.2

Joe and His Circle of Support

It began with a telephone call. "Can you help me?" the caller asked. "I'm just out of prison, and the police have already been warning everyone that I am in town. Where am I going to find a quiet place to live?" Joe, 54, had been released at warrant expiry from prison after serving a six-year sentence for sexual assault against a child. It was his eighth conviction.

Joe wanted to come to our city for several reasons. He knew us, he had met public resistance in another town when he attempted to settle there before his parole was revoked, and he suspected that he could get help in relapse prevention. We agreed to help him find accommodation, help him to find a job, and try to build a circle of friendship and support in his new city. We thought of people that we knew who could help him in each of these areas and who would be willing to work with us. We also agreed to make contact with the police.

The detectives, when we met with them, candidly said, "We don't want him here." Based on institutional reports, the police felt that Joe was likely to reoffend. There had been a lot of negative publicity recently about released prisoners reoffending, and they didn't want any of that kind of publicity for their department.

When Joe came to stay with us for the weekend while beginning the apartment search, the police quickly made his picture available to the media and warned the community of his presence among us.

The media descended upon us because we had been identified as providing support for Joe. Pickets of irate and concerned parents arrived in front of our home. After a number of angry and threatening phone calls, we finally bought a telephone answering machine.

The police mounted a plan of surveillance. They felt sure he would reoffend within a short period. They were concerned about the safety of the children in the neighbourhood, but they also wanted to ensure Joe's safety.

One of the neighbours had called the police and had a lengthy discussion with the detective. She later called to talk with me. Ann had small children and was very concerned for their safety and that of the many other children living in the area. After a discussion with her, and later with Joe, we agreed that he would meet with her to discuss her concerns. Lengthy negotiations ensued, finally resulting in a meeting proposed in a neutral site, and several other neighbours were invited to participate. The police detectives would also be present. They would be there not only as a resource but also as people who could add to the participants' feelings of security.

Joe, accompanied by two of his friends, was the first to arrive at the meeting and take a seat on the far side of the room. Soon the neighbours began to arrive. Then the detectives entered. The ground rules of the meeting were outlined. We would go around the circle to allow everyone an opportunity to share their first name and a particular concern they brought with them. We would have a statement from the neighbourhood group, followed by an opportunity for Joe to share, and from there we would move to addressing the issues presented. Only one person at a time would speak, and each speaker would follow our direction and instructions for the orderly addressing of the issues. Before the end of the meeting, we would decide together what of this meeting would be appropriate to share with other people, outside of this meeting.

As we began to go around the circle, the first person began by saying how much she appreciated the willingness of Joe and his friends to attend such a meeting. Ann outlined the questions she had heard the others discussing with her. There was a long list of questions: They wanted to know what had happened, what the sentence was, what treatment he had obtained, and what treatment he planned to receive now that he was released. "From your experience, what is the best way to avoid the behaviour you were charged with?" "How do you plan to deal with the negative reactions and anger of some individuals in the community?"

Joe responded, outlining in general terms his offences. Appreciation was expressed for the constructive method the residents had chosen to address their concerns, which he acknowledged were understandable. He indicated that he had received some treatment while in the institution and was planning to arrange suitable community-based therapy and had indeed made arrangements for that already. He had also set up an accountability system through his circle of support, by which he had daily contact with us, and we were able to make inquiry as to his faithfulness to his commitments in specific relevant areas.

We talked, and the earlier tension in the room eased as we got on with the task of problem-solving around the various issues at hand. Though all the questions were not answered, by the end of the 2 ½-hour meeting, there was a feeling of accomplishment and a readiness to move on.

Out of that meeting and others we had, some bridges were built. Neighbourhood residents, some of whom were vocally angry, began to see Joe as a person and recognized the difficulties with which he coped.

Throughout this time, Joe's circle of support met regularly with him. At least one of the circle members contacted him every day. After a year, we still talk to him daily. We took him to do his laundry, to shop for groceries and furnishings for his apartment.

The police have been partners with us in Joe's circle of support. Without the patient, humorous, understanding commitment of the detectives with whom we dealt most frequently, our efforts might not have reached this point. They came to our circle meetings. They checked in with us frequently, and we trusted their openness with us. Similarly, the police served as a buffer with the community, correcting rumours and diffusing problems.

Joe's life has settled into a comfortable pattern. He maintains a clean, comfortable apartment and has developed some close relationships. He is finding ways to spend his time and is slowly developing a small network of friends, although trust takes a long time.

Source: E. Heise, L. Horne, H. Kirkegaard, H. Nigh, I. P. Derry, and M. Yantzi, *Community Reintegration Project* (Toronto: Mennonite Central Committee, 1996), p. 14. Reprinted by permission of Mennonite Central Committee Ontario.

RESEARCH FILE 11.2

The Effectiveness of Selected Supervision/Control Strategies

Do electronic monitoring (EM) and GPS tracking reduce reoffending? There is conflicting evidence that GPS technology increases public safety, lowers rates of reoffending, or helps sex offenders successfully reintegrate back into the community.[a] Researchers examined the cost of GPS supervision for high-risk sex offenders in California by comparing the costs and performance of parolees subject to active GPS (N = 94) to those who were subject to regular non-GPS intensive supervision (N = 91) from June through November of 2005. The researchers found that it was not more cost-effective to use GPS monitoring for this population during their first year in the community, and that both groups had similar rates of parole violations.[b] A preliminary study of the use of EM with federal offenders in Canada found no impact of reoffending.[c] Studies have found that GPS programs are very time-consuming for parole officers.

Do COSAs work? Yes. Research studies of the experiences of COSA participants in Canada (including offenders) have found lower rates of reoffending and a positive view of the program by all participants. The researchers also found program participants (N = 60) sexually reoffended less severely in comparison to their previous sexual offences, although this did not hold true for the matched comparison group of non-participants (N = 60).[d] In a study of sex offenders released from confinement at the expiry of their sentence, half the sample (N = 44) participated in COSAs and the other half (N = 44) did not. The offenders were followed for nearly three years. Among the findings of the study: Compared to the offenders who did not participate in COSAs, the sex offenders who participated in the program had lower rates of sexual reoffending (83 percent reduction), other types of violent crimes (73 percent reduction), and overall reoffending (71 percent reduction).[e] A Canadian study conducted by the Church Council on Justice and Corrections also documented a return on investment valued at $4.60 for every dollar spent on COSA programs.[f]

Does CN work? Not likely. Although CN appears to have strong support from the public, the existing studies (none of them Canadian) about the impact of registration and CN on reoffending among high-risk offenders suggests CN does not work. American studies found no differences in the recidivism rates (commission of new sexual or general offences and/or violations of release conditions) of male sex offenders compared to male non-sex offenders and no deterrent value of CN laws.[g] Sex offenders have been found to view CN laws as unfair, resulting in stigmatization, vigilantism, and challenges in community reintegration, such as finding employment and developing relationships. One American study also found that sex offenders subject to notification laws were more likely than non-sex offenders to be homeless/transient, living alone, living in group homes, and not living with friends.[h]

[a] California Sex Offender Management Board, *Recommendations Report* (Sacramento, Calif.: Author, 2010), p. 48, http://www.casomb.org/docs/CASOMB%20Report%20Jan%202010_Final%20Report.pdf.

[b] M.K. Omori and S.F. Turner, "Assessing the Cost of Electronically Monitoring High-Risk Sex Offenders," Crime & Delinquency 61, no. 6 (2015), 873–94.

[c] M. Olotu, M. Beaupre, and P. Verbrugge, Evaluation Report: *Electronic Monitoring Program Pilot* (Ottawa: Correctional Service Canada, 2009), http://www.csc-scc.gc.ca/text/pa/empp/index-eng.shtml.

[d] R.J. Wilson, J.E. Picheca, and M. Prinzo, *Circles of Support and Accountability: An Evaluation of the Pilot Project in South-Central Ontario* (Ottawa: Correctional Service Canada, 2005), http://www.csc-scc.gc.ca/text/rsrch/reports/r168/r168_e.pdf.

[e] R.J. Wilson, F. Cortoni, and A.J. McWhinnie, "Circles of Support and Accountability: A Canadian National Replication of Outcome Findings," *Sexual Abuse: A Journal of Research and Treatment 21*, no. 4 (2009), 412–30.

[f] G. Duwe, "Can Circles of Support and Accountability (COSA) Work in the United States? Preliminary Results from a Randomized Experiment in Minnesota," *Sexual Abuse: A Journal of Research and Treatment 25*, no. 2 (2012), 143–65.

[g] R.G. Zevitz, "Sex Offender Community Notification: Its Role in Recidivism and Offender Reintegration," *Criminal Justice Studies 19*, no. 2 (2006), 193–208.

[h] R. Tewksbury, "Collateral Consequences of Offender Registration," *Journal of Contemporary Criminal Justice 21*, no. 1 (2005), 67–81. ; Y.N. Brannon, J.S. Levenson, T. Fortney, and J.N. Baker, "Attitudes About Community Notification: A Comparison of Sexual Offenders and the Non-Offending Public," *Sexual Abuse: A Journal of Research and Treatment 19*, no. 4 (2007), 369–79; W.G. Jennings, Z.M. Zgoba, and R. Tewksbury, "A Comparative Longitudinal Analysis of Recidivism Trajectories and Collateral Consequences for Sex and Non-Sex Offenders Released Since the Implementation of Sex Offender Registration and Community Notification," *Journal of Crime and Justice 35*, no. 3 (2012), 356–64.

SUMMARY

The re-entry of offenders into the community after serving time in custody is one of the most important, and challenging, stages of the corrections process. While society has perfected the process for removing offenders from the community, far less attention has been given to how to reintegrate them back into the community. This may be particularly challenging as many offenders were marginal prior to their conviction and incarceration. Offenders may find adjusting to life in the outside community stressful. Unique challenges are encountered by special groups of offenders, including the mentally ill and sex offenders. The majority of offenders are on some form of conditional release, and parole officers have a dual role: to provide assistance *and* oversight. Restorative justice practices such as

COSAs hold considerable promise and provide an alternative to strategies that may hinder an offender's reintegration, such as CN.

KEY POINTS REVIEW

1. To succeed, reintegration should involve continuity between the inmate's institutional programs and the services that person receives on conditional release in the community (the notion of throughcare).

2. Incarceration has a number of collateral effects, including the loss of personal relationships and social networks, the acquisition of self-defeating habits and attitudes, the loss of personal belongings, and the loss of the ability to maintain housing.

3. Persons on conditional release are subject to differing levels of supervision by corrections officials, ranging from periodic reporting to electronic monitoring, to frequent face-to-face contacts with a parole officer.

4. Parole officers have a dual role in their relations with clients: They serve as resources and confidants while also monitoring them and enforcing conditional release conditions.

5. The general approach of correctional systems is to manage the risk of sex offenders on conditional release through drug therapy, EM, CN, registration, and various supervision and monitoring strategies.

6. Statistics indicate that most federal offenders successfully complete their conditional sentences and do not reoffend prior to warrant expiry.

7. The reconviction rate for violent offences for offenders under community supervision has declined in recent years.

8. A number of factors complicate attempts to assess the effectiveness of parole.

9. CN may not be an effective strategy for ensuring the safety and security of the community and may hinder offender reintegration.

10. COSAs are an effective strategy for reducing reoffending among high-risk sex offenders.

KEY TERM QUESTIONS

1. Define **reintegration** and its objectives.

2. What is meant by **throughcare** and why is this notion important in the study of prisoner reentry?

3. How do the **pains of re-entry** and **post-incarceration syndrome (PICS)** affect offenders returning to the community?

4. Describe **community notification** and discuss the issues surrounding its use.

5. Define *suspension of conditional release* and *revocation of conditional release* and explain how these affect the status of an offender on conditional release.

6. Describe *circles of support and accountability (COSAs),* how these circles operate, and what the research suggests regarding their effectiveness.

CRITICAL THINKING EXERCISES

Critical Thinking Exercise 11.1

The National Sex Offender Registry

Currently, the National Sex Offender Registry is not accessible to the Canadian public. Online sex offender registries in the United States provide American citizens with vast amounts of information about offenders convicted of sex offences who are living in their communities. Perhaps surprisingly, survey data suggest the majority of the American public do not rely heavily on these registries and few use the information contained therein to enhance their safety through protective measures. Furthermore, empirical evidence is lacking when it comes to understanding whether sex offender registration laws are effective in reducing general or sexual reoffending, and understanding the consequences of such registries on offenders, their families, and government budgets.[89]

Your Thoughts?

1. What are your thoughts on providing the public with access to the National Sex Offender Registry?

2. What arguments could be made in support of, or in opposition to, public access to the National Sex Offender Registry?

Critical Thinking Exercise 11.2

Community Notification: Should the Practice of Community Notification be Discontinued in Canada?

Proponents of CN make these arguments: that CN will alert the neighbourhood to a potential risk, thereby reducing the likelihood of another offence; that public safety overrides any expectation the offender has for privacy; and that it protects victims. Opponents of CN counter that it is not an innovative correctional practice, but rather reflective of penal populism; that there is no evidence that it is effective at reducing reoffending; that it increases public fear and paranoia; and that it makes it difficult for offenders to reintegrate into the community and, in so doing, raises the risk of reoffending. Recent research demonstrates that while registration discourages recidivism amongst this population, public notification encourages recidivism.[90]

Your Thoughts?

    1. Which arguments do you find most persuasive and why?

CLASS/GROUP DISCUSSION EXERCISES

Class/Group Discussion Exercise 11.1

The Use, Consequences, and Perceived Effectiveness of Community Notification in Canada

Consider how your reading of a newspaper community notification or viewing of a televised community notification has altered your behaviours in the community.

Your Thoughts?

    1. Given your exposure to the practice of CN, what are your thoughts about the use of community notification as a strategy to manage high-risk offenders?

    2. How did being exposed to a CN alter your behaviour?

    3. How do you think this practice promotes public safety?

    4. How can we improve the practice?

    5. Or should it be abolished altogether?

Class/Group Discussion Exercise 11.2

Preparing for Re-entry

Assume you have been incarcerated in a CSC facility for the past 26 months and that you are nearing your statutory release date.

Your Thoughts?

    1. How do you anticipate your parents, siblings, and friends will respond to you upon release?

    2. How are you going to go about obtaining a job?

    3. Have you considered whether your university or college has regulations against admitting or providing funding to people who have a criminal record?

    4. What experiences that you have endured over the past 26 months are you going to share with your parents, siblings, and friends?

MEDIA LINKS

"The Released," *Frontline*, April 28, 2009, www.pbs.org/wgbh/pages/frontline/released/etc/synopsis.html

"Tracked: A week under GPS supervision," www.youtube.com/watch?v=QBAT07UEWug

"Circles of Support and Accountability (Part 1 of 2)," https://www.youtube.com/watch?v=bUv3BNiqrrk

"Circles of Support and Accountability (Part 2 of 2)," https://www.youtube.com/watch?v=t1E_IoMM4Jg

"No One Is Disposable: Circles of Support and Accountability (CoSA)," https://www.youtube.com/watch?v=RjioXpUk1Z4

A Hard Name, http://tvo.org/video/documentaries/a-hard-name

Out of Mind, Out of Sight: Inside the Brockville Psych, http://tvo.org/video/documentaries/out-of-mind-out-of-sight-inside-the-brockville-psych

"19facesJHSO-Luke on how JHS helped him get a second chance to succeed," John Howard Society of Ontario, https://www.youtube.com/watch?v=-iW7SKCg8Qg&feature=em-share_video_user

"John Howard Societies of Ontario – What You Need to Know \#19facesJSHO," https://www.youtube.com/watch?v=xUt-4j5Z45Y&feature=em-share_video_user

NOTES

1. A. Thurber, "Understanding Offender Reintegration," *Forum on Corrections Research 10*, no. 1 (1998), 14–18 at 14.

2. John Howard Society of Ontario, W. O'Grady, and R. Lafleur, *Reintegration in Ontario: Practices, Priorities, and Effective Models* (Toronto: John Howard Society of Ontario, 2016), http://johnhoward.on.ca/wp-content/uploads/2016/11/Reintegration-in-Ontario-Final.pdf.

3. C.T. Griffiths, Y. Dandurand, and D. Murdoch, *The Social Reintegration of Offenders and Crime Prevention* (Ottawa: National Crime Prevention Centre, Public Safety Canada, 2007), http://www.publicsafety.gc.ca/res/cp/res/soc-reint-eng.aspx.

4. K. Bumby, M. Carter, S. Gibel, L. Gilligan, and R. Stroker, *Increasing Public Safety Through Successful Offender Reentry: Evidence-Based and Emerging Practices in Corrections* (Washington, DC: Center for Effective Public Policy and Bureau of Justice Assistance, 2007), http://www.cepp.com/documents/CEPPSVORI_final.pdf; P.B. Burke, *TPC Reentry Handbook: Implementing the NIC Transition for Prison to the Community Model* (Washington, DC: National Institute of Corrections, U.S. Department of Justice, 2008), http://static/nicic.gov/Library/022669.pdf.

5. John Howard Society of Ontario et al., *Reintegration in Ontario: Practices, Priorities, and Effective Models*.

6. L. Gideon, "What Shall I Do Now? Released Offenders' Expectations for

Supervision Upon Release," *International Journal of Offender Therapy and Comparative Criminology 53*, no. 1 (2009), 43–56.

7. S. Poirier (chair), Decades of Darkness, Moving Towards the Light: A Review of the Prison System in Newfoundland and Labrador (St. John's: Government of Newfoundland and Labrador, 2008), p. 30,http://www.cbc.ca/news/pdf/nl-corrections-report-20081208.pdf.

8. Griffiths, Dandurand, and Murdoch, *The Social Reintegration of Offenders and Crime Prevention.*

9. Le Protectuer du Citoyen, *Report by the Québec Ombudsman: Toward Services That Are Better Adjusted to Detainees with Mental Disorders* (Québec City: 2011), 6, http://www.protectuerducitoyen.qc.ca/fileadmin/medias/pdf/rapports_speciaux/10-05-11_Rapport_sante_mentale_FINAL_EN.pdf.

10. M. Maguire and P. Raynor, "Offender Management in and After Prison: The End of 'End to End'?" *Criminology & Criminal Justice*, 17, no. 2 (2017), 138-57.

11. S. Maruna, "Reentry as a Rite of Passage," *Punishment and Society 13*, no. 1 (2011), 3–28.

12. A. Popovici, "Life after prison: Opting in or opting out," *The Crime Report*, May 23, 2016, http://thecrimereport.org/2016/05/23/life-after-prison-opting-in-or-opting-out/.

13. M. Borzycki, *Interventions for Prisoners Returning to the Community* (Canberra: Australian Institute of Criminology, 2005), http://www.crimeprevention.gov.au/NationalCrimePrevention Programme/Pages/Interventions_for_Prisoners_Returning_to_the_Community.aspx.

14. P.J. Murphy, L. Johnsen, and J. Murphy, *Paroled for Life: Interviews with Parolees Serving Life Sentences* (Vancouver: New Star, 2002), 166–67.

15. Poirier, *Decades of Darkness*, p. 26.

16. W.D. Bales and A.R. Piquero, "Assessing the impact of imprisonment on recidivism,"

Journal of Experimental Criminology 8, no. 1 (2012), 71–101. J.C. Cochran, D.P. Mears, and W.D. Bales, "Assessing the Effectiveness of Correctional Sanctions," *Journal of Quantitative Criminology 30*, no. 2 (2014), 317–47.

17. M.A. Ruderman, D.F. Wilson, and S. Reid, "Does Prison Crowding Predict Higher Rates of Substance Use Related Parole Violations? A Recurrent Events Multi-Level Survival Analysis," *PLoS ONE 10*, no. 10 (2015), 1–19.

18. M. Olotu, D. Luong, C. MacDonald, M. McKay, S. Heath, N. Allegri, and E. Loree, "Correctional Interventions," Chapter 1 in *Report of the Evaluation of CSC's Community Corrections* (Ottawa: Correctional Service Canada, 2011), p. 47, http://www.csc-scc.gc.ca/text/pa/ev-cci-fin/ev-cci-fin-eng.pdf.

19. Poirier, *Decades of Darkness*, p. 27.

20. John Howard Society of Ontario et al., *Reintegration in Ontario: Practices, Priorities, and Effective Models.*

21. Ibid.

22. R. Zorzi, S. Scott, D. Doherty, A. Engman, C. Lauzon, M. McGuire, and J. Ward, *Housing Options upon Discharge from Correctional Facilities* (Ottawa: Canada Mortgage and Housing Corporation, 2006), http://www.cmhc-schl.gc.ca/odpub/pdf/65340.pdf?fr=1343101698796.

23. H. Echenberg and J. Jensen, *Risk Factors for Homelessness* (Ottawa: Social Affairs Division, Parliamentary Information and Research Service, 2009), p. 2, http://www.parl.gc.ca/Content/LOP/Research Publications/prb0851-e.pdf.

24. John Howard Society of Ontario et al., *Reintegration in Ontario: Practices, Priorities, and Effective Models.*

25. Ibid.; F.E. Lutze, J.W. Rosky, and Z.K. Hamilton, "Homelessness and Re-Entry: A Multisite Outcome Evaluation of Washington State's Re-Entry Housing Program for High Risk Offenders," *Criminal Justice and Behaviour 41*, no. 4 (2013), 471–91.

26. S. Novac, J. Herner, E. Paradis, and A. Kellen, *Justice and Injustice: Homelessness, Crime, Victimization, and the Criminal Justice System*, Research Paper no. 207 (Toronto: Centre for Urban and Community Studies, University of Toronto, 2006), http://www.citiescentre.utoronto.ca/Assets/Cities+Centre+Digital+Assets/pdfs/publications/Research+Papers/207+Novac+et+al.pdf.

27. Lutze et al., "Homelessness and re-entry."

28. City of Toronto, *Street Needs Assessment Results* (Toronto: Toronto Shelter, Support, and Housing Administration, 2009), http://www.toronto.ca/legdocs/mmis/2010/cd/bgrd/backgroundfile-29123.pdf.

29. T.T. Gorski, "Post Incarceration Syndrome and Relapse," The Addiction Web Site of Terence T. Gorski (n.d.), http://www.tgorski.com/criminal_justice/cjs_pics_&_relapse.htm.

30. John Howard Society of Ontario et al., *Reintegration in Ontario: Practices, Priorities, and Effective Models*.

31. M.G. Vaughn, M. DeLisi, K.M. Beaver, B.E. Perron, and A. Abdon, "Toward a criminal justice epidemiology: Behavioral and physical health of probationers and parolees in the United States," *Journal of Criminal Justice 40*, no. 3 (2012), 165–73.

32. F.G. Kouyoumdjian, L. Kiefer, W. Wobeser, A. Gonzalez, and S.W. Hwang, "Mortality Over 12 Years of Follow-Up in People Admitted to Provincial Custody in Ontario: A Retrospective Cohort Study," *Canadian Medical Association Journal 4*, no. 2 (2016), E153–E161 at E157.

33. D. Cloud, "High mortality rate among the formerly incarcerated demands better policies," *Think Justice Blog*, June 16, 2014, https://www.vera.org/blog/high-mortality-rate-among-the-formerly-incarcerated-demands-better-policies.

34. P.A. Langan and D.J. Levin, *Recidivism of prisoners released in 1994* (Washington, DC: Bureau of Justice Statistics, 2002), https://www.bjs.gov/content/pub/pdf/rpr94.pdf.

35. B. Steiner, L.F. Travis, M.D. Makarios, and T. Brickley, "The Influence of Parole Officers' Attitudes on Supervision Practices," *Justice Quarterly 28*, no. 6 (2011), 903–27.

36. E. Gunnison and J.B. Helfgott, "Factors That Hinder Offender Reentry Success: A View from Community Corrections Officers," *International Journal of Offender Therapy and Comparative Criminology 55*, no. 2 (2011), 287–304 at 296.

37. J. Helfgott, "Ex-Offender Needs Versus Criminal Opportunity in Seattle, Washington," *Federal Probation 61*, no. 2 (1997), 12–24.

38. M. Lynch, "Waste Managers? The New Penology, Crime Fighting, and Parole Agent Identity," *Law and Society Review 32* (1998), 839–69.

39. E. Kita, "Public Safety, Psychological. no. 4 Security: A Practice-Informed Research Study Exploring How California Parole Agents Experience Their Work," *Smith College Studies in Social Work 85*, no. 1 (2015), 5–29 at 14.

40. Correctional Service Canada and National Parole Board, *National Joint Board of Investigation into the Release and Supervision of an Offender on Full Parole Charged with First-Degree Murder of a Parole Officer on October 7, 2004, in Yellowknife, Northwest Territories* (Ottawa: Author, 2006), http://www.csc-scc.gc.ca/text/pblct/ci-report05-06/report-eng.pdf.

41. "Commissioner's Directive: Community Supervision," Correctional Service Canada website, Commissioner's Directive 715-1 (2014), http://www.csc-scc.gc.ca/lois-et-reglements/715-1-cd-eng.shtml.

42. Correctional Service Canada and National Parole Board, *National Joint Board of Investigation into the Release and Supervision of an Offender on Full Parole Charged with First-Degree Murder of a Parole Officer on October 7, 2004, in Yellowknife, Northwest Territories*.

43. "CSC/NPB Release Investigation Report Into the Case of Eli Ulayuk Involved in the Murder of a Community Parole Officer in Yellowknife, NWT," Correctional Service Canada [news release], March 9, 2006, http://www.marketwired.com/press-release/csc-npb-release-investigation-report-into-case-eli-ulayuk-involved-murder-community-583722.htm

44. "Parole Reentry Court: Back in Stride," San Francisco Collaborative Courts (n.d.), http://www.courts.ca.gov/documents/SFPRC_Handbook_final.pdf; "Parole reentry court: Overview," Center for Court Innovation (n.d.), http://www.courtinnovation.org/project/parole-reentry-court.

45. E. McGrath, "Reentry Courts: Providing a Second Chance for Incarcerated Mothers and Their Children," *Family Court Review 50*, no. 1 (2012), 113–27.

46. M. Axford and R. Ruddell, "Police–Parole Partnerships in Canada: A Review of a Promising Programme," *International Journal of Police Science and Management 12*, no. 2 (2010), 274–86.

47. M.S. Martin, S.K. Dorken, A.D. Wamboldt, and S.E. Wooten, "Stopping the Revolving Door: A Meta-Analysis on the Effectiveness of Interventions for Criminally Involved Individuals with Major Mental Disorders," *American Psychological Association 36*, no. 1 (2011), 1–12.

48. Ibid.

49. J. Bonta, J. Blais, and H.A. Wilson, "A Theoretically Informed Meta-Analysis of the Risk for General and Violent Recidivism for Mentally Disordered Offenders," *Aggression and Violent Behavior 19*, no. 3 (2014), 278–87.

50. Prisoners' Legal Services, *Information for Federal Prisoners in British Columbia: Conditional Release* (Burnaby, BC: Author, 2015), p. 27, https://prisonjusticedotorg.files.wordpress.com/2012/11/federal-parole1.pdf.

51. Ibid., at 28.

52. Ibid., at 29.

53. Ibid., at 27; "Commissioner's Directive: Long-Term Supervision Order," Correctional Service Canada website, Commissioner's Directive 719 (2016), http://www.csc-scc.gc.ca/politiques-et-lois/719-cd-eng.shtml.

54. "Ste. Anne Residence: John Howard Society of Canada," Ontario Halfway House Association website (n.d.), http://halfwayhouses.ca/en/region/ohha/facility/st_annes/.

55. L. Helmus, R.K. Hanson, D. Thornton, K.M. Babchishin, and A.J.R. Harris, "Absolute Recidivism Rates Predicted by STATIC-99R and STATIC-2002 sex Offender Risk Assessment Tools Vary Across Samples: A Meta-Analysis," *Criminal Justice and Behavior, 39*, no. 9 (2012), 1148–71; M. Rettenberger, P. Briken, D. Turner, and R. Eher, "Sexual offender recidivism among a population-based prison sample," *International Journal of Offender Therapy and Comparative Criminology 59*, no. 4 (2015), 424–44.

56. R.J. Wilson, L. Stewart, T. Stirpe, M. Barrett, and J.E. Cripps, "Community-Based Sex Offender Management: Combining Parole Supervision and Treatment to Reduce Recidivism," *Canadian Journal of Criminology 42*, no. 2 (2000), 177–88.

57. M.P. Bratina, "Sex Offender Residency Requirements: An Effective Crime Prevention Strategy or a False Sense of Security?" *International Journal of Police Science and Management 15*, no. 3 (2013), 200–18.

58. Wilson et al., "Community-Based Sex Offender Management."

59. Sex Offender Information Registration Act (2004) at Section 2(1), http://laws-lois.justice.gc.ca/eng/acts/S-8.7/page-1.html\#h-4.

60. "National Sex Offender Registry: Overview," Royal Canadian Mounted Police website, last modified December 12, 2016, http://www.rcmp-grc.gc.ca/to-ot/cpcmec-ccpede/bs-sc/nsor-rnds/index-eng.htm

61. Ibid.

62. R.G. Zevitz, "Sex Offender Community Notification: Its Role in Recidivism and Offender Reintegration," *Criminal Justice Studies 19*, no. 2 (2006), 193–208.

63. W.G. Jennings, K.M. Zgoba, and R. Tewksbury, "A Comparative Longitudinal Analysis of Recidivism Trajectories and Collateral Consequences for Sex and Non-Sex Offenders Released Since the Implementation of Sex Offender Registration and Community Notification," *Journal of Crime and Justice 35*, no. 3 (2012), 356–64, D. Tolson and J. Klein, "Registration, Residency Restrictions, and Community Notification: A Social Capital Perspective on the Isolation of Registered Sex Offenders in Our Communities," *Journal of Human Behaviour in the Social Environment 25*, no. 5 (2015), 375–90; A.R. Ackerman and M. Sacks, "Can General Strain Theory be used to Explain Eecidivism Among Registered Sex Offenders?" *Journal of Criminal Justice 40*, no. 3 (2012), 187–93.

64. S. Reynolds, "Accused in Surrey teen's murder ordered to stand trial," *Surrey North Delta Leader*, February 4, 2016, http://www.peacearchnews.com/news/368248851.html; S. Dhillon, "B.C. reviews monitoring of high-risk offenders after teen's slaying," *Globe and Mail*, September 24, 2014, http://www.theglobeandmail.com/news/british-columbia/bc-reviews-monitoring-of-high-risk-offenders-after-teen-slaying/article20752628/; C. Chan, "Inside the Mind of a Monster: Accused Killer Raymond Caissie has Spent Most of his Adult Life Behind Bars," *The Province*, September 21, 2014, http://www.theprovince.com/news/inside+mind+monster+accused+killer+raymond+caissie+spent+most+adult+life+behind+bars/10226362/story.html.

65. "Correctional Services, Community Corrections: Electronic Supervision Program," Ministry of Community Safety and Correctional Services website, last modified February 8, 2016, http://www.mcscs.jus.gov.on.ca/english/corr_serv/comm_corr/elect_mon/elect_mon.html at para. 1.

66. Parole Board of Canada, *Performance Monitoring Report 2014–2015* (Ottawa: Author, 2016), p. 42, https://www.canada.ca/content/dam/canada/parole-board/migration/005/009/093/005009-3000-2015-en.pdf.

67. Corrections and Conditional Release Act (1992), Section 135(1).

68. Ibid., Section 135(6)(a)-(c).

69. Ibid., Section 135(5)(a)(i).

70. Bales and Piquero, "Assessing the Impact of Imprisonment on Recidivism"; F.T. Cullen, C.L. Jonson, and D.S. Nagin, "Prisons do not Reduce Recidivism: The High Cost of Ignoring Science," *The Prison Journal 91*, no. 3S (2011), 48S–65S.

71. S.J. Bahr, L. Harris, J.K. Fisher, and A.H. Armstrong, "Successful Reentry: What Differentiates Successful and Unsuccessful Parolees?" *International Journal of Offender Therapy and Comparative Criminology 54*, no. 5 (2010), 667–92; M. Makarios, B. Steiner, and L.T. Travis, "Examining the Predictors of Recidivism Among Men and Women Released from Prison in Ohio," *Criminal Justice and Behavior 37*, no. 12 (2010), 1377–91; C.A. Visher, S.A. Debus-Sherrill, and J. Yahner, "Employment After Prison: A Longitudinal Study of Former Prisoners," *Justice Quarterly 28*, no. 5 (2011), 698–718.

72. J.C. Cochran, "Breaches in the Wall: Imprisonment, Social Support, and Recidivism," *Journal of Research in Crime and Delinquency 51*, no. 2 (2014), 200–29 C.A. Visher and D.J. O'Connell, "Incarceration and Inmates' Self-Perceptions about Returning Home," *Journal of Criminal Justice 40*, no. 5 (2012), 386–93.

73. L. Markson, F. Losel, K. Souza, and C. Lanskey, "Male Prisoners' Family Relationships and Resilience in Resettlement," *Criminology & Criminal Justice 15*, no. 4 (2015), 423–41.

74. M.A. Koschmann and B.L. Peterson, "Rethinking Recidivism: A Communication

Approach to Prisoner Re-entry," *Journal of Applied Science* 7, no. 2 (2013), 188–207.

75. G. Duwe and B.R. Johnson, "The Effects of Prison Visits from Community Volunteers on Offender Recidivism," *The Prison Journal 96*, no. 2 (2016), 279–303.

76. L.M. Davis, R. Bozick, J.L. Steele, J. Saunders, and J.N.V. Miles, *Evaluating the Effectiveness of Correctional Education: A Meta-Analysis of Programs That Provide Education to Incarcerated Adults* (Santa Monica, Calif.: RAND Corporation, 2013), http://www.rand.org/pubs/research_reports/RR266.html.

77. S. Doherty, M. Temes, and F.I. Matheson, "An examination of the effectiveness of the National Substance Abuse Program High Intensity (NSAP-H) on institutional adjustment and post-release outcomes," Correctional Service Canada, Research at a glance R-290, February 2014, from http://www.csc-scc.gc.ca/research/005008-0290-eng.shtml; S. Doherty, M. Temes, and F.I. Matheson, "An examination of the effectiveness of the National Substance Abuse Program Moderate Intensity (NSAP-M) on institutional adjustment and post-release outcomes," Correctional Service Canada, Research at a glance R-291, February 2014, http://www.csc-scc.gc.ca/research/005008-0291-eng.shtml.

78. J. Thompson, T.K. Forrester, and L.A. Stewart, "Factors related to community supervision outcomes: Revocation," Correctional Service Canada Research Report R-304 (Ottawa: Correctional Service Canada, 2015), p. iii.

79. Ibid.

80. Ibid.

81. Langan and Levin, *Recidivism of prisoners released in 1994.*

82. Ibid.

83. Thompson et al., "Factors related to community supervision outcomes: Revocation."

84. M. Ostermann, L.M. Salerno, and J.M. Hyatt, "How Different Operationalizations of Recidivism Impact Conclusions of Effectiveness of Parole Supervision," *Journal of Research in Crime and Delinquency 52*, no. 6 (2015), 771–96.

85. A. Bates, D. Williams, C. Wilson, and R.J. Wilson, "Circles South East: The First 10 Years 2002–2012," *International Journal of Offender Therapy and Comparative Criminology 58*, no. 7 (2014), 861–85.; G. Duwe, "Can Circles of Support and Accountability (COSA) Work in the United States? Preliminary Results from a Randomized Experiment in Minnesota," *Sexual Abuse: A Journal of Research and Treatment 25*, no. 2 (2012), 143–65.

86. A. Bates, R. Saunders, and C. Wilson, "Doing Something About It: A Follow-Up Study of Sex Offenders Participating in Thames Valley Circles of Support and Accountability," *British Journal of Community Justice 5*, no. 1 (2007), 19–42; A. Bates, R. Macrae, C. Webb, and D. Williams, "Ever-Increasing Circles: A Descriptive Study of Hampshire and Thames Valley Circles of Support and Accountability 2002–2009," *Journal of Sexual Aggression 18*, no. 3 (2012), 355–73.

87. C. Wilson, "The Realities of Practice," in *A Community-Based Approach to the Reduction of Sexual Reoffending*, eds. S. Hanvey, T. Philpot, and C. Wilson (London: Jessica Kingsley, 2011), 58–71.

88. S. Hanvey, T. Philpot, and C. Wilson, eds., *A Community-Based Approach to the Reduction of Sexual Reoffending* (London: Jessica Kingsley, 2011).

89. A.J. Harris and R. Cudmore, "Community Experience with Public Sex Offender Registries in the United States: A National Survey," *Criminal Justice Policy Review*, advance online publication, January 27, 2016. 1–22.; J. Vess, A. Day, M. Powell, and J. Graffam, "International Sex Offender Registration Laws: Research and Evaluation Issues based on a Review of Current

Scientific Literature," *Police Practice and Research 15*, no. 4 (2014), 322–35.

90. A. Bain, "Please Recycle: Continuities in Punishment," *International Journal of Law, Crime, and Justice 39*, no. 2 (2011), 121–35; Y.N. Brannon, J.S. Levenson, T. Fortney, and J.N. Baker, "Attitudes About Community Notification: A Comparison of Sexual Offenders and the Non-Offending Public," *Sexual Abuse: A Journal of Research and Treatment 19*, no. 4 (2007), 369–79; G. Duwe and W. Donnay, "Impact of Megan's Law on Sex Offender Recidivism: The Minnesota Experience." *Criminology 46*, no. 2 (2008), 411–46; J.J. Prescott and J.E. Rockoff, "Do Sex Offender Registration and Notification Laws Affect Criminal Behavior?" *Journal of Law and Economics 54*, no. 1 (2011), 161–206.

PART V

SPECIAL POPULATIONS IN CORRECTIONS

Systems of corrections have a responsibility to supervise and assist a diverse population of offenders. The next three chapters focus on three special populations: women (Chapter 12), Indigenous people (Chapter 13), and youth (Chapter 14).

Correctional policy for women offenders has been driven by critical events as well as by a recognition that women's needs—and their pathways to crime—are different than for men. Indigenous persons are over-represented in the criminal justice and corrections systems. In part, this reflects the legacy of colonization and the destruction of Indigenous cultures, communities, and families. A number of specialized facilities, programs, and services have been developed in an effort to meet the unique needs of Indigenous offenders; many of these utilize Indigenous traditions and spirituality. For young offenders, there is a separate system of justice and corrections that strongly emphasizes alternatives to incarceration, including various community-based initiatives. Many of these initiatives are based on restorative justice principles.

CHAPTER 12

WOMEN OFFENDERS

CHAPTER OBJECTIVES

- Describe the profile of women offenders in corrections.
- Discuss the evolution of correctional policies for women offenders.
- Note the importance of the *Creating Choices* report and the *Arbour Report* for women's corrections.
- Discuss the dynamics of doing time in women's correctional institutions.
- Describe the pains of imprisonment for women offenders.
- Discuss the death of Ashley Smith and its implications for women's corrections.
- Discuss the issue of cross-gender staffing in women's prisons.
- Describe correctional programming for women offenders.
- Describe the challenges women offenders encounter upon release from custody.

Women offenders present unique challenges for systems of corrections. The pathways to crime for women offenders are in many ways distinct from those for male offenders, and as a result, gender-specific programs and interventions have had to be developed. A review of the correctional response to women points to instances when their human rights, including Canada's obligations under international law, have been violated.[1] Corrections File 12.1 sets out some of the general attributes of women offenders and highlights how marginalized women offenders are in Canadian society, with their extensive histories of abuse, trauma, substance abuse, socio-economic disadvantage, and mental health challenges. As many have noted, Indigenous women are the fastest-growing federal prison population across Canada.[2]

CORRECTIONS FILE 12.1

A Profile of Women Offenders in Corrections

- Women offenders account for a higher proportion of admissions to community corrections (19 percent) than institutional corrections (13 percent).
- Women offenders represent about 7 percent of offenders admitted to federal custody, 13 percent of admissions to provincial/territorial remand, and 11 percent of admissions to sentenced custody in provinces/territories.
- The number of women admitted to federal custody has increased approximately 33 percent in the past decade (at the end of fiscal year 2014–15, there were 676 women offenders in Correctional Service Canada facilities), and the number of Indigenous women admitted to federal correctional facilities has doubled during that time. Indigenous women now comprise more than one in three (36 percent) of the in-custody population of federally sentenced women.
- More and more women are being admitted to custody for violent crimes. In 2013–14, approximately 74 percent of Indigenous women were serving a sentence for a violent offence, compared to 47 percent for non-Indigenous women.
- Federally sentenced First Nations women are more likely to be serving indeterminate sentences and to be serving time for committing a violent offence than federally sentenced Métis women. This finding highlights the importance of recognizing distinct risk/needs profiles amongst the population of Indigenous women offenders.
- One in ten women are gang-affiliated, compared to one in six for male offenders.
- One in four federal women inmates have been incarcerated on drug-related charges, and HIV and HCV infection is generally higher among women inmates (e.g., HCV: 19 percent of federally sentenced women versus 1 percent of the general Canadian population).
- Women offenders generally have greater health and mental health needs and are more likely to have experienced sexual or physical victimization prior to incarceration.
- Women offenders' histories of trauma and abuse have been consistently correlated with their substance abuse and criminal behaviour.
- More than half of federally sentenced women have an identified mental health need upon admission, which is nearly double the number of men. Federally sentenced women are also more likely to be prescribed psychotropic medication than male offenders.
- Approximately four in five women offenders have a substance use problem.
- The number of federal women offenders over the age of 50 has increased over the past decade; this population accounts for 15 percent of federally sentenced women. Compared to younger women, these offenders have lower overall

(continued)

risk/needs and are less likely to have substance abuse issues, but are more likely to have personal/emotional issues.

- Women represent a small proportion (3.5 percent) of offenders serving a life/indeterminate sentence in Canada. In 2014–15, only four women had a dangerous offender designation.
- Over the past decade, federally sentenced women are more likely than federally sentenced men to be granted both day and full parole.
- Indigenous women tend to be younger (i.e., median age is 29, versus 32 for non-Indigenous women), have lower levels of education, and have higher criminogenic risk/needs profiles than non-Indigenous women.
- Federally sentenced Indigenous women continue to be over-represented in maximum-security (42 percent) and segregation placements (50 percent) while under-represented in minimum security (26 percent).

Sources: Canadian HIV/AIDS Legal Network, *Women in Prison, HIV, and Hepatitis C* (Toronto: Author, 2012), http://www.aidslaw.ca/publications/interfaces/downloadFile.php?ref=2008; D. Calverley, "Adult Correctional Services in Canada, 2008–2009," *Juristat* 30, no. 3, Catalogue no. 85-002-X (Ottawa: Statistics Canada, 2010), http://www.statcan.gc.ca/pub/85-002-x/2010003/article/11353-eng.htm; D.D. DeHart, "Pathways to Prison: Impact of Victimization in the Lives of Incarcerated Women," *Violence Against Women 14*, no. 12 (2008), 1362–81; L. Greiner and K. Allenby, *A Descriptive Profile of Older Women Offenders* (Ottawa: Correctional Service Canada, 2010), http://www.csc-scc.gc.ca/text/rsrch/; Public Safety Canada, *2015 Corrections and Conditional Release Statistical Overview* (Ottawa: Author, 2015), https://www.public-safety.gc.ca/cnt/rsrcs/pblctns/ccrso-2015/index-en.aspx; Julie Reitano, "Adult correctional statistics in Canada, 2015/2016," *Juristat* 37, no. 1, Catalogue no. 85-002-X (Ottawa: Canadian Centre for Justice Statistics, 2017), p. 15, http://www.statcan.gc.ca/pub/85-002-x/2017001/article/14700-eng.pdf; P. Saxena, N.P. Messina, and C.E. Grella, "Who Benefits from Gender-responsive Treatment? Accounting for Abuse History on Longitudinal Outcomes for Women in Prison," *Criminal Justice and Behavior 41* no. 4 (2014), 417–32. J. Beaudette, M. Cheverie, and R. Gobeil, "Aboriginal women: Profile and changing population," Correctional Service Canada, Research at a glance R-341, October 2014, http://www.csc-scc.gc.ca/research/005008-r341-eng.shtml; L.A. Stewart, J. Sapers, A. Nolan, and J. Power, "Self-Reported Health Status of Newly Admitted Federally Sentenced Men Offenders," Correctional Service Canada, Research at a glance R-332, October 2014, http://www.csc-scc.gc.ca/research/005008-r332-eng.shtml; Office of the Correctional Investigator, *Annual Report, 2015–2016* (Ottawa: Author, 2016), p. 10, http://www.oci-bec.gc.ca/cnt/rpt/pdf/annrpt/annrpt20152016-eng.pdf; S.F. MacDonald, R. Gobeil, S.M. Biro, M.B. Ritchie, and J. Curno, "Women Offenders, Substance Use, and Behaviour," Correctional Service Canada, Research at a glance R-358, January 2015, http://www.csc-scc.gc.ca/research/005008-r358-eng.shtml.

THE EVOLUTION OF CORRECTIONS POLICY FOR WOMEN OFFENDERS

Little attention has been paid to the specific issues facing women offenders on probation or to their participation in restorative justice programs and in problem-solving courts (see Chapter 5). Instead, discussions of women's corrections have tended to focus on institutions where they are incarcerated. The defining events in women's corrections have all occurred in federal correctional facilities. Note also that most of the materials on women's corrections are on federally sentenced women (FSW) although an increasing amount of research is being conducted on women in provincial/territorial corrections systems, particularly with respect to their physical and mental health care needs.

Two reports have had an especially significant impact on corrections policy for FSW. The first was **Creating Choices**, produced in 1990 by the Task Force on Federally Sentenced Women. This inquiry examined correctional policies and programs for federal women offenders. Among its recommendations were that a separate system of corrections be created for women that provided women-centred programming; that the Kingston Prison for Women be closed (which it was, in 2000); that five small regional facilities be built for women, including a healing lodge for Indigenous women; and that Correctional Service Canada (CSC) appoint a deputy commissioner for women.[3] The new women-centred correctional philosophy proposed in *Creating Choices* that was accepted by the federal government emphasized five key principles for the treatment of FSW: empowerment, meaningful and responsible choices, respect and dignity, a supportive environment, and shared responsibilities.[4]

The second influential report was produced by Madame Justice Louise Arbour.[5] It was precipitated by an incident in 1994 at the now-closed Kingston Prison for Women, discussed below.

> **Creating Choices**
> The report of the Task Force on Federally Sentenced Women that had a significant impact on the structure and operation of women's corrections.

The Incident at the Kingston Prison for Women (P4W): A Watershed Event in Women's Corrections

On April 22, 1994, a brief but violent physical confrontation took place between six inmates and several correctional officers (COs) at the Kingston Prison for Women (which has since been closed). As a result of the incident, the women were placed in segregation and criminally charged (five of the six inmates later pleaded guilty). Immediately after the incident, a high level of tension developed in the institution, compounded by the presence of a large number of overworked, overstressed, and relatively inexperienced correctional staff and COs. A lack of leadership from the prison's warden contributed to the events that unfolded over the next several days.

Two days later, on April 24, three other inmates who were housed in the segregation unit caused further disruption by slashing, taking a hostage, and attempting suicide. On April 26, COs from the institution demonstrated outside its walls, demanding that the inmates involved in the clash on April 22 be transferred to a higher-security institution.

On the evening of that same day, the warden sent an all-male institutional emergency response team (IERT) to extract eight inmates in the segregation unit from their cells and strip-search them. Six of the eight had been involved in the initial confrontation on April 22. The IERT did not complete the cell extractions until early the following morning, at which time the eight women were left in empty cells in the segregation unit. The women had been stripped (in the presence of male members of the IERT), dressed in paper gowns, and placed in restraints and leg irons. All of the cell extractions and strip searches were recorded on videotape as per routine procedure. The following evening, seven of the eight inmates were subjected to body cavity searches. Six of the women involved in the original April 22 incident then were placed in segregation for many months.

Correctional Service Canada investigated the incidents, but the report it issued left out many details. In February 1995, the report of the Office of the Correctional Investigator (OCI) was tabled in the House of Commons. This report criticized the CSC's actions, the correctional staff, and the IERT. Pressure on the federal government to take action increased when portions of the videotape, showing the cell extractions and strip searches by the IERT, were shown on national television. An independent judicial inquiry was demanded, and one was appointed in April 1995. It was headed by the Honourable Louise Arbour, a highly respected member of the Québec judiciary.

The ***Arbour Report*** was extremely critical of the actions taken by correctional staff, the IERT personnel, and the warden, stating that nearly all of the CSC's behaviour during this incident contradicted the five principles the government accepted from the *Creating Choices* report.[6] The same report sharply criticized the response of senior CSC officials. In the end, the commissioner of corrections resigned.

The inquiry's report documented numerous violations of policy, the rule of law, and institutional regulations. For example, it criticized the use of segregation, the use of force by the IERT, and the manner in which the women had been strip-searched and subjected to body-cavity searches. The same report raised serious concerns regarding whether, without intervention and monitoring, the CSC was capable of implementing the necessary reforms to ensure adherence to justice and the rule of law.

The *Arbour Report* made 14 key recommendations relating to the following: cross-gender staffing in correctional institutions for women; the use of force and of IERTs; the operations of segregation units; the needs of Indigenous women in correctional institutions; ways of ensuring accountability and adherence to the rule of law by correctional personnel; and procedures for handling inmate complaints and grievances.

The *Arbour Report* had a significant impact on the CSC's operations and on the development of women's corrections.[7] A Deputy Commissioner for Women was appointed in 1996; a use-of-force policy was developed that stipulated that all-male IERT teams were never to be used as a first response in women's correctional institutions; and it is now forbidden for male staff to be present when women inmates are being strip-searched. The report also accelerated the closing of the Prison for Women in the year 2000 and the opening of smaller, regional facilities for federal women offenders.[8]

Arbour Report
The report of an inquiry into events at the Kingston Prison for Women in April 1994, which documented violations of policy, the rule of law, and institutional regulations, and had a significant impact on the development of women's corrections.

THE CURRENT STATE OF CORRECTIONS POLICY AND PRACTICE FOR WOMEN OFFENDERS

Despite these reforms, a number of scholars have argued that CSC has failed to develop a correctional practice for women that is empowering and rehabilitative.[9] Although senior corrections officials did transform many of the recommendations from the *Creating Choices* (1990) and Arbour (1996) reports into policy, it has been argued that the experience of women offenders in institutions has remained largely unchanged and that the focus of the system is on punishment and control.[10]

The closing of the Kingston Prison for Women and the opening of smaller regional facilities across the country was heralded as a new era in women's corrections. However, in the view of feminist scholars and others, systems of corrections continue to pursue a punitive penology based on "an oppressive hierarchical structure of gender equality" in which women who resist traditional roles are viewed as a threat to male patriarchy as embodied by corrections.[11] Specifically, attention is called to how traditional views of femininity affect correctional policy and practice. Within this perspective, women offenders who commit crime ("misbehave") are severely punished. There have also been feminist criticisms of community-based programs and services, as well as calls for practices that are gender-responsive.[12]

Others dispute this interpretation, noting that the number of women committing violent offences has increased, as has the number of women who are gang-affiliated. These observers also point to the development of women-specific assessment instruments and of treatment programs that have been designed to empower women offenders.

ALTERNATIVES TO CONFINEMENT

Women offenders participate in a variety of specialized courts that are intended to divert them from the traditional criminal justice process (see Chapter 5). Women offenders generally do better on probation than their male counterparts and have lower rates of reoffending. There is some evidence that probation officers view women offenders as more challenging to supervise than male offenders.[13] These challenges often include addressing the needs of the children of women probationers, many of whom are single parents. This requires gender-specific programs and services.

DOING TIME: INSIDE WOMEN'S CORRECTIONAL FACILITIES

Women's federal institutions in Canada are multilevel, providing different levels of accommodation and supervision for FSW. Minimum and medium FSW live in housing units where the women have various responsibilities, such as cooking and cleaning. CSC recognizes the complex profiles—cognitive deficits and/or mental health issues—amongst FSW, so they operate structured living environments (SLEs) for minimum- and medium-security women prisoners who are managed by specially trained correctional staff.[14] In contrast, but like the security measures and intervention modalities that exist in men's maximum-security facilities, maximum-security FSW are housed in secure units (SUs). Note as well that Okimaw Ohci Healing Lodge (see Chapter 13 for an in-depth discussion of healing lodges) for women houses minimum- and medium-security prisoners.

The CSC recently added 114 cells for FSW by building new minimum-security units (MSUs) outside of the perimeter fencing at four of the five regional facilities for women. These MSUs were designed to facilitate participation in the mother–child program—discussed below—by increasing the bed space available for program participants.

The OCI has acknowledged that participation in the program has increased; however, the OCI identified other areas of concern with the new units and made the following recommendations: (1) more timely decision making for placement in the mother–child program; (2) increased access to the community through opportunities for temporary absences, work releases, and employment and vocational skills training, in addition to the creation of partnerships with the community to provide programming and activities for the women; and (3) appropriate access to one's case management team.[15]

Historically, scholars have given little attention to the dynamics of life inside women's correctional institutions. The research literature on inmate social systems has focused primarily on men's institutions. There are unique features of life inside women's institutions that have significant implications for the women, correctional staff, and treatment programs. These include the patterns of interaction among the women.

It appears that the pains of imprisonment may be much more severe for women offenders than for their male counterparts. This is for a number of reasons, including that many FSW are housed in facilities that are far from home, and confinement can have a strong impact on women who have experienced physical and emotional abuse as children and/or adults. Further, many are mothers who have been separated from their children. Generally speaking, research has shown that separation from one's children and families is one of the single greatest pains of imprisonment for women.[16] This is illustrated in Corrections Perspective 12.1 which presents stanzas taken from a poem written by FSW housed in the Grand Valley Institution for Women in Ontario. For additional insightful, first-person accounts of women offenders in prison, see Lamb.[17]

Women offenders adapt to life inside correctional institutions differently than men. Generally speaking, women inmates are far less likely than men to verbally and/or physically assault correctional staff, regardless of their criminal history, mental health, and addiction issues.[18] This may change with the influx of increasing numbers of women offenders convicted of violent crimes and women who are gang-affiliated.

Research has also identified a number of different types of adjustment to confinement: Some women adjust poorly to the prison regimen and remain

CORRECTIONS PERSPECTIVE 12.1

A Woman Offender's Perspective on Imprisonment

They need to humanize

Not mechanize

The more jails that we build

The more criminals we will create

The badder criminals we will create

When you're in here, you get a little institutionalized

You know, with the rules

You know everything you say is going to be put in the report

There's a lot of things I'm not used to doing anymore

Because I've been incarcerated for a long time

I'm 6 and ½ hours away from home

This is a big separation

Especially with my children

The hardest thing to maintain

Is hope

I prefer to stay here

I just feel more secure

I don't know what I'm stepping in to

I see people walking out of this place crying

Terrified

Source: Copyright © 2012 From F. Yuen, S. Arai, and D. Fortune, "Community (Dis)connection through Leisure for Women in Prison," *Leisure Sciences 34*, no. 4 (2012), 281–97. Reproduced by permission of Taylor & Francis, LLC, http://www.tandfonline.com.

entrenched in criminal thinking patterns; others are state-raised offenders who adhere to and enforce the traditional convict code; and still others access programs and resources in an effort to make significant changes in their attitudes and behaviour.[19]

The argot roles inside a correctional facility for men include "right guys," "snitches," and "square Johns" (see Chapter 8). Inside the women's prison, the argot roles include "cherries," "butches," and "tricks."[20] American researchers have also found pseudo-families are common amongst incarcerated women, and it is the relationships that women form with others that is vital to their survival in prison.[21]

These roles are not readily apparent in Canadian women's prisons, though the absence of research precludes any definitive conclusions about the structure of the social system among women inmates. Women inmates may refer to having a "street mother" or "street sister"—that is, women with whom they have had relationships in the community, often associated with gang or criminal activity (warden, federal women's prison, personal communication with C.T. Griffiths). Other differences in the dynamics inside men's and women's institutions are set out in Corrections File 12.2.

CORRECTIONS FILE 12.2

A Comparison of the Dynamics inside Men's and Women's Correctional Institutions

	Men's Institutions	**Women's Institutions**
Security	More static, particularly in maximum security	More dynamic interaction in maximum security between staff and inmates
Drugs	Generally imported from the outside	Often in-institution prescription drugs
Family visiting	Frequent; extensive use of family visitation unit; women "stand by their man"	Infrequent; men don't "stand by their women"; family visit units rarely used
Inmate interaction	Conflicts often short-lived; men internalize emotions	Conflicts endure; "assault with tongue"; emotional management a key issue
Personal relationships	Hidden; covert	Often overt

Source: Warden, federal women's prison, personal communication with C.T. Griffiths.

Violence inside Women's Institutions

The closing of the Kingston Prison for Women and the opening of smaller regional facilities across the country was heralded as a new era in women's corrections. In recent years, however, there appears to have been an increase in violence among women inmate populations. Overcrowding is often a factor in violence. During 2009–10, there was a 50 percent increase in disciplinary incidents, fights between inmates, assaults on COs, and other incidents in federal women's prisons.[22]

As in men's facilities, the social system in women's prisons appears to be changing, due in part to an increasing number of women being admitted to custody for crimes of violence. More women are self-identifying as gang-affiliated. Ten percent of women admitted to federal correctional facilities have gang ties, an increase of 85 percent between 1997 and 2012,[23] and this may lead to violence between inmates, placing correctional staff at more risk and compromising treatment efforts.

Recent American research investigating predictors of violent and non-violent victimization in women's prisons found two important predictors of victimization that mirror the findings from earlier studies. Younger women inmates are more likely to be victimized than older inmates, and women who enter prison with higher levels of education are more likely to be victimized than those who enter prison with lower levels of education.[24] The extent to which these findings apply to Canadian women's prisons is not known.

When first constructed, the regional facilities for federal women did not include maximum-security units. That changed after a series of critical incidents, including the death of Denise Fayant (see Corrections File 12.3). This incident occurred in 1996 at the then–recently opened Edmonton Institution for Women (one of the small regional facilities built for federal women offenders). At the time, minimum-, medium-, and maximum-security inmates were mixed into one population.

As discussed in Chapter 6, correctional authorities can subject offenders to segregation status, be it disciplinary segregation or administrative segregation, for a variety of reasons (e.g., for a serious disciplinary offence). Corrections File 12.4 describes the CSC's use of segregation amongst FSW over a 10-year period.

A Pain of Imprisonment: Women Inmates and Their Children

> *I have pictures of my kids under my pillow, but I don't take them out, they make me cry.*[25]

Women inmates are likely to be the sole custodial parent of their children.[26] When they are incarcerated, their children are usually cared for by relatives, most commonly grandparents. When no surrogate caretaker is available, the children may be taken in by provincial/territorial child welfare authorities and

CORRECTIONS FILE 12.3

The Murder of Denise Fayant

Thirty hours after arriving at the Edmonton Institution for Women, 21-year-old Denise Fayant was strangled by her former lover with a bathrobe sash. She died two days later in hospital. An investigation into the death, which was originally ruled a suicide, found that she had been slain by two inmates, one of whom had been her former lover and against whom she was scheduled to testify. A subsequent inquiry conducted by an Alberta Provincial Court judge found that Fayant had repeatedly told corrections officials that she would fear for her safety if they transferred her to the newly opened institution. Thirty hours after arrival, she was dead. Two inmates were later convicted and sentenced to additional federal time for the death. The investigating judge concluded that Fayant's death was a result of "callous and cavalier" actions on the part of CSC and that she was a "victim of a process intent upon implementing an untested concept to manage federally sentenced women inmates. She was the test. The process failed tragically and inhumanely. Her death was avoidable."[a] Prison officials insisted that they had been assured by inmates in the prison that no harm would come to Fayant.

Fayant's death was only one of a number of critical incidents that occurred in the Edmonton Prison for Women within four months of its opening. Others included inmate-on-inmate assaults, assaults on a nurse and a physician, a completed suicide, and two attempted suicides.

---

[a] P. Cowan and D. Sheremata, "Death in Experimental Prison Unit—'She Was Helpless,'" *Edmonton Sun*, February 9, 2000.

placed in foster care and sometimes, separated. If the period of incarceration is long and the children are young, they may be candidates for adoption. Because of these factors, the incarceration of a mother typically results in greater disruption in the lives of children than is the case if a father is incarcerated. However, parental incarceration in general has been found to affect children into their late young adulthood years, as researchers have found that those with a history of parental incarceration are more likely to engage in criminal behaviour themselves, use marijuana and alcohol heavily, experience depression, and have lower levels of educational achievement and employment earnings.[27]

Inmate mothers have varying levels of contact with their children. That contact can include day visits, overnight family visits, on-site part-time residency (i.e., extended visits on weekends and/or holidays), and live-in programs that allow the inmate-mother to have her child stay in the institution. Private family visits are generally available only in federal facilities. These visits, which allow the spouse and family members to spend up to 72 hours in a trailer unit or small house on the prison grounds, provide the opportunity for more normal parent–child interaction than is possible on a four-hour day visit.

Little research has explored the benefits of private family visits from the perspective of women prisoners, particularly in the Canadian context. However,

---

CORRECTIONS FILE 12.4

CSC and the Use of Segregation amongst Federally Sentenced Women from April 2002 to March 2012

Research examining the differences between 844 women who had been segregated and 1,858 who had not been segregated over a 10-year period leading up to March 2012 revealed the following:

- Type of segregation: involuntary (89 percent), voluntary (8 percent), and disciplinary (3 percent)
- Average length of stay: less than 10 days
- Women subject to segregation were more likely to be of higher security status, have higher static risk and dynamic risk, and be involved in institutional misconduct.
- Women subject to segregation were less likely to successfully complete programming, have high reintegration potential or motivation to engage in programming, be granted conditional release, and succeed on conditional release.

Of additional significance is that Indigenous women were more likely than their non-Indigenous counterparts to be placed in involuntary segregation and for a longer period.

Source: J. Thompson and S. Rubenfeld, "Profile of Women in Segregation," Correctional Service Canada, Research at a glance R-320, December 2013, http://www.csc-scc.gc.ca/research/005008-r320-eng.shtml.

---

women prisoners ($N = 8$) in Israel described the benefits of private family visits as minimizing the pains of imprisonment and strengthening their relationships with their partners.[28]

Mother–Child Programs

Mother–child programs generally allow infants to reside with their mothers in open living units. Despite support for mother–child programs by CSC and various provincial/territorial correctional systems, implementation has been slow and uneven across the country. The CSC fully implemented the program in 2001; children up to their fifth birthday are eligible for full-time residency, and for part-time residency until their seventh birthday.[29] Generally, participation rates have been low; as of January 2017, the CSC reported that only 10 federally sentenced women were participating in the CSC's mother–child program.[30]

Note that the new MSUs, as described above, were designed to promote participation in this program, so theoretically, participation rates should increase in the years ahead.

The government of British Columbia closed the mother–child program that was operating at the Alouette Correctional Centre for Women (ACCW) in 2008, arguing that children were not within the mandate of the organization and that the organization had concerns about the babies' safety. Interestingly, no babies had been harmed throughout the history of the program (1973–2008). In 2013, the B.C. Supreme Court ruled that this decision was unconstitutional, violating the mothers' Charter rights, and recognized that mothers have the right to care for their newborn children during the critical bonding period. While the program was reinstated in spring 2014, the first baby did not accompany its mother at ACCW until December 2015.[31] Other provinces/territories, such as Ontario, do not provide mother–child programming to its prisoners.

An unpublished study investigating the community–prison collaboration between B.C. Corrections, the Ministry of Children and Family Development (MCFD), and B.C. Women's Hospital's Fir Square Combined Care Unit that allowed mothers to have their children with them while incarcerated in a provincial correctional centre indicated that 13 babies were born to incarcerated mothers between 2005 and 2007. Only nine babies returned to the prison to stay with their mothers until their release. The mothers identified a variety of positive aspects of participating in the program, such as being able to breastfeed their babies and bond with their babies, the latter of which they viewed as a turning point in their lives. Twelve months later, seven babies were still living with their mothers, one was living with its father, one was in the care of MCFD, and a few years later, only two mothers had returned to prison.[32]

Psychological Health: Self-Injurious Behaviour (SIB) and Suicide

Recall from Chapter 8 that many inmates are at risk of engaging in self-injurious behaviour (SIB), or self-harm, as a means of coping with confinement. These behaviours may include cutting, burning, ligature use, hitting oneself, hair pulling, bone breaking, reopening of wounds, and head banging.[33] Self-harm is distinct from suicide and is most appropriately viewed as a coping mechanism that allows one to exert personal control during a time when experiencing stress.[34] This is particularly true for women offenders, who appear, as a group, to be at high risk.

A 2013 review of SIB amongst FSW conducted by the OCI revealed that chronic self-harmers (37 of the 264 women self-harmers) accounted for 35 percent of all SIB cases and Indigenous women offenders accounted for 45 percent of all cases of self-harm.[35]

Qualitative research conducted with American prisoners who engaged in repetitive self-harm ($N = 20$ [17 men; 3 women]) revealed that some prisoners were life-course persistent self-harmers who started the behaviour during childhood as a means of coping with negative childhood experiences (e.g., trauma, sexual and/or physical abuse, and/or abandonment). This means that prior to incarceration, their SIB was a fixed behaviour in their lives. However, the results also suggest that moving prisoners who engage in SIB to more restrictive environments in the prison can make the behaviours worse.[36] This finding indicates that the use of administrative segregation, which is a practice the OCI has criticized the CSC for using in response to prisoners who engage SIB, may exacerbate self-harming behaviours.

In mid-2017, CSC modified its administrative segregation policies, including the prohibition of its use for "inmates actively engaging in self-injury which is deemed likely to result in serious bodily harm or at elevated or imminent risk for suicide" and "inmates with a serious mental illness with significant impairment."[37] See the case of Ashley Smith, presented below, for an exploration of the issues around SIB and the use of administrative segregation to "manage" this behaviour.

Interviews with a sample ($N = 54$) of Canadian FSW revealed that the most common reasons for this behaviour were to deal with negative emotions and as a cry for help to draw attention to their issues.[38] In the words of an inmate in the Edmonton Institution for Women, "I sliced my arms up because my brother passed away and I didn't know what to do."[39] Increasing attention is being given to identifying women offenders who are at risk of SIB due to concern for the well-being of the offenders, correctional staff, and other inmates, and because of the operational challenges these offenders create.

The quote below, as shared by a prisoner, illustrates the seriousness and speed with which those who engage in persistent SIB can harm themselves in prison:

I did no major cutting for two months. It was the longest I ever went for and then I messed up. I cut open my intestines, took a razor and did this [respondent shows deep and significant scarring from the chest down to below the belly button]. I cut open my stomach and took out my intestines. I cut about six feet of intestines out. I grabbed my bowels and cut my bowels in half. I cut a quarter of my stomach out. I then took two pencils and one pen and sharpened them and stabbed my stomach. I swallowed my toothbrush and then I took light bulbs and grinded them up into a fine glass and put the glass in my mouth and drank it with water. I did all that in about 10 minutes.[40]

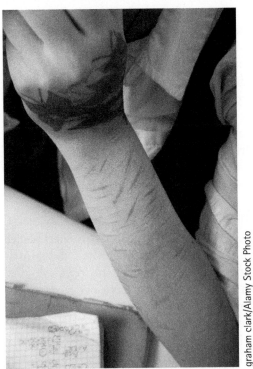

The arm of an incarcerated federally sentenced woman.

graham clark/Alamy Stock Photo

The risk of suicide, which is different from SIB, as those who engage in SIB engage in "the deliberate destruction or alteration of body tissue without conscious suicidal intent," may also be higher for women who are placed in segregation and for those who have spent lengthy periods in relative isolation from the general population.[41] The Depression Hopelessness and Suicide Screening Form, for example, is used to screen for the presence of depression and suicide risk.[42]

The Death of Ashley Smith

On October 19, 2007, 19-year-old Ashley Smith was found unconscious in her segregation cell at the Grand Valley Institution for Women. She died later that day. The official cause of death was self-initiated asphyxiation (suicide). However, a CSC report, made known in 2010, concluded that her death was accidental and the result of a desperate attempt for attention and interaction after she had been confined to isolation for many months.[43] In 2013, the Coroner's Inquest into her death deemed her death a homicide by ligature strangulation and positional asphyxia. At the time of her death, Ms. Smith was serving a sentence of six years and one month for a variety of weapons and assault offences she incurred after entering the system.

As a young offender, Ms. Smith was initially sent to the New Brunswick Youth Centre. Her initial offences were minor and included throwing crab apples at a letter carrier. During her stay in that facility, before being transferred to the Saint John Regional Correctional Centre, she accumulated more than 800 incident reports, more than 500 institutional charges, and 168 self-harm incidents.

Ms. Smith was transferred to a federal penitentiary at age 18 and during her 11½ month stay in CSC care, she was transferred 17 times between three federal correctional facilities, two treatment facilities, two external hospitals, and a provincial facility. CSC officials were not transferring Ms. Smith to address her mental health needs; rather, they transferred Ms. Smith due to cell availability and staff fatigue. Her administrative segregation status was "lifted" with each move, meaning mandatory reviews of her segregation were not completed. She was in administrative segregation during her entire confinement in the federal system. During that time, Ms. Smith engaged in numerous acts of self-injurious behaviour, resulting in many security incidents; some of these incidents involved her placement in a four-point restraint system and/or being subject to forced medication (both practices that contravene CSC policy).

The final report of the OCI (2008) found that the CSC's actions violated the law and its own policy. Specifically, it found that Ms. Smith's mental health issues had not been addressed either in the youth facility or in the federal institutions in which she had been confined. There had been no psychological assessment. The OCI concluded that her death might have been prevented had she been provided with proper care.

Among the recommendations in the OCI's final report were that the CSC comply with the law and policy in its operations, that the CSC improve its response to medical emergencies, that the CSC review its segregation policy and practices, and that the CSC ensure the delivery of adequate health care, including mental health services.[44]

A report on Ms. Smith's confinement in youth facilities was completed by the New Brunswick Ombudsman and Child and Youth Advocate,[45] and the Union of Canadian Correctional Officers prepared a report on the incident as well, criticizing what it views as a "rush to judgment" to implicate the COs involved in the incident.[46]

An investigation of the incident by the Waterloo Regional Police resulted in three COs and a supervisor being charged with criminal negligence causing death. Police documents filed in court alleged that the guards and supervisor were responsible for the death of Ashley Smith in that they were negligent in failing to come to her aid when she was in distress in her cell. Three correctional officers were fired and four other COs were suspended without pay for 90 days. The acting warden and deputy warden were also fired. However, the acting warden challenged her termination and is said to have returned to the CSC's regional offices in 2010 as a senior project manager.[47] In 2008, an Ontario judge, on recommendation from Crown counsel, dismissed all charges of criminal negligence causing death against the three COs as it was shown they had been following the directions given by their superiors.

In 2011, the family of Ashley Smith settled an $11 million lawsuit against the CSC. For a timeline of Ashley Smith's involvement in the corrections system, related documents, and interviews, refer to the video links provided at the end of the chapter.

The initial Coroner's Inquest into Ashley Smith's death collapsed in 2011 due to legal wrangling and the resignation of the coroner. On December 19, 2013, after hearing from approximately 85 witnesses over 11 months, the coroner's jury deemed Ashley Smith's death as a homicide by ligature strangulation and positional asphyxia. The Ontario coroner's jury recognized that the CSC lacks the resources required to manage prisoners with complex mental health needs, particularly women, and made 104 recommendations to the CSC. These recommendations include mandatory mental health screening for women offenders within 72 hours of admission, diverting the highest needs mentally ill offenders to provincial treatment facilities that have the resources to offer specialized care in a therapeutic environment, and prohibiting indefinite or long-term segregation for women prisoners (for the full list of recommendations, see http://www.csc-scc.gc.ca/publications/005007-9009-eng.shtml).

The CSC's 2014 response to the Coroner's Inquest has been widely criticized due to the agency's failure to address individual jury recommendations, making "it difficult to know which recommendations are endorsed or supported versus those that have been rejected, ignored or supported only in part... [Furthermore, the response] fails to support core preventative, oversight and accountability recommendations issued by the jury."[48] The CSC's response has also been criticized for failing to include a comprehensive, proactive "reform-minded correctional agenda"[49] (see http://www.csc-scc.gc.ca/publications/005007-9011-eng.shtml for the CSC's response to the Coroner's Inquest).

In the years since Ms. Smith's death, the OCI has strongly recommended that the CSC revisit the recommendations made by the coroner's jury and encourages the CSC to commit to the following recommendations:

1. Commit to move toward a restraint-free environment in federal corrections for mentally ill offenders.
2. Appoint independent patient advocates and rights advisors at each of the Regional Treatment Centres.
3. Provide for 24/7 on-site nursing services at all maximum, medium and multi-level penitentiaries.
4. Give clear and direct line authority to the Deputy Commissioner for Women for all matters relating to the care and custody of federally sentenced women.
5. Promulgate policy and practices that are more responsive to the unique needs of younger offenders (age 25 and under).
6. Establish a 5-year internal audit plan on key concerns identified in the Jury's inquest recommendations regarding legal and policy compliance.[50]

Dire outcomes will persist until such recommendations are addressed. Terry Baker, a 30-year-old woman with a history of mental health problems, committed suicide in July 2016 using the same method as Ashley Smith and in the same segregation unit. And 22-year-old Camille Strickland-Murphy, a woman with a history of self-harm and suicide attempts, committed suicide in July 2015 at the same institution, just eight days following a failed attempt.[51]

Mental Health Issues

A theme discussed throughout the text is the prevalence of mental health issues among offender populations and how correctional services manage the challenges posed by this population, such as providing treatment. Twenty-two women who had served time in federal and provincial institutions in Canada were interviewed and discussed what they perceived as the over-prescription of psychotropic drugs (also noted by the OCI) for women in prison (see Figure 12.1). The women also discussed the lack of informed consent involved in the administration and use of psychotropic drugs, as the women felt they were limited in their ability to refuse treatment, as privileges or punishments could follow (e.g., time in segregation, not being released back on parole without taking the prescription). The researchers noted the problematic lack of "separation between the carceral system and psy treatment, [resulting in] therapeutic intervention problematically [remaining] based within the realm of, and thus linked to, punishment."[52] This echoes similar criticisms made by scholars that argue the CSC equates women's needs (e.g., substance abuse, mental health, education, etc.) with risk factors and that this conflation of needs with risks results in a security-oriented, disciplinary approach in their management of offenders.[53]

Figure 12.1

Women Federal Inmates on Psychotropic Medication

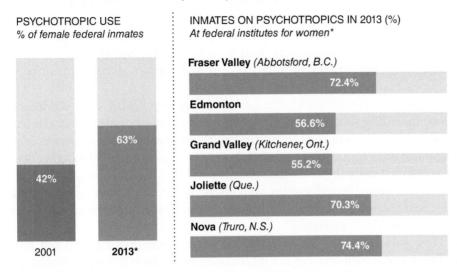

PSYCHOTROPIC USE
% of female federal inmates

2001: 42%
2013*: 63%

INMATES ON PSYCHOTROPICS IN 2013 (%)
*At federal institutes for women**

Fraser Valley *(Abbotsford, B.C.)* 72.4%
Edmonton 56.6%
Grand Valley *(Kitchener, Ont.)* 55.2%
Joliette *(Que.)* 70.3%
Nova *(Truro, N.S.)* 74.4%

* Not including 33 female inmates at Okimaw Ohci Healing Lodge in Maple Creek, Saskatchewan

Source: Figure from A. Miller, "Powerful psychotropic drug used in Canada's federal prisons," Global News, April 14, 2014. Retrieved from http://globalnews.ca/news/1271180/powerful-psychotropic-drug-used-in-canadas-federal-prisons/. Reprinted by permission of the Office of the Correctional Investigator.

The CSC has been severely criticized for its response to FSWs with mental health issues. An in-depth study of the topic found the following: (1) The CSC's mental health strategy is focused on assessment rather than treatment; (2) FSWs with mental health problems are treated as risks; (3) the CSC does not consider the women's history of abuse; and (4) women with mental health problems are often overclassified, which results in their confinement in secure environments that limit their access to programs and services.[54] In addition, many FSWs with mental health issues are moved frequently between facilities, which undermines the continuity of what little treatment is available. This occurred in the case of Ashley Smith.

The practices outlined in the sections above are viewed as violations of international law—for example, as violations of the right to health, the right not to be discriminated against, the right not to be deprived of liberty and security, and the right not to suffer cruel, inhuman, and degrading treatment.[55] Of particular concern is the absence of judicial oversight of management policies and decisions with respect to FSWs with mental health problems.

Physical Health

In addition to mental health concerns, incarcerated women also have higher HCV rates and HIV rates than women in the general population in Canada and incarcerated men. Additionally, women have unique gender-specific health care needs, such as reproductive care and gynecological care that often require immediate and ongoing attention.[56] Incarcerated women have the right to request access to different types of health care providers to address their physical health issues. However, research suggests women in provincial and territorial facilities often struggle to obtain these services due to inadequate funding, long wait lists to see health care providers because of rising prison populations, and an absence of continuity of care.[57]

There are numerous challenges in delivering health care services in prisons, including security concerns, conditions of confinement that can lead to disease transmission (e.g., overcrowding), unsafe practices in prison (e.g., intravenous drug use, tattooing), staff shortages, and frequently changing populations (particularly in provincial facilities).[58] The OCI and the John Howard Society also note the difficulties systems of corrections have in recruiting, hiring, and retaining qualified health care providers, which impedes prisoner access to health care services.[59]

The John Howard Society (JHS) observed that prisoners do not have equal access to health services in Ontario facilities, which violates national and international legislation. The JHS noted "the cyclical movement of staff, visitors, and incarcerated populations continuously entering and exiting correctional institutions has serious implications for public health," considering, for example, communicable disease transmission to family members and the community at large.[60]

The lack of access to medical care for women prisoners also has consequences for their success in the community. Researchers who examined the health care needs of women provincial prisoners in British Columbia, and followed 400 of them for up to 18 months post-release, said their data suggest that "incarcerated women's recidivism rates are directly related to their unmet health and social needs."[61] An investigation into the health of prisoners in Ontario's provincial prison system included the recommendation that women offenders be provided with access to contraceptive services while incarcerated and upon release.[62]

Another challenge for women entering provincial jails is that they might be suffering health issues due to drug withdrawal. A 21-year-old Saskatchewan inmate, Breanna Kannick, died at Regina's White Birch Female Remand Unit in August 2015 after experiencing medical distress. Her mother asserts that Breanna received inadequate medical care and should have been under medical watch due to experiencing withdrawal from heroin and morphine. A woman housed with Breanna has supposedly said that Breanna was sweating and vomiting and the guards—those whose responsibility it is to decide whether an inmate requires medical assistance—called her "pukey" saying, "Oh, you better watch out, you're gonna trip on your puke."[63] At the time of writing (late-2017), the coroner's inquiry into her death has yet to happen, so many questions remain unanswered.

Evaluation of Services for Women Offenders

In 2015, West Coast Women's Legal Education and Action Fund (LEAF) conducted a review of British Columbia's compliance with the Convention on the Elimination of All Forms of Discrimination Against Women (CEDAW), international human rights legislation that enshrines protections for women and girls, and gave the province poor or failing grades in many criminal justice–related categories. For example, the province received a D- for failing to ensure that women have access to justice, and an F in the category labelled "Women and Girls in Prison" for failing to "take steps to eliminate the increasing over-representation of Indigenous women in provincial jails or uphold many of the rights of prisoners."[64]

Various examples of successful collaborations that address the health care needs of women prisoners highlight the need to expand partnerships between corrections agencies and community health organizations. In 2010, the B.C. Cancer Agency's Screening Mammography Program screened 73 incarcerated women at a provincial correctional centre, 50 of whom had never been screened before. The B.C. Cancer Agency now visits provincial and federal correctional institutions annually. Oak Tree Clinic, a provincial referral centre, started its program in November 2008 to provide provincially incarcerated women with HIV/AIDS access to HIV care onsite, including support as they near release with hopes they can facilitate continuity of care into the community. (See also Corrections File 12.5 for discussion of another health care treatment program.)

CORRECTIONS FILE 12.5

CSC's Methadone Maintenance Treatment Program

As discussed in Chapter 6, as part of its approach to safely reintegrating offenders into Canadian society, Correctional Service Canada operates a Methadone Maintenance Treatment Program (MMTP) for federal offenders with opioid dependence. The CSC investigated the demographic characteristics and the risk/need factors of women MMTP participants ($N = 209$) who participated in the program between January 2003 and December 2008 in comparison to the remaining women prisoner population ($N = 1,879$). The CSC found that MMTP participants had higher risk and need factor ratings, lower reintegration potential and motivation levels, and lengthier criminal histories. The data analyses also revealed that women who participated in the MMTP were more likely to present mental health issues: depression (63 percent), anxiety (62 percent), and trauma resulting from physical (81 percent), mental (74 percent), and sexual abuse (67 percent). These findings demonstrate the complex risk/needs profile of FSW and the interconnected challenges the CSC must address amongst this population.

Source: M.A. MacSwain, M. Cheverie, S. Farrell-MacDonald, and S. Johnson, "Characteristics of Women Participants in the Methadone Maintenance Treatment Program," Correctional Service Canada, Research at a glance R-307, February 2014, http://www.csc-scc.gc.ca/research/005008-0307-eng.shtml.

CROSS-GENDER STAFFING IN WOMEN'S INSTITUTIONS

The incident at the Kingston Prison for Women in 1994 involved an all-male IERT extracting women inmates from their cells and stripping them of their clothing. This rekindled the debate over male staff in women's correctional facilities. Men work at all levels in Canadian women's institutions, from senior management positions down to the line level. As of 2011, men represented 68 percent of correctional officers employed across Canada, working in both men's and women's institutions.[65]

In 1998, CSC appointed a cross-gender monitor to conduct an independent review of **cross-gender staffing** in federal women's correctional facilities. The review's final report included the recommendation that male COs working in women's facilities not be permitted to carry out security functions in living and segregation units or to serve as members of cell-extraction teams.[66] An evaluation of a pilot project that involved introducing male correctional workers into front-line positions in a provincial institution for women in Saskatchewan reported positive views among inmates and staff and support for continuing the program.[67] A CSC review of the practice of employing men as CSC facilitators of women's programs also found little support for ensuring gender matching between participants and facilitators. Cross-gender program facilitation did not appear to have negative effects on women's participation or continuation in programming, or on their success in achieving treatment targets. However, there was evidence that women do psychotherapy treatment differently with women therapists.[68]

Interestingly, recent American research notes that women incarcerated in the United States are much more likely to be sexually victimized by other inmates than they are to be victimized by male staff. However, when staff members do sexually victimize women and girls, the perpetrators are overwhelmingly male.[69]

> **Cross-gender staffing**
> The practice of staffing correctional institutions with male and women officers. Most often discussed in terms of whether male COs should work inside correctional facilities for women.

TREATMENT INTERVENTIONS

Women offenders as a group have greater needs in the areas of emotional stability, marital and family relations, academic/vocational skills, and employment. Programming to target these needs is often offered using a therapeutic community approach or the cognitive behavioural approach, the latter of which was first discussed in Chapter 9.

Despite the high cost of incarcerating each federal woman offender (on average, more than $200,000), there are serious questions as to whether systems of corrections are successfully addressing the issues confronting these women. The relatively small population of FSW and their geographic dispersal on release together make it difficult to provide gender-specific health and residential services and programs.[70]

The Classification of Women Offenders

Considerable controversy has surrounded the use of assessment instruments such as the LSI-R (see Chapters 5 and 9) to assess the risk and needs of women offenders. These instruments were originally developed for use with male offenders and, it is argued, do not consider the different pathways to crime of women offenders—pathways that often include sexual abuse and victimization. This may result in women offenders being overclassified with respect to their level of risk and not having their needs identified.

Research studies have found that assessment instruments such as the LSI-R (discussed in Chapter 9) produce valid predictions of the risk that women offenders will reoffend. Indeed, it is just as valid as it is for men.[71] Even so, the prevailing view is that the assessments provided by the LSI-R, and by other instruments, could be enhanced through the use of gender-specific instruments.

For example, research investigating the predictive validity of the Level of Service/Case Management Inventory (LS/CMI) among primarily Canadian male and female offenders found that substance abuse strongly predicted recidivism for the female offenders. The results led the researchers to suggest the model should be expanded beyond the four major risk/needs factors (history of criminal behaviour; antisocial personality; antisocial attitudes, values, beliefs; and antisocial associates) to include substance abuse, which would reconfigure the model for women offenders.[72]

It has been argued that the addition of variables specifically related to women offenders would increase the predictive power of the LSI-R and other risk assessments.[73] These variables include the impact of sexual, physical, and mental/emotional victimization and the role that women's social relationships play in their involvement in criminal behaviour. One of the strongest predictors of risk, for example, is whether the woman's partner/spouse is involved in criminal activity.[74] Co-offending is an important facet of women's involvement in criminal activity and often leads to women becoming involved in more serious offences.[75] The increasing involvement of Indigenous women in gangs is one example of this.

Treatment Programs for Women Offenders and Their Effectiveness

Programming in women's corrections targets substance abuse, physical health, psychological health, education, cognitive and life skills, peer support, case management, and parenting skills. Recent meta-analyses investigating the effectiveness of the above-noted programs for women found that program participants were significantly less likely to recidivate than those who did not participate in programming.[76]

Incarcerated women are at high risk for post-traumatic stress disorder (PTSD) due to their extensive histories of physical and/or sexual trauma. Women, like men, may use poor coping mechanisms, such as abusing substances, which necessitates trauma-informed programming in correctional

CORRECTIONS PERSPECTIVE 12.2

Treatment Therapist

We have encouraged them [women] to be victims; we've encouraged them to believe that they have no control over their lives, that they have no control over the decisions that they have made; and we have to get them past that stage. And they have been victims—don't get me wrong. But we have to help all offenders to get past the victim stage and take responsibility for what they did. Women offenders do generally come from very dysfunctional backgrounds. There has been a lot of abuse. Many are addicted. And there is difficulty in accepting the fact that they have committed a criminal offence.

Source: Personal communication with C.T. Griffiths

environments.[77] While additional research is required, preliminary empirical evidence suggests that incarcerated women who participate in trauma-informed programming experience greater improvements in PTSD and depression, interpersonal relationships, and coping skills, than those who do not participate in the program.[78]

The principles of risk–need–responsivity (RNR) have been found to be equally important for male and female offenders.[79] Generally speaking, women offenders who are exposed to intensive treatment interventions have lower rates of reoffending than women who are not.[80] Several evaluations of gender-specific interventions targeting high-risk/needs women offenders in Canada have found that RNR programs may reduce reoffending.[81] Corrections File 12.6 highlights the Buffalo Sage Wellness House and the culturally and gender-sensitive programming offered to women at the facility.

Less conclusive results were found in an evaluation of the CSC's Intensive Intervention Strategy (IIS) for women offenders. This program was developed to address the needs of higher risk offenders and women with identified mental health disabilities. Two of the core components of the IIS are structured living environments (SLEs), as mentioned above, designed to support and empower minimum- and medium-security women with mental health issues or low cognitive functioning, and secure units (SUs) to address the needs of high-risk women offenders.[82] A statistical analysis of the IIS failed to indicate any changes in correctional outcomes for women participants; however, qualitative data gathered in interviews indicated that the SLEs provided women with increased coping and communication skills that helped them manage their behaviour and emotions.[83] Participation in the SU program did not appear to have any significant impact on the attitudes or behaviour of women participants.[84]

CORRECTIONS FILE 12.6

Buffalo Sage Wellness House

Buffalo Sage Wellness House (BSWH), a 16-bed Section 81 healing lodge, was built in 2010 in Edmonton, Alberta, to accommodate minimum- and medium-security FSW and women on conditional release. Women housed at BSWH are encouraged to address, among other factors, the traumas they have experienced and their broken relationships, within a culturally sensitive environment.

A process review conducted by CSC in 2015 found that of the 40 women released from BSWH since 2010, only 23 percent were revoked on conditional release with just one returning for commission of a new offence. While further research is necessary over the long term, these preliminary findings suggest the program is successfully helping women reintegrate into the community.

Source: A.J.M. Pilon, L.M. Jewell, S.J. Wormith, and P. Laboucane-Benson, "Buffalo Sage Wellness House (BSWH) Section 81 Healing Lodge Process Review," Correctional Service Canada, Research at a Glance R-371, May 2015, http://www.csc-scc.gc.ca/005/008/092/r-371-eng.pdf.

A meta-analysis of 37 studies ($N = 22,000$) conducted between 2000 and 2013 that investigated gender-informed or gender-neutral correctional interventions for women offenders found that women who participated in programming were more likely to succeed on release than non-participants. Further, the most successful interventions were those that targeted substance abuse, and gender-informed interventions were more likely than gender-neutral programs to decrease recidivism.[85]

Exploratory research conducted by the CSC examined the effect of participation in correctional programming on rates of return to custody amongst all FSW ($N = 918$) who were admitted to federal custody over an approximately four-year period and had been released on statutory release, day parole, or full parole. The study found the following:

- Twenty-seven percent ($N = 250$) of the women were revoked on release, although only 8 percent ($N = 72$) were revoked for committing a new offence.
- Participation in correctional programs, particularly in multiple programs, was beneficial for FSW.
- Three programs that were particularly beneficial for women were education, maintenance programs in the community setting, and prison visitation.[86]

Corrections File 12.7 highlights the CSC's Women Offender—High Intensity Program offered to non-Indigenous offenders. There is also an Indigenous women's offender stream. Note that the CSC recognizes the

CORRECTIONS FILE 12.7

CSC's Women Offender-High Intensity Program

Rationale: Continuation of moderate-intensity program to build on the skills acquired in that program.

Objectives:

- Learn, build upon, and practise skills—coping, problem solving, conflict resolution.
- Encourage the importance of positive and healthy relationships.
- Encourage women to work on self-management plans and address the factors related to their criminal behaviour.

Trained facilitators: Treatment program staff

Targeted population: High-needs offender with a high risk of reoffending.

Duration: Two-hour sessions; 52 group sessions and 5 individual sessions

importance of adhering to the RNR model when it comes to the provision of programs, so it matches women's risk/needs to the appropriate intensity program (e.g., the high-intensity program is longer and has more sessions).

Corrections File 12.8 provides a profile of FSW who sexually offend and the treatment programming options they have available to them through the CSC.

CORRECTIONS FILE 12.8

A Profile of Women Who Sexually Offend

CSC research investigating the characteristics of women sex offenders who entered federal custody between January 2001 and March 2010 revealed that women sexual offenders ($N = 58$) were more likely to be Caucasian, in their 30s, and under-educated; to present high risk/needs (priority areas are personal/emotional and family/marital needs); and to have histories of abuse.

The CSC offers the Women's Sex Offender Program to women at moderate to high risk to reoffend. There are 59 group sessions and 7 individual sessions that are two hours in duration and are designed to reduce crime and sexual reoffending by improving the women's coping strategies and by addressing trauma and physical health care and relationship issues.

Sources: K. Allenby, K. Taylor, and M. Cossette, "A Profile of Women Who Sexually Offend," Correctional Service Canada, Research at a glance R-274, May 2012, http://www.csc-scc.gc.ca/research/005008-0274-eng.shtml; "Women's Sex Offender Program," Correctional Service Canada website, last modified April 24, 2014, http://www.csc-scc.gc.ca/correctional-process/002001-2017-eng.shtml.

Two other gender-specific corrections programs offered to provincially sentenced incarcerated women in British Columbia are highlighted in Corrections File 12.9. These and some other gender-specific programs for women offenders have not been externally evaluated.

It is not uncommon for correctional systems—in Canada and elsewhere—to offer programming that does not adhere to the RNR model.[87] To illustrate, in early 2016, Correctional Service Canada initiated a 12- to 16-week course at the Edmonton Institution for Women to train women offenders as dog groomers. The CSC, in partnership with the Langley Animal Protection Society, also operates the Doghouse at Fraser Valley Institution for women in Abbotsford, B.C. The Doghouse provides kennel services for members of the

CORRECTIONS FILE 12.9

Two Gender-Specific Programs for Provincially Sentenced Women Offenders Incarcerated in British Columbia

Emotions Management for Women (EMWO)

Rationale	Participants develop basic techniques for managing emotions and achieving positive outcomes.
Objectives	Improve self-awareness.
Promote self-confidence.	Understand how to make healthy decisions to keep themselves and others safe.
Trained facilitators	Correctional staff in provincial correctional centres
Targeted population	Women inmates
Duration	Ten 150-minute sessions

Relationship Skills for Women (RSWO)

Rationale	Participants gain confidence in their ability to develop positive relationships and make decisions that keep themselves and other people safe.
Objectives	Promote understanding of healthy relationships.
	Promote being held accountable for behavioural choices.
	Support efforts to work on change.
Trained facilitators	Correctional staff in provincial correctional centres
Targeted population	Women inmates
Duration	Thirteen 150-minute sessions

public, training for shelter dogs that have behavioural problems, and employment training for the women prisoners who can obtain certificates in the following areas: kennel attendant, groomer's aid, canine first aid, and professional dog trainer.[88] Community groups are also involved in administering recreation activities at the Fraser Valley Institution for women; these activities include teaching women how to cook, make masks, bead, quilt, dance, and take photos, among other skills.[89]

RE-ENTRY AND LIFE AFTER PRISON

The system doesn't support reintegration … You see them being released into the community with nothing. And how surprised should we be that they reoffend?[90]

—Executive Director, Elizabeth Fry Society

Like their male counterparts, women offenders re-entering the community must attempt to find stability in their lives. This requires supportive family and friendship networks as well as access to programs and services. Finding employment may be even more challenging for women than for men, because women are less likely to have completed their education, often have little job experience, and may have to find and pay for daycare.[91] Women released from confinement may also have to address difficult issues with respect to their partners/spouses, who also may have been involved in criminal activity. This may place additional strains on women and increase the "pains of re-entry."

Women offenders may be more likely to experience gender discrimination and more stigma as ex-offenders than their male counterparts, in part because of societal attitudes toward "misbehaving women."[92] Recent CSC research ($N = 509$) suggests that Indigenous FSW typically require more extensive support than non-Indigenous women upon their release to the community in the areas of education, substance abuse, and finding and maintaining employment post-release.[93]

For inmate-mothers, the challenges may include re-establishing contact with their children, finding suitable accommodation with sufficient space, and attempting to regain custody if the children have been placed in care during the mother's confinement. Especially when the inmate-mother is the sole caregiver, child protection authorities may require that she obtain stable employment and suitable accommodation before being allowed to reapply for custody. The frustrations that mothers may encounter upon release are reflected in the following comments of an ex-offender on parole in Ontario:

I took parole to get my kids back. Parole agreed to my present location, but now the Children's Aid Society is saying it's not suitable for the kids. I can't rent before I know whether I am going to get my kids, and I can't get them back until I rent. I can't get mother's allowance until I have my kids, and without it I can't rent. I never know what I have to do for who. There are just so many hoops to jump through.[94]

It can be assumed that the challenges are even greater for women released from provincial/territorial institutions. These women, who may have extensive histories of abuse, addiction, and mental health disabilities, frequently do not have access to programs and services either while incarcerated or when released from confinement. This is a vastly under-researched area in Canadian corrections.

Surprisingly, the CSC (whose women community supervision population increased 20 percent from 2003 to 2012) and provincial/territorial corrections systems have given little attention to officially tracking the annual rates of reoffending among women released from custody. It is estimated that around 40 percent of federal women offenders will return to custody, either for a violation of release conditions or for having committed a new offence.[95] The CSC and provincial/territorial corrections systems have given even less attention to understanding women's lives while under community supervision and following their warrant expiry date.[96]

See Corrections Perspective 12.3 for a poem written by a federal woman offender incarcerated in the Grand Valley Institution for Women in Kitchener, Ontario, reflecting on her upcoming re-entry to the community. This poem highlights some of the challenges the women believe they will experience upon release into the community.

CORRECTIONS PERSPECTIVE 12.3

A Woman Offender's Concerns about Re-entry

Getting out of prison

Don't want much leisure

You can get into trouble

Need to use my free time constructively

Getting free services

You have to disclose you're an inmate

Stigma

(continued)

Never accessed it

My friend's house; everybody drunk

The only friend I have

Do I pick up the drink?

Need to find new friends

New leisure?

My son

His mother's in jail

My daughter

Told her I'm in school

My children

Rebuilding my relationship is the most important thing

How can I volunteer?

I have a record

Time changed my life forever

Taking time to volunteer makes me feel good

You judge my actions

Among the factors that appear to be associated with women's reoffending are a high-risk rating, unemployment, substance abuse, and failure to complete community-based programs.[97] Successful reintegration is facilitated by a conscious decision on the part of the woman offender to live a crime-free and drug-free life, as well as by support from families, partners/spouses, and children and by a positive relationship with their parole officer.[98]

Qualitative interviews conducted with women parolees in Colorado suggest that parole supervision can create barriers for women during re-entry. To illustrate, women in this study explained how their parole conditions and parole enforcement directed the type of employment they sought, and in some instances, cost the women their jobs. Further, parole conditions requiring that the women refrain from associating with people with criminal backgrounds often made it difficult for the women to draw on their limited social capital to assist them with their reintegration needs.[99]

A survey of CSC community parole officers ($N = 45$) was conducted in 2013 to understand the approaches and resources these officers use in supervising women in the community. The data indicate that officers rely heavily on CSC resources rather than community resources, including reporting that they use the following approaches frequently/always: maintaining frequent contact with the women (91 percent), connecting the women with psychologists (64 percent), using a team-based approach to supervision (60 percent), and using community-operated halfway houses (59 percent). Interestingly, 44 percent of the officers reported that they never used community volunteers.[100] This reflects the centralization of corrections and the decreased role of the community in correctional practices.

SUMMARY

Women offenders have a different profile than their male counterparts. Also, Canada's women's correctional system has been strongly influenced by critical incidents and investigations. Despite the development of smaller regional facilities and gender-specific treatment programs, feminist scholars and others decry the system as punitive and oppressive. Life inside women's prisons has a number of unique features, and there have been a number of high-profile incidents involving the death of women inmates. Women experience the pains of imprisonment differently from men; this is reflected in their high rates of self-injurious behaviour. A key challenge facing women upon re-entry into the community is reuniting with their children.

KEY POINTS REVIEW

1. Women offenders present unique challenges for correctional systems.
2. The profile of women offenders is changing; these changes include an increase in the number of women convicted of violent crimes and the number of women who are gang-affiliated.
3. The defining events in women's corrections have all occurred in federal correctional institutions.
4. The incident at the Kingston Prison for Women in 1994 was a watershed event in women's corrections.

5. The dynamics of life inside women's correctional institutions are different in many respects from those of men's institutions.

6. Women may experience the pains of imprisonment differently from men.

7. The death of Ashley Smith raised a number of questions about the treatment of women offenders—specifically, of women offenders with mental health issues.

8. The relatively small number of women offenders makes it a challenge to develop and deliver gender-specific programs.

9. The principles of RNR are just as important for women's treatment interventions as they are for men's.

10. Among the factors associated with reoffending among women offenders are a high-risk rating, being unemployed, having substance abuse issues, and failing to complete community-based programs.

11. Re-establishing contact with their children is a major source of stress for women offenders returning to the community.

KEY TERM QUESTIONS

1. Describe the impact of *Creating Choices* and the *Arbour Report*.

2. What issues have surrounded *cross-gender staffing* in women's correctional institutions?

CRITICAL THINKING EXERCISES

Critical Thinking Exercise 12.1

Should There Be Mother–Child Programs in Correctional Institutions?

Proponents of such programs argue that they create or strengthen the bonds between mothers and their children, provide children with health and emotional benefits through bonding and breast-feeding, provide inmate-mothers with the opportunity to learn parenting skills, and facilitate the development of prosocial attitudes and behaviours. Further, research conducted in Portugal suggests that having one's children in prison can mitigate loneliness and provide advantages, including more opportunities for recreational activities and attention from prison staff.

Critics of mother–child programs counter that they are not in the best interests of children; that the prison environment, with its attendant illicit activities such as drug use, is no place for young children; and that the prison is an artificial environment that bears little resemblance to the outside community in which the inmate-mother and her child will ultimately have to adjust.

The findings from a study in Portugal revealed that the women prisoners who did not have their children in prison with them ($N = 20$) believed the prison environment provided a lower quality of life for their children than the free community. This was expressed by Amélia, who said, "A prison is a very gloomy environment. It is not suitable; it is better for their children to be outside of it. I would like to have had her here to stop missing her, but I would never bring my daughter here." To date, there have been few published studies on mother–child programs in Canadian correctional institutions.[101]

Your Thoughts?

1. What do you think?

Critical Thinking Exercise 12.2

Should Male COs Work in Women's Prisons?

Proponents of cross-gender staffing argue that the presence of male COs helps normalize daily institutional life and provides positive relationships for women who in the past may not have been treated with respect. Opponents contend that the presence of male COs and treatment staff has a negative impact on women inmates who have histories of abuse by men and that the presence of men as front-line correctional workers increases the risk of privacy violations and sexual misconduct.[102]

Your Thoughts?

1. Can you think of other arguments in support of or opposition to cross-gender staffing?

2. What is your view on this issue?

3. If you were a woman offender in custody, would you have any difficulties with the presence of male COs?

CLASS/GROUP DISCUSSION EXERCISES

Class/Group Discussion Exercise 12.1

Correctional Officers and Ashley Smith: An Ethical Duty to Act?

The official cause of Ashley Smith's death was listed as homicide by ligature strangulation and positional asphyxia. At the time of her death, she had been in isolation for almost a year. She had an extensive history of "tying up"— wrapping nooses around her neck until she turned purple. At the Coroner's Inquest in 2013, it was revealed that the acting warden had issued an order that correctional officers were not to enter Smith's cell to cut off ligatures she had tied around her neck "as long as Smith was breathing, talking, or moving."[103] Correctional managers and COs had been reprimanded for entering her cell on previous occasions. On the day of her death, COs were right outside her cell, observing her behaviour. On one occasion, they entered briefly to determine she was still breathing, then closed the door even though the ligature was still around her neck. She subsequently self-asphyxiated. Testimony at the inquest also revealed that several of the COs had cared deeply for her, yet were constrained by their supervisor's orders who "threatened them with criminal excessive-use-of-force sanctions for entering the cell too quickly."[104]

Your Thoughts?

1. Should the correctional officers, who were outside of her cell observing her actions and who were aware of her pattern of behaviour, have ignored the order of their supervisor and intervened to prevent her from asphyxiating herself? Did they have a moral duty to intervene and cut off the ligature?

Class/Group Discussion Exercise 12.2

The Right to Visitation

The issue of overnight family visitation was recently highlighted when a woman offender convicted of a high-profile violent crime became pregnant while incarcerated. View the news broadcast, "Killer Bully Pregnant Behind Bars" (see http://globalnews.ca/video/3024239/killer-bully-pregnant-behind-bars).

Your Thoughts?

1. What are your thoughts on providing prisoners with the right to visitation with their loved ones and community supports while incarcerated?

2. Do your opinions differ based on the type of visitation (e.g., private family visits, referred to as "conjugal visits" in the news broadcast; visits held behind a glass partition; or contact visits held in a secure portion of the correctional facility)?

3. Further, do your opinions differ based on the offences for which someone has been incarcerated, or their gender?

MEDIA LINKS

"Full Story: Babies Behind Bars," https://www.youtube.com/watch?v=Jcv6dT40Fvo

"Jail Babies: Born Behind Bars (RT Documentary)," https://www.youtube.com/watch?v=dspfJKfWwCg

"Women Behind Bars," https://www.youtube.com/watch?v=XPaLFszEFDA

"How Women behind Bars Came to Be: The Michelle Lang Fellowship project," https://www.youtube.com/watch?v=kGGvr-t5xyM

"A Nation of Women Behind Bars," ABC Newss, https://www.youtube.com/watch?v=8vtudYJUzPQ

"Out of Control," *The Fifth Estate*, CBC, http://www.cbc.ca/fifth/episodes/2009-2010/out-of-control

"Behind the Wall: The Ashley Smith Story," *The Fifth Estate*, CBC, http://www.cbc.ca/fifth/episodes/2010-2011/behind-the-wall

"Inside the Legal Battle for Ashley Smith's Court Case Exhibits," *The Fifth Estate*, CBC, https://www.youtube.com/watch?v=1h-ZqhY33CQ

"Interview, Renee Acoby," *The Fifth Estate*, CBC, http://www.cbc.ca/fifth/blog/interview-renee-acoby

"Lack of Help For Mentally Ill Inmates in Canada," Global News, https://www.youtube.com/watch?v=K7fGv-oJDWg

"Report on Self-Harm in Women's Prisons (Canada)," CBC News, https://www.youtube.com/watch?v=WeQPWnCpuvY

NOTES

1. E. Bingham and R. Sutton, *Cruel, Inhuman, and Degrading? Canada's Treatment of Federally Sentenced Women with Mental Health Issues* (Toronto: International Human Rights Program, University of Toronto, 2012), http://media.thestar.topscms.com/acrobat/ba/55/3c47d5da4a599c0f879c56ebe3e6.pdf.

2. K. Pate, *Why are women Canada's fastest growing prison population; and, why should you care?* University of Western Ontario – Faculty of Law, Distinguished Speaker Series, March 18, 2011, http://www.caefs.ca/wp-content/uploads/2013/05/Why_are_women_Canadas_fastest_growing_prison_population_and_why_should_youcare.pdf; G. Malone, "Why indigenous women are Canada's fastest growing prison population," *Vice*, February 2, 2016, https://www.vice.com/en_ca/article/5gj8vb/why-indigenous-women-are-canadas-fastest-growing-prison-population; Auditor General of Canada, *Report 3 – Preparing Indigenous Offenders for Release – Service Canada* (Ottawa: Author, 2016), http://www.oag-bvg.gc.ca/internet/English/parl_oag_201611_03_e_41832.html#; J. Thompson and R. Gobeil, "Aboriginal Women: An Overview of the Correctional Process from Admission to Warrant Expiry," Correctional Service Canada, Research at a glance R-342, January 2015, http://www.csc-scc.gc.ca/research/005008-r342-eng.shtml; Office of the Correctional Investigator, *Annual Report, 2015–2016* (Ottawa: Author, 2016), http://www.oci-bec.gc.ca/cnt/rpt/pdf/annrpt/annrpt20152016-eng.pdf.

3. S. Hayman, *Imprisoning Our Sisters: The New Federal Women's Prisons in Canada* (Montréal and Kingston: McGill–Queen's University Press, 2006).

4. Task Force on Federally Sentenced Women, *Creating Choices: The Report of the Task Force on Federally Sentenced Women* (Ottawa: Correctional Service of Canada, 1990), http://www.csc-scc.gc.ca/text/prgrm/fsw/choices/toce-eng.shtml.

5. The Honourable L. Arbour (Commissioner), *Commission of Inquiry into Certain Events at the Prison for Women in Kingston* (Ottawa: Public Works and Government Services Canada, 1996), http://www.elizabethfry.ca/arbour/Arbour Report.pdf.

6. Ibid.

7. C. Glube (chair), *Moving Forward with Women's Corrections* (Ottawa: Correctional Service Canada, 2006), http://www.csc-scc.gc.ca/text/prgrm/fsw/wos29/wos29-eng.shtml.

8. Hayman, *Imprisoning Our Sisters*.

9. J. Ferrari, *Federal Female Incarceration in Canada: What Happened to Empowerment?*, M.A. thesis, 2011, Department of Sociology, Queen's University, Kingston, http://qspace.library. queensu.ca/bitstream/1974/6352/3/ Ferrari_Jacqueline_201104_MA.pdf.

10. Task Force on Federally Sentenced Women, *Creating Choices*; Ferrari, *Federal Female Incarceration in Canada.*

11. C.A. Dell, C.J. Filmore, and J.M. Kilty, "Looking Back 10 Years After the Arbour Inquiry: Ideology, Policy, Practice, and the Federal Female Offender," *Prison Journal 89*, no. 3 (2009), 286–308 at 286 and 291; S.T. Marcus-Mendoza, "Feminist Therapy Behind Bars," *Women's Studies Quarterly 32*, nos. 3–4 (2004), 49–60.

12. M. Morash, *Women on Probation and Parole: A Feminist Critique of Community Programs and Services* (Boston: Northeastern University Press, 2010).

13. M. Seng and A. Lurigio, "Probation Officers' Views on Supervising Women Probationers," *Women and Criminal Justice 16*, nos. 1–2 (2005), 65–85.

14. "Women's Facilities," Correctional Service Canada website, last modified August 15, 2013, http://www.csc-scc.gc.ca/women/002002- 0002-eng.shtml.

15. Office of the Correctional Investigator, *Annual Report, 2015–2016.*

16. C. Kruttschnitt, R. Gartner, and A. Miller, "Doing Her Own Time? Women's Responses to Prison in the Context of the Old and the New Penology," *Criminology 38*, no. 3 (2000), 681–717; S. Hulley, B. Crewe, and S. Wright, "The Gendered Pains of Imprisonment," Centre for Crime and Justice Studies, February 24, 2017, https://www.crimeandjustice.org.uk/ resources/gendered-pains-imprisonment.

17. W. Lamb, *Couldn't Keep It to Myself: Wally Lamb and the Women of York Correctional Institution* (New York: HarperCollins, 2004); W. Lamb, *I'll Fly Away: Further Testimonies from the Women of York Prison* (New York: HarperCollins, 2007).

18. M. Solinas-Saunders and M.J. Stacer, "Prison Resources and Physical/Verbal Assault in Prison: A Comparison of Male and Female Inmates," *Victims and Offenders 7*, no. 3 (2012), 279–311 at 302.

19. D.R. van Tongeren and K.J. Klebe, "Reconceptualizing Prison Adjustment: A Multidimensional Approach to Exploring Female Offenders' Adjustment to Prison Life," *Prison Journal 90*, no. 1 (2010), 48–68.

20. A. Pardue, B.A. Arrigo, and D.S. Murphy, "Sex and Sexuality in Women's Prisons: A Preliminary Typological Investigation," *Prison Journal 91*, no. 3 (2011), 279–304 at 283.

21. Kruttschnitt et al., "Doing Her Own Time? Women's Responses to Prison in the Context of the Old and the New Penology"; T.W. Foster, "Make-Believe Families: A Response of Women and Girls to the Deprivation of Imprisonment," *International Journal of Criminology and Penology 3*, no. 1 (1975), 71–78.

22. L. Stone, "Violence Spikes in Cramped Women's Prisons," *Calgary Herald*, May 25, 2010.

23. T.L. Scott, "Women Gang Inmates: A Profile," Correctional Service Canada, Research at a glance R-272, November 2012, http://www. csc-scc.gc.ca/research/005008-0272-eng.shtml.

24. K.F. Lahm, "Predictors of Violent and Nonviolent Victimization Behind Bars: An Exploration of Women Inmates," *Women & Criminal Justice 25*, no. 4 (2015), 273–91.

25. Woman Offender in Newfoundland/Labrador Correctional Centre for Women, in B. Fleming, *Alone Among the Few: A Report on Facilities and Supports for Female Offenders from Labrador* (St. John's: Office of the Citizens' Representative, Government of Newfoundland and Labrador, 2007), p. 16, http://www. citizensrep.nl.ca/pdfs/FacilitiesSupports FemaleOffendersLabrador_Report.pdf.

26. A. Brown, B. Miller, and E. Maguin, "Prevalence and Severity of Lifetime Physical and Sexual Victimization Among Incarcerated Women," *International Journal of Law and Psychiatry 22* (1999), 301–22.

27. D.P. Mears and S.E. Siennick, "Young Adult Outcomes and Life-Course Penalties of Parental Incarceration," *Journal of Research in Crime and Delinquency 53*, no. 1 (2016), 3–35.

28. T. Einat and S. Rabinovitz, "A Warm Touch in A Cold Cell: Inmates' Views on Conjugal Visits in a Maximum-Security Women's Prison in Israel," *International Journal of Offender Therapy and Comparative Criminology* 57, no. 12 (2012), 1522–45.

29. S. Brennan, "Canada's Mother-Child Program: Examining its Emergence, Usage and Current State," *Canadian Graduate Journal of Sociology and Criminology* 3, no. 1 (2014), 11–33; "Commissioner's Directive: Institutional Mother-Child Program," Correctional Service Canada website, Commissioner's Directive 768, April 18, 2016, http://www.csc-scc.gc.ca/politiques-et-lois/768-cd-eng.shtml.

30. Brennan, "Canada's Mother-Child Program"; B. Miljure, "Babies Behind Bars: Kelly Ellard One of 10 Inmates Caring for Children," CTV News Vancouver, January 19, 2017, http://bc.ctvnews.ca/babies-behind-bars-kelly-ellard-one-of-10-inmates-caring-for-children-1.3249071.

31. S. Cohen, "Mother-Baby Unit at BC Jail in-use for the First Time in Eight Years," *Vancouver Metro*, January 31, 2016, http://www.metronews.ca/news/vancouver/2016/01/31/baby-unit-at-bc-jail-in-use-for-the-first-time-in-8-years.html.

32. Unpublished paper by A. Salmon, J. Thompson, K. Murphy, et al., "Incarcerating Mothers: The Effect on Women's Health," cited in A. Granger-Brown, J.A. Buxton, L.L. Condello, D. Feder, G. Hislop, R.E. Martin, A. Salmon, M. Smith, and J. Thompson, "Collaborative Community-prison Programs for Incarcerated Women in BC," *BC Medical Journal* 54, no. 10 (2012), 509–13.

33. J. Power and A. Usher, "A Qualitative Study of Self-Injurious Behaviour in Women Offenders," Correctional Service Canada, Research at a glance R-225, July 2010, http://www.csc-scc.gc.ca/research/005008-0225-eng.shtml; H. Smith and J. Power, "Applying the Dual-Taxonomy of Offending to Self-Injury: do Offenders Exhibit Life-Course-Persistent Self-Injurious Behavior?" *Victims & Offenders* 10, no. 2 (2015), 179–213.

34. C.A. Dell, "Self-Harm Among Criminalized Women," Canadian Centre for Substance Abuse [fact sheet], 2006, http://www.ccsa.ca/Resource%20Library/ccsa-011338-2006-e.pdf#search=Self%2DHarm%20Among%20Criminalized%20Women; Smith and Power, "Applying the dual-taxonomy of offending to self-injury."

35. "Backgrounder: Self-Injury Among Federally Sentenced Women," Office of the Correctional Investigator, last modified April 28, 2014, http://www.oci-bec.gc.ca/cnt/rpt/oth-aut/oth-aut20130930info-eng.aspx.

36. Smith and Power, "Applying the dual-taxonomy of offending to self-injury."

37. Correctional Service Canada. (2017). Commissioner's Directive: Administrative Segregation. http://www.csc-scc.gc.ca/politiques-et-lois/709-cd-eng.shtml#s3

38. Power and Usher, "A Qualitative Study of Self-Injurious Behaviour in Women Offenders."

39. L. Stone, "On the Winding Road to Redemption in Canada's Women's Prison System," *Calgary Herald*, October 11, 2011, 6.

40. Smith and Power, "Applying the dual-taxonomy of offending to self-injury," p. 201.

41. A. Favazza, "Why Patients Mutilate Themselves," *Hospital and Community Psychiatry 40* (1989), 137–45; J. Martel, *Solitude and Cold Storage: Women's Journeys of Endurance in Segregation* (Edmonton: Elizabeth Fry Society of Edmonton, 1999).

42. J.F. Mills and D.F. Kroner, "Concurrent Validity and Normative Data of the Depression Hopelessness and Suicide Screening Form with Women Offenders," Correctional Service Canada, Research Brief B-47, November 2010, http://www.csc-scc.gc.ca/text/rsrch/briefs/b47/b47-eng.shtml.

43. K. Makin, "Ashley Smith's Death Was an Accident, Not Suicide, Report Says," *Globe and Mail*, October 29, 2010, A4.

44. H. Sapers, *A Preventable Death* (Ottawa: Office of the Correctional Investigator, 2008), http://www.oci-bec.gc.ca/cnt/rpt/oth-aut/oth-aut20080620-eng.aspx.

45. New Brunswick Office of the Ombudsman and Child and Youth Advocate, *Ashley Smith: A*

Report of the New Brunswick Ombudsman and Child and Youth Advocate on the Services Provided to a Youth Involved in the Youth Justice System (Fredericton: Author, 2008), http://www.gnb.ca/0073/PDF/AshleySmith-e.pdf.

46. Union of Canadian Correctional Officers, *Rush to Judgment: A Report on the Death in Custody of Ashley Smith, an Inmate at Grand Valley Institution for Women* (Ottawa: Author, 2008), http://www.ucco-sacc.csn.qc.ca/scriptorweb/scripto.asp?resultant=261990.

47. L. Stone, "Fired Ashley Smith warden back at CSC," Global News, March 19, 2013, http://globalnews.ca/news/370003/fired-ashley-smith-warden-back-at-csc/.

48. Office of the Correctional Investigator, *Annual Report of the Office of the Correctional Investigator 2014-2015* (Ottawa: Author, 2015), pp. 15, 16, http://www.oci-bec.gc.ca/cnt/rpt/pdf/annrpt/annrpt20142015-eng.pdf.

49. Ibid., p. 16.

50. Ibid.

51. H. Beaumont, "Young Women keep Killing Themselves in Canada's Jails," *Vice*, August 10, 2016, http://www.vice.com/en_ca/read/young-women-keep-killing-themselves-in-canadas-jails.

52. J.M. Kilty, "'It's Like They Don't Want You to Get Better': Psy Control of Women in the Carceral Context," *Feminism & Psychology 22*, no. 2 (2012), 162–82 at 175.

53. Ibid.

54. Bingham and Sutton, *Cruel, Inhuman, and Degrading?* p. 2.

55. Hayman, *Imprisoning Our Sisters*, p. 3.

56. A. Van Gundy and A. Baumann-Grau, *Women, Incarceration, and Human Rights Violations: Feminist Criminology and Corrections* (New York: Routledge, 2016).

57. Kilty, "'It's like they don't want you to get better.'"

58. John Howard Society of Ontario, *Fractured Care: Public Health Opportunities in Ontario's Correctional Institutions* (Toronto: Author, 2016), http://johnhoward.on.ca/wp-content/uploads/2016/04/Fractured-Care-Final.pdf.

59. Ibid.; Office of the Correctional Investigator, *Annual Report of the Office of the Correctional Investigator 2012–2013* (Ottawa: Author, 2013), http://www.oci-bec.gc.ca/cnt/rpt/pdf/annrpt/annrpt20122013-eng.pdf.

60. John Howard Society, *Fractured care*, p. 6; S.A. Kinner and E.A. Wang "The Case for Improving the Health of Ex-Prisoners," *American Journal of Public Health 104*, no. 8 (2014), 1352–55.

61. R.E. Martin, J.A. Buxton, M. Smith, and G. Hislop, "The Scope of the Problem: The Health of Incarcerated Women in BC," *BC Medical Journal 54*, no. 10 (2012), 502–8.

62. F. Kouyoumdjian, "The health status of prisoners in Ontario: Opportunities to improve population health," Paper presented at Public Health Ontario Grand Rounds, Toronto, August 16, 2016, https://www.publichealthontario.ca/en/LearningAndDevelopment/EventPresentations/Health_status_prisoners_Ontario_Kouyoumdjian_2016.pdf.

63. T. Yelland, "A Matter of Life and Death in Remand," *Briarpatch*, April 18, 2016, http://briarpatchmagazine.com/articles/view/a-matter-of-life-and-death-in-remand.

64. "2015 CEDAW Report Card," West Coast Legal Education and Action Fund, November 2015, http://www.westcoastleaf.org/wp-content/uploads/2015/11/CEDAW-Report-Card-FINAL-for-web.pdf.

65. T.H. Mahony, J. Jacob, and H. Hobson, "Women and the Criminal Justice System," in *Women in Canada: A gender-based statistical report*, 7th ed., Statistics Canada, Catalogue no. 89-503-X, June 6, 2017, http://www.statcan.gc.ca/pub/89-503-x/2015001/article/14785-eng.pdf.

66. T. Lajeunesse, C. Jefferson, U. J. Nuffield, and D. Majury, *The Cross Gender Monitoring Project: Third and Final Report* (Ottawa: Correctional Service Canada, 2000), http://www.csc-scc.gc.ca/text/prgrm/fsw/gender3/toc-eng.shtml.

67. G. Gilroy, *Evaluation of Cross-Gender Staffing Pilot Project* (Regina: Ministry of Corrections, Public Safety and Policing, Government of Saskatchewan, 2009).

68. M. Bertrand, "Evidence-Based Review of Gender-Matching in Psychotherapy to Inform Best Practices in Cross-Gender Facilitation of Women's Correctional Programming," Correctional Service Canada, Research at a glance R-288, January 2014, http://www.csc-scc.gc.ca/research/005008-0288-eng.shtml.

69. L. Stemple, A. Flores, and I.H. Meyer, "Sexual Victimization Perpetuated by Women: Federal Data Reveal Surprising Prevalence," *Aggression and Violent Behavior*, advance online publication, September 2016.

70. R.A. Sutton, "A Class Action on Behalf of Federally-Sentenced Women (FSW) with Mental Health Issues," *Canadian Graduate Journal of Sociology and Criminology 3*, no. 1 (2014), 54–70.

71. P. Smith, F. T. Cullen, and E. J. Latessa, "Can 14,737 Women be Wrong? A Meta-Analysis of the LSI-R and Recidivism for Female Offenders," *Criminology and Public Policy 8*, no. 1 (2009), 183–208.

72. D.A. Andrews, L. Guzzo, P. Raynor, R.C. Rowe, L.J. Rettinger, A. Brews, and S.J. Wormith, "Are the Major Risk/Need Factors Predictive of Both Female and Male Reoffending? A Test with the Eight Domains of the Level of Service/Case Management Inventory," *International Journal of Offender Therapy and Comparative Criminology 56*, no. 1 (2012), 113–33.

73. P. van Voorhis, E. M. Wright, E. Salisbury, and A. Bauman, "Women's Risk Factors and Their Contributions to Existing Risk/Needs Assessment," *Criminal Justice and Behavior 37*, no. 3 (2010), 261–88.

74. K. Heilbrun, D. DeMatteo, R. Fretz, J. Erickson, K. Yasuhara, and N. Anumba, "How 'Specific' Are Gender-Specific Rehabilitation Needs? An Empirical Analysis," *Criminal Justice and Behavior 35*, no. 11 (2008), 1382–97 at 1387.

75. S. Becker and J. A. McCorkel, "The Gender of Criminal Opportunity: The Impact of Male Co-Offenders on Women's Crime," *Feminist Criminology 6*, no. 2 (2011), 79–110.

76. S.J. Tripodi, S.E. Bedsoe, J.S. Kim, and K. Bender, "Effects of correctional-based programs for female inmates: A systematic review," *Research on Social Work Practice 21*, no. 1 (2011), 15–31; R. Gobeil, K. Blanchette, and L. Stewart, "A meta-analytic review of correctional interventions for women offenders," *Criminal Justice and Behavior 43*, no. 3 (2016), 301–22.

77. C.E. Grella, K. Lovinger, and U.S. Warda, "Relationships Among Trauma Exposure, Familial Characteristics, and PTSD: A Case-Control Study of Women in Prison and in the General Population," *Women & Criminal Justice 23*, no. 1 (2013), 63–79.

78. S.M. Lynch, N.M. Heath, K.C. Mathews, and G.J. Cepeda, "Seeking Safety: An Intervention for Trauma-Exposed Incarcerated Women," *Journal of Trauma & Dissociation 13*, no. 1 (2012), 88–101.

79. K. Heilbrun, D. DeMatteo, R. Fretz, J. Erickson, K. Yasuhara, and N. Anumba, "How 'Specific' Are Gender-Specific Rehabilitation Needs? An Empirical Analysis," *Criminal Justice and Behavior 35*, no. 11 (2008), 1382–97.

80. L.B. Lovins, C.T. Lowenkamp, E.J. Latessa, and P. Smith, "Application of the Risk Principle to Female Offenders," *Journal of Contemporary Criminal Justice 23*, no. 4 (2007), 383–98.

81. N. Messina, C.E. Grella, J. Cartier, and S. Torres, "A Randomized Experimental Study of Gender-Responsive Substance Abuse Treatment for Women in Prison," *Journal of Substance Abuse Treatment 38*, no. 2 (2010), 97–107; Tripodi et al., "Effects of Correctional-Based Programs for Female Inmates."

82. A. Nolan, N. Allegri, and M. Olotu, *Evaluation Report: Intensive Intervention Strategy for Women Offenders* (Ottawa: Correctional Service Canada, 2011), p. v, http://www.csc-scc.gc.ca/text/pa/ev-iiswo-394-2-88/ev-iiswo-394-2-88-eng.pdf.

83. Ibid., p. viii.

84. Ibid., p. viii.

85. Gobeil et al., "A Meta-Analytic Review of Correctional Interventions for Women Offenders."

86. G. Wilton and L. Stewart, "The Additive Effects of Participation in Multiple Correctional Interventions and Services for Federally Sentenced Women," Correctional Service Canada, Research at a glance R-369, February 2015, http://www.csc-scc.gc.ca/research/005008-0369-eng.shtml.

87. F.T. Cullen and C.L. Jonson, *Correctional Theory: Context and Consequences* (Thousand Oaks, Calif.: Sage Publications, 2016).

88. "Fraser Valley Institution Partnership," Langley Animal Protection Society website (n.d.), http://www.lapsbc.ca/about-us/special-programs/fraser-valley-institution-partnership/.

89. A. Granger-Brown, J.A. Buxton, L.L. Condello, D. Feder, G. Hislop, R.E. Martin, A. Salmon, M. Smith, and J. Thompson, "Collaborative Community-Prison Programs for Incarcerated Women in BC," *BC Medical Journal 54*, no. 10 (2012), 509–13.

90. L. Stone, "After an Inmate's Release, the Struggle Begins," *Calgary Herald*, May 25, 2012, http://www.calgaryherald.com/news/alberta/after+inmate+release+struggle+begins/5553868/story.html.

91. Glube, *Moving Forward with Women's Corrections*; R. Sampson (chair), *Report of the Correctional Service of Canada Review Panel* (Ottawa: Minister of Public Works and Government Services Canada, 2007), http://www.publicsafety.gc.ca/csc-scc/cscrprprt-eng.pdf.

92. T.P. LeBel, "'If One Doesn't get you Another One Will': Formerly Incarcerated Persons' Perceptions of Discrimination," *Prison Journal 92*, no. 1 (2011), 63–87.

93. A. McConnell, S. Rubenfeld, J. Thompson, and R. Gobeil, "A Profile of Women under Community Supervision," Correctional Service Canada, Research at a glance R-287, May 2014, http://www.csc-scc.gc.ca/research/005008-0287-eng.shtml.

94. S. Wine, *A Motherhood Issue: The Impact of Criminal Justice System Involvement on Women and Their Children* (Ottawa: Solicitor General, 1992), p. 111.

95. Stone, "After an Inmate's Release"; McConnell et al., "A Profile of Women under Community Supervision."

96. S. Pollack, "'I'm Just not Good in Relationships': Victimization Discourses and the Gendered Regulation of Criminalized Women," *Feminist Criminology 2*, no. 2 (2007), 158–73.

97. F. I. Matheson, S. Doherty, and B. A. Grant, *Women Offender Substance Abuse Programming and Community Reintegration* (Ottawa: Correctional Service of Canada, 2009), http://www.csc-scc.gc.ca/text/rsrch/reports/r202/r202-eng.shtml.

98. R. Gobiel, *Staying Out: Women's Perceptions of Challenges and Protective Factors in Community Reintegration* (Ottawa: Correctional Service Canada, 2008), http://www.csc-scc.gc.ca/text/rsrch/reports/r201/r201-eng.shtml.

99. T. Opsal, "'It's Their World, so You've just got to get Through': Women's Experience of Parole Governance," *Feminist Criminology 10*, no. 2 (2015), 188–207.

100. M.A. Lutfy and J. Thompson, "Approaches to Supervising Women Offenders in the Community," Correctional Service Canada, Research Snippet 14-09, February 2014, http://www.csc-scc.gc.ca/research/005008-rs14-09-eng.shtml.

101. A.M. Freitas, A.R. Inácio, and L. Saavedra, "Motherhood in Prison: Reconciling the Irreconcilable," *Prison Journal 96*, no. 3 (2016), 415–36 at 423.

102. Arbour, *Commission of Inquiry into Certain Events at the Prison for Women in Kingston*; Glube, *Moving Forward with Women's Corrections*; Lajeunesse et al., *The Cross Gender Monitoring Project*.

103. D. Vincent, "Ashley Smith inquest: Warden admits lack of experience," *Toronto Star*, October 2, 2013, http://www.thestar.com/news/canada/2013/10/02.ashley_smith_inquest_warden_admits_lack_of_experience.print.html.

104. C. Perkel, "Jurors Urged to find Segregation-Cell Death of Ashley Smith a Homicide," *Globe and Mail*, November 25, 2013, http://www.theglobeandmail.com/news/national/jurors-urged-to-find-segregation-cell-death-of-ashley-smith-a-homicide/article15587856/comments/.

INDIGENOUS OFFENDERS

CHAPTER OBJECTIVES

- Discuss the impact of colonization on Indigenous involvement in the criminal justice and corrections systems.
- Provide a profile of Indigenous men and women in corrections.
- Discuss the initiatives that have been taken in an attempt to reduce Indigenous over-representation in corrections.
- Discuss the role of Indigenous healing lodges and centres in corrections.
- Describe Indigenous-specific treatment interventions.
- Discuss the CSC's Continuum of Care for Indigenous offenders and Circle of Care for Indigenous women offenders.
- Discuss the challenges that Indigenous offenders experience in applying for conditional release and upon re-entry into the community.
- Discuss the effectiveness of various Indigenous-specific programs.

INDIGENOUS PEOPLES IN CANADIAN SOCIETY: THE LEGACY OF COLONIZATION

Many Indigenous people live on the margins of Canadian society. (Note: For the purposes of this discussion, the term "Indigenous" is used to include First Nations, Métis, and Inuit.) This is reflected in pervasive poverty, high rates of unemployment, low levels of formal education, substandard housing, and high death rates from accidents and violence. More than half of Indigenous students fail to graduate from high school, and the unemployment rate among Indigenous people is twice that of non-Indigenous people. Indigenous youth may be prime targets for gang recruitment, which may result in involvement in the criminal justice and corrections systems.[1]

The subordinate political and economic condition of Indigenous peoples is a consequence of their colonization by Europeans and of Canadian government policies that have exerted control over virtually every aspect of Indigenous life. Under the residential school system, Indigenous children were forcibly removed from their families, often for many years. It is well documented that Indigenous children were subject to abuse within the residential school system—physical, sexual, and psychological. Children were punished for practising their own cultures and for using their own language, resulting in feelings of shame about one's identity and a loss of cultural practices and language acquisition across generations.[2] The residential school system fractured Indigenous families, helped destroy traditional cultures and values, and shredded the fabric of many Indigenous communities.[3]

Racism and discrimination toward Indigenous people have exacerbated their marginality and vulnerability. Poverty, poor health care, higher rates of substance abuse, and inadequate educational programming and housing are all pervasive in Indigenous communities across Canada, where Third World conditions prevail. More and more Indigenous people residing in urban areas are facing significant challenges, which include finding adequate housing and accessing programs and services.[4] The intergenerational consequences of the residential school system and assimilation policies, in addition to systemic discrimination and racism, have contributed to the above factors that increase Indigenous persons' risk of involvement with the criminal justice system.[5]

The Truth and Reconciliation Commission (TRC) documented how Indigenous offenders are often in conflict with the law due to complex factors that include the intergenerational impact of residential schools.[6] In its 2015 report, the TRC called upon the provincial, territorial, and federal governments to eliminate the over-representation of Indigenous offenders in custody over the next decade and to provide funding to implement and evaluate alternatives to imprisonment that adequately address the root causes of offending. The TRC also called upon Canadian governments to reform justice and social services for offenders with fetal alcohol spectrum disorder (FASD), including a focus on providing "community, correctional, and parole resources to maximize the ability of people with FASD to live in the community."[7]

Additionally, the TRC called upon the federal government to "eliminate barriers to the creation of additional Indigenous healing lodges within the federal correctional system" and "to provide more supports for Indigenous programming in halfway houses and parole services."[8] The federal Liberal government initially agreed to implement all of the TRC's recommendations, although as of late-2017, it seems to have backed away from this. The OCI recommends that CSC appoint a deputy commissioner for Indigenous corrections to provide the type of leadership and accountability required to guide the above-noted federal correctional reform.[9] As of late-2017, this recommendation had not been acted on by the federal government.

INDIGENOUS OVER-REPRESENTATION IN THE CRIMINAL JUSTICE SYSTEM

At all stages of the criminal justice system, from arrest to incarceration, Indigenous people are over-represented in proportion to their numbers in Canada. The CSC has seen significant increases in the numbers of incarcerated Indigenous men and women.[10] In the Prairie region of the CSC, almost half of the offenders in federal custody are Indigenous.[11] Indigenous people are approximately 4.3 percent of the Canadian adult population but represent 25 percent of federal offenders and 26 percent of provincial/territorial inmates.[12]

The figure for Indigenous women in custody is even higher, representing 36 percent of federally sentenced women (FSW) and 38 percent of admissions to provincial/territorial sentenced custody.[13] Indigenous women are the fastest growing federal prison population in Canada;[14] this population nearly doubled from 2005 to 2015 when the overall population of Indigenous offenders increased by 50 percent and the general federal prison population increased by just 10 percent.[15]

The statistics for Indigenous over-representation are even more compelling in provincial/territorial correctional facilities, although there is variation across jurisdictions. In 2014–15, Indigenous offenders represented 77 percent of offenders in Saskatchewan facilities, 86 percent in Northwest Territories facilities, and 100 percent in Nunavut facilities, but just 5 percent in Québec, 4 percent in Prince Edward Island, and 11 percent in Nova Scotia and New Brunswick facilities.[16]

Indigenous youth are approximately 7 percent of the Canadian population but account for one-third of admissions to youth correctional services.[17] Data for 2014–15 in Nova Scotia highlights the over-representation of Indigenous people in that province's jails for adults and youth: Indigenous youth represented 4 percent of the population in general but 12 percent of youth incarcerated.[18] Data for 2013 in Ontario highlights that in youth custody facilities in Ontario, there are five times more Indigenous boys amongst the young male jail population than they represent in the general population, and for young Indigenous girls, their representation is ten times higher than their representation in the general population of young girls in Ontario.[19]

Compared to their non-Indigenous counterparts, Indigenous inmates are typically younger, less educated, more likely to be gang-affiliated, more likely to be suffering from FASD, have a history of substance abuse, more likely to experience mental health concerns, and more likely to have served a previous youth and/or adult sentence.[20]

Federal Indigenous offenders are more likely than non-Indigenous to be classified as maximum-level security risk.[21] A greater proportion of Indigenous men and women offenders are currently serving a sentence for a violent offence; the difference is especially evident for Indigenous versus non-Indigenous women (73.5 vs. 47.2 percent).[22] Indigenous offenders are also disproportionately designated as dangerous offenders (DOs), accounting for 31.5 percent of the 622 active DOs in Canada in 2014–15.[23] Federal Indigenous offenders are more likely to be incarcerated than on conditional release, they spend more of their prison sentences in custody before being released in the community, and they are over-represented in use of force incidents (in 2014–15, Indigenous offenders accounted for 30 percent of use-of-force incidents while comprising 25 percent of the offender population).[24]

Indigenous offenders were also over-represented in admissions to administrative segregation in 2014–15, representing 30.5 percent ($N = 6,284$) of admissions.[25] This might suggest Indigenous offenders have a more challenging time adjusting to custody. The findings from a study investigating the correctional process for Indigenous FSW suggests that Métis women are less likely than First Nations women to struggle with institutional adjustment, but when they do, challenges tend to occur earlier in their sentences.[26]

The CSC conducted a one-day snapshot of its male correctional population in 2012 to examine the unique circumstances among the Indigenous offender population (i.e., Métis, First Nations, and Inuit) and found that Inuit offenders exhibited the most stable institutional behaviour of the three groups while First Nations experienced the most difficulties.[27] This research highlights the importance of recognizing differences between groups within the larger group (i.e., Indigenous offenders).

It appears that the *Gladue* decision has done little to stem the rising tide of Indigenous over-representation in corrections systems. This is for a variety of reasons, including the absence of viable community-based alternatives. Also, the high rates of violent crime among Indigenous offenders limit the options available to criminal court judges at sentencing.

There is concern that the over-representation of Indigenous people in corrections systems will continue in both the federal and provincial/territorial systems, because the Indigenous rate of population growth is higher than for non-Indigenous populations, with the result that the Indigenous population is, overall, younger than the non-Indigenous.[28] It is also possible that the increasing focus on risk in corrections will work to the detriment of Indigenous offenders, given that many have violent offence histories and higher risk-assessment ratings.

Indigenous Women Offenders

Indigenous women are a high and growing proportion of women in remand and sentenced custody and are over-represented. Indigenous women offenders are more over-represented in the federal correctional population than their male counterparts. More than one in three (36 percent) federally incarcerated women are Indigenous.[29]

The CSC recently conducted a review of the social histories of Indigenous women and found that nearly all of the files documented traumatic histories (e.g., physical and/or sexual abuse) and substance abuse problems. Over half of the women were involved in the residential school system, having attended personally or having a family member who had.[30] CSC analyses of data collected from 2003–13 found that Indigenous women have more criminogenic backgrounds than non-Indigenous women; typically they were younger, had lower levels of education, and required programming for substance abuse, for employment, and in the emotional/personal domain.[31]

Indigenous women offenders are also over-represented in maximum-security institutions and segregation placements.[32] They are more likely to incur institutional infractions and to be assessed as higher risk when compared to non-Indigenous women.[33] Research indicates that Indigenous women in federal corrections tend to be "overclassified"—that is, given a higher than appropriate security rating.[34] This may result in less access to treatment programs and a reduced likelihood of release on parole.[35] Indigenous women are in fact less likely to receive day or full parole than non-Indigenous women and are more likely to be released on statutory release than discretionary release.[36] A profile of an Indigenous FSW is presented in Corrections File 13.1.

CORRECTIONS FILE 13.1

Profile of an Indigenous Woman Serving Time in a Federal Correctional Institution

The Indigenous woman offender is generally 27 years old with a Grade 9 education. She is also single with two or three children. She has limited education and employment skills and is usually unemployed at the time of her crime. Contributing factors that may negatively affect the life of an Indigenous woman include moving to an urban centre (isolation and loneliness); alcoholism and violence in the family home; lack of family support and supervision; lack of financial resources; and lack of opportunities to become involved in positive interactions with others.

Generally, the Indigenous offender experimented with drugs and alcohol at a young age. Often she came into conflict with the law as a youth; more recently, because of lack of intervention, she has continued into the adult system. She is likely to have left school at a young age to associate with friends who are streetwise. On the street, her abuse of drugs and alcohol continued to the point where she became a prostitute to continue her addiction. Under the influence of her associates and a negative lifestyle, she became more streetwise and committed more serious crimes such as robberies, assaults, or murder.

She may have left home because she experienced violence (whether she was abused or she witnessed abuse) and her home life became unbearable. Or she may have lived under very rigid conditions that she fled because she wanted to become independent. Or she may have been lured away by friends who were living a life of drugs, alcohol, and partying. She may have worked the streets because she needed money to live on and did not have the education, skills, and training to get a job. She may have been subjected to racism, stereotyping, and discrimination because she was Indigenous. Her experience on the streets became violent as she continued to experience sexual, emotional, and physical abuse. She probably became involved in an abusive relationship. There usually have been children born from this relationship, and the social, emotional, and economic struggle has continued. The cycle of an unhealthy family continues.

A high percentage of Indigenous women who come into conflict with the law are convicted of crimes committed while under the influence of drugs and alcohol. These contributing factors are often related to their history of physical, psychological, and emotional abuse, and they have not dealt with the effects of this abuse. This harmful way of dealing with the past history of dysfunctional behaviour may continue unless these past abuses and effects are dealt with.

Source: Facts and Figures: Aboriginal Initiatives, "Profile of an Aboriginal Woman Serving Time in a Federal Correctional Institution," http://www.csc-scc.gc.ca/text/prgrm/abinit/know/5-eng.shtml. Correctional Service Canada, 2000. Reproduced with the permission of Correctional Service of Canada.

ADDRESSING INDIGENOUS OVER-REPRESENTATION IN THE JUSTICE SYSTEM

Over the past three decades, governments, not-for-profit organizations, and Indigenous communities have made a variety of attempts to address the disproportionate involvement of Indigenous persons at all stages of the criminal justice system. These include Indigenous policing programs and autonomous Indigenous police services, diversion programs, Indigenous court worker and liaison programs, sentencing provisions (recall the *Gladue* decision), Indigenous-focused community-based corrections programs, and institutional programs designed to address the unique needs of Indigenous offenders.

An example is the Community Council Program (CCP) in Toronto, which is a diversion program that has been operating since 1992 for urban Indigenous offenders designed to reduce recidivism, increase offender responsibility, and return a greater degree of responsibility to the Indigenous community. The options offered by this program include counselling, restitution to the victim, community service hours, and referral to treatment resources.[37] While dated, an evaluation of the program found high compliance rates among CCP participants (N = 106), with 64 percent complying with all of the CCP conditions while only 30 percent did not comply at all. Further, 61 percent of the program participants had no convictions in the two-year follow-up period, and an additional 21 percent experienced a decrease in post-program convictions (as compared to the two years prior to participation in CCP).[38]

INITIATIVES IN INDIGENOUS CORRECTIONS

To address the needs of Indigenous offenders, a variety of programs have been developed by systems of corrections and also by Indigenous organizations and communities.

Indigenous Organizations

It has been argued that European methods of justice, which are predominantly adversarial, are ill suited to address Indigenous crime and that efforts should focus on programs developed by Indigenous people to address their communities' unique needs.[39]

Indigenous organizations are designing and delivering correctional services in both communities and institutions. The justice system often partners with them in delivering these services, many of which incorporate Indigenous spirituality and principles of restorative justice. These programs include sentencing circles, community mediation, and sentencing advisory committees. Many of them employ Indigenous personnel—for example, Aboriginal liaison workers.

These initiatives vary widely with regard to the types of offences and offenders; the procedures for hearing cases, reaching dispositions, and imposing sanctions; and the extent to which these programs involve justice system personnel.

Other initiatives are more independent of the justice system and are controlled by communities. In Manitoba, for example, First Nations and Métis community correctional agencies are involved in probation supervision, fine option programs, the preparation of pre-sentence reports (PSRs) for the courts, and a variety of community-based treatment programs. The Community Holistic Circle Healing Program on Hollow Water First Nation in Manitoba, profiled in Box 13.1, is one example of a community-controlled program.

Indigenous Healing Centres and Lodges

Corrections systems have made some efforts to address the specific treatment needs of Indigenous offenders. Among the more common Indigenous-specific initiatives found in correctional institutions across the country are sweat lodges, healing circles, and modules that focus on cultural awareness, substance abuse, and family violence.

Section 81 of the CCRA authorizes the federal government to enter into agreements with Indigenous communities to operate healing lodges whereby the community will take over the "care and custody" of some Indigenous inmates.

As of late-2017, the CSC funded nine healing lodges (two for women) but only operated four of them; the remaining healing lodges were managed by Indigenous communities or organizations as per Section 81 of the CCRA.[40]

Section 81 (CCRA) Authorizes the federal government to enter into agreements with Indigenous communities whereby the community assumes the "care and custody" of some Indigenous offenders upon their release from custody.

BOX 13.1

Community Holistic Circle Healing Program, Hollow Water, Manitoba

The Community Holistic Circle Healing Program was designed in the 1980s as a community-based response to the high rates of sexual and family abuse. Over the years, its mandate has expanded to other youth and adult justice cases. It includes a 13-phase process, illustrated in Figure 13.1.

The Special Gathering in the Hollow Water program is a public event. Traditional healing practices are used in an attempt to restore the community, the family, and individual peace and harmony. The offender signs a healing contract and apologizes publicly to the victims and to the community for the harm done. The circle healing process is designed to consider the needs of all of the parties to the abuse—the victim, the offender, and the community—and is directed beyond merely punishing the offender for a specific behaviour.

Source: "Compendium of Promising Practices to Reduce Violence and Increase Safety of Aboriginal Women in Canada – Compendium Annex: Detailed Practice Descriptions," Department of Justice Canada website, last modified January 7, 2015, http://www.justice.gc.ca/eng/rp-pr/cj-jp/fv-vf/annex-annexe/p132.html.

Figure 13.1

The 13 Phases of the Hollow Water Community Holistic Circle Healing Process

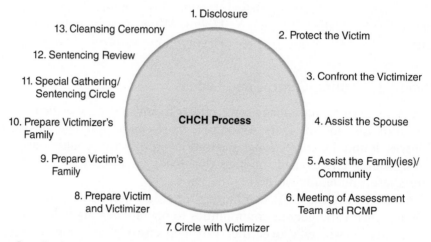

Source: From The Evaluation of Community Holistic Circle Healing: Hollow Water First Nation, Vol. 1 Final Report (p. 33). Reproduced with permission from the Manitoba Government.

The CSC manages the Okimaw Ohci Healing Lodge (Maple Creek, Saskatchewan) for minimum- and medium-security Indigenous women offenders, which incorporates Indigenous cultures and spirituality; Pê Sâkâstêw (Cree for "new beginnings" and pronounced "Bay Sah-ga-stay-o"), a minimum-security facility for male offenders near Maskwacis, Alberta, on the Samson Cree Nation; Kwìkwèxwelhp Healing Village for minimum-security male offenders located in Harris Mills, British Columbia, on Chehalis First Nation land; and Willow Creek Healing Lodge, a minimum-security facility for men that is located near Duck Lake, Saskatchewan.[41]

Under Section 81 of the CCRA, the federal government has entered into agreements with Indigenous groups across the country to develop and operate healing lodges. These include Stan Daniels Healing Lodge (Edmonton, Alberta) and the Waseskun Healing Centre, near Montréal, which follows a community-based and holistic healing model. In addition to providing services for minimum-security men, both of these lodges serve as community residential facilities for offenders on conditional release.

At healing lodges, the needs of Indigenous offenders are addressed in a holistic manner. Offenders receive individualized programming, engage with the community and Elders and partake in Indigenous teachings and ceremonies.[42] Elders play a key role in most programs. For some offenders, it is their first exposure to Indigenous cultures and beliefs.

Findings from an evaluation of O-Chi-Chak-Ko-Sipi Healing Lodge highlight the contributions the lodge makes to the local community, toward Indigenous reintegration, and toward cost savings for the CSC; however, limitations were identified, such as the lodge operating below capacity and needs in the areas of staff training and services.[43] Escapes from healing lodges, including escapes from O-Chi-Chak-Ko-Sipi Healing Lodge, Willow Creek Healing Lodge, and Pê Sâkâstêw throughout 2016 and 2017, can increase public fear and minimize public support for these minimum-security facilities due to perceived notions of ineffectiveness and poor security measures. The Pê Sâkâstêw Centre is profiled in Box 13.2.

INDIGENOUS INMATES AND TREATMENT INTERVENTIONS

> *So, prison is no place to recover. From anything, either the grief of memory, or loss, or abuse, or the diseases of addiction. But if you're Native and you can get the help to seek and find and claim your spiritual name, a lot can be changed. You can discover your destiny. Your life can bridge back to the origins of your family and people, you can seek out your colours, your clan, your spirit keepers. You may find the self you never knew you were.*[44]

Indigenous offenders generally have been found to exhibit greater criminogenic needs than non-Indigenous offenders.[45] The risk factors for chronic

---

BOX 13.2

The Pê Sâkâstêw Centre

Pê Sâkâstêw (Cree for "new beginning" and pronounced "Bay Sah-ga-stay-o") is a CSC-funded and -operated minimum-security facility, a healing lodge, near Hobbema, Alberta, on the Samson Cree Nation. Indigenous Elders are directly involved in developing the treatment programs, which focus on healing and culturally appropriate practices and include a sweat lodge. Inmates in the minimum-security facility are called *owiciiyisiwak*, which in the Cree language means "here to learn." Offenders are screened carefully before being sent to the institution and must be classified as minimum security. Also, they must demonstrate an interest in rehabilitation programs, have a genuine interest in learning more about Indigenous cultures and traditions, and have a history of positive interactions with correctional staff.

The primary objectives of the centre are to prepare the offenders for their eventual release as safe and law-abiding citizens and to encourage Indigenous community participation and organizational support of offenders' reintegration.

Source: S. Trevethan, N. Crutcher, J.P. Moore, and J. Mileto, *Pê Sâkâstêw Centre: An In-Depth Examination of a Healing Lodge for Federally Incarcerated Offenders* (Ottawa: Correctional Service Canada, 2007), http://www.csc-scc.gc.ca/text/rsrch/reports/r170/r170-eng.pdf.

A building of the Okimaw Ohci Healing Lodge for Aboriginal Women, Maple Creek, Saskatchewan

Indigenous offenders—whose deviant behaviour typically begins in childhood, escalates in the adolescent years, and continues throughout adulthood—include substance abuse, a dysfunctional family environment, and negative peer group associations.[46]

While both Indigenous and non-Indigenous federal offenders exhibit substance abuse issues, in 2012, CSC researchers found that Indigenous offenders had higher levels of dependency than non-Indigenous offenders, 56 percent versus 37 percent ($N = 15,164$), respectively.[47] Indigenous offenders are also more likely than non-Indigenous offenders to enter federal prisons unemployed and with lower levels of educational attainment.[48]

CSC researchers examined 2,273 self-report health assessment intake forms collected from newly admitted federal male offenders over six months in 2012 and found that Indigenous persons had higher rates of head injuries and blood-borne viruses than non-Indigenous persons.[49] The CSC's Addictions Research Centre examined data for Indigenous and non-Indigenous Methadone Mainte-nance Treatment Program (MMTP) participants and found "high rates of treat-ment for mental health issues and history of abuse … [for all participants but] a greater proportion of Indigenous offenders reported histories of sexual, physical, and mental abuse, as well as self-injurious behaviour and suicide attempts."[50]

Research examining the years of life lost to incarceration for Indigenous persons in comparison to non-Indigenous persons described how, federally, the Indigenous population "loses six times as many life years to incarceration as non-Aboriginal Canadians," and in B.C. provincial custody, the former "lose approximately four times as many life years to incarceration" than the latter.[51]

All of these issues require specialized programs.[52] Indigenous offenders present challenges for the correctional staff who facilitate treatment groups. One Aboriginal Correctional Program Officer stated: "A lot of inmates coming

Indigenous sweat lodge and ceremonial grounds in a federal correctional institution.

in are really young—like 19, 20, 21, 22, and they don't have their basic knowledge of having respect when an Elder comes into the room. They don't give a shit. They don't."[53]

Among the more common Indigenous-specific programs in facilities across the country are sweat lodges, healing circles, and modules that focus on cultural awareness, substance abuse, and family violence. Provincial and territorial systems of corrections have far fewer programs and services for Indigenous inmates, even though these offenders may account for as much as 90 percent of the inmate population. Given the short time that offenders are in provincial/territorial confinement, the greatest promise is for programs in the community, either post-release or as part of an alternative to confinement. Unless otherwise indicated, the programs discussed below are operated by the CSC.

The CSC's Aboriginal Corrections Continuum of Care

The CSC introduced its **Aboriginal Corrections Continuum of Care** in 2003 after extensive consultation with Indigenous stakeholders. This model begins at intake with the identification of Indigenous offenders, who are encouraged to reconnect with their communities, traditions, and cultures. It then provides programming that will enable them to cascade down to lower security levels until they receive a conditional release. Indigenous offenders are engaged throughout this process, receiving support to facilitate their successful reintegration as law-abiding citizens beyond their warrant expiry date.[54]

Aboriginal Corrections Continuum of Care An initiative of the CSC designed to connect Indigenous offenders with their communities, traditions, and cultures, beginning in the institution and continuing on conditional release in the community.

The CSC ICPM Initiative

Recall from Chapter 9 that the objectives of the new ICPM are to provide more timely access to programs upon admission, facilitate greater program enrollment, increase program completion rates, and increase the rates of discretionary conditional release.[55] This initiative is particularly important for Indigenous offenders, who, according to the Auditor General of Canada, waited, on average, five months after their admission to custody to start their correctional programs in fiscal year 2015–16, and only one-fifth of short-term offenders (those sentenced to four years or less) completed their correctional programs by the time of their first conditional release eligibility date.[56]

Corrections Perspective 13.1 provides the perspective of a CSC Aboriginal Correctional Program Officer (ACPO).

The Circle of Care for Indigenous Women Offenders

Circle of Care
A CSC program designed to provide women with coping strategies in preparation for release into the community.

The **Circle of Care** helps federal Indigenous women offenders return to their communities to live crime-free lives. It does so by helping them develop strategies to cope with daily life. Each program in the Circle of Care is assisted full-time by an Elder (the CSC is experiencing operational difficulties in meeting this objective).[57] The theme that connects all programs in the circle is healing through cultural identity. A woman's movement throughout the Circle of Care is dictated by availability, risk level, and sentence duration. Not all women will complete the cycle.

CORRECTIONS PERSPECTIVE 13.1

An Aboriginal Correctional Program Officer

As an ACPO, I work with the Elders and other case management team members, such as the institution parole officers, and ALOs to help rehabilitate Aboriginal offenders. During programs, I teach culturally appropriate healing and treatment programs to Aboriginal and Métis offenders. The Elder and I work hard to motivate and guide the Aboriginal inmates to move forward on their healing journey, which is also referred to as their path to rehabilitation. In programs, I teach the Aboriginal inmates skills and competencies, such as problem solving and challenging distorted thinking, which are necessary for a safe reintegration back into the community.

Source: Personal communication with D. Murdoch.

The circle is composed of the Program Intake Interview, the Aboriginal Women's Engagement Program, the Aboriginal Women Offender–Moderate Intensity Program, the Aboriginal Women's High Intensity Program, and the Aboriginal Women Offender–Self Management Program (Institution and Community). Depending on their risk assessment and sentence length, women sex offenders can be required to complete the Aboriginal Women Offender–Moderate Intensity Program and/or the Women's Sex Offender Program.[58]

Connections are made with Indigenous women early in their sentence to encourage them to change. Each stage of the process has different objectives, which include helping them develop healing plans, helping them understand how their thoughts affect their emotions and behaviours, encouraging them to explore their spirituality to achieve balance in their lives, and helping them access community resources.[59]

CHALLENGES IN TREATMENT FOR INDIGENOUS OFFENDERS

Indigenous offenders generally have higher risk/needs ratings than their non-Indigenous counterparts.[60] Despite this, their participation rates in treatment programs are low overall. Many Indigenous offenders are classified as high risk and are placed in maximum-security institutions where programming opportunities may be more limited.[61] Offenders who are classified as high risk and who have a history of violence may not qualify for residence in an Indigenous healing lodge.[62] Also, Indigenous inmates spend more time in administrative segregation (in 2014–15, 6.9 percent of Indigenous admissions to administrative segregation lasted more than 120 days in comparison to 5.4 percent for non-Indigenous offenders),[63] which further limits program opportunities. This may be particularly problematic in the CSC's Prairie region, where Indigenous gangs are a prominent feature of correctional institutions.[64]

In the past, the CSC has been criticized for failing to ensure that Indigenous offenders have equal access to its programs. The ICPM is designed to address this. There has also been a lack of appropriate staff to deliver Indigenous programs. Because of challenges in recruiting and retaining those staff, many institutions are forced to operate their Indigenous programs without sufficient numbers of Elders or Indigenous correctional personnel.[65] To illustrate, in his 2014–15 report, the OCI reported that the CSC is having difficulties meeting its targets for Elder involvement in correctional programs.[66]

INDIGENOUS PERSONS AND CONDITIONAL RELEASE

Indigenous inmates have lower parole grant rates than non-Indigenous inmates.[67] Relative to non-Indigenous offenders, few Indigenous offenders were released on parole in 2015–16 (31 percent versus 48 percent) and even fewer (12 percent) "had their cases prepared for a parole hearing by the time they were first eligible."[68] Additionally, Indigenous offenders had the lowest federal day parole grant rate (68 percent) although Black offenders have had the lowest federal day parole grant rate over the past five years (61 percent). However, Indigenous offenders have had the lowest federal and provincial full parole grant rates over the past five years at 17 percent and 20 percent, respectively.[69]

CSC analyses of data retrieved from a one-day snapshot of its Indigenous male correctional population in 2012 found that Inuit offenders had the most conditions imposed on their release while Métis offenders were the most likely to receive parole.[70]

Indigenous offenders also serve a higher proportion of their sentence before being released on parole, partly because of the seriousness of the crimes they have committed but also because of the lack of community supports available to them, especially in rural and remote communities.[71] In 2014–15, more than three-quarters of Indigenous offenders (83 percent) delayed their parole hearings, thereby reducing the amount of time they could spend in the community, receiving assistance and supervision prior to their warrant expiry date.[72]

Many parole-eligible Indigenous inmates do not apply for conditional release; Indigenous women who were admitted to the CSC between April 2008 and March 2010 were found to waive their right to a parole hearing more frequently than non-Indigenous women.[73] A number of reasons were cited for this, including feelings of alienation, a lack of understanding of the parole process, a lack of confidence in their ability to complete conditional release, and/or the absence of assistance in preparing their application for parole. The lack of access to Indigenous programming is another factor: If Indigenous offenders have not been able to work on their correctional plan because their institution does not provide programs for them to do so, the Parole Board of Canada (PBC) is unlikely to perceive them as a good risk.[74] For all of these reasons, Indigenous offenders are more likely than non-Indigenous inmates to be on statutory release or to be held in custody until warrant expiry.[75]

In fiscal year 2015–16, the majority (69 percent) of Indigenous offenders were released at their statutory release date, with 79 percent of these offenders entering their communities directly from maximum- or medium-security institutions. Over the past three years, the percentage of Indigenous offenders released at their statutory release date has been 18 percent higher than for non-Indigenous offenders.[76] This means Indigenous offenders are not benefiting from lengthier periods of community supervision.[77] The CSC consistently touts the value of parole, highlighting statistics that demonstrate "offenders granted day or full parole had lower rates of offending before their sentences ended than did those released at statutory release."[78]

Indigenous Inmates and the Parole Board

There may be particular difficulties between Indigenous inmate-applicants and parole boards. As of 2014–15, only 4 percent of PBC staff were Indigenous.[79] The PBC does not disclose how many board members are Indigenous, but it can be assumed that few of them are. Individual parole board members may be biased toward Indigenous people, although this has not been documented by research.

To qualify for appointment to the PBC, board members are not required to have any special knowledge of Indigenous cultures and communities. This raises the possibility of a lack of cultural sensitivity among non-Indigenous board members, as well as inequities in the hearing process, leading to poor decisions. These problems are reflected in the observations of a non-Indigenous former member of the PBC in the Prairie region:

> *When I found myself sitting opposite Samuel Grey Hawk, or Amos Morning Cloud, or Joseph Brave Bear, or when I caught the shy, uncertain eyes of a Cree-speaking teenager from the far North attempting to follow, through an interpreter, our ritualistic procedures and answer our thoroughly white middle-class questions, I felt a little like a fraud. It seemed incalculably unfair that these men had the misfortune to have to depend upon the decisions of people who might as well have come from another planet, as far as the similarities in culture and lifestyle were concerned.[80]*

Efforts have been made to address concerns about a lack of cultural sensitivity among board members. For example, they must undergo cultural sensitivity and awareness training; learn about the traditions and cultures of the Inuit, Métis, and First Nations populations; and complete training with Elders.[81] How this training is applied in parole hearings and the impact it has had on parole board decisions has not been examined.

The PBC has a number of initiatives designed to improve parole hearings for Indigenous offenders. Since 1992, federal Indigenous offenders have had the opportunity to participate in parole hearings with an Indigenous cultural adviser or partake in an Elder-assisted parole hearing.[82] The Elder may say a prayer or perform a ritual (such as smudging) to open and/or close the parole hearing. They may also provide board members with general information regarding Indigenous experiences, spirituality, traditions, and cultures as well as, hopefully, information specific to the culture of the Indigenous parole applicant. Indigenous cultural advisers and Elders are involved throughout the parole hearing but do not have authority in the release decision.

In 2014–15, only 368 parole hearings involved an Indigenous cultural advisor or Elder, which represents a decrease of 25 percent from 2010–11 when 491 such hearings were conducted. The PBC asserts this decrease is partially attributable to a change in policy whereby post-suspension hearings are now paper decisions rather than in-person reviews.[83]

There is also provision for parole hearings to be held in the community rather than the penitentiary as a means to restore the relationship between the offender and the community, thereby contributing to the "traditional sense of responsibility felt by every community member for each other and for the creatures and forces that sustain all human life."[84] **Section 84** provides an opportunity for Indigenous communities to participate in a community-assisted hearing in front of the PBC, and to propose a plan for the conditional release and reintegration of the Indigenous offender into their community. This provision also allows for offenders under a long-term supervision order (LTSO) to be supervised in an Indigenous community.[85]

While designed to enhance the involvement of Indigenous communities in the parole process, the OCI found Section 84 release plans are time-consuming and confusing and limited by the number of Indigenous community development officers to assist with the process.[86]

The Ontario Parole Board also conducts Indigenous circle hearings, which are designed to be culturally sensitive and to involve Elders. There are no evaluations, however, as to whether these hearings contribute to better decisions by parole boards or to reduced rates of reoffending among Indigenous offenders.

> **Section 84 (CCRA)**
> Provides for Indigenous communities to participate in parole hearings and propose a plan for offender reintegration, and includes a provision for Indigenous communities to supervise long-term offenders.

Indigenous Offenders on Conditional Release

In recent years, a variety of community-based services and programs for offenders on conditional release have been developed by Indigenous communities across the country. Many of these programs are grounded in traditional Indigenous cultures and spirituality and incorporate elements of restorative justice.

Several provisions in the CCRA are designed to increase the involvement of Indigenous communities in the release and reintegration of federal Indigenous offenders. As noted above, Section 81 authorizes the federal government to enter into agreements with Indigenous communities to operate healing lodges whereby the community will take over the "care and custody" of some Indigenous inmates.

Examples of these specialized community residential facilities for Indigenous persons on conditional release are the Stan Daniels Healing Centre and Waseskun Healing Centre. In Montréal, the 20-week residential program at the Waseskun Healing Centre for Indigenous men provides individual and group counselling as well as programs in life skills, conflict resolution, family awareness, and women's issues. Sweat lodges and talking circles are also offered (http://www.waseskun.net). Elders use the medicine wheel to promote balance, addressing the physical, mental, spiritual, and emotional health of each individual.[87] One resident commented on the value of one-on-one sessions with the Elders: "[They] really helped me gain ground. With the Native Elders, they have this passion, they have a different technique. They thrive off the sincerity of the individual."[88]

A major issue is the lack of community-based programs and services for Indigenous offenders from remote northern communities. This may affect the decision-making of the parole board and present challenges for those offenders who are released. A former member of the PBC recalled:

> *Sometimes the inmate was ready to go out, and if he was from a city, we would release him. Another inmate, just as ready, would be denied release simply because he was from a community in the Far North with no supports available to him—not only no work, but also no self-help group of former alcoholics, no local hospital with a mental health program, no drug counsellors, no sex offender programs.*[89]

Indigenous offenders on release may encounter unique challenges in addition to those experienced by other offenders (see Chapter 11). Many of them are from rural and remote communities, which makes it difficult for them to access programs and services. Parole supervision may be sporadic, and there may be a lack of continuity regarding their parole officers, further undermining case management. Little is known about the challenges faced by Indigenous offenders with mental health disability, FASD, and addictions upon re-entry into the community. Many will be returning to communities that are highly troubled and where there are few, if any, supports. The challenges encountered by corrections personnel in providing supervision and support for these offenders have not been studied, and they badly need to be.

Given these challenges, it is perhaps not surprising that Indigenous offenders are more likely than others to have their conditional release revoked.[90] During the time period 2010–2015, Indigenous offenders have been the least likely to complete federal day parole (85 percent successful), federal full parole (73 percent successful), and statutory release (53 percent successful). During this time, Indigenous offenders were the most likely to be revoked for a violent offence while on federal full parole (0.8 percent), provincial full parole (4.3 percent), and statutory release (2.1 percent). Indigenous offenders are also more likely to be returned to custody for technical violations of their release conditions.[91] The CSC examined the return of offenders to custody over a period of 10 to 15 years post-warrant expiry and found that Indigenous offenders were the most likely to be readmitted to federal custody for commission of a new federal offence.[92]

THE EFFECTIVENESS OF SELECTED INDIGENOUS-FOCUSED CORRECTIONAL PROGRAMS AND INTERVENTIONS

Most Indigenous-focused programs and interventions, be they community-based or in correctional facilities, require further evaluation. Various studies, typically conducted by the CSC, have focused on program dynamics and rates of return to custody. See the materials presented in Research File 13.1.

The Effectiveness of Selected Indigenous-Focused Programs/Interventions

Program/ Intervention	Approach	Outcomes
Hollow Water Community Holistic Healing Program (Hollow Water First Nation, Manitoba)	A community-based response to sexual and family abuse that uses traditional healing practices in an attempt to restore the community, the family, and individual peace and harmony.	An evaluation found that the program has increased community awareness of sexual abuse and family violence, and the rates of disclosure by offenders. It has also significantly reduced the rates of alcoholism in the community, improved educational standards, and increased services for at-risk children and youth. Impact on reoffending unknown.[a] Cost-effective in comparison to incarceration costs.
Pé Sâkâstêw Centre (Samson Cree Nation, Alberta; CSC)	A minimum-security institution (healing lodge) where federal Indigenous Elders are directly involved in developing the treatment programs, which focus on healing, culturally appropriate practices, and the use of a sweat lodge.	Research indicates that staff and residents believe the centre is effective in supporting offender reintegration into the community. The centre's residents made significant gains in many need areas following their time there and were assessed as having a higher potential for community reintegration. However, a comparable number of the centre's residents and offenders in the comparison offender group were readmitted to federal custody for new offences. Program may be becoming more effective, with recent statistics indicating that a smaller number of the centre's residents were readmitted to federal custody than in the comparison group.[b]

Program/ Intervention	Approach	Outcomes
Ma Mawi Wi Chi Itata Family Violence Program (Stony Mountain Institution, Manitoba; CSC)	A program for Indigenous inmates designed to address issues related to violent behaviour toward spouses/partners and family members.	An evaluation found high levels of inmate and staff satisfaction with the program and a widely shared view among the inmates that the program had significantly affected their behaviour, attitudes, and emotions. Impact on reoffending, post-release quality of life, and the extent to which specific issues (e.g., addiction) were addressed is unknown.[c]
CSC Aboriginal ICPM (AICPM)	Targets criminogenic factors using cognitive-behavioural strategies.	A review of the program found that Indigenous inmates had significantly higher rates of program completion and accessed their first program earlier in their sentence than in the previous year.[d] A more recent CSC evaluation conducted in 2014 noted the AICPM did not greatly assist offenders in more timely completion of correctional programs when compared to their other Indigenous-focused correctional programs; offenders waited significantly longer to enrol in and complete AICPM than other programs. Indigenous offenders who participated in AICPM, ICPM, or CSC's other correctional programs did not have significantly different rates of return to custody, with or without an offence, or for a violent offence. Those who completed AICPM or ICPM were more likely to be released on parole. When AICPM was compared to other Indigenous-focused correctional programs offered by the CSC, the AICPM group performed as well or better than those in other Indigenous-focused correctional programs.[e]

(continued)

Program/ Intervention	Approach	Outcomes
In Search of Your Warrior (Native Counselling Services of Alberta)	Intervention focused on Indigenous offenders with a history of violence; combines Western treatment approaches with traditional Indigenous spirituality in an attempt to break the cycle of violence.	An evaluation found that a significantly smaller number of offenders who had participated in the program were returned to prison for committing a violent offence within a year of being released; rates of readmission were not significantly different from those Indigenous offenders who did not participate in the program.[f]
Aboriginal Offender Substance Abuse Program (AOSAP; CSC)	A 16-week high-intensity program to address addiction using a holistic approach that considers the physical, mental, emotional, and spiritual dimensions of addiction. Sessions involve Elders and are designed to increase awareness, motivation, skill enhancement, and spirituality.	CSC conducted an evaluation with respect to post-release success up until warrant expiry and found evidence that AOSAP is an effective correctional intervention. Indigenous persons who participated in AOSAP performed better than their counterparts who participated in the mainstream substance abuse program; they also returned to the correctional system at a lower rate.[g] Findings suggest AOSAP reconnects participants with Indigenous spirituality and cultures, such as teachings and ceremonies.[h]
Tupiq program (CSC)	High-intensity, culturally based program for moderate- to high-risk Inuit sex offenders; provides teachings based on Inuit knowledge and culture, using Inuit Elders and facilitators.	Evaluation found that program participants had lower rates of general and violent recidivism than a comparison group approximately four years after they had been released from confinement.[i]

Program/Intervention	Approach	Outcomes
Pathways Units (selected CSC institutions)	Living units in federal institutions led by small teams composed of Indigenous Elders and correctional staff. The approach is grounded in Indigenous cultures and spirituality and issues, including residential schools and reserve life. Broken families are addressed through individual counselling, sweat lodge ceremonies, and other culturally based activities.	An evaluation found that Pathway participants were more likely to be transferred to lower security and had enhanced opportunities for early release than a matched group. A high level of inmate and staff support for the program. A one-year post-release review of Pathway participants ($N = 44$) with a matched group found no significant differences in outcome measures (technical revocations and new offences), although Pathway unit offenders reoffended at a lower rate than offenders in the matched group (17 percent versus 35 percent respectively).[j]
Okimaw Ohci Healing Lodge (Nekaneet First Nation in Saskatchewan; CSC)	Program for Indigenous women offenders centred on Indigenous cultures and teachings. Involvement of Elders in traditional practices, including sharing circles and sweat lodges.	An evaluation found that the lodge was an appropriate alternative to incarceration, was cost-effective compared to correctional institutions, and had established effective relationships with the local community. A number of operational difficulties, however, limited its effectiveness, including a lack of programs and the need for staff development. No data on post-release reoffending, on the impact of the program on quality of life, or on specific issues (e.g., addiction, violence).[k]
Aboriginal Community Development Officers (CSC)	Facilitate CCRA Section 84 consultations with Indigenous communities and help develop plans to help Indigenous offenders reintegrate with the community.	An evaluation found that the work of ACDOs had increased the number of Section 84 plans submitted to the PBC. There were no significant differences in reoffending between Indigenous offenders released with a Section 84 plan and a matched group with no Section 84 plan.[l]

(continued)

Program/ Intervention	Approach	Outcomes
Waseskun Healing Centre (Montréal, CSC funded, community operated)	Section 81 healing lodge. Program centred on the teachings of the medicine wheel to help offenders reintegrate with the community. Elders involved in group and one-on-one sessions.	Evaluation of the program found Waseskun is "a successful therapeutic healing community" that helps offenders address their issues. No information on the impact of the program on reoffending, quality of life, or other issues (e.g., addiction, violence).[m]

[a] J. Couture, T. Parker, R. Couture, and P. Laboucane, *A Cost–Benefit Analysis of Hollow Water's Community Holistic Circle Healing Process* (Ottawa: Solicitor General of Canada, 2001), http://www.publicsafety.gc.ca/res/cor/apc/_fl/apc-20-eng.pdf.

[b] S. Trevethan, N. Crutcher, J.P. Moore, and J. Mileto, *Pé Sâkâstêw Centre: An In-Depth Examination of a Healing Lodge for Federally Incarcerated Offenders* (Ottawa: Correctional Service Canada, 2007), http://www.csc-scc.gc.ca/text/rsrch/reports/r170/r170-eng.pdf.

[c] J. Proulx and S. Perrault, *An Evaluation of the Ma Mawi Wi Chi Itata Centre's Family Violence Program Stony Mountain Project* (Ottawa and Winnipeg: Ma Mawi Wi Chi Itata Family Violence Program, 1996).

[d] CSC, *Departmental Performance Report 2010–2011* (Ottawa: Treasury Board Secretariat, n.d.), pp. 29–31, http://www.tbs-sct.gc.ca/dpr-rmr/2010-2011/inst/pen/pen-eng.pdf.

[e] A. Bell and J. Flight, *An Evaluation of the Spirit of a Warrior Program for Woman Offenders* (Ottawa: Correctional Service Canada, 2006), http://www.csc-scc.gc.ca/text/rsrch/reports/r180/r180-eng.shtml.

[f] S. Trevethan, J.-P. Moore, and N. Allegri, *The "In Search of Your Warrior" Program for Aboriginal Offenders: A Preliminary Evaluation* (Ottawa: Correctional Service Canada, 2005), http://www.csc-scc.gc.ca/text/rsrch/reports/r172/r172-eng.shtml.

[g] D. Kunic and D. Varis, *The Aboriginal Offender Substance Abuse Program (AOSAP): Examining the Effects of Successful Completion on Post-Release Outcomes* (Ottawa: Correctional Service Canada, 2009), http://www.csc-scc.gc.ca/text/rsrch/reports/r217/r217-eng.shtml.

[h] P. Forrester, E. Trainor, S. Farrell-MacDonald, and D. Varis, "Aboriginal Offender Substance Abuse Program (AOSAP) and Cultural Engagement," Correctional Service Canada, Research Snippet 13-03, January 2013, http://www.csc-scc.gc.ca/research/005008-rs13-03-eng.shtml.

[i] L. Stewart, E. Hamilton, G. Wilton, C. Cousineau, and S. Varrette, *An Examination of the Effectiveness of Tupiq: A Culturally Specific Program for Inuit Sex Offenders* (Ottawa: Correctional Service Canada, 2009), http://www.csc-scc.gc.ca/text/rsrch/reports/r213/r213-eng.pdf.

[j] M.J. Burrowes and P. McIntyre, *Final Report—Effective Corrections Initiative—Aboriginal Reintegration* (Ottawa: Correctional Service Canada, 2004), http://www.csc-scc.gc.ca/text/pa/ev-eci-ar-394-2-32/ECI_Aboriginal_Reintegration_e.pdf.

[k] J. Wheatley and I. Roberts, *Evaluation Report: The Section 81 Agreement between the O-Chi-Chak-Ko-Sipi First Nation and the Correctional Service of Canada—The O-Chi-Chak-Ko-Sipi Healing Lodge* (Ottawa: Correctional Service Canada, 2007), http://www.csc-scc.gc.ca/text/pa/ev-ohl/ev-ohl-eng.pdf.

[l] Burrowes and McIntyre, *Final Report—Effective Corrections Initiative—Aboriginal Reintegration*.

[m] S. Bell, *The History, Lessons and Observations of Waseskun Healing Centre, a Successful Therapeutic Healing Community* (Ottawa: Public Safety Canada, 2008), http://www.publicsafety.gc.ca/res/cor/apc/_fl/apc-28-eng.pdf.

There have been no evaluations of CSC's Circle of Care or Aboriginal Corrections Continuum of Care, as they are frameworks that CSC personnel use to make referrals to the CSC's correctional programs. Individual evaluations of the programs that offenders are referred to (e.g., substance abuse programming) are found throughout this chapter and the textbook.

Note that a positive program dynamic may not translate into lower rates of reoffending once offenders are released from custody. To illustrate, an evaluation of healing lodges reported mixed results. In interviews, offenders and staff reported that healing lodges had "positive transformative effects" on offenders, modified their attitudes and behaviour, and increased their knowledge of Indigenous spirituality and cultures. However, an analysis conducted in 2011 revealed that these perceived changes did not result in improved outcomes once the offenders were released into the community.[93] The challenges of maintaining throughcare and accessing support in the community were cited as contributing to the lack of positive correctional outcomes.

The results from this study suggest that there is a disconnect between the perceptions of program staff and those of Indigenous offenders as to the benefits of such programs, including as they relate to outcomes on conditional release. It appears that whatever changes occur in the healing lodges, they do not, for whatever reason, necessarily empower Indigenous offenders to reintegrate successfully back into the community. This may be because, as noted in previous chapters, these offenders were not "integrated" into the community prior to being incarcerated.

It should also be noted that estimates of the recidivism rates among healing lodge participants vary; a 2001 CSC study found that 19 percent of program attendees recidivated upon release, whereas a 2013 CSC report claimed program completers released from three of the nine facilities had a recidivism rate of just 6 percent.[94]

SUMMARY

This chapter has examined the issues surrounding the involvement of Indigenous peoples in corrections and the initiatives that have been undertaken to address the specific needs of this group. Indigenous people are overrepresented at all stages of the criminal justice process far beyond their percentage of the national population. This is the result of a variety of historical and contemporary factors. The CSC has developed a number of Indigenous-specific programs and services; also, many Indigenous communities and organizations themselves are involved in responding to the needs of Indigenous persons in conflict with the law. Many of these programs centre on Indigenous traditions and spirituality. An absence of external evaluations often makes it difficult to assess the effectiveness of these initiatives in addressing the needs of Indigenous offenders and reducing reoffending.

KEY POINTS REVIEW

1. The subordinate political and economic position of Indigenous peoples is a consequence of their colonization by Europeans and Canadian government policies.

2. Indigenous persons are over-represented at all stages of the criminal justice system and are disproportionately represented in correctional institutions.

3. Indigenous women represent a substantial and increasing portion of women in remand and sentenced custody and are the fastest growing prison population in the CSC.

4. Indigenous communities have been active in developing alternative approaches to responding to Indigenous persons in conflict with the law, including programs based on the principles of restorative justice.

5. The CSC has developed a number of Indigenous-specific programs, many of which involve Indigenous Elders and are premised on Indigenous cultures and spirituality.

6. There are unique challenges in supervising Indigenous offenders in the community, and there has been an effort to involve Indigenous communities in this effort.

7. Indigenous offenders generally have higher treatment needs than non-Indigenous offenders.

8. Indigenous inmates are less likely than others to succeed in their applications for conditional release, and they serve a higher proportion of their sentence before being released on parole.

9. Indigenous inmates often experience difficulties when they appear before parole boards.

10. Most community-based and institutional programs for Indigenous offenders have not been evaluated externally. Further examinations are required to investigate their effectiveness in addressing the needs of offenders and their impact on reoffending.

11. To reduce the involvement of Indigenous persons in the justice and corrections systems and to effectively address the needs of Indigenous offenders, broader structural issues, such as racism, social inequality, and poverty, will need to be addressed.

KEY TERM QUESTIONS

1. Describe the *Aboriginal Corrections Continuum of Care* and the *Circle of Care* and discuss their role in Indigenous corrections.

2. What is the importance of *Section 81* and *Section 84* of the CCRA?

CRITICAL THINKING EXERCISES

Critical Thinking Exercise 13.1

Addressing the Over-Representation of Indigenous Persons in Canadian Correctional Populations

Despite a variety of initiatives over the years, the numbers of Indigenous persons involved in corrections and in correctional institutions have continued to increase.

Your Thoughts?

1. Why do you think so many Indigenous persons are involved in the corrections system?
2. What more can Canadian correctional services do to address the needs of Indigenous offenders in their care?
3. How can Indigenous communities be encouraged to get more involved in addressing this issue?
4. What social justice policies require change to curb the over-representation of Indigenous persons in Canadian correctional populations?

Critical Thinking Exercise 13.2

Indigenous Healing Lodges

View the videos *House to Home—The Buffalo Sage Wellness House* and *Journey of a Warrior—The Stan Daniels Healing Centre*, located below (see Media Links).

Your Thoughts?

1. What similarities and differences did you observe between the principles and practices at each healing lodge?
2. What benefits do you think such facilities provide Indigenous offenders? Do you think there are any disadvantages to such facilities?
3. How can the CSC encourage Indigenous communities to become involved in Section 81 agreements to operate healing lodges?

CLASS/GROUP DISCUSSION EXERCISES

Class/Group Discussion Exercise 13.1

A Case Study of One of Canada's Women Dangerous Offenders

Read the series *Life on the Instalment Plan: Is Canada's penal system for women making or breaking Renee Acoby?*, written by Marian Botsford Fraser (see: https://thewalrus.ca/life-on-the-instalment-plan/).[95]

Your Thoughts?

1. What were the main turning points in Ms. Acoby's life that you believe contributed to her involvement in criminal behaviour?

2. Do you agree with the practices the CSC has used over the years to manage Ms. Acoby? Explain.

3. Ms. Acoby was designated a dangerous offender in 2011 and received an indeterminate prison sentence. Given her violent past (including six hostage takings while incarcerated), do you believe Ms. Acoby can be reformed through services provided by the CSC?

4. If she were to be released, what conditions of supervision would you impose on Ms. Acoby? Explain.

Class/Group Discussion Exercise 13.2

Considering the Role of Elders in Corrections

Watch the video *Bringing the Grandchildren Home: Elders in Federal Correctional Facilities*, located below (see Media Links).

Your Thoughts?

1. What are your thoughts on the benefits of Elder participation in the correctional process?

2. As noted, the CSC is experiencing operational challenges in ensuring that Elders are involved in correctional programming for Indigenous offenders. How can Elders be encouraged to participate in CSC activities given the criticisms that such initiatives are a new form of colonialism?

3. Consider the role of Elders in the parole process; how might they facilitate the process for Indigenous applicants?

MEDIA LINKS

"House to Home—The Buffalo Sage Wellness House," https://www.youtube.com/watch?v=hqaGX-8TEuk

"Journey of a Warrior—The Stan Daniels Healing Centre," https://www.youtube.com/watch?v=xsqoIrKdnRk

"Bringing the Grandchildren Home: Elders in Federal Correctional Facilities," http://www.csc-scc.gc.ca/media-room/009-1009-eng.shtml

"8th Fire Dispatch: Sacred Heart Residential School—Part 1," http://www.cbc.ca/player/play/2183547330

"Inside Canada's Corrections System: Prisons: The Case of Adam Capay," http://tvo.org/video/programs/the-agenda-with-steve-paikin/inside-canadas-corrections-system

NOTES

1. Native Women's Association of Canada, *Aboriginal Women and Gangs: An Issue Paper* (Corner Brook, NL: Author, 2007), http://www.laa.gov.nl.ca/laa/naws/pdf/nwac-gangs.pdf; D. McCaskill, "Discrimination and public perceptions of Aboriginal people in Canadian Cities," 2012 UAKN Research Paper Series, http://uakn.org/fr/research-project/discrimination-and-public-perceptions-of-aboriginal-people-in-canadian-cities/.

2. D. Chansonneuve, *Addictive Behaviours among Aboriginal People in Canada* (Ottawa: Aboriginal Healing Foundation, 2007), http://www.ahf.ca/downloads/addictive-behaviours.pdf; *Final Report of the Truth and Reconciliation Commission of Canada* (Winnipeg: Author, 2015), http://www.trc.ca/websites/trcinstitution/index.php?p=890.

3. M.B. Castellano, L. Archibald, and M. Degagne, *From Truth to Reconciliation: Transforming the Legacy of Residential Schools* (Ottawa: Aboriginal Healing Foundation, 2008), http://www.ahf.ca/downloads/from-truth-to-reconciliation-transforming-the-legacy-of-residential-schools.pdf.

4. A. Webster, *Sheltering Urban Aboriginal Homeless People: Assessment of Situation and Needs* (Ottawa: Human Resources and Social Development Canada, 2007), http://pathprogram.samhsa.gov/ResourceFiles/NAFC-Homeless-Final-12-02-08%5B1%5D.pdf; Chansonneuve, *Addictive Behaviours among Aboriginal People in Canada*.

5. A. Hyatt, "Healing Through Culture for Incarcerated Aboriginal People," *First Peoples Child & Family Review 8*, no. 2 (2013), 40–53; S. Perreault, "The Incarceration of Aboriginal People in Adult Correctional Services," *Juristat 29*, no. 3, Catalogue no. 85-002-X (Ottawa: Minister of Canada, 2009) http://www.statcan.gc.ca/pub/85-002-x/2009003/article/10903-eng.htm.

6. Auditor General of Canada, *Report 3 – Preparing Indigenous Offenders for Release – Service Canada* (Ottawa: Author, 2016), http://www.oag-bvg.gc.ca/internet/English/parl_oag_201611_03_e_41832.html\#

7. *Truth and Reconciliation Commission of Canada: Calls to Action* (Winnipeg: Author, 2015), p. 4, http://www.trc.ca/websites/trcinstitution/File/2015/Findings/Calls_to_Action_English2.pdf.

8. Ibid.

9. Office of the Correctional Investigator, *Annual Report, 2015–2016* (Ottawa: Author, 2016), http://www.oci-bec.gc.ca/cnt/rpt/pdf/annrpt/annrpt20152016-eng.pdf.

10. Auditor General of Canada, *Report 3 – Preparing Indigenous Offenders for Release*.

11. Parole Board of Canada, *Performance Monitoring Report 2010–2011* (Ottawa: Author, 2011), http://pbc-clcc.gc.ca/rprts/pmr/pmr_2010_2011/index-eng.shtml.

12. Statistics Canada, "Number and distribution of the population reporting an Aboriginal identity and percentage of Aboriginal people in the population, Canada, provinces and territories, 2011 (table)," National Household Survey, 2011, https://www12.statcan.gc.ca/nhs-enm/2011/as-sa/99-011-x/2011001/tbl/tbl02-eng.cfm; Auditor General of Canada, *Report 3 – Preparing Indigenous Offenders for Release*; Office of the Correctional Investigator, *Annual Report, 2015–2016*.

13. Office of the Correctional Investigator, *Annual Report, 2015–2016*; J. Reitano, "Adult Correctional Statistics in Canada, 2014/2015," *Juristat 36*, no. 1, Catalogue no. 85-002-X (Ottawa: Minister of Industry, 2016), http://www.statcan.gc.ca/pub/85-002-x/2016001/article/14318-eng.htm.

14. J. Thompson and R. Gobeil, "Aboriginal Women: An Overview of the Correctional Process from Admission to Warrant Expiry," Correctional Service Canada, Research at a glance R-342, January 2015, http://www.csc-scc.gc.ca/research/005008-r342-eng.shtml.

15. Office of the Correctional Investigator, *Annual Report, 2015–2016*.

16. Reitano, "Adult Correctional Statistics in Canada, 2014/2015."

17. Correctional Services Program, "Youth Correctional Statistics in Canada, 2014/2015," *Juristat* 36, no. 1, Catalogue no. 85-002-X (Ottawa: Minister of Industry, 2016), http://www.statcan.gc.ca/pub/85-002-x/2016001/article/14317-eng.htm.

18. S. Luck, "Black, Indigenous Prisoners Over-Represented in Nova Scotian Jails," CBC News, May 20, 2016, http://www.cbc.ca/news/canada/nova-scotia/black-indigenous-prisoners-nova-scotia-jails-1.3591535.

19. J. Rankin, P. Winsa, and H. Ng, "Unequal Justice: Aboriginal and Black Inmates Disproportionately Fill Ontario Jails," *Toronto Star*, March 1, 2013, https://www.thestar.com/news/insight/2013/03/01/unequal_justice_aboriginal_and_black_inmates_disproportionately_fill_ontario_jails.html.

20. Assembly of First Nations, *Submission: Bill C-10 Safe Streets and Communities* Act (Ottawa: Author, 2011), http://www.afn.ca/uploads/files/parliamentary/billc-10.pdf; Auditor General of Canada, *Report 3 – Preparing Indigenous Offenders for Release*; K. Harris, "Rise in Prison Gangs Fuelling Violence, Drug Trade: Prison Population Jumps 44% in 5 Years," CBC News, October 24, 2012, http://www.cbc.ca/news/politics/story/2012/10/24/pol-gangs-prisons.html; R. Ruddell and S. Gottschall, "The Prison Adjustment of Aboriginal Offenders," *Australian & New Zealand Journal of Criminology* 47, no. 3 (2014), 336–54. Office of the Correctional Investigator, *Annual Report, 2015–2016*.

21. Office of the Correctional Investigator, *Annual Report, 2015–2016*.

22. Public Safety Canada, *2015 Corrections and Conditional Release Statistical Overview* (Ottawa: Author, 2016), http://www.publicsafety.gc.ca/res/cor/rep/_fl/2011-ccrso-eng.pdf.

23. Ibid.

24. Office of the Correctional Investigator, *Annual Report, 2015–2016*.

25. Public Safety Canada, *2015 Corrections and Conditional Release Statistical Overview*.

26. Thompson and Gobeil, "Aboriginal Women: An Overview of the Correctional Process from Admission to Warrant Expiry."

27. D. MacDonald, "Profile of Aboriginal Men Offenders: Custody and Supervision Snapshots," Correctional Service Canada, Research at a glance R-321, March 2014, http://www.csc-scc.gc.ca/research/005008-r321-eng.shtml.

28. Statistics Canada, "Projections of the Aboriginal Population and Households in Canada, 2011 to 2036," *The Daily*, September 17, 2015, http://www.statcan.gc.ca/daily-quotidien/150917/dq150917b-eng.pdf; Statistics Canada, "Aboriginal Peoples in Canada: First Nations people, Métis and Inuit," National Household Survey 2011 (Ottawa: Minister of Industry, 2013), http://www12.statcan.gc.ca/nhs-enm/2011/as-sa/99-011-x/99-011-x2011001-eng.pdf.

29. Office of the Correctional Investigator, *Annual Report, 2015–2016*; Auditor General of Canada, *Report 3 – Preparing Indigenous Offenders for Release*.

30. Correctional Service Canada, *Social Histories of Aboriginal Women Offenders*, Emerging Research Results – ERR 14-7 (May 2014), as cited in Office of the Correctional Investigator, *Annual Report, 2015–2016* (Ottawa: Author, 2016), http://www.oci-bec.gc.ca/cnt/rpt/pdf/annrpt/annrpt20152016-eng.pdf.

31. J. Beaudette, M. Cheverie, and R. Gobeil, "Aboriginal Women: Profile and Changing Population," Correctional Service Canada, Research at a glance R-341, October 2014, http://www.csc-scc.gc.ca/research/005008-r341-eng.shtml.

32. Office of the Correctional Investigator, *Annual Report, 2015–2016*.

33. Thompson and Gobeil, "Aboriginal Women: An Overview of the Correctional Process from Admission to Warrant Expiry"; Office of the Correctional Investigator, *Annual Report, 2015–2016*.

34. M. Wesley, *Marginalized: The Aboriginal Women's Experience in Federal Corrections* (Ottawa: Public Safety Canada, 2012), http://www.publicsafety.gc.ca/res/cor/apc/_fl/apc-33-eng.pdf.

35. Ibid.

36. Beaudette et al., "Aboriginal Women: Profile and Changing Population"; Thompson and Gobeil, "Aboriginal Women: An Overview of the Correctional Process from Admission to Warrant Expiry."

37. "Community Council: Background," Aboriginal Legal Services website (n.d.), http://www.aboriginallegal.ca/background.html.

38. Campbell Research Associates, *Evaluation of the Aboriginal Legal Services of Toronto Community Council Program: Final Report* (Toronto: Aboriginal Legal Services, 2000), http://www.aboriginallegal.ca/assets/alstevaluation2000.pdf.

39. D. Milward, "Making the Circle Stronger: An Effort to Buttress Aboriginal Use of Restorative Justice in Canada Against Recent Criticisms," *International Journal of Punishment and Sentencing 4*, no. 3 (2008), 124–58; L. Monchalin, "Canadian Aboriginal Peoples Victimization, Offending and Its Prevention: Gathering the Evidence," *Crime Prevention and Community Safety 12*, no. 2 (2010), 119–32.

40. Auditor General of Canada, *Report 3 – Preparing Indigenous Offenders for Release*.

41. "Correctional Service Canada Healing Lodges," Correctional Service Canada website, last modified December 12, 2016, http://www.csc-scc.gc.ca/aboriginal/002003-2000-eng.shtml.

42. M.M. Mann, *Good Intentions, Disappointing Results: A Progress Report on Federal Aboriginal Corrections* (Ottawa: Office of the Correctional Investigator, 2009), http://www.oci-bec.gc.ca/rpt/oth-aut/oth-aut20091113-eng.aspx.

43. J. Wheatley and I. Roberts, *Evaluation Report: The Section 81 Agreement between the O-Chi-Chak-Ko-Sipi First Nation and the Correctional Service of Canada—The O-Chi-Chak-Ko-Sipi Healing Lodge* (Ottawa: Correctional Service Canada, 2007), http://www.csc-scc.gc.ca/text/pa/ev-ohl/ev-ohl-eng.pdf.

44. R. Weibe and Y. Johnson, *Stolen Life: The Journey of a Cree Woman* (Toronto: Vintage Canada, 1998), 387.

45. Perreault, "The Incarceration of Aboriginal People in Adult Correctional Services."

46. A.K. Yessine and J. Bonta, "The Offending Trajectories of Youthful Aboriginal Offenders," *Canadian Journal of Criminology and Criminal Justice 51*, no. 4 (2009), 435–72.

47. P. Mullins and S.F. MacDonald, "Offender Substance Use Patterns – Aboriginal and Non-Aboriginal Offenders," Correctional Service Canada, Research Snippet 12-10, August 2012, http://www.csc-scc.gc.ca/research/005008-rs12-10-eng.shtml.

48. S. Trevethan, J.P. Moore, and C.J. Rastin, "A Profile of Aboriginal Offenders in Federal Facilities and Serving Time in the Community," *Forum on Corrections Research 14*, no. 3 (2002), 17–19, http://www.csc-scc.gc.ca/research/forum/e143/e143f-eng.shtml.

49. L. Stewart, J. Sapers, A. Nolan, and J. Power, "Self-Reported Physical Health Status of Newly Admitted Federally-Sentenced Men Offenders," Correctional Service Canada, Research at a glance R-314, February 2014, http://www.csc-scc.gc.ca/research/005008-0314-eng.shtml.

50. M.A. MacSwain and M. Cheverie, "Comparing the Mental Health Treatment and Abuse Histories of Aboriginal and Non-Aboriginal Participants of the Methadone Maintenance Treatment Program (MMTP)," Correctional Service Canada,

Research Snippet 12-08, July 2012, http://www.csc-scc.gc.ca/research/005008-rs12-8-eng.shtml

51. A. Owusu-Bempah, S. Kanters, E. Druyts, K. Toor, K.A. Muldoon, J.W. Farquhar, and E.J. Mills, "Years of Life Lost to Incarceration: Inequities between Aboriginal and Non-Aboriginal Canadians," *BMC Public Health 14* (2014), 585–91.

52. J.P. Moore, *First Nations, Métis, Inuit, and Non-Aboriginal Federal Offenders: A Comparative Profile*, Research Branch R-134 (Ottawa: Correctional Service Canada, 2003), http://www.csc-scc.gc.ca/text/rsrch/reports/r134/r134_e.pdf.

53. Personal communication with D. Murdoch.

54. Correctional Service Canada, *Strategic Plan for Aboriginal Corrections* (Ottawa: Author, 2003), http://www.csc-scc.gc.ca/aboriginal/092/002003-1000-eng.pdf.

55. Correctional Service Canada, *Revitalizing Correctional Programs to Enhance the Correctional Service of Canada's Contributions to Public Safety: Moving Towards an Integrated Correctional Program Model* (Ottawa: Author, 2011).

56. Auditor General of Canada, *Report 3 – Preparing Indigenous Offenders for Release* at paragraph 3.28.

57. Office of the Correctional Investigator, *Annual Report, 2015–2016.*

58. "National Correctional Program Referral Guidelines," Correctional Service Canada, Guideline 726-2, January 23, 2017, http://www.csc-scc.gc.ca/lois-et-reglements/726-2-gl-eng.shtml.

59. Aboriginal correctional program officer, personal communication with D. Murdoch.

60. Perreault, "The Incarceration of Aboriginal People in Adult Correctional Services."

61. Office of the Correctional Investigator, *Annual Report, 2015–2016.*

62. T. Rugge, *Risk Assessment of Male Aboriginal Offenders: A 2006 Perspective* (Ottawa: Public Safety and Emergency Preparedness Canada, 2006), http://www.publicsafety.gc.ca/res/cor/rep/_fl/abo-offen-eng.pdf.

63. Public Safety Canada, *2015 Corrections and Conditional Release Statistical Overview.*

64. Mann, *Good Intentions, Disappointing Results: A Progress Report on Federal Aboriginal Corrections.*

65. Ibid.

66. Office of the Correctional Investigator, *Annual Report, 2015–2016.*

67. Parole Board of Canada, *Performance Monitoring Report 2014–2015* (Ottawa: Author, 2015), p. 27, https://www.canada.ca/en/parole-board/corporate/transparency/reporting-to-canadians/performance-monitoring-report/2014-2015.html\#f18.

68. Auditor General of Canada, *Report 3 – Preparing Indigenous Offenders for Release* at paragraph 3.28.

69. Parole Board of Canada, *Performance Monitoring Report 2014–2015*, p. 27.

70. MacDonald, "Profile of Aboriginal Men Offenders: Custody and Supervision Snapshots."

71. Public Safety Canada Portfolio Corrections Statistics Committee, *Corrections and Conditional Release Statistical Overview, 2010–2011* (Ottawa: Author, 2011), p. 61, http://www.publicsafety.gc.ca/res/cor/rep/fl/2011-ccrso-eng.pdf; Parole Board of Canada, *Performance Monitoring Report 2014–2015*, p. 27; Public Safety Canada, *2015 Corrections and Conditional Release Statistical Overview*, p. 61; Auditor General of Canada, *Report 3 – Preparing Indigenous Offenders for Release.*

72. Auditor General of Canada, *Report 3 – Preparing Indigenous Offenders for Release.*

73. Thompson and Gobeil, "Aboriginal Women: An Overview of the Correctional Process from Admission to Warrant Expiry."

74. Mann, *Good Intentions, Disappointing Results: A Progress Report on Federal Aboriginal Corrections.*

75. Thompson and Gobeil, "Aboriginal Women: An Overview of the Correctional Process from Admission to Warrant Expiry"; Auditor General of Canada, *Report 3 – Preparing Indigenous Offenders for Release*.

76. Auditor General of Canada, *Report 3 – Preparing Indigenous Offenders for Release*; Office of the Correctional Investigator, *Annual Report, 2015–2016*.

77. Auditor General of Canada, *Report 3 – Preparing Indigenous Offenders for Release*.

78. Ibid., at paragraph 3.30.

79. Parole Board of Canada, *Performance Monitoring Report 2014–2015*.

80. L.H. Birnie, *A Rock and a Hard Place: Inside Canada's Parole Board* (Toronto: Macmillan, 1990), 195.

81. Parole Board of Canada, *From Confinement to Community: The National Parole Board and Aboriginal Offenders* (Ottawa: Author, 2007).

82. S. Turnbull, "Aboriginalising the Parole Process: 'Culturally Appropriate' Adaptations and the Canadian Federal Parole System," *Punishment & Society 16*, no. 4 (2014), 385–405.

83. Parole Board of Canada, *Performance Monitoring Report 2014–2015*.

84. Parole Board of Canada, *From Confinement to Community*.

85. "Elder-Assisted Hearings and Community-Assisted Hearings," Parole Board of Canada (n.d.), https://www.canada.ca/content/dam/canada/parole-board/migration/001/093/001-0005-02-en.pdf.

86. Office of the Correctional Investigator, *Spirit Matters: Aboriginal People and the Corrections and Conditional Release Act* (Ottawa: Author, 2012), http://www.oci-bec.gc.ca/cnt/rpt/oth-aut/oth-aut20121022-eng.aspx.

87. S. Bell, *The History, Lessons and Observations of Waseskun Healing Centre, a Successful Therapeutic Healing Community* (Ottawa: Public Safety Canada, 2008), http://www.publicsafety.gc.ca/res/cor/apc/_fl/apc-28-eng.pdf.

88. Ibid., p. 87.

89. Birnie, *A Rock and a Hard Place*, p. 195.

90. Office of the Correctional Investigator, *Annual Report, 2015–2016*.

91. Parole Board of Canada, *Performance Monitoring Report 2014–2015*; Office of the Correctional Investigator, *Annual Report, 2015–2016*.

92. Parole Board Canada. (2015). 2014–2015 Performance Monitoring Report. Retrieved from https://www.canada.ca/en/parole-board/corporate/transparency/reporting-to-canadians/performance-monitoring-report/2014-2015.html#f18

93. E. Didenko and B. Marquis, "Aboriginal Healing Lodges," Chapter 1 in *Evaluation Report: Strategies Plan for Aboriginal Corrections* (Ottawa: Correctional Service Canada, 2011), p. vii, http://www.csc-scc.gc.ca/text/pa/ev-ahl-394-2-49/healing-lodge-final-eng.pdf.

94. J. Gerson, "Dangerous offender's escape raises questions about security, effectiveness of healing lodges," *National Post*, August 17, 2016, http://news.nationalpost.com/news/canada/canadian-politics/dangerous-offenders-escape-raises-questions-about-security-effectiveness-of-healing-lodges.

95. M. Botsford Fraser, :Life on the Instalment Plan: Is Canada's penal system for women making or breaking Renée Acoby?" *The Walrus*, March 10, 2010, https://thewalrus.ca/life-on-the-instalment-plan/.

CHAPTER 14

YOUNG OFFENDERS

CHAPTER OBJECTIVES

- Discuss the evolution of youth corrections in Canada.
- Describe the profile of young offenders in Canada.
- Identify and describe noncustodial and custodial sentence options for young offenders.
- Identify and briefly describe the different types of correctional treatment programs offered to youth in custody.
- Describe the dynamics of life inside youth correctional facilities.
- Discuss restorative justice initiatives used in the youth criminal justice system.
- Discuss the importance of aftercare programs and informal social support networks.
- Discuss the effectiveness of youth justice interventions.

THE EVOLUTION OF YOUTH CORRECTIONS

Recall from the discussion in Chapter 2 that in the 1800s, young offenders were confined along with adults in institutions. Reform efforts in the late 1800s were designed to segregate youth from adults. Successive legislation, beginning in the early 20th century, reflected changing philosophies as to how best to respond to young offenders.

The first comprehensive legislation for young offenders was the **Juvenile Delinquents Act (JDA)**, enacted in 1908. This legislation set out a social welfare approach to youth crime. Youth who came into conflict with the law were viewed as misdirected—resulting from inadequate parental and social guidance—and in need of assistance and intervention to address the personal, social, and familial factors that had contributed to their offending behaviour.[1] The philosophy underlying this legislation, *parens patriae*, which is Latin for "parent of the country,"[2] gave the youth courts considerable discretion to intervene in the lives of wayward youth, including removing children from the care of their parents when the courts deemed it necessary. Further, this meant

Juvenile Delinquents Act (JDA; 1908)
Legislation centred on a social welfare approach to youth crime that gave judges considerable discretion to intervene in the lives of young offenders.

432

that youth could be subject to supervision until the authorities decided they had been rehabilitated and that sentences could be changed midway to reflect the youth's progress.[3]

The JDA, however, raised concerns about inconsistent sentencing across Canada, the lack of proportionality between the offence and sentence, the abuse of child and parental rights, and the presence of "status offences"—that is, behaviour engaged in by a youth (e.g., sexual behaviour, truancy) that would not be against the law for an adult.[4]

The **Young Offenders Act (YOA)**, enacted in 1984, attempted to balance the protection of young offenders' special needs and legal rights and freedoms with the protection of the public, while ensuring young offenders would be held accountable. The YOA was criticized for, among other things, placing too high a value on the rights and rehabilitation of youth; it was argued that this put the public at risk.[5] As discussed in Chapter 1, public sentiment influences the development of correctional policies, and in the 1990s, youth justice reform was spurred by the public's discontent with the YOA and interest in crime-control policies for young offenders.[6]

The current legislation under which the youth justice system operates is the **Youth Criminal Justice Act (YCJA)** (2003; http://laws-lois.justice.gc.ca/PDF/Y-1.5.pdf). The objectives of the youth justice system are set out in Section 3(1)(a)(i–iii) of that act and include crime prevention, rehabilitation and reintegration, and "meaningful consequences." Among other goals, the YCJA is intended to establish clear principles to guide decision-making in the youth justice system, to promote fairness in sentencing, to reduce the rate of youth incarceration through the increased use of extrajudicial measures, to reintegrate youth into their communities, and to distinguish clearly between serious

> **Young Offenders Act (YOA; 1984)** Youth legislation that attempted to balance the protection of young offenders' special needs and legal rights and freedoms with the protection of the public, while ensuring young offenders would be held accountable.

CORRECTIONS PERSPECTIVE 14.1

An Offender's Spouse

The spouse of an offender convicted of a violent crime reflects on her experience with the criminal justice and corrections system:

> *One of the overarching conclusions I drew was that if a society wants to make a pickpocketing boy into a killer and his sister into a prostitute, the best way is to put them in jail at an early age, allow them to be physically and sexually assaulted by bigger children or adults, deny them contact with anyone who might care about them, and take away opportunities for education. Then, once the child is grown, release him or her back into the community with no money, no ability to trust, no skills for getting a job, and no adults he or she can rely on.*

Source: S. Maroney, *Through the Glass* (Toronto: Doubleday Canada, 2011), p. 245.

violent offences and less serious ones, with the latter being dealt with outside of the youth courts through extrajudicial sanctions (e.g., referrals to community services and programming, warnings).[7]

The YCJA's emphasis on extrajudicial measures is intended to address young offenders' diverse needs by providing more effective and timely programming for young offenders (s. 4(b)), and to reduce the system's reliance on courts and custody to save costs.[8] The legislation reflects the belief that "youth may be more deserving of leniency due to their psychological and moral immaturity."[9] This legislation is in sharp contrast to the more punitive approaches taken by American youth justice systems.[10]

The YCJA seems to have succeeded in diverting youth from custody, as the majority (90 percent) of the approximately 8,000 young offenders supervised by youth correctional systems in Canada in 2014–15 were subject to community supervision.[11] Note as well that the youth incarceration rate has been dropping for six years straight and as of 2014–15 was 6 per 10,000.[12] The youth justice system is illustrated in Figure 14.1.

While the declining rate of youth correctional populations is positive, a concerning feature is that similar to their adult counterparts, Indigenous youth continue to be over-represented in youth correctional populations across Canada, with the greatest disparity experienced by Indigenous girls. Their over-representation as a group highlights the need to examine whether existing policies and interventions are adequately addressing the risk and protective profiles of Indigenous young offenders.[13] Further, their over-representation highlights the need to consider how police, prosecutor, and probation-officer decision making serve to limit the options that youth court judges can consider when sentencing Indigenous offenders under the YCJA.[14]

Bill C-10 and the Youth Criminal Justice System

As discussed in Chapter 2, the Conservative federal government that was in power from 2006 to 2015 passed a variety of punitive measures, including Bill C-10. One of the concerns with this bill includes the impact on Indigenous youth, who, as noted above, are over-represented in youth corrections. Also, the bill emphasizes public safety and protection, which makes it easier for judges to sentence serious and violent young offenders to a period of imprisonment and to sentence young offenders (aged 14 and older) as adults when the youth has been charged with certain offences (i.e., murder, attempted murder, manslaughter, or aggravated sexual assault).[15] Other provisions compel police agencies to keep records of extrajudicial sanctions imposed on youth to document their criminal tendencies and allow the names of young offenders to be published if they have been convicted of a violent offence.[16]

The changes that were made to the YCJA under Bill C-10 came into effect in late 2012. Some feared the policies would result in more youth being sentenced to custody as a result of the shift in focus toward public security and risk management. These fears appear to be unfounded; in the years since the changes were made, youth custody rates have continued to decline across Canada.[17]

Figure 14.1

Structure of the Youth Justice System under the YCJA

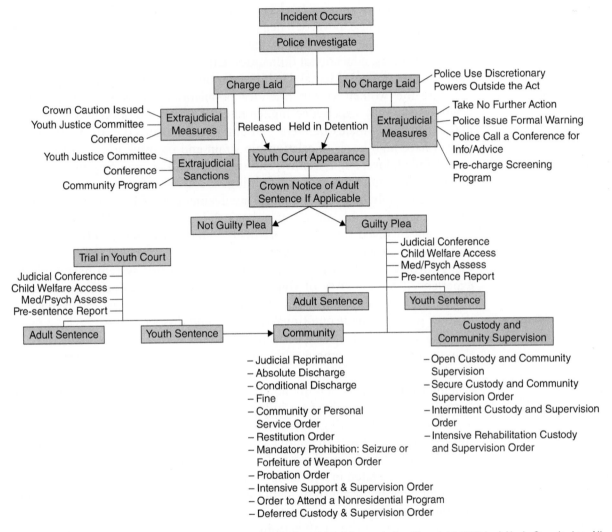

A PROFILE OF YOUNG OFFENDERS

> *Very rarely will we get someone on probation who does not have a youth record. When you look back through an offender's file, you can often see clearly that there were times in their life when they were at a crossroads when there was a need for immediate intervention, but, for whatever reason, it wasn't done.*

> —Probation officer, personal communication with C.T. Griffiths

Several key attributes of young offenders and youth crime are set out in Corrections File 14.1.

Factors that place youth at risk for involvement in delinquent behaviour include a history of antisocial behaviour, parental incarceration, drug consumption, substance abuse, poverty, a negative or disruptive family environment (e.g., involvement in the foster care system), a history of abuse, trauma exposure, delinquent peers, educational difficulties, emotional/behavioural disorders, and gang membership.[18] Mental health symptoms are typically more prevalent amongst the women young offender population.[19] Further, young female offenders typically experience higher rates of sexual, emotional, and physical abuse than young male offenders.[20] Young women involved in the youth justice system have high levels of relationship strain and multiple forms of this strain (e.g., familial, love, and frenemy), and they may end up engaging in delinquent acts (e.g., drug and substance use, fighting) as a means of coping.[21]

High levels of gang and drug involvement have been correlated with higher rates of gun use among at-risk youth in Montréal and Toronto.[22] Further, gang-involved youth are more likely to have histories of substance abuse and violent behaviour such as weapons use, and are more likely to recidivate.[23] Gang-involved youth who end up in the youth justice system have typically experienced higher rates of trauma and perpetuation-induced trauma (i.e., engaging in acts of violence) and are more likely than non gang-involved youth to show post-traumatic emotional numbing and dissociation.[24]

Having fetal alcohol spectrum disorder (FASD) also increases the risk that a youth will experiment with substances and come into contact with the youth justice system. These individuals face a variety of risks and challenges, ranging from academic, family, and mental health challenges to experiences of victimization and negative peer influences.[25]

A study investigating the risk of internalizing and externalizing disorders and service use histories of youth ($N = 152$) across Atlantic Canada found that youth who had been involved in justice services in the previous six months ($N = 73$; incarcerated in a juvenile detention centre or attended an alternative education facility for youth probationers) and youth who had been involved in mental health services in the previous six months ($N = 79$; intensive programming for mental health or addictions issues) presented similar levels of risk for mental health disorders and delinquent behaviour. Youth in the justice services group were less likely than those in the mental health services group to have accessed education, health, and mental health services.[26]

This finding highlights the need to provide youth with access to diverse services as a prevention measure to decrease the likelihood they will become involved in the youth justice system.[27]

Indigenous Young Offenders

Statistics Canada reports that in 2014–15, Indigenous youth represented 33 percent of admissions to youth correctional services while comprising only 7 percent of the youth population in these jurisdictions. Further, young female

CORRECTIONS FILE 14.1

A Profile of Youth Crime and Offenders

- Between 1984 and 2011, there was an overall decrease in the seriousness of police-reported youth crime in Canada, although it became proportionally more violent.[a]
- The rates of youth charged and cases being heard by Canadian youth courts have been declining over the past decade, due in large measure to the YCJA, which emphasizes diversion. Canadian youth courts completed the lowest number of cases (approximately 40,000) in more than two decades.
- The majority (62 percent) of youth court cases involve older youth (ages 16 and 17).
- Youth most often find themselves before the court for nonviolent offences (71 percent). The most common offences are theft, administration of justice offences (e.g., failure to appear, failure to comply with conditions of a court order), common assault, and break and enter.
- Young women offenders on average receive shorter custodial sentences than male youth.
- Probation (58 percent) and community service orders (25 percent), on their own or in combination with another type of sentence, were the most common types of sentences imposed by Canadian youth courts.
- Approximately half (51 percent) of youth serve one year or less on probation.

[a] P.J. Carrington, "Trends in the Seriousness of Youth Crime in Canada, 1984–2011," *Canadian Journal of Criminology and Criminal Justice 55*, no. 2 (2013), 293–314.

Sources: S. Alam, "Youth Court Statistics in Canada, 2013/2014," *Juristat* 35, no. 1, Catalogue no. 85-002-X (Ottawa: Minister of Industry, 2015), http://www.statcan.gc.ca/pub/85-002-x/2015001/article/14224-eng.pdf; Correctional Services Program, "Youth Correctional Statistics in Canada, 2014/2015," *Juristat* 36, no. 1, Catalogue no. 85-002-X (Ottawa: Minister of Industry, 2016), http://www.statcan.gc.ca/pub/85-002-x/2016001/article/14317-eng.htm.

Indigenous offenders represented a higher proportion (44 percent) of the admitted female young offender population than the proportion of male Indigenous youth (29 percent) amongst the admitted young male offender population.[28]

Indigenous youth in Nova Scotia, for example, represented 4 percent of the general population in 2014–15 but 12 percent of the population of youth sentenced to custody.[29] Ontario data for 2013 showed over-representation of Indigenous boys and girls in the sentenced custody population, with their representation in the sentenced custody population being five times and ten times higher, respectively, than their representation in the general population of young boys and girls in Ontario.[30]

One contributing factor to their over-representation may be the lack of community programs, resources, and extrajudicial measures in remote, rural communities.[31] Of particular concern is the plight of youth on First

Nations reserves. Indigenous youth living on reserves are charged with a criminal offence at a rate more than three times the average rate across the remainder of Canada, and they commit a greater proportion of violent and property crimes. These youth are 11 times more likely to be accused of committing homicide than non-Indigenous youth living off-reserve.[32]

The higher rates of criminal offending among the youth Indigenous population have been related to high rates of substance abuse, high rates of victimization and family violence, pervasive poverty, low educational attainment, gang membership, and high numbers of Indigenous children witnessing abuse against their mothers.[33] The risk profile of Indigenous youth increases their likelihood of engaging in criminal behaviour and becoming involved in the youth justice system.[34] Many of these risk factors relate to issues discussed in Chapter 13 with respect to the consequences of institutional racism, residential schools, and the destruction of Indigenous communities and cultures.

Indigenous youth may be prime targets for gang recruitment, resulting in their involvement in the criminal justice and corrections systems.[35] Incarcerating gang members may not be an effective way to reduce recidivism among this population, because gang members may strengthen their bonds in the prison setting, further entrenching their antisocial tendencies and criminal offending upon release.[36]

In contrast, culturally informed early prevention strategies work for at-risk Indigenous youth when they are tailored to address the risk factors that lead them to join gangs, such as the economic and social conditions of Indigenous youth, trauma and loss, and cognitive impairments (such as FASD). Culturally appropriate youth crime prevention programs offered in conjunction with programs targeting anger management, substance abuse, and family violence may be effective at decreasing Indigenous youth involvement with the criminal justice system.[37]

It should be noted that other racialized groups are over-represented in youth custodial populations. In 2014–15, Black youth were over-represented in Nova Scotian facilities; African Nova Scotians accounted for just 2 percent of the general population yet they represented 16 percent of incarcerated youth.[38] Data for 2013 in Ontario documented the over-representation of Black youth in that system; their representation in youth custodial populations was four times higher than their representation in the general population.[39]

DIVERSION

Diversion is a key feature of the YCJA. Police officers and Crown counsel can divert youth from the formal court system. Section 6(1) of the YCJA has formalized the practice of police issuing warnings and cautions and referring youth to diversion programs. Young offenders may be diverted at the pre-charge stage to community organizations whose task is to ensure that they complete specified sanctions in a given time period. Once the young offender has satisfied the requirements as laid out, the police or Crown counsel are notified and charges are not laid for the original offence.

When extrajudicial sanctions are brought at the post-charge stage, youth are diverted to formal community diversion programs. When they have met the requirements of the program, the charges are withdrawn.[40] These sanctions include offering an apology to those impacted by their offence, providing restitution or personal services to the victim(s) of the offence, completing a period of community service, participating in community programs (e.g., counselling), and/or being subject to a period of community supervision.[41]

As with adults, there is concern that diversion programs may result in net-widening, meaning that low-risk, nonviolent youth who would otherwise have received an informal warning from the police are finding themselves caught up in the justice system.[42] An examination of the Toronto Police Service Youth Referral Program (TPS-YRP) in Ontario revealed just that: Nearly 90 percent of the participants in this program would have received an informal police caution if the program did not exist.[43]

SENTENCING YOUNG OFFENDERS

The sentencing of young offenders under the YCJA has two objectives: (1) rehabilitation and reintegration of the young offender, and (2) the public's protection.[44] Sentencing tends to be progressive, so that first-time offenders are more likely to receive a community-based sanction and frequent offenders are more likely to receive an institutional sanction.[45] Sentence disparity may exist between and even within jurisdictions, with justice personnel tailoring sanctions to the circumstances, taking into account the young offender's social environment and unique risks and needs.[46] The noncustodial sentencing options for youth court judges are set out in Table 14.1.

Similar to Section 718.2(e) of the Criminal Code of Canada, first discussed in Chapter 4, the YCJA (2003) contains an equivalent sentencing principle for youth justice courts that says, "all available sanctions other than custody that are reasonable in the circumstances should be considered for all young persons, with particular attention to the circumstances of aboriginal young persons" (s. 38(2)(d)). This provision is designed to address the over-representation of young Indigenous persons in Canadian corrections systems and to eliminate sentencing disparity

Table 14.1 Noncustodial Sentence Options for Young Offenders

Sanction	Description
Judicial reprimand	A judge may issue a verbal "reprimand" to a young offender rather than an actual sentence. This is most often given to first-time offenders convicted of minor offences. These offenders do not receive a criminal record.
Absolute discharge	The youth is found guilty but is released and does not have a criminal record.
Conditional discharge	The youth is found guilty but discharged on the condition that they will follow conditions directed by the court. If the youth adheres to the conditions of the order—which may include reporting conditions—no criminal record will result.
Fine	The court can impose a fine not to exceed $1,000, which is to be paid at a time and under the conditions the court determines to be appropriate. The judge is required to consider the ability of the youth offender to pay the fine. A youth who is unable to pay it can choose to work off the fine through community service as part of a fine option program.
Compensation	The court may order the youth to pay or provide personal services to compensate for losses (e.g., loss of income or support), damage, or injuries resulting from the commission of the offence.
Restitution	The court may order the youth to make "restitution to any other person of any property obtained by the young person as a result of the commission of the offence" (YCJA, 42(2)(f)).
Community service order	The court may impose an order for the youth to perform a maximum of 240 hours of community service work. It must be completed within 12 months of the date of the order. This period of free work cannot interfere with youth's school or normal work hours. Community service orders are commonly included as a condition of probation for young offenders.

Sanction	Description
Prohibition, seizure, or forfeiture	The court may subject the youth to a prohibition, seizure, and/or forfeiture (e.g., a weapons prohibition or require the youth to forfeit proceeds gained through the commission of crime).
Probation	This is the most frequently imposed sanction in the youth courts. Around 90 percent of young offenders serving a community supervision sentence are on probation. The maximum term of probation is two years. There are mandatory conditions and often additional ones. Breach of probation is a Criminal Code offence.
Intensive support and supervision order	The provinces and territories decide whether to use this sanction. It involves more intensive programming and assistance for young offenders, as well as greater surveillance and control than youth experience on probation.
Nonresidential attendance order	A nonresidential order for a period not to exceed 240 hours over a six-month period.

Sources: S.J. Bell, *Young Offenders and Youth Justice: A Century After the Fact*, 4th ed. (Toronto: Nelson, 2012); Correctional Services Program, "Youth Correctional Statistics in Canada, 2014/2015," *Juristat* 36, no. 1, Catalogue no. 85-002-X (Ottawa: Minister of Industry, 2016), http://www.statcan.gc.ca/pub/85-002-x/2016001/article/14317-eng.htm.

that occurred within the YOA framework, where Indigenous youth were more likely than non-Indigenous youth to receive longer custodial sentences, regardless of aggravating factors (i.e., offence severity and criminal history).[47]

Youth Probation

They're so young, like they're under the age of 18 and so their lives haven't even started yet ... and they've had things happen to them or experiences that I don't even know as an adult that I could handle, so you see the resilience that a lot of these youth have, and that creates hope for me.

—Youth probation officer from Toronto[48]

As with adult corrections, the majority (90 percent) of youth under supervision in the community are on probation. Like their counterparts in the adult

Richard Gardner/Rex Features

Young offenders doing community service.

corrections systems, youth probation officers have a variety of tasks to perform: providing supervision to youth probationers; writing pre-sentence reports and attending court; making referrals to community services; and monitoring youth on bail, deferred custody, mandatory supervision, and community service. Probation officers ($N = 20$) interviewed in Toronto, Ontario, expressed a balanced approach to their work with youth, exercising both enforcement and positive, supportive roles to promote accountability and encourage youth to engage in a prosocial lifestyle.[49]

Supervising Youth on Probation

Youth probation officers typically have smaller caseloads than adult probation officers; in British Columbia, for example, they carry average caseloads of 20 youth. Probation officers may meet with the youth under their supervision at the probation office, at school, or during visits to the youths' homes. These personnel often work with other community agencies. Youth probation officers may also carry specialized probation caseloads.

In a study of youth probation officers carrying traditional caseloads and those supervising specialized caseloads—serious-violent/gang-involved young offenders and mentally disordered young offenders—in Vancouver, British Columbia, specialist officers were found to engage in more intensive supervision of their clients and make "greater use of community-based programs" to reduce their clients' risk.[50] Data analyses also demonstrated that in comparison to youth on traditional probation, the youth on specialized probation were less likely to recidivate (general and serious recidivism) and that they experienced "greater improvements in family relationships and risk assessment ratings."[51]

However, research studies have found that the level of supervision that youth receive is not as important as the risk level of the youth when it comes to predicting their risk of reoffending.[52] It is likely the specialized probation officers' greater use of programming to reduce their clients' risk profiles, rather than their increased surveillance activities, contributed to their clients performing better in the community than the traditional youth probationers.

Risk/Needs Assessments and Case Management

Two important dimensions of youth probation are risk/needs assessment and case management. The former involves determining which youth are high risk and therefore require greater supervision and more intensive intervention targeted at their identified criminogenic risks/needs (see Chapter 9 for a review of criminogenic risks/needs). Case management refers to how supervision and services will be provided to youth.[53] Many jurisdictions use assessment and case management tools informed by the risk–need–responsivity model (RNR) to assess their youth probationers' risk for reoffending and the criminogenic needs that should be targeted for intervention to reduce this risk.[54] Youth who are under an intensive support and supervision order receive more intensive programming and assistance.

Youth probation officers hold **integrated case management (ICM) conferences** with young offenders, their parents/guardians, and other support people, such as mental health workers, social workers, and specialists in FASD. The objective of ICM conferences is to establish manageable goals and benchmarks that the youth can achieve while in custody and on probation as well as after completion of their sentence. When a youth's support network has helped develop and revise the case management plan, everyone is aware of its goals and can identify their role in helping the youth achieve them.

Challenges exist in integrating RNR-informed assessment and programming into the case management process for youth probationers. Twenty-nine youth probation officers who were interviewed in Toronto, Ontario, provided insight into one such challenge: the "implementation gap."[55] The officers voiced concerns about accessing external, quality programming to address their clients' criminogenic needs; the challenges they experienced in addressing criminogenic needs that were not easy to identify, measure, or monitor; their desire to prioritize needs to ensure they did not impose too many case management goals for clients at one time, often prioritizing the high-impact

> **Integrated case management (ICM) conferences** The primary strategy used for case management of young offenders on probation.

criminogenic needs; concerns about individual responsivity issues that made it difficult for their clients to achieve success in achieving their case management goals; and the overall challenges associated with affecting change in the lives of youth whose issues are complex and diverse, and can challenge the youth's desire for change.[56]

Custodial Sentences for Young Offenders

The various custodial sentences for young offenders are summarized in Table 14.2. Only a brief description is provided for each type of sentence. A judge can also impose an adult sentence on young offenders if they are convicted of a serious offence and were at least 14 years old when they committed the offence. This means youth can be subject to mandatory minimum sentences and life imprisonment, among other adult sanctions (youth cannot be transferred to adult prisons if they have yet to turn 18).[57]

Youth in custody are likely to have experienced problems or trauma in the family home resulting in their removal and placement in youth care. Many lack positive peer, school, and adult attachments in their lives.[58] These youth are more prone than their nonincarcerated peers to substance abuse, mental health disorders, learning disabilities, and HIV.[59]

Table 14.2 **Custodial Sentences for Young Offenders**

Sanction	Description
Custody and supervision order	The community supervision period following custody is half as long as the term of custody, and the youth is subject to supervision and conditions. The total term cannot exceed two years for offences, except for those involving imprisonment for life—for which the term cannot exceed three years.
Custody and conditional supervision order	Applies to presumptive offences (e.g., man-slaughter, attempted murder). The total term of custody and conditional supervision in the community cannot exceed three years from the date of committal.
Custody and supervision order	Judges can impose a sentence of 10 years for youth convicted of first-degree murder with no more than six years in custody from the date of committal; whereas for second-degree murder, the judge can impose a sentence of seven years with a maximum of four years to be spent in custody prior to release under community supervision.
Deferral of custody and supervision	The order cannot exceed six months. It excludes cases involving presumptive offences.

Sanction	Description
Intensive rehabilitative custody and supervision order	The first portion of the sentence is served in intensive rehabilitative custody, the second under conditional supervision in the community. Maximum period of three years from the date of committal. Exception: Youth court judges can impose a 10-year sentence for youth who commit first-degree murder, seven years for youth who commit second-degree murder. Youth spend a maximum of six years in custody for first-degree murder and four years in custody for second-degree murder, serving the remainder of their sentence under conditional supervision in the community.

DOING TIME

Young offenders find imprisonment harder to take than adult offenders do, which makes a prison term a much more severe sentence for them. Making it even worse is that many young offenders lack survival strategies that might help them cope with the pains of imprisonment.[60] For youth, those pains typically include violence, the loss of freedom, and high anxiety due to severed family and social ties.[61] Violence in youth institutions may include bullying, verbal threats, theft, intimidation, physical abuse, predatory aggression, and coercion.[62]

Arlen Redekop/PROVINCE

The Burnaby Youth Detention Centre, Burnaby, British Columbia.

Displays of bravado, masculinity, and strength may be especially prevalent in youth facilities. Interviews with 350 adolescent males in Canadian custody and detention facilities revealed the ways in which hegemonic masculinity is exhibited in youth facilities: The interview subjects endorsed behaving manly, not displaying emotion, and standing up for oneself.[63] Because the "prisoner" label comes with "connotations of weakness, conformity, and the relinquishing of power," it is not surprising that "manliness becomes the primary means of adaptation and resistance" in institutional settings.[64] It seems that many of the dynamics in adult correctional institutions are also found in youth facilities. For example, a youth may hesitate to ask COs for help, out of fear that his peers will label him a "rat."[65] Also, youth may resort to aggression to achieve status within the facility.[66] Importantly, empirical evidence suggests that youth who experience negative peer influences and negative behaviour in custodial settings are more likely to engage in antisocial behaviour upon their release.[67]

Youth who have experienced many pre-custody strains, such as running away from home, being placed in foster care, and experiencing family problems (e.g., parental abuse), require support from correctional staff, as these experiences have been found to contribute to poor adjustment to the custodial environment and negative emotionality.[68] Young offenders who do not cope well within the prison environment are at a higher risk of committing suicide, as are youth with pre-existing vulnerabilities such as family instability.[69]

TREATMENT PROGRAMS

Much like in the adult system, correctional intervention with young offenders begins with an assessment to identify risks and needs and to develop an appropriate correctional plan. Correctional programs can be general, *offence*-specific, or *offender*-specific.[70] Education, counselling, and recreation programs are offered to all young offenders; *offence*-specific programs target certain offenders (e.g., sex offenders); *offender*-specific programs (e.g., for substance abuse issues) target individual risks and needs.[71] Qualified staff must deliver custodial programming in an environment characterized by positive staff–youth relationships. Research demonstrates that to do otherwise results in little more than the warehousing of youth where youth are at risk of becoming more entrenched in a delinquent lifestyle as they navigate the inmate code, which increases their likelihood of reoffending upon release into the community.[72]

Community-based interventions vary by province and territory, but probation officers everywhere refer young offenders to community services, which range from detox centres to safe houses to psychiatric assessment facilities to educational and employment resources.

In recognizing the prevalence of histories of trauma among young offender populations, various jurisdictions, including British Columbia, have recently implemented trauma-informed practices and programming into youth custodial centres. Initiating a trauma-informed approach requires that agencies address the effects of trauma on youth given that the behaviours youth use to cope with previous trauma—such as "substance abuse, interpersonal aggression, risky sexual behaviour, self-injury, gang affiliation, and running away"—put them at risk for youth justice system involvement.[73]

Examples of how to adhere to a trauma-informed model include screening youth to determine if they have a history of trauma; using culturally relevant, evidence-based practices to address exposure to trauma; and providing staff with appropriate care for the secondary trauma they experience through their work.[74] Research supports the use of trauma-informed approaches for addressing a youth's criminogenic risk and improving their likelihood of successful supervision in the community.[75]

Institutional Treatment Programs

Treatment programs in youth custodial institutions are often designed to foster a sense of agency among youth—for example, to encourage self-control and self-discipline and to teach mastery skills.[76] But the closed nature of institutions means that youth have few meaningful opportunities to apply these new tools to increase their social mobility; as a result, they may use those skills to dominate one another, which can lead to more disciplinary infractions for some youth and increased bullying and victimization for others.[77]

Another concern is that youth in secure facilities are expected to defer entirely to authority figures and the institutional structure. This does not encourage youth to take responsibility for their choices and to demonstrate their agency, which may make it harder for them to move forward upon their release in the community.[78]

Finally, youth may "do program" to show self-control, commitment to the objectives of the institution, and self-change; however, they may simply be faking it to achieve rewards by demonstrating "progress" to the administration.[79]

As mentioned, youth in institutions must confront the inmate code, the adolescent code, the pains of imprisonment, and the difficulties of adjusting to the institution. Their fear of victimization and of transgressing the inmate code may undermine treatment efforts. Research studies suggest that personal security is necessary if there is to be any hope of changing young offenders' attitudes and behaviour.[80] Other factors that may hinder the implementation and effectiveness of correctional programs for youth include these: security concerns that obstruct treatment efforts, poorly trained correctional staff, an absence of political and public support for rehabilitating young offenders, and counterproductive inmate–staff relationships.[81]

Youth who receive services (e.g., mental health services, vocational services, and the assistance of a caregiver) in custody have been found to have a decreased likelihood of recidivism in the community.[82] Further, a meta-analysis of 195 studies investigating young offender treatment programs found that youth who participated in *any* form of treatment intervention were less likely to recidivate than youth who did not.[83] Participation in treatment interventions resulted in a 9 percent decrease in recidivism, which "theoretically prevented more than 1,300 offenders from reoffending."[84]

More recent reviews of research studies reveal that control and punitive approaches (i.e., those relying on surveillance and deterrence) are less effective in reducing recidivism among young offenders than therapeutic approaches (e.g., those that involve skills building, counselling and mentoring, or restorative practices).[85]

Incarcerated young female offenders typically have higher rates of disruptive disorders, major depression, PTSD, separation anxiety, high rates of trauma exposure, and comorbid conditions (e.g., depression, substance abuse, anxiety, and suicidality) than incarcerated young male offenders.[86] The unique risk/needs profiles and characteristics of young women (as identified above) point to a need for gender-specific programming. Evidence suggests, however, that the most effective programs in reducing young offender recidivism—gender-specific or not—are comprehensive, follow the RNR model, and target multiple risk factors.[87]

Nevertheless, gender-specific programming may help achieve particular goals, such as empowerment and improved quality of life.[88] Further longitudinal research investigating girls' delinquency is required to develop effective programming for this offender population that reflects their unique socialization and development.[89]

Youth–Staff Relationships

Just as in adult facilities, COs play a prominent role in the incarceration experience for youth. Youth may require emotional support and practical assistance from staff as they adjust to life in the institution. Positive relationships with staff—those based on fairness, respect, and mutual understanding—may alleviate depression, hopelessness, and anxiety among incarcerated young offenders.[90] Staff can help create a stable and secure environment where youth do not fear for their personal security. When the rules and boundaries are consistently enforced, positive social exchanges can develop between staff and offenders.[91]

COs can demonstrate prosocial modelling for troubled youth, which may encourage the youth's resocialization.[92] Research exploring relationships between prosocial adults and juveniles in custodial institutions found that most incarcerated youth turned first to a same-sex staff member, rather than to a case manager, for assistance and advice.[93]

Positive relationships with staff can affect youth perceptions of whether they will succeed on release.[94] Youth in the "balanced" relationship category—that is, who viewed their relationships with staff positively, as being built on trust, engagement, and effective problem-solving—often anticipate succeeding on release.[95] Interviews with serious young offenders found that youth who reported having a release counsellor whose role was to assist them with their preparations for re-entry had lower recidivism rates than those who did not report having this relationship.[96]

Instead of providing positive, prosocial modelling for youth, some COs may engage in negative behaviour that breaches the trust of the youth in their care. One study of young offenders in Ontario ($N = 100$) found that when

COs put their safety at risk, it took the form of "letting bad things happen" (46 percent), jeopardizing an inmate's safety (47 percent), or bribing inmates to discipline one another (31 percent).[97] There have also been documented incidents of correctional staff abusing young offenders physically, sexually, and psychologically.[98]

Interviews with young male offenders ($N = 350$) in Canadian custody and detention centres found that youth often felt that staff were inconsistent and unfair in their decision making. One youth reported that "some staff try to make their own rules and they change them depending on what staff are here—other rules that are supposed to be enforced, they don't enforce them—so you don't know what you will get in trouble for."[99]

In 2015, the Office of the Ombudsperson in British Columbia investigated grievances made by youth held at Burnaby Youth Custody Services Centre. The youth explained how staff were subjecting them to "one-to-one" status, which required youth to be accompanied by a staff member whenever they were out of their rooms. When staff were not available, youth were often locked in their rooms—for between 30 minutes and 2 1/2 hours—which limited their access to programming and social interactions and was akin to separate confinement.[100]

RISK ASSESSMENT IN YOUTH CORRECTIONS

The principles of RNR are applied when assessing the risk and needs of young offenders and developing intervention plans for them. As noted, treatment programming that centres on the RNR model is generally effective at reducing reoffending among both young and adult offenders.[101] Risk assessment tools help practitioners classify young offenders and predict whether they will place the community at risk upon release.[102]

The **Youth Level of Service/Case Management Inventory (YLS/CMI)** is the most extensively used risk/needs measurement tool in youth justice systems.[103] It is based on RNR principles and is a variant of the Level of Service Inventory-Revised (LSI-R) used for adult offenders.[104] Youth probation officers, psychologists, social workers, youth workers, and court workers use this risk/needs assessment tool to assess a youth's risk for general recidivism, to identify the factors that require intervention, and to develop a community supervision plan.[105]

The YLS/CMI has been found to predict general recidivism among young offenders regardless of gender, Indigenous versus non-Indigenous status, or offence type.[106] It has also been found to identify the needs of young men and women offenders and so it can be used to inform recommendations for probation interventions.

Another prominent risk assessment tool used to assess adolescent offenders aged 12 to 18 years old and to develop intervention plans is the **Structured Assessment of Violent Risk in Youth (SAVRY).** The SAVRY is based on empirical evidence examining adolescent development, violence, and aggression

Youth Level of Service/Case Management Inventory (YLS/CMI) The primary risk/needs assessment instrument in youth corrections.

Structured Assessment of Violent Risk in Youth (SAVRY) A frequently used risk/needs assessment instrument in youth corrections.

among youth and comprises 24 items in three risk domains: historical risk factors, social/contextual risk factors, and individual/clinical factors.[107]

RESTORATIVE JUSTICE APPROACHES AND YOUNG OFFENDERS

As previously discussed, restorative justice initiatives bring together offenders, victims, families, and communities to mutually resolve conflicts and repair the harms that have been caused by crime. Restorative justice initiatives provide young offenders with the opportunity to make amends with those they have harmed and take responsibility for their behaviour; victims are given a voice in the process, which promotes their healing; and the community comes together to support the victims and offenders in addressing the harms that have been caused and in achieving peace in the community. Many restorative programs for young offenders are limited to first-time, nonviolent offenders, although some programs target more serious offenders.[108]

There are a variety of restorative justice initiatives across Canada designed to facilitate reparation, reconciliation, and relationship building. These may be particularly beneficial for Indigenous young offenders, who can culturally identify with these principles. Several of these initiatives are presented in Table 14.3. Note that for almost all of the initiatives, the impact on re offending is unknown, so it is difficult to assess their effectiveness at addressing the risk/needs of young offenders and in reducing reoffending.

A prominent role in restorative justice is played by **Youth Justice Committees (YJCs),** which operate across the country. YJCs provide guidance

Youth Justice Committee (YJC) Community-based committees that sponsor a variety of initiatives for youth in conflict with the law, including extrajudicial measures centred on restorative justice.

Youth Justice Committee.

© Michael Newman/PhotoEdit

Table 14.3 **Selected Restorative Justice Programs for Young Offenders**

Initiative	Participants	Approach/Outcomes
Aboriginal Youth Restorative Justice Committee (CAYRJC) (Calgary, Alberta)	Indigenous youth in conflict with the law, their families, the victims and their families, legal system personnel, and the community.	Establish a suitable and meaningful consequence for the criminal behaviour. Participants receive culturally relevant teachings from respected elders. Offer youth hope and empower them by providing meaningful opportunities to engage with experienced and knowledgeable community members.[a] Impact on reoffending unknown.
Victoria Restorative Justice Society (RJV, Victoria, B.C.)	Referrals from Victoria Police Department and Oak Bay Police, Crown counsel, Victoria Community Corrections, Insurance Corporation of BC, and members of the community. Diversion program deals with pre- or post-charge referrals; youth are held accountable without being legally convicted. Integrative Restorative Justice Program deals with referrals at the pre- or post-sentencing stage; youth have been convicted.	Trained volunteers facilitate community justice conferences, panels, victim–offender mediation (VOM), peacemaking circles. Programs include a support group for at-risk youth (Girls' Circle). RJV and the Victoria Police Department (VPD) examined the recidivism rates of the individuals ($N = 139$) referred to the program by VPD between 2011 and 2013 and who successfully completed the process. Twenty-seven youth reoffended (recidivism rate = 19.42 percent).[d]
Essex County Youth Justice Committee (YJC; Windsor, Ontario)	Alternative to formal youth court proceedings for youth aged 12 to 17 who have committed a minor offence; youth who accept responsibility and accountability for their actions.	Offenders, their families, the community volunteers (up to three on the YJC), and the victims (by choice) come together to address the harm caused, victim harm/needs, and community wellness, and how to address the above. Potential sanctions include an apology, donation to charity, volunteer work, and/or attendance at programming or a presentation. Successful completion of sanctions means the police will not lay charges, or the court will withdraw charges. Impact on reoffending unknown.[b]

(continued)

Initiative	Participants	Approach/Outcomes
Island Community Justice Society (Nova Scotia)	Referrals for family group conferences (FGC) and VOM are accepted at multiple stages of the youth justice process: pre- and post-charge (police and Crown), post-conviction/pre-sentence (judges), and post-sentence (correctional services/victims' services). Referrals for accountability meetings are from police and Crown at the pre- or post-charge stage. For youth aged 12 to 17 in conflict with the law.	Facilitate FGC, VOMs, and accountability meetings. Deliver a community service order program. Promote offender accountability to address the harms caused. Provide victims with a voice in the process, and enable community support and input. Provide victim and volunteer support services.[c] Impact on reoffending unknown.
Restorative Circles Initiative (RCI; Saskatchewan)	Pre- and post-sentencing conferences can be requested by counsel but most often recommended by judge. Feasibility assessed and then RCI facilitator works with participants (victim, offender, family, and community) to promote understanding of the process and how to contribute meaningfully.	Approximately 30 conferences held per year. Typical purpose of conference: (a) promote victim–offender understanding, and (b) plan for offender's rehabilitation and reintegration in the community. Held in circular courtroom with moveable furniture.[e] Impact on reoffending unknown.

[a] Native Counselling Services of Alberta, *Corrections and Restorative Justice* (Edmonton: Author, 2012), http://www.ncsa.ca/online/?page_id=46; Montréal Urban Aboriginal Community Strategy Network, *The Aboriginal Justice Research Project* (Montréal: Author, 2012), http://www.crime-prevention-intl.org/uploads/media/Aboriginal_Justice_Research_Project_-_Final_Report.pdf.

[b] Youth Diversion Essex County Diversion Program. *Youth Justice Committee* (n.d.), http://ecyouthdiversion.ca/programs/youth-justice-committee/.

[c] Island Community Justice Society, *Restorative Justice: How It Works* (n.d.), http://www.islandcommunityjustice.com/howitworks.html.

[d] Restorative Justice Victoria, *Restorative Justice Victoria and the Victoria Police Department: Offender Recidivism Study* (Victoria: Author, 2015), https://rjvictoria.files.wordpress.com/2011/04/recidivism-results-2015-update.pdf.

[e] S. Goldberg, "Problem-Solving in Canada's Courtrooms: A Guide to Therapeutic Justice," prepared for the National Judicial Institute (2011), http://www.sasklawcourts.ca/images/documents/Provincial_Court/Problem-Solving%20in%20Canada's%20Courtrooms.pdf.

about which extrajudicial measures would be most appropriate for individual young offenders. They also support the victim and facilitate victim–offender reconciliation; ensure community support for the young offender through services, short-term mentoring, and community supervision; and coordinate interactions between agencies (e.g., the local child protection agency and the youth criminal justice system).

YJCs may be involved in a variety of initiatives, including FGC, community/neighbourhood accountability panels, VOM/victim–offender reconciliation sessions, multidisciplinary case management conferences, and Indigenous sentencing and healing circles. Youth justice committees can produce positive changes for youth and generate return on investment. For example, the Calgary Youth Justice Society, the agency responsible for operating YJCs and that handles 70 percent of extrajudicial youth sanctions for the city of Calgary, produces a 400 percent return on investment with every $1 spent on YJCs, which results in $4 in savings going back to the community.[109]

AFTERCARE PROGRAMS

Aftercare programs are designed to address young offenders' unique needs and risks as they re-enter society. They combine community restraint elements with community service strategies to facilitate offender change and increase public safety.[110] Young female offenders may be more amenable to therapeutic interventions (e.g., formal counselling services) than young male offenders when re-entering society.[111] These findings suggest the importance of providing young women offenders with access to therapeutic community interventions to help them transition back to the community after a period of incarceration.

The research evidence demonstrates the importance of providing young offenders with aftercare programming in community settings and at a lower intensity than the youth received in institutional settings.[112] A meta-analysis of 30 studies investigating the effectiveness of aftercare programs found that programs that are well-implemented can result in reductions in recidivism for youth participants. The analyses also revealed that aftercare programming may be particularly effective for older, more mature youth, and for those whose predominant index offence was a violent offence.[113]

The Role of Informal Social Support Networks

Research suggests that informal social supports (e.g., friends and family) play a major role in the community re-entry process for young offenders. The significance of the relationships that young offenders form with their peers are important in the community re-entry process, for peers may provide young offenders with assistance such as support, camaraderie, and financial resources. However, peers may also encourage illicit behaviour, resulting in the youth returning to custody. Young offenders may thus find themselves "walking a fine line" as they limit their contacts with their old social groups so as to avoid trouble, while working to develop a new sense of identity and belonging.[114]

Mentoring is often a component of re-entry and aftercare programming; preliminary research suggests it can be effective in helping youth overcome the challenges of re-entry.[115] Social support in general—from family members and program staff—is believed to have the potential to trigger a youth's motivation to desist from crime and to maintain this motivation with the passage of time.[116] Families are able to provide financial resources, emotional support, encouragement, and potentially, employment. But the family may also pose challenges for young offenders, for the environment at home may encourage previous patterns of criminal behaviour. Also, the pressure of expectations may generate a self-fulfilling prophecy, so that some youth fall back into old patterns of illicit behaviour.[117]

Materials on the effectiveness of selected interventions are presented in Research File 14.1. Most of these interventions have not been proven effective at reducing reoffending, and it is not certain whether these interventions address the needs of young offenders.

RESEARCH FILE 14.1

The Effectiveness of Selected Youth Justice Interventions

	Strategy	Outcomes
Diversion	Designed to prevent further involvement in youth justice system. Substantial heterogeneity; programming can include the use of cautions and warnings, community service, community programming, restorative justice programming, and family interventions.	Evidence-based practices used in combination with case management, restorative justice programs, and those that involve family interventions are promising.[a] First-time young offenders who participate in diversion programs have been found to have lower rates of reoffending than first-time young offenders processed by the courts for similar offences.[b] Cautions and interventions have been found to result in greater reductions in recidivism for medium/high-risk offenders than for low-risk offenders.[c]

	Strategy	Outcomes
Boot camps	Intermediate sanction. Short-term residential program. Military model involves demanding exercise routines. Emphasis on labour, discipline, exercise, and drills. Some incorporate cognitive behavioural treatment and aftercare.	Generally do not have an impact on reoffending unless young offenders are voluntary participants. Research has found these programs to be criminogenic; participants exhibited higher recidivism rates than those subject to other forms of treatment, including discipline-oriented programs. May improve young offenders' attitudes and impact their adjustment while in the facility. Young offenders view boot camps more favourably than correctional facilities. Decreases in recidivism are more likely to occur following participation in boot camps that target risk factors through rehabilitation components.[d]
Scared Straight programs	Popular in the United States Target at-risk youth or youth who have come into conflict with the law, who are taken into correctional institutions for a "sit down" with inmates, who share their stories. Objective is to "scare youth straight" to deter youth from criminal behaviour by showing them the punitive nature of imprisonment.	Research has found that the programs are ineffective as a general or specific deterrent to future offending, and the program has been found to have a criminogenic effect on youth.[e]
Probation	The most frequently used intervention. Places youth under supervision in the community, subject to general and, often, specific conditions designed to address their risk and needs.	The effectiveness of probation is enhanced when the principles of RNR are followed (e.g., low-intensity supervision for low-risk young offenders and high-intensity supervision for higher-risk youth).[f]
Open custody and open detention facilities	Provide optimal programming opportunities for youth, prosocial role modelling opportunities, and community reintegration. Middle of the continuum between containment and reintegration.	Evaluation in Ontario found that these facilities can function as transitional programming to facilitate youth reintegration and opportunities for prosocial modelling and relationships between staff and youth.[g] Impact on reoffending unknown.

(continued)

	Strategy	Outcomes
Intensive rehabilitative custody and supervision (IRCS)	Objectives include appropriate use of courts and correctional institutions for young offenders, as well as proportionality in the youth justice system's response to the offence and offender's level of responsibility. Greater opportunities for social reintegration and rehabilitation.	IRCS has increased provincial/territorial abilities to provide programming for young serious violent offenders with mental health issues. Each jurisdiction has developed the capacity to administer IRCS sentences.[h] Impact on reoffending unknown.
Serious and Violent Offender Re-entry Initiative (SVORI) (U.S.)	Designed to improve youth access to comprehensive, integrated community services and to improve re-entry outcomes in the education, employment, health, housing, and criminal justice domains.	In one study ($N = 337$), SVORI participants were more likely to have re-entry plans, but there was no difference between SVORI and non-SVORI participants in rates of reoffending.[i]
Intensive Aftercare Programs (IAP), Denver, Las Vegas, Virginia	Attention to reintegration during incarceration. Intensive supervision and services post-release. Slow and steady transition between the institution and aftercare in the community. Objective is to reduce recidivism among high-risk parolees.[j]	Initial implementation and testing of IAP over a 12-month follow-up period found few statistically significant differences between the IAP and control groups in incidence, severity, or prevalence of reoffending.[k]
Intensive Supervision Probation (ISP), Spotlight Serious Offender Services Unit, Manitoba	Targets high-risk gang-involved young offenders. Program involves an ISP probation officer (caseload of 15), a surveillance worker, and a street mentor (if Spotlight youth choose to have one). Two components to achieve behavioural change: support-based services (e.g., mentorship, probation counselling) and deterrence-based strategies (e.g., frequent surveillance checks, intensive probation supervision).	In one study, albeit lacking methodological rigour, quantitative and qualitative analyses found Spotlight clients ($N = 57$) performed better than the comparison group of high-risk offenders ($N = 85$) on the recidivism outcomes. The researchers argued mentorship that adhered to "best practices" was the key reason to the program's success, followed by strong implementation and therapeutic integrity.[l]

^a C.S. Schwalbe, R.E. Gearing, M.J. MacKenzie, K.B. Brewer, and R. Ibrahim, "A Meta-Analysis of Experimental Studies of Diversion Programs for Juvenile Offenders," *Clinical Psychology Review 32* (2012).

^b D.K. Forgays, "Three Years of Youth Court Offender Outcomes," *Adolesence 43*, no. 171 (2008), 473–84; A.P. Logalbo and C.M. Callahan, "An Evaluation of Teen Court as a Juvenile Crime Diversion Program," *Juvenile and Family Court Journal 52*, no. 2 (2011), 1–11.

^c H.A. Wilson and R.D. Hoge, "The Effect of Youth Diversion Programs on Recidivism: A Meta-analytic Review," *Criminal Justice and Behavior 40*, no. 5 (2013), 497–518. J.M. Kretschmar, F. Butcher, D.J. Flannery, and M.I. Singer, "Diverting Juvenile Justice-involved Youth with Behavioral Health Issues from Detention: Preliminary findings from Ohio's behavioral health juvenile justice (BHJJ) initiative," *Criminal Justice Policy Review 27*, no. 3 (2016), 302-25.

^d B. Meade and B. Steiner, "The Total Effects of Boot Camps That House Juveniles: A Systematic Review of the Evidence," *Journal of Criminal Justice 38*, no. 5 (2010), 841–53; B. Steiner and A.L. Giacomazzi, "Juvenile Waiver, Boot Camp, and Recidivism in a Northwestern State," *Prison Journal 87*, no. 2 (2007), 227–40; M.W. Lipsey, "The Primary Factors that Characterize Effective Interventions with Juvenile Offenders: A Meta-Analytic Overview," *Victims & Offenders 4* (2009), 124–47, doi:10.1080/15564880802612573; B.C. Welsh and M. Rocque, "When Crime Prevention Harms: A Review of Systematic Reviews," *Journal of Experimental Criminology 10*, no. 2 (2014), 245–66.

^e P.M. Klenowski, K.J. Bell, and K.D. Dodson, "An Empirical Evaluation of Juvenile Awareness Programs in the United States: Can Juveniles Be 'Scared Straight'?", *Journal of Offender Rehabilitation 49*, no. 4 (2010), 254–72; Welsh and Rocque, "When Crime Prevention Harms."

^f D. Luong and S. Wormith, "Applying Risk/Need Assessment to Probation Practice and Its Impact on the Recidivism of Young Offenders," *Criminal Justice and Behavior 38*, no. 12 (2011), 1177–99.

^g D. Cooke and J. Finlay, *Open Detention and Open Custody in Ontario* (Toronto: 2007), http://provincialadvocate.on.ca/documents/en/Open%20Custody-OpenDetention%20Review.pdf.

^h Department of Justice Canada, *The Youth Justice Initiative Funding Components Evaluation: Final Report* (Ottawa: Evaluation Division, Office of Strategic Planning and Performance Management, 2010), http://www.justice.gc.ca/eng/pi/eval/rep-rap/11/yjifc-vfijj/yjifc-vfijj.pdf.

ⁱ P.K. Lattimore and C.A. Visher, *The Multi-Site Evaluation of the Serious and Violent Offender Re-entry Initiative* (Washington, D.C.: U.S. Department of Justice, 2009), https://www.ncjrs.gov/pdffiles1/nij/grants/230421.pdf.

^j R.G. Wiebush, D. Wagner, B. McNulty, Y. Wang, and T.N. Le, *Implementation and Outcome Evaluation of the Intensive Aftercare Program: Final Report* (Washington, D.C.: National Council on Crime and Delinquency, 2005), https://www.ncjrs.gov/pdffiles1/ojjdp/206177.pdf.

^k Wiebush et al., "Implementation and Outcome Evaluation."

^l M. Weinwrath, G. Donatelli, and M.J. Murchison, "Mentorship: A Missing Piece to Manage Juvenile Intensive Supervision Programs and Youth Gangs?" *Canadian Journal of Criminology and Criminal Justice 58*, no. 3 (2016), 291–321.

There are additional questions that can be asked with respect to the effectiveness of youth corrections, including these:

Do harsh penalties deter youth from committing crimes? In most cases, no. Research studies have found that, for a variety of reasons, punitive sanctions (including the threat to transfer young offenders to adult court) do not deter young offenders from committing crimes.[118] In one study (*N* = 53), 42 percent of the youth participants sentenced to either probation or custody indicated that their sentence would not deter them from reoffending, and 66 percent indicated that their sentence would be unlikely to deter their friends from committing the same crime.[119]

For which groups of young offenders are treatment programs most effective? The most positive outcomes tend to occur when violent and high-risk offenders are targeted for intervention. For most young offenders, the most effective correctional programs offered in the community and institutional settings are those that incorporate cognitive behaviour strategies, education, counselling, and vocational skills.[120]

THE JOURNEY OF AN EX-DANGEROUS OFFENDER

"It started out when I was at a group home, which consisted of 30 other children. I was sent there because I was labelled as being 'incorrigible' under the Juvenile Delinquents Act. This was in the late 1960s. My dad was physically abusive and so they took me away from my family. But the group home was full and I was called into the office and told that I was going to a bigger school, a school which I would learn quite a bit and would become a responsible boy. Initially I would start at a place called Bowmanville, which was kind of a reception centre for boys coming into the training school system. I would be there for approximately 10 days, and I would be classified as being too young to be there and so I was sent to a place called Coburn. Coburn Training School: what would go on in that training school for me, I felt, was probably the hardest part in my whole life, because there was a lot of discipline and discipline was really forced on you."

"I mean physically forced. We were made to sit in lockers in houses of 30 boys; each house consisted of 30 boys, and there were seven houses at the school. Everything was done military style, and we would have to sit in our lockers and if anybody, you know, acted up or something like that the house would be put onto routines. Routines sometimes consisted of running up and down fire escapes with big parkas on during the summer. This was referred to as being the sweat box, because it was summer and we would be up and down the fire escape. Some of the routines would last three or four hours. If one of the boys, or any of the boys didn't make it or fell down or gave up or whatever, the house was put on more routines. As a consequence, whoever caused the house to be put on longer routines would get beat. Sometimes the staff would suddenly get up and say he heard the telephone ring. That was the key to go and he was leaving and that some guy was going to get beat up. So at an early age we learned that fighting was part of the way of life, and that if you wanted to survive that you had to be physical, and also the fact that you weren't going to inform on anybody there, because if you did, you were a rat. So at an early age we were learning not to be a rat and also to fight. And, if somebody escaped, the whole house would be put on routines until the boy came back, providing that it was not a long period. So anyway, when this boy came back he would sometimes be put into a potato sack and tied into it. Then every-body would scramble him."

"Sometimes when visitors came they would give candy and chocolate bars and stuff like that. Well we were only allowed to have it on Friday night. So all of this candy was put away in a closet and on Friday night if the house had been good then we were able to get whatever candy we had. People like myself were unfortunate not to have visitors; so, they would have a box of candy and what they used to do is put like jelly beans or Smarties or something like that; they would give you a cup, then throw the candy in the middle of the floor. Everybody would scramble for it. So everybody was beating each other up to get a couple of candies."

"For me training school was probably, as I said earlier, the worst part of my experience with the criminal justice system. My mother and father never came to visit me, ever. Not when I was a juvenile or adult. I never saw my mother again. Due to the fact that I was very young and had just been taken away from my family and having no loved ones, I started to build this out of control kind of person, you know, in the sense that I would fight at the drop of a hat. The thing is I realized by doing that then I was protecting myself, so for my own protection I was developing these skills that as I got older would become very harmful to me, and to most other people I would come into contact with."[121]

These are the reflections of an ex-dangerous offender who entered the youth justice system as an "incorrigible" at age 7 in the 1960s under the JDA. He would go on to serve 23 years inside youth and adult correctional institutions; for his last series of offences, he would be designated a dangerous offender. His story, while perhaps extreme, is similar to those of many others who find themselves involved in the correctional system. It also highlights the difficulty of escaping what, for many, becomes a perpetual "revolving door": from the community to the justice system and (sometimes) incarceration and back into the community. The challenge for community-based and institutional correctional systems is to intervene in a positive way so as to reduce the likelihood of reoffending. When this challenge is met, the offender is helped and the community is protected.

SUMMARY

This chapter provided an overview of young offenders and youth corrections. Like their adult counterparts, the majority of youth who become involved in Canada's youth justice system have multiple needs and are often from unstable families and/or communities. The chapter examined a variety of noncustodial and custodial options as well as the effectiveness of those interventions. Concerns were expressed about the effectiveness of youth custody and of a variety of noncustodial approaches, including Scared Straight and boot camps.

KEY POINTS REVIEW

1. The Juvenile Delinquents Act (JDA) set out a social welfare approach to youth crime; youth were viewed as misdirected and in need of assistance and intervention to address the factors that contributed to their offending behaviour.

2. The Young Offenders Act (YOA) simultaneously emphasized the protection of young offenders' special needs and rights with the protection of the public and young offender accountability.

3. At the core of the Youth Criminal Justice Act (YCJA) are extrajudicial measures to reduce the incarceration rates for young offenders, particularly for those who have committed less serious offences.

4. The rates of youth charged and cases being heard by Canadian youth courts have declined over the past decade.

5. Women are less likely to become involved in the youth criminal justice system as are youth below the age of 16.

6. Factors that place youth at risk for involvement in delinquent behaviour include drug consumption, a history of abuse, delinquent peers, substance abuse, poverty, a negative or disruptive family environment, and gang membership, among others.

7. Diversion involves the police issuing warnings and cautions and referring youth to diversion programs.

8. Probation is the most frequently imposed sanction in the youth courts.

9. Youth experience a variety of pains of imprisonment, including violence, bullying, the loss of freedom, and high levels of anxiety due to severed family and social ties.

10. A variety of correctional treatment programs are offered to youth in custodial and noncustodial settings; these may be general, offence-specific, or offender-specific.

11. COs play a key role in the incarceration experience for youth; positive relationships with staff members may alleviate depression, hopelessness, and anxiety among incarcerated young offenders.

12. Treatment programming centred on the RNR model is generally effective in reducing the rates of reoffending among young offenders.

13. YJCs may be involved in family group conferences, community/neighbourhood accountability panels, victim–offender mediation/reconciliation sessions, multidisciplinary case management conferences, and Indigenous sentencing and healing circles.

14. Indigenous youth are over-represented in youth correctional populations across Canada.

15. The most effective correctional programs offered to young offenders in community and institutional settings are those that incorporate cognitive-behavioural strategies, education, and vocational skills.

KEY TERM QUESTIONS

1. Briefly describe the evolution of youth justice legislation in Canada (*Juvenile Delinquents Act*, *Young Offenders Act*, *Youth Criminal Justice Act*).

2. Identify and describe the primary goals of the *Youth Criminal Justice Act*.

3. Identify and discuss the purpose of *integrated case management conferences* in the youth probation system.

4. Describe the *Youth Level of Service/Case Management Inventory (YLS/CMI)* and the *Structured Assessment of Violent Risk in Youth (SAVRY)*.

5. What role do *Youth Justice Committees (YJCs)* play in the youth justice system in Canada?

CRITICAL THINKING EXERCISES

Critical Thinking Exercise 14.1

Publicizing the Names of Young Offenders: Should the Names of Young Offenders Be Published?

Opponents of this practice argue that publicizing the names of youth convicted of violent offences will increase the amount of public shaming that occurs and increase the youth's visibility in the community, making it more difficult for them to receive assistance and successfully integrate with the community. The provision may also violate Section 16 of the UN's *Convention on the Rights of the Child* (www2.ohchr.org/english/law/crc.htm), which addresses a child's right to privacy and to not be subjected to "interference or attacks" (s. 16(2)) "on his or her honour and reputation" (s. 16(1)), which arguably is an inevitable consequence of publicizing a young offender's name. Proponents counter that publishing the names of youth will serve as a specific and general deterrent and protect the community.

Your Thoughts?

1. What are your views on the positive and negative consequences of this practice?

Critical Thinking Exercise 14.2

FASD as a Mitigating Factor during Sentencing

Children who are exposed to alcohol in the womb may suffer permanent damage to their brain and central nervous system, which can lead to poor impulse control, mental health problems, and difficulty appreciating the nature and consequences of their actions.[122] Assume that you are defence counsel for a 15-year-old young offender who suffers from FASD and who committed three robberies in a Northern community.

Your Thoughts?

1. What would be the main arguments you present to the court?
2. What sentence would you recommend the sentencing judge impose and why?

CLASS/GROUP DISCUSSION EXERCISES

Class/Group Discussion 14.1

Sentencing Youth to Adult Sentences

A judge can impose an adult sentence on young offenders if they are convicted of a serious offence and were at least 14 years old when they committed the offence.

Your Thoughts?

1. What are your views on judges imposing adult sentences on youth who commit serious offences, such as murder, attempted murder, manslaughter, or aggravated sexual assault after their 14th birthday?
2. What are your views on a judge imposing an adult sentence of life imprisonment (which has a 25-year parole ineligibility period) on a 14-year-old youth who commits first-degree murder?

Class/Group Discussion 14.2

The Ex-dangerous Offender's Journey: What Could Have Been Done Differently?

Read the journey of the ex-dangerous offender presented at the end of this chapter; it is an all-too-familiar story, especially for offenders who are "state-raised."

Your Thoughts?

1. From the materials presented in the preceding chapters, set out what, in your view, could have been done differently that might have produced a different outcome.

MEDIA LINKS

"Young Kids, Hard Time Director's Cut," https://www.youtube.com/watch?v=g3lw6PMjj40

"Quiet Kid Learns to Cope in Prison," National Geographic, https://www.youtube.com/watch?v=PAS4uSDJe9k

"Restorative vs. Retributive Justice in Vermont and New Zealand: A Case Study Comparison," www.youtube.com/watch?v=s967kBKEJowandfeature=related

NOTES

1. L. Casavant, R. MacKay, and D. Valiquet, *Youth Justice Legislation in Canada*, Legal and Legislative Affairs Division, Library of Parliament, PRB-08-23E (Ottawa: Author, 2008), http://www.parl.gc.ca/Content/LOP/researchpublications/prb0823-e.pdf; M. Alain and J. Desrosiers, "A Fairly Short History of Youth Criminal Justice in Canada," in *Implementing and Working with the Youth Criminal Justice Act across Canada*, M. Alain, R.R. Corrado, and S. Reid, eds. (Buffalo, NY: University of Toronto Press, 2016), 23–40.

2. Alain and Desrosiers, "A Fairly Short History of Youth Criminal Justice in Canada," p. 29.

3. Casavant et al., *Youth Justice Legislation in Canada*.

4. Ibid.; S.J. Bell, *Young Offenders and Youth Justice: A Century After the Fact*, 4th ed. (Toronto: Nelson, 2012); Alain and Desrosiers, "A Fairly Short History of Youth Criminal Justice in Canada."

5. Bell, *Young Offenders and Youth Justice: A Century After the Fact.*

6. Alain and Desrosiers, "A Fairly Short History of Youth Criminal Justice in Canada."

7. J. Latimer and N. Desjardins, *The 2008 National Justice Survey: The Youth Justice System in Canada and the Youth Criminal Justice Act* (Ottawa: Department of Justice, 2009), p. 1, http://www.justice.gc.ca/eng/pi/rs/rep-rap/2008/rr08_yj1-rr08_jj1/p3.html.

8. Department of Justice Canada, *The Youth Justice Initiative Funding Components Evaluation: Final Report* (Ottawa: Evaluation Division, Office of Strategic Planning and Performance Management, 2010), http://www.justice.gc.ca/eng/pi/eval/rep-rap/11/yjifc-vfijj/yjifc-vfijj.pdf.

9. J. Umamaheswar, "Bringing Hope and Change: A Study of Youth Probation Officers in Toronto," *International Journal of Offender Therapy and Comparative Criminology* 57, no. 9 (2012), 1158–82 at 1163–4,

10. *Montgomery v. Louisiana*, 577 U. S. ____ (2016), https://www.supremecourt.gov/opinions/15pdf/14-280_3204.pdf.

11. Correctional Services Program, "Youth Correctional Statistics in Canada, 2014/2015," *Juristat* 36, no. 1, Catalogue no. 85-002-X (Ottawa: Minister of Industry, 2016), http://www.statcan.gc.ca/pub/85-002-x/2016001/article/14317-eng.htm. Note these statistics do not include daily counts for Alberta and Québec because these were not provided to Statistics Canada.

12. Ibid.

13. R.R. Corrado and A. Markwart, "Introduction. Successes and Challenges in Implementing the YCJA: A Decade Later," in *Implementing and Working with the Youth Criminal Justice Act across Canada*, M. Alain, R.R. Corrado, and S. Reid, eds. (Buffalo, NY: University of Toronto Press, 2016), 3–22.

14. N. Jackson, "Aboriginal Youth Overrepresentation in Canadian Correctional Services: Judicial and Non-judicial Actors and Influence," *Alberta Law Review* 52, no. 4 (2015), 927–47.

15. "Recent Changes to Canada's Youth Justice System," Department of Justice, September 23, 2015, http://www.justice.gc.ca/eng/cj-jp/yj-jj/tools-outils/sheets-feuillets/amend-modif.html.

16. L. Barnett, T. Dupuis, C. Kirkby, R. MacKay, J. Nicol, and J. Béchard, *Bill C-10: An Act to enact the Justice for Victims of Terrorism Act and to amend the State Immunity Act, the Criminal Code, the Controlled Drugs and Substances Act, the Corrections and Conditional Release Act, the Youth Criminal Justice Act, the Immigration and Refugee Protection Act and other Acts*, Legislative Summary of Bill C-10, Publication no. 41-1-C10-E (Ottawa: Library of Parliament, 2012), http://www.parl.gc.ca/Content/LOP/LegislativeSummaries/41/1/c10-e.pdf.

17. Correctional Services Program, "Youth Correctional Statistics in Canada, 2014/2015."

18. J. Savoie, "Youth Self-Reported Delinquency, Toronto—2006," *Juristat* 27, no. 6, Catalogue no. 85-002-XPE (Ottawa: Minister of Industry, 2007), http://www.statcan.gc.ca/pub/85-002-x/85-002-x2007006-eng.pdf; C.R. Trulson, M. DeLisi, and J.W. Marquart, "Institutional Misconduct, Delinquent Background, and Rearrest Frequency Among Serious and Violent Delinquent Offenders," *Crime and Delinquency* 57, no. 5 (2011), 709–31; D.J. Simourd and D.L. Andrews, "Correlates of Delinquency: A Look at Gender Differences," *Forum on Corrections Research* 6, no. 1 (1994), http://www.csc-scc.gc.ca/text/pblct/forum/e061/e061g-eng.shtml; D.E. Barrett, A. Katsiyannis, D. Zhang, and D. Zhang, "Delinquency & Recidivism: A Multicohort, Matched-control Study of the Role of Early Adverse Experiences, Mental Health Problems, and Disabilities," *Journal of Emotional and Behavioural Disorders* 22, no. 1 (2014), 3–15; D.M. Day, J.D. Nielsen, A.K. Ward, Y. Sun. J.S. Rosenthal, T. Duchesne, I. Bevc, and L. Rossman, "Long-term Follow-up of Criminal Activity with Adjudicated Youth in Ontario: Identifying Offence Trajectories and Predictors/correlates of Trajectory Group Membership," *Canadian Journal of Criminology and Criminal Justice* 54, no. 4 (2012), 377–413, D.P. Mears and S.E. Siennick, "Young Adult Outcomes and the Life-course Penalties of Parental Incarceration," *Journal of Research in Crime and Delinquency* 53, no. 1 (2016), 3–35,

19. T.L. Grande, J. Hallman, B. Rutledge, K. Caldwell, B. Upton, L.A. Underwood, K.M. Warren, and M. Rehfuss, "Examining Mental Health Symptoms in Male and Female Incarcerated Juveniles," *Behavioral Sciences and the Law* 30, no. 3 (2012), 365–69.

20. K.M. McCabe, A.E. Lansing, A. Garland, and R. Hough, "Differences in Psychopathology, Functional Impairment, and Familial Risk Factors among Adjudicated Delinquents," *Journal of American Academy of Child and Adolescent Psychiatry* 41, no. 7 (2002), 860–67.

21. C.A. Garcia and J. Lane, "Dealing with the Fall-out: Identifying and Addressing the Role that Relationship Strain Plays in the Lives of Girls in the Juvenile Justice System," *Journal of Criminal Justice* 40 (2012), 259–67.

22. J.E. Butters, J. Sheptycki, S. Brochu, and P.G. Erickson, "Guns and Sublethal Violence: A Comparative Study of At-Risk Youth in Two Canadian Cities," *International Criminal Justice Review* 21, no. 4 (2011), 402–26; National Crime Prevention Centre, *A Statistical Snapshot of Youth at Risk and Youth Offending in Canada* (Ottawa: Public Safety Canada, 2012), http://www.publicsafety.gc.ca/res/cp/res/ssyr-eng.aspx.

23. C.M. Chu, M. Daffern, S. Thomas, and J.Y. Lim, "Violence Risk and Gang Affiliation in Youth Offenders: A Recidivism Study," *Psychology, Crime & Law* 18, no. 3 (2012), 299–315.

24. P.K. Kerig, S.D. Chaplo, D.C. Bennett, and C.A. Modrowski, "Gang Membership, Perpetration Trauma, and Posttraumatic Stress Symptoms Among Youth in the Juvenile Justice System," *Criminal Justice and Behavior* 43, no. 5 (2015), 635–52.

25. McCreary Centre Society, *Breaking Through the Barriers: Supporting Youth with FASD Who Have Substance Abuse Challenges* (Vancouver: Author, 2014), http://www.mcs.bc.ca/pdf/breaking_through_the_barriers.pdf.

26. L. Liebenberg and M. Ungar, "A Comparison of Service use Among Youth Involved with Juvenile Justice and Mental Health," *Children and Youth Services Review* 39 (2014), 117–22.

27. Ibid.

28. Correctional Services Program, "Youth Correctional Statistics in Canada, 2014/2015."

29. S. Luck, "Black, Indigenous Prisoners Over-represented in Nova Scotian Jails," *CBC News*, May 20, 2016, http://www.cbc.ca/news/canada/nova-scotia/black-indigenous-prisoners-nova-scotia-jails-1.3591535.

30. J. Rankin, P. Winsa, and H. Ng, "Unequal Justice: Aboriginal and Black Inmates Disproportionately Fill Ontario Jails," *Toronto Star*, March 1, 2013, https://www.thestar.com/news/insight/2013/03/01/unequal_justice_aboriginal_and_black_inmates_disproportionately_fill_ontario_jails.html.

31. Bell, *Young Offenders and Youth Justice: A Century After the Fact*.

32. National Crime Prevention Centre, *A Statistical Snapshot of Youth at Risk and Youth Offending in Canada* (Ottawa: Public Safety Canada, 2012), http://www.public-safety.gc.ca/res/cp/res/ssyr-eng.aspx.

33. J. Latimer and L.C. Foss, *A One Day Snapshot of Aboriginal Youth in Custody Across Canada: Phase II*, Department of Justice Canada, Research and Statistics Division, Youth Justice Policy (Ottawa: Author, 2004), http://www.justice.gc.ca/eng/pi/rs/rep-rap/2004/yj2-jj2/yj2.pdf; M. Totten, *Preventing Aboriginal Youth Gang Involvement in Canada: A Gendered Approach*, paper prepared for the Aboriginal Policy Research Conference, 2009, http://www.nwac.ca/sites/default/files/reports/TottenAPRCGangGenderpaperFeb2609.pdf.

34. R.R. Corrado, S. Kuehn, and I. Margaritescu, "Policy Issues Regarding the Overrepresentation of Incarcerated Aboriginal Young Offenders in a Canadian Context," *Youth Justice 14*, no. 1 (2014), 40–62.

35. Native Women's Association of Canada, *Aboriginal Women and Gangs: An Issue Paper* (St. John's, NL: Author, 2007), http://www.laa.gov.nl.ca/laa/naws/pdf/nwac-gangs.pdf.

36. M. Totten, *Preventing Aboriginal Youth Gang Involvement: A Gendered Approach*, Aboriginal Policy Research Consortium International (APRCi), Paper 55, 2010, http://www.nwac.ca/sites/default/files/reports/TottenAPRCGangGenderpaperFeb2609.pdf.

37. Montreal Urban Aboriginal Community Strategy Network, *The Aboriginal Justice Research Project* (Montréal: Author, 2012), http://www.crime-prevention-intl.org/uploads/media/Aboriginal_Justice_Research_Project_-_Final_Report.pdf.

38. Luck, "Black, Indigenous Prisoners Overrepresented in Nova Scotian Jails."

39. Rankin et al., "Unequal Justice: Aboriginal and Black Inmates Disproportionately Fill Ontario Jails."

40. C.T. Greene, *Creating Consensus: An Exploration of Two Pre-Charge Diversion Programs in Canada*, PhD dissertation, University of Toronto, 2011, https://tspace.library.utoronto.ca/bitstream/1807/29733/11/Greene_Carolyn_T_201106_PhD_Thesis.pdf.

41. Bell, *Young Offenders and Youth Justice: A Century After the Fact*, p. 241.

42. Greene, *Creating Consensus*.

43. Ibid.

44. Youth Justice Committees of Ontario, *Windsor-Essex County Youth Justice Committee* (n.d.), http://www.yjcontario.ca/committees/windsor.php.

45. D.P. Mears, J.C. Cochran, S.J. Greenman, A.S. Bhati, and M.A. Greenwald, "Evidence on the Effectiveness of Juvenile Court Sanctions," *Journal of Criminal Justice 39*, no. 6 (2011), 509–20.

46. Ibid.

47. J. Latimer and L.C. Foss, "The Sentencing of Aboriginal and Non-Aboriginal Youth Under the Young Offenders Act: A Multivariate Analysis," *Canadian Journal of Criminology and Criminal Justice*, *47*, no. 3 (2005), 481–500.

48. Umamaheswar, "Bringing Hope and Change: A Study of Youth Probation Officers in Toronto," p. 1169.

49. Ibid.

50. A.M.F. Peters, *Finding an Appropriate Balance: A Comparison of Specialized and Traditional Probation Caseloads and Their Related Outcomes for Young Offenders in British Columbia*, PhD dissertation, Simon Fraser University, 2014, p. 326, http://summit.sfu.ca/item/14773.

51. Ibid.

52. R.C. Wagner, C.A. Schubert, and E.P. Mulvey, "Probation Intensity, Self-reported Offending, and Psychopathy in Juveniles on Probation for Serious Offences," *Journal of the American Academy of Psychiatry and the Law 43*, no. 2 (2012), 191–200.

53. D. Luong and S. Wormith, "Applying Risk/Need Assessment to Probation Practice and Its Impact on the Recidivism of Young Offenders," *Criminal Justice and Behavior 38*, no. 12 (2011), 1177–99.

54. Z. Haqanee, M. Peterson-Badali, and T. Skilling, "Making 'What Works' Work: Examining Probation Officers' Experiences Addressing the Criminogenic Needs of Juvenile Offenders," *Journal of Offender Rehabilitation 54* (2015), 27–59.

55. Ibid., p. 49.

56. Ibid.

57. "Sentencing of Young Persons," Department of Justice [fact sheet], March 5, 2015, http://www.justice.gc.ca/eng/cj-jp/yj-jj/tools-outils/sheets-feuillets/syp-dpaa.html.

58. B.C. Representative for Children and Youth and B.C. Office of the Provincial Health Officer, *Kids, Crime, and Care: Health and Well-Being of Children in Care: Youth Justice Experiences and Outcomes* (Victoria: Author, 2009), https://www.rcybc.ca/sites/default/files/documents/pdf/reports_publications/kids_crime_and_care.pdf.

59. N. Freudenberg, "Jails, Prisons, and the Health of Urban Populations: A Review of the Impact of the Correctional System on Community Health," *Journal of Community Health 78*, no. 2 (2009), 214–35; A.J. Sedlak and K.S. McPherson, *Youth's Needs and Services: Findings from the Survey of Youth in Residential Placement* (Washington, DC: Office of Juvenile Justice and Delinquency Prevention, 2010), https://www.ncjrs.gov/pdffiles1/ojjdp/227728.pdf.

60. J.V. Roberts, "Harmonizing the Sentencing of Youth and Adult Offenders: A Comparison of the Youth Criminal Act and Part XXII of the Criminal Code," *Canadian Journal of Criminology and Criminal Justice 46*, no. 3 (2004), 301–26; R. Maynard, "Incarcerating Youth as Justice: An In-Depth Examination of Youth, Incarceration, and Restorative Justice," *Canadian Dimension 45*, no. 5 (2011), 25–27.

61. Roberts, "Harmonizing the Sentencing of Youth and Adult Offenders"; G. Beck, "Bullying Among Young offenders in Custody," *Issues in Criminological and Legal Psychology 22* (1995), 54–70.

62. Office of the Child and Family Service Advocacy, *Review of Toronto Youth Assessment Center (TYAC)* (Toronto: Author, 2003); cf. C. Cesaroni and M. Peterson-Badali, "Understanding the Adjustment of Incarcerated Young Offenders: A Canadian Example," *Youth Justice 10*, no. 2 (2010), 107–25; and C. Cesaroni and S. Alvi, "Masculinity and Resistance in Adolescent Carceral Settings," *Canadian Journal of Criminology and Criminal Justice 52*, no. 3 (2010), 303–20.

63. Cesaroni and Alvi, "Masculinity and Resistance in Adolescent Carceral Settings."

64. Y. Jewkes, "Men Behind Bars: 'Doing' Masculinity as an Adaptation to Imprisonment," *Men and Masculinities 8*, no. 1 (2005), 61.

65. M. Peterson-Badali and C. Koegl, "Juvenile Experiences of Incarceration: The Role of Correctional Staff in Peer Violence," *Journal of Criminal Justice 29*, no. 1 (2001), 1–9.

66. Jewkes, "Men Behind Bars."

67. C.A. Schubert, E.P. Mulvey, T.A. Loughran, and S.H. Losoya, "*Perceptions of Institutional Experience and Community Outcomes for Serious Adolescent Offenders,*" *Criminal Justice and Behavior 39*, no. 1 (2012), 71–93.

68. A.M.F. Peters and R.R. Corrado, "An Examination of the Early 'Strains' of Imprisonment Among Young Offenders Incarcerated for Serious Crimes," *Journal of Juvenile Justice 2*, no. 2 (2013), 50–68.

69. A. Liebling, "Suicides in Prison: Ten Years On," *Prison Service Journal 138* (2001), 35–41.

70. Bell, *Young Offenders and Youth Justice: A Century After the Fact*.

71. Ibid., p. 321.

72. C.T. Lowenkamp, M.D. Makarios, E.J. Latessa, R. Lemke, and P. Smith, "Community Corrections Facilities for Juvenile Offenders in Ohio: An Examination of Treatment Integrity and Recidivism," *Criminal Justice and Behavior 37* (2010), 695–708.

73. E.M. Espinosa, J.R. Sorensen, and M.A. Lopez, "Youth Pathways to Placement: The Influence of Gender, Mental Health Need and Trauma on Confinement in the Juvenile Justice System," *Journal of Youth Adolescence 42* (2013), 1824–36 at 1834.

74. "Creating Trauma-Informed Systems," National Child Traumatic Stress Network (n.d.), http://www.nctsn.org/resources/topics/creating-trauma-informed-systems

75. Espinosa et al., "Youth pathways to placement."

76. A. Cox, "Doing the Programme or Doing Me? The Pains of Youth Imprisonment," *Punishment and Society 13*, no. 5 (2011), 592–610.

77. Ibid.

78. Ibid.

79. Ibid., p. 592.

80. R. McCorkle, "Living on the Edge: Fear in a Maximum Security Prison," *Journal of Offender Rehabilitation 20*, nos. 1–2 (1993), 73–91.

81. A. Kupchik, "The Correctional Experiences of Youth in Adult and Juvenile Prisons," *Justice Quarterly 24*, no. 2 (2007), 247–70.

82. Schubert et al., "Perceptions of Institutional Experience and Community Outcomes for Serious Adolescent Offenders."

83. J. Latimer, C. Dowden, and K.E. Morton-Bourgon, *Treating Youth in Conflict with the Law: A New Meta-Analysis* (Ottawa: Department of Justice, 2003), http://www.justice.gc.ca/eng/pi/rs/rep-rap/2003/rr03_yj3-rr03_jj3/rr03_yj3.pdf.

84. Ibid., p. 11.

85. M. Evans-Chase and H. Zhou, "A Systematic Review of the Juvenile Justice Literature: What is can (and cannot) Tell us about what Works with Delinquent Youth," *Crime & Delinquency 60*, no. 3 (2014), 451–70. J.R. Adler, S.K. Edwards, M. Scally, D. Gill, M.J. Puniskis, A. Gekoski, and M.A.H. Horvath, "What Works in Managing Young People who Offend? A Summary of the International Evidence," *Ministry of Justice Analytic Series*, Forensic Psychological Services at Middlesex University, 2016, https://www.gov.uk/government/uploads/system/uploads/attachment_data/file/498493/what-works-in-managing-young-people-who-offend.pdf.

86. McCabe et al., "Differences in Psychopathology"; D.W. Foy, I.K. Ritchie, and A.H. Conway, "Trauma Exposure, Post-traumatic Stress, and Comorbidities in Female Adolescent Offenders: Findings and implications from recent studies," *European Journal of Psychotraumatology 3* (2012), 1–13.

87. M.A. Zahn, J.C. Day, S.F. Mihalic, and L. Tichavsky, "Determining What Works for Girls in the Juvenile Justice System: A Summary of Evaluation Evidence," *Crime and Delinquency 55*, no. 2 (2009), 266–93; T.D. Akoensi, D. Humphreys, and F. Lösel, *What Works in Reducing Reoffending: Strengthening Transitional Approaches to Reducing Reoffending (STARR)*, European Youth Centre, Budapest, June 20–23, 2010, http://www.cepprobation.org/uploaded_files/Thomas%20Akoensi.pdf.

88. S. Peters, *Guiding Principles for Promising Female Programming: An Inventory of Best Practices* (Washington, DC: U.S. Department of Justice, Office of Juvenile Justice and Delinquency Programs, 1998); cf. D. Hubbard and B. Matthews, "Reconciling the Differences Between the 'Gender-Responsive' and the 'What Works' Literatures to Improve Services for Girls," *Crime and Delinquency 54*, no. 2 (2008), 225–58.

89. Hubbard and Matthews, "Reconciling the Differences."

90. F.H. Biggam and K.G. Power, "Social Support and Psychological Distress in a Group of Incarcerated Offenders," *International Journal of Offender Therapy and Comparative Criminology 41* (1997), 213–30; Adler et al., "What Works in Managing Young People who Offend?"

91. C. Cesaroni and M. Peterson-Badali, "Young Offenders in Custody: Risk and Adjustment," *Criminal Justice and Behaviour 32*, no. 3 (2005), 251–77; A. Liebling, D. Price, and G. Schefer, *The Prison Officer* (New York: Willan, 2011).

92. M. Inderbitzin, "A Look from the Inside: Balancing Custody and Treatment in a Juvenile Maximum-Security Facility," *International Journal of Offender Therapy and Comparative Criminology 51*, no. 3 (2007), 348–62.

93. S.C. Marsh and W.P. Evans, "Youth Perspectives on Their Relationships with Staff in Juvenile Correction Settings and Perceived Likelihood of Success on Release," *Youth Violence and Juvenile Justice 7*, no. 1 (2009), 46–67.

94. Ibid., p. 59.

95. Ibid.

96. Schubert et al., "Perceptions of Institutional Experience and Community Outcomes for Serious Adolescent Offenders."

97. A. Doob, *The Experiences of Phase II Male Young Offenders in Secure Facilities in the Province of Ontario* (Toronto: Canadian Foundation for Children, Youth and the Law, 1999); Cesaroni and Peterson-Badali, "Understanding the Adjustment of Incarcerated Young Offenders."

98. Law Commission of Canada, *Restoring Dignity: Responding to Child Abuse in Canadian Institutions* (Ottawa: Author, 2000); Cesaroni and Alvi, "Masculinity and Resistance."

99. Cesaroni and Alvi, "Masculinity and Resistance," p. 312.

100. The Office of the Ombudsperson. BC's Independent Voice for Fairness. (2015). *Unreasonable procedure in youth custody.*

Retrieved from https://bcombudsperson. ca/documents/unreasonable-procedure-youth-custody.

101. F.T. Cullen, "It's Time to Reaffirm Rehabilitation," *Criminology and Public Policy 5*, no. 4 (2006), 665–72; Akoensi, Humphreys, and Lösel, "What Works in Reducing Reoffending."

102. D. Ballucci, "Subverting and Negotiating Risk Assessment: A Case Study of the LSI in a Canadian Youth Custody Facility," *Canadian Journal of Criminology and Criminal Justice 54*, no. 2 (2012), 203–28.

103. R. D. Hoge and D.A. Andrews, *Youth Level of Service/Case Management Inventory (YLS/CMI)* (Toronto: Multi-Health Systems, 2002).

104. N.A. Vitopoulos, M. Peterson-Badali, and T.A. Skilling, "The Relationship Between Matching Service to Criminogenic Need and Recidivism in Male and Female Youth: Examining the RNR Principles in Practice," *Criminal Justice and Behavior 39*, no. 8 (2012), 1025–41; M.E. Olver, K.C. Stockdale, and J.S. Wormith, "Risk Assessment with Young Offenders: A Meta-Analysis of Three Assessment Measures," *Criminal Justice and Behavior 36*, no. 4 (2009), 329–53.

105. Olver et al., "Risk Assessment with Young Offenders."

106. Ibid.; Vitopoulos et al., "The Relationship"; C.S. Schwalbe, "A Meta-Analysis of Juvenile Justice Risk Assessment Instruments," *Criminal Justice and Behavior 35*, no. 11 (2008), 1367–81; C. Campbell, E. Onifade, A. Barnes, J. Peterson, V. Anderson, W. Davidson, and D. Gordon, "Screening Offenders: The Exploration of a Youth Level of Service/Case Management Inventory (YLS/CMI) Brief Screener," *Journal of Offender Rehabilitation 53* (2014), 19–34. M.E. Olver, K.C. Stockdale, and S.C.P. Wong, "Short and Long-term Prediction of Recidivism Using the Youth Level of Service/Case Management Inventory in a Sample of Serious Young Offenders," *Law and Human Behavior 36*, no. 4 (2012), 331–44.

107. R. Borum, P. Bartel, and A. Forth, *Structured Assessment of Violence Risk in Youth™ (SAVRY™)* (Lutz, Fla.: PAR Inc., 2012), http://www4.parinc.com/Products/Product.aspx?ProductID=SAVRY.

108. Canadian Resource Centre for Victims of Crime, *Restorative Justice in Canada: What Victims Should Know* (Ottawa: Author, 2011), http://www.rjlillooet.ca/documents/restjust.pdf.

109. "The Value of a Community-Based Approach to Youth Crime," Calgary Youth Justice Society (n.d.), http://calgaryyouthjustice.ca/what-we-do/measuring-success/.

110. J.A. Bouffard and K.J. Bergseth, "The Impact on Reentry Services on Juvenile Offenders' Recidivism," *Youth Violence and Juvenile Justice 6*, no. 3 (2008), 295–318.

111. D. Fields and L.S. Abrams, "Gender Differences in the Perceived Needs and Barriers of Youth Offenders Preparing for Community Reentry," *Child & Youth Care Forum 39* (2010), 253–69.

112. P.R. Jones and B.R. Wyant, "Target Juvenile Needs to Reduce Delinquency," *Criminology and Public Policy 6*, no. 4 (2007), 763–72.

113. R.D. Weaver and D. Campbell, "Fresh Start: A Meta-analysis of Aftercare Programs for Juvenile Offenders," *Research on Social Work Practice 25*, no. 2 (2015), 201–12, doi:10.1177/1049731514521302

114. D.J. Martinez and L.S. Abrams, "Informal Social Support Among Returning Young Offenders: A Metasynthesis of the Literature," *International Journal of Offender Therapy and Comparative Criminology 57*, no. 2 (2013), 169–90.

115. L.S. Abrams, M.L. Mizel, V. Nguyen, and A. Shlonsky, "Juvenile Reentry and Aftercare Interventions: Is Mentoring a Promising Direction?" *Journal of Evidence-Based Social Work 11*, no. 4 (2014), 404–22. P. Edwards, C. Jarrett, C. Perkins, D. Beecher, R. Steinbach, and I. Roberts, *Mediation, Mentoring and Peer Support to Reduce Youth Violence: A Systematic Review* (London, UK: London School of Hygiene & Tropical Medicine, 2015), http://whatworks.college.police.uk/About/Systematic_Review_Series/Pages/Mentoring.aspx.

116. E.A. Panuccio, J. Christian, D.J. Martinez, and M.L. Sullivan, "Social Support, Motivation, and the Process of Juvenile Re-entry: An Exploratory Analysis of Desistance," *Journal of Offender Rehabilitation 51*, no. 3 (2012), 135–60.

117. Ibid.

118. R.G. Wiebush, D. Wagner, B. McNulty, Y. Wang, and T.N. Le, *Implementation and Outcome Evaluation of the Intensive Aftercare Program: Final Report* (Washington, DC: National Council on Crime and Delinquency, 2005), https://www.ncjrs.gov/pdffiles1/ojjdp/206177.pdf.

119. Ibid.

120. Akoensi et al. "What Works in Reducing Reoffending"; D.R. Haerle, "Dosage Matters: Impact of a Violent Offender Treatment Program on Juvenile Recidivism," *Youth Violence and Juvenile Justice* (2014), 1–23. Adler et al., "What works in managing young people who offend?"

121. Personal communication with C.T. Griffiths.

122. P. Verbrugge, *Fetal alcohol spectrum disorder and the youth criminal justice system: A discussion paper* (Ottawa: Department of Justice Canada, 2003), http://www.justice.gc.ca/eng/rp-pr/cj-jp/yj-jj/rr03_yj6-rr03_jj6/rr03_yj6.pdf.

PART VI

GOING FORWARD: REFORMING CORRECTIONS

In the Preface, we promised that this text would avoid the doom and gloom that often accompanies discussions of corrections. Tracing the evolution of the response to criminal offenders over the past 200 years and identifying the obstacles to correctional change and the ongoing challenges of corrections could lead one to conclude that not much has changed. However, although systematic difficulties persist in federal and provincial/territorial corrections, there are innovative practices that have proven successful in addressing the needs of offenders and, in so doing, reducing the risk to the community.

During the years 2006–15 under the federal Conservative party, there was a move toward a punitive penology based not on evidence but rather on a "get tough" approach to crime and offenders. As of late-2017, it was uncertain what specific direction the federal Liberal government would take with respect to criminal justice and corrections, but there had already been a move to dismantle some of the key components of the punitive penology. The courts were playing a role in this as well, holding as unconstitutional a number of key legislative provisions relating to offenders.

The discussion in the concluding chapter focuses on creating effective systems of corrections: processes, programs, and services that are accountable, are transparent, adhere to the rule of law, effectively address the needs of offenders, and provide safety and security for the community.

There are both challenges and opportunities for corrections, and it is in addressing these that significant reforms will occur.

CHAPTER 15

CREATING EFFECTIVE SYSTEMS OF CORRECTIONS

CHAPTER OBJECTIVES

- Identify and discuss the challenges facing Canadian corrections.
- Identify and discuss the systemic failures of corrections that have been identified.
- Discuss the findings from audits of provincial corrections in Manitoba, British Columbia, and Ontario, and what these findings suggest about the state of corrections.
- Discuss the opportunities for corrections as the "way forward."
- Compare and contrast traditional correctional practices with evidence-based correctional practices.
- Discuss the potential and effectiveness of restorative justice as a component of the "way forward."
- Discuss the potential and limitations of privatization in corrections.
- Identify and discuss the key questions that should be asked by any observer of corrections.

In this, the final chapter, we take a step back from the specific components of the corrections process to reflect on areas where reform is required to create more effective systems of corrections. Addressing these areas will strengthen the foundations of correctional practice, increase the effectiveness of responses to criminal offenders, and better protect communities.

CHALLENGES FOR SYSTEMS OF CORRECTIONS

Correctional systems in the early 21st century face a number of challenges, many of which are discussed throughout the text. These include the challenges we address in the following sections.

Developing and Implementing Evidence-Based Correctional Policies and Programs

Evidence-based practices refer to those policies, strategies, and programs that have been shown by evaluation research to be effective in achieving specified objectives. These can be contrasted with tradition-based practices, which develop from the established routines, politics, and philosophies of agencies, organizations, and individuals—and from emotion as well. Provincial/territorial systems of corrections have struggled to implement evidence-based practices, which are more prevalent in federal corrections.

> **Evidence-based practices**
> Policies, strategies, and programs that have been shown by evaluation research to be effective in achieving specified objectives.

Addressing the Needs of Victims

In any discussion of the criminal justice and corrections systems, a key concern is that the needs of crime victims be addressed and that they not be "re-victimized" by the criminal justice and corrections process. Although federal and provincial/territorial legislation sets out the rights of victims and defines their role in the justice process, the involvement of victims is still quite limited. Many crime victims find the justice and corrections systems to be quite confusing, and they have difficulty understanding the decisions that are made and the sanctions that are imposed on their perpetrators. With respect to sentencing, for example, one study found that crime victims often confused probation with conditional sentences, and others did not understand how the judge weighed different factors in the case in reaching a decision on sentencing.[1]

Similarly, studies of problem-solving courts have found that there are challenges in engaging victims in programs and services. And although restorative justice programs are generally viewed as providing a more culturally appropriate and respectful framework within which to address crime in Indigenous communities, there may be limitations in the use of this approach for cases of violence, in particular, intimate violence.[2]

Providing Adequate Health Care for Inmates

The poor health conditions of federal and provincial/territorial offenders has been extensively documented, as has the lack of capacity in the corrections systems to effectively address these issues. Principle 9 of the United Nations Basic Principles for the Treatment of Prisoners states: "Prisoners shall have access to the health services available in the country without discrimination on the grounds of their legal situation."[3] Despite this, Canadian systems of corrections have consistently failed to provide adequate access to health services for inmates. Recall from Chapter 8 that "health issues" is the most frequent complaint filed by inmates in federal correctional facilities.

There are also ongoing challenges in hiring, and retaining, health care professionals. In Ontario, for example, a study found that 29 percent of the psychologist positions in federal institutions were vacant.[4] Both provincial

/territorial and federal institutions have also experienced challenges in utilizing new health technologies, including the use of electronic health records.[5]

Addressing the Needs of Offenders with Mental Health Issues

A key feature of Canadian corrections is the increasing number of offenders in institutions and under supervision in the community who have mental health issues.

It is estimated, for example, that 20 percent of the offenders on probation and parole in Ontario have mental health issues. The Auditor General of Ontario has criticized the Ministry of Public Safety and Correctional Services for lacking a provincial strategy to address offender mental health issues.[6] Canadian correctional facilities have been referred to as the "new asylums of the 21st century."[7] Particular concerns have been raised about the detention of migrants with mental health issues in provincial institutions and concerns that the conditions under which this group is held violates international human rights laws.[8]

The increase in the numbers of offenders with mental health issues who are involved in corrections systems is due in some measure to the failure of provincial/territorial governments to provide alternative facilities, programs, and services to persons with mental illness.

The Over-Representation of Indigenous Persons and Blacks in Canadian Prisons

The numbers of Indigenous persons and Blacks in the criminal justice system and in corrections are high and continue to rise. These groups of offenders present unique challenges for corrections with respect to the delivery of community-based and institutional programs and services. These challenges will require corrections to expand the networks of collaboration with other agencies and with community organizations. The failure to provide culturally sensitive and relevant programs and services for these offenders may result in higher rates of reoffending, continuing their over-representation in the criminal justice and corrections system.[9]

Corrections in the Canadian North

Providing correctional services and delivering programs in remote and northern regions of the country is a difficult challenge given that northern communities typically have the highest rates of crime and serious violent crime in the country.

Some small northern communities are accessible only by air (or for a brief part of the year, by sea), which makes it difficult to address the needs of offenders in these regions. Also, many small northern communities do not have full-time probation and parole officers, so justice services must be provided on a "fly-in" or "drive-in" basis. This, even though offenders in these regions may have multiple needs, including alcohol and drug addiction, mental illness, and fetal alcohol spectrum disorder (FASD).[10] Offenders who receive federal sentences or who require specialized treatment may have to be sent hundreds of kilometres from their home community, and follow-up supervision and treatment are often limited or nonexistent.

Similarly, northerners' access to mental health services is often severely limited. In the Northwest Territories, for example, there is one psychiatrist for the entire territory, and court-ordered psychiatric assessments are conducted in Alberta. For offenders with mental illness or FASD, there may be few alternatives to incarceration. Regarding the lack of resources in Nunavut, one judge remarked that "Nunavut has a psychiatric hospital. It's called BCC [Baffin Correctional Centre]."[11] A study of facilities and services for the mentally ill in the Northwest Territories concluded that "the territory's correctional system either fails even to identify prisoners with mental health problems; recognizes them but does nothing; or is simply ineffective when it does try to help. The offenders keep their heads down, their medical, mental, or addiction needs unmet, and wait for their release."[12]

The Systemic Failures of Corrections Systems

Despite the expenditure of billions of dollars, corrections still suffer from systemic failures. These are documented in the reports of the various Auditor Generals at the provincial and federal levels, the reports of the OCI, commissions of inquiry into corrections, and high-profile deaths in custody and situations in which inmates have spent lengthy periods of time in solitary confinement.

Audits have found that provincial/territorial and federal systems often fail to effectively classify inmates, to ensure that inmates have timely access to correctional programming, or to determine whether the treatment programs that are offered are effective.

The systemic failures in systems of corrections that have been identified by various inquiries and audits include the following:

- A lack of adequate systems of classification to ensure that inmate needs are identified
- A lack of capacity to adequately forecast correctional populations to ensure that sufficient housing resources and programs and services are in place
- A lack of capacity to address the needs of an increasingly diverse corrections population
- Ensuring continuity of treatment from correctional institutions to supervision in the community

- Not sufficiently addressing the needs of offenders with mental illness, addiction, and FASD
- Developing effective correctional strategies for northern and remote regions of the country
- Failing to include evaluation as a core component of any correctional program
- Keeping inmates safe during their incarceration
- Coming up short in meeting the needs of women offenders
- Experiencing challenges in addressing the needs of Indigenous offenders and Black offenders

Despite numerous commissions of inquiry into various facets of corrections, and the reports that have been produced from critical incidents and the deaths of inmates, Canadian corrections continues to be beset by systemic failures. In the discussion of solitary confinement in Chapter 7 and inmate self-harm in Chapter 8, it was noted that there continue to be significant problems in how systems of corrections are using solitary confinement and managing inmates who are at risk of self-harm. In a review of inmate suicides, the OCI stated, "A major impediment to progress appears to be the lack of immediate and substantive follow-up, especially dissemination of lessons learned from boards of investigation across a very decentralized Service."[13]

A key attribute of systems of corrections is that reforms often occur only after commissions of inquiry or critical events have occurred. And increasingly, lawsuits brought on behalf of inmates, or the inmates themselves, have forced corrections to change their policies and procedures. In recent years, inmates have sued and won court cases.

Historically, there has been only a limited capacity of corrections to initiate reforms from within the organization and to create the capacity to monitor and evaluate the outcomes of initiatives that are taken.

In many instances, the CSC has refused to implement the recommendations of the OCI and of enquiries into the deaths of inmates. Similarly, at the provincial level, the recommendations of inquiries and audits have often remained unheeded.

Audits of provincial institutional corrections in Manitoba,[14] British Columbia,[15] and Ontario [16] provide insights into the significant deficiencies that exist in the management and operations of corrections at the provincial level.

Manitoba

The province of Manitoba has the highest provincial incarceration rate in the country (213 per 100,000 population) as compared to other provinces such as Ontario (83 per 100,000) and Nova Scotia (55 per 100,000). In 2012–13, operating expenses for adult corrections were $173 million, a 129 percent increase from 2004–05. During this period, the population of incarcerated adults increased by 111 percent.

The findings of the Manitoba audit included the following:

- The planning capacity and population forecasting for institutions was inadequate, resulting in overcrowding in many institutions.
- There was no strategic infrastructure plan to address the issue of aging facilities.
- There were gaps in the planning and monitoring of adult treatment programs.
- There were problems in managing offenders in the community, with offenders not being properly supervised, offenders' rehabilitation plans requiring improvement, and a lack of management oversight of staff to ensure compliance with standards and policies.
- There was limited tracking of program offerings, offender enrollment, program completion, and outcomes.[17]

British Columbia

Similar results were obtained by an audit of provincial institutional and community corrections in British Columbia.[18] More specifically, with respect to community corrections, the B.C. Auditor found the following:[19]

- Probation officers do not consistently complete the appropriate training before supervising offenders in the community.
- Probation officers' case management work is not regularly reviewed by local managers to ensure it complies with policy.
- Probation officers do not consistently identify strategies that address offenders' risks and needs, and subsequently ensure that offenders complete assigned interventions.
- Insufficient documentation is contained in offender files, specifically as it pertains to risk/needs assessments and breach decisions, to confirm the appropriateness of probation officers' judgments.

With respect to institutional corrections, the Auditor General concluded, "Overall, we found that the Division's lack of attention to performance management, evidence-based decision making, and offender programming increase the risk to inmate, staff and public safety."[20]

Ontario

In Ontario, a 2014 audit of adult community corrections and the Ontario Parole Board found the following[21]:

- Risk assessments on offenders were not completed by probation and parole officers in a timely manner, hindering the development of correctional plans.[22]
- The ministry did not have reliable and timely information on offenders on conditional release who breached the conditions of their release or what actions were taken by probation and parole officers to address the violations.[23]

- There were significant issues in the supervision provided to offenders on conditional release; low-risk offenders were often over-supervised, and high-risk offenders were under-supervised.[24]
- The ministry did not track the availability of, and wait times for, offenders on conditional release to access treatment programs.[25]

A follow-up investigation conducted by the Auditor General of Ontario in 2016 found that many of the identified issues had not been addressed.[26] For example, no progress had been made on ensuring that high-risk offenders on probation and parole were being properly supervised; there was still no formal tracking of offenders who completed programs in the community, and no information on the effectiveness of the programs; and there was still a lack of institutional support for inmates desiring to apply for parole.

The Auditor General did find that progress had been made in ensuring correctional plans were completed in a timely manner and in ensuring oversight of the activities of probation and parole officers. Despite these improvements, concerns were expressed that 60 percent of the high-risk offenders committed new crimes during a year (2010–11) in which this was audited.[27]

A key question is, Why do these deficiencies continue to exist, despite the massive amounts of money that are spent on corrections? And, What is the solution to address these structural and operational deficiencies?

Politics and Correctional Policy and Practice

It has been argued that "crime policy is politically constituted: policy choices are driven by, and responsive to, prevailing values and interests rather than criminological knowledge."[28] This highlights the importance of examining the larger political context within which decisions about criminal justice and corrections are made.

Correctional legislation and policies are often affected by political considerations and public opinion. The legislative and policy decisions made by the federal Conservative government during the time period 2006–15 had a significant impact on the response to offenders at all stages of the corrections process, from sentencing to release from prison. The various bills that were passed were not informed by research or by the experiences of other jurisdictions (such as the United States) that had found punitive penology to be both expensive and largely ineffective.

Political agendas have also resulted in decarceration. In a case study of provincial correctional populations in Alberta, Webster and Doob found that the drive by the then-provincial government to reduce expenditures, eliminate the budget deficit, and restore public confidence in government resulted in a 32 percent decrease in institutional populations between 1993 and 1997.[29]

The case study analysis led the authors to conclude that decarceration in Alberta during this time, "was an act of political will," a "byproduct of expenditure cuts," rather than a result of enlightened correctional policy.[30]

Since 2015, the courts have found some of the legislation passed by the previous Conservative government to be unconstitutional, and its successor, the Liberals, have moved to change some of the policies that provided the foundation for the "get-tough" approach to offenders. As of late-2017, it remained uncertain as to the breadth of the changes that will occur and how this will impact systems of corrections.

The continuing systemic failures of systems of corrections to develop the capacity to ensure that the human and Charter rights of offenders are protected, to create and evaluate the effectiveness of correctional interventions in the community and in institutions, and to make the necessary structural, policy, and operations reforms to address issues that have been identified by correctional investigators, commissions of inquiry, and audits should be a priority for all correctional authorities. Only then can it be said that corrections has met its mandate to protect the community and to address the needs of offenders.

REFORMING CORRECTIONS: A WAY FORWARD

Following a spate of high-profile incidents in corrections, including the death of Ashley Smith and the failure of governments and the CSC to address systemic issues, a headline appeared: "No One Seems to Care About Prison Reform in Canada."[31]

The materials on corrections in Canada presented in this text suggest that, both historically and in contemporary times, substantive reform of corrections has remained elusive, whether due to political will, interference, and/or obstruction; a lack of effective strategic planning and evaluation by corrections services; and/or effective methods to implement reforms.

For systems of corrections to address the risk and needs of offenders more effectively, to ensure the safety of communities, and to ensure that there is a "return on investment" for correctional expenditures, a number of areas must be examined.

Despite the negativity that often surrounds discussion of corrections, there is an emerging literature pointing to strategies and interventions that can effectively address the risk and needs of criminal offenders.

Evidence-Based Policies and Programs

Historically, systems of corrections have lacked a well-developed body of empirical knowledge that could be used to formulate policies and guide programs. There is often a disconnect between correctional policy and practice and scholarly research.

One consequence of this has been the susceptibility of corrections to **panaceas**—that is, the search for a "magic bullet" that will reduce recidivism, lower costs, and deter offenders from future criminal behaviour. Systems of corrections, buffeted by a political environment that is focused strongly on penal populism, remain susceptible to simple, "quick fix" solutions that neither protect the community nor assist offenders.[32]

> **Panaceas**
> In corrections, the search for the "magic bullet" that will reduce recidivism, lower costs, and deter offenders from future criminal behaviour.

A review of initiatives over the past century reveals that systems of corrections have stumbled from one strategy to another and that most of these strategies have not achieved any of their intended objectives. Systems of corrections have been slow to adopt evidence-based strategies and to discard ineffective policies and programs. As one Canadian correctional observer has noted, "There is often a gap in public policy between evidence-based knowledge and that of politicians who represent the electorate.[33]

The challenge, for Canadians, their governments, and their systems of corrections, is to undertake the fundamental structural changes that are required so that the next 50 years of corrections do not produce the same outcomes as the present ones and so that correctional policies and practices do not continue to reel from crisis to crisis. One possibility is to give more "teeth" to the recommendations of the OCI, provincial ombudspersons and auditors, and commissions of inquiry. At present, these recommendations are not binding, and as a result, reports end up "on the shelf," only to be replicated by subsequent investigations.

This text has identified community and institution-based programs and strategies that do not help offenders and protect communities. There is plenty of research evidence that supports discontinuing a number of correctional practices, including community notification for sex offenders released into the community and (for most offenders) lengthy sentences of incarceration.

Conversely, the materials in the preceding chapters have revealed that some programs and interventions *do* work to address the needs of offenders, reduce reoffending, and protect the community. These include the Strategic Training Initiative in Community Supervision (STICS) approach in probation, the application of the risk–need–responsivity (RNR) principles in correctional treatment and programming, and the involvement of communities and families in supporting offenders.

Increasing the effectiveness of corrections will require abandoning many traditional practices. As the discussion in the text has illustrated, correctional policy and practice is often influenced more by politics and specific perspectives on crime and punishment, rather than on research on "what works."

The effectiveness of correctional programming may also be compromised by a lack of consistency in program offerings between facilities in the same jurisdictions. There is often inconsistency in the programs that are offered in correctional institutions and in the community in the same jurisdiction.[34]

There are additional challenges to promoting evidence-based practices in systems of corrections. Politicians and corrections leadership may be risk adverse and hesitant to develop and implement innovative strategies.

Early Intervention with At-Risk Youth

A key feature of systems of corrections is that many of the offenders who are in the adult corrections system have long histories of involvement in youth corrections. Recall the statements by the ex-dangerous offender in Chapters

8 and 14 who spent 23 years inside adult correctional institutions after serving numerous sentences in youth facilities. Similarly, recall the probation officer in Chapter 14 who noted that it is rare for offenders on caseload not to have had extensive involvement in the youth justice system and that there were early missed opportunities to address the issues that placed youth at risk.

Reducing the "Pains" Experienced by Offenders and Their Families

The discussion in this book has documented a variety of "pains" that many offenders experience after becoming involved in the criminal justice and corrections systems. These difficulties may be most pronounced for offenders confined in correctional institutions, although probationers, parolees, and ex-offenders and their families may struggle as well.

The offender's family may break down under the stress of incarceration and supervision in the community. The damage to the children of offenders may manifest itself in subsequent conflict with the law. There is little doubt that society (i.e., the state) has a right to sanction offenders found guilty of committing criminal offences. But it can be argued that systems of corrections have an obligation to mitigate the ancillary pains that offenders experience and the collateral damage to the families of offenders.

Addressing the Needs of Offenders

Recall that a large number of persons who come into conflict with the law are marginal with respect to their employment skills, education, and other capacities. Many are mentally ill, have a lengthy history of addiction, and have few community supports.

Do correctional systems do anything to reduce this marginality? The answer is, generally, no. Although specific interventions may reduce reoffending, there is no conclusive evidence that the marginality of offenders—that is, their substance abuse issues, homelessness, and mental illness, all of which are closely related to their conflict with the law—is being addressed successfully in the long term. Neither governments nor correctional systems compile longitudinal data to track changes in these factors among ex-offenders. For some offenders, involvement in corrections may *increase* their marginality and the likelihood of reoffending.

Special attention must be given to the needs of special groups of offenders, including Indigenous persons, Blacks, and other racialized groups. This also includes offenders suffering from FASD, trauma, addiction, and mental illness. To date, research and investigations have found systems of corrections to fall short in addressing the needs of these offenders.

Developing effective programs will require that the provinces/territories and the federal government make the necessary investment to develop, and sustain, effective treatment interventions and alternatives to confinement.

The reports of the OCI and the audits conducted at the provincial level indicate that, even with significant funding, systems of corrections have struggled to develop the capacities to ensure that the programs and services that are being delivered to offenders in community and institutional settings are effective.

Addressing the Needs of Victims

Systems of corrections have made some progress in recognizing and addressing the needs of crime victims. The evidence suggests, however, that victims are still marginalized in the criminal justice and corrections processes. Many victims do not understand how the justice and corrections systems work and have little opportunity to play a meaningful role in the response to criminal offenders. Contrast this with restorative justice programs, which provide an opportunity for crime victims to be part of the dialogue with and about offenders. Restorative justice programs provide an opportunity to address many of the issues that surround victims and the correctional process.

Acknowledging the Limits of Technology

Systems of corrections are making increasing use of technology, not only with respect to gathering and managing information but also for control and surveillance. The rise of **techno-corrections** has been accompanied by the expansion of electronic monitoring (EM) and global positioning system (GPS) to monitor offenders, and by the use of the media (including social media) to notify communities about high-risk offenders.

Techno-corrections, which includes surveillance within institutions and the GPS monitoring of offenders under supervision in the community, focuses on security and order at the possible expense of rehabilitation and treatment.[35] In correctional institutions, inmates are being more heavily restricted in their movements and are being watched over by closed-circuit televisions (CCTVs).

A study of the adoption of GPS tracking for high-risk youth in Manitoba found that probation officers had significant concerns that the use of technology had altered their role to one of monitoring, had reduced face-to-face work with youth, and had resulted in increased administrative workloads.[36]

The challenge is to ensure that systems of correction do not come to rely too heavily on technology. Techno-corrections, in themselves, do not ensure public safety. The danger is that the increasing use of technology will come at the expense of developing human and helping relationships, which have been shown to reduce reoffending and to help offenders reintegrate in the community.

Techno-corrections
The application of technology to the supervision and control of offenders.

Adhering to the Rule of Law and Respecting the Rights of Offenders

A continuing challenge for systems of corrections is to ensure that responses to offenders adhere to the rule of law and that the rights of offenders are protected. This is crucial to ensuring the legitimacy of corrections and is a fundamental requirement for a democratic society. A common thread in the various commissions of inquiry into corrections over the past 200 years has been that corrections personnel did not abide by the rule of law and the duty to act fairly.

The OCI and its provincial counterparts provide a degree of oversight into the activities of correctional systems, though their recommendations are not binding. Canadian courts are hearing more and more cases centred on inmate rights, and the resulting decisions are having a significant impact on correctional practice.

It does appear that there are instances in which Canadian corrections is in violation of UN conventions and principles with respect to inmate rights. Recall the discussion of solitary confinement in Chapter 6, wherein the negative impacts of solitary were discussed as was the detention of inmates in solitary for prolonged periods of time.

Improving the Effectiveness of Community Corrections

The majority of offenders are under some form of supervision in the community, yet only a very small portion (about 10 percent) of the $4 billion consumed by correctional systems annually is spent on community corrections. The expansion of effective community programs could be cost-effective by keeping offenders out of prison; it could also reduce risk to communities and help offenders address their needs.[37]

More research is required on community corrections. Within the current framework of probation practice, for example, there is little information about how probation officers spend their time and how effective their interventions are. From the perspective of one corrections scholar, "Probation and parole agents spend a considerable amount of time writing reports, receiving training, going to court, attending probation and parole revocation hearings, talking with program providers, all of which take time away from actually supervising their caseload."[38] The STICS model of probation practice, profiled in Chapter 5, has shown potential. It remains to be seen whether this success can be sustained and replicated in other jurisdictions.

For offenders released from custody, systems of correction struggle to provide throughcare. The challenges are especially difficult for offenders with special needs, including addicted persons and those with a mental illness or FASD. When significant community resources are absent, the likelihood of reoffending is high. Research could lead to the development of best practices of community supervision.

Reforming Correctional Institutions

Prison reform is difficult to achieve for many reasons. First, many people view prisons as places of punishment, so they may be opposed to prison reforms that entail providing treatment and rehabilitation for offenders.[39] Another major challenge can be opposition from those working within correctional systems; these individuals may feel threatened by the proposed reforms if, for example, they think the reforms will reduce their importance or change the way they have been "doing business." Consultation between reformers and correctional officials might ensure that reforms are designed and implemented in a realistic manner that accounts for the realities facing practitioners on the ground. Also, consultation with management personnel may help identify operational realities that reformers overlook; for example, those personnel may be better equipped to identify potential issues pertaining to competing demands for monetary and human resources.[40] Consultation could also secure "buy-in" from corrections staff and management, which might increase the effectiveness of reform efforts.

Financial constraints may impede reform efforts, both their implementation and their sustainability. When money and resources are scarce in correctional systems, treatment programs and services for offenders are unlikely to receive adequate funding.[41] Although reform initiatives often include resources to bring about the changes initially, ongoing maintenance of reform efforts may be impossible due to financial shortfalls in subsequent years. Also, an absence of administrative accountability may impede the thorough implementation and success of reform initiatives, for agencies may not be monitored to assess whether changes have actually been made and whether outcomes are being achieved.

A key concept in discussions of organizational change and reform is that of a **learning organization**. A learning organization has been defined as one "that is continually expanding its capacity to create its own future."[42] The organization seeks constant improvement, learning from successes as well as from initiatives that did not achieve their stated goals. A key role in this process is played by leadership, which provides a clear sense of direction and purpose and creates an organizational environment in which all personnel share a common vision.[43]

In contrast to the field of policing, little attention has been given to leadership in corrections: what makes a good prison warden, supervisor of a probation or parole office, or minister in charge of corrections at the federal and provincial/territorial levels. Primarily, correctional leaders in Canada have been the subject of extensive criticism, for not implementing the recommendations of various reports, inquiries, and audits, or in presiding over correctional institutions where critical events have occurred. This criticism is

Learning organization
The notion that a correctional service is constantly seeking improvement, learning from successes as well as from initiatives that did not achieve their intended goals.

reflected in the comments of a Canadian senator in response to a just-released report of the OCI. Among the senator's comments were that the CSC continued to fail inmates, noting that key recommendations from the inquest into the death of Ashley Smith still had not been acted on. The senator also stated, "They spent around 5 million dollars of taxpayers' money to fight the inquest."[44]

For systems of corrections to be successful requires that they, and their components, become learning organizations. The materials presented in this text suggest that, in many areas, systems of corrections in Canada have a long way to go to achieve this. Too often, systems of corrections have been reactive—responding to the latest crisis or critical incident, rather than proactively initiating innovative strategies. Similarly, there is a tendency for corrections to continue policies and programs that have been proven not to be successful in achieving their objectives.

Most disappointing, and challenging, is that these systems often do not "learn lessons" from critical incidents, which results in reoccurrences.

Even if all of these challenges are addressed, some people argue that correctional reform will be impossible without fundamental changes in society's beliefs and values.[45]

Expanding Alternatives to Confinement

A key theme in this text has been the over-representation of marginal and racialized persons in the criminal justice and corrections systems. Many persons who come into conflict with the law and who are sentenced to confinement in a correctional institution are in poverty, are afflicted with mental illness, and/or are addicted. The movement toward mass decarceration in the United States suggests that alternative programs centred on treatment and providing assistance can be effective in addressing the needs of many offenders without placing the community at risk. This has been the experience in the State of New York, where there was a 50 percent decrease in the number of persons incarcerated between the mid-1990s and 2016.[46]

Other strategies that can reduce the numbers of offenders in confinement include strengthening probation, and reducing or eliminating mandatory sentencing penalties that limit judicial discretion.[47] Systems of corrections can also invest more in assisting offenders to reintegrate back into the community and to be successful during and following community supervision. This includes developing programs and services to support offenders and their families. Specific attention should be focused on northern and remote areas of the country, which often lack services.

Addressing the Unique Challenges of Provincial/Territorial Systems of Corrections

Provincial/territorial systems of corrections face unique challenges. These are largely a consequence of the very short periods of time that offenders spend in custody, the high risk/needs of many offenders, and the difficulties of providing services in rural and remote communities.

Despite this, there is relatively little published research on community and institutional corrections at the provincial/territorial level. It cannot be assumed that research findings from federal corrections are applicable to provincial/territorial corrections. Little is known, for example, about the dynamics of life inside provincial/territorial institutions or about the effectiveness of various treatment programs. Given that most offenders in Canada fall under the jurisdiction of the provinces/territories, much more needs to be known about how these systems of corrections are operating.

Understanding the Experience of Offenders

Persons who come into conflict with the law and end up in the criminal justice system most often play a passive role in the process—restorative justice approaches being the exception. The offender, in effect, becomes a "bystander" in the proceedings and in the correctional enterprise. Interventions are too often done "to" offenders, rather than "with" offenders. Ideally, offenders should be partners in efforts to address their risk and needs and to reduce their propensity to reoffend. This is particularly important for Indigenous and Black offenders.

Systems of corrections can learn much from the experiences and views of offenders in their charge. For example, although concerns have been expressed about the increasing use of technology for the surveillance of offenders, a study of high-risk youth in Manitoba found that being placed on GPS tracking assisted them in adhering to their conditions and from reoffending.[48] As well, the findings that even offenders who are not sent to prison but are supervised in the community experience hardships are instructive for probation officers.

Corrections in the Global Community

Canadian corrections is not immune from events that are occurring on a global level. This includes the migration of large numbers of persons and the increasing risk associated with radical movements.

Thousands of non-citizens are detained in Canada every year, and it is estimated that one-third of this number are held in provincial institutions, most in Ontario. These persons have not been convicted of a criminal offence, but rather are held by the Canadian Border Services Agency (CBSA) pending a hearing on their immigration status or removal from the country. The situation of detainees has been referred to as a "legal black hole," since neither the corrections service nor the CBSA has clearly defined authority over the conditions of confinement.[49]

Another issue is the impact of radicalized offenders on prison populations. A study (N = 89) of Canadian offenders from various religious backgrounds found that Muslim inmates scored much higher than Christian and atheist inmates on a scale designed to measure religious attitudes and beliefs and ideologies of Middle Eastern extremists.[50] This raises the spectre that offenders with these beliefs may radicalize other inmates with whom they have contact in correctional institutions. Researchers and police and security agencies have documented the connection between criminality and terrorist activities among jihadists.[51]

Despite this, neither the federal nor provincial/territorial corrections have a strategic plan in place to prevent and detect the radicalization of inmates.[52] Among the recommendations that have been made are that correctional authorities educate staff to be aware of efforts by certain inmates to radicalize others, identifying and isolating offenders who pose a risk to radicalize others, and that corrections systems develop a deradicalization strategy to assist offenders to successfully reintegrate back into the community.[53]

Moving Away from a Punitive Penology

In Chapter 2, it was noted that during the time of the federal Conservative government (2006–15), a punitive penology was developed. This was reflected in legislation and policy. The adoption of this approach to offenders occurred just as the United States was moving to reduce the number of offenders in correctional institutions, expanding community-based programs and services, and increasing the use of alternatives to confinement.

It should be noted, however, that there were many long-standing punitive features of Canadian corrections (some extending back to the Kingston Penitentiary in the early 1800s) prior to the actions of the Conservative government. The lack of programs and services for offenders, the high numbers of vulnerable and marginal persons and Indigenous offenders in prison, and the extensive use of solitary confinement have been documented for decades and, in some cases, centuries.

Expanding Effective Interventions: What Works in Corrections

Despite the challenges faced by systems of corrections, including resistance to reforms and to addressing substantive issues that have been identified by external reviews, there are correctional strategies and interventions that have been proven to be effective, including the following:

- The use of RNR principles as the basis for correctional interventions
- The STICS model for probation practice

- Restorative justice approaches, which can take a number of forms, including Circles of Support and Accountability (COSAs)

Although there is the risk of "comparing apples and oranges," it is useful to consider successful correctional policies and programs from other jurisdictions. These are often referred to as **best practices**.

Recall from the programs reviewed in the various Research Files throughout the text that while many created positive program dynamics, this was not translated into reduced rates of reoffending. This suggests that much more attention must be given to throughcare—ensuring that positive gains achieved in confinement are used as a foundation for success upon release into the community. This will require programs and services to assist offenders with the challenges that are encountered in re-entry.

The jury is still out on the effectiveness of some initiatives, including the various problem-solving courts discussed in Chapter 4. These courts hold considerable promise; however, an absence of evaluations precludes a determination of their effectiveness. It has been noted several times in this book that lack of evaluation often makes it impossible to assess the effectiveness of specific interventions.

There is a recognition that corrections occupies a unique place in the criminal justice process. For example, the senior management and staff in correctional institutions do not determine which offenders, in what numbers, are sent to confinement; nor, in large measure, do they determine when an offender leaves the facility. The over-representation of Indigenous and Black Canadians in correctional institutions present challenges for programming, as does the increasing number of offenders with mental illnesses and offenders with post-traumatic stress disorder (PTSD). That said, the materials in this text have demonstrated that there are programs that work with offenders if certain protocols are followed.

> **Best practices**
> Organizational, administrative, and operational strategies that are effective in addressing the needs of offenders and keeping communities safe.

Corrections as a Restorative Process: Time for a Rethink?

Note, in particular, the finding from evaluation studies that restorative justice seems to work best with more serious offenders and in cases involving serious, violent crime. This suggests that there is considerable potential for using it at all stages of the justice system. In 2015, the province of Manitoba enacted the Restorative Justice Act, designed to integrate restorative justice into the response to offenders.[54] Among other provisions, the act created an advisory council composed of community and government representatives to oversee the implementation of a five-year strategic plan that included funding for new mental health and drug courts, support for restorative justice programs on First Nations reserves, and enhancing support for victims.

Restorative justice is an alternative framework for holding offenders accountable while at the same time addressing the needs of victims and the community—and the offenders themselves.

As the discussion in the preceding chapters has illustrated, Canadian corrections is far from a restorative process. Both in the community and in correctional institutions, offenders are managed in ways that often do more harm than good, that do not hold offenders accountable for their behaviour, and that often increases their likelihood of reoffending.

Mobilizing the Community: Maintaining Human and Helping Relationships

Correctional systems have long been susceptible to penal populism, whereby politicians point to public pressure as their justification for enacting tougher laws and correctional policies. Meanwhile, criminal justice and corrections authorities have done little to educate the public about the system and the offenders it houses. Too often, this has placed the public in a reactive role in which there is little support for corrections initiatives.

The success of COSAs, which target high-risk offenders, illustrates the potential for criminal justice professionals, working with community residents, to reduce reoffending among high-risk offenders. There is a vast, untapped reservoir in the community that, if mobilized and supported, could play a significant role in the corrections process.

The success of COSAs is evidence that human and helping relationships with ex-offenders (even high-risk ones) can be at least as effective as interventions based on risk assessment instruments, or supervision based on surveillance and control.

Developing Models of Correctional Practice for a Diverse Society

Diversity is a defining characteristic of Canada. Cultural diversity poses challenges to the criminal justice system and to systems of corrections as well. Canada is a multicultural society, yet we know very little about the experiences of Indo-Canadian offenders, Black offenders, or offenders from "newcomer" groups.

Similarly, little attention has been paid to the challenges faced by probation officers, COs, treatment personnel, parole boards, and parole officers when it comes to supervising and making decisions about these groups of offenders. Language and cultural barriers, community resistance and suspicion, and a lack of knowledge about the cultures and communities of minority offenders can all undermine intervention efforts. There has been no research, for example, on the role that mosques or Sikh temples might play in helping offenders return to the community on conditional release, or on the potential for community-based alternatives, programs, and services.

Police services across Canada have made the recruitment of visible and cultural minorities a priority. Corrections should do the same and, like their police counterparts, publish information on the ethnicity of their personnel to track these changes.

More Research on Canadian Corrections

In reading this text, it will no doubt have been noticed that for many of the topics, the materials are from the United States or other jurisdictions. Notably, the Canadian scholars Owusu-Bempah and Wortley have cited the lack of research on the experience of Black offenders in the Canadian criminal justice system and the study of why this group is increasingly overrepresented in admissions to correctional institutions.[55] Similarly, there is a paucity of research on the decision-making of the provincial parole boards in Ontario and Québec and the Parole Board of Canada that would provide insights into the role of these boards in the over-representation of Indigenous persons, Blacks, and other marginalized groups in correctional facilities. And while the raw statistics suggest that there is bias against Indigenous and minority inmates inside the walls—for example, in the use of force by correctional officers—this has not been validated by independent research studies. Observers have noted that the de facto prohibition against gathering race-based statistics has hindered the study of racial differences in criminal justice and corrections outcomes.[56]

This is a consequence of the comparative lack of Canadian research on corrections, particularly on provincial/territorial systems of corrections. There is a dire need for independent research on all facets of the Canadian corrections system, preferably conducted by university-based scholars who bring a critical eye and sound methodological frameworks to the studies.

There has not been, historically, a strong tradition of scholarly inquiry into various facets of Canadian corrections. This has been due, in part, to a lack of amenability of corrections to research projects conducted by university-based scholars. Access to correctional populations and to corrections personnel has been limited.[57] Access is generally controlled through the research and/or policy branch of the particular correctional service, and there may be barriers to access as well as censorship of study findings.[58] Much of the research on federal corrections has been conducted by the CSC, and most of the provincial/territorial corrections systems have little capacity to conduct evaluative research. This has resulted in a too-heavy reliance on research studies conducted in the United states and, to a lesser extent, in the United Kingdom and Oceania.

While there are notable exceptions, including the work of Dr. Rose Ricciardelli of Memorial University of Newfoundland and Dr. Michael Weinrath's research on federal offenders and correctional officers,[59] in comparison to their police counterparts, correctional agencies and institutions have remained largely inaccessible to researchers. Too often, what materials are gathered are often in the context of an inquiry into a critical event, an audit or a commission of inquiry.

IS PRIVATIZATION THE ANSWER?

Recent years have witnessed the increasing involvement of the private sector in corrections services in a number of international jurisdictions. This has been driven primarily by the ongoing fiscal crisis facing governments rather than by evidence-based practices. Private, for-profit companies are involved today in a variety of corrections activities, including monitoring offenders on electronic surveillance, operating institutions (in the United Kingdom and the United States), and supervising offenders completing community service as a condition of probation (in the United Kingdom).[60]

Nearly 70 percent of probation services in England and Wales are provided by 21 private community rehabilitation companies (CRCs), with the remainder provided by the National Probation Service (NPS). The privatization of probation in the United Kingdom, however, has been surrounded by controversy. In addition to massive layoffs of probation officers, a number of CRCs have failed audits, and there are ongoing challenges in having two probation services, one private and one public. Further, there is no evidence that the rates of reoffending by offenders on probation has declined.[61] And there is widespread pessimism that the situation will improve.[62]

To date, Canadian corrections has not been beset with the move toward privatization that has occurred in the policing realm or in corrections in other jurisdictions. For many years, the United States and the United Kingdom have been contracting with private, for-profit companies to build and operate prisons. The Government of Ontario experimented with privatization in 2001, when a private company was contracted to operate a maximum-security mega-jail in Penetanguishene under a five-year contract. A subsequent evaluation found that the company had complied with its contractual obligations to the province; maintained the required standards for health care, security, and safety; and in doing so, saved the province around $23 million in operating expenses. This was in comparison to a mega-jail that had been constructed at the same time and was operated by the province. For reasons that were never made clear, the private-sector contract was not renewed.[63]

Researchers have cautioned that debate over privatization of prisons has "been long on ideology and assumptions and short on empirical research" and there are calls for more in depth analysis.[64] More specifically, it has been argued that despite the long history of private corrections in the United States, little is known about the conditions under which public and private corrections produce the best outcomes with the least harmful effects.[65]

Research studies conducted in other jurisdictions, including the United States and England, suggest that, generally speaking, the performance of private prisons is much the same as that of public prisons and that there is no conclusive evidence of cost savings.[66] A U.K. study did find that private prisons performed better on those factors that could be directly measured, including confinement conditions and inmate activities, whereas the publicly operated prisons performed better on those dimensions that are more difficult to measure, such as levels of order in the facilities.

On the other hand, the outcome of privatizing some probation services in the United Kingdom has not been encouraging. A report by Her Majesty's Inspectorate of Probation found significant shortcomings in probation supervision by private contractors. This included unmanageable caseloads, inexperienced probation officers, and poor management and oversight.[67] As a consequence, the investigation found that many probationers were not seen for weeks or months and some not at all. Further, there was no evidence that the supervision services provided by the private contractor had reduced reoffending.[68]

THE UNIQUE POSITION OF CORRECTIONS IN THE CRIMINAL JUSTICE SYSTEM

Corrections is but one component of the criminal justice system, which itself is beset with numerous problems.[69] One report has described the criminal

THE PRIVATIZATION OF THE PENAL SYSTEM

Jack Ziegler/The New Yorker Collection/www.cartoonbank.com

justice system as being, with a few exceptions, "slow, inefficient, and costly," and in which there is a "justice deficit: a large and growing gap between the aspirations of the justice system and its actual performance."[70]

And the role of corrections is unique. Systems of corrections have no control over the numbers, and attributes, of the offenders that enter its "doors," and very little over when offenders "exit" corrections. These factors are determined in large measure by law and policy, the activities of police, the charging practices and decisions of Crown counsel, and the sentencing decisions of judges. The police and criminal courts spend very little time with individual offenders during the criminal justice process. By contrast, corrections must provide programs and services over a longer term, be it in the community or in institutional settings.

That said, there is sufficient evidence to indicate what does not work in community and institutional corrections and the programs and services that have proven to be successful in addressing the needs of offenders, ensuring their rights, and keeping communities safe.

KEY QUESTIONS GOING FORWARD

It was noted at the outset of this text that corrections is a dynamic enterprise and that the response to crime and criminal offenders at any one point in time is influenced by politics, perspectives on crime and punishment, and the public, among others. Corrections has long been surrounded by controversy and is likely to continue to be a focal point for debate and discussion.

The informed observer should bring an open mind and a critical eye to discussions of corrections. Key questions surrounding corrections in the early 21st century that should be addressed include the following:

- Are correctional policies and operations evidence based and informed by best practices?
- Are systems of corrections cost-effective?
- What is the potential, and limitations, of privatizing corrections programs and services?
- What initiatives can be taken to better address the needs of persons in remand and those sentenced to provincial/territorial institutions, albeit for very short periods of time?
- What processes can be put in place to reduce political influences on correctional policy and practice?
- How can it be determined that corrections provides value for money?
- What capacities will systems of corrections require to address radicalized offenders and to prevent the potential radicalization of inmates in correctional institutions?

- How will the increasing pressures to adopt high technology in corrections be managed so as to ensure that the rights of offenders and their families are protected?
- How can the unique challenges of delivering corrections programs and services in northern and remote communities be best addressed?
- What structures and processes need to be put in place to ensure that correctional policy and practice is driven by best practices and are evidence based?

FINAL THOUGHTS

As promised, this text will end on a positive note. Increasingly, prison administrators and corrections staff are being held accountable to the rule of law, and inmates have recourse through grievance procedures and the courts for perceived injustices. The living conditions of inmates have improved dramatically. New regional facilities have been built for federal women offenders; facilities that incorporate elements of Indigenous cultures and spirituality have been established for Indigenous offenders; and at several minimum- and medium-security facilities, new architectural designs have allowed inmates to live in apartment-like residences.

Significantly, much of this change has been precipitated by reports of the OCI and ombudspersons at the provincial/territorial levels. Several of the various commissions of inquiry have resulted in improvements to correctional institutions for both inmates and personnel. This, in conjunction with the impact of politics suggests that systems of corrections, in themselves, have not proven capable of initiating and sustaining reforms. Rather, to the extent that change has occurred, it has often been driven by external forces. It is an open question as to whether privatizing portions of corrections would result in increased efficiency and effectiveness. The experience of the United States and the United Kingdom suggests that this issue is highly charged, and to date, the results have been less than promising.

However, Canadian prisons continue to be beset by violence. Also, persons who are under supervision, whether in the community or in confinement, are still overwhelmingly from vulnerable groups at the lower strata of society. Corrections systems (and the criminal justice system generally) continue to be populated by an "underclass" on the economic and social margins of society; many of these people are afflicted by mental illness, addiction, homelessness, and poverty.

The demands on corrections are likely to accelerate in the coming years. Responding to these demands will require vision and, in many cases, a departure from traditional correctional practice. The materials in this text have documented the "what is" of corrections; the task going forward is to move toward "what should be" and, in so doing, increase the effectiveness of corrections, which, in turn, will be beneficial for offenders, victims, and the community.

SUMMARY

This chapter has identified and discussed the challenges and opportunities that systems of corrections face in becoming more effective at responding to criminal offenders and protecting the community. A key requirement is that corrections move toward the use of evidence-based practices, although a number of obstacles will be encountered. Similarly, there is a need to reduce the pains experienced by offenders and their families, to improve the effectiveness of strategies designed to address the needs of offenders, to focus greater attention on the needs of crime victims, and to acknowledge the limits of technology.

Throughout history, systems of corrections have struggled to adhere to the rule of law and to abide by the duty to act fairly in their responses to offenders. While the OCI and provincial ombudspersons provide a certain level of oversight, their recommendations are not binding. It is the courts that provide a measure of accountability.

Strategies such as probation and parole have been in place for more than a century. The majority of offenders are under some form of supervision in the community, yet community corrections receives only a very small portion of overall corrections budgets. There is an urgent need for evidence-based practices such as the STICS initiative in probation.

Canada is a multicultural society, yet little is known about the experiences of offenders from visible and cultural minorities, their families, and the potential role their communities could play in reintegration.

Systems of corrections must discard ineffective strategies, expand effective interventions, explore the potential for integrating restorative justice approaches with the corrections process, and develop strategies for mobilizing community residents as change agents. There are a number of questions that can be asked about corrections by observers with a critical eye.

KEY POINTS REVIEW

1. Historically, systems of corrections have lacked a well-developed body of empirical knowledge that could inform policy and practice.

2. Systems of corrections are subject to panaceas—the "magic bullet" that will reduce recidivism, lower costs, and deter offenders from future criminal behaviour.

3. There are challenges in implementing evidence-based practices in corrections, but there are also strategies for overcoming these challenges.

4. Offenders and their families experience a number of "pains" that should be reduced for corrections to become more effective.

5. It is unlikely that systems of corrections are effective at reducing the marginality of most offenders.

6. Despite various initiatives, crime victims are largely marginalized in the criminal justice and corrections processes.

7. There is a danger that overreliance on the use of technology for supervision and control in corrections will undermine human and helping relationships.

8. Systems of corrections have faced challenges in adhering to the rule of law and in fulfilling their obligation to act fairly in the treatment of offenders.

9. The expansion of community-based corrections could reduce costs, help offenders address their needs, and reduce the risks to the community.

10. There is a need to develop models of correctional practice that consider the diversity of Canadian society.

11. Reforming correctional institutions is a difficult task that will require extensive consultations with all stakeholders.

12. Provincial/territorial systems of corrections face unique challenges as a consequence of short custodial times, the presence of high-needs/high-risk offenders, and a lack of resources.

13. To increase effectiveness, systems of corrections should discard ineffective strategies and expand effective interventions.

14. There is considerable potential to expand the use of restorative justice approaches in corrections.

15. To increase effectiveness, systems of corrections should facilitate the proactive involvement of the community.

KEY TERM QUESTIONS

1. What is meant when it is said that systems of corrections are subject to *panaceas*?

2. What are the challenges of an overreliance on *techno-corrections*?

3. What is meant by corrections as a *learning organization* and how is this related to reforming systems of corrections?

4. What are *best practices* and why are they important in any study of corrections?

CRITICAL THINKING EXERCISES

Critical Thinking Exercise 15.1

The Continuing Evolution of Perspectives on Crime and Punishment

In Chapter 1, it was noted that perspectives of crime, offenders, and the response to persons in conflict with the law are often influenced by politics. As of late-2017 when this text was published, the courts had negated a number of key components of the "get-tough" legislation of the previous Conservative government.

Your Thoughts?

1. At the time you are reading this text, what additional changes have occurred in the views of crime and offenders, and of the most appropriate response to persons in conflict with the law? What examples can be used to illustrate the changes that have occurred? To what extent has the "get-tough" approach of the previous Conservative government been altered?

2. How would you characterize the current approach of the federal government to crime and criminal offenders?

Critical Thinking Exercise 15.2

Should There Be Private-Sector Involvement in Correctional Institutions?

The discussion surrounding the involvement of the private sector in corrections revolves around the following: whether this approach (1) is a faster and cheaper way for corrections systems to add capacity, (2) reduces operating costs, (3) improves the quality of service provided to inmates, (4) reduces rates of reoffending, and (5) relieves government of the responsibility to sanction offenders.

Proponents argue that private prisons are (1) more cost-effective than "public" prisons, (2) more accountable to monitoring and review, and (3) more flexible and able to expand physical capacity and programs more quickly than government-operated facilities. Critics counter that (1) any savings are due to cutbacks in services and programs for inmates, and lower wages paid to nonunion employees; (2) punishment for profit is unethical; and (3) private prisons are part of the prison–industrial complex, which should be curtailed.

Your Thoughts?

1. What are the strengths and limitations of the arguments that are made by proponents and opponents to increasing private-sector involvement in corrections?

2. What is your position on this issue, and why?

CLASS/GROUP DISCUSSION EXERCISES

Class/Group Discussion 15.1

Evidence-Based Correctional Practice

Throughout the text, there have been a number of examples where correctional policies and programs are not evidence based. A body of literature is emerging about what works in correctional practice and what does not. Proponents of evidence-based practices argue that corrections policies and programs should be based on what research has shown makes correctional systems more accountable and effective. Critics of this approach counter that correctional professionals are in the best position to determine which policies and programs are most appropriate for their particular jurisdiction and circumstances.

Your Thoughts?

1. What is your view of the positions put forth by the proponents of evidence-based corrections?

Class/Group Discussion 15.2

Have Punishments Really Changed over the Years?

In a discussion of crime and justice, the British criminologist Alan Bain stated: "[In] relation to crime and punishment I would argue that a change in development has not taken place, that society (and by definition punishment) remains in a state of confusion; changes reflecting little more than a renaming and recycling, of institutional roles and practices which make it more appealing to the public in terms of a 'tough on crime' rhetoric, and which seek to reduce an unhealthy fear of crime…. The punishments we observe are little more than a reflection of the past."[71]

Your Thoughts?

1. Knowing what you know now about corrections, what is your response to Bain's statement?

MEDIA LINKS

"Politics & Media: Will Privatising Probation Services Help Cut Re-Offending?" https://www.youtube.com/watch?v=aX9WnkGN7oM

"Private Probation Companies," Full Frontal with Samantha Bee, https://www.youtube.com/watch?v=RD1JxL5QfzI

"Private prisons: How US corporations make money out of locking you up," https://www.youtube.com/watch?v=hQxtRcfBIXY

"My Four Months as a Private Prison Guard: Part One," https://www.youtube.com/watch?v=cBiqRGXog4w

"My Four Months as a Private Prison Guard, Part Two," https://www.youtube.com/watch?v=E4EMf9hhU6Y

"My Four Months as a Private Prison Guard, Part Three," https://www.youtube.com/watch?v=MJ_cIFtqSP0

"My Four Months as a Private Prison Guard, Part Four," https://www.youtube.com/watch?v=yLauiFJrWAY

"My Four Months as a Private Prison Guard, Part Five," https://www.youtube.com/watch?v=n5edUGv3A1o

"My Four Months as a Private Prison Guard, Part Six," https://www.youtube.com/watch?v=1lqmiWgm3nI

NOTES

1. J.V. Roberts and K. Roach, *Community-Based Sentencing: The Perspectives of Crime Victims* (Ottawa: Research and Statistics, Department of Justice, 2004).

2. J. Dickson-Gilmore, "Whither Restorativeness? Restorative Justice and the Challenge of Intimate Violence in Aboriginal Communities," *Canadian Journal of Criminology and Criminal Justice 56*, no. 4 (2014), 417-46; National Judicial Institute, *Problem-Solving in Canada's Courtrooms* (Ottawa: Author, 2011), http://www.sasklawcourts.ca/images/documents/Provincial_Court/Problem-Solving%20in%20Canada's%20Courtrooms.pdf.

3. John Howard Society of Ontario, *Fractured Care: Public Health Opportunities in Ontario's Correctional Institutions* (Toronto: Author, 2016), p. 11, http://johnhoward.on.ca/wp-content/uploads/2016/04/Fractured-Care-Final.pdf.

4. Ibid.

5. Ibid., p. 13.

6. Office of the Auditor General of Ontario, "Adult Community Corrections and Ontario Parole Board," *Annual Report 2014*, Chapter 3 (Toronto: Author, 2014), p. 68, http://www.auditor.on.ca/en/content/annualreports/arreports/en14/301en14.pdf.

7. S. Kirkey, "Canada's Mental Health System is Turning Prisons into 'Asylums of the 21st Century': Report," *National Post*, May 7, 2012, http://news.nationalpost.com/news/canada/canadas-mental-health-system-is-turning-prisons-into-asylums-of-the-21st-century-report.

8. J. Gros and P. van Groll, *"We Have No Rights": Arbitrary Imprisonment and Cruel Treatment of Migrants with Mental Health Issues in Canada* (Toronto: University of Toronto Faculty of Law, 2015), http://ihrp.law.utoronto.ca/utfl_file/count/PUBLICATIONS/IHRP%20We%20Have%20No%20Rights%20Report%20web%2020170615.pdf.

9. A. Owusu-Bempah and S. Wortley, "Race, Crime, and Criminal Justice in Canada," in *The Oxford Handbook of Ethnicity, Crime, and Immigration*, S.M. Bucerius and M. Tonry, eds. (New York: Oxford University Press, 2014), 281–319 at 309.

10. L. Burd, D.K. Fast, J. Conry, and A. Williams, "Fetal Alcohol Spectrum Disorder as a Marker for Increased Risk of Involvement with Correction Systems," *Journal of Psychiatry and Law 38*, no. 4 (2010), 559–83.

11. K. Murphy, "Mental Health Crisis Overflows into Jail Cells," *nunatsiaqonline.ca*, May 17, 2002, http://www.nunatsiaqonline.ca/archives/nunavut020517/news/nunavut/20517_10.html.

12. L. McKeon, "The Prisoner Dilemma," *This Magazine*, June 1, 2010, p. 8, http://this.org/magazine/2010/06/01/nwt-prisoners-mental-health.

13. Office of the Correctional Investigator of Canada, *A Three Year Review of Federal Inmate Suicides (2011–2014)*, (Ottawa: Author, 2014), p. 28, http://www.oci-bec.gc.ca/cnt/rpt/pdf/oth-aut/oth-aut20140910-eng.pdf.

14. Office of the Auditor General Manitoba, *Managing the Province's Adult Offenders* (Winnipeg: Author, 2014), http://www.oag.mb.ca/wp-content/uploads/2014/03/Chapter-6-Managing-the-Provinces-Adult-Offenders-Web.pdf.

15. Office of the Auditor General of British Columbia, *An Audit of the Adult Custody Division's Correctional Facilities and Programs* (Victoria: Author, 2015), https://www.bcauditor.com/sites/default/files/publications/2015/special/report/AGBC%20Corrections%20report%20FINAL.pdf.

16. Office of the Auditor General of Ontario, *Annual Report 2014*.

17. Office of the Auditor General Manitoba, *Managing the Province's Adult Offenders*.

18. Office of the Auditor General of British Columbia, *Effectiveness of BC Community Corrections* (Victoria: Author, 2011), http://www.bcauditor.com/sites/default/files/publications/2011/report_10/report/OAGBC-BC-Community-Corrections%20for%20print.pdf; Office of the Auditor General of British Columbia, *An Audit of the Adult Custody Division's Correctional Facilities and Programs*.

19. Office of the Auditor General of British Columbia, *Effectiveness of BC Community Corrections*, p. 8.

20. Office of the Auditor General of British Columbia, *An Audit of the Adult Custody Division's Correctional Facilities and Programs*.

21. Office of the Auditor General of Ontario, "Adult Community Corrections and Ontario Parole Board."

22. Ibid., p. 67.

23. Ibid., p. 68

24. Ibid.

25. Ibid.

26. Office of the Auditor General of Ontario, "Adult Community Corrections and Ontario Parole Board Follow-Up on VFM Section 3.01, 2014 Annual Report," *Annual Report 2016: Follow-Up Reports on Value-for-Money Audits* (Toronto: Author, 2016), http://www.auditor.on.ca/en/content/annualreports/arreports/en16/v2_101en16.pdf.

27. Ibid.; D. Reevely, "Ontario's Probation System in Shambles, Auditor Reports," *Ottawa Citizen*, December 12, 2014, http://ottawacitizen.com/news/national/reevely-ontarios-probation-system-in-shambles-auditor-reports.

28. W. Lyons and S. Scheingold, "The Politics of Crime and Punishment," *The Nature of Crime: Continuity and Change*, in E. Jefferis and R. Titus, eds. (Washington, D.C.: Department of Justice, 2000), 103–49, https://www.ncjrs.gov/criminal_justice2000/vol_1/02c.pdf.

29. C.M. Webster and A.N. Doob, "Penal Reform 'Canadian Style': Fiscal Responsibility and Decarceration in Alberta, Canada," *Punishment & Society 16*, no. 1 (2014), 3–31.

30. Ibid., p. 22.

31. S. Goodyear, "No One Seems to Care About Prison Reform in Canada," *Vice News*, October 1, 2015, https://news.vice.com/article/no-one-seems-to-care-about-prison-reform-in-canada.

32. A.J. Harris and A.J. Lurigio, "Introduction to Special Issue on Sex Offenses and Offenders: Toward Evidence-based Public Policy," *Criminal Justice and Behavior 37*, no. 5 (2010), 477–81 at 480.

33. I. Zinger, "Human Rights and Federal Corrections: A Commentary on a Decade of Tough on Crime Policies in Canada," *Canadian Journal of Criminology and Criminal Justice 58*, no. 4 (2016), 609–27 at 614.

34. Office of the Auditor General Manitoba, *Managing the Province's Adult Offenders*, p. 274.

35. M. Welch, *Corrections: A Critical Approach*, 3rd ed. (New York: Routledge, 2011).

36. A. Willoughby and M. Nellis, "'You Cannot Really Hide': Experiences of Probation Officers and Young Offenders with GPS Tracing in Winnipeg, Canada," *Journal of Technology in Human Services 34*, no. 1 (2016), 63–81.

37. A.L. Solomon, J.W.L. Osborne, L. Winterfield, B. Elderbroom, P. Burke, R.P. Sroker, E.E. Rhine, and W.D. Burrell, *Putting Public Safety First: 13 Parole Strategies to Enhance Reentry Outcomes* (Washington, DC: Urban Institute, 2008), http://www.urban.org/sites/default/files/alfresco/publication-pdfs/411800-Putting-Public-Safety-First--Strategies-for-Successful-Supervision-and-Reentry-Policy-Brief-.PDF.

38. J.L. Ross, "Debunking the Myths of American Corrections: An Exploratory Analysis," *Critical Criminology 20*, no. 4 (2012), 409–27.

39. K. Hannah-Moffat, "Creating Choices: Reflecting on Choices," in *Women and Punishment: The Struggle for Justice*, P. Carlen, ed. (London, UK: Willan, 2002).

40. H. Toch, *Corrections: A Humanistic Approach* (Albany, NY: Harrow and Heston, 1997).

41. J.B. Jacobs, "Prison Reform amid the Ruins of Prisoners' Rights," in *The Future of Imprisonment*, M. Tonry, ed. (New York: Oxford University Press, 2004).

42. P.M. Senge, *The Fifth Discipline: The Art and Practice of the Learning Organization* (New York: Doubleday, 1990) p. 14.

43. M. Kiefer, *The Corrections Learning Organization* (Washington, DC: National Institute of Corrections, 2016), https://s3.amazonaws.com/static.nicic.gov/Library/032739.pdf.

44. Cited in H. Senoran, "Senator Runciman Calls Correctional Services Out for Bad Leadership," *CKWS Newswatch*, March 25, 2016, http://ucco-sacc-csn.ca/2016/03/26/senator-runciman-calls-correctional-services-out-for-bad-leadership/.

45. N. Shover, *Sociology of American Corrections* (Homewood: Dorsey Press, 1979).

46. J.A. Greene and V. Schiraldi, "Better by Half: The New York City Story of Winning Large-Scale Decarceration While Increasing Public Safety," *Federal Sentencing Reporter 29*, no. 1 (2016), 22–38.

47. T.R. Clear and D. Schrantz, "Strategies for Reducing Prison Populations," *The Prison Journal 91*, no. 3 (2011), 138S–195S.

48. Willoughby and Nellis, "You Cannot Really Hide."

49. Gros and van Groll, *We Have No Rights*, p. 5.

50. W. Loza, "The Prevalence of Middle Eastern Extremist Ideologies Among Some Canadian Offenders," *Journal of Interpersonal Violence 25*, no. 5 (2010), 919–28.

51. R. Basra, P.R. Neumann, and C. Brunner, *Criminal Pasts, Terrorist Futures: European Jihadists and the New Crime-Terror Nexus* (Brussels: The International Centre for the Study of Radicalisation and Political Violence, 2016), http://icsr.info/wp-content/uploads/2016/10/ICSR-Report-Criminal-Pasts-Terrorist-Futures-European-Jihadists-and-the-New-Crime-Terror-Nexus.pdf.

52. K. Harris, "Radicalization a Growing Risk in Canadian Prisons, Experts Warn," CBC News, January 22, 2015, http://www.cbc.ca/news/politics/radicalization-a-growing-risk-in-canadian-prisons-experts-warn-1.2928373.

53. A. Wilner, *From Rehabilitation to Recruitment: Stopping the Spread of Terrorist Doctrines Within Our Prisons Before It Becomes a National Security Problem* (Ottawa: The Macdonald Laurier Institute, 2010), p. 4, http://www.macdonald-laurier.ca/files/pdf/FromRehabilitation-ToRecruitment.pdf.

54. "Manitoba proclaims first-of-its-kind Restorative Justice Act," CBC News, November 18, 2015, http://www.cbc.ca/news/canada/manitoba/restorative-justice-act-manitoba-proclaimed-1.3324095.

55. Owusu-Bempah and Wortley, "Race, Crime, and Criminal Justice in Canada."

56. Ibid., p. 309.

57. T.M. Watson, "Research Access Barriers as Reputational Risk Management: A Case Study of Censorship in Corrections," *Canadian Journal of Criminology and Criminal Justice 57*, no. 3 (2015), 330–62.

58. Ibid.

59. R. Ricciardelli, *Surviving Incarceration: Inside Canadian Prisons* (Waterloo, ON: Wilfred Laurier Press, 2014); M. Weinrath, *Behind the Walls: Inmates and Correctional Officers on the State of Canadian Prisons* (Vancouver: UBC Press, 2016).

60. A. Travis, "Two Companies to Run More Than Half of Privatised Probation Services," *The*

Guardian, October 29, 2014, https://www.theguardian.com/uk-news/2014/oct/29/justice-probation-contracts-private-companies.

61. G. Kirton and C. Guillaume, *Employment Relations and Working Conditions in Probation After Transforming Rehabilitation* (London: National Association of Probation Officers, 2015), https://www.napo.org.uk/; T. Rutter, "Privatised Probation Staff: Stressed, Deskilled and Facing Job Cuts," *The Guardian*, February 23, 2016, https://www.theguardian.com/public-leaders-network/2016/feb/23/privatisation-probation-service-stressed-job-cuts.

62. J. Deering, "A Future for Probation?" *The Howard Journal of Crime and Justice 53*, no. 1 (2014), 1015.

63. Ontario Ministry of Community Safety and Correctional Services, *Central North Correctional Centre Review and Comparison to Central East Correctional Centre* (Toronto: Author, 2006), http://www.privateci.org/private_pics/CNCC.pdf.

64. A.M. Lindsey, D.P. Mears, and J.C. Cochran, "The Privatization Debate: A Conceptual Framework for Improving (Public and Private) Corrections," *Journal of Contemporary Criminal Justice 32*, no. 4 (2016), 308–27 at 320.

65. Ibid., p. 323.

66. B.W. Lundahl, C. Kunz, C. Brownell, N. Harris, and R.V. Fleet, "Prison Privatization: A Meta-Analysis of Cost and Quality of Confinement Indicators," *Research on Social Work Practice 19*, no. 4 (2009), 383–94.

67. Her Majesty's Inspectorate of Probation, *Quality & Impact Inspection. The Effectiveness of Probation Work in the North of London* (London, UK: Author, 2016), https://www.justiceinspectorates.gov.uk/hmiprobation/wp-content/uploads/sites/5/2016/12/North-of-London-QI.pdf.

68. Ibid., p. 4.

69. C.T. Griffiths, *Canadian Police Work*, 4th ed. (Toronto: Nelson, 2016).

70. B. Perrin and R. Audas, *Report Card on the Criminal Justice System: Evaluating Canada's Justice Deficit* (Ottawa: Macdonald Laurier Institute, 2016), p. 4, http://www.macdonald-laurier.ca/files/pdf/JusticeReportCard_F4.pdf.

71. A. Bain, "Please Recycle: Continuities in Punishment," *International Journal of Law, Crime, and Justice 39*, no. 2 (2011), 121–35. p. 131

GLOSSARY OF KEY TERMS

Aboriginal Corrections Continuum of Care: An initiative of Correctional Service Canada designed to connect Indigenous offenders with their communities, traditions, and cultures, beginning in the institution and continuing on conditional release in the community. **(p. 411)**

Absolute discharge: A sentencing option wherein the offender is found guilty, but is technically not convicted. **(p. 77)**

Administrative segregation: The separation of an inmate to prevent association with other inmates, when specific legal requirements are met, other than pursuant to a disciplinary decision. **(p. 157)**

Arbour Report: The report of an inquiry into events at the Kingston Prison for Women in April 1994, which documented violations of policy, the rule of law, and institutional regulations, and had a significant impact on the development of women's corrections. **(p. 366)**

Assessment for Decision: A document prepared by an institutional or community parole officer that addresses the offender's criminal and conditional release history, institutional and community behaviour, correctional plan progress and offender engagement, release plan and supervision strategy, and their recommendations for conditional release and special conditions. **(p. 299)**

Auburn model (for prisons): A system that allowed prisoners to work and eat together during the day and housed them in individual cells at night. **(p. 24)**

Bail: The release of a person who has been charged with a criminal offence, prior to trial or to sentencing. **(p. 149)**

Best practices: Organizational, administrative, and operational strategies that are effective in addressing the needs of offenders and keeping communities safe. **(p. 488)**

Brown Commission: An investigation into the operations of Kingston Penitentiary that condemned the use of corporal punishment and emphasized the need for rehabilitation. **(p. 24)**

Canadian Charter of Rights and Freedoms: The primary law of the land, which guarantees basic rights and freedoms for citizens, including convicted offenders. **(p. 45)**

Carceral: That portion of systems of corrections relating to confinement in correctional institutions. **(p. 50)**

Case management: The process by which the needs and abilities of offenders are matched with correctional programs and services. **(p. 245)**

Circle of Care: A Correctional Service Canada program designed to provide women with coping strategies in preparation for release into the community. **(p. 412)**

Circle sentencing: An approach to sentencing based on the principles of restorative justice. **(p. 88)**

Circles of Support and Accountability (COSAs): Community-based committees composed of criminal justice personnel and community members that provide mentoring for high-risk sex offenders whose sentences have expired. **(p. 343)**

Classical (conservative) school: A perspective on criminal offenders and punishment based on the view that offenders exercise free will and engage in criminal behaviour as a result of rational choice, and that punishment must be swift, certain, and severe. **(p. 10)**

Classification: Using various assessment instruments to categorize inmates in order to determine the appropriate security level and programs. **(p. 243)**

Cold turkey release: The discharge of an offender at the end of a sentence when no conditional release or supervision is possible, such as when an offender has served their entire sentence in federal custody, or when provincial/territorial offenders are released early due to earned remission. **(p. 284)**

Community notification: The practice, usually carried out by police agencies, of making a public announcement that a high-risk offender has taken up residence in an area. **(p. 337)**

Community strategy guide: A document prepared by probation and parole officers (in Ontario and Québec) or community parole officers for the parole board and containing information on the feasibility of the inmate-applicant's proposed community plan in terms of the level of supervision required, employment/residential/education plans, and the availability of community resources. **(p. 298)**

Concurrent sentences: Sentences that are amalgamated and served simultaneously. **(p. 76)**

Conditional discharge: A sentencing option wherein the offender is found guilty and released upon condition that they comply with the conditions of a probation order for three years, at which time the conviction is removed from the offender's record. **(p. 77)**

Conditional sentence: A sentence imposed on an offender who would otherwise be incarcerated for a period of less than two years but whose risk is determined to be manageable in the community. **(p. 108)**

Consecutive sentences: Sentences that run separately and are completed one after the other. **(p. 76)**

Constitution Act (1867): Legislation that includes provisions that define the responsibilities of the federal and provincial/territorial governments with respect to criminal justice. **(p. 45)**

Continuity of supervision: The requirement that, to be effective, offenders be supervised by the same probation officer during their term of probation. **(p. 119)**

Continuum of correctional institutions: The differences in institutional environments among correctional institutions located at either end of the security spectrum—minimum to maximum. **(p. 142)**

Correctional agenda (of correctional officers): The activities of correctional officers as change agents using their authority to help inmates cope with the problems of living in confinement. **(p. 185)**

Correctional plan: A key component of the case management process that determines the offender's initial institution placement, specific treatment or training opportunities, and preparation for release. **(p. 251)**

Corrections: The structures, policies, and programs to punish, treat, and supervise persons convicted of criminal offences. **(p. 3)**

Corrections and Conditional Release Act (CCRA): The primary legislation under which the federal system of corrections operates. **(p. 45)**

Creating Choices: The report of the Task Force on Federally Sentenced Women that had a significant impact on the structure and operation of women's corrections. **(p. 365)**

Criminal Code: Federal legislation that sets out the criminal laws of Canada and the procedures for administering justice. **(p. 45)**

Criminogenic risk factors: Risk/needs factors that contribute to a person's propensity to commit criminal offences, including substance abuse problems and the acceptance of antisocial values. See also dynamic risk factors. **(p. 248)**

Critical incident stress debriefing (CISD): A procedure for assisting COs following a critical incident. **(p. 196)**

Critical (radical) school: A perspective on crime, offenders, and punishment that highlights the role of economics, politics, power, and oppression in the formulation of laws and the administration of justice. **(p. 11)**

Cross-gender staffing: The practice of staffing correctional institutions with male and women officers. Most often discussed in terms of whether male COs should work inside correctional facilities for women. **(p. 382)**

Custodial agenda (of correctional officers): The activities of correctional officers that centre on control and enforcement of regulations. **(p. 185)**

Dangerous offender: A designation made by the judge after conviction that can result in an indeterminate term of imprisonment in a federal correctional institution. **(p. 81)**

Day parole: The authority granted by a parole board that provides an opportunity for inmates to be at large to complete community-based activities in preparation for full release (e.g., for job search) while returning at night to an institution or, more typically, to a community residential facility or halfway house. **(p. 287)**

Deprivation theory: An explanation that holds that the inmate social system develops as a consequence of inmates' attempts to mitigate the pains of imprisonment. **(p. 215)**

Detention during the period of statutory release: A decision by the Parole Board of Canada (after an application by Correctional Service Canada) that a federal inmate be denied statutory release and be detained in the institution until warrant expiry date. **(p. 288)**

Differential amenability to treatment: The notion that, for a variety of reasons, not all inmates are receptive to treatment, and/or, that they require interventions tailored to meet their specific needs, abilities, and interests. **(p. 256)**

Differential treatment availability: The recognition that, within systems of corrections, not all inmates have equal access to treatment programs. **(p. 261)**

Differential treatment effectiveness: The requirement that, to be effective, treatment interventions be multifaceted and matched to the specific needs of individual offenders. **(p. 255)**

Disciplinary segregation: An inmate is placed in solitary confinement after being found in violation of an institutional rule. **(p. 157)**

Diversion: Programs designed to keep offenders from being processed further into the formal criminal justice system. **(p. 105)**

Duty to act fairly: The obligation of corrections to ensure that offenders are treated fairly by corrections personnel. Also, the right of inmates to be heard and to have an impartial hearing. **(p. 50)**

Dynamic risk factors: Attributes of the offender that can be altered through intervention, including level of education, employment skills, addiction issues, and cognitive thinking abilities. **(p. 248)**

Dynamic security: A variety of ongoing, meaningful interactions between staff and inmates. **(p. 140)**

Earned remission date: A provision that allows incarcerated provincial/territorial offenders to earn early release through good behaviour at a rate of 15 days for every month served. **(p. 288)**

Electronic monitoring (EM): A correctional strategy that involves using electronic equipment to ensure that the conditions of supervision are fulfilled. **(p. 107)**

Evidence-based practices: Policies, strategies, and programs that have been shown by evaluation research to be effective in achieving specified objectives. **(p. 473)**

Fetal Alcohol Spectrum Disorder (FASD): A condition of mental impairment due to the birth mother drinking alcohol while pregnant. **(p. 153)**

Fine: A sentencing option wherein the offender must pay a specific amount of money within a specified time, or face the prospect of imprisonment for fine default. **(p. 77)**

Full parole: The authority granted by a parole board for an inmate to be at large under supervision in the community for the remainder of their sentence. **(p. 287)**

General deterrence: An objective of sentencing designed to deter others from engaging in criminal conduct. **(p. 74)**

Importation theory: An explanation that holds that the inmate social system develops as a consequence of pre-prison attitudes and behaviours that are brought by inmates into the institution. **(p. 215)**

Inmate code: A set of behavioural rules that govern interactions among inmates and with institutional staff. **(p. 216)**

Inmate social system: The patterns of interaction and the relationships that exist among inmates confined in correctional institutions; often referred to as the *inmate subculture*. **(p. 215)**

Institutionalized: Inmates who have become prisonized to such a degree that they are unable to function in the outside, free community. **(p. 215)**

Integrated case management (ICM) conferences: The primary strategy used for case management of young offenders on probation. **(p. 443)**

Integrated Correctional Program Model (ICPM): An interdisciplinary approach to correctional programming operated by Correctional Service Canada. **(p. 252)**

Integration model (of the inmate social system): An explanation of inmate behaviour inside correctional institutions that considers both the environmental features of the institution and the attributes of the individual offender as affecting behaviour. **(p. 215)**

Intensive supervision probation (ISP): An intermediate sanction (between the minimal supervision of traditional probation and incarceration) that generally includes reduced caseloads for probation officers, increased surveillance, treatment interventions, and efforts to ensure that probationers are employed. **(p. 122)**

Interdiction strategies: Efforts to reduce the use of illegal drugs and other high-risk behaviours in order to prevent HIV/AIDS and other infectious diseases. **(p. 162)**

Intermediate sanctions: A wide range of correctional programs that generally fall between probation and incarceration, although specific initiatives may include either of these penalties as well. **(p. 106)**

Intermittent sentences: Sentences that are served on a "part-time" basis, generally on weekends. **(p. 76)**

Judicial determination: An order by the sentencing judge that the offender serve one-half of their sentence, or 10 years, whichever is less before being eligible to apply for parole. **(p. 81)**

Judicial recognizance: An order of the court, often referred to as a peace bond, that requires the offender (most often sex offenders) to adhere to set conditions beyond the expiry of their sentence, including most often avoiding places where there are children. **(p. 289)**

Juvenile Delinquents Act (JDA; 1908): Legislation centred on a social welfare approach to youth crime that gave judges considerate discretion to intervene in the lives of young offenders. **(p. 432)**

Learning organization: The notion that a correctional service is constantly seeking improvement, learning from successes as well as from initiatives that did not achieve their intended goals. **(p. 484)**

Long-term offender: A designation under Section 752 or 753 of the Criminal Code that requires the offender to spend up to 10 years under supervision following the expiry of their sentence. **(p. 81)**

Mature coping: A positive approach taken by inmates to adjust to life inside correctional institutions. **(p. 225)**

Maximum-security institutions: Federal correctional institutions with a highly controlled institutional environment. **(p. 139)**

Medical model of corrections: The view that criminal offenders were ill—physically, mentally and/or socially—and that treatment and diagnosis would ensure rehabilitation. **(p. 28)**

Medium-security institutions: Federal correctional facilities that have a less highly controlled institutional environment than maximum-security institutions and in which the inmates have more freedom of movement. **(p. 139)**

Minimum-security institutions: Federal correctional facilities that generally have no perimeter fencing and allow unrestricted inmate movement except at night. **(p. 139)**

Moral architecture: The term used to describe the design of the first penitentiary in Canada, the intent of which was to reflect themes of order and morality. **(p. 24)**

Motivational interviewing (MI): An interview technique used by probation officers designed to empower offenders to change their attitudes and behaviour. **(p. 120)**

Multilevel institutions: Federal correctional institutions that contain one or more security levels (minimum, medium, and maximum) in the same facility or on the same grounds **(p. 140)**

Need principle: To be effective, correctional interventions must address the criminogenic needs of offenders. **(p. 116)**

Net-widening: A potential, unanticipated consequence of diversion programs in which persons who would otherwise have been released outright by the police or not charged by Crown counsel are involved in the justice system. **(p. 106)**

NIMBY (not in my back yard) syndrome: The resistance of community residents to efforts of corrections systems to locate programming and residences for offenders in the community. **(p. 63)**

Noncarceral: That portion of systems of corrections relating to offenders in non-institutional settings. **(p. 50)**

Normative code of behaviour (among correctional officers): The behavioural rules that guide interaction and contribute to solidarity among correctional officers. **(p. 180)**

One-chance statutory release: When CSC recommends to PBC detention during the period of statutory release but the PBC decides to release the offender who has been convicted of serious crime(s) at their statutory release date, wherein if the offender is revoked, they must complete the remainder of their sentence in prison. **(p. 288)**

Pains of imprisonment: The deprivations experienced by inmates confined in correctional institutions, including the loss of autonomy, privacy, security, and freedom of movement and association. **(p. 214)**

Pains of probation: The emotional and economic challenges that probationers may experience while under probation supervision in the community. **(p. 127)**

Pains of re-entry: The difficulties that inmates released from correctional institutions encounter in attempting to adjust to life in the outside, free community. **(p. 326)**

Panaceas: In corrections, the search for the "magic bullet" that will reduce recidivism, lower costs, and deter offenders from future criminal behaviour. **(p. 479)**

Parole certificate: A document that contains the standard and, often, special conditions of a conditional release. **(p. 304)**

Penal populism: Corrections policies that are formulated in pursuit of political objectives, often in the absence of an informed public or in spite of public opinion, and that are centred on being "tough on crime." **(p. 15)**

Pennsylvania model (for prisons): A separate and silent system in which prisoners were completely isolated from one another, eating, working, and sleeping in separate cells. **(p. 24)**

Positivist (liberal) school: A perspective on criminal offenders and punishment based on the view that criminal behaviour is determined and that offenders require individualized treatment. **(p. 11)**

Post-incarceration syndrome (PICS): A condition of offenders in custody and in the community that is caused by prolonged exposure to the dynamics of life inside correctional institutions. **(p. 328)**

Post-traumatic stress disorder (PTSD): An extreme form of critical incident stress that includes nightmares, hypervigilance, intrusive thoughts, and other forms of psychological distress. **(p. 195)**

Pre-sentence report (PSR): A document prepared by the probation officer for the sentencing judge that contains information on the convicted offender, including socio-biographical information, offence history, victim impact, and risk assessments. **(p. 113)**

Prevention strategies: Efforts to prevent and reduce high-risk behaviour among inmates and to reduce the levels of infection of HIV/AIDS and other infectious diseases. **(p. 161)**

Prisonization: The process by which inmates become socialized into the norms, values, and culture of the prison. **(p. 215)**

Probation: A sentence imposed on an offender by a criminal court judge that provides for the supervision of the offender in the community by a probation officer, either as an alter-native to custody or in conjunction with a period of incarceration. **(p. 109)**

Problem-solving courts: Specialized courts designed to divert offenders with special needs from the criminal justice system. **(p. 86)**

Program drift: The extent to which a treatment program as delivered has moved away from the original design, with a potential impact on program effectiveness. **(p. 262)**

Program fidelity: The extent to which a treatment program is delivered in accordance with the original program design. **(p. 262)**

Punishment: Inflicting a consequence or penalty for wrongdoing, or the consequence or penalty itself. **(p. 6)**

Punitive penology: A response to criminal offenders characterized by severe criminal sanctions, including "tough-on-crime" legislation. **(p. 15)**

***R. v. Gladue*:** A decision by the SCC that held that in cases where a term of incarceration would normally be imposed, judges must consider the unique circumstances of Indigenous people. **(p. 80)**

Recidivism rates: The number of offenders released from confinement who, once released from confinement, are returned to prison. **(p. 265)**

Reintegration: The process whereby an inmate is prepared for and released into the community after serving time in prison. **(p. 323)**

Remand: The status of accused persons who have been charged but have been denied bail and are awaiting trial or have been found guilty and are awaiting sentencing. **(pp. 56, 149)**

Responsivity principle: Correctional interventions should be matched to the learning styles of individual offenders. **(p. 117)**

Restorative justice: An approach to responding to offenders based on the principle that criminal behaviour injures victims, communities, and offenders, and that all of these parties should be involved in efforts to address the causes of the behaviour and its consequences. **(p. 64)**

Revocation of conditional release: A decision by a releasing authority, such as a parole board, made in connection with an offender whose release has been suspended. **(p. 339)**

Risk principle: Correctional interventions are most effective when matched with the offender's level of risk, and higher risk offenders benefit from interventions more than medium- and low-risk offenders. **(p. 116)**

Rule of law: The requirement that governments, as well as individuals, be subject to and abide by the law. **(p. 50)**

Section 81 (CCRA): Authorizes the federal government to enter into agreements with Indigenous communities whereby the community assumes the "care and custody" of some Indigenous offenders upon their release from custody. **(p. 407)**

Section 84 (CCRA): Provides for Indigenous communities to participate in parole hearings and propose a plan for offender reintegration, and includes a provision for Indigenous communities to supervise long-term offenders. **(p. 416)**

Segregation: The physical isolation of individuals who are confined to their cells for 22–24 hours a day; also often referred to as *solitary confinement*. **(p. 157)**

Self-injurious behaviour (SIB): Deliberate self-inflicted bodily harm or disfigurement. **(p. 226)**

Social (or argot) roles: Roles that inmates assume based on their friendship networks, sentence length, and other factors related to their criminal history and activities in the institution. **(p. 217)**

Special Handling Unit (SHU): A federal correctional facility that houses inmates who pose such a high risk to inmates and staff that they cannot be confined in maximum-security institutions. **(p. 139)**

Specific deterrence: An objective of sentencing designed to deter the offender from future criminal conduct. **(p. 74)**

State-raised offenders: Inmates who have spent most of their youth and adult lives confined in correctional institutions. **(p. 215)**

Static risk factors: Attributes of the offender that predict the likelihood of recidivism and that are not amenable to change, including criminal history, prior convictions, seriousness of prior offences, and performance on previous conditional releases. **(p. 248)**

Static security: Fixed security apparatus in correctional institutions, including fixed security posts to which correctional officers are assigned, such as a control room. **(p. 140)**

Status degradation ceremonies: The processing of offenders into correctional institutions whereby the offender is psychologically and materially stripped of possessions that identify him or her as a member of the "free society." **(p. 212)**

Statutory release: A provision that allows incarcerated federal offenders to be released at the two-thirds point in their sentence (unless PBC accepts CSC's recommendation to detain an offender during their period of statutory release) and to serve the remaining one-third of their sentence under supervision in the community. **(p. 287)**

Structured Assessment of Violent Risk in Youth (SAVRY): A frequently used risk/needs assessment instrument in youth corrections. **(p. 449)**

Suspended sentence: The offender is convicted of the offence, but the imposition of the sentence is suspended pending successful completion of a period of probation. **(p. 77)**

Suspension of conditional release: A process initiated by the supervising parole officer (or in some instances by the parole board) in cases where the releasee has allegedly failed to abide by the conditions of release, is believed to be at risk of breaching a condition, or is at risk of re-offending. **(p. 339)**

Techno-corrections: The application of technology to the supervision and control of offenders. **(p. 482)**

Temporary absences (TAs): A type of conditional release that allows an inmate to leave the institution for a reason that adheres to their correctional plan, including for employment and education. May be either escorted or unescorted, or a work release. **(p. 286)**

Therapeutic integrity: The importance of the training, skill sets, and supervision of treatment staff for the effectiveness of correctional treatment programs. **(p. 262)**

Therapeutic justice: The use of the law and the authority of the court as change agents in promoting the health and well-being of offenders. **(p. 87)**

Throughcare: The notion that there should be continuity between institutional treatment programs and community-based services for offenders. **(p. 263)**

Total institution: Correctional institutions, mental hospitals, and other facilities characterized by a highly structured environment in which all movements of the inmates/patients are controlled 24 hours a day by staff. **(p. 141)**

Two-year rule: The basis for the division of responsibility for convicted offenders between the federal and provincial/territorial governments. **(p. 54)**

Unit management model: The supervisory arrangement in many provincial/territorial correctional institutions. **(p. 145)**

Warrant expiry date: The end of an offender's sentence as imposed by the courts at the time of sentencing. **(p. 284)**

Work release: A type of conditional release that allows inmates to leave the institution to participate in community-service or employment opportunities. **(p. 286)**

Young Offenders Act (YOA; 1984): Youth legislation that attempted to balance the protection of young offenders' special needs and legal rights and freedoms with the protection of the public, while ensuring young offenders would be held accountable. **(p. 433)**

Youth Criminal Justice Act (YCJA; 2003): The legislative framework for the youth justice system that applies to young persons aged 12–17; it has, as one of its key principles, the use of extrajudicial measures for less serious offences to reduce the rates of incarceration of young offenders. **(p. 434)**

Youth Justice Committee (YJC): Community-based committees that sponsor a variety of initiatives for youth in conflict with the law, including extrajudicial measures centred on restorative justice. **(p. 450)**

Youth Level of Service/Case Management Inventory (YLS/CMI): The primary risk/needs assessment instrument in youth corrections. **(p. 449)**

INDEX

Note: Page numbers followed by *f* and *t* denote figures and tables. Boldface page numbers denote key terms.

Abolition of Early Parole Act, 29
Aboriginal Community Development Officers, 421*t*
Aboriginal Correctional Program Officer, 411
Aboriginal Corrections Continuum of Care, **411**
Aboriginal Cultural Adviser, 415
Aboriginal Offender Substance Abuse Program
    (AOSAP), 420*t*
Aboriginal Youth Restorative Justice Committee
    (CAYRJC), 451*t*
Absolute discharge, **77**–440*t*
Accountability
        of corrections systems, 147
Accountability and concern, rule of law, 49–50
Act to Provide for the Conditional Liberation of
    Penitentiary Convicts, 283
Administrative segregation, **157**
Adult correctional services, 52*f*
Adult offenders, PSRs on, 113
Adult probation, 110
Aftercare programs for young offenders,
    453–8
Age of Enlightenment, 6
Aggravating circumstances, 83
American-style approach, 28
Appeal Court, 68, 76
Arbour inquiry, **366**
Arbour, Louise, 366
Arbour Report, **366**
Assessment for Decision, **299**
Auburn model, **24**, 33
Auditors, 57

Baffin Correction Centre (BCC), 148, 149
Bail, **149**
Beccaria, Cesare, 10, 11
Bentham, Jeremy, 10
Best practices, **498**
Bill C-10, 29–30, 108, 109, 231, 433
Black offenders, 209
Black offenders, correctional officers and, 177
Bloody Code, 5
Board of Investigation (BOI), 332
Bodily fluids, attacks with, 198
Bona Fide Occupational Requirements (BFOR), 177
Boot camps, 455*t*
British Columbia, provincial institutional
    corrections, 476
Brown Commission, **24**, 36

Calgary Remand Centre (CRC), 150
California correctional institutions, 16
Canadian Charter of Rights and Freedoms,
    45, 193
Canadian Court system, outline of, 73
Canadian Human Rights Tribunal, 50
Canadian North, corrections in, 474–5
Canadian prison architecture, 32–5
Canadian public, corrections and, 62–4
Canadian society, Indigenous peoples, 401–2

Case law precedent, 83
Case management, 191, 245–54
    classification tools and techniques, 247
    correctional plan and, 251
    goals of, 245–6
    IPOs and, 246–7
    phases of, 246
    risk and needs profiles of offenders,
        247–51
    youth probation, 441–2
Catholic Church, 4
Certificate, parole, 304–5
Circle healing process, 407
Circle of Care Program, 412–13
Circle sentencing, **88**–92
Circles of Support and Accountability (COSAs),
    343–50, 488
        conceptual model of, 345*f*
        principles of, 344*f*
        success of, 489
Citizen's Advisory Committees (CACs), 60–2
Classical (conservative) school, **10**
Classification, 243–5, 245*f*
    assessments and, 243–5, 245*f*
    dynamic risk factors, 247, 248
    tools and techniques, 247
Coercive power, 187
Cold turkey release, **284**
Collaborative Justice Program, 92–4
Colonization, legacy of, 401–2
Commissions of inquiry, 28
    corrections, 36–9
Community
    corrections, 104, 483
    institutional programs, involvement in, 254
    intermediate sanctions and, 106–7
    offender and, 325
Community assessment (CA), 298
Community assistance, innovations in, 341
Community-based interventions, young
    offenders, 446
Community-based treatment programs, 299
Community corrections, 51
Community corrections liaison officers
    (CCLOs), 334
Community corrections organizations, clients and
    service providers on, 341–2
Community Council Program, 406
Community Holistic Circle Healing Program,
    407–9
Community justice, 92–4
Community notification (CN), 336–7
Community re-entry process for young
    offenders, 453
Community residences, 139
Community service
    young offenders, 440
Community Service Order, 440*t*
Community strategy guide, **298**
Compensation, 440*t*

Concurrent sentences, **76**
Conditional discharge, 69*t*, 440*t*
Conditional release, 284–5
    effectiveness of, 309–10
    eligibility dates for, 288
    purpose and principles of, 283–4
    revocation of, 339–40
    success/failure on, 340–2
    suspension of, 339–40
    types of, 284–90
    victims and, 305–7
Conditional sentence orders (CSOs),
    107, 108
Conditional sentences, **108**–9
    defined, 108–9
    justices and, 108
Confinement, offenders in, 485
Consecutive sentences, **76**
Conservatism, 308
Constitution Act (1867), 45
Contemporary Canadian corrections
    correctional process, 46–8
    legislative framework of corrections, 44–6
    structure of
        correctional jurisdiction, split in, 54
        federal system of corrections, 55
Continuity of supervision, **119**
Continuum of correctional institutions, **142**
Convention on the Elimination of All Forms of
    Discrimination Against Women (CEDAW), 381
Conway v. Canada, 197
Corporal punishment, 3, 24
Correctional camps, 139
Correctional centres, 139
Correctional change, 3
Correctional institutions, 32. *See also* Prisons
    accountability, 147
    attributes of, 140–2
    California, 16
    "closed" nature of, 190
    conditions in, 148
    cross-gender staffing, 382
    Deputy Commissioner for Women, 365, 366
    disorder and disturbances, preventing, 156–7
    effectiveness of incarceration, 145–7, 163–5
    elderly inmates, 151
    external and internal environments of, 141*f*
    FASD, offender with, 153–4
    federal, 144*f*
    health issues and infectious diseases, 160–3
    inmates gangs, 155–6
    inmates safety, 156
    interdiction strategies, 162–3
    legislation and policy requirements, 146–7
    maximum/medium/minimum-security, 139
    mental health issues, 151–3
    mentally ill offenders, 151–2
    multilevel institutions, 139–40
    offender profile, changing, 150
    operating and managing challenges, 146–57
    overcrowding of, 154–5, 379
    prevention strategies, 161–2
    reforming, 484–5
    remand populations, growth in, 149–50
    rule of law and justice, 147

    security, 140
    staff, management of, 147–8
    trauma, offenders suffering from, 153
    types of, 139
Correctional interventions, effective, 479
Correctional jurisdiction, split in, 54
Correctional officers (COs), 365, 377
    attitudes toward inmates, 181
    civil/criminal liability of, 188
    correctional agenda of, **185**
    correctional officer unions, role of, 198–9
    discretion and decision making, 186–7
    dualists, 181–2
    at Edmonton Institution for Women, 379,
        383, 395
    employee assistance programs, 196
    ethics, professionalism, and corruption,
        190–1
    exercise and abuse of power, 187–8
    generational differences and commitment, 159
    impact of critical incidents on, 195–7
    incarceration experience for youth, 458
    inmates and, 183–7, 185*f*
    job satisfaction and commitment, 192
    moral relativists, 182
    multiple tasks of, 194
    murder of, 196, 197
    orientations of, 181, 182
    personal life of, 194
    personal security and, 192–3
    prison administration and, 191
    prison conditions and, 195
    provincial/territorial training, 178–9
    punishers, 182
    recruitment and training of, 177–9
    relationship patterns among, 180–1
    roles and responsibilities, 176–7
    shift work and, 195
    socialization of, 179–80
    solidarity among, 180
    stress and, 192–7
    support and respect for, 193
    testing inmates, 193
    training, inadequate, 194
    treatment staff and, 191–2
    typology of, 181–2
    unions, 18
    use-of-force incidents, 188–9
    women as, 197–8
    women-centred training course, 178
Correctional plan, **251**
Correctional process, 46–8
Correctional programs
    young offenders, 456
Correctional Service of Canada (CSC), 46, 49, 55,
    139, 329, 332–3, 342
    assessment centres, 243
    ICPM initiative, 412
    IIS for women offenders, 392
    Integrated Correctional Program Model,
        252–3
    mother–child programs by, 373–4
    parole officer, 332
Correctional systems
    techniques of, 336

Correctional treatment
    conditions for, 256–9
    doing time and doing treatment, 260
    effectiveness measurement of, 265
    ethics of, 263–4
    expectations of rehabilitation, 260–1
    inmate access to programs, 261–2
    interventions, effectiveness of, 264–71
    mandatory, 264
    "nothing works" *vs.* "some things work," 266
    obstacles to effective, 260–3
    potential obstacles to, 260–3
    principles of, 255
    program drift, 262–3
    program fidelity, 262–3
    punishment *vs.* treatment, 260
    therapeutic integrity, 262–3
    throughcare, 263
    working procedure of, 264–5
Corrections
    Canadian Corrections, research on, 490
    in Canadian North, 474–5
    and Canadian public, 62–3
    challenges for systems of, 472–9
    commissions of inquiry, 36–9
    COSAs and, 489
    costs of, 57
    creating effective systems of, 472
    criminal justice system, 492–3
    in democratic society, 49–50
    diverse society practice and, 489
    effective interventions, 487–8
    in England, 4
    evidence-based correctional policies and
        programs, 473
    global community, 486–7
    goals of, 48–9
    health care for inmates, 473–4
    needs of offenders with mental health
        issues, 474
    needs of victims, 473
    noncarceral and carceral components,
        50–1
    over-representation of Indigenous persons
        and Blacks, 474
    philosophies of, 33–5
    philosophy for criminal offenders, 52
    politics and correctional policy and
        practice, 478–9
    privatization, 491–2
    provincial/territorial, 331
    provincial/territorial corrections, 55–6
    punitive penology, 487
    reflections on history, 39
    restorative justice, 64–6
    as restorative justice, 488–9
    swinging pendulum of Canadian, 28–31
    systemic failures, 475–8
    women offenders, profile of, 371–2
    youth, evolution of, 432–5
Corrections and Conditional Release Act
    (CCRA), 29, 45, 231
    purpose and principles of, 283–4
    Section 81 of, 415
    Section 100 of, 283

Section 102 of, 284
    Section 147 of, 307
Corrections policy for women offenders,
    364–5
Corrections systems, 401, 404, 405
    over-representation of Indigenous
        offenders, 402
Counselling, probation officers, 113*t*
Courts
    problem-solving, 473
    re-entry, 333
Creating Choices, **365,** 367
Crime
    early days, 3–6
    perspectives on, 6–9
Crime victims, 305
    in conditional release, role of, 305
    needs of, 473
Criminal behaviour, electronic monitoring
    and, 107–8
Criminal Code, 29, 45
    conditional sentences and, 108–9
    death penalty and, 227
    purpose of sentencing and, 73–4
    Section 718 of, 73
    Section 718.2(e) of, 80
    Section 731 of, 109
    Section 743.6 of, 81
    Section 810.1 of, 289
    sentencing and, 76–9, 81
Criminal Court
    and circle sentencing principles, difference
        between, 88, 89*t*
    judges, 82
Criminal justice funnel, 48
Criminal justice system, 47, 492–3
    classical school, 10
    corrections as subsystem of, 52–3
    Indigenous over-representation, 402–05
Criminogenic risk factors, **248**
Critical incident stress debriefing (CISD), **196**
Critical (radical) school, **11**
Cross-gender staffing, **382**
CSC. *See* Correctional Service of Canada (CSC)
CSC Aboriginal ICPM (AICPM), 419
CSOs. *See* Conditional sentence orders (CSOs)
Cultural diversity, correctional practice
    for, 489
Custodial agenda of correctional officers, **185**
Custodial sentences for young offenders, 444
Custody Rating Scale, 249

Day parole, **287,** 293
Death penalty, 3, 16, 81
Decarceration, 18
Decarceration in the United States, 15–18
Denunciation, 74
Depression Hopelessness and Suicide Screening
    Form, 383–4
Deprivation theory, **215**
Detention centres, 139
Detention during the period of statutory release, **288**
Differential amenability to treatment, **256**
Differential treatment availability, **261**
Differential treatment effectiveness, **255**

Disciplinary segregation, **157**
Diverse clientele, supervising, 125–6
Diverse society, correctional practice for, 489
Diversion programs, **105**–6
    YCJA, 439
    Youth Justice Interventions, 454*t*
DOs (dangerous offenders), **81**–2
    ex-dangerous offender, journey of, 458–9
Double-bunking inmates, 154
Drugs
    inmates and, 150, 161
    inmates' visitors and, 225
    in prison, 224–5
    trafficking, 190
Duty to act fairly, 50, 483
Dynamic risk factors, **248**
Dynamic security, **140**

Early 21st century
    swinging pendulum of Canadian
        corrections, 29–31
Earned remission date, **288**
Ecclesiastical prisons, 4
Economic condition of Indigenous Peoples, 401
Edmonton Institution for Women, 371, 375, 387
Edmonton Prison for Women, 161
Elderly inmates, 151
Electronic Monitoring (EM), **107**–8
    Global Positioning System and, 108*f*, 337
Eliminating Pardons for Serious Crimes Act, 29
EM. *See* Electronic monitoring (EM)
Emotions Management for Women (EMWO), 387
Enforcement, probation officers, 113*t*
England, corrections in, 4
Essay on Crime and Punishments (Beccaria), 10
Essex County Youth Justice Committee,
    461*t*–462*t*
Ethics, of treatment programs, 263–4
European methods of justice, 406
Evidence-based practices, **473**
Exchange power, COs, 187
Ex-dangerous offender, journey of, 458–9
Expenditures for corrections, 57, 59
Expert power, COs, 187

Family support for young offenders, 453
Family visit programs, 215, 229, 230
FASD. *See* Fetal alcohol spectrum disorder (FASD)
Federal correctional facilities, security levels, 139
Federal correctional institution, 405–6
Federal Court, 208
Federal day/full parole, grant rates for, 293*f*
Federal Indigenous offenders, 403, 412, 416–7
Federal inmates, 296
Federally-sentenced women (FSW), 365, 368
Federal Minister of Justice, 29
Federal offenders, 32, 284–5
    sentencing milestones for, 285, 285*f*
Federal prisons, 30
Federal sex offenders, 289–90
Federal women offenders, 32, 36, 363, 365, 371
Ferri, Enrico, 11
Fetal Alcohol Spectrum Disorder (FASD), 56,
    153–4, 436

Fine, 440*t*
First Nations and Métis community involvement
    in corrections, 92, 404, 407, 410, 415
Floating prison, 5, 5*f*
Full parole, **287**, 291, 294, 301

Garafalo, Raffaelo, 11
General deterrence, **74**
Get tough approach, 308
Gladue decision, 412, 414
Global Positioning System (GPS), 108*f*, 337
Global Positioning System monitoring
    components, 108
Goffman, Erving, 141
Good Lives Model, 252
GPS. *See* Global Positioning System (GPS)
Grand Valley Institution for Women, 32
Grant rates, 293*f*
Grievance system, 231
Griffiths, C. T., 326, 329

Harm reduction programs, 162
HCV. *See* Hepatitis C virus (HCV)
Health issues and infectious diseases, 160–1
Hedonistic calculus, 10
Hegemonic masculinity, 456
Hells Angels, 190
Hepatitis C virus (HCV), 162, 371, 387
High-risk offenders, 284, 299, 331–2, 334
    CN and, 336
    restorative, reintegrative practice for,
        343–5
    treatment programs for, 252, 323
HIV/AIDS, 193
    high-risk behaviour, 161–2
    interdiction strategies, 162–3
    prevention strategies, 161–2
Hollow Water Community Holistic Circle
    Healing Process, 408*f*, 418
        Healing Process, 48*f*
Howard, John, 6
Hulk prison, 5, 5*f*
Human rights and corrections, 49

ICM conferences. *See* Integrated Case
    Management (ICM) conferences
ICPM. *See* Integrated Correctional Program
    Model (ICPM)
IERT. *See* Institutional Emergency Response
    Team (IERT)
Importation theory, **215**
Imprisonment
    pains of, 215, 224, 225
    punishment by, 3
Incapacitation, 74
Incarcerated young women offenders, 448
Incarceration, 10, 211–12
    alternatives to, 104
    effectiveness of, 163–5
Indigenous circle hearings, 416
Indigenous corrections, initiatives in,
    406–409
Indigenous-focused programs/interventions,
    effectiveness of, 417–18

Indigenous healing centres and lodges, 407–9
Indigenous inmates, 253
    Aboriginal Corrections Continuum of Care, 411
    conditional release, parole-eligible, 413–14
    gangs, 155
    High-Intensity Program for, 413
    ICPM initiative, 412
    Moderate-Intensity Program for, 413
    and parole board, 415–16
    and treatment interventions, 409–11
Indigenous offenders, 83, 113
    community corrections, 407
    and conditional release, 416–17
    judicial determination and, 81
    risk factors for, 409
    sentencing, 80
    treatment programs for, 409, 413
Indigenous organizations, 406–7
Indigenous peoples in Canadian society, 401–2
Indigenous sentencing, 80
Indigenous-specific programs, 407, 423
Indigenous young offenders, 436–8
Indiginous women offenders, 412–13
Industrial Revolution, 4
Infectious diseases, health issues and, 160–1
Informal social support networks, role of, 453–8
Inmate code, **216**–18
Inmates
    access to library materials, 59
    appeals, 307
    code of, 180
    community service projects, 255
    coping strategies of, 210
    correctional plan, 257
    disorder and disturbances, preventing, 156–7
    doing time and doing treatment, 260
    drugs and, 224–5
    families of, 228–31
    federal, 296
    gangs and, 155–6, 367–69
    general profile of, 207–8
    grievances and complaints, 231
    health of, 374–380
    HIV/AIDS (*See* HIV/AIDS)
    Indigenous, 253
    as institutionalized, 215
    LGBTQ, 216
    loss of liberty and, 214
    in Manitoba Penitentiary, 27
    mature coping by, 225
    mental illness, 295
    networks and, 217
    niches and, 218
    pains of imprisonment, 214–15
    and parole hearings, 301–4
    participation and program completion, low rates of, 262
    population, profile of, 207–10, 210*f*
    rape among, 225
    safety of, 156
    searches of, 225
    sexual coercion among, 221–2
    sexual gratification among, 225

    SIB and, 226
    smuggling and, 224
    social roles and, 223
    social system of, 223–4
    state-raised, 227–8, 329
    status and power among, 218–19
    status degradation ceremonies and, 212
    status restoration and, 212
    in Toronto-area jails, 328
    treatment interventions, 409–13
    urine samples, 225
    violence and exploitation among, 219–22
    vocabulary, 217
Inmate social system, **215**
Inmate subculture, 215
Institutional Emergency Response Team (IERT), 365
Institutionalized, **216**
Institutional parole officers (IPOs), 246
Institutional Treatment Programs, 447–8
Integrated Case Management (ICM) conferences, **443**
Integrated Correctional Program Model (ICPM), **252**, 325
Intensive Aftercare Programs (IAP), 456*t*
Intensive Intervention Strategy (IIS), 384
Intensive rehabilitative custody and supervision (IRCS), 445*t*, 456*t*
Intensive supervision probation (ISP), **122**, 128
Intensive Support and Supervision Order, 451
Intensive support units (ISUs), 162
Interdiction strategies, 162–3, **162–3**
Intermediate sanctions, **106**–7
    conditional sentences and, 108–9
    EM and, 107–8
Intermittent sentences, **76**, 77*t*
International agreements and conventions, 46
Ipeelee, Manasie, 80
IPOs. *See* Institutional parole officers (IPOs)
Island Community Justice Society, 452*t*

Jails, 25, 139
JDA. *See* Juvenile Delinquents Act (JDA)
John Howard Society, 6
Judges, conditional sentences and, 108
Judicial determination, **81**
Judicial recognizances, **289**–90
Judicial recommendations, 95
Judicial reprimand, 450*t*
Justice
    correctional institutions, 147
Juvenile awareness program, 457
Juvenile Delinquents Act (JDA), **432**, 433, 459

Kerr, Jason, 220
Kingston Penitentiary, 23, 32, 36, 148, 219
    Brown Commission, **24**
    goals of, 24
Kingston Prison for Women, 146, 365–6, 371, 382

Law, rule of. *See* Rule of law
Leaders, role of, 142

Learning organization, **484**
Legislative bills, 29
Legislative framework of corrections, 44–6
　　Canadian Charter of Rights and Freedoms, 45
　　Criminal Code, 45
　　provincial and territorial corrections
　　　legislation, 46
Legitimate power, COs, 187
Level of Service/Case Management Inventory
　　(LS/CMI), 117, 249
Level of Service Inventory-Revised (LSI-R), 117,
　383, 449
　　Ontario Revision, 203, 249
Liberal school, 11
Life imprisonment, 81
Life sentences, 184, 227
Local jails, 25
Lombroso, Cesare, 11
Long-term confinement, 227
Long-term inmates, 154
Long-term offenders, **81–2**
Long-term supervision order, 416
Low-risk offenders, 340
LS/CMI. *See* Level of Service/Case Management
　Inventory (LS/CMI)
LSI-R. *See* Level of Service Inventory-Revised
　(LSI-R)

Maconochie, Alexander, 282, 283
Male inmates, 24
Ma Mawi Wi Chi Itata Family Violence
　Program in Stony Mountain Institution, 427
Manitoba Penitentiary
　　daily menu for inmates in, 27
　　symbol of discipline in, 26–7
Manitoba, provincial institutional corrections in,
　486–7
Mark system, 283
Martinson, Robert, 266
Marx, Karl, 11, 12
Mature coping, **225**
Maximum security institutions, **139**
Medical model of corrections, 28
Medium security institutions, **139**
Mental health issues, women offenders,
　386–7
Mental health strategy, 151
Mental illness for inmates, 295
Mentally ill offenders, 151–2
　　parole and, 334
Methadone maintenance program, 325
Middle Ages, 3
Minimum security institutions, **139**
Ministry of Correctional Services Act, 46
Mitigating circumstances, 83
Moderate-Intensity Program, 413
Modern prisons, 32
Moral architecture, **24**
Mother–child programs, 368, 373–4
Motivational interviewing (MI), **120**
M2 programs, 254
Multilevel institutions, **139**
Multi-Target program, 252
Murder
　　of correctional officers, 195, 197
　　of inmates, 227
　　sentencing for, 81

National Parole Board (NPB), 283
Native Counselling Service of Alberta
　(NCSA), 62, 420
Need principle, **116**
Net widening, **106**
NIMBY (not in my back yard) syndrome, 63–4
Noncustodial sentence for young offenders, 440
Nonresidential Attendance Order, 441*t*
Nonviolent federal offenders, 290
Nova Institution for Women, 178–9
NPB. *See* National Parole Board (NPB)

O-Chi-Chak-Ko-Sipi Healing Lodge, 408, 409
Offence, victim of, 305
Offender
　　ex-dangerous, journey of, 458–9
Offender Intake Assessment (OIA), 245
Offender Management System, 249
Offenders
　　classification of, 244
　　community and, 317
　　community corrections and, 481–2
　　conditional release, 327–8
　　conditional sentences, 108–9
　　confinement, 495
　　contact and intervention, 124–5
　　criminal, 10, 13
　　dangerous, 81–2
　　diversion programs, 105–6
　　electronic monitoring and, 107–8
　　experience of, 486
　　federal, 32
　　with Fetal Alcohol Spectrum Disorder, 153–4
　　grievances and complaints, 231
　　and incarceration, 163–5
　　in ISP programs, 122
　　mentally ill, 151–2, 334
　　needs of, 474
　　pains, 481
　　parole officers and supervision of, 329–3
　　perspectives on, 6–9
　　populations on parole, 333–9
　　and probation, 109–11
　　problem-solving courts and, 105, 106
　　profile, changing, 150
　　reintegration process for, 323–6
　　restorative process, 488
　　risk and needs profiles of, 247–51
　　state-raised, 216, 227–9
　　treatment needs, 247
Office of the Correctional Investigator (OCI),
　45, 211
OIA. *See* Offender Intake Assessment (OIA)
Okimaw Ohci Healing Lodge, 408, 421*t*
Ombudsman
　　federal, 231
One-chance statutory release, **288**
Ontario, adult community corrections in, 477–8
Ontario Court of Appeal, 80
Ontario Parole Board, 305, 416
Ontario, penitentiary in, 23
Open custody

facility for young offenders, 118
  and open detention facilities, 455*t*
Ottawa–Carleton judicial district, 92
Overcrowding in correctional institutions, 154–5
Owiciiyisiwak, 409

Pains of imprisonment, **214**–15
Pains of probation, 127, **127**
Pains of re-entry, **326**–7, 329
Panaceas, **479**
Pargeter, Louise, 332
Parole, 491, 493, 494
  applicant's documents/files and, 298–9
  day, 287, 291–3, 309
  full, 285, 287, 291, 301
  hearings, inmates and, 301–4
  low grant rates for, 296
  proposed community plan, 298
  special offender populations on, 333–9
Parole Act, 283
Parole and Earned Release Board (Ont.), 305
Parole Board of Canada (PBC), 46, 56, 283
Parole boards
  decision making of, 307–10
  feedback to, 308–9
  hearings, inmates and, 301–4
  Indigenous inmates, 423–4
  inmate appeals, 307
  members, appointment of, 307
  Ontario's, 315–16
Parole certificate, **304**–5
Parole decision making, 315–16
Parole eligibility date, 284–5, 296
Parole officer, 329–3
  activities of, 331
  safety of, 332–3
Parole supervision, 329–33
  dual function of, 331–2
  innovations in, 341
Pathways units, 421
PBC. *See* Parole Board of Canada (PBC)
PC. *See* Protective custody (PC)
Pedophiles, 289
Penal populism, **15**, 479, 489
Penitentiaries. *See also* Prisons
  architecture, 32–5
  Auburn model, **24**, 33
  bells and, 26–7
  food in, 27
  Pennsylvania model, **24**
Penitentiary Act, 27
Pennsylvania model, **24**
Pê Sâkâstêw Centre, 409, 418*t*
Physical health, women offenders, 379–80
Police
  circle of support and, 344–347
  community notification and (*See* community
    notification (CN)), 337
  sex offender registries, 336–337
Political enterprise, corrections as, 52
Positivist (liberal) school, **11**
Post incarceration syndrome (PICS), **328**
Post-traumatic stress disorder (PTSD), **195**
Post-World War II Corrections, 28
Pre-employment training, 112

Pre-release planning, 295–6
Pre-sentence reports (PSR), 83, **113**, 113*t*
Prevention/intervention programs, 448
Prevention strategies, 161–2
Prison Gate Section of the Salvation Army, 283
Prisonization, **215**
Prison reform, 494
Prison regulations, breaches of, 24
Prisons, 3. *See also* Correctional institutions
  architecture, eras of, 32–5
  architecture, functions and symbolism of, 32
  Auburn model for, **24**
  "big box," 32
  conflicting goals of, 140
  drugs in, 224
  entering, 212
  federal, 28
  as "home," 227–8
  neighbourhood housing, 35
  Pennsylvania model for, **24**
  as political and public institutions, 141
  provincial, 25
  re-entry and life after, 396–9
  reforms, 6, 27–8
  as total institutions, 141–2
Prison sentence, 326
Private, not-for-profit agencies, 61*t*–62*t*
Privatization, 501–2
Probation, 77*t*, 109, 441–5, 441*t*, 477, 478, 480, 483
  breach of, 110
  collaborative partnerships, 128
  defined, **109**
  effectiveness of, 127–30
  experiences of, 126–7
  supervision, 452–3
  youth, 451–4
Probationers
  experience of, 126–7
  needs and risks of, 125
  programs for, 121–2
Probation officers
  activities of, 113*t*
  caseloads, 124
  contact and intervention, 124–5
  core component of, 117, 118
  discretion, 118
  dual role of, 118
  efforts of, 120
  recruitment and training of, 111–12
  role and responsibilities of, 112–15
  safety, 123–4
  stress levels of, 123
  supervision, 118–21
  workloads, 124
  youth, 452
Probation practice
  challenges in, 122–6
  in remote and northern regions, 125–126
  RNR application to, 120
Probation supervision, 118–21
  clientele, 125
  gender in, 119
Problem-solving courts, 105, 106, 473, 488
Professional power, COs, 187
Program drift, 262–3

Program fidelity, 262–3
Proposed release plan, 298, 299
Protecting Canadians by Ending Sentence
  Discounts for Multiple Murders Act, 29
Protective custody (PC), 213, 218
Province of Ontario, 56, 140, 154, 160
Provincial and territorial corrections
  legislation, 46
Provincial correctional systems, 139
Provincial ombudspersons, 57–60, 60*t*
Provincial parole boards, 284, 304, 309
Provincial prisons, 25
Provincial/territorial correctional systems,
  offenders in, 245
Provincial/territorial governments of correction
  systems, 139, 152
Provincial/territorial inmates, 304
  release options for, 286–8
Provincial/territorial institutions, 251–5
Provincial/territorial programs, 334
Provincial/territorial systems
  challenges of, 496
PSR. *See* Pre-sentence reports (PSR)
Psychological assessments, 83
Psychopathy check list, 249
Punishment
  corporal, 24
  early days, 3–6
  by imprisonment, 4
  objectives of, 13–14, 14*t*
  perspectives on, 6–13
  treatment *vs.*, 260
Punitive corrections, 15
Punitive penology, 15

Quasi-judicial tribunals, integrity and
  impartiality of, 313

Radical school, 11
Recidivism
  conditional release and, 284, 339
  reintegration and, 284, 323
Recidivism rates, **265**
Re-entry courts, 333
Reforming corrections
  community corrections effectiveness, 486
  confinement, 485
  effective interventions, 487–8
  evidence-based policies and
    programs, 479–80
  experience of offenders, 486
  in global community, 486–7
  needs of offenders, 491–2
  needs of victims, 482
  provincial/territorial systems, 485
  punitive penology, 487–8
  reforming correctional institutions, 484–5
  rule of law, 486
  technology limits, 482
  youth at risk, early intervention, 480–1
Rehabilitation, 74
Reintegration, 323–6
  goal of, 323
  parole supervision and, 329–3
  process of, 323–6

recidivism and, 323
re-entry pain and, 326–7
Relationship Skills for Women Offenders
  (RSWO), 395
Release
  cold turkey, 284
  conditional (*See* Conditional release)
  criteria for, 308
  statutory, 287, 291, 292, 305
Release plan, 323
Remand, **149**
Remand centres, 139, 150
Remand populations, growth in, 56, 149–50
Remission, 282, 288
Reoffending, 343
Research
  on abuse of power, 187–8
  on alternatives to confinement, 127–30
  on COSAs, 348
  on women correctional officers, 197
  on inmate social system, 223–4
Residential school system for Indigenous
  children, 401
Restitution, 440*t*
Restorative Circles Initiative, 452*t*
Restorative justice, 64–5, 65*f*, 66*t*, 75, 106, 488–9
  circle sentencing, **88**–92
  corrections as, 488–9
  programs, 473, 482
  programs for young offenders, 450–3
Restorative Justice Act, 488
Retribution, sentencing and, 74
Retributive *vs.* restorative justice principles, 66
Revocation of conditional release, 339–40
Reward power, COs, 187
Risk assessment
  instruments, 248–9
  in youth corrections, 449–50
Risk factors
  criminogenic, 248
  dynamic, 244, 248
  static, 248
Risk/needs assessment, youth probation, 443–4
Risk/needs measurement tool in youth justice
  systems, 449–50
Risk–need–responsivity (RNR), 252, 480
  principles of, 384, 449–50
  to probation practice, application of, 119–20,
    128
Royal Commission. *See* Commissions of inquiry
Rule of law, 50, 147, 493
R. v. Gladue, **80**
R. v. Ipeelee, 80
R. v. Kerr, 220
R. v. Proulx, 109

Safe Streets and Communities Act, 29
Sanctions, 10
  alternative, community and, 106
  alternatives to incarceration, 130
  intermediate, 106–7
SARA. *See* Spousal Assault Risk Assessment
  (SARA)
Saskatchewan provincial institution, 196
Scared Straight programs, 455*t*

Section 81 (CCRA), **407**
Section 84 (CCRA), **416**
Section 718.2(e) of the Criminal Code, 80, 83
Section 810.1 of the Criminal Code, 289
Secure units (SUs), 368, 384
Security Reclassification Scale for men and women, 249
Segregation, **157**
Seizure/forfeiture, 451*t*
Self-injurious behaviour (SIB), **226**
    psychological health and, 374–6
Sentences, 207, 215, 218, 227
    conditional (*See* Conditional sentences)
    length of, 82
    mandatory, 81
Sentencing
    circle, **88**–92
    denunciation, 74
    effectiveness of, 94–5
    factors considered in, 83
    goals of, 74–5
    incapacitation, 74
    Indigenous offenders, 80
    options in, 76–82, 77*t*
    proportionality, 75
    purpose/principles of, 73–4
    rehabilitation, 74
    retribution, 74
Sentencing, young offenders
    custodial sentences, 444
    noncustodial sentence options, 440*t*–441*t*
    youth probation, 441–2
"Separate and silent" system, 24
Serious and Violent Offender Re-entry Initiative (SVORI), 456*t*
Service coordination, 113, 113*t*
Sex offender program, 252
Sex offender registries, 338–9
Sex Offender Risk Assessment (SORA), 117
Sex offenders
    community notification, 336–7
    COSAs and, 343–5
    GPS and electronic monitoring, 337
    judicial recognizances for, 289–90
    managing the risks of, 336
    parole and, 336
    parole supervision and, 336
    sex offender registries, 338–9
    statutory release, 317
    treatment programs, 253–4
Sexual harassment, 197
Sexual offences, 82, 218
SIB. *See* Self-injurious behaviour (SIB)
Smith, Ashley, 376–8, 479
Smith, Henry, 24
Social roles, **223**
Society of Captives, 214
Solitary confinement, **157**
Special Handling Unit (SHU), **139**
Specific deterrence, **74**
Split personality of corrections, 49
Spousal Assault Risk Assessment (SARA), 117, 249
State-raised offenders, 164–5, **216**, 329
STATIC-99, 249
STATIC-2002, 249

Static risk factors, **248**
Static security, **140**
Statistical Information on Recidivism Scale Revised, 249
Status degradation ceremonies, **212**
Statutory release, **287**, 291, 292, 305
    detention during the period of, 288
Strategic Training Initiative in Community Corrections (STICS)
    model, 483
Structured Assessment of Violent Risk in Youth (SAVRY), 449
Structured living environments (SLEs), 368, 384
Subordinate political condition of Indigenous Peoples, 401
Suicide, 374–8
Suicides, 226
    young offenders, 456
Supervision orders, 82
    types of, 115–16
Supervision, per day and annual costs of, 58*t*
Supervision, probation, 110, 118–21
    gender in, 119
Supreme Court of Canada, 220
    conditional sentences, probation and, 108
    women correctional officers and, 197
SUs. *See* Secure units (SUs)
Suspended sentence, 77*t*
Suspension of conditional release, **339**
Swinging pendulum of Canadian corrections, 28–31
Sykes, Gresham, 214

Task Force on Federally Sentenced Women, 373
Techno-corrections, **482**
Temporary absences, **286**
Therapeutic integrity, **262**
Three-strikes laws, 16
Throughcare, **263**, 325–6
Ticket of Leave Act, 283
Toronto-area jails, inmates in, 328
Total institution, **141**
Treatment centres, 140
Treatment programs, 251–5
    anger management, 251
    community-based, 299
    community involvement in, 254
    community service projects, 255
    doing time and, 260
    effectiveness measurement of, 265
    ethics of, 263–4
    ICPM, 252
    Indigenous inmates and, 409–13
    for Indigenous offenders, effectiveness of, 417–423, 418*t*
    mandatory, 264
    obstacles to effective, 260–3
    parolee in, 305
    principles of, 265
    program drift, 262
    program fidelity, 262
    right to refuse, 264
    for sex offenders, 253–4
    staff, correctional officers and, 191
    substance abuse, 251
    therapeutic integrity, 262

Treatment programs (*continued*)
    throughcare, 262
    for women offenders, 391–6
    for young offenders, 457–8
    in youth custodial institutions, 457–8
Truth in Sentencing Act, 29
Tuberculosis, 193
Tupiq program, 428

Ulayuk, Eli, 332
Union of Canadian Correctional Officers
    (UCCO), 198
United States
    decarceration, 13–15
    fiscal crisis in, 10
Unit Management Model, **145**
UN's Convention on the Rights of the Child,
    Section 16 of, **471**
Urban Indigenous offenders, diversion program
    for, 414
U.S. Supreme Court, 16
Utilitarian sentencing goals, 74

Victim impact statements, 83
Victim-offender mediation (VOM) programs, 106
Victim-offender reconciliation (VOR)
    programs, 106
Victims
    and conditional release, 305–7
    crime, 482, 492
    inmates as, 220–1
    of offence, 305
    offenders, 75
    written submission to parole board, 306
Victoria Restorative Justice Society, 451*t*
Violence in youth institutions, 445
Violence Prevention Program (VPP)
    components of, 121
    inmate's responses in, 258
Violent offenders, 219–22
Voltaire, 10
VOM programs. *See* Victim-offender mediation
    (VOM) programs
VOR programs. *See* Victim-offender
    reconciliation (VOR) programs
VPP. *See* Violence Prevention Program (VPP)

Wardens staff, management of, 147
Warrant expiry date, **284**, 291, 334
Waseskun Healing Centre, 408, 416
Women Indigenous offenders, 404–5
Women inmates
    and children, 371–4
    in Manitoba Penitentiary, 27
Women offenders, 32, 36
    classification of, 383

correctional facilities, 367–81
    in corrections, profile, 363–64
    evolution of corrections policy for, 364–65
    gender-specific programs for, 387
    treatment interventions, 382–8
    treatment programs for, 383–8
Women offenders, young
    aftercare programs, 453
    characteristics of, 448
Women's correctional institutions, 367–70
    cross-gender staffing in, 382
    dynamics inside men's and, 370
    violence inside, 371
Women's prisons, male COs in, 382
Women probation officers
    stress levels of, 123
Work release, **286**
W2 programs, 254
"Wrap-around model," 342

YCJA. *See* Youth Criminal Justice Act (YCJA)
YJCs. *See* Youth Justice Committees (YJCs)
YLS/CMI. *See* Youth Level of Service/Case
    Management Inventory (YLS/CMI)
Young offenders
    aftercare programs for, 453–8
    community re-entry process for, 453
    community service, 446
    custodial sentences for, 444–5
    diversion, 438–9
    Indigenous, 436–8, 439
    profile of, 435–6
    publicizing the names of, 461
    restorative justice approaches, 450–3
    role of informal social support networks,
        453–8
    sentencing of, 439–41
    suicides, 446
    treatment programs for, 446–9
Young Offenders Act (YOA), **433**
Youth corrections
    effectiveness of, 457
    evolution of, 432–5
    provincial/territorial systems of, 459
    risk assessment in, 449–50
Youth crime, profile of, 437
Youth Criminal Justice Act (YCJA), **433**, 435*f*
Youth Criminal Justice System, 434–5, 435*f*
Youth institutions, violence in, 435
Youth Justice Committees (YJCs), **450**
Youth justice interventions, effectiveness of, 454–7
Youth justice systems, risk/needs measurement
    tool in, 449
Youth Level of Service/Case Management
    Inventory (YLS/CMI), 113, **450**
Youth probation, 449
Youth–staff relationships, 448–9
Yukon communities, 88